FRANCO CORELLI

OPERA BIOGRAPHY SERIES, NO. 17

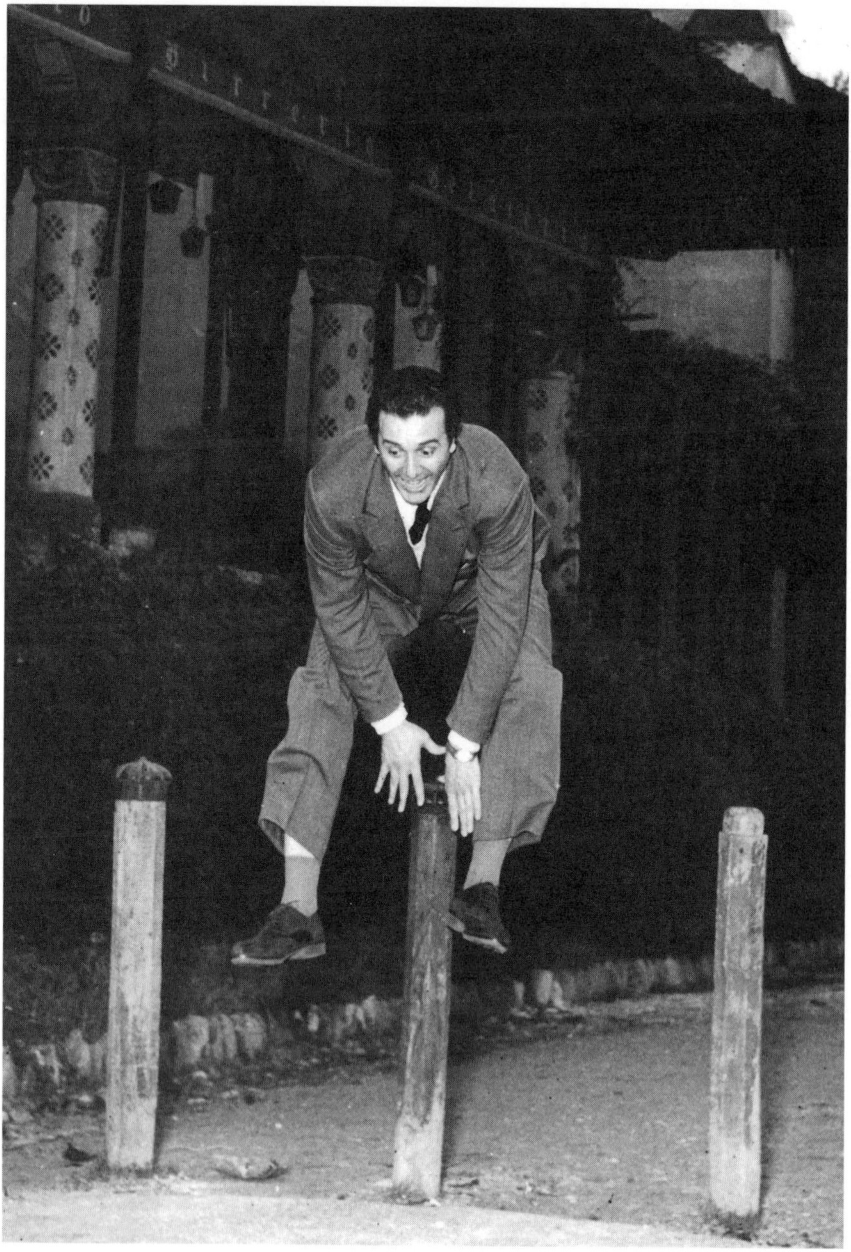

Franco Corelli

Prince of Tenors

René Seghers

with a foreword by Marco Corelli

AMADEUS PRESS

AMADEUS PRESS
AN IMPRINT OF HAL LEONARD CORPORATION
NEW YORK

FRONTISPIECE: Franco Corelli riding on a cloud while visiting Turin's medieval castle at the Valentino park in November 1955, in between his *Tosca* performances at the Teatro Carignano and his first Cetra recordings. (Photo: Courtesy of Arrigo Michelini)

© Copyright 2008 by René Seghers

All rights reserved. No part of this book may be reproduced in any form, without written permission, except by a newspaper or magazine reviewer who wishes to quote brief passages in connection with a review.

Published in 2008 by Amadeus Press
An Imprint of Hal Leonard Corporation
19 West 21st Street, New York, NY 10010

Printed in the United States of America

Book design by Mark Lerner

Library of Congress Cataloging-in-Publication Data is available upon request.
ISBN: 978-1-57647-163-6

www.amadeuspress.com

In memory of Annegreet Haisma
February 23, 1977–July 12, 2006

For being my girlfriend for seven years, for monitoring my
business throughout the years of research, and for making this
possible in many other ways

Contents

Acknowledgments ix
Foreword xiii
Preface xv

Chapter 1 • 1921–1925
The Land of Pergolesi, Spontini, and Rossini 1

Chapter 2 • 1926–1939
Childhood and Teenage Years 8

Chapter 3 • 1940–1945
A World in Flames 20

Chapter 4 • 1946–1949
The Call of the Muse 31

Chapter 5 • 1950
Choosing Music 41

Chapter 6 • 1951
Vincerò! 45

Chapter 7 • 1952–1954
The Conquest of Rome 52

Chapter 8 • 1955–1957
Forging the Voice 102

Chapter 9 • 1958–1959
Il Divo 141

Chapter 10 • 1960
The Road to the Metropolitan 177

Chapter 11 • 1961
Prince of Tenors 195

Chapter 12 • 1962
"The World's Greatest Tenor" 241

Chapter 13 • 1963
"Acclaimed the World's Greatest Tenor" 269

Chapter 14 • 1964
Toward a Lyric Repertoire   289

Chapter 15 • 1965
Mixed Emotions   318

Chapter 16 • 1966
The Best-Fed Tenor in the World!   329

Chapter 17 • 1967
Italy Greets the Prodigal Son   345

Chapter 18 • 1968–1969
The Years of Transition   366

Chapter 19 • 1970–1975
Defending the Throne   385

Chapter 20 • 1976–1981
Dunque è proprio finita?   442

Chapter 21 • 1982–1989
Headed for the Future   451

Chapter 22 • 1990–1994
"Opera Fanatic"   455

Chapter 23 • 1995–2000
Silent Years   462

Chapter 24 • 2001–2002
New Life, New Muse   466

Chapter 25 • 2003
Tu che a Dio spiegasti l'ali   468

Chapter 26 • 2004–2007
In Memoriam   474

Epilogue   478

Appendix: Short Corelli Family Tree   481
Notes   483
Index   519

Acknowledgments

SPECIAL THANKS TO

Bruce Badger (knowledgeable collector and voice specialist,
reader, documents—especially hundreds of rare recordings)
Monica CiuCiu (Italian translations and sacrifice)
Anna Corelli (logistics, great cooking)
Franco Corelli (interview, inspiration)
Graziano Corelli (logistics, invaluable documents)
Loretta Corelli (interviews, invaluable documents)
Marco Corelli (for everything, friendship)
Donald DiGrazia (invaluable documents, revealing information)
Gemma Giacomini (invaluable documents, touching information)
Alessandro Grati (invaluable documents, revealing information)
Merle Hubbard (invaluable documents,
incredibly entertaining information)
Chiara Liuti (too many translations, documents,
logistics, love—*tutti*)
Tony Locantro (invaluable documents, reader)
Mario G. Lucchesi (extremely convenient logistics)
Alessandra Malusardi (invaluable Teatro dell'Opera
documents and kind help)
Marcella Marchetti (invaluable documents, loving memories)
Arrigo Michelini (incredible photos, reminiscenses, and kindness)
Jan Neckers (great authority on the career of Franco Corelli,
excellent historian, invaluable reader, documents)
Birgit Nilsson (documents, interviews, correspondence—
my ears still hurt!)
John Pennino (invaluable documents, logistics, critical reader)
Alessandro Scaravelli (invaluable documents,
insightful information)

Bart Spek (Russian translations are one thing,
but the entire Buljigin book . . . wow)
Robert Tuggle (invaluable documents, logistics,
exceptional permissions)
Gianluca Turricchia (Italian translations,
final Italian corrections, patience)
Judith van den Berg (Italian translations and the only
human being who ever made me beg)
Rudi van den Bulck (a great authority on the life and career of
Mario Del Monaco, reader, documents, devil's advocate)
Claire Winterholler (great authority on the career of Franco
Corelli, invaluable reader, merciless corrector, documents)
Luigi Zoboli (invaluable documents,
revealing information, logistics, humor)

❖❖❖❖❖

I am further indebted to those who contributed in many different ways, such as establishing contacts; helping with research; providing authorizations and tips; giving interviews or providing me with unpublished interviews; selling memorabilia to me outside eBay; and contributing articles, photographs, and documents of all sorts: Frank Abe, Sonia Allende, Lucine Amara, Davide Annachini, Charles Anthony, Nazarreno Antinori, Juan José Arias Dávalos, Dick Bak, Bianca Maria Barbadori, Davide Barbone, Kristie Beliza, Roberta Berni, Moreno Bucci, Andrea and Ingeborg Bucolier, Alexei Buljigin, George Burr, Paola Busoli, Victor Callegari, Cosimo Capani, Anita Cerquetti, Jill Chase, Walter Colombo, Ada Colzani, Cliff Cremer, Mayrwin Curtis, Mary Curtis-Verna, Janet De Jesus-Sulimowicz, Giancarlo Del Monaco, Michael Delos, Pierfranco Delprino, Joost de Man, Marijke Dessing, Jaap Deutekom, Giulio Di Marco, Virginia Eckman, Isabel Ferreira, William Fiorelli, Mosè Franco, Ed Frank, Mirella Freni, Giuliano Giaccaglia, Marco Gianotti, Giorgio Gualerzi, Gian Giacomo Guelfi, Jean-Jacques Hanine, Kenn Harris, Jörg Hillebrand, Guido Ingaramo, Paul Jaretzki, Wouter Klein, Patricia Kolakowska, Giampieri Lamberto, Bruno La Rooij, Fred London, Alessandra Malusardi, Maria Manganaro, Robleto Merolla, Charles Mintzer, Anna Moffo, Gilda Morelli, Nana Mouskouri, Leopoldo Mucci, Alsie Murdoch, Asun Noriega, Magda Olivero, Rolf Orth, Lucia Palianti, Mario Panzini, Luciano Pavarotti, Alberto Podesti,

Rita Poli, Federica Pompili, Vera Ramer, Andrey Ryzhov, Romolo Ricci, Katia Ricciarelli, Charlie Riecker, Tony Russo, Bruno Sammartino, Harry W. Saunders, Elisabetta Savoca, Luigi Settembretti, Giulietta Simionato, Peter Simons, Giuliani Solari, Antonietta Stella, Joan Sutherland, Luke Syson, Jaume Tribo, Gabriella Tucci, Frans van der Beek, Ellie van Santen, Karl van Zoggel, Giulia Visci, Franca Warden, and Stefan Zucker.

Many thanks also to Alitalia; Archives of the Maggio Musicale, Firenze; Archives of the Metropolitan Opera House, New York; Archivio Periodici RCS; Arena di Verona; Asociación Bilbaína de Amigos de la Ópera Bilbao; Biblioteca Nacional Portugal; Conservatory "Gioacchino Rossini," Pesaro; Daewoo; EMI; ENIT Amsterdam; Fono Forum; Grand Hotel; Hachette Rusconi Publishing Group; Mondadori Publishing Group; Museo Teatro "Giuseppe Verdi," Trieste; Musica e Dischi; the New York Public Library; Pioneer Press; RCS Publishing Group; Teatro alla Scala, Milan; Teatro delle Muse, Ancona; Teatro San Carlo, Naples; Teatro Liceu, Barcelona; Tourism Agency of Ancona; Tourism Agency of Firenze; and Tourism Agency of Pesaro.

I also feel I should acknowledge some people at Amadues Press with whom the contact has been very intense. First of all, there is John Cerullo, the only publisher I ever approached for this book—he decided to publish it while I was still busy explaining the ins and outs. Then there is Jessica Burr, the project editor, who was my very considerate intermediary there for nearly a year. Last but not least, there is Barbara Norton, my copy editor. Barbara was simply always right—molto grazie!

Additional thanks to Gilberto Starone, Federico Rota, and Frank Hamilton. Starone will always remain the first to have drawn up a Corelli career chronology. His effort (published in Marina Boagno's *Franco Corelli: A Man, a Voice*) was impressive by pre-Internet standards. The same goes for Rota's tapeology (published in the same book's first edition). Thanks to them, Frank Hamilton and I had a reference point. Hamilton then expanded upon their pioneering work through painstaking further research, and he made the results freely available to all online. The strictly chronological order and the scope of this book made a comprehensive chronology chapter superfluous (performance and recording information is separately listed where these performances are being discussed in the text). However, I have substantially expanded the list of performances and recordings previously cited and have corrected or expanded cast lists and data wherever possible. The main sources used for these—apart from information provided by the theaters concerned, vintage performance programs, and original recordings—were the countless performance reviews and articles quoted throughout the book. Unless mentioned otherwise, listed recordings that were hitherto unknown are recordings I have actually heard.

René Seghers

Foreword

These pages retrace the life and the career of my beloved cousin Franco Corelli. I had the pleasure and the great honor to share part of his life adventures and a number of the successes that have made him a legend in twentieth-century opera. The intent of these pages, however, is to create an honest picture of the human side of Franco Corelli rather than another portrait of the artist. His greatness will be there, but also his weaknesses, his private interests, and, naturally, the many colorful anecdotes. That is a rare chance, for few ever got to know him intimately.

Within the family, we always considered all these things private, even "secret." But when I met the author of this book in April 2004, he gradually convinced me that it was time to let my cousin's present and future fans know the marvelous human being behind the artist. The beauty of any given voice is a gift from God, something that proves His very existence. Franco himself used to say that he had been chosen by a divine entity not just to be "a voice among others," as he used to call himself, but a voice that, among other things, conveyed to his audiences the soul and the deeper emotions of the characters he used to portray. And into them he poured his own despairs, his hopes, his emotions. He had to make many sacrifices before he became the acclaimed Franco Corelli that the world remembers today, both in his life and with respect to his nature, because unlike some of his colleagues, Franco was shy and reserved. The Franco I knew was very human, with all a human being's anxieties, emotions, dreams, hopes, affections and, above all, a genuine love for his family.

During my encounters with the author I have asked myself many times, would Franco have agreed to all this? Would he have allowed me to reveal so much of his intimate life, about which he had always been so discreet? Over the three-year period that I cooperated with the author, I frequently felt embarrassed when I recalled certain facts. But I came to believe it would serve Franco's memory well for people to know his very human side in order to better understand and appreciate all of what he accomplished professionally. After all, the two were so very intertwined. And also, in the end, I was comforted by the perfectionism and the deep sensibility of my interlocutor. He was right in pointing out that if I hadn't opened my reminiscences to the world, all this would have been lost forever. At one point, I even felt Seghers's rush taking hold of me, for indeed, there was not a day to waste to secure the direct testimonies of the childhood friends and fellow artists from the early years who were still alive! For the love of Franco, I want to thank all of them here for making possible this monumental testimony of my cousin's life and art.

Marco Corelli
December 12, 2007

Preface

I don't have that many secrets, it's just that people ask me the same questions over and over again: the "high heel duel" with Hines during Eracle, *the swordfight with Christoff in* Don Carlo, *my quarrel with a spectator during* Trovatore, *and the biting of Nilsson in* Turandot. *Today it seems as if my life revolved around these events, but they were of minor importance to my life. Just four nights—I'd be more than happy to talk to you about the other seventy-six years.*
    Franco Corelli to the author, Vienna, December 19, 1997

Franco Corelli. The name represents triumph and sacrifice, physical strength tempered by emotional weakness, a modest character that was punctuated by outrageous behavior—in short, all one could wish for in a tenor. And yet we know almost nothing of him apart from his stage appearances. The major aim of this book is to paint a picture of Franco Corelli, the man, in his private and professional life.

    The idea for the book was sparked by a meeting with Corelli in December 1997 in Vienna, where he was supposed to make a onetime comeback appearance with a few songs in the context of a tenor gala including Nicolai Gedda, José Cura, Peter Seiffert, and Vladimir Galouzine. In the end, Corelli did not sing, but he granted me an interview, during which we discussed the writing of a comprehensive, personal, and intimate biography with him, to which he agreed. As often happens with such spontaneous expressions of enthusiasm, nothing came of it. I ran into him again in New York in May 2000, when he entered the opera-friendly Caffè Taci restaurant (then still on the Upper West Side) where I was having dinner. Upon his arrival, the audience—forgive me, those present there for dinner—rose from their seats and gave him a standing ovation. Suddenly I was confronted with the full visceral impact of the Corelli phenomenon. Back home I started collecting vintage article clippings and discovered that all these supposed inhibitions about publicly revealing his personal life that he allegedly had were not there in the 1950s and 1960s. During that time he had happily chatted away about his childhood, his parents, the army—and he welcomed reporters and photographers into his home. He even posed for fashion shoots together with his wife, Loretta. Her recipes of his favorite dishes graced dozens of magazines, and he even commented on the beginnings of their love affair.

My job as a freelance writer on opera topics gave me plenty of access to opera performers, and by 2001 I was routinely asking singers such as Joan Sutherland about their encounters with Corelli. In the second half of 2003, with the larger part of the research completed and the first chapters already written, I got in touch with my contact at EMI, in order to arrange a meeting with the man himself. A few days later EMI's Jeroen van Riel informed me that Corelli had meanwhile suffered from a heart attack and no longer had his full capacities. A few months later, on October 29, 2003, he died. His death made me realize that there was no time to lose in contacting the remaining friends from his childhood in Ancona, Italy. I knew no one in that city but developed what I thought was a brilliant plan: I would ask elderly people on the street if they knew someone who had known Corelli. Within a couple of hours, that plan should lead me to the answers to my remaining questions. And it did. With a little give and take and the help of the Teatro delle Muse and the local newspapers, I eventually ended up in a branch of the bank where Franco's cousin Marco Corelli had his office. He looked at me with a suspicious eye: "We people of Ancona keep to ourselves. You can ask me anything about my cousin's career, but nothing about his private life. That he guarded jealously."

I shrugged my shoulders and replied that, according to me, Franco was an open book. Mr. Corelli looked at me as if I had completely lost my mind. So I took a handful of magazines from my bag and showed him pictures of Franco posing as Tarzan, seminude in Verona, laughing his heart out backstage, showing off his home and his wife, and talking about it all endlessly. After I had been in his office about ten minutes, Marco interrupted me, opening his drawer: "I will show you something. These are letters, twenty, thirty or more, all from people who asked me to open up my private archive on Franco for the books they wanted to write about him. But I never answered those letters, because I was waiting for you." He rose from his chair, escorted me to his car, and took me on a trip down memory lane, off to the places of Franco's childhood. We drove to the Teatro delle Muse, the Bellini choir, the arcades where he would listen to the echo of his young voice and to the Lazaretto, where the Stamura boating house is—just in front of the building where he was born, overlooking the Adriatic Sea. From those emerald waters emerged shadows of a past long gone. His father and mother, uncles and aunts, his grandparents and childhood friends, all smiled at us, and the clock moved backward to the day when an ancient ship approached the shores of a *terra incognita*: "Italy! Italy!"

CHAPTER 1 ❖ 1921–1925

The Land of Pergolesi, Spontini, and Rossini

Visions of Aeneas permeate the mind when we read of the exiled Greek Syracusians who roamed the Adriatic Sea in 387 B.C. Unlike the peregrinations of the great Trojan, the hardships of the roving Syracusians did not survive in testimonies as imaginative as those of Homer. Yet, it is easy to imagine their joy upon finally spotting land, halfway down the Adriatic coast of the Italian peninsula, and it was there that they settled. The local population called them "Dori," and by the time their settlement became a Roman city, they had wholly merged with the natives in the area, although their origins were still apparent in the name they had bestowed upon their settlement—Ankon, Greek for "elbow," referring to the shape of a promontory that jutted into the sea and formed a natural harbor between two hills. The spiritual counterpart of that promontory was the Temple of Venus, rising high above the settlement atop Mount Guasco, on the very spot where the cathedral of Ancona stands today. From there the ancient Romans watched the marvel of nature the gods had bestowed upon the city: although Ancona faces east, from the top of the mountain one can see the sun rise and set over the sea. Caesar occupied the city, and Trajan strengthened its harbor, which ultimately made it one of the five powers of the Pentapoli Marittima in the Byzantine era. The early Middle Ages brought Goths, Lombards, and Saracens to its soil until the Holy Roman Empire of the German Nation claimed it and made it the center of the region known as the Marches, but Ancona kept its freedom through varying alliances until it became part of the Papal States in 1532. The annexation more or less closed the region off from the outside world for a number of centuries; it is this isolation that is said to have caused the legendary reserve of the Marches' inhabitants today. People from the Marches keep to themselves. Perhaps that is also why they loved (and love) music so much, a love that produced the composers Giovanni Battista Pergolesi, Gaspare Spontini, and Gioacchino Rossini, all of whom were born in the Marches in the eighteenth century. Rossini was firmly established on the operatic throne when, in 1827, his *Aureliano in Palmira* and *Riccardo e Zoraide* opened Ancona's splendid new Teatro delle Muse.

✦✦✦✦✦

One would like to believe the Corelli family legend that traces their genealogy back to the renowned seventeenth-century composer Arcangelo Corelli, but Arcangelo never married and died childless. These inconvenient facts leave only the possibility of a link through one of Arcangelo's brothers, Don Ippolito, Domenico, or Giacinto. The first known Corellis of interest to this book are Carlo Corelli and his wife, Gertrude, who gave birth to Luigi Corelli in Rimini in 1821. In 1849 Luigi, a soldier, married Antonia Puliti (born in 1825), who gave birth to a son in Ancona on December 12, 1858. That child, Augusto, arrived just in time for the liberation of Ancona by the Piedmontese in 1860, when General Enrico Cialdini brought the city out of its economically devastating position as a Papal State and into the Italian union. Judging from the fact that Augusto, one of the few among his eight brothers and sisters (one of whom, Francesco, was adopted) to survive infancy, began working at the harbor at a very early age, his family seems to have been of modest means. In earlier times, that would have been the end of young Augusto's story. However, the change of regime and the opening up of commerce in the harbor brought plenty of work to Ancona. Although it wasn't Augusto's favorite pastime, he worked hard in order to help provide for his family. Only after work was he able to give in to his one indulgence: an unbridled passion for singing. He and his friends copied the style of the great singers of the time that they had heard at the Teatro delle Muse, and they tested themselves in local groups (some of which Augusto helped to found) such as the Giuseppe Verdi Chorus.

Whenever there was an opportunity, Augusto's virile tenor voice graced churches, street corners, cafés, and the balcony under which he sent forth serenades to the adorable Leonilde Sbarbati. It would have added a lovely operatic touch if there had been reports of Romeo and Juliet–like overtures, with difficult obstacles in Augusto's way, but the truth was Leonilde welcomed his attentions, and she married the twenty-four-year-old Augusto when she was eighteen. The couple rented a house in Via del Pozzetto 2, where their first child, Corrado, arrived on July 11, 1882. The family's happiness was short-lived: Corrado died within a year of his birth. When their second child, Beatrice Virginia Corinna, died at the age of three in September 1887, the couple were inconsolable. Their grief is reflected in the name of their third child, Corrado Attilio Fernando, born on August 20, 1886, and named after their dead son. With yet another baby on the way, the family moved to a house at Fortress Square 4, located at the base of the city's fortress on the hill of Capodimonte, overlooking the sea. Their fourth child, Remo Pilade Adriano, was born on November 10, 1887, and around that same time the house was renamed Via Capodimonte 69. There, on December 29, 1889, the couple welcomed their fifth child, named Corinna Elvira Adelia in honor of the daughter who had died two years earlier.[1]

Leonilde and Augusto were now blessed with three healthy children, followed by another one on December 21, 1891, Rossilla Quartilla, nicknamed Bice (again after their deceased daughter). By the time Viero Dario Aldo arrived on February 14, 1894, Augusto had managed to work himself up to a management position, which he relinquished in 1895 in order to start his own business selling household products. Therefore, when the couple's last child, Dora Alma Vanda, was born on September 21, 1896, it was under different circumstances: their street had once more been renamed and was now Via Cialdini 77 (in honor of the general who had liberated the Marches), and the family business was failing, due to Augusto's inexperience. In those difficult moments, when his family expected him to return to his former job, Augusto made a decision that would change his life: at the advanced age of thirty-eight, he decided to follow his heart and pursue a career as a professional opera singer.

In any other period he probably would have failed, but the late 1890s were the very culmination of opera as a living art. With *La Bohème*,[2] Giacomo Puccini had just caught up with the creator of verismo, Pietro Mascagni. Umberto Giordano's *Andrea Chénier* followed in the same vein, and suddenly the entire world was clamoring for the latest compositions of these sensational new composers. Italian opera troupes proliferated, traveling the continents in order to supply the demand for fresh voices. Augusto, in spite of his passion for cigars, is said to have had a fairly beautiful tenor voice, virile and expressive, with a romantic, sensual edge. Together with some singing friends, he quickly managed to build himself a local reputation as a *comprimario* singer.

Eventually he joined tours taking him to such exotic places as Brazil, Argentina, and Mexico, from which he would return with ponchos and sombreros for the children.[3]

The Argentine tour was the high point of Augusto's career, culminating in a number of performances under the baton of Arturo Toscanini. With his career blossoming, Augusto's family prospered as well. The Corellis moved to a spacious second-floor apartment in the prestigious Via Aurelio Saffi 10 building (located precisely where Ancona's Grand Hotel Palace stands today), just around the corner from the Teatro delle Muse. There the family enjoyed a spectacular view of the port and the mesmerizing turquoise Adriatic Sea. In time Augusto's sons managed to secure good jobs at the shipyards of Ancona, no more than a few hundred yards from the family's home. Corrado eventually rose from naval designer to head of the assembly department. Remo became chief of the technical facilities office (logistics), and Viero was entrusted with heading up the ship drafting department. Even Dora worked there, while Bice started a trattoria opposite the Corelli house in Via Aurelio Saffi.[4]

1913: A Corelli in Love

In 1913 Remo asked for the hand of Natalina "Adria" Marchetti, five years his junior. She readily accepted, and they married in 1914. Their first child, Ubaldo, called Aldo or Bibi, was born the same year in their Archi district apartment in the Marchetti family's building, located in Via del Gazometro 12 (later renamed Via Mamiani 16). The Adriatic Sea was just thirty-two yards from the building's entrance, and the hill of Capodimonte rose abruptly behind it. By 1916 Aldo had been joined by a sister, Liliana. The young Corelli family lived in fairly comfortable middle-class conditions. Adria managed the household and took care of the children while Remo guided his growing family safely through World War I and the political changes that followed.[5]

1921: The Birth of Dario "Franco" Corelli

Unaware of politics and oblivious to Enrico Caruso's final days in New York (owing to his illness, he would soon leave for Naples, where he died on August

Left: Dario Franco Corelli's birth certificate. His birth was officially reported by his grandfather Augusto, whose profession as a singer is noted on the certificate. *Right*: Dario Franco Corelli as a baby, 1921. (Photos: Courtesy of Marco Corelli)

2), to the early successes of his later idol and fellow Marchegiano Beniamino Gigli, and to Puccini's beginning the composition of *Turandot*, the third child of Remo and Adria came into the world on April 8, 1921.[6] They named him Dario, but he was called Franco.[7] Dario Franco was born into a family that was doing fairly well for post–World War I Italy, when large numbers of Italians were still emigrating to northern European countries in search of work. The rise to power of Benito Mussolini, which began less than a month before Dario Franco's birth, soon brought new self-esteem to the war-shattered country. Mussolini managed to improve the economy and, on the strength of a nationalistic policy with a socialist edge, developed an effective policy against communism, which was then on the rise.

With their positions in the local shipyard, the Corelli families must have been aware of the shifting political sands, but their attention, their very lives, gravitated more toward matters musical. Corinna and Bice sang in church, while Dario Franco's uncles Corrado and Viero were both fine tenors active on the same local scale that Augusto had been before he turned professional. The uncles sang in Ancona's Croma Chorus, and Viero regularly bought scores of the latest *romanzas* in the Bucchi sisters' store in Corso Garibaldi. These pieces, opera or operetta arias or popular songs, would be rehearsed with friends who played guitar, mandolin, or violin. In a time when people didn't have radio, the troupe seized every opportunity in the evenings and during festivities to perform those pieces in the town center. More than once these excursions would end beneath the window of Viero's brother Remo, with whom he had a special bond and who would always, even if just roused from sleep, come to the window and listen to his younger brother.[8]

1923: The Death of a Tenor

In a family as involved with music as the Corellis, family gatherings never failed to recall the heroic travels of its beloved patriarch. When Augusto Corelli died of acute pneumonia on August 20, 1923, at age sixty-five, Dario Franco was only two years old, too young to be left with any personal memories of his illustrious grandfather. However, Augusto's legend lived on in the stories told by the little boy's uncles and aunts. It seems that Bibi's own passion for music was inherited more from his grandfather Augusto and his uncles Corrado and Viero than from his own father. Remo was a rather strict and serious man of the old school; he was just about the only Corelli family member who didn't sing.[9]

Dario Franco Corelli at age four, already sporting a tennis racket. (Photo: Courtesy of Marco Corelli)

❖❖❖❖❖

Dario Franco certainly had a happy infancy, spoiled by aunts and uncles from both sides of the family—the inevitable fate of the youngest. His angelic, curly-haired looks may well have contributed further to that fate. They clearly came from Adria, a beautiful woman, born into a fairly well-to-do family. Her family's economic success was largely due to their Sant' Antonio Horse Exchange, which had prospered since the 1860s and was now run by Adria's brother Vitaliano "Taglià" Marchetti and their mother, Giuseppa, whom everybody called Nonna Peppa. As for Dario Franco, he soon developed a lively, creative, and industrious personality. His protective, warm-hearted mother had a soft spot for him, to judge by what, many years later, he recalled her telling him: "Franco, your brother is a daredevil, your sister tells on others, but you, you are my friendly little frog." Alas, a mother's eye isn't always the most objective.[10]

CHAPTER 2 ❖ 1926–1939

Childhood and Teenage Years

1926: Joyriding!

Perhaps from a desire to outshine his older brother, or simply out of curiosity, one day five-year-old Dario Franco decided to try his Uncle Taglià's truck when no one was around. The result of his first shot at driving was his earliest concrete memory: "The truck was loaded with hay. I managed to put it in motion, starting a crazy joyride that ended [with me] crashing right into a store at the bottom of a hill, destroying the window and the interior of the

The Corellis around 1926. From left to right: Bibi, Remo, Dario Franco, and Liliana. (Photo: Courtesy of Marco Corelli)

shop that I rammed there."[1] While elsewhere Arturo Toscanini prepared for the posthumous world premiere of Puccini's *Turandot* with Rosa Raisa and Miguel Fleta, in 1926 there was little in the young hothead's development that pointed toward a future beyond the average provincial Italian boy's expectations. Apart from the fact that he seemed about the only one in the family except for his father who was definitely not born to sing, he was also rather slow in developing. Remo and Adria kept him home for a year longer than usual, postponing his enrollment in elementary school until he was seven.[2]

We Meet the Marchettis

Dario Franco's life at that time revolved mostly around his neighborhood friends and his mother's family, the Marchettis. They were living in an apartment right below the Corellis' on the Marchetti family property, and his oldest and best friend was his cousin Marco, the son of Vera and Taglià Marchetti. Taglià and Vera also had a daughter, Marcella, born in 1926. Marcella's earliest memories begin with two pictures of her with her brother Marco and her cousin Dario Franco, one at First Communion and one at Ancona's beach. In the photos, the young Corelli is at their side, a shy, friendly child, afraid of the camera. Pictures can be deceiving, Marcella acknowledges, noting Dario Franco's big, innocent eyes that seem to reflect nothing but cherubs and well-behaved choirboys: "He wasn't like that at all! Franco was a reckless guy! He climbed trees and didn't listen to anyone. His mother often got angry with him—that is, if she could catch him. He was very lively, and you could find him anywhere except at home!"[3]

On the beach: Marco Marchetti, Marcella Marchetti, and Dario Franco Corelli, ca. 1930. (Courtesy of Marcella Marchetti)

Rifle Range

The dilemmas that Dario Franco faced around 1931 were enormous: some adults were forcing him to go to school, when he knew without a doubt that he could be a great warrior in the Roman Empire! Or at least a great hunter! The ten-year-old hero welcomed a few days visiting his mother's sister Caterina and her husband, Attilio Morichi, because the Morichi farm in nearby Falconara was a perfect place for the boy to demonstrate once and for all that he was able to provide for himself and his family. There was plenty of game, and his uncle had a rifle. As Franco later told the story: "So, I stole my uncle's hunting rifle and went out to shoot the pigeons and the sparrows in the public gardens outside their property, right under the nose of the police." Before the police noticed him, though, he actually managed to pull the trigger. The result was disastrous: the shower of shot grazed his face, and the barrel of the rifle kicked back against his forehead, resulting in a serious cut more than two inches long going upward from his right eyebrow. "In shooting myself I injured my face quite badly [on the right side], and this is why ever since I have wanted photos of me taken from the other side."[4]

Although he was more careful thereafter, his boldness regularly forced his parents to take precautions. No spanking hurt him as much as being grounded, which prevented him from organizing late-night swimming contests or battles with the boys from "above"—the Capodimonte gang. On the hill's flanks they would frequently throw stones at each other or play "hit the soldier" or "one-two-three *palin palotta*," during which they would attack each other with sticks. Less aggressive means of amusement were their frequent visits to Santì Reginelli in the Archi district, where there was a mechanical puppet theater, with puppets that parodied local politicians or other well-known characters. But the highlight of the year was always the few days when the circus came to town. Franco would cajole his uncles into taking him, for he loved the animals, the actors' costumes, and the trapeze artists.[5]

✦✦✦✦✦

A more introverted side to Dario Franco's character manifested itself about the same time when, at age ten, his ear opened to music for the first time: "I was visiting a church in a neighboring town. It was very still and when the organ's sad voice began to resonate through the silence, I could hear such suffering trapped inside the melody I felt myself go empty inside."[6] This inclination toward religion and religious music is a little-known side of Dario Franco. He was very cautious about it and never showed it in public, but even as a boy he would light candles in church.[7]

Ubaldo "Bibi" Corelli

When Dario Franco was about twelve years old, his brother Bibi quit school in order to study singing as a baritone at the Accademia Nazionale di Santa Cecilia in Rome. Although both Bibi and Liliana had taken piano lessons, with their parents' blessing, neither Remo nor Adria was pleased with their eldest son's choice of vocation. Adria was especially unhappy, for music didn't seem a very reliable profession. In addition, Bibi soon proved susceptible to the temptations of life in the big city. According to Marcella Marchetti, "Bibi was quite a spendthrift, and every time he came back home he asked his mother for money. You know how that works with boys, especially in this case, as his father was very stingy!"[8] Later, the smallest signs of Dario Franco's developing passion for singing were quashed by his mother, who would find an excuse to silence him on every occasion. Her most famous line was: "Not so loud, not so loud, Franco! You'll wake up the neighbors!"[9]

The Athlete

Dario Franco's singing during his early teens was nothing that could be taken at all seriously; his love of music was expressed freely only in church. In later years he remembered having to accompany his parents to the Teatro delle Muse, when Aureliano Pertile was singing there in *Un Ballo in Maschera* in October 1933, as genuine torture. Even though his uncles Corrado and Viero were singing in the chorus, Dario Franco claimed he survived only when he discovered how comfortable the theater's seats were for a boy determined to catch some extra hours of sleep; if only he could do that in school as well![10]

If he showed any signs of a vocation, it wasn't singing, but sports. Dario Franco became a member of the Stamura boating club, located in the Lazzaretto right in front of the Corelli apartment in Via Mamiani. The Lazzaretto, a pentagon-shaped architectural masterpiece by Vanvitelli, was designed as a sea fortress for the defense of the Papal States. After the fortress lost its function, it eventually became a quarantine facility, hence its current name. In Dario Franco's teenage years it served yet another purpose, however, when it was used as a cigarette factory of the very type that Bizet depicts in the first act of *Carmen*.

The right side part of the Lazzaretto was reserved for SEF Stamura, the Society of Physical Education. Giampieri Lamberto, five years younger than Dario Franco but an early sports enthusiast at Stamura, was sure Dario Franco was going to be a great athlete. Singing, however, was certainly the last thing on his mind: "He may have chimed in when we were singing songs over campfires on the beach at night, but otherwise us guys came here to plunge in the sea! We went rowing, splashing, teasing girls. Dario Franco even did a little boxing and played tennis from time to time in front of the Lazzaretto, after the railroad workers had finished their shift there."[11]

Marcella Marchetti's older brother Marco often looked after her, so she spent quite a lot of time with him and with his friends, Dario Franco and Gastone Traù, on the beach: "We mostly went near the cliff, about a mile away from our block. Dario Franco was a very good swimmer and soon developed an athletic body." Just how close the Corelli and the Marchetti children were is illustrated by the bridge that their parents built from the garden in front of the house to the Corelli apartment.[12]

1932–1938: Homework, Headaches, Houses

As is so often the case with lively, athletic teenagers, Dario Franco's high school obligations fared less well than his physical development. Said Marcella Marchetti:

> When he had to do his homework, Liliana, who was very good in Latin, helped him, while his mother stayed near, a little broom placed provocatively on the table. And she would use this broom on him, whenever she saw that he was distracted, for he was a daydreamer! Franco needed a little stimulation when it came to pointing him toward the right direction. Perhaps Adria had more influence on him than his father also, because he loved her very much. Not

that he was a difficult kid, by no means: he was easily distracted but also very easygoing; I actually got along better with him than with my own brother, who was more reserved.[13]

The kind of boy Marcella Marchetti describes may well have needed a particularly watchful eye at times, and on occasion his father preferred to take him along instead of leaving him at home alone. One day Dario Franco had to accompany his father to the office of the family lawyer, Fernando Tambroni. Remo warned his son to remain quietly seated in the lawyer's waiting room, but when Remo stayed away too long, Dario Franco started sending clear messages of boredom through the closed door of Tambroni's office. He may have begun humming the lines of "Ch'ella mi creda" softly at first, but soon belted out the tune, which he had apparently picked up from one of his uncles or from their record collection. Remo was not amused and rushed over to teach the young rascal a lesson in patience. Tambroni intervened: "Remo, let the boy sing! He has a fine voice. Tell me son, do you perhaps wish to become a tenor when you are big?" Dario Franco, still bored and also a little embarrassed, answered in the way only children do: "Yes, sir, Mr. Lawyer, as soon as you become a secretary of state!"[14]

Beyond his parents' watchful eyes, Dario Franco built a little empire for himself out in the streets. He was the ringleader of the boys his age. He would decide what games they would play and who had to do what, with himself featuring prominently in the most daring acts. At age fourteen, while playing in his uncle's stables at Sant' Antonio, he ordered his "recruits" to move a haystack, in spite of his Uncle Taglià and Aunt Peppa's repeated admonishments to stop. The haystack became the center of their games, and Dario Franco installed himself at its top. He lost his balance and fell to the ground, landing hard on the side of his head. He suffered a severe concussion and lost consciousness for several minutes. Though there is no medical proof of it, the family always maintained that he later suffered from sudden mood changes as a result of the injury, especially when he felt under pressure.[15]

◆◆◆◆◆

The year 1935 brought a decisive change in the relationship between the Marchettis and the Corellis, when the main source of income for the Marchettis, the Sant' Antonio horse exchange, collapsed under the rapidly decreasing demand for horse-driven transport. To blame were both the changing times and perhaps also the general economic crises following the Wall Street crash of October 1929. Benito Mussolini, now firmly in power, had surprisingly managed to lessen the impact of that crash on Italy's economy. For the Marchettis, however, it didn't help, and in order to keep the Via Mamiani building, Remo Corelli took it upon himself to come up with the 78,000 lire they needed. He borrowed 38,000 lire from his brother Viero, another 20,000 came from selling the family trattoria, and the remaining 20,000 came from his personal savings.[16]

1936: School's Out!

Thanks to a certain Massimo Pizzi, who "happened" to be sitting next to Dario Franco when they took their final math tests and let him copy his answers, Dario Franco graduated from Francesco Podesti High in 1936. Alas, the leader of the pack in the Archi district was a slow student, with his mind still set on other things. Music was not one of them, however, in spite of the fact that he was increasingly surrounded by it now that his brother was well on his way to following in his grandfather Augusto's footsteps as a professional singer. Meanwhile Corrado, who had the more dramatic tenor voice, had long since reformed local musical life. He was a founder of the Corale Vincenzo Bellini (Vincenzo Bellini Chorus), with which the Croma Chorus, where Viero sang, eventually merged. With the best members of both choruses united in one group, the Vincenzo Bellini Chorus soon became the Marches' most prominent chorus, residing within the Teatro delle Muse and participating in its performances.[17]

Meanwhile, life in general had changed enormously over the past twenty years. Fascism became the predominant force in Europe. Adolf Hitler rose to absolute power in Germany. Mussolini backed up General Francisco Franco in Spain and used chemical weapons and mass executions to pursue his aggressive goals in Ethiopia. The full impact of Il Duce's reign became visible in Ancona when the Italian government passed anti-Semitic legislation. Because it had been one of the three cities in the Papal State where Jews were allowed to trade, Ancona had a large Jewish population, and the effects of the new laws were felt when the Jewish Anconetan shoe manufacturer of the then-famous Lola brand had to surrender his business to the Fascists.[18] All this probably loomed less large for the teenagers of the young Dario Franco's crowd than the new marvels that the arrival of radio and cinema brought to town: "There were two kinds of cinema heroes that impressed me. As a boy, the Roman warrior type of Cecil B. DeMille's *Cleopatra*—which is probably where I got my obsession for shiny armor and feathered helmets—and as a teenager, Johnny Weissmuller, the Tarzan of the '30s."[19] Weissmuller, a five-time Olympic medalist in swimming, remained Dario Franco's idol for years.

Corelli's singing activities at the time mostly fell into the dutiful category, such as joining in countless times with "Fischia il sasso," known as the "Inno del Balilla," one of the Fascist hymns that all children in schools and sports organizations had to sing before their activities could begin. Dario Franco, who, like nearly everyone else, participated in the Fascist youth movement called the Balilla, was no exception.[20] Some of these songs, like the "Giovinezza" (composed by Giuseppe Blanc to a text by Nino Oxilia in 1908–9), were written long before the Fascist movement was born. Blanc also composed "Fischia il sasso," though the exact date is not known; even if it was composed during Mussolini's rise to power, however, the choral setting and juvenile, marching rhythm of "Fischia il sasso" bears a strong resemblance to the kinds of tunes Boy Scouts might sing around the campfire. The more aggressive "stone-throwing" part of the text is linked to a legendary young hero of the Portorian revolution of 1746 named Balilla and is reminiscent of the biblical story of David and Goliath (as well as of Franco's own childhood games on Capodimonte). The central themes are virtue, friendship, pride, and respect for one's mother –virtues that Fascism, like most other cultures, indeed strongly promoted:

Fischia il sasso, il nome squilla	The stone is whizzing, the name is ringing
del ragazzo di Portoria,	of the boy from Portoria
e l'intrepido Balilla	and the courageous Balilla
sta gigante nella storia . . .	a giant in history . . .
Era bronzo quel mortaio	That bronze mortar
che nel fango sprofondò	was sinking in the mud
ma il ragazzo fu d'acciaio	but the kid, with his iron will,
e la madre liberò.	liberated his mother.
Fiero l'occhio, svelto il passo,	Proud his look, quick his step,
chiaro il grido del valore:	clear resounds the call of virtue:

ai nemici in fronte il sasso,	send a stone to the enemy,
agli amici, tutto il cor!	but give all your heart to your friends!

Giuseppe Blanc, "Inno del Balilla"

If there was a major change in Franco's life during these years, it was due to the marriage of his sister Liliana to Carlo Morichi, the grandson of Attilio and Caterina. The couple tied the knot on April 24, 1938, after which they moved to Via Imperiali in Rome, leaving Franco alone with his parents. (Bibi had married Elisa Rinaldi the year before, on April 22, 1937, but the impact on his younger brother had been minimal, for Bibi was already living in Rome. Bibi's career at the time was considered very promising. He is said to have participated in early broadcasts by EIAR, the forerunner of the present Italian Broadcast Corparation RAI, although that could only have been in concerts, for his name doesn't appear in the EIAR chronology for complete operas throughout the 1930s.)

1939: The First Call of the Muse

Franco's mother's efforts to keep him away from the various Muses were successful enough until early in 1939, when Franco met a Muse before whom even Adria had to bow: "I confess that my youth passed under a sign of recklessness. That is, except with girls. I mean the ones I liked. Sure, I was the ringleader and we used to set all the girls' hearts on fire, all but the ones I was interested in. The ones I liked all had bourgeois ideals and they categorically detested me. There was one particular girl, a redhead named Norma...."

As time passed and Norma continued to avoid his glances, Franco lost himself entirely in the shape of her back. He tried every trick in the book, even arranging to be officially praised for his efforts by the secretary of the Gioventù Italiana Littorio, the sports federation to which the water-polo team he swam for reported—all to no avail. In despair, he finally came up with one last plan: "Blushing excessively and stuttering hopelessly, I asked her for help with my Latin homework. That finally awoke her motherly, protective instincts. So, it was my systematic failure in Latin that ultimately threw her into my arms after all!"[21]

Though their relationship began with all the feverish passion of youth, Franco's affair with Norma was short-lived, and he soon returned to his usual activities near the Stamura boathouse and the seaside. There he and his friends staked their claim to a place dubbed "Beach of the Brutes," which good girls were expected to avoid. Nevertheless, the evening dances he and his friends Gastone Traù, Marco Marchetti, and Giordano Giaccaglia organized were well attended. Even Bibi, when visiting Ancona, sometimes joined them. According to the later recollections of Traù and Giordano Giaccaglia, Franco was still not one to join the others in song. On the contrary, he had lost some of his earlier wildness and begun to develop a more introverted, almost shy personality.[22]

1939: *Amor fatal*

Later in the year, with his mind all set on the sort of life that a popular bachelor of his age could enjoy, Franco suddenly noticed a group of girls, sisters on their way to college. Their school was located at a convent near the Piazza Roma, and Franco felt instantly attracted to the most beautiful of them, Iride Monina. She returned his feelings, but she came from a prominent family in Ancona, and her parents were opposed to the match. However, the Moninas didn't make Franco feel unwanted. As Iride's daughter recalls, they genuinely liked him but considered him ill suited as a candidate for marriage because he came from the Archi district—not the best part of town.[23]

Franco and Iride's relationship was based on a profound and sincere love, but it was troubled from the start by excessive jealousy. When Iride accompanied Franco to the beach in a revealing swimsuit, for example, he could explode and demand that she put on some clothes. Sex in that pre–birth control era could have permanent consequences, so Iride's grandmother vigilantly watched the couple whenever they were alone in the Moninas' house. Not that they were ever truly alone: the entire family lived there, together with a number of servants.

Ancona's climate provided plenty of occasions for the pair to be together outside either the Corelli or the Monina household. Giuliano Giaccaglia (the brother of Franco's friend Giordano Giaccaglia), although three years younger than Franco, befriended him through Marco Marchetti. Together with their circle of friends, including Giuliano's future wife and Iride, they frequently went to Falconara by tram, from which they would go by taxi or bicycle to Marina di Montemarciano. Recalled Giuliano:

Iride Monina (in a decent swimsuit) and Franco Corelli at the beach, Ancona. (Photo: Courtesy of Gemma Giacomini)

There was an isolated villa belonging to my girlfriend's parents. It had a piano and a gramophone, and we danced there till breakfast. There was a guy who played the piano, and even Franco gave his voice a try at times, but without any pretensions. His voice already had a certain ring. I remember that once, when we were playing cards and he was already out of the game, he suddenly stood up and started to sing some aria with a truly *great* voice. We asked him which bolt of lightning had struck him![24]

The Summer of 1939: On Lisping

Over the summer Franco and his friends would sometimes cool off around the fountain in the immediate vicinity of the fish market. Once, while playing on the edge of the fountain's basin, a friend slithered up from the water and knocked Franco off his feet. He fell flat against the concrete edge of the basin, hitting his mouth and breaking a number of teeth. An Anconetan dentist by the name of Tullio Moroni fixed the extensive damage to Franco's mouth. Still, the accident proved the basis for lifelong dental problems, gingivitis, and inflammations of his oral cavity; Moroni would see a lot of Franco throughout his career.[25] According to Franco's family, the accident was the cause of his problems with pronouncing the letters *s* and *z*, yielding off and on a slight lisp that ultimately became an intrinsic feature of his singing.[26]

September–December 1939: On the Eve of War

During the course of 1939, neither the marvels of the latest Johnny Weissmuller movie, *Tarzan Finds a Son*, nor his new girlfriend, Iride Monina, could distract Franco to the point of being blind to very turbulent times. In addition to Adolf Hitler's invasion of Czechoslovakia, Italy had annexed Albany just four days after Franco's eighteenth birthday. In the months that followed, more and more boys from Ancona were being drafted. The Anconetan shipyards were increasingly being converted into construction sites for Mussolini's naval fleet. When Hitler invaded Poland in September, Great Britain declared war on Germany, and most of Europe was forced to choose sides.

CHAPTER 3   ❖   1940–1945

A World in Flames

1940: Swimming Champs

During most of 1940, life went on more or less normally for the majority of Italians, with the nation seemingly in a celebratory mood over the striking early successes of Mussolini's aggressive foreign policy. On April 28, with Germany on the verge of a total war with its neighboring countries on all sides, Franco even managed to attend a regular performance of Pietro Mascagni's *L'Amico Fritz* with Augusto Ferrauto in the title role, although the greatest impact on Franco came from the evening's young baritone—Tito Gobbi.[1] If Franco is to be taken at his word that he saw only two operas during his youth, then this is the one he attended with the Monina family. Like most of the Corellis, the Moninas loved music: Iride played the piano; her mother, the violin; and the whole family loved opera. Franco must have been inspired by the public's enthusiasm, because during the curtain calls he suddenly turned to Iride and said: "One day you'll see me on that stage, because I am going to be a singer."[2]

On May 13 the young Gobbi fan received an exemption from compulsory military service, which enabled him to take his final exams at the Francesco Podesti Institute. He received his certification on May 31. When Mussolini joined the Nazis on June 10, Franco was drafted into the military reserves, with instructions to report for compulsory training on June 13. On June 11, before he had even had time to pack his bags, the letter drafting him into full military service arrived, followed immediately by one exempting him from service, probably because he had enlisted in the Polytechnical Institute of Bologna for advanced engineering studies.[3] His sports activities with a water-polo team that was preparing for the June National Youth Swimming Championships, organized by the Fascist movement, may have contributed further to his dispensation.[4]

Franco Corelli (far left) and Giuliano Giaccaglia (bottom row, second from right) on the Stamura swimming team. (Photo: Courtesy of Giuliano Giaccaglia)

Also among the Anconetan water-polo delegation was Giuliano Giaccaglia: "If you think about the war starting on June 10 and the championships being held in July, it was an odd moment. But hey, we finished in sixth place, although we didn't have swimming facilities where we could train for the competition, apart from the sea. . . . We started training barely a month before the championship. We would train mostly by ourselves, as for teams there was only the relay race. Franco was in the 100-meter freestyle, and I participated in competitive diving."[5]

Corelli left the team shortly after the July championship to begin working as a naval draftsman in his Uncle Viero's department on August 26. While there, he worked on the construction of the battleships *Pompeo Magno*, *Mitragliere*, and *Bombardiere*. Italy meanwhile reveled in Mussolini's victories over British Somaliland. The nation fully supported the war until November, when the Italian fleet was destroyed overnight at Taranto and the Greeks defeated Italy's 9th Army as if it had never existed. With the war taking a turn for the worse, promising young "engineers" like Franco Corelli were no longer safe from the draft.

1941: Under Arms

Franco's contribution to Italy's battleships should not be overestimated. His employment at the shipyard ended on February 26, 1941, when the army draft caught up with him. With the war taking an increasingly bad turn for Italy, there was little time to prepare, and so he found himself on the platforms of Ancona's railway station at 2:00 A.M. on the 27th. His friends Alessandro Grati, Guido Berti, and Giordano Giaccaglia were there as well, bound for the same train to the 133rd Artillery Regiment in Mantua. Thanks to their studies, they were destined to become officers, although that sort of detail didn't faze them at the time. Recalled Gratti: "We weren't nervous at all. War? We had no clue as to what it meant. We never talked about politics. The four of us left together from the railway station in an atmosphere of gaiety and happiness. We felt like genuine heroes! Just look at the photographs! We started as corporals and, after three months, we would be promoted to sergeants!"[6]

The new soldiers' routine was predictable. In the morning there were exercises, and by 5:00 P.M. they were off duty. After checkout they could stay out until 9:00 or 9:30 P.M. However, the corporal who had to supervise the recruits deferred to them, because as officer trainees they were destined to surpass him in rank. That allowed the recruits more freedom than they otherwise would have enjoyed. Nevertheless, in the evenings, after they returned to their barracks, silence reigned. Grati confirmed Franco's own testimony regarding the awakening of his musical awareness around this time:[7]

> In such moments of silence it could happen that Corelli would say: "Sandro, let's do a little song. . . ." "You start," I would answer. But he would never give in easily, saying, "But Sandro, I need your help! Do you know *Cavalleria Rusticana*?" I did, and from one thing came another, with Franco saying, "Sandro, caro, then you sing the part of the mother and I will do Turiddu. . . ." Well, I knew that "part," as Mama Lucia has hardly four words to sing! "*Avanti*," he would say, and we would start.

The other men were so bored in the evenings that singing became a regular distraction, with Franco inviting them to sing.

Mantua, 1941: Recruits Grati and Corelli proudly posing with the "company car." (Courtesy of Alessandro Grati)

And he would sing it again, "Mamma, quel vino e' generoso. . . ." Imagine his drill! He kept his hand near mine, and when my cue was due, he touched me so I could finish. I still remember the lines: "Perché parli così?" And the others would applaud us until he sang that aria again and again. Sure, he was untrained, but I remember that we already speculated about his voice, although he didn't think anything of it himself. For Franco it was just a way to kill time. But the voice that we heard in Mantua definitely had a ring to it, something that was already a little bit the Corelli voice.[8]

On March 16, around 2:00 A.M., Grati was awakened by sounds coming from the bed next to him. In spite of the darkness, he could see Franco coughing. His hands, face, and pillow were smeared with blood. Grati rushed to his duet partner's aid, bringing towels to stop the bleeding. Supported by their alarmed friends Berti and Monina (a relative of Iride's), Grati demanded that his friend be taken to the first-aid station. On March 21 Franco was sent to a military hospital in Verona for further examination. He returned to his regiment, but after he fell ill again on the 25th, he was once more sent to Verona on the 27th, from which he emerged with his army discharge, for reasons described in his military files as a "preventive health measure."[9]

While Grati and his friends were sent off to different regiments in Italy, Franco returned to the arms of his beloved Iride, whose family had meanwhile evacuated to Aspio, between Camerano and Osimo Station, because the Anconetan port was becoming a target for Allied bombings. In order to keep himself occupied, Franco started a small business repairing bicycles and copying technical drawings, because there weren't any print shops left operating in town. Overall, this was a tranquil period for him, with few worries and a healthy outdoor life. Also, because his livelihood required him to do quite a lot of bicycling, he was soon in better physical condition than ever.[10]

Mantua, 1941: Grati, Monina, Berti, and Franco in their Italian Army uniforms, complete with machine guns, swinging loosely around their shoulders, looking like film-noir antiheroes. (Photo: Courtesy of Alessandro Grati)

1942: *Ossessione*

The attack on Pearl Harbor brought the United States into the war, although in 1942 this had little impact on daily life in Italy except for a decline in the national economy. As men with substantial positions in the military shipyard, the Corellis weren't doing too badly. Still unmarried, Viero lived in the large ten-room building with his mother, Leonilde Sbarbati, where Franco sometimes used to invite friends (his uncle gladly left him the keys) when he needed an occasional place to party. Meanwhile, radio had conquered the world, and Franco increasingly indulged himself in the many operatic programs that were broadcast at the time:

> In Ancona there was this obsession with the bel canto, the choral societies were flourishing, just like today, and there would be fervent discussions on

the last performance of [Beniamino] Gigli or [Giacomo] Lauri-Volpi that we heard on the radio. These were discussions between informed people who knew all about volume, emission, diaphragm, high notes with head resonance or breath support. Due to my usual pride, to my desire to stand out at any time and on any occasion, I eventually started to sing myself, competing with friends or serenading the girls, based on "Vivere, Mamma" and "Torna piccina mia." I was singing like a dog, rough, disagreeable, and the only thing I liked was making long, monotonous, and irritating high notes. In this way I found my destiny, although I wasn't aware of it at the time.[11]

Naturally, the career Franco's brother Bibi was making for himself in Rome and the adventures he told his friends back home about were influential as well. Though a married man, Bibi enjoyed a certain reputation with the women. When opera performances decreased rapidly owing to the war, he had turned to participating in traveling cabarets performing revues with the likes of Carlo Campanini, Walter Chiari, and Nuto Navarrini. Bibi found he could make up to 5,000 lire an evening, at a time when the song "If I Could Make 1,000 Lire a Month" was a hit.[12]

Because Bibi had some contacts with Cinecittà, it has been suggested that he may even have been the one to point Luchino Visconti toward Ancona as the location for his first film, *Ossessione*. Based on the James M. Cain novel *The Postman Always Rings Twice*, the movie was immediately condemned as morally inappropriate, and the Fascists destroyed the negatives. Visconti managed to save a copy, though, and the scenes shot in Ancona's harbor area represent the only filmed glimpses of the actual environment Franco Corelli was living in at that time. Indeed, he may have been in the area during the filming; Ancona's young people would have wanted to be around for something as extraordinary as the making of a movie in their own hometown.

Franco continued his excursions with Iride and other couples, occasionally picnicking near Loreto or heading off toward Pesaro in the north or the splendid Mount Conero to the south. Iride later remembered it as a strange world, with the war on one side and the gaiety and innocence of youth on the other: "Threatening bombings on one day, roasted pork and Chianti wine on the next in our house, whenever my uncle Walter, who was of a more lighthearted, libertine nature, threw one of his renowned banquets."[13] Meanwhile, Franco kept selling bicycles to support himself, for he didn't want to be a burden on his family.

1943: Air Raids on Ancona and Evacuation

The year 1943 was a turning point in the war for Italy, and Ancona suffered as well. Operatic performances in the Teatro delle Muse came to a halt on May 27 because of the increasing numbers of Allied air raids on Ancona, which also led to the evacuation of the population. Remo's family was evacuated to Aspio, near where Iride's family had been relocated. The first major attack on Ancona followed in the wake of the curious political situation that had General Dwight Eisenhower revealing that a truce had been agreed upon with the Italians on September 8, which led the Nazis to occupy the whole north of Italy, stopping at a defensive line above Naples. The Nazis liberated Mussolini, who proclaimed a Fascist republic in the German-occupied territory (the king and his government had fled to the unoccupied south). Healthy young men such as Franco Corelli could be seized by the occupying Nazis at any moment. They preemptively detained many Italian soldiers, among them Carlo Bergonzi and Giuseppe Taddei. Giuseppe Di Stefano fled to Switzerland in order to escape; Mario Del Monaco was allowed to continue his career in Fascist Italy.[14] However, either Corelli's membership in the Italian Sportsmen's Union or the documents that proved his exemption from the army kept him out of harm's way, and he is said to have made himself useful in the Monina household: he protected the women from the increasingly aggressive German soldiers when the Monina men who had not been drafted were away at work. (The Moninas' business was cattle trading and slaughterhouses, so they fared well in spite of the war.)[15]

❖❖❖❖❖

On October 10 the Allied forces carried out their first major air raid on Ancona, followed by a second one on the 13th, which left the city in ruins. Miraculously, the cathedral and the Teatro delle Muse remained standing, although one misguided bomb pierced the roof of the Muse, exploding onstage and ruining the theater's entire interior. After those three days of bombing, Alessandro Grati, who had returned to Ancona after the Italian army was dissolved in April, ceased to feel like a hero: "We only understood the true meaning of the war when the first bombardments of Ancona started."[16]

1944: Evacuated

The Allies landed south of Rome in January 1944. From then on the Germans were fighting a losing battle. By that summer people were allowed to return to their houses, or what remained of them. Ancona had suffered severely, the harbor area almost completely shattered. Though the historical Lazzaretto had largely survived, the Corellis' home in Via Mamiani hadn't, and the family—Remo, Adria, and Franco—were forced to remain in their temporary lodgings. There were shortages of everything, in Ancona as well as elsewhere in Italy and all across Europe, and the city immediately became the center of an infamous smuggling route, which brought lots of contraband into town. The smugglers showed off their fast money in a flashy lifestyle. Some even owned Studebakers, the first American cars ever to be seen in Ancona, which made quite an impression at the time.[17]

1945: A Working-Class Hero

The end of the war brought unforeseen opportunities for the law-abiding as well, most notably for the *geometra* (one who measures houses, streets, etc.) Franco Corelli. Large parts of the city had to be rebuilt from scratch, and on February 24, 1945, Franco joined the ranks of the city administration (with help from Iride's grandfather Gino). The town hall was destroyed in a bombing raid, so the city's offices were relocated in the gym of the Carlo Faiani Elementary School. Franco's job was to visit the damaged buildings all over town and take inventory of the destruction.[18] All in all it proved to be a very untroubled episode in his life. He had an excellent group of colleagues in his fellow *geometri* Fausto Lanternari and Ivo Rotelli and the engineer Alberto Podesti (the great-grandson of the renowned painter Francesco Podesti), who was in charge of the department. It was a job that gave Franco great personal satisfaction: he felt useful and saw the results of his work whenever he walked back along a road that he had assessed and reported on. A Corelli trait that would serve him well all his life revealed itself in these days when Franco proved to be a wise manager of his hard-earned money. Following his father's example, he saved as much as he could.

The beginning of 1945 brought a few other changes as well. In January Remo's mother died. The family subsequently moved to a large house in Via Fazioli 1, where they lived together with Viero Corelli, who had just married Rachele Gambardella.

July 18, 1945: "Ch'ella mi creda libero e lontano"

Meanwhile the reminders of the war in Europe were being eliminated rapidly, beginning with Mussolini's execution on April 28, followed by Hitler's suicide two days later. While the war continued in the Pacific, Ancona already began to celebrate its liberation. By chance, that celebration would liberate something in Franco Corelli that had been trying to get out since the days when he spontaneously burst into song among his fellow soldiers in Mantua: his love for singing. On July 18, liberation day, the Muse came to him by an unidentified messenger:

> In '45, when the Americans came, with all their clichéd thinking about the singing Italy, there was a custom of throwing parties in all the city neighborhoods. And one evening, when the program in ours was a little thin, someone sent a small boy for me: "Franco," he started yelling at my window, "Come sing 'Ch'ella mi creda.'" This was the only aria I knew well. I went, I sang, and I triumphed. It was my first public concert, and the applause went to my head. In this way I became infected with the mania of singing.[19]

Ch'ella mi creda libero e lontano,	May she believe me roaming free and far away
sopra una nuova via di redenzione!...	on a new path of redemption!...
Aspetterà ch'io torni...	She will wait for me to come back...
E passeranno i giorni,	Days will pass,
ed io non tornerò...	and I won't come...
Minnie, della mia vita unico fiore,	Minnie, the one and only beauty in my life,
Minnie, che m'hai voluto tanto bene!	Minnie, my one and only love!

Giacomo Puccini, *La Fanciulla del West*

❖❖❖❖❖

The end of the war finally arrived with the dropping of two atomic bombs in Japan in early August 1945. For anyone charged with rebuilding a war-ravaged city, as Corelli, Lanternari, Rotelli, and Podesti were, the effect the bombs had on Japan must have been shocking, although Franco had problems of his own closer to home to resolve. His brother's career having rapidly deteriorated during the war years owing to Bibi's rather careless lifestyle, Franco's parents were now firmly opposed to their youngest son's sudden desire to study singing: "They wanted me to continue my accursed studies in engineering. As my father was practically born in the shipyard, he just wanted me to follow in his footsteps."[20]

Iride's reminiscences serve to demonstrate how strongly the Muse had affected Franco by 1945: he asked her to run away from Ancona with him so he could pursue his operatic ambitions. But Iride, a conventional, well-brought-up girl with her mind set on raising a family within the secure boundaries of the kind of life she was used to, refused.[21] For the time being, Franco had no choice but to comply with her wishes and those of his parents. Yet, from this moment on, reports of him singing rapidly increase. According to his boss, Alberto Podesti, he would readily join them in the evenings, when Martini played the violin, Biagi the bass, and Franco sang Neapolitan songs.

But when it came to his employee's professional singing ambitions, Podesti was crystal clear: "It was not the right time for such distractions."[22]

❖❖❖❖❖

The war brought about my discovery of the singer Corelli. Circumstance made me move to a house in his vicinity. It was then and there that we met in the house of a pianist.
    Carlo Federico Scaravelli, "Private Recollections"

Franco actually knew Carlo Scaravelli from school; both had completed the *geometra* course in the Francesco Podesti Institute. Carlo was two years his senior, so the two had had little contact at the time. By 1946, however, they were effectively colleagues, although Franco's job was with city hall whereas Carlo worked for the provincial government.[23] One day that year, Franco left his house and passed by the window of the Cionci sisters' home. One sister was a pianist and the other a violinist; both gave music lessons. Carlo Scaravelli recalls: "Franco heard singing coming from the pianist's house, and because he knew her, he dropped in while I happened to be there. That was our first meeting, during which I asked him if his voice was as good as the voices of his family. He answered that his voice was so ugly, that his family asked him to shut up whenever he opened his mouth to the point where they actually scolded him at times." Scaravelli had heard that story before and nevertheless insisted that Bibi's brother sing something. Franco relented and sang "Celeste Aida" for Scaravelli and the Cionci sisters. Said Scaravelli: "I was not yet properly trained myself, but I immediately realized that his was a big, powerful, and most accurate instrument—a voice that had a theatrical dimension in it, a genuine personality that destined him for a career as a singer."[24]

Franco and Scaravelli soon struck up a friendship, and for a while Franco evaded his parents' opposition to singing by taking some harmless private lessons on a semi-amateur level with the Cionci sisters in his spare time. In spite of having a good number of unusual top notes, he was still uncertain about his true voice and gravitated toward the baritone register.[25]

CHAPTER 4 ❖ 1946–1949

The Call of the Muse

Early 1946: A Love Compromised

Along with Franco's awakening interest in singing, some familiar features of his character at the height of his celebrity were now beginning to materialize: as he matured and the years passed, the number of his close friends diminished. Alessandro Grati describes this process as a normal one for all of them: "After the war we all went our separate ways, as happens in general between childhood friends. They get jobs, obligations, they marry and have children." This was exactly what was expected to happen between Franco and Iride. They had been seeing each other for several years now, and the logical next step was to marry.[1]

Ultimately, though, their jealous natures proved incompatible. In addition, the couple's mothers didn't get along. Iride's mother, Maria, was ambivalent. Whereas the difference between the families' social standing had over time ceased to matter, she now worried about what the relationship was doing to her daughter's emotional state: the fights between the two lovers were way beyond what could be considered normal. Iride's daughter Gemma recalls:

> My mother told me about an episode that concerned a brothel, then called a "house of tolerance," in the Via della Loggia. At times you could see these women going in or out of the house, and naturally the men would look at them in passing. Anyone would understand, but my mother was so madly in love with Franco that it actually hurt if he even glanced at another woman on the street. And vice versa! Really, there weren't many true perfumes or makeup products then, but if he smelled even a hint of scented soap on her, he had a fit, because that was bound to attract other men! It was a love worthy of a movie, a passion that burned too brightly to last for a long time.[2]

One day in the first months of 1946, Franco suddenly decided he had had his fill. Tired of the whole situation, he proposed a separation. The devastated Iride ran to her mother, who—surprisingly—supported her, accusing Franco of adultery. She rushed to the Corelli home, demanding an explanation from Viero's then extremely pregnant wife, Rachele, who happened to answer the door and who protected Franco as he ducked down the hallway behind her, trying to avoid getting involved in the confrontation.[3] Maria demanded nothing less than a marriage, on the grounds that Franco had compromised her daughter.[4]

◆◆◆◆◆

After Iride, Franco kept away from serious relationships as long as he lived in Ancona. He had caused enough problems as it was, and furthermore, he feared his strict father. On top of that, there was local public opinion to be reckoned with, as well as the remarks of the angry Moninas, whom he would run into from time to time. Romolo Ricci, one of Franco's acquaintances, recalled how Iride's mother confronted Corelli once on the street, beating him with her umbrella and scolding him for "talking to another girl"—a full year after her daughter and Franco had broken up.[5]

April–June 1946: The Beginning of a New Age

Upsetting as the breakup between Franco and Iride may have been, this period after the war was first and foremost a period of renewal. With the families of Remo and Viero now living together, the dawn of a new age was symbolized by the arrival of another Corelli: Marco. The first child of Viero and Rachele was born on April 16, exactly eight days after Franco's birthday. Said Marco: "That provided food for jokes, because eight is said to be the fool's number in Italy, which left me twice as crazy as he was." Because the families were living in such close proximity, Franco was aware of all the details surrounding the child's birth, and they made a strong impression on him, not least because Rachele's pregnancy was so difficult.[6]

◆◆◆◆◆

For Italy, the new age arrived when the nationwide protest against King Vittorio Emanuele III of Savoy, considered a collaborator during the war, resulted in a referendum over whether Italy should remain a kingdom. In a final attempt to save the crown, Vittorio Emanuele III abdicated in favor of Umberto II. On June 2, 12,700,000 Italians voted to create an Italian republic, defeating the 10,700,00 who voted to retain their monarchy. Following the loss, Umberto and his family went to live in exile.[7]

November 1946: Baritenor at the Rossini Conservatory of Pesaro

None of those who shared their childhood memories with me had any recollection of Franco studying at the conservatory in Pesaro. Corelli himself always denied having attended regular classes. Yet the mysterious entry in Antonio Brancati's heavy volume on the Pesaro Conservatory, where Franco is listed as having entered as a student in 1946, was confirmed by the conservatory's archives.[8] Franco, yielding to his friend Carlo Scaravelli's relentless pleas to join him at the conservatory, formally requested admission in a letter dated September 28, 1946.[9] The request was granted, and in November the two friends entered the class of a Pesaro native, the prominent tenor Umberto Macnez. Macnez had just begun his first and only year as a teacher in Pesaro.

Corelli did not enroll as a tenor, however. Weighing his options, he decided to follow in the footsteps of his brother and Scaravelli and submitted himself as a baritone. That mistake was corrected at an early audition by the conservatory's Maestro Fradelloni, who pointed out to Franco that he was really a tenor. This classification was more consistent with the spontaneous, instinctive singing he had done among friends, in the military, and before small groups in earlier years.

Not that it mattered much, because Franco's conservatory experience ended almost as soon as it had begun; he was expelled from Macnez's class because he attended too few sessions.[10] That outcome was fairly predictable, for he still was working full time. His enrollment was more a case of following Scaravelli's urging and his own vague desires than actually realizing what it would take to succeed at a conservatory and committing himself to it. The urge to sing was genuine, though, and, once more persuaded by Scaravelli, he shifted from the conservatory to Rinalda Pavoni for further vocal training. His later claim of never having attended formal lessons should be seen in light of the fact that he went to Pavoni as a private student in her home in Ancona. Location seems to have been the main reason he chose her as his teacher: it was the only way to combine his musical studies with his job in the city. Any remaining confusion over Corelli's formal training primarily concerns the duration of his studies with Pavoni, which he sometimes mentioned as having lasted eight months,[11] sometimes three months.[12] Scaravelli suggests the shorter period is accurate and confirms the well-known result of Franco's studies with Pavoni, whose teachings of "mask placement" didn't work for him.[13]

Corelli maintained throughout that this failure was not necessarily Pavoni's fault. He felt the technique she taught was valid, but he had failed to place the upper notes higher in the mask while continuing to sustain them in the diaphragm, as the technique required. His mistake was trying to reach the upper notes by placing his larynx ever higher, in order to build each high note on top of the previous one. The inevitable result was a loss of breath support, and in order to reach those notes without loss of volume, he started "squeezing his throat in order to push the note out." This ultimately affected his vocal cords to the point where he lost his upper range.[14]

In an effort to make the best of the situation, he stopped singing for about two months. Taking a practical approach to the problem, he then decided that

On holiday: Franco Corelli, Liliana Corelli, and Marcella Marchetti, Bressanone, July–August 1948. An interesting glimpse of Franco's leisure time is given to us by Marcella Marchetti, who joined Franco and Liliana on a summer trip to Corinna Corelli's country house in Bressanone: "We went there for holiday only that one time. Franco liked walking, and during that holiday he often went for long walks, or we would play games—there is a picture with us playing ping-pong. But things were no longer the same after we were separated through the bombs. Everyone went in different directions, and Franco became increasingly focused on his singing aspirations. He became more serious as a person, making fewer jokes." The last observation may have had something to do with his mother's illness. She had been diagnosed earlier in the year with breast cancer and had undergone a mastectomy, which only temporarily slowed the development of the disease. It soon became apparent that the cancer had already progressed beyond the point of treatment, and Adria never recovered.[18] (Courtesy of Marcella Marchetti)

his best option was to move down to the baritone register again, where he didn't need his upper range. That "rest" proved to be a fine medicine for his throat. After some time, the high notes mysteriously returned.[15]

1947: Alone Within the Muse

The year 1947 brought Franco a most fortunate misfortune when, in spite of the enormous amount of reconstruction work left to do in town, he was fired from his job. The official grounds given were a disagreement on wages and conditions, but according to his boss, Podesti, the truth was a little different. Franco originally had obtained the job through the help of Iride's grandfather. When Iride finally gave up hope of a reconciliation with Corelli, she began seeing another man and became engaged. Her new fiancé worked in the building opposite Franco's, and the two men could actually stare at each other as they worked at their desks. To resolve that irritation, Iride's grandfather decided to pull the same strings he'd used to secure Franco's job to force Franco out of that job.[16] With time on his hands, Corelli walked past the Teatro delle Muse one day and discovered a hole in the wall that led to the interior of the building. Claudia Gentile described in *Il Messaggero* what happened next:

> The curtain was still there, as were the seats and the walls of velvet and gold. A ray of light fell through an opening in the roof, and in the silence that ruled the tormented building, the young voice of Franco Corelli filled the auditorium, greeted by the fluttering wings of the surprised doves. He sang alone, testing a voice already powerful and special. He proceeded to sing in the room that had been occupied by the Bellini Chorus, right above the arcade on the Piazza del Papa. From its windows the Muses could be seen.[17]

1949: In the Bars and the Cafés

Every moment there was a discussion about voice, about the style of the singing, about "portamento," especially about the technique of the voice.
    Franco Corelli on Ancona, "Opera Fanatic" broadcast, February 3, 1990

Franco and Carlo Scaravelli began frequenting the Bellini and the Croma choruses, although Franco never became a member for the usual family reasons (Adria disapproved). However, by now he was actively participating in the heated discussions on singers in the local cafés, where he became known as "Il Bello del Garelli"—Mr. Handsome from Garelli (the most popular café in town).[19] At times they would also drink coffee under the porticos of Piazza Cavour at the Caffè Roulette (today called Caffè Rico), where they were joined by the poet Mario Panzini, Davide Barbone, the baritone Rolando Giacchetti, the tenor Lucio Borgnognoni, or even Bibi, whenever he came to town.[20] Apart from singing or discussing singing, these fine young men enjoyed an occasional practical joke. Recalls Carlo's son Alessandro Scaravelli: "Barbone was very short, Corelli extremely tall, but nevertheless they borrowed each other's clothes and went walking along the streets; imagine Barbone in Corelli's long sleeves, with the crotch of his pants hanging down to his knees!"[21]

From there Corelli would return home, stopping by Giordano's *pasticceria* to buy some caramels for young Marco, to whom he tried to teach the Children's Chorus from Bizet's *Carmen*.[22] Once Marco was sound asleep, Franco might even go out again for an evening stroll that could wind up with the four friends vocalizing in the entrance halls of buildings, where they could listen to their own voices echoing from the walls.[23] Alessandro Scaravelli maintains that they were never scolded: people realized that they weren't trying to disturb anyone but rather were practicing, in much the same way young people practice soccer on the streets today.[24] However, at age twenty-eight or older, neither Franco nor his friends were still regarded as boys; time was starting to press.

February 1949: An Unexpected Competition

Franco Corelli followed a comfortable routine in the early weeks of 1949, commuting to his studies in Bologna, then returning home and meeting up with his friends Giacchetti, Scaravelli, and Barbone. They would gather in each other's homes to sing or go to Caffè Roulette or Garelli and discuss singing. Was Caruso better than Pertile, Lauri-Volpi, or Gigli? How did they achieve those high notes? Where was opera going? Where were they going?

Well, they were going to Florence! Because one day, right there in front of them, the newspaper was open to a page that invited them to enroll in Florence's Maggio Musicale voice competition. Scaravelli, Barbone, and Giacchetti jumped at the opportunity, while Franco merely welcomed the thought of venturing into unknown territory. He waved off any thought of competing because he felt insufficiently trained. He changed his mind only because his friends made participation part of a bet: the one who went the furthest had to treat the others to their usual fare in the café for a full five days. Winning by losing! That was a temptation Franco could not resist. When the day of competition arrived, he rented a car and drove Scaravelli and Barbone to Florence,[25] leaving behind Giacchetti, who at the last minute was unable to make it.

Upon arrival, and on his way to win the bet, Franco readily succumbed to Florence's temptations: "I almost missed the audition chasing a girl! When I finally arrived at the Teatro Communale, I was all sweaty and had no scores. When the examiners asked me what I intended to sing, with the boldness of one who had nothing to lose I replied, 'Se quel guerrier io fossi!'"[26] The opening lines of the recitative to Verdi's "Celeste Aida" fit the occasion to perfection: "Se quel guerrier io fossi / se il mio sogno si avverasse" (If I were to be the soldier chosen, if my dream were to be fulfilled).

Scaravelli and Barbone were immediately sent home,[27] but the jury was divided when it came to Franco. One juror, Francesco Siciliani, a composer and the general manager of the Teatro Communale and the Maggio Musicale, referred to the timbre of his *mezza voce* and a certain ring in the B-flat. While his friends were already ordering drinks in Franco's name at the nearest bar, their tenor friend was invited to sing a little more. Unprepared as he was, he chose a lightweight piece made very popular by Gino Bechi's hit version, "La strada nel bosco":

Le prime stelle in cielo brillano già	Stars are shining up in the sky
Tra i biancospini il vento mormora e va	Among the hawthorn trees wind is murmuring
Sembra un'incanto il bosco sotto la luna	Under the moon the wood looks enchanted
Favole appassionate narra per te	It's telling you tales of passion
Vieni c'è una strada nel bosco	Come, there is a path through the wood
Il suo nome conosco	I know its name
Vuoi conoscerlo tu?	Do you want to know it too?

Cesare Andrea Bixio, "La strada nel bosco"

With that, Franco passed through to yet another round, actually reaching the finals. Barbone and Scaravelli were not there to witness it, and because the Maggio Musicale no longer has any records of the auditions, Franco has the last word regarding what came next. He recalled singing "Giunto sul passo estremo" from Boito's *Mefistofele*:

Giunto sul passo estremo	Come across the very last step
Della più estrema, età,	Of the very last age,
In un sogno supremo	In a superb dream
Sì bea l'anima già	I feel my soul rejoicing

Arrigo Boito, *Mefistofele*

He chose the piece in part because he was very comfortable with the aria's highest note, the A-flat. On this occasion, though, his attempt to play it safe backfired: "I sang with a big, shrill, shouting voice."[28]

After the competition Franco returned to his engineering studies in Bologna, sure all was lost and thinking of ways to pay for his friends' drinks. He was unprepared for what happened next. A visitor knocked on the door of his Bolognese lodging: "It was Maestro Ildebrando Pizzetti, the president of the Florence jury! He asked me to come to his hotel for another audition!" As it turned out, Siciliani had been so convinced of Franco's talents that he had persuaded Pizzetti to give the tenor another chance, outside of the competition. Pizzetti had no problem convincing the commission to award Corelli a special study allowance for a three-month course in Florence. He recommended that Franco work with Maestro Gentile there.[29]

1949: The Student "Teacher"

Franco, you with this enormous voice! With those high notes and the family tradition! You have everything! And you don't want to sing?
    Carlo Scaravelli, as related by Alessandro Scaravelli, interview, Ancona, June 11, 2004

While Franco resumed his studies at the Polytechnical Institute in Bologna, Carlo Scaravelli continued his musical studies. He kept pushing his friend to work on his voice, yet Franco hesitated. Taking regular classes meant giving up his studies, which, given his so-far discouraging results, seemed a big risk to both him and his parents. What ultimately won him over was the former Pesaro Conservatory student Mario Del Monaco, whose fame had been rising swiftly since his debuts at La Scala in 1944 and at Covent Garden and the Arena di Verona in 1946. His victories culminated in a sensational La Scala *Andrea Chénier* premiere on March 6, 1949, which further boosted the already considerable local fame of Del Monaco's teacher, Arturo Melocchi. Coincidentally, at the time Scaravelli was studying with Melocchi, with stunning results. Del Monaco's example and Scaravelli's progress eventually persuaded Franco to at least speak with Melocchi.[30]

The testimonials about Melocchi, as a man and as a teacher, passed along directly by his pupils and preserved for posterity in the letters he sent to their parents, either border on religious devotion or depict him as a throat wrecker.[31] The few photos that survive of him (as well as a fascinating recorded lesson he gave the tenor Gastone Limarilli) show him as a serious, fragile man with considerable charisma; Franco was impressed enough when he met with Melocchi in person to pursue some instruction. The only problem was that he couldn't simply quit his studies, nor could he ignore his family's wishes. And so Scaravelli and Corelli developed a plan of attack: when Carlo returned from Melocchi's lessons in Pesaro, Franco would wait for him at the Ancona railway station. They would then go to the war-ravaged ruin that had been the Corelli house in Via Mamiani, which was still uninhabited. There they could practice without disturbing anyone. On the way, Carlo would explain the new lessons, and once they arrived Franco would try to put them into practice. This went on for all of 1949, meaning that Scaravelli ultimately became Franco Corelli's actual vocal teacher.[32]

Interestingly, Franco's main interest in studying singing was based on the simple fact that he didn't understand his own voice; at least, he wasn't able to bend it completely to his will, which fascinated him.[33] He was well aware of his vocal potential, particularly with respect to volume and vocal coloring, but he felt that above A-flat he sounded like a screaming cat. Melocchi's technique of lowering the larynx provided a possible remedy. It aimed at giving the breath ample passage through an open throat, allowing for maximum breath support. When singing within the larynx, the voice receives the greatest amplification from the large resonance chambers in the upper chest and lower jaw.

This enhances the volume. Unfortunately, it also demands vocal cords of steel, as numerous singers who lost their voices trying to sing this way discovered. Fortunately, thanks to his genes and his athletic training, Franco had the precise physical characteristics to make the technique work for him. Still, when Scaravelli predicted that he would become one of the best singers in the world, Franco responded, "Shut up!"[34]

Nevertheless, on September 9, 1949, Franco wrote a letter to Siciliani in which he expressed his hope of starting his studies in Florence in October of that year.[35] Ultimately, however, he did not. In a letter dated December 23, 1949, he mentions to Siciliani that, referring to their previous telephone conversations, he thinks it best to try his luck in Rome. This sudden change of plan, he writes, was made on economic grounds—perhaps because of the presence there of his brother and his Aunt Dora, who provided him with free housing and various other kinds of help.[36]

CHAPTER 5 ❖ 1950

Choosing Music

April 15, 1950: The Franco and Bibi Corelli Recordings

Corelli's desire to start his musical studies in Rome indicates that he first entered the Spoleto voice competition sometime between December 1949 and January 1950.[1] Judging from his earlier plan to start his studies in Florence by October 1949, it seems that he was very close to abandoning his studies at the Polytechnical Institute in Bologna.

The only obstacle in his way was his mother's veto. A complicating factor was that Bibi was in the middle of the process of leaving his wife, Elisa, which made the profession of a singer seem less honorable than ever. Over the past thirteen years, Elisa had had a hard time accepting Bibi's frequent absences during his traveling engagements, and that finally brought about a permanent separation (not a formal divorce, which was impossible to obtain in Italy then).[2] But when Adria—persuaded by Remo, who in turn had been persuaded by Liliana, who had believed in Franco's vocal dreams from the start—at last gave Franco her consent, he could devote himself to his true vocation.

Liliana also seems to have been especially instrumental in the process of dealing with Franco's already omnipresent nerves. It is said that when her younger brother failed to fill out the forms for the first Spoleto voice contest, she took matters in her own hands, completing and sending in the application in his name. Said Franco: "When I received the acceptance letter, she almost forced me onto the train to compete. I sang 'Il fior che avevi a me tu dato' from *Carmen* and the first tenor aria from *Il Trovatore*."[3] Elsewhere he remarked, "The result was even worse than in Florence: I was immediately rejected. That was it; the idea of becoming a tenor became an obsession."[4]

> April 15, 1950
> Milan (private recordings, S.T.E.A. Vox, 78 rpm)
> Disc 1: Giordano: *Fedora* "Amor ti vieta." Puccini: *Madama Butterfly* "Addio, fiorito asil"
> Disc 2: Giordano: *Andrea Chénier* "Un dì all'azzurro spazio," "Sì! fui soldato!" Ponchielli: *La Gioconda* "Enzo Grimaldo, principe di Santafior" (with Ubaldo Corelli)
> Disc 3: Puccini: *Tosca* "Recondita armonia" [matrix destroyed]

One of the things that got the better of Franco on the day of that competition was the knowledge that his idol Beniamino Gigli was on the jury. Franco was paralyzed with fear, although Gigli himself had no doubts about the young singer's potential. The great tenor, universally acclaimed as Caruso's true heir, assured Franco that there would be a future for him as a singer if he studied seriously: "Why are you wasting time on studying something that many people can do, when you could make a fortune with your true talent!"[5]

Siciliani proved equally encouraging and welcomed the prodigal son back after Franco wrote him a letter, dated January 28, 1950, in which he detailed his misfortunes in having lost the Spoleto voice contest, the prize for which was to study in Rome.[6]

February–May 1950: Florence, Centro di Avviamento al Teatro Lirico

By February 1950 Franco therefore began to fight for his chance in Florence. And with good prospects, for the responsibility that Siciliani and Pizzetti had bestowed upon him was more than honored by the very eager student.[7] Just how seriously Franco took his vocal studies is shown by the five surviving arias that he recorded in Milan on April 15, 1950. His partner and accompanist was none other than his brother Bibi, who watched over Franco to make sure that he didn't make the same mistakes Bibi himself had made. In his good years Bibi had had a fine dark baritone voice with a tenorial ring in the high notes. But owing to his lack of discipline, his voice abandoned him very early. The first documentary evidence of his voice that has surfaced to date is the recording of the Act I duet from *La Gioconda* with Franco. Although only thirty-six, Bibi was clearly already past his vocal prime and cannot be evaluated fairly on the basis of this recording.

The session recordings reveal two very interesting things about the immature Franco Corelli voice. The first is that he was right when he maintained that he was born with a voice that was very unstable at the top, where it sometimes took on a quality that indeed approached shouting. The second is that there are certain vocal characteristics that clearly announce the later Franco Corelli, including the ring, the intrinsic metallic, dark-copper color of the middle voice, and the presence of a solid foundation upon which a major voice could be built. But apart from those characteristics, these rediscovered recordings, which miraculously survived time and destruction while in the care of Corelli's friend Mario Panzini,[8] vividly demonstrate that he had a lot of work to do to overcome his vocal deficits.

Most people are unpleasantly surprised the first time they hear their recorded voice, but for Franco the recordings were such an utter and horrifying shock when he first played them back that he refused to record again as long as his voice remained as unruly and ugly as he thought it sounded here. At the same time, these records provided him with his first means of comparison with the recordings of the singers on whom he had been modeling himself—Enrico Caruso, Aureliano Pertile, and Beniamino Gigli. Suddenly Franco was able to visualize the gap between his achievements and the finished artistry of established tenors. The question was how to cross the ravine when there was no bridge. The answer was as easy as it was impossible: build one.

May 16, 1950: *Addio alla madre*

If Remo ever met with his son on the small piazza Porta Pia to talk about Franco's musical aspirations, Adria would shout from the window that the pasta was ready.
    Marco Corelli, interview, August 22, 2004

With his musical dreams materializing and his life seemingly on track, fate intervened in the worst possible way, when, on May 16, Franco's mother finally lost her two-year battle with cancer. He fell into a serious depression and vowed

Franco's mother, Natalina "Adria" Corelli, remembered by all who knew her for her gentle soul and captivating beauty. (Photo: Courtesy of Marco Corelli)

not to rest until he could sing Verdi's Requiem for her in Ancona's cathedral. Until that day he would wear only black ties in her memory.

Liliana tried to persuade him to resume his singing studies but, for a number of months, to no avail. From there on the stories about what happened next diverge. One thing is certain, though: Franco did not remain inconsolable until the next year's voice competition in Spoleto, for he himself actually wrote a letter to Siciliani, dated November 27, 1950, in which he asks when the next courses in Florence will start, because he wants to resume his studies there.[9] This he did by the end of the year.[10]

CHAPTER 6 ❖ 1951

Vincerò!

1951: Last Chance

If it was indeed Liliana who reminded Franco of an open invitation from Guido Sampaoli, director of the Teatro dell'Opera in Rome and the Lirico Sperimentale Spoleto (Sampaoli had urged the young tenor to participate in the Lirico Sperimentale voice competition again, after hearing Franco singing while the maestro was eating his lunch in Rome's conservatory's cafeteria), she found her brother less enthusiastic than might be expected. At the time, he may well have been happy with his studies in Florence, and/or he may still have been disappointed over his earlier failure in Spoleto. So it was once more his sister who filled out and posted the entry forms for him.

When the big day arrived, fate once more seemed to plot against Franco, when he awoke running a high fever, due to a late case of the mumps.[1] In Franco's mind, any competition was therefore out of the question, but Liliana simply kicked him out of bed: "You're thirty years old, this is your very last chance! Whatever happens today is in the hands of God, but you will get on that train!"[2]

She helped him get up and ready and pushed him on board the train. Arriving in Spoleto late, he hastily wrote his legal name, Dario, in the participants' book, then crossed through "Dario" and wrote "Franco Corelli" instead.[3] He also subtracted a year from his age. His chosen aria was the one that had brought him luck before, in Florence, "Celeste Aida." Recalled Corelli: "Totally naive. 'Celeste Aida' is not just very difficult, it is incredibly difficult! But what did I know? I had seen two operas in my life and had started singing seriously only about a year and a half before."[4]

With no time to reconsider, Franco was immediately propelled into the audition. There, much to his own surprise, something extraordinary happened: "That day was blessed by, what can I say—a Grace. Never in my life did I manage to sing that aria like I sang it then. That *romanza* ends with a high B-flat, and I shall never forget the B-flat that came out of my throat . . . there was no end to it. I never managed to sing it like that again, but I won the contest with it!"[5] Anita Cerquetti, a participant in the competition, witnessed Franco's audition: "We had to sing one after the other, and I remember well the rumor that Corelli and I would win. For that reason I was curious and listened to him. Well . . . it was hard to miss his voice! You could immediately recognize its potential."[6]

✦✦✦✦✦

A few days later Corelli received a letter from the president of the festival, Adriano Belli, which he later recalled as "a beautiful letter from a very sympathetic man. He was on first-name terms with all students! And he wrote me: 'Dear Franco, dear Corelli, I can tell you that you have won Spoleto and that you will debut this very year in *Aida*.'" Upon reading those words, courage failed the ill-prepared hero of the contest: "A crisis started to manifest itself. I panicked because I had no idea how to achieve the task ahead of me. I mean. . . . I only knew four *romanzas* and nothing else."[7]

Anita Cerquetti received a similar letter informing her that she was scheduled as Franco's Aida. Her preparation too had been far from ideal. After having been "discovered" at seventeen while singing at a wedding party, she was sent to study, after which she won the same 1951 Spoleto contest in the soprano category. But whereas Franco panicked upon winning, success made Cerquetti nearly overconfident. "I would open my mouth and the voice would be there; it has always been that way."[8]

1951: The Emergence of Franco Corelli, Tenor

Studying in Rome
In spite of his misgivings about the task he faced, Franco went to Rome, where he lived with his Aunt Dora and her husband, Giovanni Magni, at Via Gaetano Moroni 8. From there he went to his daily lessons in the master course that was

a part of his Spoleto prize. Typically, his first memories of that period were of those lessons: "There was a fantastic atmosphere and truly great names: Maestro Luigi Ricci and Maestro Bertelli."[9]

Anita Cerquetti, in her inimitable way, took a much more practical approach to her task and her tutors:

> That *Aida* was practically the first opera I ever saw. So Ziino was as good a maestro to me as any given Tom, Dick, or Harry. He prepared me and was as perfect as the first teacher can be, because he took away my nerves. At your debut that is more important than anything else. But Franco kept on saying that he didn't want to sing it. I told him that with his voice and stage presence, he could handle it. The maestro even told him that he was born to sing that part! But at a certain point he answered: 'That may be, but I don't feel ready for it now!'"[10]

After less than three months of rehearsals,[11] even Ziino came to agree that things weren't going too well. On Bertelli's advice, Franco went back to Ancona for a two-week break in order to get back on his feet. The family discussed Franco's options, and his father urged him to go back to his engineering studies. But Liliana and his uncles argued that he had come too close to give up now. Viero and Corrado suggested that he investigate a less difficult part. Because he already knew the Flower Aria from *Carmen*, they eventually agreed that the Bizet opera might be a suitable alternative.

The only one who remained doubtful was Franco himself, so Scaravelli took him to Mario Scoponi, an ear, nose, and throat specialist in Ancona. When Scoponi began examining his patient, Franco proved to have little knowledge of anatomy—he thought he had six or seven vocal cords. When the doctor corrected him, he couldn't believe it: "So I make all that noise with only two vocal cords?!" Scoponi gave him some books to study, and Franco returned home relieved, having obtained "near medical approval!" He continued to visit Scoponi from then on; the doctor became a friend with whom Franco would discuss the physical aspects of his profession. Ultimately, these discussions taught him how to control his gag reflex (he would occasionally inspect his throat with his fingers or direct medicines to his vocal cords). But the most important reason for his continuing visits was that Scoponi didn't charge him! Said Franco: "Only because you don't want money, I can be sure that what you say is true. I would never trust one who asked for money, because it is in their interest to invent defects."[12]

♦♦♦♦♦

At home Franco took up the score of *Carmen* and spent the next ten days studying his part: "In *Aida* you need legato, you need bel canto, you need style. I lacked the technique, and I was too young for it. *Carmen* is much more an opera of impulse, temperament."[13] Elsewhere he added: "I am generally nervous, but *Carmen* made me feel at ease. Among the three aces in my sleeve, this was the opera that first came to my rescue!"[14] Well prepared, he returned to Spoleto and suggested the change of operas to Bertelli, who agreed. The only one who regretted the substitution was Anita Cerquetti, who was to have been his Aida: "Looking back, it was a great pity, for now I had to sing Aida to a tenor [Paolo Ascià] who started and finished his career then and there."[15]

The Spoleto Festival

The atmosphere in Spoleto just before its fifth summer opera festival season opened with *Carmen* was crackling with anticipation. Finally the young singers, all new to the public except for Lucia Danieli,[16] who had won the year before, were going to have a turn at spinning the wheel of fortune. The excitement was enhanced by a number of circumstances, such as a telegram from the living legend and honorary president of the Lirico Sperimentale, Beniamino Gigli, who had committed himself generously to the youngsters. Then, too, Italy longed for something new, something that could help wipe out the memories of the war.[17] The Spoleto contest, under the guidance of its intendant, the seventy-three-year-old lawyer Adriano Belli,[18] had gained a reputation for finding fine voices. Expectations ran especially high because it was the festival's fifth anniversary, and everything had been programmed on a grander scale than ever before.[19]

As for the young singers, they had left a period of extremely hard work behind them and were all now meticulously prepared. An insightful and beautifully written article on the circumstances surrounding their debut appeared in *Il Momento*. It described how the aspiring singers arrived in the mountain city that was to be the gateway to either the fulfillment or the eclipse of their ambitions—to glory or failure. Everyone knew the names of the stars that had been discovered in Spoleto's Festival Lirico Sperimentale performances, but a still greater number of candidates had been forgotten. There was no middle of the road in the highest art: "So, dear youngsters of the Teatro Nuovo, cheer up! In these days your studies will be put to the test, but the public of Spoleto stands united behind you. They will follow you carefully during your artistic careers, they will tremble with you and take part in your successes. . . . And during the evenings to come, they will encourage you with all their hearts."[20]

The day before the first performance, Gigli's telegram to the young singers arrived from Rio de Janeiro, and in it he stressed the importance of their task: "From this test of every single one of you, art and Italy itself are awaiting new forces to build up and maintain our worldwide supremacy, which your involved president encourages with an open heart."[21]

August 26–September 12, 1951: Corelli's Debut[22]

The sense of anticipation reached fever pitch on the evening of the *Carmen* performance. The Rome Opera House had sent its director of mechanical and electrical services, and the famous dancer Attilia Radice had accepted the task of producing the choreography, starring herself as *prima ballerina assoluta*.[23] Many notables were in attendance, among them the under-secretary of state, Giulio Andreotti, and the Swiss representatives of the Montreux Festival, Manuel Roch (general manager) and Alfred Vogelsang (mayor of Montreux).[24] The last two were present to investigate the possibility of bringing the Spoleto Festival performances to Montreux, which filled the Italians with pride.[25]

> August 26 and 30; September 7 and 12, 1951
> **Georges Bizet:** *Carmen*
> **Spoleto, Teatro Nuovo**
> Lucia Danieli (*Carmen*), Franco Corelli (*Don José*), Ofelia Di Marco (*Micaëla*), Manuel Spatafora (*Escamillo*), Oberdan Traica (*Dancaïro*), Gino Pasquale (*Il Remendado*), Giorgio Onesti (*Zuniga*), Dante Mascitti (*Moralès*), Adriana Pupella (*Frasquita*), Gabriella Contessa (*Mercedes*), cond. Ottavio Ziino; chorus master, Mario Chierici; stage director, Riccardo Picozzi; choreographer and prima ballerina, Attilia Radice

The performance turned into a triumph for the young singers, whose careful preparation was readily acknowledged by the press. Lucia Danieli confirmed her rapidly growing status as a mezzo of merit with a moving psychological portrait of the heroine that was based on superb vocality and a well-defined balance between the passionate and the lyrical elements of the character.[26] And the charming and sweet-voiced Ofelia Di Marco received a triumphant solo curtain call for her performance of Micaëla's Act III aria.[27]

With that, it is time to consider the tenor.

The reporter for *Il Popolo* observed that Italians are always waiting for a new tenor to step out of the shadows, adding that Italy might just have found one: "Corelli has considerable capacities. He can easily reach the high notes. The tenor voice is a very difficult one, but the Don José of yesterday stands a good chance of becoming famous."[28] *Il Momento* agreed, and *L'Unita* added that his singing had been a splendid crescendo from the duet of the first act to the Flower Aria, which was rendered with the precise amount of expressivity to arouse the audience to a state of delirium. The public demanded an encore but Corelli refused, and with that a tradition was born.[29] *Il Tempo*'s reporter agreed with the previous authors, although he considered the tenor's singing still to be too "physical."[30]

Besides Danieli, Corelli, and Di Marco, there was also praise for the rest of the cast, the wonderful scenery, and the superb choreography. In the last act, where Corelli made his most striking impression, light and color harmonized perfectly with the music, for which the conductor was praised. Even the chorus master was singled out.

The performance was deemed a triumph. The critic of *Il Momento* actually gave up reviewing from Act III on, claiming he'd been too caught up in the drama of the spectacle.[31] *Il Tempo* summarized the event in its headline: "Special Correspondents and Art Critics Applaud at the Opera Season of the Sperimentale."[32]

❖❖❖❖❖

Today we can hardly imagine critics attending second, let alone third performances, but the Spoleto Festival of 1951 was one of those rare occasions: "We judged the first performance of *Carmen* worthy of the greatest opera theaters. Today, after the second performance, we can safely say that the performance came out superior to some performances staged in the great theaters."[33] The main credits went to Ziino, who received an unprecedented ovation when he entered the pit for the third performance. The success of Danieli's Carmen was confirmed, Di Marco rose to great lyrical heights as Micaëla, and Corelli and Spatafora were again recognized.[34]

October–December 1951: House Tenor of the Teatro dell'Opera

After the fourth and final staging of *Carmen* on August 12, Corelli's world turned overnight into the world of a tenor bound for glory when he was rewarded for his efforts with a contract as house tenor at Rome's prestigious Teatro dell'Opera. It filled him with pride as much as fear, for he felt he might fall short of such high expectations. His life had changed overnight from the quiet promenades of Ancona and the Caffè Roulette to the big-city life of Rome, where he rented a three-room apartment in the Via Santa Croce. In between his obligations, he traveled to Ancona, where he continued to work with Scaravelli and look up some friends. Naturally, things were different. Old friendships weren't forgotten, but life had given its Anconetan actors different parts to play. And yet, the involvement of Franco's family initially increased, for they were very protective and would stand by him in Rome whenever possible; if Bibi couldn't be backstage, Remo or Liliana would occasionally take the train to the Teatro dell'Opera. And if they couldn't, Viero and Corrado occasionally went over to support their nephew. Surely the young Corelli brothers had some adventures together in the Italian capital that evoked memories of their childhood years in Ancona,[35] but there was little time for extracurricular activities. At almost thirty-one years of age, Franco's chance of a lifetime was at hand, whether or not he felt ready. Franco decided to make the best of it and win over the hard-to-please Roman audiences while studying right before their eyes.

CHAPTER 7 ❖ 1952–1954

The Conquest of Rome

January 3–February 9, 1952: An Ardent Romeo

The tenor wasn't the only one having trouble with the critics. Perhaps Zandonai's misfortune was a surplus of genius, which compelled him to write in an extremely individualistic, intimate, and intellectual style. His creations are far from the sentimental mold and represent a clear break with the verismo repertoire of the 1890s. The score evokes the Verona captured on canvas by the famous painters of the fifteenth-century Veronese School—not surprising, because rather than turning to Shakespeare, Zandonai based his libretto on the original short story by the Veronese writer Luigi Da Porto (1485–1529). At times *Giulietta e Romeo* combines echoes of Giuseppe Verdi's *Otello* and *Simon Boccanegra* with the musical abundance of Pietro Mascagni's medieval legend *Isabeau* and the brilliant orchestral colors of Igor Stravinsky and Maurice Ravel.[1] Although the sensual atmosphere and some specific musical themes are a little too reminiscent of Zandonai's earlier opera *Francesca da Rimini*, as critics pointed out at the time, some pages are truly unforgettable, beginning with the exalted love duet between the two lovers in the first act, "Romeo! Giulietta! . . . Deh! Bel fioretto!" The duet leads into a steady crescendo to the third act, where Romeo hides in Mantua.

January 31; February 3 and 9, 1952
Riccardo Zandonai: *Giulietta e Romeo*
Rome, Teatro dell'Opera
Mercedes Fortunati (*Giulietta*), Franco Corelli (*Romeo*), Mafalda Micheluzzi (*Isabella*), Afro Poli (*Tebaldo*), Enzo Guagni (*Il Cantatore*), Loretta Di Lelio (*a Woman, Third Maid*), cond. Ottavio Ziino

The plot takes its fatal turn when a minstrel reveals Giulietta's death in a song that inspires Romeo to his emotionally charged "Giulietta mia!" In despair, he mounts a horse and rides through a storm in the middle of the night to Verona, depicted musically in the famous instrumental "Cavalcade." Standing before the tomb of the Capulets, he bursts into his great aria "Giulietta! Son io!," which brings Giulietta back to life just long enough for the lovers to sing the concluding duet of love and death, "Ahimè! La morte!"

The opera's complexity lies in the delicate musical writing, which focuses on the medieval setting. It does not aim for the more straightforward verismo idiom. Therefore, *Giulietta e Romeo* can't come to life without an involved audience and a superb cast. The last demand was effectively met at the world premiere on February 14, 1922, when Miguel Fleta and Gilda Dalla Rizza were the principals in Rome's Teatro dell'Opera (in the presence of both Benito Mussolini and Crown Prince Umberto). Almost exactly thirty years later, on January 31, 1952, it was Franco Corelli who took on Fleta's mantle in the same theater. Fleta recorded Romeo's aria (Preiser CD 89002; Aria 2CD 1021) shortly after he created the part, and there can be little doubt that Corelli studied it, as was his habit, although he was still a long way from mastering Fleta's technical accomplishments in the field of *filature* (the spinning of a note into infinity) and *messa di voce* (the diminishing of the volume on a single note, only to let it swell after a moment of magic when the voice seems about to disappear). Apart from these baroque stylistic features— no longer associated with this music today—the part of Romeo seems to have

Mercedes Fortunati and Franco Corelli in Zandonai's *Giulietta e Romeo*, Teatro dell'Opera, Rome, 1952. Corelli recalled in a 1975 article in *Oggi Illustrato*: "After one of my first Romeos was not very much appreciated by the critics, Maestro Guido Sampaoli, director of the Teatro dell'Opera, came to my dressing room and said: 'They have it wrong, my boy, you just go out there and sing and you'll have a great career.'"[2] (Photo: Courtesy of the Teatro dell'Opera)

been written with Corelli in mind. Vocally, he could rely largely on the strong center of his voice and its unusual declamatory power in this role. Theatrically, he may actually have been able to compete with the real Romeo when it came to conquering the heart of Giulietta. Perhaps he gave the doomed lover more contrast later on, as we can sense from his 1972 recording of the duet from Zandonai's *Francesca da Rimini* (Decca 475 522-2), but the Rome audience had the advantage of hearing his trumpetlike voice with all its fresh and youthful unbridled passion.

At the premiere on the evening of January 31, Ottavio Ziino received the lion's share of the laurels for his achievement in blending the ensemble. Mercedes Fortunati was singled out by most critics for her clear, fluent, and passionate singing as Giulietta.[3] The young tenor received encouraging reviews for his instinctive, pure musicality as well as his ability to bring out certain accents that usually passed unnoticed; in short, his singing was deemed "expressive." In the melodic parts a hint of his later elegance and legato must have been present as well, although the power of his voice garnered most of the attention. His singing was declared "broad, warm, and vibrant,"[4] and his easy passage to the high register was as impressive as his good looks.[5] These qualities and his youthful ardor made up for his vocal defects, which were merely noted as areas for the young tenor to work on. In *Il Paese*, Enrico Fondi wrote that he should work toward a more refined emission.[6] *Giustizia*'s Franco De Luca was of the same opinion, stating that with careful study, Corelli could achieve superb results,[7] an opinion shared by the critic of *Globo*: "Once he gains experience . . . he'll be a voice and an actor that we can rely on."[8] Corelli's acting met with a more mixed reception. *Il Tempo*'s G. Pan thought that he acted the part of Romeo with bold self-confidence,[9] whereas Fondi was of the opinion that there was a certain awkwardness in the young tenor's stage deportment.[10]

When it came to the rest of the cast, Afro Poli's Tebaldo, Mafalda Micheluzzi's youthful Isabella,[11] and Enzo Guagni's excellent minstrel were all well received,[12] while *L'Osservatore Romano* singled out for praise the *comprimaria* diva of 1940s film fame—Loretta Di Lelio.[13]

❖❖❖❖❖

With such largely positive reviews, why would Corelli recall only the encouraging words of Guido Sampaoli, which clearly indicate that the tenor remembered his Romeo debut as a near failure? To find the answer to this puzzling recollection, one needs to note that Corelli's career came to an abrupt halt after his third Romeo: he went four months without a single performance. What had been true for Anita Cerquetti, who also learned to sing on the job, certainly was doubly true for Franco, who didn't even have her musical background in playing an instrument to help him along the way. He had to work hard in order to progress and make the best of his natural qualities. Having had only a rudimentary technique at his disposal at the outset of his career, he largely mastered his first two roles by sheer determination and willpower. While this enabled him to survive in the moment, he would increasingly find himself finishing these operas tired and with an inflamed throat. The matter became sufficiently serious for him to consult a doctor after the third Romeo. An examination revealed that he had developed a node on his vocal cords and would need surgery to remove it.[14] Said Loretta: "He was worried his voice could be damaged for good."[15]

Following the surgery, Corelli had to remain silent for months; even speaking was restricted to an absolute minimum. When he was finally able to test his voice and found it very much as he had left it, he knew that his former approach to singing was no longer an option. Thus was born his obsessive search for knowledge and understanding of his voice as an instrument.[16] He was fortunate in that the Teatro dell'Opera provided an environment with all the facilities and means for him to learn. Moreover, in its director, Guido Sampaoli, he found a friend, mentor, and promoter who believed in him and sustained him whenever his insecurities manifested themselves. Sampaoli wisely gave Corelli all the time he needed to recover from the surgery and then let the young singer work his way back to performing in a low-profile role debut as Maurizio in Cilea's *Adriana Lecouvreur*, coming in only for the last performance. While studying the part, Corelli seized the opportunity to make up for his earlier neglect of opera as an entertaining art form; what once had been a dreaded childhood obligation held him spellbound when he attended Bellini's *I Puritani*, with Giacomo Lauri-Volpi and Maria Callas, in early May. Recalled Corelli:

> Today it's easy to sing, . . . but when I began to sing it was very hard, because the theater was full of wonderful artists, with beautiful voices, beautiful style—when I heard Callas and Lauri-Volpi sing in *Puritani*, my God! It was the end of this world! . . . The beautiful fight between these two artists, the high notes of Lauri-Volpi, ringing! The beautiful legato, the purity of his voice, the style of Callas![17]

He soon found out how those spectacular results were achieved; even if some singers had been blessed with great instruments, none of them was born able to sing Elvira or Arturo without first learning the required technique. If the artistry of Lauri-Volpi and Callas was still a bit of a mystery to Corelli, a mere glance at the conductors of his day revealed one of the keys to success: he saw them working around the clock, preparing both the orchestra and the singers. But that, Corelli discovered, was not even their main job: "More than once I went to Maestro Santini, Maestro Capuana, Maestro Votto... and every time I went they were studying! Always studying!"[18]

May 8, 1952: *La dolcissima effigie*

Though more popular than Zandonai's *Giulietta e Romeo*, Cilea's masterpiece also has both its supporters and its detractors. Its defenders praise the delicate orchestration and a number of vocal highlights, while its critics maintain that the music is too repetitive and is wasted on cardboard characters. Maurizio is not considered a very difficult role from the vocal point of view, but it requires imaginative phrasing and enough sweet accents to make the sensitive character come alive. Given his recent surgery, the debut represented a victory in and of itself for Corelli, although it remained an isolated performance. And yet he had plenty to be proud of: his name appeared on the bill right next to that of the most famous soprano of the 1940s, Maria Caniglia, the regular partner of the very tenor whose judgment he had feared so much when he first entered the Spoleto contest, Beniamino Gigli (who had preceded Corelli in this run of *Adriana Lecouvreur* at the Rome opera). And then there was Tito Gobbi, the already world-famous baritone and movie star, whom Corelli had seen on the

---

May 8, 1952

Francesco Cilea: *Adriana Lecouvreur*

Rome, Teatro dell'Opera

Maria Caniglia (*Adriana Lecouvreur*), Franco Corelli (*Maurizio*), Maria Benedetti (*the Princess of Bouillon*), Tito Gobbi (*Michonnet*), Giulio Tomei (*the Prince of Bouillon*), Loretta Di Lelio (*Mademoiselle Jouvenot*), cond. Vincenzo Bellezza

stage of the Teatro delle Muse during the war years. Admittedly, he couldn't begin to match their refined singing in Maurizio's lyrical music, but whatever Corelli still lacked in vocal flexibility and interpretative skills, he made up for with his good looks and a masculine vocalism that was already having an effect on audiences. Later he would mold Maurizio to perfection, but the reason this early role-debut performance proved to be the most important of his life had nothing to do with his vocalism or stage skills. Remembered Corelli: "During the rehearsals I saw a young artist, rather myopic, who, from out of the shadows, hesitantly descended the dressing room stairs; so I took her hand and accompanied her to the stage."[19]

The young artist whose hand he had taken was to sing the minor part of Mademoiselle Jouvenot, but her emergence from the backstage shadows made a bigger impact on Maurizio's heart than his famous Adriana did onstage. The name of this petite redheaded *madamigella* was Loretta Di Lelio, and, for better or worse, she was destined to be the love of his life. His burgeoning feelings are neatly captured in his famous poetic exclamation of *La dolcissima effigie*:

... sorridente	In your sweet, smiling countenance I
	see again the features
in te rivedo della madre cara;	of my beloved mother;
nel tuo cor della mia patria	through your heart I breathe again
dolce, preclara l'aura ribevo,	the sweet, radiant air of my fatherland
che m'aprì la mente	that revived my sanity
Bella tu sei come la mia bandiera	You are as beautiful as my banner
delle pugne fiammante entro i vapor;	ablaze in the turmoil of battle
tu sei, gioconda, come la chimera	You are, joyful one, as a vision
della Gloria, promessa al vincitor...	of glory, promised to the winner...
Bella tu sei, tu sei gioconda...	Beautiful you are, you are joyful...
Sì!... Amor mi fa poeta.	Yes!... Love made me a poet.

Francesco Cilea, *Adriana Lecouvreur*

Rumors have abounded about Loretta, beginning with the suggestion that she was illegitimate. The truth, as revealed in her birth certificate, is a little different. Indeed, her birth certificate reveals that her mother, Ida Rosselini, was not yet married to the bass Umberto Di Lelio when she gave birth to a baby daughter in Montecatini Terme: "Umberto Di Lelio, 24, artist, living in

Rome, has declared that at 1:10 of July 27, 1918, at Via Benedetto Casati 9, Bagni di Montecatini, from his union with a woman not married to him, . . . a girl was born that he has shown to me and given the names Anna Laura Augusta Giorgina."[20] The baby's status changed within a week, when the bond between Umberto and Ida was legalized through their marriage of August 3, 1918.[21]

Perhaps these circumstances of her birth were enough in Roman Catholic Italy of the 1920s through the 1960s to make a woman like Loretta want to avoid candor on the subject; then, too, she may just have been playing the hide-your-age game, for few women like to be reminded that they are older than their male partners. In fact, she was less than three years Franco's senior,[22] although she had enjoyed a successful *comprimaria* career for over a decade, since her debut at the Teatro dell'Opera in 1941. Her voice (a soprano, although she sang minor mezzo parts from time to time) was not of the highest quality, but she compensated with a pleasant stage appearance and a great sense of musical culture. Consequently, she secured numerous engagements for herself throughout Italy in such *comprimaria* parts as Flora in *La Traviata*, Ines in *Il Trovatore*, and Kate Pinkerton in *Madama Butterfly*. At the time she met Corelli, her most notable achievements were her 1947 performances in two films of Donizetti operas, as Giannetta in the renowned version of *L'Elisir d'Amore* and as Alisa in *Lucia di Lammermoor*. In both she was surrounded by an all-star cast that included Mario Filippeschi, Italo Tajo, Tito Gobbi, and Nelly Corradi (while a very young Gina Lollobrigida can be seen in the chorus of *L'Elisir*).[23]

More important than that modicum of movie-star fame as a supporting artist was the fact that as the daughter of Di Lelio, a renowned bass, she had grown up in the heart of the operatic world. As a child she had seen and heard at close range both composers and singers whom Franco knew only from books and recordings. She was also familiar with contract negotiations and the various tricks of the trade that mattered in building a successful career. This early education in music and the inner workings of the world of opera provided a vast reservoir of experience and knowledge from which Franco would draw as he made his way up the career ladder in an intensely competitive field.

None of this mattered yet, though, because from the moment he first touched her hand to lead her down the stairs, he was captivated. He fell in love with all that focused passion so characteristic of him, with a love that went far beyond the immediate erotic spell that she cast over him. They had much in common. He had lost his mother at a relatively early age; she had lost her father at a similarly young age. Umberto Di Lelio was only fifty-two when he died in 1946, unable to witness his daughter's major successes on the silver screen, just as Franco's mother had missed her son's earliest successes. Both singers had emerged from World War II and the difficult immediate postwar years unmarried, although Loretta had been engaged when she met Franco and also was rumored to have had an affair with Tito Gobbi. Here they were, two single Italian singers falling in love at ages thirty-one and thirty-four. Their personalities complemented and sustained each other's needs, and Loretta's engagement to a man who had nothing in common with her lifestyle as an opera singer couldn't withstand destiny: she and Franco were clearly meant to be.[24] However, the young woman from Montecatini Terme was not lightly conquered. According to Loretta, he had already spotted her during the earlier *Romeo* rehearsals, and in contrast to Franco's poetic memories of their first contact at the *Adriana* rehearsal, Loretta was unenthusiastic: "In his first approaches he acted quite weird, and I wasn't in the mood to talk to him."[25]

✦✦✦✦✦

Fortunately for Franco, he had an ace up his sleeve when he repeated the act he had played with that other redhead, his high-school crush Norma: he asked Loretta for advice on vocal matters, which she readily provided. Their lessons quickly "progressed," and they soon established a relationship. Initially they kept it secret, but once Loretta broke off her engagement to the other man, she and Franco were more open. However, for reasons unknown they continued to conceal their relationship from his family in Ancona.[26]

Throughout the 1950s Loretta would accompany Franco to nearly every occasion, gradually becoming all the good and bad things that have been said about her: his driving force, his stimulus, and the real reason we were able to have Franco Corelli the tenor at all, for she would literally push him onstage whenever he was too afraid to go out there. She had found him in a difficult moment, when the sheer impossibility of his task threatened to overwhelm him, and she provided him with an environment in which he could progress: "I immediately started working with him, coaching him, helping him, teaching him, until the point where I ended up feeding him. As for the *Adriana* performance, I performed my two small parts there in such a way that I could sustain his performance. He felt much more secure in this way."[27]

July–August 1952: Seducing Carmens

Given his insecurities and limitations, the tenor in love was perhaps ill prepared for immediate success. It happened, nevertheless—much to his own surprise: "In a few months I found myself on top of a wave of success without first having spent even a day in the provinces." Others might have had mixed feelings about some of the nonmusical reasons for this success, but Franco couldn't care less. He blessed the good fortune that had given him qualities that compensated to some extent for what he considered to be technical handicaps and vocal defects: "More than a voice, I was a significant stage presence; directors and managers soon started to realize that, from the shadows of their boxes, the ladies were salaciously applauding this tenor who knew how to get away with some vocal shortcomings, all because of a certain vague resemblance to Rock Hudson."[28]

As the end of the Rome season approached, Franco's calendar filled with bookings for an extensive summer festival tour that assured these festival impresarios of a handsome Don José with a voice that stood a good chance of being heard in their open-air theaters. These performances confirmed the points made in earlier reviews, although the first performances in Rome's Terme di Caracalla did meet with some fierce negative criticism from the press. Fortunately, Corelli's contribution was thought to be the exception, and he garnered the usual encouraging reviews and compliments over his good looks.[29] Other protagonists were judged to be less than perfect, starting with Pia Tassinari. Corelli thought she was great,[30] but the critics found that the former soprano couldn't meet the lower vocal demands of the role.[31] The performances in the open-air theaters of Civitavecchia, Terracina, and Cagliari, where Miriam Pirazzini stepped in as Carmen, were reviewed more favorably. And when the experienced Giulietta Simionato brought her acclaimed star power as well as her appealing mix of warm femininity and intimate vocal expressiveness to the role in Trieste's Castello di San Giusto and Turin, Italian audiences hailed their quintessential Carmen of the decade.[32] Corelli benefited from the improved cast and felt that career advances came more easily for him after the Caracalla performances. There he had discovered that his voice was tailor-made for Italy's large open-air theaters, where it could expand freely.[33]

Simionato soon proved an important figure in Franco's early career. She practically took him under her wing, singing *Carmen* with him almost wher-

The very first thing that Franco bought from his earnings was this brown Lancia Aurelia, which came in handy for the first tour. (Photo: Courtesy of Arrigo Michelini)

ever she appeared in that role, and in spite of the acclaim over Corelli's later pairings with Maria Callas, Renata Tebaldi, or Birgit Nilsson, she was his most significant partner in the coming decade (not counting his love affair with his new Lancia Aurelia, his first car and the one that firmly established his passion for driving). On a more personal level, Simionato's friendship gravitated rather toward Loretta, with whom she felt at ease throughout: "Loretta was a special woman, a good friend, who followed Franco everywhere." Admittedly, that last habit also prevented Simionato from getting to know Franco on a more personal level: "He would always call me 'Signora,' never 'Giulietta.' That is, if he spoke at all, because he was always preserving his voice. We had little personal contact other than during rehearsals. But we did wonderful things onstage together, especially in *Carmen*."[34]

Summer 1952: Dreams of La Scala and the Met

Discoveries: that is the word that comes to mind when one hears Corelli say that he didn't understand his voice in these first years. This ongoing uncertainty made him an eager and introspective student. He would ask nearly anyone in the business for comments on his singing. It was almost masochistic: What was his worst note? His worst mistake? How he could he get rid of the ugly color on a certain note?[35] Then he would ask about other important issues: What was *La Scala* like? Whom did one need to know in the opera world? How should one deal with critics? These were all important issues, any of which could be decisive in walking the thin line between success and failure. Finding answers to these questions in the cutthroat atmosphere of opera in the 1950s was critical; throughout his career, although he would entrust some people with handling specific affairs, he never really had a manager. In his apprentice year there was little to discuss regarding financial matters. His contract for the upcoming 1952–53 season stipulated that his services would be obtained at the rate of 130,000 lire ($208) monthly, with a repertoire that would be decided upon by the management. He was required to be at the theater's disposal as a contract singer whose duties included his upcoming debuts in Bellini's *Norma* and Guerrini's *Enea*, while serving as the understudy for Giordano's *Fedora*, Verdi's *Don Carlo*, and Puccini's *Manon Lescaut*. The first-class train tickets between Ancona and Rome that the management guaranteed him show that he was still very much attached to his family. And with an $80 bonus for each performance outside his regular contract, he was prepared to sing nearly anything during this early period—especially over the summer, because festivals paid a little better. (The summer program at the Terme di Caracalla the previous July had brought him a princely fee of $125 per performance).[36]

With such financial and artistic constraints, any young artist would be on the lookout to improve his lot. Despite his limited repertoire, Franco's stentorian voice had led Italy's scouts straight to his mentors. Through the intercession of the illustrious "vocal coach and singers' broker" Liduino Bonardi, Corelli even auditioned for the Metropolitan Opera House in New York.[37] This Met audition materialized for reasons that lead straight to the heart of the operatic world of that era. The emerging new generation of young vocalists was mirrored by a similar shift toward youth in the management of opera houses.

The Austrian impresario Rudolf Bing's initial encounters with the world of opera had been in Austria and Germany, after which he had been trained in the organization of festivals such as Glyndebourne and the Edinburgh International Festival. He took over the direction of the Metropolitan Opera in 1950. Cautious because of his status as a foreigner in a country where nationalist tendencies were strong, Bing focused on effecting changes that would transform the house into a professional, modern opera venue.[38] For this he needed the support of the public. Opinions on his policies regarding singers tend to be diametrically opposed. One camp argued that he neglected American artists in favor of foreign ones, while the other camp proclaimed him a true advocate for homegrown singers.

To judge from his memoir *5000 Nights at the Opera*, Bing's own position was in fact somewhere in between. He not only overcame his initial misgivings about the so-called Chicago convention, which forced him to employ a certain number of American soloists, but also grew to value them as the backbone of the Met. On the other hand, he felt the need for a steady injection of European singers. One of his early actions as general manager of the Met was to approach the Italo-German Roberto Bauer,[39] whom Bing knew from his days in Europe and who had achieved a reputation as a specialist in voices. Also renowned for his invaluable 1947 catalog of acoustic recordings,[40] Bauer was an authority on historical singers and a household name in the collector's world. Bing called on him for advice on European singers.[41] At first he would simply query Bauer about a certain singer or a certain theater. After a while he began asking Bauer to go here and there to check on something or other. By June 1952 Bauer had organized the first Metropolitan Opera audition in Rome, at the studio of Liduino Bonardi. In *5000 Nights at the Opera*, Bing recalls how Bonardi, whom at first sight he had deemed a friendly old rogue, soon proved to be a waste of time; each of the thirty or thirty-one singers who were auditioning turned out to be worse than the one before. Said Bing to Bonardi: "Did you present these to [Antonio] Ghiringhelli [La Scala's intendant] as well?" Bonardi, throwing his hands in the air, answered something that translates most accurately into "Of course not."[42]

Rogues will be rogues, and because Bonardi was an impresario in the nineteenth-century sense of the term, Ghiringhelli eventually had to hear these singers as well. Corelli went to the La Scala audition with few expectations: "I only went to La Scala because I could see Loretta in Milan. As far as the audition was concerned, I was really unprepared." After he sang a voice said: "Thank you, sir, you can go. We have your address. Next."[43] Had the audition ended on that note, Corelli might have taken it as lightly as Tucci, who also participated in the audition and still grins when she recalls that day: "We came, we sang, and were rejected."[44] The young tenor's feelings changed when, on his way out, he ran into Ghiringhelli, who, it was said, had contributed some of his personal funds to rebuild the bombed-out theater. Ghiringhelli asked Franco if he was the young lad who had just been singing: "What is your true profession, young man? Listen carefully to me, for I am going to give you some good advice: return to your engineering studies. You see, singing is a hard and difficult challenge. These days you need exceptional talents to succeed." Corelli felt humiliated: "His words sounded like a final verdict with no possibilities left for appeal."[45]

Ghiringhelli's discouraging comments sound a little over the top, though, considering the tenor's encouraging press reports. Carlo Scaravelli, himself a successful participant at this audition, remembered it a little differently: according to him, Corelli made the cut to the final ten singers from an original group of ninety. That landed him an offer from an unidentified theater to be an understudy in a production of *Andrea Chénier*. Disappointed, Corelli refused; that was not what he had in mind when he auditioned for La Scala. Like Callas before him, he was determined to conquer the Milanese temple on his own terms.

Scaravelli also declined an offer that resulted from the audition. Just when all that he had strived for was about to materialize, his modesty and recognition of the risks involved in a professional singer's career made him reconsider. Concluding that his responsibilities as a husband and father required him to choose the greater security provided by his emerging career as an architect, Scaravelli decided to limit his ambitions as a singer and teacher to the local scene.[46]

❖❖❖❖❖

Regardless of the outcome of both the Metropolitan and the La Scala auditions, Corelli reached the United States after all in 1952, when *Musical America* was the first American magazine to publish a review of one of his Italian performances.[47] Moreover, a few months later he had his revenge against Ghiringhelli when La Scala asked him repeatedly to be the cover artist for one of their stars. Corelli cynically wondered whether, now that his first successes were beginning to appear in the papers, they had forgotten that terrible singer from the audition just a few months before. Suddenly it was Ghiringhelli's turn to experience rejection when the insulted "lad" turned down the impresario's offers one by one.[48]

December 14–28, 1952: The False Dimitri

Being a member of a repertory theater inevitably means having to sing roles as assigned by management according not only to the singer's own abilities but also to the theater's needs. For Corelli, that meant gaining experience in a wide variety of roles, some of which were very much out of the standard repertoire then, such as the False Dimitri in Modest Mussorgsky's masterpiece *Boris Godunov*. Roman audiences and critics alike were struck by the opera's beauties when the Teatro dell'Opera revived it in December 1952. The work was deemed inimitable and a welcome antithesis to Wagner's pomp. The libretto's haunting story line could have made Boito envious for its perfect measure, while the music would have been an eye-opener for Mascagni, Leoncavallo, and Catalani in the early 1890s—but that was long before Feodor Chaliapin popularized it at the dawn of the twentieth century. Instead, Italy had to wait for its first Mussorgsky until the early 1930s, when Italian audiences could relate to the sincere and impulsive nature of the Russian people and their dedicated inclination toward mystery, preserved in the work's hymnlike tone. Tancredi Pasero popularized the hapless ruler, but it wasn't until Boris Christoff exchanged the cloak of Pimen for the mantle of the tsar that the work's deepest mysteries were revealed.

At the time Christoff appeared as Boris Godunov at the Teatro dell'Opera opposite Franco Corelli's False Dimitri, the bass had just reached his prime. His sculpted legato, fine diction, and imposing timbre melded into a shattering performance. Corelli came off second best: "Together with Christoff Franco Corelli must be mentioned for the generous vocal means with which he performed the restless and ambiguous figure of the False Dimitri."[49] His abundant voice and beautiful, piercing notes stood out, though the need for further sculpting at this early stage in his career could still be observed:[50] "A tenor of excellent vocal means, who should continue to refine his art, for he merely hinted at shaping his powerful metal into the required eloquent phrases."[51] Di Lelio's Xenia was

December 14, 16, 20, and 28, 1952
Modest Mussorgsky: *Boris Godounov*
Rome, Teatro dell'Opera
Boris Christoff (*Boris Godounov*), Antonio Zerbini (*Pimen*), Franco Corelli (*Grigori, or the False Dmitri*), Loretta Di Lelio (*Xenia*), Miriam Pirazzini (*Marina*), Vito De Taranto, Robert Silva [December 16] (*Varlaam*), Petre Munteanu (*Prince Sciuisky*), Gino Del Signore (*Missail*), cond. Vittorio Gui

singled out, along with Petre Munteanu's diabolic rendering of Prince Shuiski, Vito De Taranto's lively Varlaam, Zerbini's austere Pimen, Miriam Pirazzini's Marina, the always excellent chorus, and the conductor, Vittorio Gui.[52]

None of the *Boris Godunov* performances were recorded, but the Rodzinski recording of February 23, 1952 (GOP CD 66316),[53] with both Christoff and Loretta Di Lelio in the cast, gives a fair idea of what theatergoers might have experienced at the Teatro dell'Opera that December.

March 11–15, 1953: The Flight from Troy

We believe that it is no coincidence that the management of the Teatro dell'Opera decided to produce the work of two composers [Adriano Lualdi and Guido Guerrini] *who harbor a specific political and moral conviction . . . , resulting in the improper and insulting belief that they are victims themselves, as illustrated by Guerrini's introduction to* Enea, *where he writes that he still has no clue why he was imprisoned in the Collescipoli camp in 1944. He describes his position in Terni as "A prisoner without guilt in a destroyed fatherland." Well done, Guerrini, you betrayed your country in collaborating with the enemy [the Germans] and you don't even realize it!*
    Ennio Melchiorre, *Avanti!,* **March 12, 1953**

In composing his opera, Guerrini worked closely with the librettist while both were imprisoned in 1944 for collaborating with the Germans,[54] the ultimate suggestion being that they envisioned their former Duce, Benito Mussolini, as Enea, and the defeated Italian Fascist regime as the Trojans. That left themselves as the last bastion of decency. Guerrini protested right away that the press was prejudiced toward new operas and asked that critics not judge *Enea* until they had seen a second or third performance. G. Pan played with Guerrini's a priori accusations in *Il Tempo*, where he actually sighed with relief when, quite unexpectedly, he found he liked the opening scene.[55] It took place in a Troy that was under siege and in flames, at the base of the temple of Demeter, where the vanquished Trojans were begging for their lives in a striking mixed chorus that captured the atmosphere of despair to perfection. From there things took a wrong turn, wrote Ennio

Melchiorre in *Avanti!*: the opera became increasingly rhetorical and eventually disintegrated.[56]

Gino Scaglia, in *L'Ora del Popolo*, pointed to Guerrini's academic background: one couldn't expect a professor like that to come up with anything better than academic, artificial music. The lion's share of the blame, though, was reserved for the "mythical libretto." *Enea* cobbled together a disjointed and unrelated array of chapters from Virgil's *Aeneid*, yet omitted the most theatrical and emotional parts (such as the meeting between the living Dido and Aeneas).[57] The public witnessed the pillaging of Troy and the apparition of Creusa's ghost, who briefly predicts her husband Enea's future. What followed were Enea's flight from the city and his conversation with the Sibyl of Cuma, culminating in Enea's central aria, "E' apparsa una colomba!" After all that, the voices of Orfeo (Corelli) and Euridice are heard in an interlude:

THE VOICE OF ORFEO

Pietà, pietà del misero amatore.	Have pity, pity on the miserable lover.
Pietà vi prenda, o spiriti infernali!	Have pity, o infernal spirits!
Quaggiù mi ha scorto solamente amore.	Down here only love smiled upon me
Venuto son quaggiù con le sue ali.	I arrived down here on its wings.
Lasciate questo miserel passare	Let this miserable man pass through.
C'ha il ciel nimico e tutti gli elementi.	Heaven is hostile to him and so are all the elements.
O come potrò mai lacrimar tanto	O how could my eyes ever produce enough tears
Che sempre pianga il mio mortale affanno?	For this mortal soul's eternal grief?

THE VOICE OF EURIDICE

Ohimè, che il troppo amore	Alas! The excesses of love
N'ha disfatti ambe due.	Defeated the two of us.
Ecco ch'i' ti son tolta a gran furore,	Here I am, taken from you with fury.
Nè sono ormai più tua.	From now on I'm no longer yours.
Ben tendo a te le braccia, ma non vale,	I am stretching out my arms to reach you, but in vain,
Chè indietro son tirata. Orfeo mio, vale!	Because I'm being pulled back. My Orfeo, farewell!

Lyrics by Angelo Poliziano/Adolfo Angeli, reprinted courtesy of the Teatro dell'Opera

Act II continues with Enea's arrival in the Elysian Fields, where he sees Orfeo and Euridice; all the Greek heroes of the past; his late father, Anchise; and finally, his former lover Dido. From there the libretto moves to the events that follow the Trojans' arrival in Latium, culminating in a brief scene and duel between Enea and Turno, king of the Rutuli (Corelli), over the hand of Lavinia, daughter of the king of Latium. Enea is victorious, and the opera ends in general rejoicing, with the hero founding a city in her name on the very spot where he killed Turno.

With the composer's focus on epic exterior events rather than human emotions, it is hardly surprising that *Enea* made little impact apart from the acclaimed sets and costumes and the sheer vocal achievements of Christoff, Stella, Pirazzini, and Corelli.[58] According to the critics of *L'Ora del Popolo, Avanti!, Il Tempo,* and *Il Mondo*, Guerrini was applauded politely after each act=but without much genuine enthusiasm. Only Franco De Luca of Popolo di Roma took Guerrini's side, judging the work a masterpiece that suffered merely from bad staging, ridiculous costumes, indifferent singers (except for Christoff and Antonio Zerbini in the *comprimario* part of Anchise), and a crippled libretto. Poor Angeli, the librettist! Not only did he suffer attacks from Guerrini's friends and foes alike, but the benefit of the doubt about his political inclinations was denied him by his own first name: Adolfo.[59]

Corelli's feelings about the music and about his parts of Turno and Orfeo are unknown. Antonietta Stella and Gian Giacomo Guelfi dismissed it as one of the things that had to be done at the outset of their careers.[60] And yet, those diverse criticisms make one curious about the actual music. Fortunately, a rare

---

March 11 and 15, 1953
Guido Guerrini: *Enea*
Rome, Teatro dell'Opera
Boris Christoff (*Enea*), Ofelia Di Marco (*Julo*), Franco Corelli (*Orfeo, Turno*), Orietta Moscucci (*Euridice*), Antonio Zerbini (*Anchise*), Antonietta Stella (*Creusa, Didone, Lavinia*), Gino Del Signore (*Acate*), Miriam Pirazzini (*the Sybil of Cuma*), Carlo Platania (*Drance; an Old Man*), Fernando Valentini (*Museo*), Bruno Sbalchiero (*a Priest*), Clara Betner (*a Priestess*), Loretta Di Lelio (*one of the Four Women*), cond. Emidio Tieri

Franco Corelli, looking the part as Turno, king of the Rutuli. (Photo: Courtesy of the Teatro dell'Opera)

RAI recording from January 14, 1960, does exist,[61] revealing that *Enea* is a curious attempt to combine Ildebrando Pizzetti's post-veristic idiom with the theories and the atmosphere of Gluckian opera. Its major flaw is indeed, as most critics noted, a lack of melodic invention, resulting in endless, monotonous recitatives. The dreamlike, lyrical interlude of Orfeo and Euridice was unfortunately cut from the recording, as was Orfeo's fascinating "Hymn to Apollo" (sung with a chorus of poets). Corelli's part of Turno is a very pragmatic but insignificant *comprimario* part, which culminates in his duel with Enea. Unfortunately, that duel was set to instrumental music alone, apart from a one line oath in which Turno and Enea accept the conditions of the duel. The libretto provides a spectacular, gladiator-like setting for the duel, which is not altogether matched by the music. Moreover, the choice to score the leading role of Enea for baritone seems to have been rather academically inspired indeed, and when it comes to choosing sides among the critics, one will observe that G. Pan wouldn't even have had the chance to judge a third performance at the Teatro dell'Opera, as Guerrini had requested: like so many other postwar novelties, the work received but two performances in all. Giorgio Vigolo summarized both the political muddle and the opera most imaginatively when he labeled the work "a veritable Trojan Horse!"[62]

April 9–18, 1953: Holding His Ground Against the White Army

Critical comparisons between the masterpieces of Wagner, the Dionysian Teuton, and Bellini, the Apollonian bel canto composer, were inevitable, and they appeared in rather poetic language in periodicals of the day, with *Norma* coming out on top. Although the critics loved Wagner, they considered *Norma* a masterpiece beyond compare. Bellini's chef d'oeuvre was considered one of those mysterious creations of mankind that cuts straight to the heart, with the main weight resting heavily on the shoulders of the protagonist, in this case Maria Callas. No critic failed to note the diva's dramatic qualities in what was rapidly becoming her signature role, though some judged her vocal texture less pure than desired for the "Casta diva." That quibble aside, *Il Mondo*'s Giorgio Vigolo had to evoke images of Bellini's age to describe the impact of the pairing of Callas and Barbieri. The contrast between their voices and the emotional

> April 9, 12, 15, and 18, 1953
> Vincenzo Bellini: *Norma*
> Rome, Teatro dell'Opera
> Maria Callas (*Norma*), Franco Corelli (*Pollione*), Fedora Barbieri (*Adalgisa*), Giulio Neri (*Oroveso*), Paolo Caroli (*Flavio*), cond. Gabriele Santini

intensity of their duets left even Vigolo speechless.[63] To describe Callas's appearance, *Paese Sera* turned to the majestic paintings of Nicolas Poussin, so cold, so splendidly opulent.[64]

The critics were not the only ones impressed by Callas; these performances were an eye-opener for her Pollione. Callas brought out the best in Corelli, who recognized he had to surpass himself in order simply to hold his own. Her finished mastery of the art of bel canto was one of the examples upon which he sought to model his own voice, although he wasn't yet capable of following her lead fully. He still had his hands full with trimming his voice to appropriate volumes while maintaining a smooth legato line and blending his registers. Nevertheless, it is significant that this initial performance with Callas marks not only the first of many with the diva, but also the point at which the usual encouraging reviews finally are exchanged for unqualified praise of the young tenor's efforts. *Giornale d'Italia* mentions that he explored his many talents to the fullest, and they praised his noble and focused timbre.[65] *Momento Sera* wrote that Franco's "beautiful voice, with all of its warmth and powerful timbre, sounded with the utmost security."[66] *Il Tempo* first quoted Bellini himself, who didn't like the duet between Adalgisa and Pollione, and then stated that Corelli was interesting to listen to even there.[67] To top it all off, Giorgio Vigolo, much to his own surprise, concluded that the Pollione of the evening turned out to be "a genuine tenor, who stood his ground and fought his way to the core of the battle with the sword of his voice."[68]

Such reviews were balanced by *Il Globo*'s criticism that Corelli's performance was "a little uneven," yet even that critic acknowledged that Corelli had achieved the complexity of his character "better than anyone heard before."[69] The worst of his reviews came in *Paese Sera*, whose critic remarked that the Pollione might have achieved even more by limiting his powers instead of releasing them so opulently.[70] In comparison, although she was most often singled out for mention in the reviews, Callas also received the roughest treatment when G. Pan wrote: "Power, not purity. The interpretation of this role asks for complete mastery of bel canto and expressive means. Maria Callas possesses the former, not the latter. This means that Norma is beyond her powers.... From her aggressive throat erupted a 'Casta diva' full of bristles, instead of chaste purity."[71]

You can't please everyone. Callas, like Corelli, was a singer you either loved or hated. If such conflicting reviews are confusing, Vigolo's final words on the first Callas-Corelli *Norma* put them in perspective and provide a fitting summary: "We would prefer to go to this [*Norma*] night after night rather than suffer the depths of boredom at other Teatro dell'Opera performances."[72]

❖❖❖❖❖

Although most critics focused on Callas, the mezzo, Fedora Barbieri, had her eye trained on certain aesthetic values of the production, most notably Franco's legs. She was infatuated with their beauty and nicknamed him "Coscia d'Oro" (Golden Thighs). The nickname became a favorite in the Italian press.[73] Vigolo proved less prophetic on this than on vocal matters: he compared Franco's long legs and slender ankles to "the wooden legs of a stilt-walker."[74]

May 26–June 2, 1953: *War and Peace*

Corelli's debut in Prokofiev's *Guerra e Pace* is important both because this performance yielded the earliest example of Franco Corelli's voice in a complete opera live recording and because it represents the highly successful, though unofficial, world premiere of Prokofiev's chef d'oeuvre—unofficial because the Soviets had prevented the opera's premiere in its completed form in 1947, when parallels were drawn between the libretto and the political situation during the war. Officially, of course, the work was condemned for dramatic weakness and lack of melody. Confronted with nothing but two student performances and no possibility of a genuine premiere, Prokofiev managed to get the score smuggled out of the Soviet Union, entrusting it to an American editor while hoping for a premiere in another country.[75] The memoirs of Halina Rodzinski, the conductor's wife, vividly describe the outcome. At a Valentine's Day dinner meeting in 1953, the intendant of the Florence May Festival, Francesco Siciliani, told the Rodzinskis that he wanted to produce Prokofiev's *War and Peace* with Leopold Stokowski, who had demanded a full year to prepare it. Artur Rodzinski seized the opportunity and promised the work for the upcoming May Festival. Siciliani, doubting Rodzinski's ability to pull off such a feat, countered that he would not even be able to get his hands on the score on such short notice. However, Siciliani knew that La Scala was negotiating the rights with Prokofiev's representatives and liked the idea of stealing the prestigious opera house's thunder.

With the full support and financial aid of the Italian Ministry of Culture, an agreement with Prokofiev's representatives in New York was reached. Pressed for time and filled with anticipation, Siciliani and Rodzinski anxiously awaited the score; when it finally arrived, they literally ripped the wrappings off the package. What followed was disappointing. Siciliani judged the score mediocre, while Rodzinski adopted a more practical approach: "Oh, I don't know. We can prune here, drop that scene altogether." Halina Rodzinski describes the ensuing process of cut-and-paste as equal to making a *Reader's Digest* condensation: "In itself a barbaric act, but in the case of *War and Peace*, a blessing."[76] Prokofiev had died on March 5, so whatever objections he might have made were not the opera house's main concern.

As if to make up for the butchering of the score, Siciliani spared neither cost nor effort. The best possible singers were recruited from the ranks of both acclaimed stars and Italy's finest young talents, such as Rosanna Carteri, Italo

Franco Corelli as Piero Besukov in the world premiere of Prokofiev's *Guerra e pace* at the Maggio Musicale in May 1953. (Photo: Courtesy of Arrigo Michelini)

> May 26, 29, and 31; June 2, 1953
> Sergei Prokofiev: *Guerra e pace*
> Florence, Teatro Communale
> Rosanna Carteri (*Natascia*), Ettore Bastianini (*Andrea*), Franco Corelli (*Piero Besukov*), Vittoria Calma (*Sonia*), Italo Tajo (*Rostov, General Kutusov*), Marinella Meli (*Maria Bolkonsky*), Fernando Corena (*Prince Bolkonsky*), Cesy Broggini (*Elena Besukov*), Mirto Picchi (*Anatolio*), Fedora Barbieri (*Maria Akrosimova*), Renato Capecchi (*Dolokov, General Davout*), Fernando Corena (*Balàga*), Anselmo Colzani (*Denisov*), Piero De Palma (*Fiodor, Dementi*), Giulio Fioravanti (*a French Captain*), cond. Artur Rodzinski

Tajo, Mirto Picchi, Fedora Barbieri, Renato Capecchi, Fernando Corena, and Anselmo Colzani. The very young Piero De Palma joined the forty soloists required. With thirty-eight of the roles cast, only the key roles of Piero Besukov and Andrey Balkonsky remained. For Balkonsky, Rodzinski remembered a young baritone who had sung in his recent *Pique Dame* performances—Ettore Bastianini—and moved quickly to engage him. Then began a feverish hunt for a Piero, and here their luck seemed to run out. Rodzinski despaired when Siciliani had to leave on business with no Besukov in place to rehearse. When the intendant returned, however, out of the blue he presented Rodzinski with their Besukov: "I found him in the dining car on the train. He's tall, too good looking for the part, but with a wig and eyeglasses he might do."

"Can he sing?" Rodzinski wanted to know.

"He has a lovely voice and could even develop into something great," was Siciliani's evaluation.

"I take your word," Rodzinski answered, and the Pierre was put to work. Because Siciliani had "discovered" Maria Callas, Renata Tebaldi, and a host of equally great artists and voices, Rodzinski believed the tenor Franco Corelli just possibly might work out.[77]

✦✦✦✦✦

What is perhaps most surprising in this early Corelli performance is his ability to deliver a solid stylistic portrayal of Besukov's restless character. The music had none of the heights that Corelli still feared, and his inborn legato stands out as much as his explosive, nervous drive; in comparison, the acclaimed tenor Mirto Picchi can barely hold his own. Bastianini's renowned qualities are already suggested, but he is not yet as dominant as he would become in just a few more years. Rosanna Carteri is a moving Natascia; her soprano voice contrasts to great effect with Fedora Barbieri's Akrosimova, who treats the score as if it were the next Verdi masterpiece, throwing her luscious dark Italian mezzo into the depths to stunning effect. Among the forty soloists, only Corelli matches her passionate approach, his uninhibited, trumpeting voice vibrating as if dancing barefoot on coals.

Such a star-studded cast was bound to make headlines, and the critical acclaim for performance and opera alike proved Siciliani and the Rodzinskis wrong in their judgment of the work. Despite the quickly organized Italian-language production, *War and Peace* emerged from the May Festival as an acclaimed masterpiece along the epic outlines of Tolstoy's great novel. The dramatic impact of the composition and the libretto was strikingly underscored by the real hero of the performance, Artur Rodzinski. *The New York Times* wrote: "What the performance had in sensitivity and power it owed to Artur Rodzinski.... It was the creative conducting of a great man of the musical theatre, and it was a happy thing to see how much of the evening, next to the huge success of the opera itself, became a personal triumph for Rodzinski."

Rodzinski's qualities can be heard in the surviving recording, which allows us to hear a haunting musical arc from the first measures until the final scene, where a stunning instrumental pandemonium illustrates the madness of the legendary Napoleonic-Russian War of 1812 to striking effect. All this wild and exciting music was matched by the stage action, where Rodzinski had insisted upon a real horse for Kutusov and a highly realistic way of letting Moscow burn down to cinders. With such spectacular features, accidents were bound to happen. Wrote Halina Rodzinski: "Moscow burned satisfactorily until the smoke got trapped in a sudden draft and nearly choked and blinded the players in the pit. The snow fell slowly at first; then a flake-filled bag suspended overhead broke, and an avalanche all but buried a troop of retreating French soldiers."[78]

July 2–September 6, 1953: Replacing Gigli

When the Spoleto theater designed its master schedule for 1953, it hoped to repeat the coup from the previous year, with the beloved Beniamino Gigli opening the season as Canio in Leoncavallo's *Pagliacci*. Gigli gladly consented again; he was honorary president of Pesaro's Lirico Sperimentale and considered the town his second home. However, there was one small detail still to be worked out as the first performance approached, and it concerned his daughter Rina. From the late 1940s onward, Gigli had tried to advance her singing career by having her engaged whenever he was engaged, wherever possible. Unfortunately, Rina lacked her father's stellar vocal qualities. However, by hanging on to her father's coattails for dear life, she managed to sing a few performances at Rome's Teatro dell'Opera in 1952. With that prestigious engagement on her résumé, Gigli expected additional performances for the 1953 season and asked the management what parts they had in mind for his daughter.[79] When his not-so-subtle request met with a flat refusal, he angrily canceled the Spoleto *Pagliacci* and vowed never to sing there or in Rome's Teatro dell'Opera again. He even tried to get the management fired, and when the truth of the matter became public, the papers rewarded him with a reminder of a Giacinto Gallina comedy and a Gioacchino Belli sonnet, both cautionary tales about the overprotective love of a father for his daughter.[80]

Facing the problem of finding an acceptable Canio on short notice, the Spoleto management turned to Corelli, who had successfully debuted in the part just two months earlier with the Teatro dell'Opera. In spite of a persistent cold that would trouble him for four months—a legacy from his *Carmen*

July 2 and 6, 1953
Ruggero Leoncavallo: *Pagliacci*
Rome, Terme di Caracalla
Franco Corelli (*Canio*), Clara Petrella (*Nedda*), Aldo Protti (*Tonio*), Adelio Zagonara (*Beppe*), Mario Borriello (*Silvio*), cond. Giuseppe Morelli

September 6, 1953
Ruggero Leoncavallo: *Pagliacci*
Spoleto, Teatro Nuovo
Franco Corelli (*Canio*), Lisetta Pinnarò (*Nedda*), Umberto Borghi (*Tonio*), Renato Ercolani (*Beppe*), Renzo Scorsoni (*Silvio*), cond. Ottavio Ziino

performances in the Castello Lombardo at Enna, located high on a Sicilian mountaintop[81]—he accepted the engagement and achieved an unprecedented success. According to the local press, the performances went so well without the contribution of the great Gigli that all discussions of the venerable tenor's cancellation ended then and there. *Corriere del Teatro* was the first paper ever to mention a phenomenon that would follow Corelli from now on: his festival performances were the only ones that were *tutto esaurito* (all sold out). The public welcomed him with warm applause after his first impressive notes on "A ventrite ore," then again at "No, Pagliaccio non son!," and finally at the dramatic conclusion of the opera. The next morning, *Giornale d'Italia* and a string of other newspapers wasted no time in recognizing Corelli as one of Italy's best tenors.[82] Their praise may have been a little excessive, but it documents the moment from which the Corelli cult emerged. Once more Spoleto proved instrumental in advancing his career.

September 12, 1953: On Meeting Verdi

In Ravenna, while performing in *Carmen*, Corelli had the opportunity to see Giuseppe Verdi's *Aida*, which was scheduled in between his own performances. But events took an unexpected turn when the Radamès became indisposed and the management called upon Corelli, who earlier had agreed to cover the part although he had never before performed it onstage, to step in. The tenor, by now feeling as though he held the world in the palm of his hand, kept his promise and debuted in the part, although he was largely unprepared. This fact was not lost on the press, which later reported that he knew nothing more of the score than "Celeste Aida" and the final duet.[83]

> **September 12, 1953**
> **Giuseppe Verdi:** *Aida*
> **Ravenna, Piazza J. F. Kennedy (open-air theater)**
> Caterina Mancini (*Aida*), Franco Corelli (*Radamès*), Elena Nicolai (*Amneris*), Giulio Neri (*Ramfis*), Plinio Clabassi (*the King of Egypt*), Aldo Protti (*Amonasro*), Loretta Di Lelio (*a Priestess*), cond. Angelo Questa

The cast consisted of a splendid array of Italian voices in their prime, including Loretta Di Lelio, from whom Corelli was by now almost inseparable. She took care of any tenorial nerves, although Corelli was not in fact as ignorant of the score as the press said (after all, he had studied *Aida* in Spoleto, where he even did some rehearsals with Anita Cerquetti before switching to *Carmen*). A late report that he managed to pull it off by turning his back to the audience whenever he didn't know the words, which were then sung by other cast members,[84] is surely an exaggeration, but there can be no doubt that the prompter had to see him through most of the part. That he regarded this premature Radamès debut primarily as a friendly gesture toward the management and his indisposed colleague can be gleaned from the letter to his Amneris, Elena Nicolai, when she was preparing her autobiography: "Dear Signora Elena, your letter . . . brought back so many wonderful memories of the beginnings of my artistic career. . . . I remember my appearance with you in my very first *Aida* in Ravenna, when I sang without any stage preparation, caused by the extraordinary circumstance of having to step in for another tenor in the middle of two appearances in *Carmen*."[85]

November 19–29, 1953: The Bull and the Tigress

While the Rome *Norma*s from seven months earlier marked the first meeting between Corelli and Callas, it is this performance from Trieste that is remembered because it was the first of his encounters with Callas that lives on through a recording (and the second recorded example of his voice in live performance at all). Of the actual performance, the critic from the *Messaggero Veneto* wrote:

> Last night's spectacle harbored a surprise in the shape of a young, well-built, and ringing tenor voice. Franco Corelli already had presented his calling card in the form of extraordinary vocal material in the *Carmen* at the Castle of San Giusto, but at the time he still lacked a marked style. We will not say that he has already reached the top, but it is certainly true that his splendid high notes already framed an intelligent and harmonious portrayal. Impeccable on the stage, Franco Corelli presented us with an almost perfect Pollione, for which he was applauded endlessly.[86]

Unfortunately, large portions of the performance are missing from the master recording, among them Corelli's entire entrance scene. This tempted an

> November 19, 22, 24, and 29, 1953
> Vincenzo Bellini: *Norma*
> Trieste, Teatro Giuseppe Verdi
> Maria Callas (*Norma*), Franco Corelli (*Pollione*), Elena Nicolai (*Adalgisa*), Boris Christoff (*Oroveso*), Raimondo Botteghelli (*Flavio*), cond. Antonino Votto

unknown engineer to recreate the performance by substituting bits from other *Norma* recordings for the missing parts, creating a misleading amalgam, advertised as the complete Trieste performance, that eventually made it to the market on the Melodram label. In particular, the insertion of Mario Del Monaco's voice instead of Corelli's in the phrase "Io fremo!" (just before "Im mia man, alfin tu sei") raised some eyebrows, as does the use of such different voices as those of Miriam Pirazzini, Giulietta Simionato, and Fedora Barbieri to fill in some gaps for Elena Nicolai.[87] Divina Records has issued a beautiful pressing of the complete recorded sections in a well-documented CD (DNN-3).

❖❖❖❖❖

Corelli's progress after his 1950 recordings is clear from the countless press reports on his performances in the years between his debut and this Trieste *Norma*. Even so, few would have believed him capable of genuine *pianissimo* singing in 1953, which he truly does in "Qual più di noi fallì?" There were also plenty of places where he could stand out with the required power, such as at the end of the Act I duet with Adalgisa, on "E il tu Dio sfidar saprò." His belted-out fortissimo A-flat on "Ch'io mi sveni innanzia a te" at the end of the Act III duet "In mia man alfin tu sei" even constitutes his first documented vocal (mini-)battle with a diva: Corelli holds the note a little longer than Callas does. Nevertheless, Callas emerged triumphant from the premiere. Corelli came off second best, but left both Christoff and Nicolai in the dust.

December 19–23, 1953: *Carmen*

The style revealed in the extended excerpts that survive on tape of the notorious December 19, 1952, *Carmen* performance in Naples is a throwback when compared to the *Norma* performance from Trieste. The reasons for this re-

> **December 19 and 23, 1953**
> **Georges Bizet:** *Carmen*
> **Naples, Teatro San Carlo**
> Giulietta Simionato, Pia Tassinari [December 23] (*Carmen*), Franco Corelli (*Don José*), Sena Jurinac (*Micaëla*), Ugo Savarese, Giuseppe Taddei [December 23] (*Escamillo*), cond. Artur Rodzinski

gression lie in part in events that preceded the performances, described entertainingly in Halina Rodzinski's memoirs. They reduce to an understatement the oft-repeated observation that the San Carlo Orchestra was never a very disciplined bunch: "The musicians would not concentrate and chattered incessantly. When Artur was on the edge of erupting angrily, the concertmaster explained that the blue sky and the warm sun were too seductive for the men to concentrate." The sublimely clueless intendant also had to be reckoned with; when Rodzinski once proposed to him that they do *Tristan and Isolde*, the intendant responded that to offer both operas in the same season would be too costly: "We'll do *Tristano* this season, *Isotta* the next."[89]

Ingrid Bergman, rehearsing for Arthur Honegger's *Jeanne d'Arc au Bûcher*, stopped by with her husband, Roberto Rossellini. Enchanted with *Carmen*'s music, she told Rodzinski that she would love to sing the part. Replied Rodzinski, "How I wish you could!" That was a jibe at Inge Borkh, a German beauty who was Rodzinski's original Carmen for this production. She had arrived in Naples in style with her husband, Alexander Welitsch, who was to sing Escamillo, in tow. She knew next to nothing of her part, while her husband only mouthed his words, never singing louder than sotto voce. Tempers flared when Rodzinski, with only two rehearsals left, forced him to

Franco Corelli and Sena Jurinac as Micaëla and Don José in *Carmen*, Naples, December 19, 1953. (Photo: Courtesy of the Teatro San Carlo)

sing out over an impossibly fast tempo. The *torero* threatened to throw a chair at the conductor's head if he tried that tempo in performance. Halina Rodzinski then persuaded the management to replace the German Carmen and her "pet bullfighter," and Simionato and Savarese stepped in.[90]

With these new prizefighters, Rodzinski gave the Naples audience a *Carmen* with all the emotions of a true bullfight, imposing no limits on the artists' freedom to show off their voices. The predictable grandstanding was neatly matched by the stampede in the orchestra pit, as can be heard on the incomplete recording released during the LP era on Edizione Lirica (EL001 2).[91] Those who prefer the French style may criticize Simionato's vulgar and egocentric Carmen as well as Corelli's passionate, nearly demented Don José, but this was very much what *Carmen* was about in the Italian provinces in the early 1950s. The performance sent the public into a frenzy, and the press could find no fault with it. Simionato was praised for her vocal and theatrical approach, while Corelli was judged a splendid Don José, "whose virile voice and efficient dramatic accents met with the approval of the audience."[92] Given that even his offstage entry on "Alto là! Chi va la! Prode d'Alcalà!" was belted out with a stentorian voice that only Mario Del Monaco could have matched, it was a good thing that someone had thought to supply a Strauss-and-Wagner soprano for the more lyrical part: Sena Jurinac was judged "a gorgeous Micaëla."[93]

January 28–February 3, 1954: *Romulus*

The challenge of being a singer facing an audience probably has not changed since opera's invention, but the challenge of being a composer of Italian operas after Puccini's *Turandot* is a different matter. In the early 1950s a composer's stylistic options, if his name was not Prokofiev or Britten, were between the relatively popular postmodern neo-nostalgia of Menotti and Malipiero and the revolutionary twelve-tone style that followed tonal music. Salvatore Allegra seems to have been of the school of Menotti and Malipiero,[94] which makes *Il Tempo*'s review of the Roman premiere of *Romulus* all the more surprising:

> The indecent muddle performed yesterday evening at the Teatro dell'Opera under the name of *Romulus* sounded like an offense. An offense not only against the art, which, in this case, is not worth mentioning, but an offense

against the very name of Rome. Because, with the same level of ridiculousness and of presumption, they aimed to take the heroic splendors of Rome's origins onto the stage. An unbecoming performance, in spite of the holy memories that are both religion and poetry to our people. Responsible are, first of all, the curators of our Artistic Heritage. As its first citizen, the mayor of Rome should feel offended by this insult to the city and to the Theater, of which he is president by law.[95]

Other reviews, however, suggest that Allegra, like Guerrini before him, was caught in the middle of a political debate. *Il Quotidiano* judged the music "genuine,"[96] and *Il Secolo* described Allegra as a composer who nurtured his music from the flowers that blossomed between the purest romanticism and verismo. According to the same critic, *Romulus* was a subtle crescendo from the pastoral theme at the beginning of the first act to the third, which was considered inspired: "It is definitely an opera where the creative genius of the Maestro gives complete freedom to the singers' souls, bringing the characters to life with fluent and fitting music that matches the poetic text."[97]

In order to make up one's mind about those opposite views, it is necessary to listen to a recording of it, and in fact a rare 1962 RAI recording exists, featuring Luigi Infantino as Remo.[98] There Allegra's hyperdramatic music proves to be heavily influenced by the great epic film music scores of the day, combined with incidental echoes of Rimsky-Korsakov's instrumental colors and the vocal and orchestral spirit of Mascagni's middle period (*Parisina, Isabeau*). The latter influence is so obvious, one could label him a Mascagni imitator. That particular mixture of borrowed styles, however, blends ideally with Emidio Mucci's libretto, which revives the mythical figure of Romolo, founder of Rome, in a Gabriele D'Annunzio–like idiom.

> **January 28 and 31; February 3, 1954**
> **Salvatore Allegra: Romulus**
> **Rome, Teatro dell'Opera**
> Gian Giacomo Guelfi (*Romolo*), Franco Corelli (*Remo*), Elisabetta Barbato (*Flora*), Maria Benedetti (*Tarpeja*), Augusto Romani (*Faustolo*), Carlo Platania (*a Sentinel*), Margherita Bagni (*the Soul of Queen Silvia*), cond. Oliviero De Fabritiis

THE CONQUEST OF ROME • 83

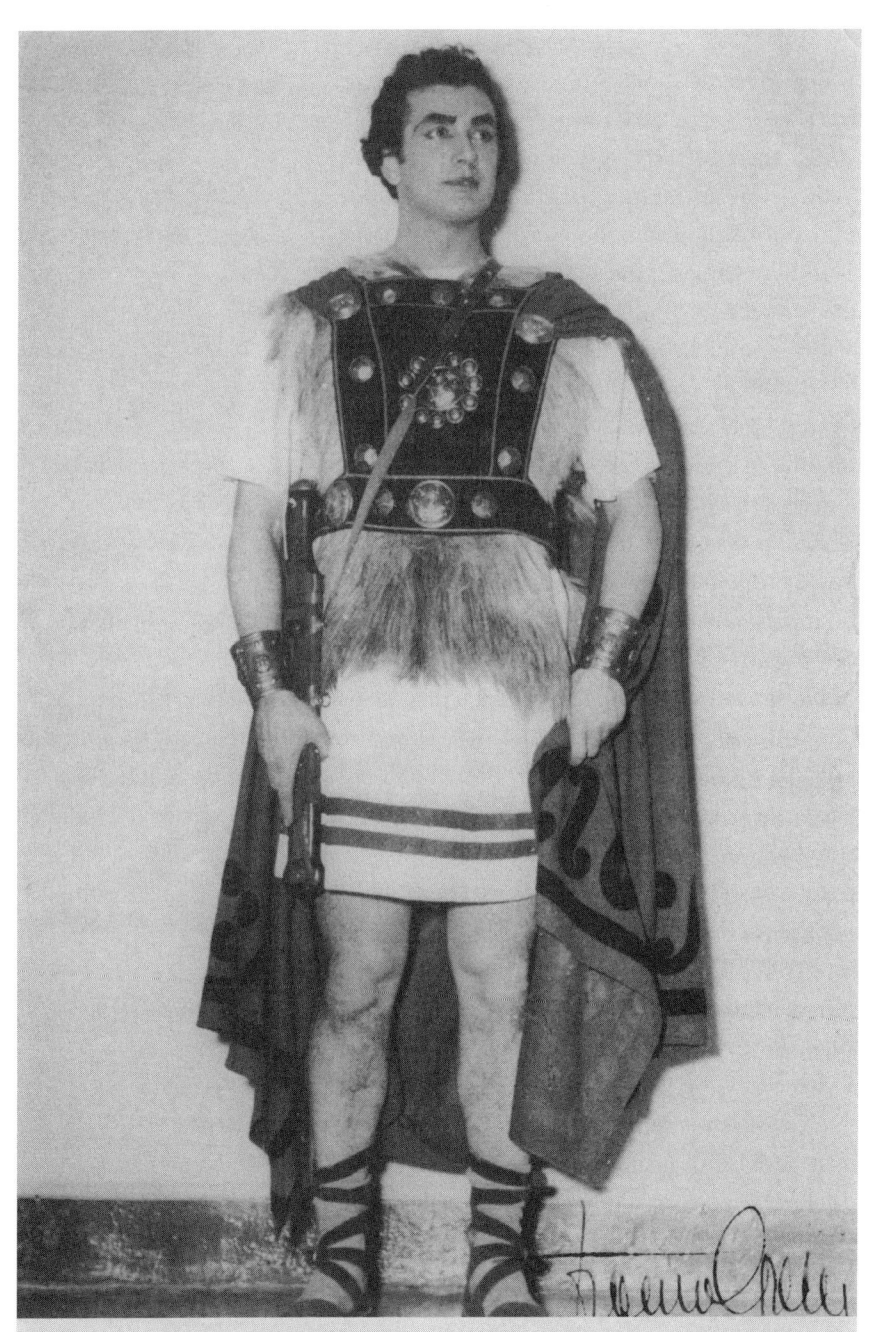

One of the rarest of all photos of Corelli: as Remo in Salvatore Allegra's *Romulus*. (Photo: Courtesy of the Teatro dell'Opera and Arrigo Michelini)

The first act is largely conceived around an apparition: the ghost of the twins' mother, Queen Silvia, reveals their identity as demigods, predicts the appearance of a flower from the sea, and envisions a new city on the banks of the Tiber. Flora (the predicted "flower") then appears to Romolo and tells him to found the city on the Palatine Hill. Remo prefers the slope of the Aventine Hill, so the brothers ask the gods for a sign to settle the matter. When twelve eagles appear to Romolo but only six to Remo, Romolo considers the matter closed, though Remo refuses to accept the decision in his arioso "Sull'Aventino più lieti gli uccelli."

The killing of Remo (Corelli) by Romolo (Gian Giacomo Guelfi, left). (Photo: Courtesy of the Teatro dell'Opera)

The second act focuses on the fatal dispute between the twin brothers. Following Romolo's order to abduct the Sabine women, Remo returns with the intent to govern the city—alone. The act culminates in Remo's agitated aria "A Numitore, dal fratello Amulio," after which Romolo kills him in a duel. Judging from Luigi Infantino's 1962 recording of the declamatory aria, and with an eye to the type of poetry that is employed here, it is not hard to imagine the impact that the young Corelli voice made here:

A Numitore, dal fratello Amulio,	Wasn't it Amulio who took the scepter and crown
tolti non furono scettro e corona?	away from his brother Numitore?
E con violenza, dalla città d'Alba,	And wasn't the piteous king,
non fu discacciato il re misero?	violently driven from the city of Alba?
Questo le sacre parole di nostra Madre: ricordi?	These were the sacred words of our Mother: do you remember?
E andai—bello è combattere—con un pugno di prodi.	And I went—it's beautiful to fight— with a fistful of courage.
Ma nella lotta, sopraffatto e dalle funi avvinto,	But in the battle, I was overpowered, bound with ropes,
fui gittato in un'orrida caverna.	and thrown in a horrible cave.

O madre! Madre! Invoco dal profondo.	O, mother! Mother! I'm begging from the depths.
Poi come zanne di lupo i miei denti recidono la stretta.	Then like wolves' fangs my teeth cut through the hold.
Balzo, mi avvento, gli sgherri di guaria, attero.	I jumped up and knocked down the guards.
È notte . . . il cuore nella gola mi palpita;	It's night . . . my heart beats in my throat;
Pènetro nella regia . . . m'inoltro . . .	I penetrate into the King's palace . . . I pass through . . .
Ecco lui! . . . alzo l'arma, la bacio, e nel suo petto l'immergo.	There he is! . . . I lift my weapon, I kiss it, and I stab it into his chest.
M'ispirò—grido esultante— giustizia, o Madre, giustizia!	I was inspired—I shouted with joy— justice Mother, justice!

(Lyrics by Emidio Mucci, reprinted courtesy of the Teatro dell'Opera)

The final act brings a poetic account of Tarpeia's betrayal of the Capitol to the vengeful Sabines, Romolo's victory, and a long concluding hymn to Rome. That nationalistic focus, rendered in a muscular style, much in line with the old Italian regime's taste, may have inspired *Il Tempo*'s critic to condemn the opera in such bitter words.

Although the title role was written for baritone, the tenor, Remo, is by far the toughest part from a vocal point of view. It was written in a murderous tessitura with numerous B-flats, As, and Gs, and it easily constitutes the most challenging role Corelli had performed to date, and perhaps ever. To his credit, he came off with honors, after Guelfi, who was considered to have been outstanding. In addition, Elisabetta Barbato, Maria Benedetti, and Oliviero De Fabritiis were all said to have carried out their tasks with the utmost care.[99]

April 4–13, 1954: A Close Encounter with Giuseppe Verdi

When asked about the composer most suited to his voice, Corelli frequently answered, "Giuseppe Verdi." True though that may have been in later years, he wasn't a born Verdian. Not only *Aida* but also Verdi's complex *Don Carlo* posed a challenge to Corelli at this early stage in his career. The tenor part is written in a high, dramatic tessitura, while at the same time it asks for exceptionally sensitive, lyrical phrasing. If ever there was a Verdi tenor role that called for the full range of the art of bel canto and its elements of legato, shading, *morbidezza* (the tragic coloring of certain notes), and all the other vocal graces, it is *Don Carlo*. The press, still hoping for the next Verdi or Puccini to step out of the shades, actually labeled the opera a textbook example for modern composers: "It is music from the past, but incredibly beautiful Italian music, still vibrant and alive with balanced melodies. Verdi's music reflects his inborn vocal spirit to maximum effect. A full eighty-seven years after the Paris premiere, the fearless Swan of Busseto still rises with head and shoulders above all others."[100]

The cast succeeded in reviving Verdi's relatively unpopular masterpiece, with Gobbi and the regal Christoff dividing the first honors. Their distinctive timbres, finished vocal artistry, and superb acting left nothing to be desired. Mancini had just reached the apex of her prime and would never be better. Because this fine trio were repeating their parts from the year before,[101] they had a little advantage over the cast's only newcomer, who celebrated his true Verdi debut in the difficult title role. But Corelli held his own in his most challenging task to date. The

Corelli at his debut in Verdi's *Don Carlo*, Rome, April 1954. (Photo: Courtesy of the Teatro dell'Opera and Arrigo Michelini)

April 4, 7, 10, and 13, 1954

Giuseppe Verdi: *Don Carlo*

Rome, Teatro dell'Opera

Franco Corelli (*Don Carlo*), Caterina Mancini (*Elisabetta di Valois*), Elena Nicolai (*Princess d'Eboli*), Boris Christoff (*Filippo II*), Giulio Neri (*the Grand Inquisitor*), Tito Gobbi (*Rodrigo*), Loretta Di Lelio (*Tebaldo*), Ines Bardini (*a Heavenly Voice*), cond. Gabriele Santini

opinion of *Il Paese* was almost touching; its critic observed that the tenor tried almost too hard to give his very best: "Corelli was so overly noble that he almost sacrificed his voice over it. He forced and abused it too much."[102] That brings up another interesting aspect of the early Corelli voice: his initial problems with the blending of registers between his middle voice and his high range.[103] *Il Quotidiano* suggested the usual remedy: "He needs to study and gain experience."[104]

◆◆◆◆◆

Despite the experienced coaching of Gabriele Santini, singing Verdi proved to be a process of trial and error for Corelli, which could sometimes lead to surprising results. Corelli readily confirmed the opinion of the critic of *Il Paese*, who observed that he sang with too much force, arriving a little tired at the end: "I remember one night, I had a little phrase on an A-flat, not a very high note, but a particularly difficult one, and when I arrived at this A-flat in 'Ed io la mancero,' my voice slipped from its full, round sound to a thin sound, because I was tired. But at least I managed to keep this thin sound." Corelli left the stage worried, but afterward people congratulated him for the beautiful little note that he had spun out so enchantingly. Said Corelli, "This is how I discovered the art of the pianissimo."[105]

Most critics, however, simply raved over Corelli's now evident abilities. *Il Secolo* marveled at his volume and praised him for the way he mastered the technical demands of this difficult role.[106] *D'Italia* judged him a noble, serious, and intelligent artist, with beautiful vocal means.[107] *Il Messaggero* heard fiery accents in a versatile voice,[108] and *Avanti!* predicted that the young Don Carlo would become a tenor people would talk about.[109] There was praise also for the Santini, for Elena Nicolai's Eboli, and for Loretta Di Lelio's Tebaldo, "a fresh, graceful voice."[110]

April 17–26, 1954: Cristoforo Villibaldo "Knight" von Gluck

I dream of embracing the music, to use the poetry to express the situations of the story without interrupting the action or diminishing its impact with empty ornaments.

  Christoph Willibald von Gluck, at the beginning of the composition of
  Iphigénie en Aulide

Like a fierce banner in battle, *Iphigénie en Aulide* was presented to the French public on April 19, 1774. The crowd fell into two camps: those who preferred Italian opera and those who hailed Gluck as Jean-Philippe Rameau's true heir. Queen Marie Antoinette and the philosopher-composer Jean-Jacques Rousseau were with the latter. As an Italian opera, after all, *Ifigenia in Aulide* conquered Italy in 1818, and a full 136 years later the Roman critics were still short of words to describe the opera's splendor when it was performed in the Teatro dell'Opera. The press judged Gluck Verdi's equal, both as the son of a farmer and as a decisive force in the search for dramatic truth. The list of superlatives for the opera was endless: marble, a fresco filled with tragic pathos, mythical, chaste, sober, intimate, sincere, revolutionary, and "a great relief after the performances of Hans Werner Henze's *Boulevard Solitude*, which had harassed the public shortly before."[111] The anti-Henze critic came close to proclaiming "Cristoforo Villibaldo" a veritable son of Italy, although one critic duly noted that Gluck's music

Achille in Gluck's *Ifigenia in Aulide* is one of the most overlooked parts among Corelli's early debuts. Apart from the circumstance that here, as in most of the operas until this point, both photographs and recordings were thought to have been lost, Corelli fans also tend to favor his more popular repertoire. Corelli himself remembered Achille as one of the most difficult roles he ever performed, because of its numerous high notes. This unique photo was privately made and then given to his friend Arrigo Michelini. (Photo: Courtesy of Arrigo Michelini)

was less revolutionary than claimed. His operas were firmly embedded in the eighteenth-century French tradition, and *Ifigenia in Aulide* features an abundant number of ballets, a Rameauesque set of sweet duettinos and graceful arias, and a sugary approach to dramatic scenes, culminating in the inevitable

> **April 17, 19, 22, and 26, 1954**
> **Christoph Willibald "Ritter" von Gluck: *Ifigenia in Aulide***
> **Rome, Teatro dell'Opera**
> Boris Christoff (*Agamennone*), Franco Corelli (*Achille*), Marcella Pobbe (*Ifigenia*), Elena Nicolai (*Clitennestra*), Silvio Maionica (*Calcante*), Alfredo Colella (*Argante*), Ines Bardini (*Diana*), Silvia Bertona (a *Slave Girl*), Orietta Moscucci (a *Greek Woman*), cond. Gabriele Santini.

happy ending. Wrote the critic for *Paese Sera*: "Dressed in classical clothes they are dancing passacaglias."[112]

In between the dances Agamennone pledges to Diana to sacrifice his daughter Ifigenia. Her mother, Clitennestra, and Clitennestra's lover, Achille, try to prevent it. When they fail, the usual deus ex machina appears to guarantee the happy ending. The part of Achille, written for a very high tenor, was (somewhat surprisingly) given to Corelli, the Agamennone was Boris Christoff, the Clitennestra was Elena Nicolai, and the Ifigenia was sung by Marcella Pobbe, who was enjoying one of her very best years. Apart from the usual single negative review, all critics proclaimed the performances a veritable triumph for Gluck, in spite of the alien performance style. Public and critics alike gladly sacrificed historical accuracy for the abundant vocal splendor onstage, and this time it was Corelli who came out on top: "Franco Corelli has really convinced us (a) because of the clarity of his singing, which was expressed in the appropriate style, and (b) because of the sober allure of his stage movements."[113] Others followed suit, judging his performance "heroic," "balanced," and "ardent" in its rendering of the proud and energetic Achille.[114]

Curiously, *Il Mondo* considered Corelli perfect for the role because it was so central. Corelli considered Achille one of the two most difficult roles he ever sang. Not only would he never sing it again, but he maintained that he couldn't have done so later on account of all the B-naturals, which were very taxing because of the way they were written, after a series of high Gs, A-flats, or A-naturals.[115] There is no doubt that Achille, written for a high tenor of the French school who was expected to take his upper notes in *voix mixte* or *falsetto*, is a murderous part when sung with the blazing high notes in the full voice that Corelli used. On the other hand, he was allowed a number of cuts in critical places, and outside his three arias, a trio, and a modest duet, for the most part he had only to survive some shortened recitatives. But in the arias "Crudelle, no, già mai," "Rival del mio valor," and "Cadra, Calcante sì cadra," he had to show his mettle. Still, the general consensus today is that Corelli's early years were limited by a short top. Corelli himself later in life maintained that he had his high notes from the very beginning, although he didn't always feel secure enough to deliver them at will.[116]

Apart from the high notes, the classical style bewildered Corelli, who found Gluck uncongenial to his more passionate musical nature. Nevertheless, Corelli's admirers who treasure the Callas live recordings of Gluck's *Alceste* and *Ifigenia in Tauride* lament this particular performance as one of the most heartbreaking omissions from his recorded legacy—not only because of the loss of that handful of heroic tenorial top notes, but also because of the majestic Agamennone of Boris Christoff, the touching Ifigenia of Marcella Pobbe, and the fitting Elena Nicolai as Clitennestra. The loss of the visual aspect is likewise lamented, for Herbert Graf's direction was unanimously praised, and if there was disagreement over the subtlety of the choreography and the procession of soldiers,[117] the various descriptions strongly suggested that they were at least spectacular.

May 6–11, 1954: Bauer to Bing on Enrico di Braunschwig

In spite of the admiration that Weber, Rossini, Schumann, Liszt, Meyerbeer, Berlioz, and Wagner had for Gaspare Spontini,[118] his star has dimmed considerably since their day. Forced to give up his position in the post-Napoleonic Paris of 1819, Spontini nevertheless managed to transport the Napoleonic idiom to the Prussian Royal Court in Berlin, where Friedrich Wilhelm III welcomed him as court composer. Spontini rewarded the king with some of his most exquisite works, among which *Agnes von Hohenstaufen* stands out. The opera breathes Gluck, while the vocal and orchestral texture owe much to Luigi Cherubini; they link *Agnese* to the classical era, which had peaked thirty years before the work was premiered in its entirety in June 1829 (the first act had been given in May 1827). Despite its initial success in Berlin, the opera stood little chance against the revolutionary, romantic German style defined by Weber's *Der Freischütz* and Marschner's *Der Vampyr*, operas that were the sensation of the day.[119]

> May 6, 9, and 11, 1954
> Gaspare Spontini: *Agnese di Hohenstaufen*
> Florence, XVII Maggio Musicale, Teatro Communale
> Lucille Udovick (*Agnese di Hohenstaufen*), Franco Corelli (*Enrico di Braunschwig*), Gian Giacomo Guelfi (*Emperor Enrico VI*), Dorothy Dow (*Irmengarda*), Francesco Albanese (*Filippo di Hohenstaufen*), Enzo Mascherini (*the Duke of Borgogna*), Anselmo Colzani (*Enrico the Lion*), Arnold van Mill (*the Archbishop of Magonza*), cond. Vittorio Gui

Agnes von Hohenstaufen in particular and Spontini in general benefited from the urgent need to find new operatic repertoire in the early 1950s, when it was beginning to dawn on the public that new masterpieces would no longer appear regularly. Mascagni, Cilea, and Zandonai had died in the preceding decade, and theaters were starting a hunt for forgotten composers and masterpieces. In a time when recordings were still exceedingly scarce, a legendary score such as *Agnes*, in an Italian adaptation, was bound to draw crowds.

And so it happened that after a century of silence, Enrico di Braunschwig fell in love with Agnese di Hohenstaufen again, in spite of the fact that she was promised to the king of France by Emperor Henry VI. Enrico, son of the rebellious Henry the Lion, assaults his rival and is arrested. The king demands satisfaction by duel with Enrico, which doesn't prevent the latter from secretly marrying his beloved Agnese. When the course of events finally threatens to get Enrico killed, his father bursts into the castle and offers peace, to general rejoicing.

The dramatic story line almost matched the one Siciliani had in mind for the Maggio Musicale premiere, which clearly aimed to steal some of the thunder of the upcoming La Scala revival of Spontini's *La Vestale*. The added asset of having La Scala's lead Vestale, Maria Callas, for the title role was to have made his coup complete. That plan fell through when the diva demanded 800,000 lire per night. Siciliani saved the situation, as he so often had, by making a star out of an unknown—in this case, Lucille Udovick.

◆◆◆◆◆

Regarding the eve of the Berlin world premiere, rumor had it that *Agnese di Hohenstaufen* lasted a full ten hours, divided over two days. Such regal proportions were of course no longer possible in the postwar Italian republic; the Italian adaptation was cut to four and a half hours, including intermissions.[120]

Roberto Bauer was among the audience and relayed the Udovick hype in his report to Rudolf Bing. Dorothy Dow and Francesco Albanese were judged passable, whereas the much more difficult of the two tenor parts was sung, or shouted, by Corelli, often with unclear intonation. Wrote Bauer:

> I can't find any pleasure in Franco Corelli and judge the voice badly carried, and of not such good quality that one could forget about this. In addition he appears to be totally unmusical. All there is to him is a maddening arrogance and then he puts it on very thick and through that he even manages to make some impact. The voice is loud but not very beautiful and I don't believe that he can sing very long in this fashion.[121]

All the other critics, though, believed Corelli had sung a splendid Enrico di Braunschwig, an evaluation confirmed by the recording. The combination of his stamina and his baritonal quality provided just the right sort of weight for the role, while his romantic qualities are striking in broad-winged melodic sections such as the *Trovatore*-like opening serenade "A chi affidar poss'io" and the arioso "Quest'occhio inebriato."

✦✦✦✦✦

Bauer was more favorably impressed by Corelli's friend and colleague Gian Giacomo Guelfi, whose expansive voice seemed limitless. His truly imperial Enrico VI immediately secured him a summer audition with Bing.[122] But Bauer could no longer completely ignore the emerging Corelli cult, and he recommended Franco for an audition as well, on

Franco Corelli as Enrico di Braunschwig in Spontini's *Agnese di Hohenstaufen*, Teatro Communale, Bologna, May 1954. (Photo: Courtesy of Arrigo Michelini)

> **July 27 and 29, 1954**
> Giacomo Puccini: *Tosca*
> San Remo, Teatro delle Palme
> Elisabetta Barbato (*Tosca*), Franco Corelli (*Cavaradossi*), Enzo Mascherini (*Scarpia*), cond. Oliviero De Fabritiis

the grounds of his popularity alone. However, when he approached the singer in June, he found that the terms of their relationship had somehow changed; the tenor flatly told him that he had progressed beyond having to audition.[123] In fact, Corelli didn't give a damn about the Met. His immense fear of flying made appearing in the United States little more than an exotic dream, and besides, he had his hands full with his upcoming debut as Mario Cavaradossi in *Tosca*, set for San Remo's Teatro delle Palme on July 27 and 29. It was his first Puccini role and an instant success, which he took from San Remo to Fermo's Teatro dell'Aquila in his native province, Le Marche. A few *Carmen*s in the Terme di Caracalla and Messina preceded the end of his summer activities, when he reprised his Cavaradossi in the Teatro Duse in Bologna in September.

September 26, 1954: Television Star

As with Besukov in *Guerra e Pace*, Corelli's Canio in *Pagliacci* is a part for which the tenor lacked the *physique du rôle*, for he is supposed to be the older, ugly one betrayed by his beautiful young wife, Nedda, who lusts after the handsome Silvio. But that handicap is easily forgotten in the barrage of tumultuous emotions unfolding before the eyes of the television audience. This *Pagliacci*, preserved on DVD (Hardy Classic Video, DVD HDC 4016), has all that Canio promises the spectators at the beginning of the opera: "Un grande spettacolo!"

> **September 26, 1954**
> Ruggero Leoncavallo: *Pagliacci*
> Milan (black-and-white telecast)
> Franco Corelli (*Canio*), Mafalda Micheluzzi (*Nedda*), Tito Gobbi (*Tonio*), Mario Carlin (*Beppe*), Lino Puglisi (*Silvio*), cond. Alfredo Simonetto

Corelli acts the part brilliantly, thanks no doubt to a director who understood the importance of credible gestures—it looks as though he designed a ballet for Canio's arms and hands. The same can be said of his facial expression; the anger in his eyes expressed while singing "Un tal gioco" appears truly genuine and is matched by a stunning vocal presence. Still, prime honors go to Tito Gobbi, who turns Tonio into the vocal brother of Iago, as if to prove that Leoncavallo's melodies were not born of a sudden verismo rain falling on the Mediterranean peninsula. As an actor, Gobbi is the living image of the wretched Tonio—despised, submissive, vengeful. What a pity that all that vocal splendor was wasted on a lightweight Nedda, who apparently was beyond coaching.

1954: "PeCorelli"

A pronounced vibrato is a characteristic of many Mediterranean singers. Its most renowned exponents were Fernando De Lucia and the young Giacomo Lauri-Volpi.[124] Whereas a pronounced, rapid vibrato was De Lucia's vocal signature throughout his career, Lauri-Volpi largely managed to reduce his in later years. Together with Aureliano Pertile and a handful of other early twentieth-century tenors, they were the last of the nineteenth-century line of tenors referred to as "caprini"—goatlike. The fact that American and English critics of the fin de siècle rejected this "excessive" vibrato may well have contributed to the gradual extinction of that bloodline. The most notable exception among major postwar tenors was the young Corelli. This characteristic was perfectly fine in Italy, where no critic ever scolded him for his strong vibrato, until his colleague and competitor Mario Del Monaco started ridiculing him for it when he labeled the man he saw as a runner-up to his tenor throne "PeCorelli"—Corelli the Sheep.

Giancarlo Del Monaco, the tenor's son, recalls how the story arose: "It was not a joke my father invented, but rather my uncle Alberto, my father's youngest brother."[125] The nickname quickly spread among the galleries through the Del Monaco claque, who teased Corelli with it so cruelly that even late in life he had difficulty speaking about it. Effectively, the Del Monacos' joke marks the beginning of Corelli's long-running adversarial relationship with his idol and rival. However, Corelli always differentiated between the humiliating joke and the technical aspects of his vibrato. Interestingly, he probably discovered his pronounced vibrato only when he started to record, because the very notion of it is absent from the hundreds of performance reviews published in the years following his debut. They occasionally mentioned a "vibrant" voice in the sense that it trumpeted or had presence, that it was piercing and tantalizing, but never that it suffered from excessive vibrato. Because his more serious recording career began with the televised *Pagliacci*, where the vibrato is very apparent, his own awareness of this characteristic in a negative sense may be pinpointed to September 1954.[126] In his own words, he was downright shocked to discover that he had this *caprino* and set out to eliminate the defect, which he regarded as the result of a faulty emission of his breath: "I was not using my breath well. It was somehow dispersed. . . . It was a vibrato that came from a certain physical force. When I sang in the beginning, I never thought where to place a note; I opened my mouth and I sang. That is not singing with technique, that is natural singing."[127]

✦✦✦✦✦

By chance or by design, the Del Monacos' degrading remark coincided with rumors that Corelli had been asked to open La Scala's upcoming season.[128] Though they may not have had the intention of preventing that, it is a striking moment, especially considering that La Scala didn't plan very far ahead due to their system of *stagioni*—a fixed run of performances of a certain opera that would not be repeated later on. That allowed for more freedom than the Metropolitan's repertory system, which involved house singers. At La Scala the repertoire could be established on a much shorter term, and casts could be picked at the last minute. As late as September, Ghiringhelli—advised by Callas, Votto, and Visconti—approached Corelli for the upcoming December production of Spontini's *La Vestale*, which was to open the season. But if La Scala's chief had expected to be received with open arms, he was soon brought down to earth. Corelli was riding high, looking back on an incredibly successful year that had started with his debut in Parma, where people had waited in line for a full thirty hours to get tickets for his January 9 performance of *Norma* with Caterina Mancini. There was little doubt in the tenor's mind that the press reports of this exceptional case of "Corelli-itis" had landed on the desk of La Scala's intendant as well, just as his participation in the *Pagliacci* film would not have passed unnoticed. Still carrying a grudge over Ghiringhelli's condescending and dismissive remarks after the 1952 audition, he decided that it was payback time and demanded a scandalous amount of money for his debut: "More than double what I had ever received in the Teatro dell'Opera or any other theater."[129]

After a full month passed with no response from management, Corelli feared he had overplayed his hand. But just when he started to despair, he received word that his demands would be met: "I was going to open La Scala with the highest fee ever paid to a *débutant*."[130]

December 7–18, 1954: The Marlon Brando of D Major

If Callas had taken a liking to Corelli from their first appearance in the Rome *Norma*s, she became all the more aware of her handsome young Pollione during the triumphant *Norma*s in Trieste. From there to the equally supportive part of Licinio in Gasparo Spontini's *La Vestale* was but a small step. The story lines are very similar up to the end, where the vestal virgin Giulia accuses herself. (The most striking difference is Spontini's happy ending.) Like *Norma*, *La Vestale* is clearly a vehicle for the soprano lead. Revived by Rosa Ponselle in 1925, it was almost a natural choice for Callas in 1954, when her voice fit the dramatic music like a glove. Licinio was originally composed for Adolphe Nourrit, the illustrious predecessor to the breed of dramatic tenors (though he didn't sing it at the work's premiere). The part consists largely of effective but hardly impressive declamatory music in which the tenor spends most of his time singing around the center of the staff, with hardly any melodic legato phrases like the ones that enliven the part of Enrico in Spontini's *Agnese di Hohenstaufen*. Licinio's only true solo, "Giulia fia ver che mora!," is more a declamatory outburst than an aria.

The opera has a neoclassical score and an atmosphere somewhere between Cherubini's *Medea* and Bell-

Corelli as Licinio in *La Vestale*, Teatro alla Scala, December 1954. (Photo: Erio Piccagliani. Courtesy of the Teatro alla Scala)

ini's *Norma*. However, to label it "a neoclassic *Norma*," as Luchino Visconti did,[131] is backward: Spontini's chef d'oeuvre precedes Bellini's work by a full twenty-four years, and *Norma* is rather *La Vestale* on a grand scale. Both Bellini and Donizetti fondly remembered Spontini's score when it was their turn to produce melodrama after melodrama, as would Verdi. At its 1807 premiere it enchanted the Empress Joséphine, and it even became Napoleon's favorite opera once he returned to Paris. In spite of all that, it wouldn't have been the most likely choice for a prestigious opening night at La Scala without the added glamour of Maria Callas in the title role.

It was at her side that Corelli opened his very first La Scala season on the evening of December 7, 1954:

> I was trembling with fear. Maria Callas as protagonist, Antonino Votto as conductor, Luchino Visconti as director. Visconti was the one who wanted me as Licinio. He had heard me a few months before in Rome, in *Norma*. I should better say "seen" than "heard." Visconti was looking for a classical, beautifully sculptured athlete who would resemble a gladiator or a Roman general to put next to Callas. That was certainly one of the reasons he selected me, though not the only one. But even if it was, I am convinced that physical beauty is an advantage for an artist and it should be put to good use, just as any given vocal qualities, a certain temperament, or a fine high C-natural should.[132]

His physical appearance may have helped, but Ghiringhelli and company would never have acceded to Corelli's demands on the basis of his looks alone. Clearly his vocal abilities had progressed. Visconti had Callas and Votto on his side in deeming this young singer a match for her temperament both vocally and visually in a certain repertoire. Corelli always retained fond memories of Votto,

December 7, 9, 12, 16, and 18, 1954
Gaspare Spontini: *La Vestale*
Milan, Teatro alla Scala
Maria Callas (*Giulia*), Franco Corelli (*Licinio*), Enzo Sordello (*Cinna*), Nicola Rossi Lemeni (*the High Priest*), Ebe Stignani (*the High Vestal Virgin*), cond. Antonino Votto; stage director, Luchino Visconti; stage designer, Nicola Benois.

who supported him throughout and helped the singers considerably: "I have a particular devotion for him. I remember him stretching out his hand from the podium, looking at me with his shining, kind eyes, with his half smile, itself an incentive for the singer. And if he told you, 'OK, Corelli, it's OK if you want to relax, . . .' then you started again with fresh energy, you felt like a lion."[133]

In turn, Luchino Visconti was to Corelli what he had been to Callas before, instructing him in how to use his body, how to stand, to walk, to move, to kneel, to rise and face the public. Visconti paid special attention to the duet, where he even corrected Corelli's right thumb: "My thumbs are overlarge and bent, and he didn't want that to be noticed. 'Just put your arms around her'—he insisted—'touch Maria, don't worry, in this way those fingers will be hidden in the folds of her costume.' Then he turned to her: 'Look, Maria, Corelli is striking here, you must raise yourself and turn your back to the audience, allow him to sing with his face turned toward the public.'" In addition, Visconti made Corelli try at least five different capes, looking for the one that would be the most imposing and effective onstage. Said Corelli: "It was the heaviest, I got tired wearing it on my shoulders. Yet I wish I had given more, I wish I had learned more."[134]

The combination of a great theatrical talent and innovative, film-oriented staging, not to mention noble ancestry (he was a grandchild of Duke Guido Visconti, intendant of La Scala at the turn of the century), gave Visconti, who debuted as director at La Scala with this production, just the right credentials to win over a new generation. A good ten years after the war, the public longed for the glamour of the past. Together with Piero Zuffi, Visconti, taking for their inspiration the imperial neoclassical paintings of Andrea Appiani the Elder, designed three-dimensional sets, erected large white marble pillars, and designed breathtaking mass scenes and processions in which priestesses dressed in stunning neoclassical robes carried garlands of roses. The gestures were largely modeled upon illustrious French tragediennes and the paintings of Canova, David, and Ingres, who summed up what Visconti believed to be the essence of Greek tragedy.[135] So much artistic drive usually needs an outlet; Visconti had a reputation for being rather vulgar in private, as well as openly homosexual. Whereas Callas tried to cope with the first, she completely ignored his sexual identity. Said Visconti: "At some point Maria began to fall in love with me. It was a stupid thing, all in her mind."[136] All the same, Callas's feelings didn't help things as far as rehearsals were concerned. Visconti remembers: "Like so many

The rehearsals for *La Vestale* were an eye-opener for Corelli. Luchino Visconti, who can be seen here with Callas and Corelli, explained to Franco how to stand, walk, move, and kneel and rise again. (Photo: Courtesy of the Teatro alla Scala and Erio Piccagliani)

Greeks she had a possessive streak, and there were many jealous scenes. She hated Corelli because he was handsome. It made her nervous, she was wary of handsome people. She was always watching to see that I didn't give him more attention than her."[137] This precise quote may have inspired Arianna Stassinopoulos to write that Visconti, in turn, was in love with Corelli.[138] Stassinopoulos explicitly mentions that Visconti's affection for Corelli was a one-way street, but this little retouching of Ardoin and Fitzgerald's much more sober story has been the source of a number of unfounded rumors concerning the tenor's private life.[139]

Another factor adding luster to both the *La Vestale* rehearsals and the premiere was the presence of the legendary Arturo Toscanini, the famous conductor who had participated as a cellist in the world premiere of Verdi's *Otello* in 1887. Although, at his age, Toscanini couldn't clearly see what Visconti was doing, his ears were still fine: "I find this Callas woman very good, a beautiful voice and an interesting artist, but her diction is unintelligible. With the tenor I understand every word. This is important, for opera is theater and the words are more important than the music." Visconti was shocked at this last remark, but when he asked again the maestro confirmed it.[140] When Toscanini finally ran into Corelli, he shook his hand and congratulated him on his splendid diction and considerable volume: "My dear boy, you just keep going like that, don't change anything. Just strive to become a little more bright and a little bit darker at the same time. For a voice like yours, I would have to go back many, many years and even if I did, I might not find one. Don't let anyone destroy it."[141]

Callas's feelings for Visconti emerged at a moment where she had lost a significant amount of weight in the space of a few months. As the vestal virgin, she appeared before the stunned Milanese audience in the shape of an elegant, slender, Audrey Hepburn–like swan. Suddenly she matched Corelli onstage in beauty, and together they made an incredible pair. As for the tenor, he had little trouble with the role. The tessitura does not go beyond high A, which marks the part as tailored to the voices of the traditional baritone-tenors of the past. *Musica e Dischi* added that he sang and acted immaculately: "His recitatives were noble, his voice robust and worthy of La Scala, ready for greater challenges; we believe that he could become a first-choice Don Carlo or Samson in the future." *Corriere della Sera* praised his fluent singing, and Eugenio Gara ultimately put all those flattering words into a heartfelt crescendo: "Corelli had everything in order, having a warm, full, substantial voice, and, what really matters, a profound commitment to what he was doing—the firm connection of sound, gesture, and words. . . . The audience immediately became fond of him. The ladies, and this is good, had the feeling they had found what they were looking for: the Marlon Brando of the key of D major."[142]

◆◆◆◆◆

Just how important the *Vestale* premiere was for Corelli's career is clear from Bauer's report to Bing. Both had disliked the tenor at the 1952 audition. Bauer had despised him as Dimitri and Don José in 1953 and judged him only a little bit better in *Agnese di Hohenstaufen*. Much to his own surprise, he found himself reporting that the singer's Licinio was quite good. Given that it isn't much of a part for an aspiring tenor, he judged Corelli to be the best of this cast, for "all [the] others were so lousy that someone who would sing at least a little bit good, would stand out easily." The other reason he was suddenly recommending Corelli as a last resort, in case their first choice for tenor couldn't be had, was of course Franco's good looks.[143]

Unfortunately for Bauer and Bing, Corelli was now riding very high, with money and offers flowing in from all sides. He was very much aware of his new value and ridiculed Bauer when he tried to tempt Corelli once again to audition for Bing: "I don't need any audition. Besides, I am not interested in America, as they pay too lousy. And when you earn a lot, you have to pay 50% tax and I don't like the idea of working for the American government." Bauer and Bing, still unaware that Corelli had no intention of ever stepping onto an airplane, now began to calculate what it would take to get Corelli to New York, both financially and with respect to Italian operatic politics. Wrote Bauer: "He is under the protection of *Maestro* Sampaoli and Liduino [Bonardi] and I know that they never gave him out to any theater below lit. [*lire*] 300,000 ($480). And then he has this contract with them, where he has to pay each of them 33% of his earnings."[144]

CHAPTER 8 ❖ 1955–1957

Forging the Voice

January–March 1955: *La Fanciulla del West*

His real career started in 1955.
  Loretta Corelli, interview, Milan, January 26, 2007

The instant success of Corelli at his debut in Puccini's *La Fanciulla del West* is hardly surprising today, where Dick Johnson has become something of a connoisseur's choice among Corelli roles. The complex and vocally taxing part fit his heroic-dramatic voice and his vocal temperament like a glove. Whereas most tenors had either the stamina for the four B-flats in "Or son sei mesi," or the lovelorn ro-

---

January 26, 28, and 30; February 1, 1955
Giacomo Puccini: *La Fanciulla del West*
Venice, Teatro la Fenice
Elisabetta Barbato (*Minnie*), Franco Corelli (*Dick Johnson/Ramerrez*), Gian Giacomo Guelfi (*Jack Rance*), Mariano Caruso (*Nick*), Ivo Vinco (*Jake Wallace*), cond. Oliviero De Fabritiis

Early 1955
Milan, RAI (radio broadcast)
Puccini: *La Fanciulla del West* "Or son sei mesi"

March 15, 1955
Milan, RAI (radio broadcast)
Massenet: *Werther* "Ah, non mi ridestar"
Cond. Mario Rossi

manticism for the cantilena in "Ch'ella mi creda," or the tenderness for certain passages in Johnson's duet with Minnie, Corelli had it all. That combination proved a winning number, especially in this opera, where he also could act out his passionate love for westerns. Recordings from just a few years later fully support Giuseppe Pugliese's assertion that Corelli succeeded in wringing a maximum of passion from the role even though the character he portrays is far from the average opera hero. His characterization was immediately recognized as "fearless.... Beautifully sung, convincing, measured, lively, and solid as a rock in the high register."[1]

Fanciulla also provided the material for his first RAI radio recital, which included the aria "Or son sei mesi." The most intriguing part of this recital, however, was the dedication to no less a personage than the secretary of state, Fernando Tambroni—the same family lawyer who had once stopped Franco's father from punishing the twelve-year-old boy who had disrupted the two men's meeting by belting out "Ch'ella mi creda." Corelli told him: "Well, Mr. Secretary of State, I kept my promise: you became a secretary of state and here I am, a tenor!"[2]

❖❖❖❖❖

With triumphs rapidly accumulating one after the other, it suddenly seemed as if the whole operatic world had begun to chase after Corelli. On the eve of his first foreign appearances, the Metropolitan Opera was distressed over the rumor (which turned out to be unfounded) that one of the leading booking agencies, Fox-Kelly, had secured Corelli's services for the Chicago Lyric Opera (which they had founded), with an exclusivity clause preventing him from appearing elsewhere in the United States. Bing immediately asked Bauer to investigate the matter, threatening retaliation against Fox-Kelly if the rumor was true.[3] If Corelli was to come to the United States, it would have to be through the Metropolitan, even though they despised him! Bing's nerves were so frayed he felt he had to judge Corelli himself. And since Muhammad was no longer prepared to come to the mountain, Bauer scheduled Bing to visit some of Corelli's summer rehearsals.[4]

April–August 1955: The Conquests of Portugal and Verona

In the beginning there was very little in common between Del Monaco and Franco.

Loretta Corelli, interview, Milan, January 27, 2007

> **April 29 and May 1, 1955**
> **Georges Bizet:** *Carmen*
> **Lisbon, Teatro de São Carlos**
> Giulietta Simionato (*Carmen*), Franco Corelli (*Don José*), Anselmo Colzani (*Escamillo*), Marcella Pobbe (*Micaëla*), cond. Oliviero De Fabritiis
>
> **July 24 and 30, 1955**
> **Georges Bizet:** *Carmen*
> **Verona, Arena di Verona**
> Giulietta Simionato (*Carmen*), Franco Corelli (*Don José*), Anselmo Colzani (*Escamillo*), Raffaella Ferrari (*Micaëla*), cond. Antonino Votto
>
> **August 8, 13, 15, and 18, 1955**
> **Giuseppe Verdi:** *Aida*
> **Verona, Arena di Verona**
> Antonietta Stella (*Aida*), Franco Corelli (*Radamès*), Adriana Lazzarini (*Amneris*), Giulio Neri (*Ramfis*), Aldo Protti (*Amonasro*), Silvio Maionica (*the King of Egypt*), cond. Francesco Molinari-Pradelli

The importance of Corelli's two Portuguese Don Josés lies more in the fact that they represent his first appearances outside Italy than in the facts that the critic for *O Seculo* claimed to have witnessed one of the greatest Josés ever to grace the stage there and that *Diaro de Noticias* predicted a great future for the tenor[5]—a prediction that materialized with a summer series of *Norma*s in Ravenna, Florence, and Rome, after which a *Pagliacci* in Thienne (Vicenza, Italy, with Loretta promoted to the role of Nedda) propelled him into one of his most cherished debuts, the one in the Arena di Verona. There his sensational José almost won out over Del Monaco's Otello in a local newspaper's competition for best performer of the season. Del Monaco came out on top, but it was a narrow victory, and in spite of his previous jokes about "PeCorelli," he was now on notice of serious competition.[6]

Gratifying as this must have been for Franco, the true revelation of his Veronese debut was his follow-up performances there as Radamès in *Aida*, which Corelli considered his true debut in the opera. Facing the daunting role of Radamès in front of 25,000 spectators in that frightening outdoor arena, practically the home base of that particular opera, was his greatest challenge to date. Says Marco Corelli: "To succeed in the higher tessitura and certain difficult passages, he needed to find a way to project his voice efficiently, especially in those large theaters. By then he had discovered this 'imaginary wall' toward which he could project in a way that would ensure that his voice would emerge more balanced, without also straining his voice."[7]

✦✦✦✦✦

Negotiating a part and mastering it to perfection are two different things. Corelli still needed to adapt further to the tessitura and the heavy orchestration of late Verdi, but he was clearly on the right track; his electric performance was noticed, as were his equally impressive seminude promotional shots. Those pictures also came just in time for two teenage Corelli fans, Arrigo Michelini and Camilla Merzi. Said Michelini:

> I was pretty mad at Corelli, because I had written him numerous times about how much I loved his voice and that I would like to receive a photograph. But he never answered a single one of these letters, although Camilla and I completely adored him as an artist. His Veronese performances were the first ones where I actually saw him live, and it was magnificent. Still, I confronted him about his impolite behavior when I ran into him in town the next day. I remember I was pretty angry. He, in turn, seemed really upset by our accusations and invited us to come to his hotel after the next day's performance. There he gave us some photos, and from then on we kept in touch—at first through letters, but later we would visit him backstage, and eventually we became very close friends. Franco was glad to have us in the theater because he felt stronger knowing that he had support in the auditorium.

Corelli liked his new friends so much that he ended up copying his archives for them: each would have two copies of any photos made for the other. Thanks to that practice, an array of photos from the early 1950s survives today. Nor was their treasure trove limited to photos: a feather of Corelli's helmet from the costume for his *Aida* debut ended up in Michelini's collection—signed, of course, because Franco had to sign each and every single object that Michelini and Merzi acquired. Said Michelini: "Sometimes he gave us that sad look when he had to sign something again, but that was only to tease us. Well, perhaps

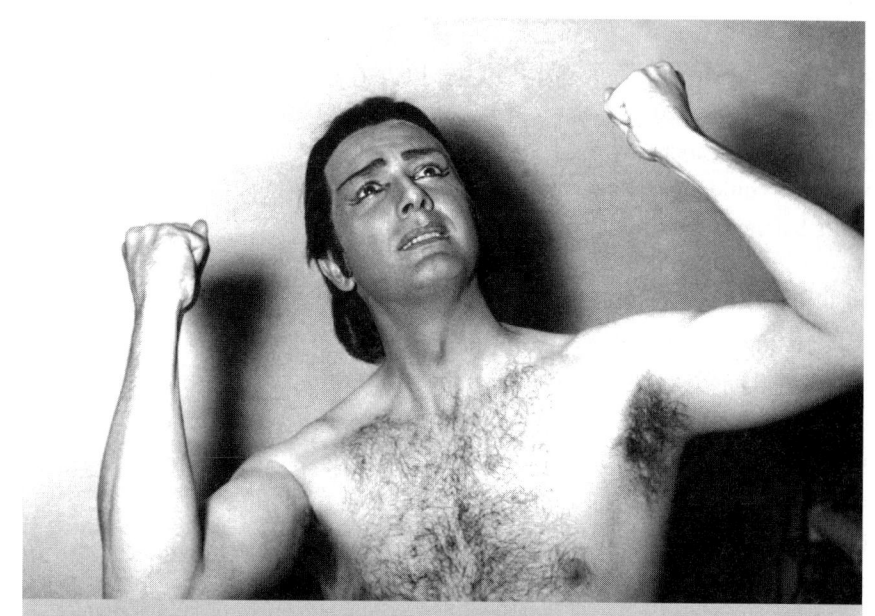

Radamès at the Arena di Verona, July 24, 1955. Initially shot without much fanfare, this and other seminude dressing-room pictures were instantly seized by the Arena's press office and actually made it into both the newspapers and the Arena's posters and programs. (Photo: Courtesy of the Arena di Verona)

he shook his head a little more on the days when we made him sign twenty pictures in a row."[8]

September–November, 1955: First *Tosca*, Then Naples

A black-and-white 1955 telecast of *Tosca* provides an interesting peek at Corelli's early stage appearances. Marina Boagno observed that it was not every day we see Cavaradossi enter by swinging off the painter's scaffolding, and some would add that this is not only his best filmed Cavaradossi but also one of his best from a vocal point of view. In contrast, the 1955 Naples *Aida*, Corelli's first recorded Radamès, provides an interesting look at his initial difficulties with the part. At the last minute Corelli had generously granted the plea of the San Carlo management to step in for his indisposed colleague Mario Del Monaco. The setting looked promising enough, with a mise-en-scène that aimed to outdo all earlier stagings. Unfortunately, Del Monaco's very loyal Naples fan

> September 24, 1955
> Giacomo Puccini: *Tosca*
> Milan, RAI Television (black-and-white telecast)
> Renata Heredia Capnist (*Tosca*), Franco Corelli (*Cavaradossi*), Carlo Tagliabue (*Scarpia*), cond. Antonino Votto
>
> November 24 and 26, 1955
> Giuseppe Verdi: *Aida*
> Naples, Teatro San Carlo
> Antonietta Stella (*Aida*), Franco Corelli (*Radamès*), Fedora Barbieri (*Amneris*), Mario Petri, Giuseppe Modesti (*Ramfis*), Anselmo Colzani (*Amonasro*), cond. Vittorio Gui

base had paid to see *him*, not the grand staging, and they prepared a merciless "welcome" for their hero's rival. This hostility may partially account for Corelli's overly nervous beginning, with an uneven, almost shouted "Celeste Aida" lacking in any of the required poetry. *Opera News* subsequently presented him to its readers as a "bitter disappointment," but the recording doesn't confirm that assessment. There can be no doubt about the opening aria, which presents one of his worst recorded moments, but he soon managed to subdue his nerves, and after the aria his fine B-flats contrasted beautifully with his unexpectedly tender singing in the finale. It wasn't enough to win the audience over, though; instead of the valiant savior it was young Antonietta Stella who made a name for herself in this production, with Corelli's virtues noticed merely in an aside: "A rich, beautiful, and strangely appealing voice, . . . but probably due to his youth and to excusable nervousness, he was awkward."[9]

Corelli's Veronese *Aida* debut presented an early example of a so-called boot fight. Here Giulio Neri falls victim to Corelli's abundantly feathered helmet. (Photo: Courtesy of the Arena di Verona)

December 26–28, 1955: A Handel Renaissance

A little-known story about the Roman *Giulio Cesare* performances concerns a conflict that emerged between Corelli on one side and Gianandrea Gavazzeni, Piero Zuffi, and Margherita Wallmann on the other. The set director, Giovanni Crociani, had managed to create a ray of sunlight to fall on the tomb of the Pharaoh, when Sesto exploded: "The sun is mine! It should follow me. . . . I won't sing if the sun doesn't follow me!" When they tried to explain to him the logic of having the sun on the tomb, Corelli, now very much aware of his new position as an emerging major tenor, suddenly imposed his will upon the production team: "You can have all the logic you want, as long as the sun illuminates and follows me."[10]

The Teatro dell'Opera gala premiere, on St. Stephen's Day, was truly an historical one, if only because it represented the first staged performance of *Giulio Cesare* in Italy, a work hitherto only given in concert form. The local chic crowd attended, including President Giovanni Gronchi; his wife, Carla; and a good portion of the parliament, all greeted by Goffredo Mameli's national anthem.[11] No expense was spared for the production, and its success was such that it actually ranks as one of the pillars supporting the worldwide Handel revival that began in the 1950s. Librettist and composer had provided a thrilling montage of events and arias, culminating in the glorious music written for Cleopatra, who is at the center of the action. Corelli, in the part of Sesto, son of Cornelia and Pompey, has only marginal importance. Even so, he is given some fine opportunities to stand out, as can be heard on the recording that exists of this performance (2-CD set, Andromeda, ANDRCD5079). His part begins with the vengeful "Vanni sono i lamenti" after Caesar has confronted him and his mother

---

December 26 and 28, 1955
George Frideric Handel: *Giulio Cesare*
Rome, Teatro dell'Opera
Boris Christoff (*Giulio Cesare*), Fedora Barbieri (*Cornelia*), Franco Corelli (*Sesto*), Mario Petri (*Tolomeo*), Onelia Fineschi (*Cleopatra*), Antonio Cassinelli (*Achillas*), Ferruccio Mazzoli (*Nireno*), cond. Gianandrea Gavazzeni; director, Margherita Wallmann; scenographer, Piero Zuffi

Left: Franco Corelli as Dick Johnson in Puccini's *La Fanciulla del West*, Trieste, Teatro Giuseppe Verdi, November 30, 1955. According to one reviewer: "*Fanciulla* took off with daring bravery, leading us toward the land of vocal plenty, where three young, passionate artists threw themselves into the action with voices as gorgeous as they were fearless." V. T., "*La Fanciulla del West*," *Il Piccolo*, December 1, 1955. (Photo: Courtesy of the Museo Teatro Giuseppe Verdi) *Right*: Corelli in his role debut as Sesto in the Roman production of *Giulio Cesare*, December 1955. (Photo: Courtesy of the Teatro dell'Opera)

with the severed head of Caesar's enemy Pompey. When mother and son discuss the possibilities of revenge, Cleopatra comes to their aid, hoping to ascend to the throne when her brother Ptolemy is killed. This culminates in the tragic duet between Cornelia and Sesto, "Son nata a sospirar," where they lament their fate after Ptolemy has suggested that Cornelia should marry Achillas—the man who beheaded her husband. With Cleopatra falling in love with Caesar in Act II, matters go from bad to worse; when Sesto finds his mother about to take her own life, he swears to avenge her in the poisonous aria "L'angue offeso." The aria has a sumptuous slow section where Corelli truly gets to the emotional core of his character, finishing on a blazing G. In the third act, Sesto avenges his father and, together with his mother, pledges loyalty to Giulio Cesare, who is himself celebrating his bond with his beloved Cleopatra. Corelli was praised for his timbre and the presence he brought to the part: "His voice molded to the stylistic demands of the part, with just the right amount of energy and expressivity. This was accentuated by his well-proportioned stage movements."[12] Similarly praised were a number of fellow giants, both vocally and in inches: at six feet one inch Franco was actually the third in line after Christoff and Mario Petri, both of whom measured six feet three inches.[13]

The most striking aspect of the performance was arguably Zuffi's Cinemascope-like setting of it, as Fernando L. Lunghi described it in *Giornale d'Italia*: a broad stage with a stairway running toward a terrace that overlooked the African sea. The baroque props and the effective lighting worked magic, just as the glittering embroidered gold-and-purple costumes contrasted beautifully with the sober brown and gray of the slave girls' costumes. Within that setting, Wallmann created stage movements that resembled a classical painting coming to three-dimensional life. Even the auditorium matched the action on stage; each box had been lavishly decorated with pink carnations.[14] Because no Italian critic ever seems to agree with his colleagues, the opinion of Piccinelli in *Momento Sera* should not be omitted here. He judged the opera a tasteless "revue" made up of the sort of rotten surrealism that increasingly bothered him in modern performance practice: "They aimed at creating a super spectacle that wholly despises good taste and is wholly contradictory to the austere, classical style of Handel's score."[15]

November–December 1955: Cetra

Cetra, that priceless recording company when it came to landing new local operatic talent, must have been pleasantly surprised at the unequivocal praise their new tenor's first recordings won. Not only in Italy, but even in countries as remote from the center of the operatic world as the Netherlands, Corelli hit the mark. Leo Riemens, coauthor of the invaluable Kutsch-Riemens *Großes Sänger-Lexikon* (Great Singers' Lexicon) and respected critic for the Netherlands' only classical review publication, *Luister*, presented the newcomer to the public:

> The first Cetra recording of the young Franco Corelli caught me off guard. I was so surprised that I wrote a very enthusiastic review of it in *Luister*. And rightfully so, because this recording debut proved him to be more than just

> **November 22, 1955**
> Turin (Cetra recording)
> Arturo Buzzi-Peccia: "Lolita." Agustín Lara: "Granada"
> Cond. Gian Stellari
>
> **December 15, 1955**
> Turin (Cetra recording)
> Puccini: *La Fanciulla del West* "Una parola sola . . . Or son sei mesi"; *Turandot* "Non piangere Liù," "Nessun dorma." Cilea: *Adriana Lecouvreur* "La dolcissima effigie," "L'anima ho stanca"
> Cond. Arturo Basile
>
> **December 30, 1955**
> Turin (Cetra recording)
> Gaetano Errico Pennino: "Pecchè?" Nino Piccinelli: "Canción moresca"
> Cond. Alberto Bonocore
>
> **January 11, 1956**
> Turin (Cetra recording)
> Gaetano Donizetti: *La Favorita* "Una vergin, un angiol di Dio." Puccini: *Tosca* "Recondita armonia," "E lucevan le stelle"; *La Fanciulla del West* "Ch'ella mi creda libero e lontano"
> Cond. Fulvio Vernizzi

the possessor of splendid raw material, but also capable of handling it. He was truly an artist and a great musician. Two characteristics that don't generally come together with a tenor voice! He had the volume of Del Monaco, the brilliant tone of Björling, the finished phrasing of Martinelli, the technique of Pertile, and the copious, organlike sound of Caruso.[16]

The arias are fairly polished throughout, and even Corelli himself was completely satisfied with his efforts in "La dolcissima effigie."[17] The four extremely rare songs that have yet to be reissued are of lesser value, if not downright disappointing. "Granada" has very sloppy phrasing, and one can almost see his eyes as he struggles with the score, divided between conductor and words on the page. Never would he be that sloppy in studio recordings again or permit himself to indulge in such odd high notes. In turn, "Lolita" is impossibly slow, the musical structure on the verge of disintegration, his voice inflexibly heavy, and once more Corelli sounds as if he is sight-reading. Not surprisingly, these two songs marked his first and last encounter with the conductor Gian Stellari, who was replaced by Alberto Bonocore for Corelli's second song recital. With Bonocore things improved considerably, although "Canción moresca" still sounds a little unprepared. On the other hand, it has some tender vocal phrasing and hints at the singer's potential in popular Italian song. In a sense, this potential is realized in "Pecchè?" Here is that quintessential mellifluous tone quality, with a slight hint of Gigli's sob and that heartbreaking, innate tear in his voice that truly captures the song's desperate, lovelorn quality.

April 27, 1956: Romeo in Portugal

Apart from a number of repeat performances over February and March of *Carmen* and *Aida* in Venice, the most interesting novelty of the first months of 1956 was Corelli's first radio concert in the Martini and Rossi series on January 16. Coupled with the lovely-voiced Rosanna Carteri, he gave Italian radio audiences a taste of his Chénier and José, and joined Carteri in a beautiful duet from *Adriana Lecouvreur*, all of which can still be appreciated through the surviving artifact of the broadcast. In the field of live recordings, 1956 is a turning point: an increasing number of performances were being captured through surviving broadcasts or pirate recordings, such as the legendary opening night of *La Fanciulla del West* at La Scala on 4 April. When two friends of the Dutch critic Leo Riemens returned home from the premiere, Riemens recounted their bewilderment: "They returned filled with joy and judged him a step up in comparison with the two other tenors [Del Monaco and Di Stefano] they had heard on their journey."[18]

The recording of the premiere makes plain the reason for the enthusiasm of Riemens's friend: on this hot-blooded Scala night, with Gigliola Frazzoni as a challenging Minnie, Dick Johnson came to life. Corelli's voice boiled over with a raw intensity as affecting as it was dangerous. This might explain the curious phenomenon that critics reflecting on these recordings in later years scolded him for this kind of vocal display, although a good number of fans prefer these

> January 16, 1956
> Grandi Concerti Martini and Rossi
> Milan, RAI Studio
> Rosanna Carteri, Franco Corelli (singing *Andrea Chénier* "Un dì all'azzurro spazio"; *Carmen* "Il fior che avevi a me tu dato"; *Adriana Lecouvreur* "La dolcissima effigie"), cond. Oliviero De Fabritiis
>
> April 4, 7, 11, and 15, 1956
> Giacomo Puccini: *La Fanciulla del West*
> Milan, Teatro alla Scala
> Gigliola Frazzoni (*Minnie*), Tito Gobbi (*Jack Rance*), Franco Corelli (*Dick Johnson/Ramerrez*), cond. Antonino Votto
>
> April 27 and 29, 1956
> Riccardo Zandonai: *Giulietta e Romeo*
> Lisbon, Teatro de São Carlos
> Maria Curtis-Verna (*Giulietta*), Franco Corelli (*Romeo*), Jeda Valtriani (*Isabella*), Rodolfo Azzolini (*Tebaldo*), Piero De Palma (*Il Cantatore, Gregorio*), Loretta Di Lelio (a *Woman; First Maid*), cond. Oliviero De Fabritiis

high-risk 1950s recordings to the later, more refined ones. Just to be able to hear that trumpeting, stentorian voice is cathartic for fans of exciting singing.

It is easy to imagine the effect on São Carlos audiences when this sensational voice traveled from Milan to Portugal for two revivals of *Giulietta e Romeo*. The role of Romeo in Zandonai's second-best-known opera did not inspire the best of memories in Corelli, who remembered his debut in it as a difficult struggle. And yet there were occasionally offers, even concrete plans, for him to reappear in it. Because those plans never materialized, these Lisbon audiences were the last ones to see him in a part that seems to have been nearly ideal for him at the time. His Giulietta, Mary Curtis-Verna, maintained that Corelli had little to worry about in the part that he now easily dominated, but she didn't think much of the role itself: "The cut of the part was not such that you could feel you had something in your hands to work with . . . that's why the opera is not done very often." One salient detail: the São Carlos tickets for the two performances of *Giulietta e Romeo* were priced so high that ordinary people couldn't attend. Said Curtis-Verna: "There was another theater for them to go to, and they did this on purpose. The São Carlos was like a jewel box . . . it was gorgeous."[19]

May 21–June 3, 1956: *Fedora*

The revival of that eternal Sarah Bernhardt vehicle, Sardou's *Fedora*, in the operatic adaptation by Arturo Collauti and Umberto Giordano was the number-one operatic event of 1956. It initiated a long-lasting reconciliation between the protagonists, who had not appeared together since *La Vestale*, when Callas became enraged over the tenor's popularity with men she desired herself.

Both Corelli and Callas knew they reached greater heights when performing with a challenging partner, and in a way they were birds of a feather; both tormented souls, prisoners, perhaps even slaves of their respective careers. They were also blessed with unique yet well-matched voices, fiery temperaments, and an unfailing instinct for the sort of musicianship that could bring the house down. The difference was that Callas, though more than two and a half years younger than Corelli, had taken up singing a full thirteen years before the tenor started to investigate his vocal resources seriously. In a certain sense, *Fedora* represents the apex of her career, whereas for Corelli it was simply another major step up in standing and learning: "No one can imagine what it meant to me, a virtual beginner on the stage, only in my second year at La Scala, to work with Callas. I learned so much—how to see—how to improve myself. Maria was extremely thoughtful with me and tried to make everything easy. And she did."[20]

The scenic preparations of the opera, with its lavish Russian aristocratic setting, were entrusted to the able hands of the Russian stage director Tatiana Pavlova and her henchman, the scenic designer Nicola Benois. The sets were imaginative, with phantasmagoric accumulations of Russian folklore and noble splendor, blending into a set that would have filled even Giordano with proud surprise—in spite of the fact that the second act plays in Paris and the third act in Switzerland. In the first act Callas wore a *kokoshnik*, an aristocratic Russian headdress that belonged to an earlier period but was put to use here just because she looked stunning in it.[21] In striking contrast were Corelli's famous suit and austere hairdo.

FORGING THE VOICE • 115

> May 21, 23, 27, and 30; June 1 and 3, 1956
> Umberto Giordano: *Fedora*
> Milan, Teatro alla Scala
> Maria Callas (*Princess Fedora Romazov*), Franco Corelli (*Count Loris Ipanov*), Silvana Zanolli (*Countess Olga Sukarev*), Anselmo Colzani (*Count Giovanni de Siriex*), Enzo Cassata (*Dimitri*), Mariano Caruso (*Désiré*), Gino Del Signore (*Baron Rouvel*), Paolo Montarsolo (*Cirillo*), Michele Cazzato (*Borov*), Eraldo Coda (*Gretch*), Giuseppe Morresi (*Lorek*), cond. Gianandrea Gavazzeni

The many photos of the premiere that have surfaced almost compensate for the absence of a recording. They clearly show the delight and the seriousness with which both principals worked on the opera. For Corelli it was a revelation to work with Callas again. Her total involvement inspired him so much that he found himself absorbed in the opera as he had never been absorbed in anything before. Their joint efforts actually reached a point where even Pavlova stepped back when soprano and tenor worked out the gestures of the third act between themselves— on instinct, on feeling. Said Corelli: "I felt it a duty to respond, to work deeply, as never before, in a way I really did not fully comprehend, but which I strongly sensed."[22]

His involvement moved Corelli to suggest that where Fedora confessed to having been the cause of all Loris's misery, he seize her by her hair in anger. Callas embraced the idea and fastened her hair. When Loris subsequently denied her pardon, swearing revenge with his angry outburst "I crush you, you serpent, along with your hate!,"

Corelli describes the scene: "Act III is set in Switzerland, and begins as a romantic idyll, with Fedora and Loris strolling into the garden of their chalet. We had a charming little pantomime in which Maria sat in a swing and I pushed her. Very lovely." John Ardoin and Gerald Fitzgerald, *Callas* (London: Thames and Hudson, 1974). (Photo: Erio Piccagliani)

he pulled her hair backward and dragged her around the stage. Then, when he let go, he turned away, covering his tormented, grief-stricken face in his hands. At that point Fedora, in despair, drank the poison concealed in her crucifix. Said Corelli: "When I realized what she had done, in shock I tried to carry her into the chalet, but as we reached the steps she was so near death I gently sank there with her in my arms. Here Maria uttered those final lines so movingly":

Ho freddo,	I feel cold.
quanto freddo.	so cold.
Loris, riscaldami tu.	Loris, warm me in your embrace.
Vorrei ancora un po' del tuo amor.	I am longing for a last bit of your love.[23]

All that made even Corelli lament the missing recording himself, although Loretta has been rumored to have taped it partially from the wings. Yet the couple always denied this in public,[24] and Corelli himself said that he wished he had it: "We had rehearsed four weeks to achieve such effects. . . . The full value of the opera came forth. This *Fedora* could have been filmed as it was—perfect. Maria had helped me so much during the rehearsals that we completely interlocked. That's the word for it. Interlocked."[25]

❖❖❖❖❖

The critics, however, quibbled over whether Callas was suited for this verismo part and over the value of the opera itself. Some judged it Giordano's masterpiece, others called it operatic kitsch. *Corriere della Sera* readily admitted that Callas was all you could wish for as Fedora, from the voice to the melodramatic poses, from the costumes to the shuddering death scene. Corelli's vocal endowment was hailed as well. Still, this premiere was not universally acclaimed,[26] and one wonders why it became one of the great operatic myths of the 1950s. The eternal discussion over the rumored pirate recording has certainly helped, but there must have been more to it. Whatever the technically oriented critics wrote, there was something in these performances that made an unforgettable impact on the audience. Recalls Mary Curtis-Verna: "That *Fedora* was probably the greatest production I have ever seen with Callas. When it was over, I simply couldn't leave my seat. I didn't want to talk to anybody. The whole evening was so complete. Corelli was good, but she was really the one that stood out. She was tremendous. I probably have never seen another performance like that in my life. Everything was right."[27]

1956: On Balance

The successful La Scala reunion between tenor and diva seemed a possible starting point for a new operatic team, especially now that Giuseppe Di Stefano had recorded a studio *Traviata* with Antonietta Stella instead of with Callas in mid-1955. Although they had performed together in the months after the recording was made, relationships between the diva and her former EMI partner seemed clouded from January 1956 until after the Callas-Corelli *Fedora* run, a period during which they did not appear or record together. Corelli certainly opened prospects beyond the possibilities of Di Stefano, who was essentially a lyric tenor, but by 1956 Corelli's Cetra contract prevented him from appearing in any EMI recording. The main question, then, is why Cetra didn't employ him more widely in its own projects—especially given the international press's enthusiastic support for Corelli's recordings of arias from *Lucia di Lammermoor*, *I Lombardi*, and *Rigoletto* (Cetra, EPO 0327) and from *Un Ballo in Maschera* and *Fedora* (Cetra, EPO 0328).[28] Bruno Slawitz of *Musica e Dischi* openly pleaded that Franco be considered for a programmed first recording of Puccini's *Edgar*. In the same article he mentioned Cetra's plans for recordings of Mascagni's *Guglielmo Ratcliff* and *Iris*, which were well within the capabilities of the recording company now

July 1, 1956
Turin (Cetra recording)
Donizetti: *Lucia di Lammermoor* "Tombe degli avi miei . . . Fra poco a me ricovero." Verdi: *I Lombardi* "La mia letizia infondere"; *Rigoletto* "La donna è mobile"; **Un Ballo in Maschera* "Forse la soglie attinse . . . Ma se m'è forza perderti." Giordano: *Fedora* "Amor ti vieta"*
Cond. Arturo Basile, *Alfredo Simonetto

that it had assured itself of the services of such singers as Corelli and Gianni Raimondi.[29]

❖❖❖❖❖

With those and a number of other plans, a new golden era of recordings and performances of forgotten masterpieces that had been waiting decades for the appropriate voices seemed at hand. Unfortunately, none of Slawitz's speculations materialized, and Corelli himself became far more discriminating, many say excessively so, when selecting new roles, both with recordings and in the theater.[30]

June–August 1956: Making Movies

Comparing the *Carmen* telecast to a film production shot on location such as Carmine Gallone's *Tosca* is perhaps unfair, especially when the first is in black and white and the second in color. The dilemma faced by television producers, who must work within a comparatively low budget, is also twice as problematic as the one faced by movie producers, who habitually dub actors' voices: privilege looks over voice, or accept a fat soprano and an inappropriate tenor? Opera singers with sex appeal who come across well on either television or the silver screen are rare birds. *Carmen*'s producer, Franco Enriquez, was fortunate enough in Corelli's José, but Belén Amparán clearly presented more beauty than voice. Alas, theatrical acting and television close-ups are seldom a good fit (Corelli's Canio in the *Pagliacci* telecast was a notable exception), and the *Carmen* production suffered from some serious overacting (even on Corelli's part, especially toward the end, although one can easily grasp the effect of this José in the theater).

The Gallone *Tosca* was vocally much better, although the acting was only marginally so. That was largely due to Gallone's solution to deal with the visual impact of his older Tosca, Maria Caniglia: the American soprano Franca Duval was selected to act and lip-synch Caniglia's part. The movie enjoyed a full worldwide release, complete with gala premieres and printed programs, which outside Italy focused entirely on the Brooklyn-born, titian-haired, topaz-eyed beauty Duval and her march toward La Scala, which had culminated in Ghiringhelli's offering her the role of Sonia in Sutermeister's *Raskolnikov*. What re-

> June 13, 1956
> Georges Bizet: *Carmen*
> Milan, RAI Television (black-and-white telecast)
> Belén Amparán (*Carmen*), Franco Corelli (*Don José*), Anselmo Colzani (*Escamillo*), Elda Ribetti (*Micaëla*), cond. Nino Sanzogno, dir. Franco Enriquez
>
> 1956
> Giacomo Puccini: *Tosca*
> Rome, Cinecittà, Cinemascope/Eastman Color
> Maria Caniglia/*Franca Duval (*Tosca*), Franco Corelli (*Cavaradossi*), Gian Giacomo Guelfi/*Afro Poli (*Scarpia*), Vito De Taranto (*the Sacristan*), (Ub)aldo (Co)relli (*Sciarrone*), cond. Oliviero De Fabritiis; director, Carmine Gallone; choreographer, Attilia Radice
> *Acting the part only

mains is a drop-dead gorgeous Tosca with acting skills that fall short of those of a Barbie doll. An obscure seven-inch EP from two years later with arias from *La Traviata, I Vespri Siciliani, Suor Angelica,* and *Idomeneo* (Cetra, EPC 1486/7) reveals that Duval actually had a fine voice. Perhaps she would have been more at ease on screen lip-synching to her own voice rather than Caniglia's.

The poor choice of Duval was almost matched by the intriguing substitution as Scarpia of Afro Poli, who lip-synched to Guelfi's voice. The substitution of Caniglia at least made sense, but why would either Poli or Guelfi accept such humiliating conditions? In an interview, Guelfi mentioned that he was just beginning then and hadn't given it any thought—when Gallone asks you to appear in the sound track of a prestigious movie release, you jump at the chance! One might also argue that in his younger years he may not have had the right looks for Scarpia, but for a singer as celebrated as Poli to be asked to act the role but not sing it was clearly not a compliment.

◆◆◆◆◆

Surprisingly little is known about the genesis of the Gallone *Tosca,* which presumably was shot at the Cinecittà studios during the early summer of 1956. And there has been speculation about how Corelli landed his leading role, some going as far as to suggest that Gallone asked Franco's brother Ubaldo if he knew a suitable tenor when Mario Del Monaco's fee proved a step too high. The story that Ubaldo suggested a brother who was then unknown to the director is hard to accept, however, because Gallone would had to have been deaf and blind to have been unaware of the 1954 *Pagliacci* telecast, the *La Vestale* premiere at La Scala of the same year, and the televised *Tosca* of 1955. Marco Corelli sheds some light on the matter, saying that Franco's fear of mistakes made him reluctant to accept such invitations: "If he made a mistake, it would be there forever, and so he was very reluctant with respect to movies. Gallone then asked Ubaldo to help convince Franco to sing in the movie."[31]

Ubaldo was rewarded for his services with the part of Sciarrone but in Italy was billed as Aldo Relli to avoid allegations of nepotism (in the American and English programs he was regularly billed as Aldo Corelli). Ubaldo's voice was clearly at its very end when the film was shot, but the pairing of the brothers in the torture scene of the second act gives us a few electrifying shots.

Franco acts fairly convincingly for the larger part of his role, but the movie is not Gallone's masterpiece. In spite of the on-location filming, the sets often look artificial, an impression exacerbated by far-from-ideal camera direction; how one can film "E lucevan le stelle" focusing until the phrase "disciogliea dai veli" on a streetlamp instead of on the tormented Cavaradossi while he sings one of his major set pieces is inexplicable. The film is at best a B movie with great singing, although Caniglia sounds perhaps a bit too old for her part. In addition to the soundtrack, the publicity photo stills deserve to be singled out: Duval may not be a Tosca, but when she doesn't have to move, she looks every bit like the Attavanti Cavaradossi envisions as the Madonna in his painting.

June–August 1956: *Suprema Confessione*

Whether Corelli's appearance in Sergio Corbucci's long-lost *Suprema Confessione* was a by-product of the Gallone *Tosca* or the other way around,[32] the film is a fascinating Corelli document from the early days of his career. In the movie, the conductor Marco Neri meets the mysterious blonde beauty Elisa on

> *Suprema Confessione (Non c'è pace per chi ama)*
> Produced by Sergio Corbucci and Sante Chimirri for GEA Cinematografica
> Filmed in Rome
> Franco Corelli (*as himself, singing* Donizetti: *Lucia di Lammermoor,* "Fra poco a me ricovero." Meyerbeer: *L'Africana* "Mi batte il cor . . . O paradiso"), Massimo Serato (*Marco Neri*), Anna Maria Ferrero (*Lisa*), Andrea Checchi (*Don Diego*), Piero Lulli (*Franz*), Sonja Ziemann (*Giovanna*), Arnoldo Foà (*Armando*), Massimo Giuliani (*Carlo, son of Lisa and Marco*), cond. Carlo Franci; director, Sergio Corbucci

a flight back to Rome, falls in love, and soon marries her. Just when all seems to be going well, a stranger confronts Elisa with her shady past. The scene changes to a concert hall, where Neri rehearses *Lucia di Lammermoor* with the famous tenor Franco Corelli, who sings all of "Fra poco a me ricovero." Elisa confides her shameful secret—she used to be the partner of the drug dealer Franz, who has now shown up in order to blackmail her—to Neri's brother, the priest Don Diego, who forgives her. Then, while Neri is conducting Meyerbeer's *L'Africana* in the theater—with Corelli singing "Mi batte il cor . . . O paradiso"—Franz is arrested publicly in the company of the pregnant Elisa. In the end, all is forgiven, and the movie ends on the last, climactic bars of Neri conducting the overture to *Tannhäuser*.

Although *Suprema Confessione* may hardly merit a DVD release, Corelli's part in it is truly historic. Here we actually see him, in vibrant voice and heroic manner, singing two pieces that are destined to remain among his best filmed performances. For purposes of the script, the Donizetti piece was filmed in black and white as a rehearsal, although Corelli sings it in one piece (interrupted in the middle section by dialogue from the actors). To see him sing it is of course a treasure, because we don't have even a photo of his Met Edgardo, but the true sensation here is clearly the Meyerbeer aria. Not only is it staged, in full costume and in color, but it features him years before he became associated with this heroic repertoire. Moreover, apart from a concert performance very late in his career, nothing of his known Meyerbeer ventures was captured on film.[33]

November–December 1956: The *Forza* and *Aida* Recordings

The highlights recording of *La Forza del Destino* shows Corelli as not yet the equal of his rivals Del Monaco and Di Stefano, who were at the time still unchallenged as Alvaro. It was Corelli's first Alvaro, though, so this is hardly surprising. The *Aida* recording benefited from his experiences in the role, but in spite of the eleven times Corelli had sung Radamès since his Arena debut earlier in the year, the Cetra studio recording process did not go smoothly. According to his Aida, Mary Curtis-Verna, Corelli was never satisfied: "We took takes and retakes; he took many, many retakes. He must have recorded the aria umpteen times. And then he and Loretta, who sang the High Priestess, would go off by themselves and analyze everything all over again."[35]

Once the recording was released (in June 1957), Bruno Slawitz of *Musica e Dischi* wrote that Corelli hit the mark in "Celeste Aida" and in the fire and flames of the third act, but he almost regretted that it was "only" *Aida*. As Slawitz listened, he already was dreaming of Corelli's Osaka (in Mascagni's

---

November 14, 18, and 23, 1956
Giuseppe Verdi: *Aida*
Trieste, Teatro Giuseppe Verdi
Anna Maria Rovere (*Aida*), Franco Corelli (*Radamès*), Giulio Neri (*Ramfis*), Dora Minarchi (*Amneris*), Gian Giacomo Guelfi (*Amonasro*), cond. Antonino Votto

November 27, 1956
Giuseppe Verdi: *La Forza del Destino* (highlights)
Turin (Cetra recording)
Gian Giacomo Guelfi (*Don Carlo di Vargas*), Franco Corelli (*Don Alvaro*), cond. Arturo Basile

December 18, 1956
Giuseppe Verdi: *Aida*
Turin (Cetra recording)
Mary Curtis-Verna (*Aida*), Franco Corelli (*Radamès*), Antonio Zerbini (*the King of Egypt*), Miriam Pirazzini (*Amneris*), Giulio Neri (*Ramfis*), Gian Giacomo Guelfi (*Amonasro*), cond. Angelo Questa

Iris), followed by Manrico (in Verdi's *Trovatore*) and Meyerbeer's Raul or Vasco da Gama.[36] In the Netherlands, Leo Riemens followed suit in predicting that Corelli would become the greatest *heldentenor* of the 1960s, although he thought it would be a wise move if the singer remained a little longer within more lyrical repertoire.[37] Giancarlo Landini met the two critics halfway when he wrote that he was intrigued by the tenor's Tristanesque approach to this Verdi masterpiece, with Corelli foreshadowing the "Liebestod" right from the beginning. Landini was less enthusiastic about the rest of the cast, especially the conductor.[38] On the other hand, Slawitz judged this to be the best *Aida* set ever,[39] and the controversial recording ultimately became a collector's item.

To return from Radamès to the Sesto of *Giulio Cesare* called for a dramatic shift, but what tenor can pick and choose his Scala roles at will after barely five years of singing? Still, it is interesting to see Corelli continuing to contribute to the Handel revival in this once more very Italian cast consisting of Nicola Rossi Lemeni (born in Istanbul but raised in Italy), Giulietta Simionato, Mario Petri, and the Romanian Virginia Zeani. A bit of Handel can't hurt when it comes to developing vocal refinement, and the part's brevity may have made it attractive to Franco: he was struggling to manage his increasingly busy performance and recording schedules without harming his instrument by singing too much.

1956: Palazzo Corelli

Franco's friends in the '50s? He had no friends, unless you mean his childhood friend Carlo Scaravelli.
    Loretta Corelli, interview, Milan, January 27, 2007

Despite Corelli's skyrocketing career, Ancona saw quite a bit of its native son in 1956, because this was the year in which he embarked on rebuilding the Corellis' Via Mamiani home, which had been demolished in the war.[40] The restoration was finally completed in December 1958.[41] The long planning and proceedings since the house's demolition after the war seem to have resulted in some tension and disagreement between the Corelli clan and the Marchetti family (who had owned the building up until 1935). The dispute played a part in the distance that developed after the war between Franco and his cousin and childhood friend Marco Marchetti.[42]

Although Franco and most of his childhood friends had drifted apart over the years, his friendship with Carlo Scaravelli continued as it had since they first met. Franco went to see Carlo whenever he was in Ancona, where he often consulted his friend on vocal matters. Scaravelli had chosen another direction in life, but his love for the theater was such that he continued to perform in the region, once even in a season at the Teatro della Fiera where his name appeared in the same advertisement as Giuseppe Di Stefano's. His main involvement in opera, however, was as a voice teacher, and his most famous pupil continued to consult him whenever he was in Ancona. Franco's visits to Scaravelli's house left a lasting impression on a small member of the latter's household, Carlo's son Alessandro, ten years old in 1956: "I used to hide behind the piano . . . because I was infatuated with opera and music in general. When regular students came, you would feel normal vibrations while they sang, but when Franco came, the lamp would shake. You couldn't stay in there. I had to leave the room." Another of Alessandro's tantalizing reminiscences concerns some duet recordings that Franco and his father once made in a private recording session: "They went to Rome and recorded together. I still have the ones my father cut as a solo artist, but, unfortunately, I lost the ones they made together."[43]

January 10–20, 1957: *Pagliacci*

The La Scala *Pagliacci* premiere of January 10, 1957 represents a critical moment in Corelli's career—not because the performance was another triumph, but because it was a total failure, and one of the tenor's own making. He attended only one rehearsal, the dress rehearsal the night before the premiere. Normally, a singer can have an off night and survive one way or another, but this time the

---

January 10, 12, 15, and 20, 1957
Ruggero Leoncavallo: *Pagliacci*
Milan, Teatro alla Scala
Franco Corelli (*Canio*), Eugenia Ratti, Gigliola Frazzoni [January 12, 15], Cesy Broggini [January 20] (*Nedda*), Romano Roma, Aldo Protti [January 20] (*Tonio*), Luigi Alva (*Beppe*), Enzo Sordello (*Silvio*), cond. Nino Sanzogno

tenor's troubles went beyond acceptable limits. Corelli sang out of tune, repeatedly came in too early, took shortcuts to where he should have been, and so on, to the point where the conductor stopped conducting. Corelli readily acknowledged that he was very bad that night and, in looking back, still wrung his hands when he recalled Nino Sanzogno's response: "Just when I need him most, he put his face down in the score and leave me to finish alone."[44]

Stupendous photo, disastrous performance, admitted Corelli: "I sang very bad that night, very bad." Robert Daley, "The Greatest Tenor," *Life*, December 15, 1967. (Photo: Erio Piccagliani)

According to Robert Daley, at the conclusion of this *Pagliacci*, there was no applause, not a sound, and when the curtain fell, there was no curtain call, not one. The very next day Corelli went to La Scala to cancel his remaining contracts.[45] This was but a single element of the master plan for dealing with his defeat; he seriously contemplated ending his career then and there, for sheer shame and fear that such a disgrace could befall him again. Ghiringhelli refused to accept the cancellations, but Loretta had to use every trick in the book, from his moral obligation to the public and management to his obligation to himself and those who were dear to him, to convince him to continue. If there ever was a decisive moment in Corelli's career, then this is the one for which his fans owe Loretta; whatever else one may say, without her his career might actually have ended that opening night.

The second performance was scheduled for January 12, and Franco devoted all of the available time remaining to prepare himself as well as possible. That evening, he avenged himself for his earlier mishap, scoring an undisputed triumph in what was still regarded as a signature Corelli role.[46]

January–April 1957: Cetra

Corelli's Cetra aria recordings made between January and April 1957 are a treasure trove. His voice unfolds with unbridled romanticism, immaculate legato, and a sensitive edge that at the time was arguably matched only by Björling and Di Stefano. These recitals reflect the full range of his voice in that period. The arias from *Il Trovatore* and *Ernani* show him on the brink of entering into the heroic repertoire. Elsewhere he reveals his possibilities in the more lyric repertoire, such as in the *Werther* duet and the arias from *Mefistofele* and *Lodoletta* and the *Fedora* "Mia madre . . . Vedi io piango." In between, he stakes his claim as the true heir to the nineteenth-century baritonal tenors of the *voix sombrée* in *Pollione*'s "Meco all altar di venere" and to a certain extent also in *Otello*'s "Esultate." That declamatory piece is executed with vigor and all the youthful ardor that a voice can bring to it; if ever there was a time for Corelli to have recorded *Otello*, 1957 would have been a very fine year for it.

Fans often blame Cetra for not seizing the opportunity to record *Otello* as a whole at a time when Corelli seemed ready to record about anything. However, Cetra had recorded *Otello* with Carlos Guichandot in the title role, one year before signing Corelli. The real question here is, why did Cetra never record him in any other complete operas at all, besides that one single *Aida*? A look at the list of recorded arias in these Corelli recitals may provide some answers. One of the gems is the hauntingly beautiful duet from *Werther*, where Loretta delivers the opening lines "Dividerci dobbiam." These few lines are the prelude to something that surely would have tempted any other recording companies to sign him up for a complete recording at once. Again, fate was against him: Cetra had just released its acclaimed *Werther* with Pia Tassinari and Ferruccio Tagliavini. Furthermore, their catalog already featured a *Cavalleria/Pagliacci* with the young Carlo Bergonzi as Canio. The same goes for *Mefistofele*, released with again Tagliavini. Cetra's *Lucia di Lammermoor* with Giovanni Malipiero was celebrated at the time (and a connoisseur's pick today), but apart from that, any new *Lucia* stood little chance against EMI's brilliant Callas–Di Stefano release of 1953. The same sad scenario was repeated with *Norma* and other suitable titles: the relatively minor Cetra catalog even featured a 1951 *I Lombardi* and a 1952 Giacinto Prandelli–Maria Caniglia *Fedora*! Andrea Chénier and the Duke of Mantua in *Rigoletto*, roles Corelli planned to perform on stage, were likewise recorded shortly before he was signed by Cetra. Unlike other recording company executives, Cetra's general manager, Edgardo Trinelli, hardly ever allowed for an expensive genuine studio rerecording aimed at merely improving on existing recordings from the Cetra catalog (with the exception of the Corelli *Aida*). Of all the operas that were in Corelli's repertoire or within his reach during his years

January 21, 1957[47]
Turin (Cetra recording)
Massenet: *Werther* "Dividerci dobbiam" (with Loretta Di Lelio as Carlotta)
Cond. Arturo Basile

February 5, 1957
Turin (Cetra recording)
Verdi: *Ernani* "Mercé diletti amici . . . Come rugiada cespite"; *Il Trovatore* "Quale d'armi fragor . . . Ah sì, ben mio . . . Di quella pira" (with Loretta Di Lelio as Leonora)
Cond. Arturo Basile

February 6, 1957
Turin (Cetra recording)
Verdi: *Otello* "Dio fulgor della buffera . . . Esultate"; *Il Trovatore* "Deserto sulla terra"; *La Forza del Destino* "La vita è inferno all'infelice . . . O tu che in seno agli angeli"
Cond. Arturo Basile

April 5, 1957
Turin (Cetra recording)
Bizet: *Carmen* "Il fior." Massenet: *Werther* "Ah, non mi ridestar." Boito: *Mefistofele* "Giunto sul passo estremo." Leoncavallo: *Pagliacci* "Recitar . . . Vesti la giubba," "No, Pagliaccio non son." Mascagni: *Cavalleria Rusticana* "Mamma quel vina è generoso"; *Lodoletta* "Se Franz dicesse il vero! . . . Lodoletta è fuggita." Giordano: *Andrea Chénier* "Colpito qui m'avete . . . Un dì all'azzurro spazio," "Come un bel dì di maggio"; *Fedora* "Mia madre . . . Vedi io piango"
Cond. Arturo Basile

April 18, 1957
Georges Bizet: *Carmen* (highlights; in Italian)
Turin (Cetra recording)
Franco Corelli (*Don José*), Gian Giacomo Guelfi (*Escamillo*), Pia Tassinari (*Carmen*), Margherita Benetti (*Micaëla*), cond. Arturo Basile

> **Around 1957**
> Gaetano Lama: "Silenzio cantatore"
> RAI Television (black-and-white telecast)
>
> **Around 1957**
> Giuliani/Bonavolonta: "La leggenda di guerra (La madre dell'Alpino)"
> RAI Television (black-and-white telecast)

with Cetra, only Zandonai's *Giulietta e Romeo* would have been a realistic option (an opera that by now Corelli counted among the ones he treasured most).[48]

✦✦✦✦✦

Missed opportunities and wishful thinking aside, one can occasionally be lucky enough to have one's dreams come true, as with the completely forgotten television broadcasts of "Silenzio cantatore" and "La leggenda di guerra." The picture actually suggests a Corelli of earlier years, but the voice is unmistakably of mature Cetra quality. The "Silenzio cantatore" is delivered in the context of a typical Italian television revue. Lovely as that work is, though, the "Leggenda di guerra" is the true discovery here: Corelli in repertoire never before or after heard from him! And staged, with the tenor in the uniform of an Italian World War I soldier, seated miserably between his pals in the regiment, singing another famous farewell to his mother:

"È giorno di battaglia	"It is the day of the battle
per il mio figlio alpin.	for my son, the alpinist.
Mio dio! fa che ritorni	Dear God! Let him return safely
qui con me nella casetta	to me in this little house
ad allietarmi i giorni	to fill my days with joy
o me ne morirò."	or else I will die."
. . .	
"Madre, tu	"Mother, you
il figlio tuo non chiamar più	should never call your son again,
sul mio altar,	on my altar,
la gioventù seppe immolar . . .	youth has sacrificed itself . . .

Ei dorme quaggiù	He sleeps down here
né si desterà mai più!	never to wake up again!
Madre, tu	Mother, you
lo rivedrai lassù."	shall see him back up there."

Giulani/Bonavolantà, "La leggenda di guerra (La madre dell'alpino)"

March 3–10, 1957: *Chénier*

Andrea Chénier *opened the doors to the high repertoire for me. It is one of the characters that I have truly "lived." There I surrendered myself to a passion that was so overpowering, that I lost control over my voice.*

    Franco Corelli, in Chiara Milani, "Corelli, un ritorno tra gli applausi,"
    Il Piccolo, October 25, 1999

In March 1957 Corelli added *Andrea Chénier* to his repertoire when he debuted as the doomed poet at the Teatro San Carlo of Naples. His interpretation of the title role was an immediate success. Corelli was almost as powerful as Del Monaco, his rival in the role, but had greater poetic appeal; the heroic-romantic vocalism fitted him like a glove. In *Chénier* Corelli found everything he craved in opera: those beautiful, passionate melodic phrases he loved combined with innate romanticism and tragedy. Finally, it was also composed in a range with which Corelli now felt increasingly comfortable, a range bridging the gap from, say, Don José to the more heroic demands of Verdi's Manrico. From Naples, Corelli took his new trump card to Palermo, where his success was confirmed. While in Sicily he also added new luster to his now three-year-old interpretation of the title role in *Don Carlo.*

> **March 3, 6, and 10, 1957**
> **Umberto Giordano:** *Andrea Chénier*
> **Naples, Teatro San Carlo**
> Franco Corelli (*Andrea Chénier*), Gian Giacomo Guelfi (*Carlo Gérard*), Anna Maria Rovere/Mara Coleva (*Maddalena di Coigny*), cond. Alberto Erede/Pasquale De Angelis

April–May 1957: Gabriele Adorno and Russia Revisited

After bringing his acclaimed Chénier to Lisbon's eager audiences, Corelli seized the opportunity to test himself in a part that would frequently be discussed with theaters as he moved forward in his career, but that he would never sing again: only the Portuguese had the privilege of witnessing him as Gabriele Adorno in Verdi's *Simon Boccanegra*. To date, the performances testify to his early inclination toward a more lyric-romantic repertoire, although not everything went smoothly, if we are to believe Tito Gobbi's reminiscences. At the premiere, all went well enough, with *Diario de Noticias* proclaiming the performance unsurpassable, thanks to the emotional direction of conductor Vittorio Gui and the finished art of Tito Gobbi. Boris Christoff and Marcella Pobbe were likewise singled out as excellent, whereas Corelli garnered a string of compliments for his voice that had everything one could hope for in a tenor: plentitude, sensitive phrasing, and "brio."[49]

In his book *Tito Gobbi on His World of Italian Opera*, Gobbi recalls a disastrous development during a *Simon Boccanegra* performance when Corelli (whom Gobbi does not mention by name) lost either his voice or the text in mid-performance. Because *Diario de Noticias* doesn't mention any interruption, this could only have happened during the second performance, which the press did not attend. According to Gobbi, the performance went well until the middle of the ensemble that ends with Boccanegra's passionate call for peace. At the moment Adorno surrenders his sword to the Doge, Boccanegra and Adorno have to look directly and intensely at each other before Adorno is removed by the guards. Recalled Gobbi:

> The tenor having raised his sword against me on the words, "Pel cielo! Uom possente sei tu" (By heaven! You are the man in power) just continued to stare at me in such wide-eyed horror that I thought the place must be on fire. Then, drawing near to me, he whispered hoarsely, "I've lost my voice." Grasping the situation, I cast a terrible glance upon him, and with an authoritative gesture, indicated to the guards that they should remove him. Amelia's aria, my plea for peace—all continued without a tenor. But at the beginning of the grand finale I saw, to my amazement, an Adorno with a different face and heard the beautiful phrase, "Amelia e salva, e m'ama!" (Amelia is safe and loves me) soar triumphantly to the roof.[50]

> **April 25 and 28, 1957**
> **Giuseppe Verdi: *Simon Boccanegra***
> **Lisbon, Teatro de São Carlos**
> Tito Gobbi (*Simon Boccanegra*), Marcella Pobbe (*Maria Boccanegra*), Boris Christoff (*Jacopo Fiesco*), Giampiero Malaspina (*Paolo Albiani*),Vito Susca (*Pietro*), Franco Corelli (*Gabriele Adorno*), Loretta Di Lelio (*a Maid of Amelia*), Piero De Palma (*Captain of the Crossbow Regiment*), cond. Vittorio Gui
>
> **May 3 and 5, 1957**
> **Modest Mussorgsky: *Kovantchina***
> **Lisbon, Teatro de São Carlos**
> Marcella Pobbe (*Emma*), Amalia Pini (*Marfa*), Franco Corelli (*Prince Andrea Kovantsky*), Gianni dal Ferro (*Prince Vassili Golitzin*), Giampiero Malaspina (*Schiakloviti*), Raffaele Arié (*Prince Ivan Kovantsky*), Boris Christoff (*Dositeo*), Piero De Palma (*Escrivao*), cond. Vittorio Gui
>
> **May 4, 1957**
> **Concert**
> **Lisboa, Teatro de São Carlos**
> Franco Corelli (singing Bizet: *Carmen* "Il fior che avevi a me tu dato." Puccini: *Turandot* "Nessun dorma," "Non piangere, Liù"; *Tosca* "E lucevan le stelle"), Gianni dal Ferro, Jeda Valtriani, Giampiero Malaspina, Marcella Pobbe, Amalia Pini, Raffaele Arié, Marcella Pobbe, Giampiero Mastromei; accompanists, Mario Pellegrini, Carlo Pasquali

The audience erupted in applause. Carlo Cossutta, who happened to have been sitting in the audience, had rushed backstage to offer his help, in spite of the fact that he had never sung that opera on stage before (in fact, according to Kutsch-Riemens he had not yet sung any opera anywhere: Cossutta's official stage debut took place the *following* year). According to Gobbi, Cossutta was immediately taken up on his offer and finished the performance with the help of Gobbi's directions and the producer's miming of the words from the wings.[51] Thereafter, Gabriele Adorno would pop up in repertoire discussions from time to time, but after this devastating experience Corelli hesitated to appear in the part again, leaving these two performances as unique and unrecorded rarities in his career (apart from his 1956 Cetra recording of Gabriele Adorno's aria "Sento avvampar nell'anima").

♦♦♦♦♦

There are always less gratifying parts that one accepts during the earlier part of one's career, usually owing to the combination of financial reward and little effort in terms of vocal demands and study—Andrea Kovantsky is certainly not the most difficult tenor role. Nonetheless, Corelli's Russian biographer Alexei Buljigin regrets the lack of a recording, because Franco's voice had precisely the qualities that lent prominence to this secondary part. As was to be expected, Boris Christoff scored such a triumph in Lisbon that hardly a word was wasted on the rest of the cast. From Corelli's perspective, that made Kovantsky a part that he would not repeat.

Following a final concert, the whole team waved goodbye to the enthusiastic Portuguese audience, which could look back at a most unusual aspect of Corelli's career.

♦♦♦♦♦

Leaving the *Boccanegra* experience behind him, Corelli spent the months of May and June expanding his fledgling international career to the point of conquering Europe. First, there was the important debut in Madrid (with *Tosca* and *Aida*), where Loretta remembered the audience as the most critical in the world: "They remember all the old singers and constantly make comparisons between a modern singer and someone they heard twenty-five, or even fifty years ago."[52] Next came his historic first appearance in Vienna, where his four performances as Radamès made him an instant local favorite. Then Corelli moved on to a debut that was perhaps no more important than the ones in Vienna and Madrid but that was destined to become a reference point in his career because of the dashing recording that remains of it: his Covent Garden debut as Mario Cavaradossi on June 27.

June 27–July 3, 1957: Covent Garden

In Italy the audiences are always severe and rather rigid. They sit with raised guns waiting for you to make a mistake. The Germans are more

Left: Franco Corelli as Gabriele Adorno in Verdi's *Simon Boccanegra*, Teatro Nacional de São Carlos, Lisbon, April 25 and 28, 1957. (Photo: Courtesy of the Biblioteca Nacional de Portugal) *Right*: Corelli as Andrea Kovantsky in Mussorgsky's *Kovantchina*, Lisbon, May 3, 1958. (Photo: Courtesy of Arrigo Michelini)

sympathetic; they applaud everything. The English on the other hand, don't applaud until the end of the act, so you never know where you are.
   Loretta Corelli, "Musical Events: A Great Night," *The New Yorker*, February 4, 1961

Again and again it has been written that the Anglo-Saxons never warmed up to the art of Franco Corelli. That makes it all the more surprising that among sixteen reviews of his Covent Garden debut, even the worst—Andrew Porter's for *The Financial Times*, in which the writer noted, but forgave, some undesirable idiosyncracies[53]—was encouraging.

Porter's fellow critics, however, hailed the production. The thirty-year-old conductor Alexander Gibson was judged a revelation, Milanov a soprano of

> **June 27; July 1 and 3, 1957**
> **Giacomo Puccini: *Tosca***
> **London, Royal Opera House, Covent Garden**
> Zinka Milanov (*Tosca*), Franco Corelli (*Cavaradossi*), Gian Giacomo Guelfi (*Scarpia*), Michael Langdon (*Angelotti*), Forbes Robinson (*the Sacristan*), David Tree (*Spoletta*), cond. Alexander Gibson

finished artistry, and Guelfi a baritone who shot out "vocal thunderbolts" matched only by Corelli's shameless play to the galleries. British and American critics were the first ones to find the right words for the emerging Corelli hype. Instead of sticking to the technical side of the matter, as Italian critics had done up to this point, they focused on Corelli's crowd-pleasing aspects: "The wow of the evening was Franco Corelli as Cavaradossi—that rare bird, an Italian tenor who looked like something off the roof of the Sistine Chapel. I liked his vibrant, very loud 'spinto' delivery and his lust for lung busters at the top; not merely 'not flubbed,' but *gloried* in. This is singing that makes the fifth gallery at La Scala go wild."[54]

Even Porter found complementary qualities that made up for Corelli's vocal indulgence: "Corelli is that rare thing. . . . He has a Radamès-sized voice, not sweet, not really lyrical, but very big and not at all unpleasant in quality. He showed himself something of an artist in all those passages where he was not holding the limelight; but in the arias and big solo utterances he outdid Del Monaco in his tenacious clinging to every possible high note."[55]

All this can be appreciated when listening to Covent Garden's own recording of this memorable evening—one of the most treasured among Corelli fans, who have always disagreed with the tenor himself, who once dismissed it as belonging to his early period, where the flicker vibrato he so despised still featured prominently.[56] His fans tend to value his vibrancy, much as did Philip

On the ferry to *Inghilterra*, June 1957. (Photo: Courtesy of Arrigo Michelini)

On July 17, 1957, Corelli was given the decoration of the Gnoccolara by the civic and provincial authorities of Verona. The origin of the Papà del Gnocco festival dates back to the sixteenth century, when Verona suffered poverty and destruction after several wars unleashed by the pope against Venice and France. A small group of wealthy citizens organized a distribution of gnocchi to the poor in the area of Verona's San Zeno Cathedral. The Veronese later created a Santa Claus–like festival character whose staff is a giant fork with a gnocchi on top.[58] (Courtesy of the Arena di Verona)

Hope-Wallace in *The Guardian*, who thought it something that "add[ed] . . . to the 'squillante' quality so much desired by Italian audiences from their Puccini singers."[57]

July 24–28, 1957: Family Matters in Pesaro

On the eve of June 24, Pesaro's Sports Palace was transformed into the Teatro dei Tremila. The occasion was the return of Franco Corelli to his native province of Le Marche. Unusual measures such as the redirection of traffic on the nearby Adriatic highway were taken to prevent any disturbances. As a tribute to Pesaro's most famous son, Giaocchino Rossini, the overture to his opera *Semiramide* was played immediately before Bizet's *Carmen*. The most impor-

> July 24 and 28, 1957
> Georges Bizet: *Carmen*
> Pesaro, Palazzo dello Sport
> Franco Corelli (*Don José*), Anselmo Colzani (*Escamillo*), Miriam Pirazzini (*Carmen*), Annabianca Meletti (*Micaëla*), Loretta Di Lelio (*Frasquita*), cond. Napoleone Annovazzi

tant aspect of the event for the Corelli family, however, was their introduction to Franco's fiancée. He had never even mentioned Loretta to his family in Ancona, according to Marco Corelli, then ten years old. He remembers the introduction: "I had the sense that she was a woman who knew the operatic world well. She clearly wanted to be essential and of vital importance to Franco's career and life, and she was very kind to me then."[59]

September 16–21, 1957: Opera in Bilbao

Opera in 1957 Bilbao was far from ideal, for it had no performing venue dedicated or even well suited to opera, but the local buffs consoled themselves with highly anticipated appearances that season of the undisputed star of the early 1950s, the tenor Giuseppe Di Stefano. His performances in *L'Elisir d'Amore* and *Pagliacci* were considered worthy replacements for a number of canceled performances by Mario Del Monaco. However, it was not to be. While the upcoming Spanish tenor Alfredo Kraus was making his *Rigoletto* debut there, a telegram arrived announcing Di Stefano's indisposi-

As Pollione in Bellini's *Norma*, Verona, July 18, 1957. Corelli loved children but never had any, owing to a very late case of mumps he contracted right before the 1951 Spoleto voice competition. Winning that competition launched his career. (Photo: Courtesy of the Arena di Verona)

tion, accompanied by a doctor's statement. The public, suspecting a set-up (rumor had it that Di Stefano was never even contracted for these appearances), protested vigorously, but that didn't bring Di Stefano any closer to the ancient city. A series of frantic telephone calls eventually led to replacements being found: Juan Oncina was engaged for *L'Elisir*, and "a certain Franco Corelli," already booked for *Carmen* and *Tosca*, agreed to take over *Pagliacci*. Unfortunately, Franco made a few major mistakes in "Vesti la giubba," due, he said, to the fact that he could barely hear the orchestra in the improvised theater. The attempt to fix the problem with microphones and loudspeakers didn't prove to be much help. However, the tenor survived, thanks to his enormous abilities: "His mighty voice filled the scene, lending his character an extraordinary dramatic quality, which was loudly welcomed by the audience." Although Canio was thus excused, Tonio had little trouble with the bad acoustics of the auditorium: this was unanimously judged Ettore Bastianini's evening. Corelli avenged

September 16, 1957
Ruggero Leoncavallo: *Pagliacci*
Bilbao, Teatro Coliseo Albia
Franco Corelli (*Canio*), Aureliana Beltrami (*Nedda*), Ettore Bastianini (*Tonio*), Vittorio Pandano (*Beppe*), Renato Cesari (*Silvio*), cond. Nicola Rescigno

September 18, 1957
Georges Bizet: *Carmen*
Bilbao, Teatro Coliseo Albia
Belén Amparán (*Carmen*), Franco Corelli (*Don José*), Aureliana Beltrami (*Micaëla*), Antonio Campo (*Escamillo*), Pierluigi Latinucci (*Le Dancaïre*), Vittorio Pandano (*Le Remendado*), Franco Ventriglia (*Zuniga*), Juan Rico (*Moralès*), Loretta Di Lelio (*Frasquita*), Pilar Torres (*Mercédès*), cond. Argeo Quadri

September 21, 1957
Giacomo Puccini: *Tosca*
Bilbao, Teatro Coliseo Albia
Margherita Roberti (*Tosca*), Franco Corelli (*Cavaradossi*), Giuseppe Taddei (*Scarpia*), cond. Argeo Quadri

himself two days later when he triumphed as Don José opposite his *Carmen* film costar Belén Amparán.

September 24–27, 1957: Franco and Franco

I can imagine you are aware of the difficulties of convincing artists of this high level to take on the enormous extra effort and travel difficulties to come to Oviedo. However, this year I am bringing a company like never before: Carteri, Frazzoni, Zanolli, Bergonzi, Corelli, Di Stefano, Poggi . . . what else? Not even Madrid has ever had so many stars!
  Impresario Fabio Ronchi to the mayor of Oviedo, June 21, 1957

The tenth season of the Bilbao opera festival was organized by the team of Don Julio Vallaure and Fernandez Peña, who didn't bat an eye at the criticisms leveled at their impresario Fabio Ronchi over Di Stefano's cancellation. Vallaure simply labeled the occasion a festival of great tenors. He had a point there, with the likes of Gianni Poggi, Franco Corelli (at a top fee of 70,000 pesetas a performance), and Carlo Bergonzi, who had to repeat "E lucevan le stelle" no fewer than three times. Corelli had his own personal triumph when he inaugu-

> September 24, 1957
> Georges Bizet: *Carmen*
> Oviedo, Teatro Campoamor
> Belén Amparán (*Carmen*), Franco Corelli (*Don José*), Jeda Valtriani (*Micaëla*), Anselmo Colzani (*Escamillo*), Ernesto Vezzosi (*Le Dancaïre*), Franco Taino (*Le Remendado*), Gino Belloni (*Zuniga*), Antonio Montini (*Moralès*), Loretta Di Lelio (*Frasquita*), Fernanda Cadoni (*Mercédès*), cond. Nello Santi
>
> September 27, 1957
> Umberto Giordano: *Fedora*
> Oviedo, Teatro Campoamor
> Nora De Rosa (*Princess Fedora Romazov*), Franco Corelli (*Count Loris Ipanov*), Loretta Di Lelio (*Countess Olga Sukarev*), Enzo Sordello (*Count Giovanni de Siriex*), cond. Nello Santi

rated the new city street lights at the mayor's side. Vallaure's biggest problem was probably how to get enough flowers for decorating the theater, until someone whispered in his ear that the Caudillo, General Franco himself, would attend that evening. An untimely honor: the general's favorite tenor, Corelli, was at that moment busy gargling at the Hotel Principado, owing to an incipient inflammation of his throat that raised the specter of a cancellation. Vallaure rushed to the hotel, where he exchanged impressions with a Dr. Florez, who then accompanied him to see Corelli:

> We were discussing the results when the mayor called me. After having talked to him, facing the news of General Franco's imminent arrival, I returned immediately to Corelli's suite. I let him know that the head of state would be present at the performance of *Carmen*, and that it was necessary to pull himself together immediately. His reaction was surprising: he jumped out of bed and ran to get the score. At the performance, he was colossal.[60]

Franco and Franco; Il Divo meets El Caudillo at the *Carmen* premiere, Oviedo, September 24, 1957. From left to right: Jeda Valtriani, General Francisco Franco, conductor Nello Santi, Franco Corelli, and Belén Amparán (the three individuals in the back row on the left and the two on the far right are unidentified). (Photo: Courtesy of the Fundación Ópera Oviedo)

The press chimed in with Vallaure, noting moments of extraordinary expressive power in the duet and never-ending applause.[61] Amparán fared less well. One paper printed that she was a fine Carmen; others judged her voice a poor instrument with nice colors, a mezzo-soprano who still had a lot of studying to do before she could seriously consider a part as demanding as Carmen. Corelli probably couldn't have cared less; he was rewarded for his own vocal sacrifice when, after the performance, he had his picture taken with the Spanish dictator, who had arrived at the theater accompanied by his wife.

If Ronchi's troupe was merely plagued at the early festival performances, *Fedora* turned out to be cursed by a broader calamity: an influenza epidemic. The small role of Cirilo had to be cut altogether when Ugo Novelli didn't recover in time. Otherwise, however, the opera was performed with passion and even brilliance. Corelli offered a warm-voiced Loris that was called shining and dominant, although he was criticized for his constant fortissimo and lack of coloring. The veteran Nora De Rosa was commended for her temperament, expressivity, and warmth, while Loretta Di Lelio, these days routinely engaged as part of the Franco signing package, received praise as Olga.[62]

CHAPTER 9 ❖ 1958–1959

Il Divo

January 2–11, 1958: The Tale of the Three Cs

Public acclaim is one measure of success, but the best way to hit the big time is to be involved in a scandal, preferably an international one. At the dawn of 1958, shortly before Corelli's fourth opera-house pairing with Maria Callas, fate stepped in. Callas had recently met Aristotle Onassis, who was opening her eyes wider and wider to worldly pleasures. On New Year's Eve, 1957, she was spotted "drinking champagne" in the Roman nightclub Circolo degli Sacchi. This has often been cited as evidence of her new jet-set lifestyle, although she certainly had some reason to celebrate. Apart from the occasion—who doesn't celebrate New Year's Eve?—it had been quite a special day, even for Callas. In addition to having sung at the dress rehearsal for the upcoming *Norma* premiere, she also visited the RAI studios in Rome. There, around 9:00 p.m., she sang "Casta diva" for Italy's contribution to one of the very first pan-European telecasts—at the time a unique technical accomplishment, because it involved a simultaneous chain of broadcasts across the countries served by Eurovision.[1] After that television appearance, which brought Callas's art to tens of millions of Europeans, she went to dinner with friends, staying out until after 1:00 a.m.[2] That well-deserved dinner seems to have been what the press dubbed "the party," with the champagne being nothing more than the normal New Year's Eve toast at midnight.

Neither of these events would have been an issue had Maria not awakened the next morning with her voice gone. She had suffered from a cold for days and asked the Rome Opera to either postpone the premiere or have an understudy ready. "No one can replace Callas," was the management's answer, and the January 2 premiere, a major A-list event in Rome, could not be postponed. Everyone who mattered in Italy was present at the star-spangled gala. President Giovanni

> **January 2, 4, 8, and 11, 1958**
> **Vincenzo Bellini: *Norma***
> **Rome, Teatro dell'Opera**
> Maria Callas [January 2, part of Act I only], Anita Cerquetti (*Norma*), Franco Corelli (*Pollione*), Miriam Pirazzini, Fedora Barbieri [January 8, 11] (*Adalgisa*), Giulio Neri (*Oroveso*), Piero De Palma (*Flavio*), cond. Gabriele Santini

Gronchi added almost royal luster, and the cinema divas Gina Lollobrigida and Silvana Pampanini were major attractions among the audience of luminaries. They witnessed a legendary night that was a turning point for the careers of both Callas and Corelli: while Corelli and his Adalgisa, Miriam Pirazzini, were still fully engaged in their Act I love duet, Callas was informing the management that she was ill and couldn't continue to sing. With no understudy around, the management desperately tried to persuade her to save the night, arguing that this was a moment when any singer simply had to make a sacrifice.[3]

When Corelli left the stage, he could follow the unfolding drama from his dressing room right next to the diva's:

> She wanted to relax a little more when the theater management pressed her to begin the next scene. But she was really a little sick and didn't feel like she could continue because of this, as she couldn't give her best in this condition. Some vase was thrown, some chair also, this is true. She began to scream and little by little she lost her voice completely and a little tragedy emerged. But afterwards she came out very, very elegant, looking as if nothing had happened.[4]

Thus Callas walked out of the Teatro dell'Opera in the middle of a live broadcast, leaving the public and the president in their seats, where they waited for over an hour for her to return to the stage.[5] The infuriated management canceled Callas's contract for the remaining *Norma*s, which resulted in a lawsuit. (Many years later the diva prevailed in the courts and was awarded damages.)

✧✧✧✧✧

The laws of balance require that where one person loses, another will win. In this case, the first winner was Corelli, whose name and photo traveled to every corner of the world in the slipstream of the turmoil. The second winner was Anita Cerquetti, who stepped in to save the remaining performances:

> Maestro Sampaoli, the artistic director of the Teatro dell'Opera, asked me to study that Norma long before the Rome premiere. I answered that I would start working on it as soon as he gave me the contract. When I read that they were going to do it with Callas, I accepted a standing offer from the Teatro San Carlo in Naples, where they also wanted me for Norma. When Callas canceled, Sampaoli turned to me, and I can't deny that I felt a certain amount of satisfaction at having him at my mercy. When he wanted to explain the situation, I told him that it was better if he kept his mouth shut, as I didn't like to be manipulated. I simply accepted, and so it happened that on Thursday I sang Norma in Naples, on Saturday in Rome, on Sunday in Naples, and from there back to Rome again. The first Rome performance with me and Franco turned out to be a very important one for me. Not only because of the recording that remains or what it did for my career, but also for the public's reaction. They greeted me and the others with "Hurrah for Italy! Hurrah for Italian singers! Thanks, Anita!" Alas, they were quite angry with Callas, as they felt she had walked out on them.[6]

There were a few other important aspects of the performance, remembered a proud Corelli: "As Pollione I was seven feet two inches high, from the shoes to the waving-plumed helmet!"[7]

January 23–February 1, 1958: Swordfight

If Sampaoli thought the Callas walkout was scandal enough for an entire career, he must have been stunned when the next one hit his theater only a few weeks later. In this case, it was a special type of swordfight during the rehearsals that caught the attention of the global press. According to the eyewitness quoted by *Il Piccolo*, rehearsals had been tense from the beginning, because Corelli was said to have refused to greet the bass, Boris Christoff, backstage.[8] During a rehearsal of the auto-da-fé scene, at the point where Don Carlo draws his sword in order to defend the Flemish, singing, "Sarò tuo salvator, popol fiammingo, io sol!," tempers got out of hand. Christoff was standing behind

> **January 23 and 26; February 1, 1958**
> **Giuseppe Verdi: *Don Carlo***
> **Rome, Teatro dell'Opera**
> Franco Corelli (*Don Carlo*), Mario Petri (*Filippo II*), Tito Gobbi (*Rodrigo*), Antonietta Stella, Mara Coleva [February 1] (*Elisabetta di Valois*), Caterina Mancini (*Princess d'Eboli*), Giulio Neri (*the Grand Inquisitor*), cond. Gabriele Santini

Corelli, a little higher on the stage, when suddenly he roared that Corelli was stealing his scene by deliberately blocking him from the public's view. Remembered Corelli:

> Following the libretto, the king had to burst into a rage against his son, while singing, "Signor, sostegni del mio trono, disarmato ei sia!" Christoff was supposed to take a sword from the captain of the guard and attack me. And so he did, but with unbounded rage. I merely awaited him, motionless, while exposing my own blade. Fierce curses flew through the air and blades sparked, while the deputies of Flanders tried to intervene.[9]

To which he later added: "Once disarmed, we turned from swordfighters into boxers."[10] Tito Gobbi came to the rescue: "I stepped hastily forward to prevent a serious accident. Posa restores calm with four well-placed E-flats—tremendous and very effective. Then he quietly disarms the prince."[11] Said Corelli: "The bass then ran off, swearing that he wouldn't be back. Who was right and who was wrong? Well, they replaced Christoff, didn't they?"[12]

◆◆◆◆◆

A fantastic story, although *Il Piccolo*'s eyewitness remembered it somewhat more colorfully, saying that Corelli, instead of merely throwing his sword on the ground, threw it at Christoff's feet (after Sampaoli intervened). At that the bass started swearing at the tenor, storming toward him and slapping Corelli's thigh with the flat side of his sword. According to some reports, Christoff actually returned to the rehearsals; he walked out again only after the press started taking Corelli's side and management refused to support him. (Rome Opera's official position was that it was a personal matter and didn't concern them.)

IL DIVO • 145

Insulted, the bass withdrew and was replaced by Mario Petri. When nothing further was heard of Christoff's published threat to sue Corelli and the Teatro dell'Opera after the latter had accused him of breach of contract, Corelli emerged as the big winner in the public's eyes.[13] Much more significant than the incident was the worldwide press coverage, which once again brought his name before the public. These news stories landed squarely on the desk of Rudolf Bing in New York. Remarkably, Roberto Bauer, who passed the clippings to Bing, took Corelli's side: "I can't see how Carlo can rob Filippo of his success there, especially after Filippo's great regal scene. Although Corelli and Christoff are both truly fine characters!"[14]

Corelli was "severely injured" after his encounter with Boris Christoff during the *Don Carlo* rehearsals at the Teatro dell'Opera in January 1958. (Photo: Courtesy of Arrigo Michelini)

1958: New Voice, Failing Looks

When it came to being in all the right places, 1958 was a banner year for Franco Corelli. In spite of the fact that Bauer loathed the Corellis (as he already called them though they were not yet married), he reluctantly acknowledged that in Italy Franco was now more in demand than either Del Monaco or Di Stefano. Not only did Corelli's fee begin to surpass his rivals', but his shameless demand for $2,000 per night exceeded the limits of even the Metropolitan Opera House, where Callas and Del Monaco then sang for a fee of $1,500 per performance.[15] Scandals and Loretta's negotiating skills notwithstanding, the key to explaining Corelli's rise in status after 1957 is his vocal progress. His trial-and-error method of studying had finally led him to discover the ideal placement for his voice, which led to a significant diminishing of his pronounced vibrato and

The wounded Corelli playing solitaire. This and the previous photo show a less well-known side of the temperamental tenor: the clown, the joker who used to amuse his friends at campfires or in the army. The incident with Christoff may have lasted hardly a minute, but Corelli clearly cherished it as much as if not more than the press. (Photo: Courtesy of Arrigo Michelini)

a smoother vocal emission. These accomplishments enabled him to convey a multitude of colors in his voice, in addition to which Corelli began to counterbalance his stentorian voice with a Gigli-like, innate tear that fit the romantic repertoire. His legato improved greatly, and an emerging interest in *mezza voce* singing combined with the development of a rudimentary diminuendo, *messa di voce*, and a number of other vocal embellishments added much to the vocal impact of his Chénier and Cavaradossi. Said Corelli: "I began in a voice not so interesting, but I tried little by little to make my voice more beautiful, with some added sentiment inside—if possible genuine, simple."[16]

On the other side of the vocal palette, his improved top notes brought such high-lying *lirico spinto* parts as Manrico and Calaf within reach. Now he had only to put his technique in the service of an improved expressivity.

♦♦♦♦♦

With his voice on the right track, Corelli suddenly had to come to terms with his physique when the movie producer Alfredo Panone came to check him out as a possible replacement for Mario Lanza in a film with the working title *Silent Melody*. Lanza tended to gain weight, which he would then struggle to lose when it came time for filming. On this occasion, when he failed to slim down quickly enough, they reached a point of no return. Both Panone and the screenwriter, Andrew Solt, were impressed with Corelli's good looks when they visited him in Milan. The fact that he spoke no English whatsoever was considered but a minor problem. However, when Corelli's generous smile revealed too much of his gums during the conversation, both men looked at each other and knew it was over. Said Solt: "The look resembled that of a horse. While we could teach him his lines in English, or at worst dub him, there was nothing we could do to lower his upper lip when he smiled." Haunted by Corelli's smile, they went straight back to the overweight Lanza, who was sent off to Germany to undergo "twilight sleep therapy" in a sanatorium for the alcoholic and the obese. Franco stayed in Milan.[17] A pity, for the film's story about a tenor notorious for his temperament, unpredictability, and cancellations who finally finds peace of mind in the arms of a deaf girl was certainly, though loosely, based as much upon Corelli's life as on Lanza's.

March–April 1958: From Naples to China and Back to Brussels

A bootleg recording of the March 6, 1958, *Tosca* from Naples that surfaced recently turned out to be the missing link between the old and the new Corelli voice. Most traces of the former quick vibrato are gone, and the tenor starts painting a completely new, heroic-romantic picture, albeit with some surprising retouches. He received ample support from Renata Tebaldi and Tito Gobbi, both of whom were in the best vocal shape of their lives, before an ecstatic San Carlo audience. Applause after "Recondita armonia" is one thing, but to have single phrases and high notes cheered with ovations such as the one Corelli received after his high B-natural at the end of "Scarpia? Bigotta satiro" is quite something else. The duet shortly before that moment appears to take place on

> **March 6, 9, and 23, 1958**
> **Giacomo Puccini: *Tosca***
> **Naples, Teatro San Carlo**
> Renata Tebaldi (*Tosca*), Franco Corelli (*Cavaradossi*), Tito Gobbi,
> Ettore Bastianini, Piero Guelfi (*Scarpia*), Leo Pudis (*the Sacristan*),
> cond. Ugo Rapalo
>
> **March 15 (black-and-white telecast), 18, and 20, 1958**
> **Giuseppe Verdi: *La Forza del Destino***
> **Naples, Teatro San Carlo**
> Renata Tebaldi (*Leonora di Vargas*), Franco Corelli (*Don Alvaro*),
> Ettore Bastianini (*Don Carlo di Vargas*), Oralia Domínguez
> (*Preziosilla*), Giovanni Amodeo, Giorgio Algorta [March 20] (*the
> Marquis of Calatrava*), Boris Christoff (*Priest Guardiano*), Renato
> Capecchi (*Brother Melitone*), cond. Francesco Molinari-Pradelli
>
> **April 12 and 14, 1958**
> **Giacomo Puccini: *Turandot***
> **Pisa, Teatro Communale Giuseppe Verdi**
> Anita Corridori (*Turandot*), Franco Corelli (*Calaf*), Ferdinando Lidonni
> (*Timur*), Lifia Coppola (*Liù*), cond. Mario Cordone
>
> **April 20, 1958**
> **Flemish Public Radio and Television**
> **Brussels, Grand Expo Auditorium (opening concert on the
> occasion of the World's Fair in Brussels)**
> Franco Corelli (singing Puccini: *Tosca* "Recondita armonia."
> Donizetti: *La Favorita* "Una vergin, un angiol di Dio." Puccini:
> *Turandot* "Nessun dorma." Lara: "Granada" [encore, with piano]),
> Hazel Scott, Vico Torriani, George Melachrino, cond. Fernand Terby

a new vocal plane, one where gravity does not hamper the free unfolding of voices. In the second act, Cavaradossi's "Vittoria!" is catapulted to the point of boomeranging back to his throat at the final note, but his hoarseness in the "L'alba vince appar" that immediately follows goes unnoticed under the subsequent ovation. Subsequently, "E lucevan le stelle" is attacked more cautiously. Only at the very end of it does he show his mettle, trying to impress foremost through his first recorded attempt at a diminuendo on "Disciogliea dai veli." It is not yet in focus, developing a sharp edge that serves to show that this vocal coup was something not easily wrought from his throat. Whether because of the diminuendo, the powerful ending, or the applause, Tebaldi rises to the occasion and throws out a powerful high C before "O dolci mani." This sends the public into yet another frenzy and catapults Corelli back into the heroic mold. Not even Del Monaco recorded "O dolci mani" as (inappropriately) loud as our tenor sings it here. Surprisingly, Tebaldi comes out on top, her high notes solid as a rock. Even Gobbi adapts to the "playing to the galleries" mode engulfing him and gives a towering, heroic Scarpia, sung effortlessly at the top of his lungs.

Corelli with Arrigo Michelini at his role debut as Calaf in Pisa, April 12, 1958. (Photo: Courtesy of Arrigo Michelini)

A good week later, when stepping onto the San Carlo stage for the televised performance of *La Forza del Destino*, the "recruits" were more disciplined. Corelli, Tebaldi, and now Bastianini gave a lesson in operatic singing that still stands as a textbook example of their art form. Also joining the cast was Boris Christoff. The warmth of the scene in the DVD release of this telecast where Father Guardiano meets Alvaro at the entrance of the cloister nonetheless is no proof of a reconciliation of the animosity with which Christoff and Corelli regarded the other after *Don Carlo*. Far more telling is the fact that they never again met onstage.

After a last Neapolitan *Tosca* on March 23, Corelli took three full weeks to prepare himself for his imminent debut as Calaf in Puccini's *Turandot*. Role debuts like this for Corelli would increasingly take on a low profile, try-out character, occurring outside the view of the Milanese critics and the demanding public of Italy's great operatic centers. Pisa was granted the honor of Corelli's Calaf debut, after which he appeared for an impromptu concert at the Brussels World's Fair. (The fair also gave the city its Atomium—Brussels's answer to Paris's Eiffel Tower.)

Because the Flemish Broadcasting Corporation, VRT, later erased the master tapes of the broadcast,[18] the World's Fair concert might have been forgotten completely had not Corelli's encore piece, Lara's "Granada," been recently rediscovered among the legacy of the Flemish tenor Frans Meesters, who taped extensively for Flemish radio.[19] Today, the "Granada" from Brussels constitutes Corelli's first extant live concert recording; the photo of the occasion is treasured for the post-concert coupling of Corelli with the bebop diva Hazel Scott.

May 19–31, 1958: *Il Pirata*

Mounting *Il Pirata* in 1958 was hardly a logical choice. Apart from a revival with Beniamino Gigli in 1935, it had already fallen out of the standard repertoire in the 1850s. But the 1950s' Bellini revival had critics and public eagerly anticipating the production, which offered old and new favorites in the major roles, although the critics had reservations about the work's dramatic structure.[20] The opera begins with the exiled pirate Gualtiero's return to his native soil after having been shipwrecked in a storm. In his challenging opening aria, "Nel furor delle tempeste," he sings of his home and his love for Imogene. When the pirate reveals himself to Imogene in the lengthy duet "Se un giorno," the action commences. He learns of her forced marriage to his enemy, Ernesto, and when their child enters, Gualtiero threatens to kill it on the spot. He is stopped only by Imogene's tears. This dramatic weakness largely sealed the fate of *Il Pirata*, because no audience could ever sympathize with Gualtiero the child murderer. The subsequent killing of Imogene's husband makes more sense, but Gualtiero's surrendering himself like a lamb to his mortal enemies

> May 19, 22, 25, 28, and 31, 1958
> Vincenzo Bellini: *Il Pirata*
> Milan, Teatro alla Scala
> Maria Callas (*Imogene*), Franco Corelli (*Gualtiero*), Ettore Bastianini (*Ernesto*), Luigi Rumbo (*Itulbo*), Plinio Clabassi (*Goffredo*), Angela Vercelli (*Adele*), cond. Antonino Votto; stage director, Franco Enriquez; scenery, Nicola Benois and Piero Zuffi

leaves Imogene's mad scene hanging in midair. The task of providing sets for the crippled story was entrusted to Nicola Benois and Piero Zuffi. They created a sequence of ruins, beaches, and dark palaces in a gloomy, atmospheric light that was judged splendid by *Corriere della Sera* and particularly mediocre by John Ardoin.[21]

Corelli threatening to kill Imogene's son. (Photo: Erio Piccagliani. Courtesy of the Teatro alla Scala)

A general sense of the atmosphere is still perceptible in Erio Piccagliani's production stills. The dim lighting, together with the impact of the work's music, guaranteed *Il Pirata*'s success at its La Scala revival. By 1958 multimedia had started to shift opera's emphasis to the visual aspects, providing a counterpart to the vocal achievements of opera's most beloved stars. The La Scala production provided all of that in abundance, beginning with the triumvirate of Callas, Corelli, and Bastianini and continuing through the conductor's clever cuts. There were some disputes over the direction, but whatever evil caricature the stage director had made of Ernesto in an attempt to make Gualtiero's fury more acceptable was answered by Bastianini with sheer vocal beauty. As the pirate, Corelli sang boldly, although *Corriere della Sera*'s Franco Abbiati wished for a little more discipline and the sort of refinement with which Bellini was traditionally associated[22]—a rather curious remark, considering the opera had been performed only once since the 1850s. In Corelli's case, the style to draw upon would be his own Pollione. The Roman proconsul is far closer to Gualtiero than the melancholic, lovelorn tenors in Bellini's *La Sonnambula* and *I Puritani* that Abbiati seems to refer to, although Gigli's unique 1935 rendering may well have surpassed Corelli's in gracefulness. In turn, Gigli is unlikely to have brought the sort of fireworks to Gualtiero's lines that Corelli did with his pantherlike 1958 voice. His new and thunderous top notes made him ideal for the dark and merciless pirate captain and left the distinguished critic Rodolfo Celletti

A towering, very high-heeled Corelli with Callas in Bellini's *Il Pirata*, Teatro alla Scala, May 1958. (Photo: Erio Piccagliani. Courtesy of the Teatro alla Scala)

"stupefied."[23] Bruno Slawitz noted Corelli's effectiveness in both the vocal and the stage demands of the impossible role, praising the hint of melancholy combined with the tenor's newly acquired quality of innate sensuality. And Slawitz didn't stop there: "In the spellbinding final act aria 'Tu vedrai la sventura,' he proved that he could actually sing in the sense of combining technique with noble expression."[24]

According to Slawitz, Callas was truly convincing only in the final scene, surpassing all with a mad scene that she delivered as if her life depended upon it.[25] In a certain sense, that was true. After the Rome walkout, Italian theaters appeared to have united against the diva, who was to be taught a lesson or two. When, during the *Pirata* run, Ghiringhelli refused to deny the rumors that he didn't want her back, Callas announced that she would not return to La Scala as long as it was under the same management. During the final cabaletta of the last *Pirata* performance, where she envisions the scaffold on which Gualtiero is to die in "Là . . . vedete . . . il palco funesto" (There . . . see . . . the fatal scaffold), she aimed her outstretched arm at Ghiringhelli's box (*palco* can mean either "scaffold" or "box"). That brought the house down. When Callas's curtain calls threatened to turn into a public demonstration, the curtain mysteriously fell during her fourth bow. A large number of security guards popped up from nowhere and ushered everyone out.[26] Unfortunately, the rumored *Pirata* recording has never surfaced. Corelli always denied having owned a copy himself, though it was supposedly taped by Loretta from the wings.[27]

July–August 1958: Taking Turns with Lauri-Volpi

During the late summer of 1958, Corelli alternated between the summer festivals of Verona and the Terme di Caracalla (a festival under the management of Rome's Teatro dell'Opera). Although Caracalla's intendant, Guido Sampaoli, had no roles for Loretta there (in spite of her explicit request),[28] Corelli did not pull out of his performances. In fact, he showed great flexibility allowing Giuseppe

> **July 6 and 11, 1958**
> Leoncavallo: *Pagliacci*
> **Rome, Terme di Caracalla**
> Franco Corelli (*Canio*), Vera Montanari (*Nedda*), Aldo Protti (*Tonio*), Adelio Zagonara (*Beppe*), Ferdinando Lidonni (*Silvio*), cond. Ottavio Ziino
>
> **July 13 and 17; August 21, 26, and 31, 1958**
> Verdi: *Aida*
> **Rome, Terme di Caracalla**
> Antonietta Stella, Simona dall'Argine [July 21, 26, 31] (*Aida*), Franco Corelli (*Radamès*), Miriam Pirazzini, Dora Minarchi [July 21], Adriana Lazzarini [July 26, 31] (*Amneris*), cond. Franco Ghione, Alberto Paoletti [July 21]
>
> **July 24, 26, and 29; August 5, 12, and 14, 1958**
> Puccini: *Turandot*
> **Verona, Arena di Verona**
> Frances Yeend, Anita Corridori [August 5, 12, 14] (*Turandot*), Franco Corelli (*Calaf*), Rosanna Carteri, Marina Cucchio [August 5] (*Liù*), cond. Antonino Votto

> **August 2, 6, and 9, 1958**
> Verdi: *Aida*
> Verona, Arena di Verona
> Leontyne Price, Antonietta Stella [August 9] (*Aida*), Franco Corelli (*Radamès*), Fedora Barbieri (*Amneris*), cond. Tulio Serafin
>
> **August 17, 1958**
> Puccini: *Turandot*
> Rome, Terme di Caracalla
> Lucille Udovick (*Turandot*), Franco Corelli (*Calaf*), Pina Malgarini (*Liù*), cond. Vincenzo Bellezza
>
> **August 23 and 28, 1958**
> Puccini: *Tosca*
> Rome, Terme di Caracalla
> Luciana Bertolli (*Tosca*), Franco Corelli (*Cavaradossi*), Gian Giacomo Guelfi (*Scarpia*), cond. Angelo Questa

Di Stefano to have the opening-night *Pagliacci* (in the Teatro dell'Opera). He also agreed to alternate with Del Monaco in the Veronese *Turandot*s, though Del Monaco ultimately declined the offer. Because the June 28 opening night had been granted to Giacomo Lauri-Volpi, it was with the veteran tenor, at the time a merciless critic of Corelli, that Franco alternated as Calaf.[29] A first, not yet significant meeting between the two probably took place in between Lauri-Volpi's four Arena performances. By now, Corelli's technique had significantly progressed, and his Calaf and Radamès met with the expected rave reviews.

November 6, 1958: Manrico and the Grapevine

Corelli put some effort into learning the part of Manrico. Immediately after the summer festivals he told Sampaoli that he was able to study the role only after he was forced to cancel his studies of Giuseppe Hagenbach in Alfredo Catalani's *La Wally* in January 1958, owing to the fact that the premiere was canceled. Corelli then asked Sampaoli to release him from his Rome Opera winter season *Fedora*s so he could rise to the challenge of Manrico: "As you know, it is anything

With Maria Luisa Nache at his Manrico role debut in Bologna, November 6, 1958. (Photo: Courtesy of Arrigo Michelini)

but easy to fully master *Trovatore*. I therefore am forced to dedicate a certain amount of time to a repertoire with higher tessitura and I have to take all the time necessary to let it fully resound in my throat."[30]

Despite his efforts, Corelli did not arrive in Bologna in optimal form for his role debut as Manrico, although the critic Adone Zecchi writes that he managed rather well, including being asked for, and rewarding the audience with, an encore of a lowered "Di quella pira."[31] Still, Corelli's encore on the season's opening night could not make up for his being forced by the laryngitis that had bothered him on the first night to cancel the next two performances.

◆◆◆◆◆

Corelli took advantage of Manrico's unexpected time off to stir things up on the other side of the world. Even though the Met's attempts thus far to obtain his services had been in vain, Franco and Loretta clearly took pride and pleasure in broadcasting Bing's interest, claiming that Franco had been contracted by the Met and adding a few bucks on top of Bing's actual offer. Such padding had an explosive effect on the Met's current tenor roster. In the middle of his Met negotiations, Carlo Bergonzi suddenly began telling Roberto Bauer that Vienna and La Scala now paid him the same as they paid Del Monaco, Di Stefano, and Corelli.[32] The thought of Corelli coming to the Met was bad enough, but the idea that Corelli was again receiving more money than he brought on some un-Bergonziesque fortissimos.

> **November 6, 1958**
> Verdi: *Il Trovatore*
> **Bologna, Teatro Communale**
> Franco Corelli (*Manrico*), Maria Luisa Nache (*Leonora*), Dino Dondi (*Count di Luna*), Adriana Lazzarini (*Azucena*), cond. Franco Capuana

More irritated by Corelli's behavior than ever before, Bing hastened to write Bauer: "Bob Herman tells me about your letter and Mr. Corelli's statement that he has been offered $2,500 per performance. I hope you have already told Bergonzi that this is a complete and utter invention. You know better than anyone that I do not like Mr. Corelli's singing, that I think he is unmusical and conceited, that his voice is not very good and that in fact I have never made any kind of offer to him."[33] Bauer was so delighted with Bing's scornful reproach of Corelli that he took it and ran straight to Liduino Bonardi, who was already a little displeased with Corelli's "performance" in Bologna.[34] If the Met could only put one over on Corelli, just once, what a Christmas gift that would be!

December 7–23, 1958: Capturing Calaf

When the Stockholm Opera asked me to do a new role, I was pressed for time and looked for something simple. So I picked Turandot, the shortest and easiest part for soprano I could find.
Birgit Nilsson, telephone interview, April 10, 2005

For the opening of the 1958–59 season La Scala mounted *Turandot* for Birgit Nilsson and the surprising Calaf of Giuseppe Di Stefano. The more likely prospect for Calaf, Mario Del Monaco, was unavailable, owing to his engagement at the Met. Unexpectedly, Di Stefano triumphed, as one critic wrote, playing each and every trick in his book in order to match Birgit Nilsson's enormous vocal output. "Pippo" added a lovelorn, tragic element and a voice of velvet to create a more humanized prince, as opposed to Del Monaco's more brutal characterization. Said Nilsson: "Di Stefano had a much larger voice than his records suggest. He was a little uncertain at the high notes, but he had a tear in his voice and he was wonderful. Perhaps Calaf wasn't for him, but I loved him, I loved to sing with him."[35]

Unfortunately, singing with Di Stefano was not an option on December 23, when the tenor canceled due to illness. Fortunately for Ghiringhelli, although Corelli had never sung the role at La Scala, he was in the middle of preparations for filming the RAI-TV *Turandot* in Milan. Said Corelli:

> One evening I received a phone call with the request to substitute for Di Stefano. If not, they would have to cancel the performance altogether. I said, "Yes," went

> **December 7 and 17, 1958**
> **Giacomo Puccini: *Turandot***
> **Milan, Teatro alla Scala**
> Birgit Nilsson (*Turandot*), Angelo Mercuriali (*Altoum*), Giuseppe Modesti (*Timur*), Giuseppe Di Stefano [December 7], Franco Corelli (*Calaf*), Rosanna Carteri (*Liù*), Renato Capecchi (*Ping*), Mario Ferrara (*Pang*), Piero De Palma (*Pong*), cond. Antonino Votto
>
> **December 23, 1958**
> **Giacomo Puccini: *Turandot***
> **Milan, RAI Television (black-and-white telecast)**
> Lucille Udovick (*Turandot*), Franco Corelli (*Calaf*), Nino Del Sole (*Altoum*), Plinio Clabassi (*Timur*), Renata Mattioli (*Liù*), Mario Borriello (*Ping*), Mario Carlin (*Pang*), Renato Ercolani (*Pong*), cond. Fernando Previtali

to the theater, and sang the part. That was my first encounter with Nilsson. . . . I noticed immediately that she had an enormous breath span, and that she liked to linger on notes to the point where others should have been singing theirs. But on this specific evening everything stayed within acceptable limits.[36]

December 29, 1958–January 7, 1959: The Story of Illo and Hercules

I was unaware of the complex my height was giving our tenor from Ancona until the bootmaker came to my dressing room to fit my boots. I suddenly realized that Lucia, my wife, was measuring the heels of my boots with her fingers and was asking the bootmaker to add at least three inches to my height. I began to protest. "Calm yourself, darling," she said, smiling very sweetly, "I know what I am doing." She had been tipped off that Franco, stewing over my size, had insisted on extra-high heels for his boots.
Jerome Hines, *Great Singers on Great Singing*, 1983

The Battle of the Boots between Jerome Hines and Franco Corelli, who was adamant about being the tallest singer on stage, has grown so famous that it overshadows the historical importance of *Eracle*'s being performed in honor of the bicentennial of Handel's death. La Scala's decision to mount the oratorio met with some raised eyebrows, but the Italians judged the difference between *Eracle* and any of the composer's opera serias not significant enough for Italians to rob themselves of a fully staged spectacle. The experimental approach can also be deduced from the choice of singers, who were selected on the basis of their general operatic reputations rather than their specific Handelian accomplishments, which were virtually nonexistent. (Apart from a limited tradition in Great Britain, there simply was no Handel canon in the 1950s.) The primary importance of the La Scala revival by the likes of Hines, Schwarzkopf, Barbieri, Corelli, and Bastianini is that it proved Handel could be performed successfully. That helped to pave the way for a greater Handel renaissance and the development of a more historically informed baroque opera style, although Corelli's importance in the emerging Handel renaissance should not be exaggerated. Illo is even more of a minor character than was Sesto in the earlier *Giulio Cesare* revivals. His languid and sweet moments appear in only three

Corelli as Illo in Handel's *Eracle*, La Scala, December 29, 1958. (Photo: Erio Piccagliani. Courtesy of the Teatro alla Scala)

December 29, 1958; January 1, 5, and 7, 1959
George Frideric Handel: *Eracle*
Milan, Teatro alla Scala

Jerome Hines (*Eracle*), Fedora Barbieri (*Deianira*), Franco Corelli (*Illo*), Elisabeth Schwarzkopf (*Iole*), Ettore Bastianini (*Lica*), Agostino Ferrin (*a Priest of Giove*), cond. Lovro von Matačić

short arias and a duet, beginning with the rhythmically varied arioso "Io sento, sento il Dio," which combines heroic inflections with reflective moments. In the more famous lament "Dalla sfere celestiale," his newfound vocal colors make for a striking interpretation, but the inevitable happy ending, with its jubilant baroque-style love duet, is not his métier. In the end, Corelli made his contribution to the Handel renaissance on a mix of Spontini and instinct. He was well aware of his limitations: "The operas of 'style' were not my strongest points. I consider myself a tenor *eroico romantico* because I like the moments of languidness, sweetness. I love some moments when you have to pour out the voice. *Eracle* asked for a lot of style, and there were not many moments where you could pour out the voice. Vocally I could manage, but this music is not for my temperament."[37]

❖❖❖❖❖

There were other moments in the opera where Corelli had to leave the honors to others, most notably to Hines. Once Corelli learned, after meeting Hines in rehearsals, that the bass was almost three inches taller than himself, he pleaded with Hines not to wear high heels. Meanwhile, he "forgot" to inform Hines of his own intention to order heels high enough to ensure his own physical dominance on stage. When Hines saw his wife indicating higher heels to the La Scala bootmaker, an old acquaintance of hers, he at first refused—he thought he was tall enough as it was. But the bootmaker had told her of Corelli's plans, and she insisted. Said Hines: "Following that, Corelli walked on stage a towering 6 foot 7 and found me waiting for him at 6 foot 10."[38] Corelli immediately returned to the bootmaker to order still higher heels for the next performance.

❖❖❖❖❖

Pride, vanity—perhaps he simply needed those three inches over Hines to catch a glimpse of the very tangible fruits of his money and labor in Ancona, where the reconstruction work on the Palazzo Corelli was finally completed in December 1958. He had made it taller too—there were two extra levels on top of the old building. When he mentioned the completed renovations to a reporter for *Alba*, C. Bianchi, he reminded her of his deceased mother, whose death he still mourned. Wrote Bianchi: "This son's devotion is heartbreaking, and Franco Corelli is also convinced that his successes, his moments of glory, have been watched over by the angelic woman who bore him."[39]

January 4–31, 1959: An Unpaid Bill and a Secret Liù

Although Corelli had sung in Parma's golden theater before, his status as the public's favorite there rests on this *Turandot* premiere. Afterward, the triumphant tenor invited all journalists present to have dinner with him in a local restaurant. That evening was the first encounter of *Oggi*'s Maurizio Chierici with the singer:

> Gathered around a majestic table with lavish dishes, the conversations grew longer and longer, until all present lost count concerning the number of courses that were being served. Suddenly Corelli rose to his feet and said: "I have to get back to Milan. It's almost morning." He saluted us and left elegantly, just as an English gentleman would have done. We looked at one another. Who had paid the bill? No one. A little sadly, we walked to the counter to take care of it. "What a guy, this Corelli!"[40]

Once again singing Calaf, Franco had an unexpected surprise later that month while singing opposite Lucille Udovick. Ilva Ligabue had suddenly fallen ill, which threatened to render the production Liù-less. The substitution of Liù was so last-minute that the cast wasn't even notified. Unrecognizable under the heavy Chinese makeup and hairdo, she only "introduced" herself to Calaf onstage: "When I fell to my knees at the beginning of 'Signore ascolta,' his

---

January 4, 1959
Giacomo Puccini: *Turandot*
Parma, Teatro Regio
Anita Corridori (*Turandot*), Franco Corelli (*Calaf*), Rina Terzi (*Liù*), Armando Benzi (*Altoum*), Alfonso Marchica (*Timur*), cond. Vincenzo Bellezza

January 17, 20, 25, 28, and 31, 1959
Giacomo Puccini: *Turandot*
Palermo, Teatro Massimo
Lucille Udovick (*Turandot*), Franco Corelli (*Calaf*), Ilva Ligabue, Magda Olivero [date unknown], Elisabetta Fusco [date unknown] (*Liù*), Armando Benzi (*Altoum*), Ivo Vinco (*Timur*), cond. Ottavio Ziino

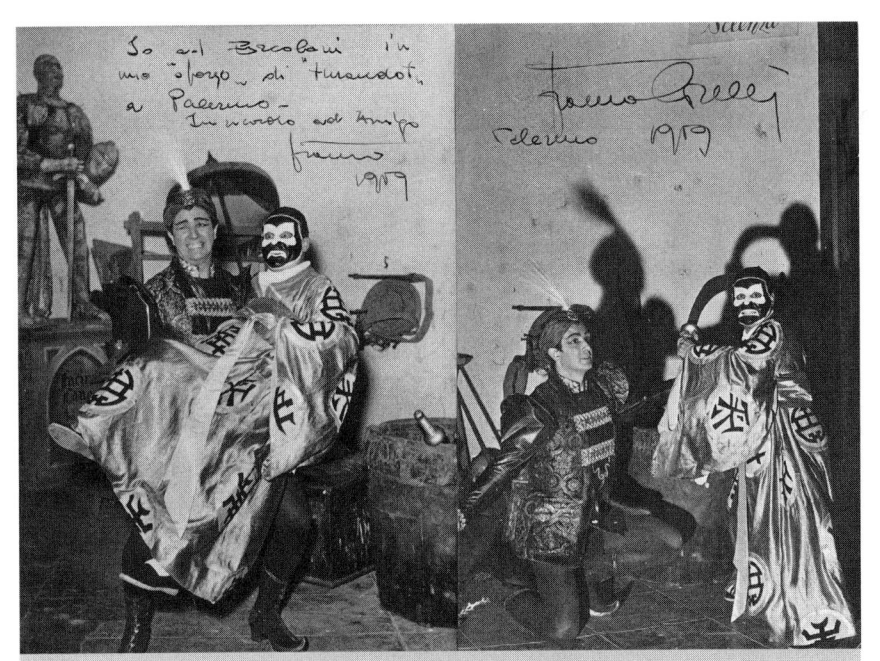

"I am so nervous, ... so serious, ... always studying, ... no life, no friends—where is my doctor?" These pictures present the other Corelli, the one his friends knew, enjoying some leisure time with Pang (Renato Ercolani) in between rehearsals for his Palermo *Turandots*, January 17–31, 1959. (Photo: Courtesy of Arrigo Michelini)

face expressed both confusion and surprise ... he knew this voice but it was not the one of Ligabue. Ah, he was already a marvelous Prince then! He had this elegance, also in his voice, and the *romanza*, 'Nessun dorma'! God, how beautiful that was! A halo of sound that came out from his mouth."[41]

Thus, Calaf solved an unexpected first-act riddle scene, identifying the unknown slave girl who appeared from under the makeup as none other than the renowned soprano Magda Olivero, who in 1939 had recorded the part of Liù in the very first complete recording of Puccini's final work.

February 25–April 12, 1959: On Boos, Bises, and Barks for Ernani

It's the same old song repeating itself over and over again. Young talents aren't much appreciated by the Kings of Old, nor by their fans. What happens in the boxes of La Scala is, to say the least, curious. And I have five years experience there to back up what I am saying. Someone shouts "Bravo," another "Boo!" Someone calls for a "Bis," another shouts "Dog!"

Franco Corelli, "Sono il tenore più alto ma voglio diventare il più grande," *Oggi*, March 12, 1959

Merely coping with the role of Ernani is completely different from striving to equal and even surpass any previous renderings of the part by your immediate rivals. As can be heard on Corelli's earlier Cetra recording of "Come rugiada al cespite," he was very much aware of the standard set by Gino Penno and Mario Del Monaco, to whom Corelli was likely to be compared at La Scala. The pressure that resulted from those demands made him touchy and hard to handle at times. Claques pro and con, a headache, a cough from his dog, the idea that something felt a little strange in his own throat, all seemed to affect Corelli's nervous condition before a performance more than the challenge of singing the opera.

La Scala's premiere of *Ernani* was a resounding success. In his book *Grandi voci*, Rodolfo Celletti wrote of this Ernani as a statuesque figure dressed in a black cloak, evoking memories of gloomy Meyerbeerian heroes. He mentioned a ringing voice combined with impressive phrasing, as effective in the middle voice as in the high notes. Still, the quote that opens this section provides an interesting side light to this *Ernani* premiere: it refers to the practice at La Scala in these years of having audience galleries split up into sections that fervently favored particular stars. Singers either paid cash or gave free tickets to claques to shout the required "Bravos." Corelli always denied participating in these

February 25 and 28; March 3, 5, and 8; April 12, 1959
Giuseppe Verdi: *Ernani*
Milan, Teatro alla Scala (inauguration of the Thirty-seventh Fiera di Milano)
Franco Corelli (*Ernani*), Ettore Bastianini, Diego Dondi [March 3], Cornell MacNeil [March 5] (*Don Carlo*), Nicola Rossi-Lemeni, Nicola Zaccaria [March 3, 8; April 12] (*Don Ruy Gomez de Silva*), Margherita Roberti (*Elvira*), Biancamaria Casoni (*Giovanna*), Piero De Palma (*Don Riccardo*), Alfredo Giacomotti (*Jago*), cond. Gianandrea Gavazzeni

practices, and we can take him at his word: it was in fact Loretta who made the necessary arrangements to counterattack an expected anti-Corelli demonstration by paid Del Monaco fans.[42] Corelli still sometimes lost his temper over the habitual booing: "I know each and every single one of these antagonists, some even by name: Signora Margherita, Signor Antonio et cetera. One of them was particularly on my mind. I caught him just after the *Ernani* premiere, writing slander next to my name on a poster in front of the theater. I couldn't hold back and grabbed his collar. Action, reaction, bang! Not too violent, though—you couldn't really call it a crime."[43]

March 12, 1959: "PeCorelli" Challenges Del Monaco

The tenors of the time were Corelli and Del Monaco, the others were . . . on another level. I prefer Del Monaco to Di Stefano, but between Del Monaco and Franco I prefer Franco. On the whole he was more "tenor," beautiful, with a beautiful voice—he was complete, he had everything.
  Anita Cerquetti, interview, Rome, January 14, 2005

Corelli's by this time greatly increased self-esteem is reflected not only in his physical approach to enemy claques, but also in the way he settled another score that was long overdue: his feud with Del Monaco. In the middle of the *Ernani* run, *Oggi* gave him the chance to set the balance to rights in a piece of his own entitled "I Am the Tallest Tenor, but I Aim to Become the Greatest." There he stressed that the picture of him as a serious and hardworking artist is the one that "objective" and "good-hearted" opera managers and colleagues had rightfully painted of him—even if "certain colleagues" had chosen a different approach:

> The most illustrious one among them has even changed my last name, by applying some "popular mockery," I assume inspired by Aristophanes: instead of Corelli he calls me "PeCorelli." With that, he refers to a vibrato in my voice five years ago, when I was a mere débutant who couldn't always cope with the emotion or fear of performances. Today I can reflect on this calmly and accept the joke, as it was about something that is now completely eliminated, as any given critic will confirm.[44]

What are we to make of Corelli? Well, according to the man himself, his true makeup was that of a singer who simply accepted colleagues who refused to greet him and so on; a modest man who stuck notes on the paintings in his house that said things such as, "Dear Franco, don't be a jerk! Don't hurt your throat by singing too much." Wrote Corelli: "I need these notes, I read them whenever I study, day in and day out. . . . I have to, because now that I have found the passage to the highest notes, I have to be careful, because I am easily carried away by my own enthusiasm." This sympathetic vocal enthusiasm was clearly matched by his pride when he wrote that his days as the third man behind Di Stefano and Del Monaco were over. They could no longer frustrate him with their pestering, and their mockery of him was in vain, for he chose to learn from them, his "enemies," because he had nothing but admiration for them: "I have played Mario Del Monaco's recording of 'Testa adorata' from Leoncavallo's *La Bohème* so often, that it has turned completely gray."[45] How friendly can a post-"PeCorelli" tenor get!

A few words from Del Monaco's son Giancarlo may serve to explain the extremes between which Corelli's opinions on his rival swung: "My father was already world-famous at the time; he didn't need the publicity. In retrospect, I am convinced that it was Loretta who fueled this feud in the press from the start. She managed him, and this rivalry made good publicity. It lent Franco's name a certain amount of notoriety."[46]

March 12–22, 1959: A Royal Fan

By 1959 *Turandot* and *Trovatore* had become Corelli's two most celebrated parts, for which he was in demand all over Europe. By now his physical appearance was clearly seen as a nice extra perk alongside his renowned voice, instead of the other way around. This was confirmed when he was walking through the streets of Lisbon after his last *Turandot* there. Out of the blue the driver of a passing car hit the brakes, stopping just behind him. Alarmed, Corelli turned his head to see what was going on when someone approached him with open arms, asking why he looked so worried. Recalled Corelli:

> I was shocked. In front of me was Umberto of Savoy [the last king of Italy, living in exile]. "Majesty," I stuttered, but before I could continue he lent me his arm. I told him of my fears regarding the upcoming *Trovatore* performance,

> **March 12 and 15, 1959**
> **Giacomo Puccini: *Turandot***
> **Lisbon, Teatro de São Carlos**
> Inge Borkh (*Turandot*), Armando Guerreiro (*Altoum*), Alessandro Maddalena (*Timur*), Franco Corelli (*Calaf*), Nicoletta Panni (*Liù*), Carlo Meliciani (*Ping*), Cesare Masini Sperti (*Pang*), Franco Ricciardi (*Pong*), Loretta Di Lelio (*First Maid*), cond. Antonino Votto
>
> **March 22, 1959**
> **Giuseppe Verdi: *Il Trovatore***
> **Lisbon, Teatro de São Carlos**
> Franco Corelli (*Manrico*), Régine Crespin (*Leonora*), Ettore Bastianini (*Count di Luna*), Lucia Danieli (*Azucena*), Silvio Maionica (*Ferrando*), Loretta Di Lelio (*Ines*), Franco Ricciardi (*Ruiz*), cond. Antonino Votto

and he told me: "You are just as good as you are tall. Tonight I will be there to cheer you on! And tomorrow I'll be awaiting you in my villa, to celebrate your success." When I walked him to his car, I could not bid him goodbye without tears in my eyes.[47]

March 28–April 4, 1959: A New Life

The Genovese *Trovatore*, with its three performances, is one of only three productions in which Corelli would be paired with the Turkish soprano Leyla Gencer. These *Trovatore*s are also of interest as the last documented stage performances of Loretta Di Lelio. Her involvement in his career had developed to the point where her backstage support was needed more than her presence onstage. Her decision to leave the stage may have been made easier because at the age of forty-one her career prospects as a *comprimaria* were no longer very promising.[48] If it was a sacrifice or risk at all to put her entire fate in Franco's hands, it was foremost because they were still unmarried. Franco was not very troubled by this, for he recognized the turbulent nature of their relationship. His nerves, her domineering character, and the constant career pressure made their lives not altogether enviable, but in the end he took the blame for that turbulence upon himself, at least in public:

> **March 28 and 30; April 4, 1959**
> **Giuseppe Verdi:** *Il Trovatore*
> **Genoa, Teatro Carlo Felice**
> Franco Corelli (*Manrico*), Leyla Gencer (*Leonora*), Anselmo Colzani (*Count di Luna*), Fedora Barbieri (*Azucena*), Agostino Ferrin (*Ferrando*), Loretta Di Lelio (*Ines*), cond. Oliviero De Fabritiis

Loretta dedicated—in fact, sacrificed—her entire life to me, and I am rewarding her with the worst egoism. An egoism that is another aspect of the concern and dissatisfaction that seizes me when I face a demanding challenge. This concern makes me become tyrannical, irritable, and despotic. She manages to get some peace and quiet only during the days off, when we go to the countryside. There my fears, the pressing demands for pills or hot-water bottles, stop persecuting her.[49]

May 1959: In Need of Corelli

When Bauer reported to the Met possible new peccadilloes by Mario Del Monaco, who was falsely accused of having exposed himself at a window to passersby,[50] Bing realized that he was taking a great risk depending on just one star tenor. A mere six months after his anti-Corelli letter to Bauer over the Bergonzi salary feud, Bing felt that he could no longer ignore Corelli's immense successes in Italy and the rest of Europe. Bergonzi's apparent fear of the prospect of Corelli's arrival at the Met seems also to have opened Bing's eyes to Corelli's true value. By now even Bauer admitted that there was undeniable value in his recent La Scala Manricos: "Corelli sang extremely loud and sure and had an enormous success. I must admit that he has bettered a lot."[51] With all that in mind, the Metropolitan Opera initiated negotiations with the reluctant tenor. Or rather, they tried to start negotiations with him, while Bonardi, possibly backed by La Scala, played cat-and-mouse with them, even arranging a meeting between Corelli and Bing, which the tenor did not attend.[52] Did Bonardi plan it this way, or did Corelli just not show up? Future negotiations suggest that the Met pair thought it was the former.

June 23, 1959: Corelli Meets de Gaulle

The gala for Charles de Gaulle at La Scala celebrated a century of fraternity between France and Italy, beginning with the Risorgimento (which had led to the unification of Italy) in 1859. The gala proved to be a magnificent event. La Scala was completely decorated with stems of gladiolus, and the public was perhaps the most elegant one that ever assembled at the theater. Even Bauer completely succumbed to the glamour of the event: "On principle I am against all dictators or semi dictators, but I must say that de Gaulle looked most sympathetic and behaved most charmingly."[53]

The musical highlight of the evening was the performance of the third act of *Ernani*, where Bauer judged Bastianini in top form, Corelli very good, and Gabriela Tucci "supposedly good," as he couldn't hear her in the ensembles.[54] Tucci, who never sang Elvira again, was actually surprised to sing there herself. But to get somewhere one needed the right contacts, and in spite of the difficulties he posed for the Met, her manager, Liduino Bonardi, was clearly the one you needed in Italy. The gala impressed her: "It was very well prepared. We actually rehearsed, there were costumes made and everything. Highly unusual for a single act! We were introduced to de Gaulle afterward, when we went up to the presidential box. Besides de Gaulle, Gronchi, the Italian president, and their respective wives were there as well—that was an evening to remember."[55]

> June 23, 1959
> Milan, Teatro alla Scala
> Gala in honor of the president of the French republic, Charles de Gaulle
> Giuseppe Verdi: *Ernani* (Act III)
> Franco Corelli (*Ernani*), Ettore Bastianini (*Don Carlo*), Nicola Rossi Lemeni (*Don Ruy Gomez de Silva*), Gabriella Tucci (*Elvira*), cond. Gianandrea Gavazzeni

August 7, 1959: EMI

One would think being stood up by a tenor would leave any manager angry enough not even to consider that tenor's name ever again. Apparently, though, it only whetted Bing's appetite. On July 3 he asked Bauer about Corelli: "Could you get to him? Will you be able to get through to him before you leave? I simply need him for an extended period in the 1960–61 season." Bing even suggested getting the conductor Erich Leinsdorf to intervene when it came to thwarting Bonardi's plans,[56] but that proved unnecessary. On July 13 Bonardi suddenly informed Bauer that Corelli had expressed an interest in singing at the Metropolitan after all. If Bing and Bauer attributed this sudden change in Corelli's attitude to a veritable deus ex machina, they were not yet aware of her identity: Electric and Musical Industries, also known as EMI. By 1959 the voice of their former star tenor, Giuseppe Di Stefano, had deteriorated to the point where he was no longer an option. Just like Bing, they were in need of a new tenor with sales potential, although EMI's need was arguably more immediate.

EMI began negotiating with Corelli in 1959 while he was still under contract to Cetra. Corelli drove a hard bargain, but EMI's officials pointed out in no uncertain terms that operatic and vocal records were primarily sold in the United States, and in order to make it there you simply had to be on the Metropolitan Opera's roster. In negotiating with their artists EMI always emphasized a key point: it can be well worth accepting a few dollars less per performance at that theater in order to secure the potential royalties gained from large record sales. Bonardi, in a sudden change of strategy, told Bauer that Corelli himself had already suggested that he might be more generous toward the Met than to others: "Perhaps one can't ask the same from the Metropolitan as from Chicago or San Francisco."[57]

His Met negotiations now in full swing, Corelli signed an exclusive contract with EMI that included an option under which he was allowed to record three operas for another company, apart from the titles reserved to EMI: *Aida, Il Trovatore, Cavalleria Rusticana, Pagliacci, La Forza del Destino, Norma, Otello,* and *Tosca.*

The contract spanned three years, from August 7, 1959, to August 7, 1962, with two renewal options of one year each. It was agreed that EMI would record a minimum of four of the reserved titles.[58]

✦✦✦✦✦

With the EMI contract in his pocket, Corelli entered into serious negotiations with the Met. Remarkably, he agreed to deal directly with Bauer in secret instead of through his cunning spokesman/manager/advisor Bonardi.[59] The negotiations now began to have less to do with opera than with soap opera, with Bing telling Bauer to whisper in Corelli's ear that Mario Del Monaco had fooled Corelli into believing that Bing paid him $2,500 per performance in the hope that Corelli would demand the same, causing Bing to refuse to hire him. Bing's maximum was still $1,500 per performance, but he offered to raise the number of Corelli's guaranteed performances to twenty-eight, which would yield him an additional $3,000. He then threw in an extra $100 for expenses per performance on the Metropolitan's spring tour on the condition that Corelli pay his wife's travel costs. In addition, Bing offered to raise the transatlantic travel expenses to $2,000, which guaranteed a first-class return trip for two. As was his custom, Bing coupled his generosity with a subtle threat. Now aware of Corelli's freshly signed EMI contract, he played the royalties card in reverse: "Tell him that he should not risk all for the sake of another few dollars."[60]

If this reads like the beginning of a quick deal, it most certainly was not. Opera singers and theater managements had raised fighting over the very last penny to a high art. The tactics employed by singers were matched by Bing's various means of getting his way. Money mattered, always, but when they came to the duration of the tour in the second year of Corelli's contract (even while the first year was still under negotiation), Bing suggested a compromise when Corelli wanted twelve weeks instead of the sixteen that Bing had requested. At that point, Bing suddenly drew out his wallet, promising to raise Corelli's travel expenses from $2,000 to $4,000 for the second year (on the condition that he could write it in the contract as "twice $2,000 for two trips," even though Corelli would only have to make one trip. Likewise, he asked Bauer to inform Corelli that it was impossible to put the term "tax-free" into his contract: "Will he trust my and your word that he will get his fee tax-free?").[61]

Those tactics may seem clever, but they included risks for future negotiations and proved downright counterproductive in Corelli's case. The tenor's only response to the extra $2,000 offered in travel expenses for the second year was to demand them for the first year as well.

◆◆◆◆◆

The skirmishes continued on the artistic level. Bing asked for *Manon Lescaut*, but after a brief look at the part Corelli rejected it, offering to sing *Un Ballo in Maschera* instead (which was not included in the season under discussion). It is just short of a miracle that Bauer, who was in the middle of all this backstage wheeling and dealing, didn't lose heart along the way. Incredibly, he believed things could have been far worse: "If you leave out the fact that, like all Italians, he really cares for money (and indeed he gets everything he wants over here), it is also a fact that he is much less difficult in the contract negotiations than many others."[62]

September 3–22, 1959: Too Hot to Handle

Money may have been an important issue in Corelli's career, but the critics from Bilbao and Oviedo duly noted how he obtained his legendary fees: by singing better and better. After taking Bilbao's Teatro Coliseo Albia audience by storm, Corelli conquered the Spanish crowd in Oviedo's pride and joy, the majestic new gold-trimmed Teatro Campoamor: "His splendid voice has gained in brilliance, clarity, and security in all registers, especially in the high register, where he demonstrates incredible qualities and ease. . . . After 'Di quella pira' he received a prolonged ovation that couldn't possibly have been more deserved. . . . His Manrico was a creation of unsurpassable artistic quality."[63] Good news for fans: a recording of the performance recently surfaced (highlights, made public through a free online download).

Unfortunately for the Met, Bauer's next scheduled contract negotiation meeting with Corelli (in Milan shortly after the Oviedo triumph) had to be postponed owing to a major hurricane that struck Ancona on September 5, 1959. The catastrophe killed ten people and destroyed a number of houses, enough to make Corelli run home to see what was left of his newly completed Palazzo Corelli. Though the damage proved to be no more than a little water in the basement, upon his return to Milan Corelli was not in the best of spirits. Going for the very last dime over dinner with Bauer, the singer squarely refused the proposed option for a second Met season—and rightly. After all, the proposed "option" was nothing more than Bing's opt-out in case Corelli did not hit it off with American audiences. The tenor was aiming for a long-term engagement with the Met, but on more equitable terms. If he couldn't get a fair two-year contract, he would try the opposite tactic: "When I succeed, we will surely reach an agreement."[64] That scenario was of course Bing's worst nightmare, for he knew there would be no limit to the tenor's demands should he successfully establish himself as the public's favorite.

Bilbao, Teatro Coliseo Albia
September 3, 1959
Giuseppe Verdi: *Il Trovatore*
Franco Corelli (*Manrico*), Margherita Roberti (*Leonora*), Fedora Barbieri (*Azucena*), Ettore Bastianini (*Count di Luna*), cond. Manno Wolf-Ferrari

Bilbao, Teatro Coliseo Albia
September 7, 1959
Giuseppe Verdi: *Aida*
Margherita Roberti (*Aida*), Franco Corelli (*Radamès*), Fedora Barbieri (*Amneris*), Giuseppe Modesti (*Ramfis*), Ettore Bastianini (*Amonasro*), cond. Manno Wolf-Ferrari

Bilbao, Teatro Coliseo Albia
September 12, 1959
Giacomo Puccini: *Turandot*
Gertrude Grob-Prandl (*Turandot*), Franco Corelli (*Calaf*), Gabriella Tucci (*Liù*), cond. Manno Wolf-Ferrari

Oviedo, Teatro Campoamor
September 17, 1959
Giuseppe Verdi: *Il Trovatore*
Franco Corelli (*Manrico*), Maria Luisa Nache (*Leonora*), Gina Consolandi (*Azucena*), Aldo Protti (*Count di Luna*), cond. Manno Wolf-Ferrari

Oviedo, Teatro Campoamor
September 22, 1959
Giacomo Puccini: *Tosca*
Maria Luisa Nache (*Tosca*), Franco Corelli (*Cavaradossi*), Aldo Protti (*Scarpia*), cond. Franco Patanè

In the midst of those difficult negotiations, Ghiringhelli raised the stakes by offering Corelli on behalf of La Scala the incredible sum of 1,200,000 lire—close to $2,000 per performance.[65] Confronted with that offer, a desperate Bing tried to convince Bauer of his own reasonableness by pointing out that Corelli was offered terms for his first-year Met contract that no other singer in history had obtained. How could this Corelli even begin to expect that the Met would blindly offer him the same terms for a second season? Bing had but one trump card left: "You can assure him that Del Monaco has not one cent more than we have now offered him. On the contrary!"[66] With that remark, he made a conscious choice of Corelli over Del Monaco, who had been the Met's number-one draw throughout the 1950s. Three days later, when the negotiations stalled over the last $100, Bing was finally on his knees: "Please add to Corelli that really I beg of him not to be so small minded for the second year because of $100 extra. This is just a ridiculous amount for someone in his income class. At the same time, the Association's rules make it impossible for me to grant his request unless I want to be dismissed from my job, and this may not yet be his intention."[67]

Poor Bing. He didn't know he was begging of the wrong person. The real question was not what Corelli wanted—it was what Loretta wanted. From the moment Corelli agreed to negotiate with Bauer without the omnipresent Bonardi, she presented herself as his manager. Option or contract, to her it was the same. There was no doubt in her mind that Franco would be a success in New York. She was against both deals, for she considered either variant a matter of "mortgaging the future too far ahead." Naturally, she wanted to demonstrate their "good will," so she gladly promised Bauer an option of four to six weeks for the second season. But anything more would simply cost them too much money on lost engagements of a more lucrative nature. Bauer sighed to Bing that Loretta showed him incredible offers from Paris, where he was offered more than $1,000 per performance above the Met's top fee. And worse, even provincial Italian theaters such as those in Bari and Brescia were currently outbidding La Scala. Said Bauer: "I am afraid that no argument can convince Corelli. This moment is his finest hour—as Callas had hers here a few years ago. They pay him those sums because his name alone suffices to sell out the house down to the very last seat."[68]

A normal person would have given up then and there, but Bing simply asked whether Corelli could arrive earlier for the opening of the 1960–61 season, in which case he would guarantee him six extra performances. Unfortunately, Corelli had meanwhile agreed to open La Scala with either Meyerbeer's *Gli Ugonotti* or Rossini's *Guglielmo Tell*. Bauer readily understood that such a premiere was destined to become the crowning glory of the tenor's career to date and judged it unlikely that Corelli would be able to arrive earlier at the Met because he would have to sing all La Scala performances: "With all those high Cs I wouldn't know of any present tenor who could substitute for him."[69]

The result of this new blow to the interminable negotiations with Bing was that the Met's general manager became obsessed with the idea of getting this tenor. Furthermore, he was at the same time in danger of losing Del Monaco, who was not amused at the thought of having to face the former "PeCorelli" at the Met. In vain, Bauer tried to point out to him that no tenor could ever sing all performances at the Met by himself and that in any case Corelli and Del Monaco had different repertoires. But Del Monaco would have none of it. In the end, he demanded all or nothing. Said Bauer: "He informed me that should Corelli get a new production, he would take back his promise to come for the whole 1961–62 season including the tour." In response, Bauer reminded Del Monaco that the latter had canceled a whole string of productions intended for him, such as *Manon Lescaut*, *Il Trovatore*, and *Aida*. Then Bauer dropped a bomb with a slow fuse: when Del Monaco asked Bauer what new productions the Met had planned, he mentioned *Falstaff*, *Nabucco*, and *Elisir d'Amore*, all operas with no parts for either of the rival tenors. Meanwhile, his report to Bing spelled out something quite different: "Naturally, I was very careful not to mention the word *Turandot*."[70]

Bauer's repertoire tactics for the 1961–62 season proved in vain. Bing had already discussed *Turandot* with Del Monaco earlier, in the presence of the tenor's wife, Rina, and Bob Herman, Bing's right-hand man. As with the canceled 1958 Caracalla performances, Del Monaco was not interested in the part at the Met. And yet Bing understood perfectly well that Del Monaco's attitude would change if he knew the truth about Bing's plan: "Obviously you will not tell him that we had offered it to Corelli long before this discussion with Del Monaco."[71]

November 26–December 9, 1959: Behind the Scenes at the Great *Adriana Lecouvreur*

I had been in retirement for nine years when, at the end of 1950, the Sonzogno publishing house told me that Maestro Cilea was critically ill. He had asked them to get me to promise that I would sing his Adriana Lecouvreur again, so that he could part from this world with peace of

mind. He saw in me the incarnation of his most beloved creation, and I returned to the world of opera for Cilea alone.
    Magda Olivero, interview, Milan, January 12, 2005

One frustrating matter in the negotiations between the Met and Corelli was the series of undisputed triumphs that the tenor began to accumulate almost from the beginning of those negotiations. First, he scored an immense success with his Calaf in Bologna, wiping out any memory of his ill-fated Manrico debut there. Then he scored one of his greatest victories to date with an unsurpassed Maurizio, sung with the quintessential Adriana, Magda Olivero. Interestingly, the opera was basically a last-minute substitute for Verdi's *Aida*, which the ailing Renata Tebaldi no longer trusted herself to sing. Corelli, who had not sung the part of Maurizio for years, was displeased with the change but relented as a courtesy to the management and Renata, who had even gained the respect of the usually defensive Loretta.[72] Olivero herself maintains that the *Adriana* had been planned from the beginning, with her in the title role. But when she returned her contract because she had fallen ill and had to undergo an operation, Tebaldi, who was also in Naples and scheduled to sing *Aida*, seized the opportunity to switch roles because she found Adriana far less taxing than *Aida*. Tebaldi then participated in the *Adriana* preparations up until the final dress rehearsal on November 26, after which she became indisposed herself. In despair, the theater management returned to Olivero: "It was almost a month after my operation when the San Carlo management phoned me, asking if I was able to sing yet. So, I packed my bags and, with my sister's help, I went to Naples, where I sang on the very evening of my arrival. It was perhaps the greatest success of my entire career."[73]

Olivero's strength as Adriana consisted of her unique mastery of the *recitar cantando*, the art of transitioning between singing and acting. Olivero's finished artistry was paired with a unique dramatic ability that combined Callas's expressiveness with an intimate style that was at home in the Neapolitan *Adriana* environment,[74] where she had three splendid costars in Ettore Bastianini, Giulietta Simionato, and Corelli. The tenor may not have been as lyrical as Beniamino Gigli had been when he sang Maurizio to Olivero's Adriana in the 1930s, but Corelli's looks made her melt all the same. Says Olivero:

> It was impossible for Adriana not to love him. He was so handsome! And I took care of him, of his nerves. He would say to me that he would die should

he have to wait in the wings for just five minutes. He tried anything to cope with that fear. He would usually show up only at the very last minute, so he wouldn't have time to think about what was awaiting him, sometimes with his makeup done at home! Then he tried injections, infusions, tranquilizers, and medicines to the extent that I thought it couldn't be good for his health. But I gave him the feeling that he had a friend next to him. I never did anything that could have put him in an awkward position and he truly appreciated that."[75]

The importance of the *Adriana* premiere is clear from the way the Italian press treated this essentially Neapolitan affair. It received wide coverage, complete with television interviews with all of the principals, all raving about their future plans at the Met. Bastianini proudly announced his return to America, and Simionato expressed her desire to stay there for a long time, referring to her triumphant last season there. With his colleagues boasting about their future American engagements, Corelli let the cat out of the bag and proudly announced his status as the Met's newest tenor star. Bing was furious: he had planned to issue a statement at a more appropriate moment—actually, to drop a bomb on both the press and La Scala. After all, Bonardi and Ghiringhelli had been completely unaware of the negotiations between Bauer and their protégé.

From Bauer's report, there can be no doubt that Bonardi and Ghiringhelli were in a state of cold war with Bing over Corelli: Bonardi had sworn to Bauer that the Met would never get him. But Bauer pardoned Corelli's slip of the tongue before the tenor even got a chance to apologize himself: "Corelli let it

---

November 26 and 28; December 1, 6, and 9, 1959

Francesco Cilea: *Adriana Lecouvreur*

Naples, Teatro San Carlo

Renata Tebaldi [dress rehearsal only], Magda Olivero [November 28], Gigliola Frazzoni [probably December 1, 6, 9] (*Adriana Lecouvreur*), Franco Corelli (*Maurizio*), Giulietta Simionato (*the Princess of Bouillon*), Ettore Bastianini (*Michonnet*), Antonio Cassinelli (*the Prince of Bouillon*), Mariano Caruso (*the Abbot of Chazeuil*), Rosanna Zerbini (*Mademoiselle Jouvenot*), Anna Di Stasio (*Mademoiselle Dangeville*), Renato Ercolani (*Poisson*), Augusto Frati (*Quinault*), cond. Mario Rossi

all out in the middle of all this *Adriana* euphoria, where he scored an incredible triumph indeed. . . . He gets better and better from opera to opera now. I actually heard him singing piano, and he modulates with artful taste. At present he is beyond doubt the greatest Italian tenor around and well on his way to becoming the greatest tenor in the world."[76] With that off his chest, he had found the right passage to Corelli's reluctant heart. On December 12, Bauer was finally able to send an affirmative telegram to Bing: "Corelli completely settled. Photos on their way."[77]

CHAPTER 10 ◈ 1960

The Road to the Metropolitan

January 8–31, 1960: Mario Chénier

In the first act he turned towards me after having embellished the romanza and he would say those lines: "Udite, non conoscete amore?" He would say them in a way that gave me gooseflesh, and I would be transformed. He would drug me. I was hypnotized by his way of handling the sentence and by his hands. . . . I was a passionate person by nature, but he would charge me, he would give me more.

   Gigliola Frazzoni on Corelli's Chénier, in Marina Boagno and Gilberto Starone, *Corelli: A Man, a Voice*, 1996

Looking at the chain of events revolving around La Scala's *Andrea Chénier* run, one begins to understand why the ancient Greeks believed in gods who used mankind as living toys. In spite of heavy snows and slippery roads, Corelli drove all the way from Rome to Milan in order to make it to his *Andrea Chénier* rehearsals at La Scala. It took him an entire day of fighting the winter weather to get there, and there was a heavy hidden cost to that journey: an embryonic cold.[1] His condition quickly worsened to the point that his appearance on opening night was out of the question. La Scala panicked. To shift the premiere at that point was not an option, and yet there was no adequate replacement on hand. According to Bauer, Carlo Bergonzi was offered a fortune to take over for Corelli, but he said he was obligated elsewhere and archly informed Ghiringhelli that he was renowned for keeping his contracts (which, if Bauer's claim is true, was adding insult to injury, because Bergonzi gave no performances at all between January 3 and January 23). Ghiringhelli next turned to Mario Del Monaco, who at the time was suffering severely from hemorrhoids. The effort

> **January 8, 11, 15, 17, 20, 24, 28, and 31, 1960**
> **Umberto Giordano:** *Andrea Chénier*
> **Milan, Teatro alla Scala**
> Mario Del Monaco [January 8], Franco Corelli (*Andrea Chénier*), Ettore Bastianini, Ugo Savarese [January 24, 28, 31] (*Carlo Gérard*), Renata Tebaldi, Gigliola Frazzoni [January 28, 31] (*Maddalena di Coigny*), Edda Vincenzi, Elisabetta Fusco [January 11, 24, 28, 31] (*Bersi*), Aurora Cattelani (*Countess di Coigny*), Fiorenza Cossotto (*Old Madelon*), cond. Gianandrea Gavazzeni

of performing had been causing significant bleeding for some time, and his doctor had informed him that an operation was unavoidable. However, because the scheduling of his surgery allowed it, he acceded to La Scala's plea to save the *Chénier* premiere. In a truly heroic effort, at the cost of great pain and a terrifying loss of blood, he managed to save the day for Ghiringhelli.[2] If ever something proved Bing's point about wanting two heavyweight champions on the roster, it was this evening. Unfortunately for Bing, that very premiere was also the precise moment when he lost Del Monaco. Disappointed by Bing and Bauer's treatment of him, pessimistic over his illness, and frightened by the prospect of a complex operation, he suddenly turned in his entire contract for the upcoming season, yielding both the second-night La Scala *Chénier* and the Met to his rival.[3]

⋆⋆⋆⋆⋆

On the second night, Corelli established himself as a warm, poetic, and moving Chénier in an ensemble that was not altogether in top form. Gianandrea Gavazzeni's direction was considered rather loud and one-dimensional. Renata Tebaldi suffered from exhaustion and was pleading with Bauer to cut some of her programmed Met performances. Said Bauer to Bing: "I have to admit that she was very mediocre in the *Chénier* next to Corelli. He himself was hardly in optima forma, but he had an easy job outsinging her as he did."[4]

⋆⋆⋆⋆⋆

Illnesses, insecurities, depression—all these things can suddenly evaporate when an ensemble clicks during a performance. By the fourth evening, Tebaldi had miraculously regained her former splendor, and a completely cured Corelli confirmed his position as the world's leading Chénier.[5]

February 1, 1960: On Prima Donnas

After Del Monaco's departure things went from bad to worse for the Met. He never had the surgery, preferring expensive injections instead—injections he might have been given as easily in New York as in Belgrade, where he suddenly popped up performing in *Carmen* and *Pagliacci* to great acclaim. Bauer proposed that Bing sue Del Monaco for breach of contract on the grounds that the singer had gotten out of his contract under false pretenses. However, a lawsuit would prevent Del Monaco from ever appearing in the United States again, which was likely to backfire if the Met ran into trouble with their latest trump card. Wrote Bauer: "Corelli is an equally hysterical *prima donna*.... I believe it might be to our advantage if we could continue to play Del Monaco off against Corelli.... In that way we can keep Corelli in check-position whenever we want."[6]

February 13, 1960: Fighting the Audience

Among those eternally recycled stories that lend spice to a singer's reputation, this particular *Trovatore* premiere stands out in Corelli's career. To begin with, opening night was on the 13th. The artists were nervous because the difficult Neapolitan audience had vivid memories of *Trovatore*s with the tenors Beniamino Gigli, Giacomo Lauri-Volpi, and Gino Penno, and such sopranos as Gina Cigna and Maria Callas. To make matters worse, the audience wasn't focused and the smatterings of applause didn't come at the right times, which prompted irritated spectators to make repeated calls for silence.[7] The result was a certain tension in the air, in the midst of which Corelli prepared for his usual Neapolitan battle with the strong fan base of the local favorite, Mario Del Monaco. His fans were likely to categorically boo Corelli during each and every performance regardless of how he sang.[8]

During the second act, a youthful fan of the Azucena of the evening, seated in the dress circle, took an offensive attitude toward Manrico. From his gestures it was clear that as far as he was concerned Verdi might as well have cut the tenor's part from this scene altogether, including the "Mal regendo" and his line in the concluding duet, "Perigliarti ancor," even though it was a thrilling performance that won over the rest of the audience.[9] Barbieri and Corelli were taking their curtain calls together when a loud baritone voice suddenly shouted: "Barbieri alone! Alone!" Corelli, disturbed, looked up but decided to let it go,[10] until the same voice rang out with a disgusted "Va via! Get out!" It was a phrase usually reserved for dogs.[11] The enraged Corelli leapt off the stage and started running toward the corridor that gave passage to the auditorium, trying to get to the wretched spectator. Pasquale Di Costanzo, a Naples police officer, was in the audience and jumped from his seat to prevent Manrico from doing something that would require an official response. The insulted tenor meanwhile forced his way through the crowded backstage corridors, shield in hand, his sword swinging violently from his hip. Mario Falconi, a reporter for *Tempo*, which ran the only firsthand account of the incident, remembers that Corelli's eyes shot fire, and he looked like the wrath of God. Bystanders were stunned; where was he going? Word of a duel spread, though no one could tell where or with whom. So naturally, they had to go find out.[12]

By the time Corelli reached the box at dress-circle level, he was followed by a crowd of gypsies, monks, firemen, men in tails, and women in evening gowns, all led by the police officer. Corelli didn't wait for the curious procession that ran after him. With his shoulder he forced open the door of the box and charged in. Seconds later a medical student, Mario Improta, was involuntarily thrust into the role of Count di Luna. Feeling an angry hand on his shoulder, he didn't even have time to react before Franco's hand shot to his sword, at which point Di Costanzo seized him, assisted by some of the theater personnel.[13] "Corelli, please don't do this . . . you will go to the jail!" they shouted in panic.[14] Overpowered, Corelli had to let go, but his anger was far from quenched. Infuriated, he shouted at Improta: "I will wait for you outside!"[15]

February 13, 1960
Giuseppe Verdi: *Il Trovatore*
Napoli, Teatro San Carlo
Mirella Parutto (*Leonora*), Franco Corelli (*Manrico*), Fedora Barbieri (*Azucena*), Gian Giacomo Guelfi (*Count di Luna*), Giuseppe Modesti (*Ferrando*), cond. Gabriele Santini, Pasquale De Angelis

In northern European settings, such an incident might end a performance then and there, but Italian opera in Italy, especially in Naples, is intended to generate heightened emotions. And so, after a fifty-minute break, the performance continued, with the police officer's seat empty; Di Costanzo had posted himself in the wings to prevent any repeated mingling of opera and reality.[16]

The brawlers were still at daggers drawn when the curtain came down. Improta was ready to take up the gauntlet and meet Manrico outside. The San Carlo management tried to convince their reckless star that he faced a serious lawsuit for assault while pleading with Improta and his family to forgive Corelli. Improta made them beg a little bit before he agreed to accept the apologies of the tenor, who was of course at fault. A calmed-down Corelli readily admitted this: "*Trovatore* is one of my very best operas and in the duet with Barbieri I gave my very, very best. When I heard that voice afterward shouting for her to step to the front alone, I felt as if my very existence ended then and there."[17]

All ended with the very agreeable Neapolitan tradition of *tralaluci* and wine, and the story goes that Corelli and Improta actually became good friends later.[18]

In Corelli's San Carlo dressing room, peace is established between Corelli and the twenty-two-year-old Mario Improta. (Author's collection)

March 21–April 3, 1960: On Claques

One *Turandot* performance in this period gives a particularly telling look into Italian opera practices of the time and the beginning of the rivalry between Nilsson and Corelli. After their first chance meeting onstage due to Di Stefano's last-minute indisposition, this official La Scala run planned for the now famous pair threatened to begin without the tenor when Corelli demanded that Nilsson stick a little more closely to what Puccini had written in the score:

At the dress rehearsal, we arrived at the high C in "Ardente," at the end of the second act. Just before it, the soprano has to sing a prolonged G, but Nilsson held it even past the point where I had to begin singing, "No, no, principessa altera." I was so concentrated on this phrase, because I wanted to hold back a little there, that I interrupted the rehearsal. I told Votto: "If the lady holds that note like that again I will walk out immediately." Votto communicated this to Nilsson and asked me to do it again, but because of the stress my throat was clenched and I produced a stupid sort of childlike cry, instead of the required high C.[19]

At the premiere and during the rest of the run, all was in balance. Corelli's and Nilsson's claques were equally strong, and honors were evenly distributed between the two protagonists. Except for the Liù, Bauer witnessed a great performance, with two optional high Cs from Corelli in the second act.[20] No further problems occurred until the evening performance of April 3, when Corelli's claque had been hired away by Joan Sutherland, who was singing in Genoa. Bauer, who had by now progressed from talent scout and manager to mental coach and lifeguard for Met stars in Italy, went to Sutherland's matinee performance in Genoa. In spite of the distance, he managed to drive back in time for Corelli's evening performance in Milan, where he had to look out for Bing's other interests. But with Corelli's claque in Genoa, Nilsson's fans easily outshouted Corelli's supporters and even demanded that she take a solo bow. Wrote Bauer: "I had fear that he would bite someone again! But he handled it in an intelligent manner and came out again and again as a real trouper."[21]

A glimpse of Corelli's vocal approach to Calaf onstage at this time can be heard from the pirate recording that surfaced of his March 1 radio broadcast in Monte Carlo immediately preceding the April La Scala one. Corelli is less disciplined than he would be in a major theater, but he is definitely in stupendous voice and treats the opera as if it were a vocal boxing contest. That sort of singing is indeed intended for the galleries, who rewarded him with such

March 21, 24, 27, and 31; April 3 and 6, 1960
Giacomo Puccini: *Turandot*
Milan, Teatro alla Scala
Birgit Nilsson (*Turandot*), Franco Corelli (*Calaf*), cond. Antonino Votto

ovations that he uncharacteristically gave in to their request for an encore of "Nessun dorma."

April 26–July 7, 1960: Spring, Summer, and a Recording

Following the Monte Carlo and Milan *Turandot*s, Corelli participated in a (for him) fairly routine run of *Carmen*s at La Scala in April featuring Gloria Lane in the title role. From there he went on to La Fenice in Venice for a May series of *Forza del Destino*s and more *Turandot*s, one of which was broadcast over the radio. Regrettably, copies of the broadcast never materialized, although the earlier one from Monte Carlo largely compensates for this loss (in spite of the missing first few minutes of the performance). More celebrated moments of his early 1960 schedule that can be relived today by way of a recording came in his two June performances of *Andrea Chénier* in Vienna under Lovro von Matačić, a disciple of Herbert von Karajan's. The recorded performance of June 26 ranks very high on the list of Corelli's recorded portrayals of Chénier, and there is the added attraction of Tebaldi, who is more imaginative than Stella was in the Naples recording from November 1958. Corelli's impact on this particular night is perhaps best illustrated by a story of a spectator, Martina Arroyo, then

> **June 26 and 29, 1960**
> **Umberto Giordano: *Andrea Chénier***
> **Vienna, State Opera**
> Franco Corelli (*Andrea Chénier*), Ettore Bastianini (*Carlo Gérard*), Renata Tebaldi (*Maddalena di Coigny*), Margareta Sjöstedt (*Bersi*), Elisabeth Höngen (*Countess di Coigny*), Hilde Konetzni (*Old Madelon*), Kostas Paskalis (*Pietro Fléville*), Alois Pernerstorfer (*Mathieu*), Renato Ercolani (*Spy*), Harald Pröglhöf (*Butler*), cond. Lovro von Matačić
>
> **July 3–7, 1960**
> **Ruggero Leoncavallo: *Pagliacci***
> **Milan, Teatro alla Scala (EMI recording)**
> Franco Corelli (*Canio*), Lucine Amara (*Nedda*), Tito Gobbi (*Tonio*), Mario Spina (*Beppe*), Mario Zanasi (*Silvio*), cond. Lovro von Matačić

in Vienna for her upcoming audition with Karajan himself: "Tebaldi was singing, Bastianini, and a gentleman I didn't know, Mr. Corelli. The performance was so great, and I was so floored by this gentleman, Mr. Corelli, that we screamed and we yelled and the next day I couldn't sing the audition because I was hoarse." Arroyo, famous for her wit, went on to thank Corelli for having thus saved her career, a clear reference to Karajan's reputation as a throat wrecker.[22]

"Ridi, Pagliaccio. . . ." Corelli dresses. (Courtesy of the Teatro alla Scala)

✦✦✦✦✦

Corelli used the summer following the Viennese *Chénier*s to consolidate his increasingly demanding repertoire. His first Met schedule arrived by mail and included a reinstalled role debut in *Manon Lescaut* (scheduled for February 6, 1961), *Il Trovatore* (January 27), *Turandot* (February 24), *Aida* (March 9), and an intriguing *Carmen* in French (April 12).[23] He was still wrestling privately with *Ugonotti*, *Guglielmo Tell*, and now also *Poliuto*. But first came his July 20 recording of *Pagliacci* for EMI (released on Columbia records in the United States)[24] with the American soprano Lucine Amara as Nedda. Presumably she was hired with an eye to capturing the American market, with EMI for once trying to make a star rather than hire one. Unfortunately, though, things did not turn out as the record company had hoped: Amara's Nedda was widely regarded as unimaginative and a major reason for the uneven recording.

July 31–August 23, 1960: Facing Minnie

In Verona, when he came onstage during the first act of Fanciulla, *all dressed in black, with the saddle. . . . I shall never forget that sight.*
    Magda Olivero, interview, Milan, January 12, 2005

During the Veronese *Fanciulla del West* rehearsals there was a scene in the first act where Dick Johnson was on Minnie's left side—a natural position for a tenor and a soprano, according to his Minnie. At a certain point Corelli asked Olivero: "Excuse me, Signora, would you let me stand on the other side?" Olivero answered that it was all the same to her and changed places, although she had no idea why he preferred to have her on his left instead of his right: "Maybe the change gave him his voice, who knows. He was so nervous, especially when he faced a high note. I remember a point in the same act where we had to dance and he said: 'Heavens! Now I have to sing that high note . . . and now that I have to sing it, that note doesn't come to me! I can't manage.'" Olivero assured him that he had been singing perfectly well until then and that he didn't have to worry, but to no avail. Only when he sat down on the table and Minnie turned her back to the audience did Olivero manage to work the required miracle: "I smiled at him, he looked up at me and launched that note—splendidly!"

Apart from these psychological matters, Olivero's most vivid memories are of his voice and his stage personality. According to her, their voices blended beautifully, and Corelli was the epitome of Dick Johnson: "In the duets there was a union between us that transmitted to the audience. Finally I had a tenor like him to sing with, one who cared for musical details—in fact, he cared for stage details as well! Although he was taller than me, he kept experimenting with the height of his boot heels in order to achieve the most picturesque visual balance between us."[25] With her aristocratic self-assuredness, Olivero could

July 31; August 3, 7, 10, and 13, 1960
Giacomo Puccini: *La Fanciulla del West*
Verona, Arena di Verona
Magda Olivero (*Minnie*), Franco Corelli (*Dick Johnson/Ramerrez*), Gian Giacomo Guelfi (*Jack Rance*), Piero De Palma (*Nick*), cond. Oliviero De Fabritiis

August 20 and 23, 1960
Giacomo Puccini: *Tosca*
Rome, Terme di Caracalla
Magda Olivero (*Tosca*), Franco Corelli (*Cavaradossi*), Gian Giacomo Guelfi (*Scarpia*), Vito De Taranto (*the Sacristan*), cond. Armando La Rosa Parodi

only smile at Franco's insecurities. Fights such as the ones he had with Christoff over trivial matters would never materialize with a responsive partner such as herself; she would simply give way.

◆◆◆◆◆

Olivero's two *Tosca*s with Corelli as Cavaradossi followed, just a week after the last Veronese *Fanciulla*. The *Tosca*s were performed at the end of the summer season in Rome's Terme di Caracalla. Once more they eluded the pirates. Olivero and Corelli never met onstage again, and their joint *Adriana Lecouvreur* from the year before remains the only recorded opera to capture their voices together.

August 1960: Photo Model

Sometime in 1960 Corelli gave in to the pleas of the editors of *Grand Hotel* magazine, who had asked him to star in their famous line of *fotoromanze*, the soap opera–style "photo novels" that dominated the magazine. The fact that the owner of the magazine was a family member, albeit a remote one, may have helped persuade the tenor to lend his face and fame to this romantic genre, aimed at stimulating the fantasies of women of all ages. The proposed title was *Andrea Chénier*, his costar the ravishing soprano Marcella Pobbe. Little is known about the production process, but the fact that the *Chénier* series began running with four pages per issue starting from the time it was announced in the August 13 issue suggests a production date during Franco's summer holidays.

> **August 13–December, 1960**
> **Andrea Chénier**
> **Photonovel for *Grand Hotel* (After Illica and Giordano)**
> Franco Corelli (*Andrea Chénier*), Marcella Pobbe (*Maddalena*), Alberto Farnese (*Gérard*), Maria Fie' (*Bersi*); director, Sirio Magni; producer, Arminda Tencalla; photographer, A. Domingo; special effects, Grazia Irene; scenery, Tonj Camatta; costumes, Sartoria Werther; hairdresser, Silvano Rocchettil; footwear, Arditi.

THE ROAD TO THE METROPOLITAN • 187

> **In the realm of a love like ours, time ceases to exist, everything around you ceases to exist, nothing is important anymore... Only you and me remain...**

> **Again... tell me again that our love is all that matters. Your words sink into my heart as drops of water in the desert.**

> **Can you see that star, appearing in heaven?... Her pure light scorns the mud of this earth. In the same way our love stands above all, reaching out beyond the sublime.**

> **Sweet words that happily echo into the depressing silence of this prison... Then the weak light of the moon makes way for the bright light of day: Maddalena and Andrea understand that the moment to part has arrived.**

> **Morning has arrived, Maddalena; you must leave. I don't want you to see me on the condemned prisoner's wagon.**

> **I beg you, hold me just a little bit longer.**

> **You would only increase your torment and mine. Go, and pray for me.**

> **Give me one more kiss... our last kiss.**

> **...And with that kiss, an idea enters Maddalena's mind.**

A page from a *Grand Hotel* issue of *Andrea Chénier*. (Courtesy of *Grand Hotel*/Casa Editrice Universo)

Some people judged his appearance in these rather lowbrow but wildly popular publications odd; however, there were several good reasons for it. For one, he was a photo enthusiast himself, who, contrary to what many have claimed, loved posing (he had Loretta pose him for each and every performance, in order to have a shot of himself in full costume). But apart from that, he sincerely believed in the need to engage the next generation in opera and felt that the popular genre of photo novels might stir an interest among an audience not yet involved with opera.[26] Naturally, Corelli also had his own inimitable defensive line at the ready when Maria Rusconi discussed the matter with him in *Tempo*: "I did it for all the girls who adore me: I had to do something for them in return."[27]

All in all he had little to be ashamed of; the publisher had spared neither cost nor effort and managed to realize an excellent blend between Domingo's lavish photography and what seems to be added backgrounds and drawn-in secondary characters here and there. *Andrea Chénier* alone runs for a full fifty-four pages, at a rate of approximately four pages per issue. It had 351 photographs in all—an average of 6.5 photographs per page. In them, Corelli can be seen remonstrating against the nobility when he first meets Maddalena. He then visits her in the middle of the night, masked with a sort of Venetian Carnival mask. From there, the drama takes its inevitable course, with a strong emphasis on romance. There are numerous photos of Corelli holding the swooning Pobbe. A suggestive little love scene in the fields proves to be a nice precursor to the final passionate kiss in prison.

September 1960: Prima Donna

Corelli was the real star, with his wife calling two hours late that he couldn't sing. We were all waiting for him; he was the real prima donna.
    Christa Ludwig, "Voices," BBC Radio

With the fruits of his new modeling career possibly on tables in various EMI waiting rooms, Corelli met with Walter Legge, Callas, Christa Ludwig, and Tulio Serafin in September 1960 for the historic recording of what would be Callas's second studio *Norma*. Corelli was in top form and a vast improvement over Mario Filippeschi's one-dimensional proconsul in the first, legendary Callas *Norma*, recorded in mono in 1954, but six years later Callas exhibits audible signs of wear and tear. According to the critics, she compensated for this with a deepened sense of tragedy, making the heroine more vulnerable and touching

> September 5–12, 1960
> Vincenzo Bellini: *Norma*
> Milan, Teatro alla Scala (EMI recording)
> Maria Callas (*Norma*), Franco Corelli (*Pollione*), Christa Ludwig (*Adalgisa*), Nicola Zaccaria (*Oroveso*), Piero De Palma (*Flavio*), cond. Tulio Serafin

than ever before. And yet, this stereo *Norma* has never replaced the mono set in the hearts of home audiences.

September–October 1960: Doing It His Way

During the month following the *Norma* recording, difficulties arose over the programmed repertoire for the upcoming Met season. Corelli again refused to do *Manon Lescaut*, which he judged ill suited to his voice. Bing responded by explaining that he had a repertory opera house to run, where everything depended upon reliability. Corelli shot back that not only was he canceling the *Manon Lescaut*s, he also was refusing to sing "in between Radamèses." Such difficult parts he reserved for *stagione* theaters, such as La Scala, where specific operas were performed in sequence, so that he did not have to shift up and down in tessitura from one part to another. Corelli also was cutting *Carmen* from the roster, because singing it in French meant learning it all over again and he felt he had enough on his hands with *Trovatore* and *Turandot*. Bing agreed—on the condition that he substitute *Simon Boccanegra* and *Don Carlo*, in addition to which Corelli had to sing Radamès on tour. Corelli refused but offered to sing *Butterfly* or a couple of *Trovatore*s instead; even *Don Carlo* would be all right on tour. Bing despaired. He already had sold those *Aida* performances and engaged the proper singers, and mounting the lightweight *Butterfly* with the powerful *Aida* cast was an outrage. So he got around Corelli's maneuverings by accepting the tenor's offer "on the condition that Corelli . . . accept half the fee." And so, regrettably, Corelli never sang Pinkerton because he was judged "too expensive" for it.

In the end, Bing met Corelli halfway, or perhaps even a bit further, by accepting *Don Carlo*. But when the tenor started the game all over again, claiming that *Don Carlo* was just impossible for him, Bing pitched a fit. He explained to his tenor in Italian that there was a limit to which any friendship could be stretched. Corelli immediately apologized. Whereas Del Monaco and Callas had proved incapable of recognizing Bing's limits (and vice versa), Corelli and Bing somehow pulled off a delicate balancing act, continually managing to meet each other in the middle of a tightrope.[28]

December 7, 1960–January 15, 1961: Poliuto

On stage I am a lion, but before ... what a terror! The audience thinks of me as an operatic character, bold and confident in life as on stage. But I am very timid. And from this shyness stems the fear: a terrible fear of the confrontation with the public, a fear which consumes my nervous system and makes me approach the performance as a battlefield. Yet, once I step out of the shadows behind the scenery and the lights of the stage surround me, my nervous tension miraculously vanishes and a supreme serenity infuses me, I could even call it a state of grace, which makes me lucid and aware of my performance at all moments. These are the only truly happy moments of my days, where no worries, no doubts, and no uncertainties cross my mind.

    Franco Corelli, in "Sulla scena sono un leone," *Arianna*, February 1961

Alfa Romeos and Ferraris replaced the horse-drawn gilded coaches of days of yore on this starry night at La Scala. Elegantly gowned women enveloped in mink, ermine, chinchilla, and delicate perfumes clung to the arms of important men in tails. There were Princess Grace and Prince Rainier of Monaco, ravishing in gold-embroidered white, accompanied by the Prince Pierre de Polignac; the Begum Aga Khan, majestic in a gold-embroidered corsage; the ubiquitous Elsa Maxwell; and, finally, Aristotle Onassis, Callas's lover, arriving all alone and gazing out at the scene from behind dark sunglasses. Even before the curtain opened it was clear that this was going to be one of the most memorable operatic events of the 1960s. The filmed newsreel footage of the premiere shows the extent to which La Scala was still linked with the epoch of Rossini, Stendhal, and Verdi as the epicenter of Italy's high society. The gilded La Scala doors seemed to transport those present to the distant days when

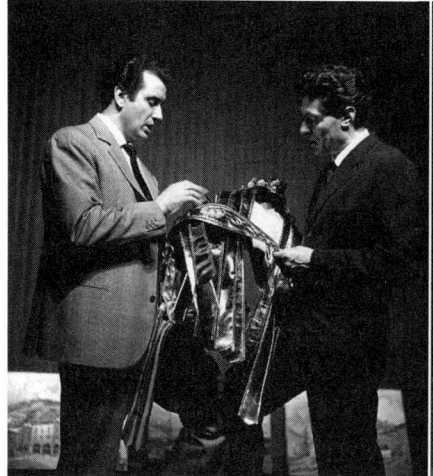

Left: It has been said that Corelli didn't like rehearsals, but he still prepared himself like few other tenors. He took great care with his costumes and the visual aspects of the stage direction, as can be seen in this photograph of his preparations for *Poliuto*, Milan, November 1960. *Right*: Corelli as Poliuto, Act I, December 7, 1960. (Photos: Erio Piccagliani. Courtesy of the Teatro alla Scala)

Tamberlick and his successor Tamagno sang their Poliutos; some spectators had actually witnessed Pertile or Gigli wearing the mantle of the convert. However, few spoke of tenors on this night, where all attention turned toward Maria Callas's return to La Scala. The soprano had been absent for two and a half years, since the legendary *Il Pirata* run with her friend Corelli where she had publicly defied La Scala's intendant, Ghiringhelli. Would there be another scandal on this night?

Actually, La Scala was already in the midst of a scandal. The director and set designer Luchino Visconti had walked out on the *Poliuto* production, not for any reason related to opera, but rather because of the Italian film censors, who had just banned one of his more notorious film projects. Visconti vowed not to set foot in a state-subsidized theater again.[29] La Scala's opening night was in fact a scandal averted, for it had been unclear whether the production would be performed at all, given that government budget cuts at all state-subsidized theaters had recently interfered with opening nights in Bologna and Naples. La Scala was due for a similar strike, but the politicians gave in to the demands of the strikers at the last minute, fearing the commotion that would arise if the historic opening night on St. Ambrose's Day, December 7, were canceled or suspended.[30]

> **December 7, 10, 14, 18, 21, 26, and 29, 1960; January 15, 1961**
> **Gaetano Donizetti: *Poliuto***
> **Milan, Teatro alla Scala**
> Maria Callas, Leyla Gencer [December 26, 29; January 15] (*Paolina*), Franco Corelli (*Poliuto*), Ettore Bastianini (*Severo*), Nicola Zaccaria, Agostino Ferrin [January 15] (*Callistene*), Rinaldo Pelizzoni (*Felice*), Piero De Palma (*Nearco*), cond. Antonino Votto; stage director, Herbert Graf; stage director and scenery, Nicola Benois

As the auditorium filled, all eyes were glued in vain on the box where President Giovanni Gronchi was expected to appear. This evening he settled the score for the Rome premiere of *Norma* in 1958, where Callas had walked out on him after the first act. At 8:55 P.M., 3,200 lorgnettes turned from the empty presidential box to the pit. A storm of applause rained down upon Antonino Votto,[31] who bowed his head before raising his baton.

Donizetti's rarely performed *Poliuto* is a spectacular opera in the Meyerbeerian mold, including a finale with Christians who are to be fed to the lions. When the curtain parted, the glitter and glamour of La Scala made way for Decius's court in Mytilene around 250 A.D. The splendid temples and terraces and the spirit of ancient Rome were recreated on the stage, the site of the conversion to Christianity of the Armenian nobleman Poliuto. From the instant he set foot onstage, Corelli was the incarnation of the convert. His rendering of "D'un'alma troppo fervida" stunned the audience; the familiar dark-bronze hue of his voice was suddenly gilded with 14-karat gold and topped by notes of mesmerizing brilliance. As for Callas, Harold Rosenthal took the serious route in his review for *Opera*, but *Paris Match*, whose reporter's impressions have already been noted, took an eloquent French approach to the diva's first-act appearance:

> Her haughty bearing in that white cape gave her the curves of the ancient Pharos [the Lighthouse of Alexandria, one of the seven wonders of the ancient world], a piece of tulle rolled into a necklace around her throat, almost concealing an ill-conceived baroque hairstyle, tied up in bows. She acted with measured, noble gestures and walked out right up to the footlights, where she hurled denunciations, her eyes blazing, her mouth open like the muse of

tragedy, toward the Christians, as if they had become her personal enemies. Who cares if her voice is not her voice of old; what matters is that she is there. From the last seat just under the roof to the very first an ovation was bestowed upon her.[32]

At the first intermission Callas dominated the conversation. All marveled at her weight, now down to 139 pounds (22 more than three years earlier, but what's a pound or two among fans?), and her salary: 40 million French francs (about $500,000) per year from EMI royalties, 3 million per recital.[33] Despite the captivating Callas, in the second act the true triumph was Poliuto's. In his great aria "Sfolgorò divino raggio" Corelli confirmed his now undisputed reputation as the last of that ultra-rare breed of unchained dramatic tenors in the mold of Adolphe Nourrit and Gilbert Louis Duprez, both linked to *Poliuto*'s world premiere. After Ettore Bastianini responded to Corelli's aria with a superbly sculpted opening of the trio "La sacrilega parola," the audience held its breath for the challenge Callas faced in her entry line, "Qual preghiera al ciel discioglio?" The amazed audience heard the purest emotions and most subtle phrasing pour from her lips. Corelli then echoed her subtle inflections in his entry, "Dell iniqua, del protervo," which still stands as the culmination of his art. The subsequent unison finale was described as an operatic thriller that would be remembered as long as memories of opera performances exist. And that was only the second act.[34]

The third act led the audience to the cave in which the persecuted Christians were hiding. Reunited with Paolina, Poliuto refuses to renounce his new faith in a magical rendition of the duet "Ah! fuggi da morte." Paolina decides to convert as well, and they march toward the lions and heavenly bliss in "Il suon dell'arpe angeliche." Upon the final notes of the opera, the stupefied audience erupted in an ovation that turned this night into one of those handful that defined La Scala and opera in the twentieth century. The *Paris Match* reporter moved toward the stage to focus on Corelli: "His joy is understandable. Sure, he owed this break to Callas, but he is the one who has won everything in this opening night, during which he redirected his competitors Mario Del Monaco and Giuseppe Di Stefano back to their earthly realms. With all the vanity and the egoism that is a tenor's own, he has taken all and everything."[35]

✦✦✦✦✦

When the applause subsided and I was alone in my dressing room, I had a long, intensive moment of meditation and I realized for the first time that my career had changed my personality and my psychological makeup.

Franco Corelli, "Sulla scena sono un leone, ma prima . . . che paura!," *Arianna*, February 1961

Against the background of these new insights into his own personality, it didn't take long before Corelli was able to formulate a fitting explanation for his success, the key of which was to be seen in his very nervousness. His nerves, says Corelli, were always his cross and his blessing, for they propelled him onward: "Poliuto raised so many vocal difficulties that few tenors ever truly mastered it. Directly proportional to it was my heroic momentum on stage, that made me come out victorious, should you allow me to use such flattering words." In addition to his immediate triumph at his debut in the role, he also cherished the high Ds that he interpolated in the production's final performance, when Leyla Gencer took over from Callas and he no longer needed to hold back.[36]

CHAPTER 11 ❖ 1961

Prince of Tenors

January 18–19, 1961: *Il Matrimonio Segreto*

If we are to die, we will at least die married!
  Franco to Loretta a few days before embarking on his first-ever airplane
  trip to go to the United States and the Met; interviews with Loretta Corelli,
  Milan, January 27, 2007, and Marco Corelli, Ancona, August 16–17, 2004

The year 1961 began with Corelli's inauguration of the Parma season with Verdi's *Il Trovatore*. There Corelli fever reached new heights: one ardent female admirer, Camilla Merzi, presented him with a carnation she had managed to pick up during a 1957 performance in the Arena di Verona. It was the very carnation that Corelli had caressed that night, as a reminder of his beloved Carmen; if he would please sign one of the leaves? Touched, Corelli readily complied.[1] This endearing Parma *Trovatore* interlude left only one professional obligation between Franco and his upcoming Metropolitan Opera debut: a final *Poliuto* at La Scala opposite Leyla Gencer. Corelli would have preferred sailing to New York right after his Parma performances, but Ghiringhelli's insistence that he sing this last *Poliuto* forced him to book a transatlantic flight—and his fear of flying was real and severe. Corelli's worry over the upcoming trip may have made him more tense than usual; at any rate, he was very much on edge when he encountered La Scala's substitute chorus master, Romano Gandolfi, in the corridor. The unfortunate maestro had recently dared to comment on the Parma *Trovatore*s in a newspaper interview where he judged Bergonzi's Manrico superior to Corelli's, and this public pronouncement had become a fishbone in Corelli's throat. Impulsively, he seized the opportunity to settle the score: "Maestro, are you still convinced that Bergonzi's *Trovatore* is better than mine?" When Gandolfi answered, "Certainly, you know that very well," the tenor grabbed him by the throat. The encounter might have turned out very badly if bystanders hadn't intervened. The scandal was such that it reached the Soviet Union, where *Izvestia* published an account of it.[2]

Corelli's remaining obstacle was finding a way to assuage his fear of flying, especially now that Loretta suddenly refused to accompany him because they were not married (it is said that she had no desire to face the Americans as his mistress). The prospect of having to fly alone and to survive in New York City all by himself was simply too much for Franco.[3] In fact, his nightmares over the idea of leaving terra firma were such that he himself ultimately insisted on marrying Loretta before they left: "If we are to die, we will at least die married!"[4]

On January 16, five days before their departure, the couple tied the knot in Rome. They were married by a priest at 8:50 A.M. in the Church of Santa Maria in Via.[5] The ceremony took place under extraordinary circumstances, for the marriage was never published, as is obligatory in Italy. But Nino Ciotti, the official of the civil administration who married Loretta and Franco for the State on January 18, agreed to write in the document that, per dispensation of the twelfth of that month, the couple was "excused" from the obligation of having to publish their marriage,"[6] although the validity of such an exception is questionable from a legal point of view. A precise reason for the lack of publication is not given in the documents, but a short glance over them reveals a few interesting facts—among them the couple's actual birthdates.

Concealing Corelli's birthdate became an odd game over the years. The correct date was more or less a public secret, but Corelli avoided candor on the subject. He provided a different age for himself in nearly every interview (astoundingly, he even managed to whittle his age down by two years on his American immigration documents).[7] Nonetheless, Loretta readily provided the correct date of the marriage when asked in 2004 and had no problem commenting on their "secret" marriage: "A secret? Who says that? Everybody knows we were married. January 16, 1961. What is the secret?"[8]

Apart from the age matter, it seems that hiding things became something of a little game for the couple, just as her "profession," as stated on the marriage certificate, attests to a sense of humor: *casalinga*—a housewife.

January 19–26, 1961: New York, New York

The Met has always been the dream of every singer.
  Birgit Nilsson, telephone interview, April 10, 2005

On the American side, Bing had done all he possibly could to ease his new star tenor's nerves, beginning with paying the airfare for Corelli's new friend, Roberto—not for a second had it crossed the tenor's mind that Bauer had a job in Italy. Bing didn't complain; even before his relationship with Corelli began, he had resorted to a whatever-it-takes attitude. And with Bauer at hand to help Corelli through his first weeks, the added cost might turn out to be a good investment. After all, Franco didn't speak a single word of English, and he had no friends in New York whatsoever except for Loretta and himself, "Sir Rudolfo." Bing readily acknowledged all this in his memoirs: "Without Bauer we couldn't possibly have captured Corelli. He accompanied him to New York and held his hand, whenever he threatened to explode."[9]

Bing also absorbed the costs for Franco's excess luggage (he had brought his entire wardrobe and camera equipment), which added another $800 to the bill.[10] After all, Bing had been the one who had asked the Corellis to bring Franco's Radamès costume to save money (Corelli had eventually agreed to the *Aida*s). Loretta then cunningly gave Bing an option: pay the excess luggage charge, or pay for a Radamès costume designer.[11]

❖❖❖❖❖

Franco's fear of flying literally evaporated into thin air when he took some sleeping pills upon boarding the plane in Italy. He immediately dozed off and woke up, still on January 21 but now in New York,[12] where Bing was the first to welcome him, his now lawfully wedded wife, and Bauer. There was little time to recover from the long flight: Franco's debut was scheduled for six days from the moment he first set foot on American soil. From the airport, the Corellis and their forty suitcases were taken straight to their suite in the Essex House, a Central Park South hotel where the Bings were longtime residents. Once ensconced in his new quarters, Corelli received reporters in a silk robe, a T-shirt, blue pajama bottoms, and floppy black leather slippers. They inquired about his notorious temperament, about his relationship with Callas, and about his popularity with women. Loretta answered questions about the last subject: "I am always nice to his lady fans. They are part of his career."[13]

January 27, 1961: A Double-Barreled Debut

Grand opera, temporarily absent from the Metropolitan Opera, returned there last night with the season's first performance of Verdi's Il Trovatore *and the simultaneous debuts of Leontyne Price and Franco Corelli.*
   Harold C. Schonberg, "Opera: Two Debuts in *Il Trovatore*,"
   The New York Times, January 2, 1961

The public interest in Corelli's upcoming Met debut was considerable. But he had not counted on a factor that was totally out of his control: the simultaneous debut of the African American soprano from Mississippi, Leontyne Price. Corelli most likely was oblivious to the racial aspect of the attention that surrounded her Met debut. After all, he had recently sung with Price under fairly normal conditions in Verona. There she had definitely made an impact as his Aida and as his *Trovatore* Leonora. In Italy, her color was welcomed as something exotic, even "authentic" for her portrayal of the enslaved Ethiopian princess. Not so in New York, where, as a black girl from the South appearing at the Met in Verdi's *Trovatore* as the lily-white Leonora, Price occupied a highly controversial cultural position that attracted the kind of national attention not generally afforded opera in the United States.[14] However, her Italian triumphs, the changing times, and Bing's outspoken opposition to racism had paved

Franco Corelli and Louis Melançon (1901–1974). Melançon was the Met's outstanding house photographer from 1947 to 1950 and then from 1956 until his death—almost the entire period Corelli sang there. (Photo: Courtesy of the Metropolitan Opera Archives)

> January 27; February 4, 8, and 18, 1961
> Giuseppe Verdi: *Il Trovatore*
> Metropolitan Opera House, New York
> Leontyne Price, Lucine Amara [February 18] (*Leonora*), Franco Corelli (*Manrico*), Irene Dalis, Jean Madeira [February 8], Nell Rankin [February 18] (*Azucena*), Robert Merrill, Mario Sereni [February 4, 18] (*Count di Luna*), cond. Fausto Cleva

her way to the Met. Bing met with some resistance from the Met's board, but his stubborn determination to go ahead with the experiment proved to be one of the best decisions of his career.

On the evening of the performance, the atmosphere was tense. Leontyne Price, blessed with resplendent looks, was at her absolute vocal peak at the time of the *Trovatore* debut. When she made her stage entrance under the moonlight in the first act, clad in a pearl-studded green gown and wearing a commanding golden headdress,[15] she received an unprecedented ovation, both a tribute to a beloved artist and an acknowledgment of a historic appearance by a black singer in a leading role on the Met stage. Her entrance aria, "Tacea la notte placida," was deemed by the audience worthy of the hype: "Howls of delight and a roar of applause pursued her into the wings at the close of her first aria. 'Ascolta!' she cried. They did; and they found what they heard to be worth stopping the show for."[16] Her voice was fresh, silvery, and full-bodied all at the same time. Luscious and warm, at times even "hot," it was as much made for Verdi as for Corelli. Manrico, dressed in a velvet tunic and tights that displayed his famous thighs to full effect,[17] counterattacked with his offstage aria, "Deserto sulla terra," with a delivery that was considered a model of breath support.[18] After the "Di quella pira" Bing greeted him backstage. Remembered Corelli: "He embraced me and said: 'The doors of the Metropolitan have opened themselves for you. We are going to take some wonderful walks together.'"[19]

In spite of the general enthusiasm for the performance, the task of analyzing it in terms of vocal achievements seems to have been the sole preserve of Harold C. Schonberg of *The New York Times*. His overall impression was a balanced one: "Everybody sang out. Sometimes the singing was glorious, sometimes it was lacking in finesse, but at all times everybody was giving all he or she had. Thus nobody in the audience was bored. It was an exciting night."[20]

Unfortunately for Corelli, much of the credit for that excitement went to Price. The tenor felt robbed of his anticipated triumph in light of her sensational appearance on the Metropolitan Opera stage. Price received more coverage than Corelli in the reviews, all of which hailed her vocal technique. Several critics noted that she even took the trills as written, while also being a competent actress.[21] According to Schonberg: "No soprano makes a career of acting. Voice is what counts, and voice is what Miss Price has. And it is not all florid singing on her part. In the convent scene she took some fine-spun phrases in a ravishing pianissimo. And her top is exceptionally secure. She does not lunge for notes, attacking them from underneath and sliding into them."[22]

With a key New York critic so focused on technical matters and so enthusiastic about Price's ability to attack notes straight on, Corelli had a very severe judge in Schonberg from the outset. The critic's principal question after acknowledging Manrico's good looks was whether this cross between John Barrymore and Errol Flynn could sing. The answer was affirmative, if with some reservations:

> It is a large-sized voice but not an especially suave instrument, and it tends to be produced explosively. It has something of an exciting animal drive about it, and when Mr. Corelli lets loose, he can dominate the ensemble. The nature of his upper register remains to be determined. He did take the D-flat in the Second Act, but the ending of "Di quella pira" was transposed down, and he was unable to take the climactic note in one breath.[23]

If Schonberg's final comments were ever translated into Italian for Corelli, the reigning star tenor of La Scala, of Italy, and of the rest of Europe must have felt himself dragged back to the stage of the Rome Opera as a new singer a full eight to ten years earlier: "The guess here is that Mr. Corelli could develop into an exceptional tenor, but his art does need some refining and polishing."[24] That was certainly not the Met debut Corelli had expected. Moreover, a few catcalls had emerged between loud cheers for him at the end of the second and third acts. They were truly undeserved; he was audibly nervous, but he had given all he had, and that was quite a lot. Schonberg immediately sensed the generalized sentiment behind those catcalls, which Corelli also experienced at La Scala and in Naples: "There is something about his work that greatly excited the audience, pro and con."[25]

While all of the critics agreed that his was a very successful Met debut, bordering on triumphant, just as all agreed that this was a very exciting *Trovatore*, Corelli was beside himself with anger and frustration. The very first thing he did when he woke up the next morning was storm in on a cheerful Bing and his staff, all in excellent spirits over the sensational "double-barreled debut,"[26] as the press had labeled it. The critics tried hard to outdo one another: "Pinza appeal back into opera," one declared, while dubbing the two protagonists "Skylark and Golden Calves."[27] To the Met staff's chagrin, Corelli had a totally different perception of the outcome of the previous evening. Recalled Bing: "I cannot describe the combination of blandishment and threat I had to use on Franco Corelli after his debut at the house, which unfortunately occurred on the same evening as Leontyne Price's debut, which meant that the press paid virtually no attention to him."[28] Thanks to his experience with singers' psychology, Bing eventually managed to calm the Italian hothead down, convincing him that his time would come on the second night, when the novelty of Price's historic debut would be gone.[29] And Price? She had nothing but the sweetest words for her Manrico: "I just love Franco, he has such gorgeous legs."[30]

Corelli looks uncertain as Bing the diplomat divides handshakes equally between Corelli and Leontyne Price after their sensational Met debut. (Photo: Louis Melançon. Courtesy of the Metropolitan Opera Archives)

❖❖❖❖❖

Depending on one's point of view, the second performance was not a felicitous one either, because an overenthusiastic Corelli sprained his ankle when he retreated a little too carelessly after his Act I curtain calls. Such trivia, of course, couldn't possibly stop a true Italian tenor from getting his fair share of applause: Corelli still managed to limp out for two more ovations.[31] When it was announced that the six-foot one-inch, 200-pound singer would continue the performance in spite of his agony, he was wildly cheered again and became the center of attention, just as Bing had predicted.[32] He actually made the front page of *The New York Times* the next day, happily pointing at his swollen ankle and beaming that he couldn't have garnered that kind of publicity if he had hired a whole public relations agency.[33]

March 1961: Two Italians in New York

I do like America a great deal, much more than I expected; it is so far from home and the family.
    Franco Corelli, in F.S., "Matinée Idol," *Opera News,* March 4, 1961

Most first-time visitors to New York marvel at the sights, and the Corellis were no different. In 1961 huge skyscrapers were virtually unknown in Europe. Then there was the snow. Threatening as the cold may have been to Franco's voice, he simply loved the blanket that covered the city: "It's so pretty! So white!" One report wrote that when he looked out over Central Park from the window of his hotel room, his brown eyes gleamed with the mischief of a youngster about to launch a snowball.[34] In this and other interviews, both Corellis sparkled with exuberance. They showed no reserve in their dealings with American journalists. If they weren't "disposed" to talk about Franco's youth, it was but a pose, for they certainly told and retold the story of his earliest beginnings, from his lost voice as a student up through his work as a *geometra*. They even played with the photographers: Franco was a fanatic amateur photographer with thirteen cameras of his own. When he started to take pictures of Dale Haven of the *New York Herald Tribune*, Loretta took on the journalist's role, teasing Haven with questions like, "How do you like Italy? You like Italian men? Do Italian women seem more free, like Americans today?"[35]

Once the gunsmoke of the double-barreled debut cleared, Franco and Loretta in New York were like two children let loose in Disneyland. Loretta would cook dinner for journalists they had never met before; Corelli would receive them in his pajamas, telling them that he didn't smoke, drink, or attend parties, all while beaming from ear to ear and proposing a toast to the photographer with a large glass of grappa.[36] His hobbies were happily discussed. Loretta told them: "We

Left: Franco and Loretta in the United States, 1961. (Photo: Louis Melançon. Courtesy of the Metropolitan Opera Archives). *Right:* "I don't drink, don't smoke," Franco told the readers of *Opera News*, while proposing a toast on the accompanying photo. He certainly was not a heavy drinker, but his house bar showed that he at least had some "taste." (Photo: Erio Piccagliani. Courtesy of the Teatro alla Scala)

collect old opera records and new cars. Right now we have a beige-and-turquoise Lincoln Continental, a grey Jaguar and a white Alfa Romeo Giulietta. We're going to have to sell the Lincoln though, because the heater gives off some sort of vapor that bothers Franco's throat." Her choice of a replacement car—a Ford Thunderbird, vetoed by Franco—shows how thoroughly she had adapted to living in America.[37]

January–June 1961: "Ah! Matilde!"

Offers for Otello continue to come in, and one day I will certainly sing it, but right now I feel too young for it. And then I would also like to fulfill the potential of my current repertoire before I enter the domain of the Heldentenors with Otello.

    Franco Corelli, in Giovanna Kessler, *Opernwelt*, "Sterne am Opernhimmel," February 1964

If Franco had the last word about cars, it clearly was Loretta who decided what he was going to sing and what he wasn't. Not only did she explain why

Corelli and the camera's eye; according to his close friend Andrea Bucolier, he was more a collector of cameras than an active photographer, but he certainly liked to pose as a photographer. (Photo: Courtesy of the Teatro alla Scala)

there could be no question of singing *Otello* at that moment, but she was also perfectly right. There can be no doubt that he would have been a splendid Otello by this time, just as he would have been a wonderful Samson, a part EMI had recently offered to him for a set that was eventually made with Jon Vickers and Rita Gorr.[38] The question was, at what cost? Over the past three years, Franco had expanded his voice to an impressive two and a half octaves, adding three notes at the top without losing a single one on the bottom. A heavy *Otello* performance schedule would have cost him the agility for *Poliuto* and certain other operas he currently was studying, such as Raul in Meyerbeer's *Gli Ugonotti*, the Duke in Verdi's *Rigoletto*, and Arnoldo in Rossini's *Guglielmo Tell*, roles that were on his mind for future La Scala (*Ugonotti, Tell*) and Met performances (*Rigoletto*).[39] Loretta knew such rare treasures could not be squandered: "Today, while he is still young, Franco is using his very high range. Later he will do other roles which require the darker, slightly lower voice."[40]

Loretta also had a perfectly reasonable rationale for their choices, for Del Monaco was a high-caliber alternative for Otello, yet there were none for Poliuto, Raul, and Arnoldo. Between performances, Corelli was actively studying the latter two roles, and he used the recordings from his Poliuto studies at the piano to investigate certain notes. If Raul was a challenge, then Arnoldo was a dare. The extreme tessitura, plus twenty-eight blazing high Cs and two high C-sharps, make the part unfit for mere mortals. In terms of high B-flats and high Cs, his opening duet with the baritone "Ah! Matilde" equals the efforts expended in all of Acts I and II of *Turandot* combined. In *Tell*, Arnoldo's intense duet with the soprano is but the prelude to the breathtaking "Troncar suoi di," while "Corriam voliam" harbors no fewer than six high Cs if performed uncut and seven if the tenor ends on the unwritten one that became the traditional performance practice in France. And that cabaletta is only the afterglow following his big aria "O muto asil," which itself includes several B-flats and a naked, sustained, and unaccompanied high C.

"Troncar suoi dì quell'empio ardiva...." Corelli recorded many of his private rehearsals, among which the complete tenor parts of *Guglielmo Tell* and *Manon Lescaut* are the greatest treasures. This particular photo seems to show him listening to a playback. (Photo: Erio Piccagliani. Courtesy of the Teatro alla Scala)

> January–June 1961
> **Gioacchino Rossini:** *Guglielmo Tell*
> **Piano rehearsals**
> **Complete tenor role including: "Avver comun con essi ... Ah! Matilde," "Al campo volo—Onor m'attende ... Troncar suoi dì," "O muto asil ... Corriam, voliam"**
> Franco Corelli (*Arnoldo*); vocal coach, Loretta Corelli; pianist and vocal coach, unidentified (presumably Arnoldo Schiavoni)

As thrilled as people may now be to learn that parts of Corelli's *Tell* rehearsals are preserved on tape, the singing is in no way a finished performance. The *Tell* tapes are best judged in comparison with the surviving fragments of his Manrico and Poliuto studies, and not with his performances. The Corelli voice at home was not the voice we know from the theater. In comparison, the Poliuto and the Manrico rehearsals at times display the Corelli voice in full bloom, clad in the velvet cloak it had in actual performance, but this brilliant mantle did not represent his voice in its natural state. Said Corelli:

> Each year you understand the mystery of the voice a little better and only after many years can you begin to understand where your voice can go. Then you start thinking of interpretations, possible colors that you can give it. Before going to sleep I spend hours just thinking about my voice, about the ideal road to take. Singing must pursue you, must live inside you and blossom. Those few hours on the stage don't do the job, it is the constant research in between, the discipline, the never ending sacrifice. I needed to eliminate a certain inflexibility and found my qualities in the ligature. Studying Caruso's record made me discover a more beautiful color and eventually I succeeded in becoming a romantic tenor.[41]

All that, combined with the expansion of his voice in a theatrical acoustic, defined the Corelli miracle, but in the dry environment of his rehearsal room at home, the voice doesn't get to bloom for sheer lack of space in which to expand. Furthermore, Corelli is not concerned here with delivering a finished portrait. These studies are just that—sketches for what would become finished oil paintings with respect to Poliuto and Manrico, and what remained a sketch in the case of Arnoldo. His cautious attempts at the highest notes merely serve to convince himself that he could manage them onstage, and the Arnoldo rehearsals leave us very much in the dark as to whether he actually could have realized the role on stage. Still, it is clear from the study tapes that this was to have been the most overpowering and utterly romantic Arnoldo ever to have graced the operatic stage. The way he breathes life into "Ah! Matilde" draws us in, and he rises to full Poliuto splendor in the sumptuous legato bars of "Troncar suoi di." Elsewhere there are insightful, sweet, or dramatic accents in usually overlooked passages, such as in "Al campo volo—Onor m'attende." Phrase by phrase he repeats and fortifies or shifts his approach to a passage until he arrives at the conclusion with "O muto asil... Corriam, voliam." There the stentorian nineteenth-century tradition of Duprez and Tamagno is combined with the gilded copper color and the intrinsic humanity of the Corelli voice. Much more than Otello, Arnoldo was conceived by Corelli to become the crowning glory of his career.[42]

✦✦✦✦✦

Corelli's studies were not limited to the vocal aspects of a work; accordingly, he had Loretta film his performances from the wings in order to improve his stage deportment.[43] Perhaps he was more content with his stage appearance, for he seldom expressed enthusiasm over his own voice after listening to any given tape of a performance: "Perhaps those who visit the theater hear another voice than the one I hear on tape." This degree of self-criticism was no mere pose. In between his intense and often frustrating studies, he would dream about a way out, about getting into some swimming competition and plunging into the sea; even hanging out seemed a very desirable pastime to him, and he had always been a passionate dancer![44]

✦✦✦✦✦

After his visit to the Corellis, the *Herald Tribune*'s Dale Haven marveled at Loretta's many unexpected talents. She programmed her husband's career, and she was both a protective wife and a clever public-relations person. And one should not forget her importance as a performance coach and cook. On the afternoon of a performance, she would prepare Franco a raw beefsteak with lemon, salad, and maybe a little cheese. Then she would follow him to the performance, watch him from the wings, and take care of his needs post-performance: "After the opera, he has a real meal that I fix for him—that is, if he has sung very well."[45]

Could one ask for more? Well, she was also a state-of-the-art manager! Said Loretta: "He tells me how much money he wants and I ask for it—but I ask more than he says. That's the important part of being a manager."[46]

February 24–April 11, 1961: Beating Beaton

With the February 1961 premiere of *Turandot*, the conductor Leopold Stokowski arrived at the pinnacle of the New York opera scene in spectacular fashion.

> February 24; March 4, 9, 13, and 21 [Philadelphia];
> March 24 and 29; April 8 and 11
> Giacomo Puccini: *Turandot*
> New York, Metropolitan Opera House
> Birgit Nilsson (*Turandot*), Franco Corelli, Giulio Gari [March 29, Acts II and III] *(Calaf)*, Anna Moffo, Teresa Stratas [March 9, 13], Lucine Amara [March 24], Leontyne Price [March 21, 29], Licia Albanese [April 8] (*Liù*), Alessio De Paolis (*Emperor Altoum*), Bonaldo Giaiotti, William Wildermann [March 21, 24, 29; April 8] (*Timur*), Frank Guarrera (*Ping*), Robert Nagy (*Pang*), Charles Anthony, Gabor Carelli [March 24] (*Pong*), cond. Leopold Stokowski; chorus master, Kurt Herbert Adler; stage direction created by Yoshio Aoyama; staged by Nathaniel Merrill; set and costume designer, Cecil Beaton

Bing hired Stokowski for his fame and glamour, as a "stunt conductor" who might bring additional luster to the already lavish premiere. The outcome soon proved a mixed bag. Corelli adored "Stoky," ranking him among his three favorite conductors, along with Karajan and Votto.[47] The showman in Stokowski seems to have understood Corelli's inclination to "go for the gold." He seems never to have complained about Corelli's singing to the galleries, and he managed to put the tenor at ease. Nilsson, for her part, belittled the conductor. Stokowski was famous for "conducting with his fingertips," which greatly irritated her, for she never knew where she was with this "mere indicator."[48] As for Bing, he regretted hiring Stokowski almost before the ink on the contract had dried because of Stokowski's public recommendations about how to clean up the mess he found himself in at the Met.

Stokowski couldn't have cared less. It almost seemed as if he regarded the invitation to conduct as an honor for the Met, where he deigned to enter the world of opera for this little cameo. And a fake opera at that! Completely convinced of his own views and much to the bewilderment of Bing and his staff, he once used the Met Guild magazine *Opera News* to point out that none of the orchestral writing in *Turandot* was in Puccini's hand: "Whoever made it did not understand the difference between accompanying voices and solo orchestration. At performances I have, as far as I could, held down the volume of sound when the orchestra accompanied the solo voices or the chorus. It has been very difficult, because the orchestration is much too thick."⁴⁹

Whereas Stokowski and Corelli clicked from the very first moment, the tenor's first encounter with the star designer Cecil Beaton was less successful. Beaton's rather superior English persona and his Chinese prince were headed on a collision course from the start. Corelli was well aware of Beaton's status as photographer of the British royal family and the official escort of Greta Garbo, at whose side Beaton had appeared in public just a month before the *Turandot* rehearsals began. But that didn't help Corelli in the least when it came to his personal needs: "I had asked for two different costumes for Calaf, one for the first and one for the second act. Beaton answered with Olympian calm, 'No, we cannot do that.' I repeated the request a number of times, to his eternal 'No.' As any good Italian would, I then lost my temper and hammered on the table with my fist. 'Get me a second costume, or I won't sing.'"⁵⁰

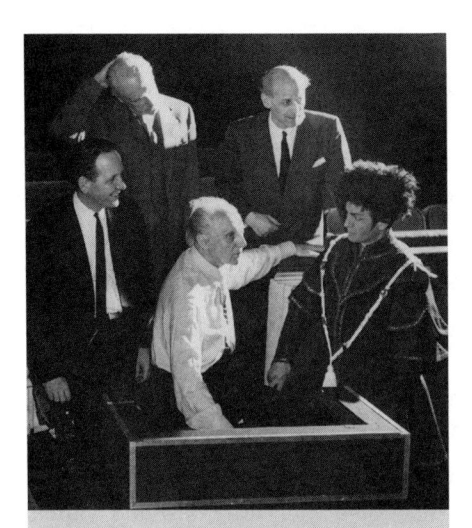

From left to right: Nathaniel Merrill, Cecil Beaton, Leopold Stokowski, Rudolf Bing, and Corelli. Stokowski's dazzling "insights" into conducting opera, not to mention his views on Puccini and the Met's internal affairs, caused quite a stir during *Turandot*'s run. In an *Opera News* interview of February 24, 1962, titled "What's Wrong with Opera?," he made his insights public: "I do not think the orchestration is by Puccini; it is by another hand. Whoever made it did not understand the difference between accompanying voices and solo orchestration." (Photo: Louis Melançon. Courtesy of the Metropolitan Opera Archives)

Beaton seems to have maintained his sangfroid while Corelli raged in front of him, but he exploded once the singer was out the door: "Then it was Beaton, deeply offended, who lost his control and went into a state of total hysteria." At that point the gossip maven Elsa Maxwell, always hovering around and sometimes involving herself in potential operatic or other scandals, intervened when she ran into Corelli after that evening's dinner at Colony, a famed Manhattan restaurant. Maxwell told Corelli that she had heard him during the rehearsals and that he was excellent—so beautiful that she was in love with him. Then, with a disgusted gesture toward Beaton (who was apparently also dining at the

Colony), she added: "In this country it is better to get what you want through a friendly manner, and should that fail, you still have time to show your iron fist." Franco followed her advice: "I offered my apologies to Beaton, sending him a bouquet of twenty-four red roses. He replied with a letter to my wife and me that read, 'I love you both.'"[51]

Nilsson had less colorful memories of the period leading up to the actual premiere performance, for she suffered from a severe cold that forced her to skip most of the rehearsals.[52] When she attended, she was forced to sing sotto voce, which apparently lulled Corelli to sleep even though he knew from experience what she was capable of. Things changed from the dress rehearsal on, though. The freshly recruited Merle Hubbard, who was active in the Met's rehearsal department, saw Nilsson in her royal position forty feet upstage suddenly open her mouth: "Out came this incredible laser beam of sound. Corelli got a look of terror on his face, turned around to make sure he had heard what he thought he had, and then opened his throat to make those stentorian sounds that only he could make in order to match Nilsson when she went up high."[53]

❖❖❖❖❖

The premiere was one of the most memorable in the history of the Met. Ultimately, Stokowski garnered kudos just for showing up. The barely-seventy-eight-years-young conductor had recently suffered an injury while roughhousing with his young child in the family's New York apartment. On the night of the premiere, his slow progress toward the conductor's stand created a roar of approval before a single note sounded. Ovations were the order of the evening, and the musical grandeur was matched by Beaton's splendid, colorful sets and costumes. The tragedy of stage director Yoshio Aoyama's death from a heart attack during the preparations (Nathaniel Merrill had stepped in on short notice and finished the production according to Aoyama's concept) further helped to create one of those magical moments for which opera will always be remembered.[54] Even Harold C. Schonberg was so swept away by the production that he more or less forgave Stokowski for "improving" Puccini's score by reducing the full orchestral accompaniment in a part of "In questa reggia" to the timpani alone. Corelli took Schonberg by surprise as well, for there had been little in his earlier Manrico to suggested the kind of resplendent singing he demonstrated as Calaf. Nilsson was nothing short of a revelation; the soprano Mary Curtis-Verna, in the audience that night, thought she heard a Boeing 747 take off as Nilsson launched her big notes. Said Curtis-Verna: "Then came Corelli's answer; what are those things they launch at Cape Canaveral?"[55]

◆◆◆◆◆

Triumph and defeat in opera singing are separated from each other by a thin fold. Today's victory can be tomorrow's defeat. On the evening of March 30, Corelli had to give up after the first act of *Turandot*, felled by laryngitis. Giulio Gari finished the performance, while Bing sent Franco a letter wishing him a swift recovery and informing him that he wouldn't apply the usual pro rata payment terms, which entitled Franco to only a third of his fee. Considering his efforts, his protégé could count on full payment. That sort of considerate gesture was precisely what his prize tenor needed to get back in shape.

March 16, 1961: JFK

When the United States held an official commemoration of the unification of Italy in the Library of Congress, Renata Tebaldi and Franco Corelli were selected to represent their homeland in song. The event was attended not only by the president and first lady, but also by the Italian ambassador, Manlio Brosio.[56] The program was short, with the focus on singing for and meeting the president. Loretta freely commented on the occasion afterward. Appearing with Franco next to John and Jackie Kennedy filled her with pride in a typically feminine way: "I returned from Washington in the best of spirits because the blue-and-white hat I had bought in Ancona outdid the one that Jacqueline Kennedy was wearing."[57]

Franco and Renata received as commemorative gifts the president's portrait with a dedication attached to it. Then Kennedy introduced Franco to his wife:

> March 16, 1961
> Concert on behalf of the Centennial of the Unity of Italy
> Washington, D.C., Library of Congress (NBC telecast)
> Verdi: *I Lombardi* "La mia letizia infondere" (Corelli); *La Forza del Destino* "Pace, pace, mio Dio!" (Tebaldi). Giordano: *Andrea Chénier* "Vicino a te s'acqueta" (Corelli and Tebaldi)
> Renata Tebaldi, Franco Corelli

"Here is a fan of yours! Why don't you tell him, honey? You're the one who speaks Italian." The first lady rewarded those assembled with her famous smile and then uttered a most Italianate "Yes," to the amusement of all.[58] Franco's reply was courtly: he wondered whether the Grand Canyon, which he hoped to visit during his upcoming Metropolitan Opera tour, could show him anything that matched Mrs. Kennedy's charm.[59]

◆◆◆◆◆

Corelli had just one little obligation left: his imminent Met debut in Verdi's *Don Carlo*. In a fatherly tone, Bing expressed his worries over both the tenor's lack of interest in the production (Corelli claimed he didn't have time to attend more than two acts of the running production) and his disastrous stage rehearsals.[60] The reception of *Don Carlo* was a draw: the critics were critical, the audience ecstatic. Eric Salzman's esteemed review of Corelli's Don Carlo tells it all. In his opinion, the tenor's performance might have been more genuinely impressive if his efforts had not been so exclusively directed at flinging notes out to the gallery: "Six feet worth of heroic shouting was all very fine but the art of musical and dramatic characterization demands just a wee bit more in the way of phrasing and right notes."[61]

The paradox of such reviews is that Corelli's fans ultimately learned to read them in reverse, for they merely confirmed what the fans craved most from their favorite. Even Bing, who always had an eye to the Met's bank balance, couldn't suppress a smile over the repeated accusations of singing to the gallery. Critics didn't necessarily sell tickets, and Corelli had meanwhile confirmed his European reputation as "Mr. Esaurito [Sold Out]."

April 19–May 30, 1961: The Metropolitan Spring Tour

Tra-La! It's Opera Week.
  Cleveland Press-News, April 24, 1961

The Metropolitan Spring Tour! Few European singers had ever heard of it, and once they experienced the tour, they usually did everything in their power to avoid it in the future. Enduring the most difficult performance and living conditions, traveling in uncomfortable trains with decided sanitary limitations

Franco and Loretta on the verge of conquering America (Met Spring Tour, 1961). (Photo: Louis Melançon. Courtesy of the Metropolitan Opera Archives)

(unless one agreed to fly on local airlines in vintage cramped planes), all in order to perform in what Europeans clearly considered the provinces. In comparison, no amount of money in the early 1960s could have lured a Birgit Nilsson, a Leonie Rysanek, or a Giuseppe Di Stefano to perform in, say, Pesaro, unless they had a personal tie with that particular town (as was the case with Corelli). Year in and year out, Bing had to cajole, plead, negotiate, and blackmail his premier artists into accepting the tour assignments. He sometimes simply threatened not to renew their Met general contract if they didn't accept.

Bing had no choice in the matter. He had inherited the tour as a full-blown, highly regarded American institution. Expensive and scarcely profitable, the tour nevertheless added greatly to the Met's prestige as a national institution. It helped to create new opera fans in the hinterlands and made a substantial cultural contribution to the country. The last function included sponsor parties at each stop where local denizens and donors looked forward to mingling with the Met stars and top brass. Attendance was nearly obligatory and often was viewed as the height of the social season of the tour cities. These gatherings also typically were fundraisers. Benefactors expected value for money, in terms of both performances and star power. Sending Corelli's and Nilsson's understudies to Memphis was possible only if there were at least two other operas sporting a first-rate cast. Naturally, this was not the official view that Bing gave to the press and to America. Outside his office he played the often rewarding part of the general manager who gave the country's most glittering provincial audiences precisely what they craved: glamorous opera in the grand old style. An echo of this can be seen in the fact that papers from Boston and Cleveland to St. Louis and Atlanta regularly devoted more space to the prominent guests than to the singers and the operas. The press hardly made an effort to hide it either, outdoing each other in articles with titles such as "Party, Supper Dance Top Off Met Opera Opening"[62] or "Met Audience Nearly Equals *Turandot*'s Glittering Splendor."[63] Not that the stars had anything to complain about, because when they were discussed, it would be in tones of unstinted enthusiasm. In city after city, the arrival of the stars created a genuine Met fever.

April 19, 1961: Let's Get Physical

He kept his notes very, very long, and you know, I tried to keep them also very long. It was like a bullfight onstage.
  Birgit Nilsson, interview, April 10, 2005

Eh . . . I would have liked to bite her!
  A smiling Franco Corelli, "Opera Fanatic" broadcast, February 3, 1990

Bing's first problem with his tour roster of eight orchestral conductors, five assistant conductors, twenty sopranos, five mezzos, seventeen tenors, nine baritones, eight basses, a corps de ballet of thirty-eight, a chorus of eighty, and an orchestra of ninety-two members was to get the Corellis from point A to point B, for they refused to fly with the company. With Franco speaking no English whatsoever and Loretta just a little, Bing foresaw catastrophic complications when trains had to be switched in the middle of nowhere. So he entrusted Merle Hubbard with the task of accompanying the couple. Said the freshly appointed "tour manager": "Guide, nursemaid, keeper, I could call it what I wanted as long as I didn't leave them out of my sight. So we set off for Boston. . . . Franco, Loretta, their poodle, Loris, a great deal of luggage, and no small amount of Italian foodstuffs at the ready at all times."[64]

On April 17 they arrived in Boston, where Franco was to open the Met's seventy-third Spring Tour singing Calaf to Nilsson's Turandot. Their rivalry, both real and carefully promoted, was firmly established by now, although each was convinced that the other had the upper hand. Nilsson, who felt particularly strong that night, regarded Boston as a new game, providing her with new chances to beat out her rival. Things went as usual until the point where Corelli

> **April 19, 1961**
> **Giacomo Puccini:** *Turandot*
> **Boston, John B. Hynes Civic Auditorium (Met Spring Tour)**
> Birgit Nilsson (*Turandot*), Franco Corelli *(Calaf)*, Lucine Amara (*Liù*), Alessio De Paolis (*Emperor Altoum*), Bonaldo Giaiotti (*Timur*), Frank Guarrera (*Ping*), Robert Nagy (*Pang*), Charles Anthony (*Pong*), cond. Leopold Stokowski

moved to the front of the stage, as was his habit before the "No, no, principessa altera" section at the end of the second act, where he used to relish taking his optional high C on "ardente." As he began moving downstage, Nilsson started her final notes, asking Calaf if he really wanted her as cold as ice, and there it happened. Recalled Nilsson: "He had been kicking me so long with his long notes, and I finally saw a chance to settle the score and give it to him!"[65] Said Corelli: "She sang the 'Rillutante fremente' and this 'freme-e-e-e-e-e-e-e-e-e-e-e-e-' went on and on and on to the point where my 'No, no principessa altera' became a duet. I finished my few lines and left."[66]

With Calaf gone prematurely, Nilsson finished the last minutes all by herself, although neither Stokowski,[67] the audience, nor the critics noticed the change. Only a single critic noticed that Corelli didn't take his curtain call. Corelli couldn't care less. He stomped into his dressing room, where he exploded with anger. He started pacing around like a caged tiger, screaming and hammering the walls with his fists: "I really lost it then and placed a tremendous punch to the table, that fortunately was not all that robust. It gave way to my hand as it crashed into the table. Blood sprang from my hand, splattering all around. Loris panicked and started barking, Loretta was crying and screaming." At that point Bing entered, having been alerted by the backstage crew, and was horrified to see a bleeding and shouting Corelli and a hysterical Loretta screaming for an ambulance and shrieking that Nilsson had ruined her husband's career. All through the scene the dog barked tirelessly.[68] Even Bing lost his head and started screaming that it was a catastrophe, the performance would have to be canceled.[69]

The intermission stretched from twenty-five to a full forty minutes. Finally Corelli calmed down enough to listen to Bing's pleas. The general manager, always at his best in a crisis, then came up with one of his most inventive solutions ever. He turned to Corelli and said: "Listen, Franco. I know how you can settle the score. You know that spot in the third act where you have to kiss her. . . . Suppose you would bite her instead."[70] Immediately a boyish gleam came into Franco's eyes. Beaming a broad smile, he rushed off to the stage while Bing, claiming that he had to get back to New York, retreated from the theater for fear of what would happen at the bite. Fortunately for Nilsson, that spot was toward the end of the opera, and by the time it arrived,[71] the very idea of biting her had restored her Calaf's good humor. When Turandot ultimately surrendered, he treated her to a more subtle surprise:

CALAF

È l'alba! E amore nasce col sole!   Dawn is here! Love is born from the sun!

CHILDREN

Tutto è santo! Che dolcezza nel tuo pianto!   All is holy! You cry for tenderness!

TURANDOT

Che nessun mi veda, la mia gloria è finita!   Let no one see me, my glory is finished!

At that point Calaf had to sing, "No! Essa incomincia!" (No, your glory just began!), but instead he sang, "Sì! È finita!" (Yes, it is over!).[72]

Nilsson was thunderstruck. Afterward she ran into Merrill and told him of the extraordinary change to Giuseppe Adami and Renato Simioni's text. Merrill then explained to her the turmoil she had created with her triumph over Franco at the finale of the second act.[73] Nilsson could appreciate a joke, even if it was on her. Later she sent a legendary telegram to Rudolf Bing: "Muss die kommende Vorstellungen absagen stop schwere Bissverletzung stop Birgit" (Have to cancel all coming performances stop severe bite wounds stop Birgit).[74]

Bing, in whom Birgit Nilsson had found a lively verbal sparring partner since her arrival at the Met, immediately saw the public-relations value of the telegram and leaked to the press that Nilsson had written that she had contracted rabies. From there the story became world famous. For Corelli and Nilsson, the notoriety of the story in the press became the basis of their professional friendship.[75] However, Nilsson, who held the singer Corelli in high esteem, never learned to appreciate Corelli's sense of humor: "Hojotoho—nonono, not very much!"[76]

> April 26, 1961
>
> Giacomo Puccini: *Turandot*
>
> Cleveland, Public Auditorium (Met Spring Tour)
>
> Birgit Nilsson (*Turandot*), Franco Corelli *(Calaf)*, Lucine Amara (*Liù*), Alessio De Paolis (*Emperor Altoum*), Bonaldo Giaiotti (*Timur*), Frank Guarrera (*Ping*), Robert Nagy (*Pang*), Charles Anthony (*Pong*), cond. Leopold Stokowski

April 26, 1961: No Love Letters from Cleveland

Cleveland greeted the arrival of the Met's matinee idol with great enthusiasm. The media acquainted the public with the tenor's love life, and Loretta gleefully chimed in, claiming that he received love letters from young Italian and French girls, but none from American teenagers, who apparently respected his marital status and restricted themselves to humbly applying for signed photographs. Wasn't she afraid that a rival might appear and take her husband away from her? Said Loretta: "Franco won't leave me. Where else will he find a wife who works like me? He needs me and he loves me. He has no interest in looking further." At that point, the anonymous journalist noted that not even a housemaid would ever get the chance to look at Mrs. Corelli's husband from close up. Despite their position in one of the top income-tax brackets, they had no maid, no laundrywoman, no seamstress, not even a general go-between. All that was taken care of personally by Loretta. Dinners out were equally rare: they usually locked themselves in their hotel room, where they would cook and dine in private.[77] Their dinner conversations were not always a candlelight affair, adds Merle Hubbard; at times the walls of their hotel room looked as if they had been playing games with the spaghetti.[78]

May 1, 1961: Cold in Atlanta

Fair as Apollo and cross as a wet hen, Franco Corelli came South after New York's heinous winter and, standing in the terminal station, shivered.... Friday night was chill and damp and the grand young man scowled in disapproval.
    Frank Daniel, "Met Idol Corelli Shivers Here," *Atlanta Journal,*
    April 28–29, 1961

> May 1, 1961
> Giacomo Puccini: *Turandot*
> Atlanta, Civic Auditorium (Met Spring Tour)
> Birgit Nilsson (*Turandot*), Franco Corelli *(Calaf)*, Lucine Amara (*Liù*), Alessio De Paolis (*Emperor Altoum*), Bonaldo Giaiotti (*Timur*), Frank Guarrera (*Ping*), Robert Nagy (*Pang*), Charles Anthony (*Pong*), cond. Leopold Stokowski

After the cold New York winter, Corelli looked forward to sunny Atlanta. He was terribly disappointed when local reporters greeted him, his wife, his poodle, and a mountain of luggage on an unexpectedly chilly train platform. Corelli's very first words to the welcoming committee were that he couldn't possibly sing under such conditions. He had felt cold ever since he left Italy, and he'd had his fill. The press just laughed his complaints off, saying that anybody familiar with opera tenors knew that he wouldn't miss an appearance even if Atlanta developed glaciers before Monday night. And they were right: Franco's temper was soon swept away under a blanket of love and then,[79] on May 1, the sun returned to Atlanta, and he warmed up to the city.

Atlanta was in for another kind of Corelli premiere that was perhaps not as important as his opera performance there, but certainly more tasty, for Loretta gave one of her soon-to-be-famous Italian recipes to the *Atlanta Constitution*, which presented it as a major feature story on the opera star's diet with a headline that claimed, "Corelli Doesn't Sacrifice Food for Song—Still Eats High-Caloried Italian Dishes." Corelli maintained that pasta asciutta and risotto Milanese filled up the hole in his stomach. Then Loretta proudly presented the reporter, Patricia Deaton, with a creation of her own that substituted for the usual antipasto: tiny segments of orange and lemon, soaked in a little olive oil for about an hour. Just before serving, ripe black Italian olives were added. Deaton tried it and judged the resulting flavor "somewhat piquant, subtle and hard to define." Reading that careful description, one might prefer to go straight for the main course:

Loretta's Rice Salad

4 cups rice, cooked

2 large ripe tomatoes

2 tablespoons capers

1 lemon

1 teaspoon fresh basil (1½ teaspoons dried)

2 (6-oz.) cans tuna, undrained

Freshly ground black pepper

Flake the tuna, combine it with the cooked rice, stir in the oil from the fish, and then cut the tomatoes into bite-sized pieces and add them. Sprinkle the mixture with the capers, basil, and pepper. After that, squeeze the lemon over it all and toss the magic potion just enough to combine ingredients and flavors.

Loretta had some dinner tips for singers as well: "When Franco has a performance, he has lunch at 2:00 in the afternoon. This avoids any cramping or uneasy situations during the performance."[80]

May 9–10, 1961: Wet Feet in St. Louis

A lot of water had to flow under the bridge before Aida and Radamès could die in peace under the roof of St. Louis's Kiel Auditorium. The highway from Birmingham to St. Louis was struck by the worst flooding in memory, and the only train allowed to pass through was the "special" Met train. Said Merle Hubbard: "We sailed along and at one point I looked out from an open platform door only to notice that the tracks and the lower part of the wheels were underwater."[81]

When the eighteen cars carrying the personnel and sets finally arrived in St. Louis, it was 6:15 P.M. With *Aida* scheduled at 8:00, the chorus ran to the theater in an attempt to make the curtain time. Said Hubbard: "*Aida* requires full

---

May 10, 1961

Giuseppe Verdi: *Aida*

St. Louis, Kiel Auditorium (Met Spring Tour)

Birgit Nilsson (*Aida*), Franco Corelli (*Radamès*), Irene Dalis (*Amneris*), Ezio Flagello (*the King of Egypt*), Bonaldo Giaiotti (*Ramfis*), Robert Merrill (*Amonasro*), cond. Nino Verchi

body makeup for all concerned, but they came on stage in two tones. Gradually more and more Egypt-colored participants could be seen, all of course to the horror of the management."[82]

Corelli and his Aida, Birgit Nilsson, had arrived in St. Louis earlier, so there was no makeup problem for them. But Corelli had a different surprise in store for management and audience alike. No one in U.S. theaters had yet seen his European Radamès costume, the one he had brought from Italy. Its most essential part was a short-skirted suit of silver armor that showed off his legs to their best advantage. With it he wore massive silver bracelets, bicep rings, and a pageboy-length blue-black wig. His silver sandals made him look even taller and more beautiful than before.[83]

His Aida paid little attention to this stunning sight. Backstage between scenes she stammered in broken English to Hubbard: "Look, look, he 'as a spung attached to his bracelet!" Hubbard didn't quite get it but was happy to see she was having a good time. Nilsson then repeated her comment, adding that the "spung" was "for to make wet his mouth." Wet sponges! Corelli had several of them on each bracelet so he could wet his throat when needed.

This obsession with treating a dry throat soon led to a playful game between Franco and Birgit in which she would move the sponges, which he had placed strategically around the stage, so that he couldn't find them. Corelli eventually found a place where even Nilsson couldn't get to them. Said Nilsson: "Once he put his hand under his pants, where he started to fool around. I stared at what he was doing and then, just before his high C was due, he suddenly took it out with a sponge in it. He sucked it dry, threw it to a chorus lady, and then he hit that high C like no one else. I almost fell flat for laughing."[84]

✦✦✦✦✦

The local press had their own adventure with the Corellis when Alvin H. Goldstein interviewed them for the *St. Louis Post-Dispatch*. Goldstein spoke no Italian whatsoever and had to rely on Corelli's press manager, a certain "Count Rasponi." The count served as an intermediary between Goldstein and the Corellis, who seemed to quarrel over the answers in heated Italian. With the preliminaries and the career retrospective out of the way, Rasponi translated some questions to the couple about interesting adventures in their artistic life. The Corellis started in on long Italian phrases accompanied by wild gesticulations, and Goldstein feared things would get out of hand. Only Count Rasponi's bored look during these arguments reassured him that everything was normal; when the couple paused to take a breath, Rasponi would tell Goldstein: "They say no. Nothing unusual." To make up for the difference in length between what they had been talking about and the brevity of his translation, he would occasionally add: "I am only telling you the answer, not what they are arguing about."[85]

May 12–13, 1961: Singing for the Dog in Chicago

If the St. Louis adventure was a lot to handle for a tour manager, Chicago surpassed all that Hubbard had ever encountered in his life. The city's brand-new McCormick Exposition Center opened with an *Aida* featuring Leonie Rysanek and Eugenio Fernandi in Corelli's stead. First, Rysanek ended up at odds with Fernandi. Then the corps de ballet, dressed in little to nothing, found themselves freezing in the wings—the heating and air conditioning system had not yet been tested. All ended in total disaster when, between set changes, the theater filled with carbon monoxide from the bevy of trucks parked underground that carried the stage scenery. After dealing with the various physical emergencies, Hubbard sent a crying and thoroughly upset Rysanek off to her hotel. He finally dozed off while watching television in his room at the Pick Congress on Michigan Avenue. In the middle of the night, with the light on and the television blaring, the phone rang. It was Rudolf Bing, exhorting him to get over to Corelli's hotel, where something had happened to his dog. Hubbard, in a state of shock from the unexpected wake-up call but otherwise still fully dressed, pulled himself together and went downstairs, where he met Charlie Riecker, Bing's assistant. Riecker invited Hubbard to join him in the

---

May 13, 1961

Giacomo Puccini: *Turandot*

Chicago, McCormick Exposition Center (Met Spring Tour)

Birgit Nilsson (*Turandot*), Franco Corelli (*Calaf*), Lucine Amara (*Liù*), Alessio De Paolis (*Emperor Altoum*), Bonaldo Giaiotti (*Timur*), Frank Guarrera (*Ping*), Robert Nagy (*Pang*), Charles Anthony (*Pong*), cond. Kurt Herbert Adler

bar, and the confused and groggy Hubbard accepted. Revived by the drink, Hubbard suddenly remembered why he was awake—the dog! Immediately he raced down Michigan Avenue to the Blackstone Hotel, where the Corellis were encamped—literally. Said Hubbard: "I got to their floor and found Loretta hysterically crying on a love seat by the elevator. When I went into their suite, I found all of the furniture turned over and arranged in such a way that Loris could not get under anything and hide. Franco was on his hands and knees, trying to console the dog, weeping and out of control." It was 2:00 A.M. Hubbard's first thought was for the fast-approaching performance: Franco had to sing *Turandot* in just sixteen hours.[86]

At 3.00 A.M. the hotel manager miraculously found a veterinarian prepared to come over. Either the good fellow was an ardent opera lover or he was bribed by Hubbard, who confessed he would have given the man anything at that moment. While waiting for the vet with the crying Corellis, Hubbard decided that now it was his turn to wake up Bing. He called him at 3:45 A.M., for no particular reason except that he thought that Bing's voice might calm Franco down. Instead of being irritated, Bing once more showed his exceptional weakness for Franco. He was very glad that Merle had called and instantly managed to calm Franco down. Then the vet arrived. He turned first not to Loris, but to Loretta, and gave her a sedative. He then examined the dog, who was now having convulsions. Miraculously, the veterinarian managed to stop the seizures, and poor little Loris fell asleep immediately.[87]

Hubbard then returned to his hotel and a very short time later woke up to a happier day until his immediate supervisor informed him that the little dog had hemorrhaged around 5.30 A.M. and the Corellis had taken him to the local veterinary hospital. That morning Victoria de los Angeles canceled her matinee performance, leaving her cover, Laurel Hurley, to face a sold-out audience that included Claudia Cassidy, the famous Chicago hatchet woman, whose sole focus seemed to be to write devastating reviews of Met performances. Fortunately, that wasn't Hubbard's responsibility anymore, because his supervisor had just sent him off to get some much-needed sleep.

Just after he dozed off, the phone rang again. It was Bing. Corelli had canceled his evening performance. Said Bing: "Go to his hotel and get him to the theater by whatever means required." A few minutes later a pale and exhausted Corelli faced Hubbard, his newest friend, and stammered, "Non posso cantare" (I can't sing). Hubbard then promised him the first thing that came to mind and finished with a dramatic crescendo, saying, "I will never leave your side."

Corelli eventually went to the theater, where dressers and makeup designers had their materials ready for him. Bing had ordered the only piano around, the one in Nilsson's dressing room, to be moved to Franco's so someone could play his opening lines in order to get the tenor tuned. Nilsson wasn't pleased, although over the phone Bing asked her to be extra gentle with Franco because of the dog. The soprano, never at loss for a tart remark, at once proved her unfailing wit: "Mr. Bing, I would rather be a dog in your house than a singer."[88]

When the piano was rolled into Corelli's dressing room, the door was purposely left ajar so that the tenor could see his cover, Giulio Gari, strolling up and down, waiting for his chance—a trick often employed in such situations; but even this ruse failed. Corelli remained inconsolable, and when the opera began. Hubbard took Franco's arm and led him toward the stage. Franco protested, insisting that he couldn't sing. Hubbard took his hand, looked him in the eye, and said without a shred of guilt: "Franco, canto per il cane!" (Sing for the dog!). Tears welled up in Franco's eyes, and he said, "Provo!" (I'll try!).[89]

The press understandably noticed some unevenness in Franco's overall performance that night. The *Chicago American* still characterized Corelli's stage presence as part peacock, part panther, and always imperious: "He has a genuinely heroic tenor, not perfectly produced or controlled at every moment, but extraordinarily exciting. Perfection is dull if predictable: Mr. Corelli, by never seeming quite a predictable singer, is never for a moment dull."[90]

May 21–22, 1961: Calling the Dog from Detroit

For his Detroit performances, Franco had to be sent ahead. Because a change of trains was involved, Bing sent Hubbard to accompany the Met's precious gem and his wife. When the trio finally arrived in Detroit, Franco refused to leave the train station until he had spoken to Loris, who was still confined to the animal hospital back in Chicago. Hubbard managed to find a phone in the train station and called the hospital. When the vet came on the line, Hubbard told him: "Franco would like to speak to his dog. Can you please put him on the line?"[91]

A whimper from Loris somehow satisfied Franco, and all was well again, especially once Franco managed to obtain a discount on a shiny white Cadillac. It

> **May 22, 1961**
> **Giacomo Puccini:** *Turandot*
> **Detroit, Masonic Temple Auditorium (Met Spring Tour)**
> Birgit Nilsson (*Turandot*), Franco Corelli (*Calaf*), Lucine Amara (*Liù*), Alessio De Paolis (*Emperor Altoum*), Bonaldo Giaiotti (*Timur*), Frank Guarrera (*Ping*), Robert Nagy (*Pang*), Charles Anthony (*Pong*), cond. Kurt Herbert Adler
>
> **May 26, 1961**
> **Giuseppe Verdi:** *Aida*
> **Detroit, Masonic Temple Auditorium (Met Spring Tour)**
> Birgit Nilsson (*Aida*), Franco Corelli (*Radamès*), Mignon Dunn (*Amneris*), Ezio Flagello (*the King of Egypt*), Norman Scott (*Ramfis*), Frank Guarrera (*Amonasro*), cond. Nino Verchi

seemed a perfect compromise between the Ford Thunderbird Loretta wanted and the Lincoln Continental he had previously preferred. Said Corelli to Lenore Romney, the wife of American Motors' president, George Romney: "Next year I will buy a Rambler as well . . . possibly a Chrysler too!"[92]

❖❖❖❖❖

While Franco was learning the difference between Chryslers, Ramblers, and Fords, Bing seized the opportunity to make a historic splash himself. He announced to the Detroit audience (which put the one at La Scala's *Poliuto* premiere to shame with an even more ostentatious display of jewelry and expensive fashions) that the seventy-third Met tour would be the last one performed before segregated audiences. Just a few days earlier he had received a telegram from Martin Luther King, Jr., protesting the segregation in certain opera houses on the Met tour. Bing's initial response was merely diplomatic. But mindful of Price's successful debut and her scheduled tour performances over the next season, he decided it was time to do things right. He organized a press conference in Detroit and declared that all Met performances would have equal entrance and ticket facilities for all, or there would be no more glittering opening nights.[93]

Having solved that little problem, Bing had but one last request from Franco to deal with: could his new friend Merle drive the Corellis back to New York in their brand-new, snow-white Cadillac? Said Hubbard: "Was I lucky that he asked it after the performance! With no show at risk, Bing replied: 'Sorry, I am afraid I need Merle here.'"[94] A passionate driver, Corelli somehow managed to do it himself, for he made it to his last spring appearance as Calaf in Toronto on time before boarding a ship for Italy and his summer festival performances in Venice as Andrea Chénier.

June–July 1961: The First EMI Recital Recordings

The Corellis received Bing in Milan when he dropped in during his off-season holidays. A little later Franco received his Met schedule for the 1962–63 season, which seemed to revolve around the return of *Adriana Lecouvreur*. Adriana

> June–July 1961
> London, Kingsway Hall (EMI recording)
> *Operatic Arias by Franco Corelli*
> Giordano: *Andrea Chénier* "Colpito qui m'avete... Un dì all'azzurro spazio." Donizetti: *La Favorita* "Favorita del re!... Spirto gentil." Puccini: *Tosca* "Recondita armonia." Bellini: *I Puritani* "A te, o cara." Puccini: *Manon Lescaut* "Donna non vidi mai." Cilea: *Adriana Lecouvreur* "L'anima ho stanca." Puccini: *Turandot* "Nessun dorma." Meyerbeer: *Gli Ugonotti* "Non lungi dalle torre... Bianca al par." Giordano: *Andrea Chénier* "Come un bel dì di maggio." Puccini: *Tosca* "E lucevan le stelle." Ponchielli: *La Gioconda* "Cielo e mar."
> Philharmonia Orchestra, cond. Franco Ferraris

> July 1961
> London, Abbey Road, Studio 1 (EMI recording)
> *Franco Corelli Sings Neapolitan Songs*
> Cardillo: "Core 'ngrato." De Curtis: "Senza nisciuno." Tortorella: "Addà turnà." D'Annibale: "O paese d' 'o sole." Pennino: "Pecchè?" Traditional: "Fenesta che lucive." Ernesto Tagliaferri: "Piscatore 'e Pusilleco." De Curtis: "Tu, ca' nun chiagne!" Di Capua: "I' te vurria vasà"; "Torna a Surriento."
> Philharmonia Orchestra, cond. Franco Ferraris

was an opera Renata Tebaldi had blackmailed out of Bing with the threat of not returning to the Met if Bing refused to schedule it.[95] With additional *Turandot*s and *Aida*s and a new production of *La Gioconda* in his pocket,[96] Franco lobbied for two distinguished colleagues. He mentioned that Bastianini was ready to rejoin the Met ranks,[97] and Franco also offered his help in talking Callas into doing an opening night as Carmen to his Don José.[98]

With that intriguing parting gift, the Corellis sailed to London, where Franco was due to record in late June and early July. Scheduled for his first two EMI solo albums were operatic arias in Kingsway Hall and a Neapolitan song recital in Studio 1, Abbey Road.

The aria recital mixed his established roles with those he was currently studying (*Gli Ugonotti* and *I Puritani*) and ones he was considering, such as *Manon Lescaut* and *La Favorita*. With that repertoire, one hardly misses arias from *Tell* or Meyerbeer's *Le Prophète*, which Corelli also was investigating.[99] Among the recorded items, the *Ugonotti* aria is a gem that would have been a thrilling preview of his scheduled La Scala revival of the part of Raul de Nangis had it been released before that premiere instead of after.

The second album, *Franco Corelli Sings Neapolitan Songs*, is less universally acclaimed, although it was an instant smash hit. If there were doubts, they definitely were not about his vocal endowment. Stylistically there will always be something one can hold against non-Neapolitans in this repertoire. Corelli's voice in these songs is commanding, passionate, and emotionally charged, but lacking in the authoritative style and subtle modulations of, say, Tito Schipa.[100]

August 1961: Slow Hand

He often clashed with directors or conductors, especially when they conducted too slowly. Most of all if they were foreign—perhaps they had more difficulties "feeling" the story and the Italian temperament in that particular moment.

Marco Corelli, interview, Ancona, January 17, 2005

Sixty-eight-year-old Fabien Sevitzky came to Verona from Indianapolis, where he was a respected symphony conductor. In a small way as a visiting conductor, he had something in common with Leopold Stokowski, although arriving

> **July 25, 27, and 30; August 2, 5, 9, 12, and 15, 1961**
> **Georges Bizet:** *Carmen*
> **Verona, Arena di Verona**
> Giulietta Simionato (*Carmen*), Franco Corelli (*Don José*), Ettore Bastianini (*Escamillo*), Virgilio Carbonari (*Il Dancaïro*), Renata Scotto (*Micaëla*), Piero De Palma (*Il Remendado*), Alessandro Maddalena (*Zuniga*), Guglielmo Ferrara (*Moralès*), Adalina Grigolato (*Frasquita*), Aurora Cattelani (*Mercédès*), cond. Fabien Sevitzky (rehearsals only) and Francesco Molinari-Pradelli

in New York as a world-famous conductor was very different from arriving in Verona as the toast of Indianapolis. On the afternoon of August 25, the Don José stopped the *Carmen* rehearsals, claiming that the tempo was too slow for him to sing. Sevitzky argued that his tempo for the Flower Aria was "what Bizet had in mind," which prompted Franco to respond that he couldn't sing it that way: "Either you play a comfortable tempo or you find yourself another tenor." With that, he walked off the stage. Several other artists took Corelli's side and joined him in his complaint. Sevitzky maintained that he conducted what Bizet had written and if the singers couldn't deliver that, he wouldn't conduct them, and so he took his leave.[101]

Pride is often a poor counselor. Franco later apologized, admitting that the incident had escalated out of control because of his own ego.[102] In the end, right and wrong are determined by the winners. When 15,000 spectators cheered on Corelli and company,[103] it was clear that Sevitzky's hope of returning to Verona under "better conditions" was

Doing his own stage makeup before the Veronese *Carmen*s, July and August 1961. In the background on the right can be seen the head of one of his numerous stuffed toys—his good-luck charms. (Photo: Epoca. Courtesy of the Mondadori Group)

wishful thinking. If today his name is remembered outside Indianapolis or the United States, it is mainly because Corelli forced his early departure from the Italian summer opera festival.

As turbulently as things had started with Sevitzky's departure, so did they end when a terrible thunderstorm unleashed itself over Verona during the fourth act of the very last *Carmen* performance. *Opera* and the Flemish magazine *Het Rijk van de Vrouw* (Women's Empire) reported on the proceedings when gale-force winds dislodged much of the gigantic scenery during the final duet, causing near-panic in the large audience. Alarmed by both the crashing noise and the reaction of the public, Corelli and Simionato looked behind them. When they saw the scenery crashing down on them, with fire already visible in the back of the stage, they ran for their lives and barely escaped. A member of the chorus was injured, and an elderly Swiss visitor died on the way to the hospital after being overcome in the crush of people.[104]

❖❖❖❖❖

When it came to adjusting to a situation, Bing could have taught Sevitzky a lesson or two when it came to Corelli. Despite artistic success, the Met in the 1960s was not in optimum form, especially financially, and it faced crippling strikes from its labor unions. In such situations, Bing counted on his friends. It was a card he never hesitated to play: "We are of course planning for the 1962–63 season, and I sincerely hope that you can make yourself available—it is now that I need the help and support of those friends on whom I have to rely most heavily. With kind regards, also to your wife, yours sincerely, Rudolf Bing."[105] What friend could possibly refuse such a request?

August 1961: An Athlete Punished

Dear Franco, don't be a fool. Don't ruin your voice by singing high Cs for hours in a row.—A friend who loves you.
Don't be afraid, you're great!
  "Reminder notes" on the walls of Corelli's Milanese home, quoted in Aldo Falivena, "Corelli è un atleto in castigo," *Epoca*, August 27, 1961

An interesting aspect of Corelli's life is the contrast between his unpredictable backstage behavior and his private life. It is clear from reading contemporary articles that the jet-set press thrived on both the stage and the personal scandals surrounding Callas, Di Stefano, or Del Monaco. Yet although Franco's stage antics were covered, it seems as if there simply weren't any scandals to find in the private life of the Corellis. *Epoca*'s Aldo Falivena attributed this to his modest household, which lacked the usual entourage of doctors, secretaries, and colorful weirdos that opera singers somehow seem to gather around them; no clerks, no gossip. His seemingly ascetic lifestyle consisted of a programmed diet served on a schedule between performance preparations, further enhancing a stable image.

An athlete punished. . . . Some days even the scent of a fresh rainfall couldn't bring a smile to the outdoors-loving Franco's face. (Photo: Epoca. Courtesy of the Mondadori Group)

Candid press photos of the tenor further reinforced that image; his favorite color for suits was a somber grey. Understandably, he was nostalgic for his own glory days in Ancona, when he would dream of equaling Johnny Weismuller at the Olympics and onscreen. Falivena explains the singer's dilemma: "Since he started singing, it is as if he is being punished. He has an athletic build, but can't practice sports as much as he would like; he loves the outdoor life, but is forced to stay at home all day to study scores."[106]

Pale, locked in his house, if not always to study, then for fear of catching a cold, writing himself such reminders as those at the beginning of this section—one could actually pity the most sought after tenor of the 1960s. But what else would he like to do? What does he value in life? Said Corelli: "The scent of wet fields after rainfall." Falivena adds that Corelli considered finding

Loretta to be his luckiest break. The interviewer describes her as speaking with the direct honesty of a simple, loving heart and at the same time with the logic of an intelligent and experienced woman: "Corelli, if given the chance, would probably give her a curtain call." When Corelli embraces her, Falivena describes them as resembling two happily married doves. Said Corelli: "She is my 'treasure,' you see?"

Once more, Loretta is portrayed as the one who takes care of everything in his life, from seeing to it that he is not disturbed to answering the letters from his female fans, "without blinking or blushing over the content." Falivena even names her as the one who sews on his buttons and combs his wig before he goes onstage! In individual interviews, such descriptions have some charm, but the repeated mentions of Loretta's total control over Franco's life, from interview to interview, also start to become a little painful to read—who would enjoy such a life? At this point in his career, she even started answering questions that he should have answered himself, such as the one Falivena asks about the confusion over Franco's age. Said Loretta: "My husband is young, very young, but the career of a tenor is difficult and long and it is better if people don't know his real age. At times the public can be cruel and why should one encourage them to say: 'Oh, that tenor is so and so old, etc.' I am sure you agree that all that matters is whether he is singing well."[107]

Once the photographer arrived, Loretta proved her value yet again: "Please, take him from the right. My husband's profile is more beautiful from that side." With that, Corelli suddenly takes an interest and responds—about whether it is true that he deliberately oiled his famous *coscia d'oro* to make them appear even better on stage? Answered Corelli: "I take care of my body; what on earth could people have against that? I'll tell you a secret: did you know that many Italian theaters now design their new costumes to my measurements?"[108]

September–October 1961: The Lost EMI *Bohème* and the Clash of the Titans

I would make a bad Rodolfo in La Bohème, *because my voice is too big, and you would have to use some sort of Wagnerian soprano as Mimì.*

Franco Corelli, with a somewhat surprising quote in Alan Rich, "Mythless Corelli," *The Sunday Times,* **February 11, 1962**

Although during this period the expectations of Corelli for heroic repertoire were at their peak, he went to Rome in order to record Puccini's *La Bohème* for EMI, with Victoria de los Angeles as Mimì. Unfortunately, the September 1961 session collapsed when the soprano became indisposed,[109] a setback that mattered but little to Franco at a time when he had the world at his feet. In the euphoria of his success, it seemed as if he had lifetimes left to complete any unfinished business. Rather than on his Mimì, his mind was set on Raul, Arnoldo, possibly even Jean de Leyden and the ongoing *Carmen* discussions with Callas. It was to further the last project that he took to alternating with Bauer over dinner dates with La Divina. On one occasion he even came to the aid of Bauer and Bing when problems arose with his good friend Tebaldi, who was about to cancel her contract with the Met. Corelli blamed this development on bad advice from her lover, Arturo Basile. Had Bing but asked his friend Franco to speak with her earlier, the problem would never have occurred!

Corelli had his loyalties among conductors as well and suggested that Bing hire Gavazzeni or De Fabritiis for him. After all, Ghiringhelli allowed him his pick of conductors and soprano leads. (This was how the new Prince of Tenors defined the current state of affairs in opera.) He had very good reasons for wanting to have things his way. Modern opera careers required complex and ingenious negotiating of travel requirements, airplane schedules, and other details in order for the singer to get from one lucrative engagement to the next on time. Having his preferred conductors and sopranos meant that he could do more performances with fewer rehearsals. Money mattered to all singers, especially to Italian singers at the top level. Theater directors naturally blamed this on greed, but from the singer's point of view things looked entirely different. A singer's career ends when his voice is gone, which could be in thirty years or tomorrow. Because their alternative careers weren't likely to grant them the lifestyle to which they had become accustomed, and because they had little in the way of pensions at the time, most of them simply tried to secure the future as quickly and as well as they could. Having rival theaters compete for a singer

---

September 1961

Giacomo Puccini: *La Bohème*

Rome, Teatro dell'Opera (EMI recording)

Franco Corelli (*Rodolfo*), Victoria de los Angeles (*Mimì*)

was a good setup for him or her. An ideal one was animosity between their respective managements, such as existed between the general managers of the Met and La Scala.

Both Bing and Ghiringhelli were despotic by nature and not inclined to let artists get the upper hand. If it came to an open war, such as both were engaged in with Callas, the singer would lose, much in the way Del Monaco had begun to when he started drifting dangerously off course with Bing. Bad timing played a role as well: when Del Monaco finally reached an agreement with Bing over his return to the Met in the 1962–63 season as Otello, the no longer supremely reigning King of Tenors was so happy that he immediately put word of his return out on the street, adding that the Met had offered him the next season's opening night. That was an ill-advised move: Bing and Bauer had not informed Franco of their plans with his rival, out of sheer fear that it might affect their ongoing negotiations with the now omnipotent Prince. Bauer therefore crawled to Corelli on shaking knees. At the earliest moment of rumors of Del Monaco's return, as early as July, Corelli had responded by giving a little press conference of his own, where he bluntly announced that he was eventually going to open the new Met, currently under construction at Lincoln Center, as . . . Otello! (This despite the fact that his current Met negotiations didn't run beyond opening the 1962–63 season as Chénier). That left Bauer to convince each rival that it was all wishful thinking on the other tenor's part. An opening night! There had been no such offer! Just a few *Otello*s, that was all. At that point Franco showed a side of himself that left Bing and Bauer flabbergasted—a vulnerable, human side that would emerge from time to time and endear him to them. Instead of erupting in anger, he supported his rival's return in the friendliest of tones. Moreover, as "a friend of Bing" and fully aware of the Met's current financial problems, the goodhearted Anconetano came up with a superb, unheard-of suggestion of his own: "Why don't you let us open the Met together. Give *Cavalleria Rusticana* and *Pagliacci* for opening night. Let Mario sing the Pagliacci and I'll do the Turiddu."[110]

It is pointless to speculate on what opportunities were lost when Bing and Bauer dropped the matter out of fear of Del Monaco's reaction. So afraid were they of a clash of the titans if the two rivals ran into each other during the season that they actually planned to organize it in such a way the two men wouldn't be in New York at the same time. Beyond that, Bing's and Bauer's minds were set not on a *Cav/Pag* double bill, but on Mario's "prestigious" *Otello mille-e-tre*.[111]

Bauer calculated that Del Monaco would eventually bend to the Met's will, because he needed to return to the Met in order to rescue his collapsing U.S. record sales.[112] For the time being, however, Del Monaco refused to bend, and as if the devil slept between them, Corelli came up with precisely the same exorbitant new financial demands Del Monaco had made, flaunting offers from Spain, Vienna, and the Italian provinces that ran more than double the Met's fees. Salzburg paid him $3,000 for *Il Trovatore*, Venice was good for $3,200, and the Philadelphia Lyric Opera and also some German and Scandinavian opera houses offered him contracts for $4,500 per performance. He bluntly turned down an incredible offer from Paris "because he didn't like it there."[113]

October 1961: On Double Bookings and *Trovatores* After Midnight

Corelli had begun to encounter some unexpected hostility as a result of his singing too well, when he had a woman's shoes thrown at him in Verona after the audience had started throwing hats, programs, and whatever was at hand because he refused to do encores.[114] With that "tribute," he went with the Rome Opera to Berlin's Theater of the West, where he sang what some considered his best Manrico to date. Again the audience refused to let him go, this time simply refusing to go home themselves. Said Corelli: "Certain customs vary from house to house. . . . At La Scala, as at the Metropolitan, we never sing encores. Good. In Berlin, however, the audience simply refused to go home after *Trovatore*, . . . so we wheeled a piano on stage and I sang Italian folk songs until long after midnight."[115]

Reading of his incredibly successful performances in this period, one almost feels sorry for Bing; no off night ever arrived to bring "Mr. Sold Out" back down to earth. Loretta and Franco kept directing Bauer's attention to the weekly financial losses they would have to bear if they were to accept the Met's extended offer for the whole 1962–63 season and the tour, which added up to a small fortune. At the same time, Franco understood very well that Bing couldn't raise his fee without getting other stars on his back, so he suggested that Bing adopt Ghiringhelli's way of handling this delicate matter: La Scala

> October 1 and 3, 1961
> Giuseppe Verdi: *Il Trovatore*
> Berlin, Theater des Westens
> Mirella Parutto (*Leonora*), Franco Corelli (*Manrico*), Fedora Barbieri (*Azucena*), Ettore Bastianini (*Count di Luna*), Agostino Ferrin (*Ferrando*), Anna Marcangeli (*Ines*), cond. Oliviero De Fabritiis

paid him for an unsung performance after each fourth performance. Loyal as he was, he would even help his friends for less, but then he could only grant them three weeks and no tour at all.[116]

✦✦✦✦✦

While Franco dashed from Berlin to Barcelona for a few *Tosca*s, Bing panicked. In vain, he fired off letters to his star tenor filled with calculations of tax refunds and pleas for solidarity, until finally God sent him a veritable deus ex machina when Corelli himself ran into trouble. He had previously accepted La Scala's offer for the opening of their Verdi memorial season, assuming it was going to be in 1963–64. As it turned out, La Scala celebrated it a full year ahead of the actual anniversary—in the middle of his Met commitment.[117] Corelli then relented and agreed to sing for less and to do the tour, up to and including the very last day of it, if Bing would only let him out for a couple of weeks to fulfill his La Scala obligations. From that moment on, Bing held all the cards, leaving Corelli to plead and beg. The tenor even brought his personal financial affairs into the mix. He had recently acquired a piece of land in Italy, and in order to cover the purchase price, he had asked Ghiringhelli for a large advance, so he owed the manager some loyalty.

With Corelli now eager to please, Bing had his hands free to concentrate on his problems with the labor unions and with keeping his other tenors in check. Specifically, he had to secure the further services of Richard Tucker, who was the next to sour over Corelli's popularity with the public and press.[118] Tucker, who (like most tenors) was convinced he was the greatest tenor in the world,[119] even went so far as to hint that the reason he was not so highly esteemed as Corelli was the public's anti-Semitism. His direct grudge grew out of Corelli's interference with his own plans for *Il Trovatore* and *Aida*. After Björling and Del Monaco, Tucker had carefully prepared these roles as pillars of his future Met career, only to see his efforts crumble when Corelli conquered the Met overnight. Tucker deeply resented Bing's unconcealed favoritism toward Corelli. The fact that Corelli got away with unheard-of divo behavior just because Bing thought that he "looked like God" felt to Tucker like a betrayal,[120] and in response he sought to substantially cut back his performances.

Bing's response was twofold. First, he wrote long letters to Tucker in which he assured him of his undisputed position as "one of the world's leading tenors."[121] Next, he went back to Del Monaco, because he simply didn't want to risk having to rely on Corelli alone.

Del Monaco, who in response to the lingering Met negotiations had booked out completely with fabulous engagements, still showed interest in the offer for *Otello* at the Met.[122] There were just a few minor problems to be resolved. For one, he had learned that Corelli would open the 1962–63 season with *Chénier*. That was a part that only he, Del Monaco, or perhaps Tucker, was allowed to sing. Corelli's voice, Del Monaco told Bauer, was mere "tin" compared to his own solid gold.

With that, believing that Bing couldn't mount *Otello* without him, Del Monaco had laid his cards on the table. When Bauer pointed out that there were alternatives, Del Monaco responded that Vickers and McCracken were nothing but *comprimari* who *might* sing Cassio to his Otello—though they were still inferior. All this was vented in a forty-minute telephone tornado filled with B-flat accusations, which he concluded by raising his fee to a high D. Del Monaco said regally that if Bing and Bauer didn't let him open the season, they could all go to hell. Predictably, that ended the matter.[123] Del Monaco canceled his signed contract and went on to show parts of his correspondence with the Met to the press, boasting that Bing couldn't afford him. Infuriated, Bing issued a hostile press release in which he stated that the real reason for renouncing Del Monaco was that he had demanded that Bing fire Corelli. Naturally, he would accept no such demands—there was only one king at the Met.[124]

❖❖❖❖❖

In between these affairs, Bing had a ball trifling with the man who, after King Bing, was fittingly left with the title "Prince of Tenors" at the Met. He even squeezed some *Pagliacci*s from Corelli, an opera that his prizefighter still resented. Bing clearly enjoyed the game now that negotiations had shifted in his favor, thanks to the tenor's inadvertent overbooking. A full year of skirmishes ensued over the very last minute of Corelli's departure from the Met and subsequent return from La Scala, with Bing going so far as to urge him to talk some sense into Ghiringhelli. But denying the tenor his prestigious and unique double opening was never an option. As meek as he had become, Corelli made it perfectly clear that the managements involved should never force him to choose between two personal loyalties. Not that there was any need, for Bing and Bauer secretly relished the extra publicity and prestige the double openings would bring to his future Met appearances.

December 1961–January 1961: *Canzoni Napoletane no. 2*

From New York, the Corellis journeyed to Milan, where Franco recorded his second song recital album (not released until the next year, in order to leave enough time between this record and the previous song recording). Cut in between his La Scala performances, this second recital provided another string of popular gems to which his dramatic voice truly brought some sex appeal instead of the usual soft-voiced romantic approach.[125] He had boasted earlier, in response to a Detroit reporter's question, that he would sing *Carmen* in French.[126]

> December 1961
> Milan (EMI recording)
> *Canzoni Napoletane no. 2*
> Falvo: "Dicitencello vuie." Falvo "Guapparia." Lama: "Silenzio cantatore." De Curtis: "Voce 'e notte." Gambardella: "O marenariello." Valente and Tagliaferri: "Passione." Di Capua: "O sole mio." Cannio: "O surdato 'nnammurato." Tosti: "'A vucchella." Valente: "Torna!" Cioffi: "Na sera 'e maggio." Valente: "Addio, mia bella Napoli."
> Cond. Franco Ferraris
>
> January 9, 1962
> Milan (EMI recording)
> Renato Cairone: "Pourquoi fermer ton coeur?" Luigi Denza: "Si tu m'aimais."
> Cond. Franco Ferraris

His alleged recordings of Cairone's "Pourquoi fermer ton coeur?" and Denza's "Si tu m'aimais," listed by Gilberto Starone as having been released on an Italian seven-inch 45 rpm record (La Voce del Padrone, VdP 7RO3131), show his intentions. This seven-inch disc was never reissued in any format—a pity, for "Si tu m'aimais" provides the only extant example of Corelli in the song at all.[127]

December 7–26, 1961: The Battle of Legnano

Owing to their different operating systems and their different positions toward native and foreign singers, La Scala could never be compared to the Met. Ghiringhelli created stars, who were then lured away by Bing, who had no place for beginners. La Scala was also by far the more adventurous theater with respect to repertoire. In Corelli's case, the Met relied almost completely on his established warhorses, whereas Ghiringhelli and La Scala's conductor, Gianandrea Gavazzeni, pushed the tenor from one creation to the next, combining the great *lirico spinto* parts with legendary operas that were revived only because Corelli was there to sing them. For the 1961–62 season he added Arrigo in Verdi's *La Battaglia di Legnano* to his Milanese scalps, a production that had originally been intended for Mario Del Monaco. The opera had not been mounted at La Scala since 1916, when the patriotic subject seemed appropriate in the context of the war against the Austro-Hungarian Empire. Beginning and ending with "Eviva Italia!" and presenting the whole unification of Italy in between, the work had been a resounding success in 1849 when it was first presented in Rome. The third-act oath in the crypt of the Sant' Ambrogio basilica even evoked shouts from

> December 7, 10, 13, 16, 19, 23, and 26, 1961
> Giuseppe Verdi: *La Battaglia di Legnano*
> Milan, Teatro alla Scala
> Franco Corelli (*Arrigo*), Antonietta Stella (*Lida*), Ettore Bastianini (*Rolando*), Marco Stefanoni *(Federico Barbarossa)*, Silvio Maionica (*Primo Console di Milano*), Agostino Ferrin (*Secondo Console di Milano*), Antonio Zerbini (*Il Podestà di Como*), Virgilio Carbonari (*Marcovaldo*), Aurora Cattelani (*Imelda*), cond. Gianandrea Gavazzeni

the galleries, swearing to drive the occupying tyrants to the far side of the Alps.

What had worked in Rome worked doubly well in Milan, where Frederick Barbarossa evoked some of the bitterest memories of the city's history. The city had been conquered and ruined by him twice during the second half of the twelfth century and the population humiliated. That served to bring the Milanese into an alliance with their former enemies, which resulted on May 29, 1176, in the Battle of Legnano, where Frederick Barbarossa was finally defeated by the Lombard alliance. Though the critics were divided as to the musical merits of Verdi's version of this heroic episode in Lombardy's history, the Maggio Musicale telecast of the year before with Gastone Limarilli as Arrigo had turned out to be one of the operatic highlights of the year. The Cetra recording of a decade before was a public favorite in Italy, so expectations for the upcoming *Battaglia di Legnano* were once again at fever pitch. Ghiringhelli presented the Milanese nobility with an incomparable spectacle, including a scene with an elevated bridge that would not have been out of place in the real event. The costumes were lavish, and the patriotic effect was amplified through rivers of banners of the Lega alliance, a magnificent view of Lake Como, and a pompous entry by Barbarossa himself, dressed in a crown and mantle and bearing a scepter in a sinister reminder of the days of the Holy Roman Empire of the German Nation.

Corelli taking the oath as Arrigo in Verdi's *La Battaglia di Legnano*, Teatro alla Scala, December 7, 1961. (Photo: Erio Piccagliani. Courtesy of the Teatro alla Scala)

As can still be heard on the recording of this event, Gavazzeni captured the scenic atmosphere in his orchestra, giving ample space to Verdi's brass section and the bombastic orchestral tuttis. Bruno Slawitz praised the golden trio of Corelli, Stella, and Agostino Ferrin, though he noticed a loss of warmth in Bastianini's voice. With respect to Corelli, Slawitz smiled over the Americanization of the publicity machine, with its extensive reports on Corelli's wounded fist. Fortunately, the honorary decoration he received from Milan's city council on behalf of his La Scala efforts surely made up for any lingering physical pain.[128] The sacrifice he made in accepting the part of Arrigo, which he judged too low for his voice, was largely rewarded by the dazzling performance reviews: "His personality justifies his fame and his phrasing lends just the right accent to each and every single syllable. His performance was another pure, honest and deserved success." Corelli was also praised for his skill as a stunt man. In the third act, he jumped blindfolded from the tower—without a safety net.[129]

Christmas 1961: O Holy Night

Christmas fell between Franco's last La Scala *Battaglia* and some personal affairs, such as the Corellis' visit to Bauer on Christmas Eve. A stunned Roberto faithfully wrote to his boss how the evening came to pass. The Corellis were friendlier than ever, enjoying themselves until 2:30 A.M., but there were of course some matters to discuss. Franco contemplated acquiring a home in New York, an idea Bauer supported wholeheartedly; any European with money should seek to find himself a fixed point in the United States, because after two world wars God only knew what more could befall Europe. What he didn't tell Franco, but did write to Bing, was that with Franco living in New York, Bing could almost be sure of the tenor's continuing services. For his part, Corelli still had high hopes of securing Callas for *Carmen*, if only he didn't have to sing those damned *Pagliacci*.... Accepting them was his biggest mistake ever, unless one were to take his wretched EMI recording of the same work into account. Wrote Bauer: "He finds it terrible and when he recently played parts of the recording for me, he never stopped criticizing his singing there."[130]

By now the Corellis believed themselves to have a true friendship with Bauer, whom they invited to the opening of the season in Parma, where Franco and Renata Tebaldi were invited as guests of honor. Bauer's true feelings about the Corellis notwithstanding, he couldn't possibly refuse, and at the performance he was impressed with a side of the tenor he had never witnessed before. The tenor singing in that evening's *Don Carlo* was a hopeless case altogether, but during the intermission the conductor, Arturo Basile, and the theater manager assured their guests of honor that the American soprano, Giulia Barrera, was really good but unfortunately was indisposed. When the gallery started to roar and the first catcalls rained down on the poor woman, Franco insisted that someone had to stand up for her. Said the sincerely worried Corelli: "If no one explains what is wrong, her Italian career ends tonight." Tebaldi was asked to address the audience because she was from the area, but she shied away. Franco then stepped to the fore, asking the public's indulgence: Barrera had agreed to sing only in order to let the opening night take place at all—no replacement was available. After Barrera's great aria, the Corellis loudly initiated an ovation for the soprano all by themselves. Bauer was touched: "I don't think many stars would have made such a nice gesture!"

CHAPTER 12 ❖ 1962

"The World's Greatest Tenor"

January 1962: Good Spirits

This seems to be my Cavaradossi year, but really, anyone can bring down the house with those high B-flats in "Vittoria," even if he's stupid.
   Franco Corelli, quoted in Alan Rich, "Mythless Corelli," *The Sunday Times*, February 11, 1962

The year 1962 started out wonderfully for Corelli. Bing informed him through Bauer that he was prepared to relieve him of the accursed two Canios in *Pagliacci*—on the condition, of course, that he sign the contract then and there. Corelli had driven things to the limit as far as concessions were concerned.[1] Even so, he managed to coax an additional two "unsung performances" out of Bing (setting a dangerous precedent for the Met's future). In turn, Corelli gave up his struggle for extra travel expenses when Bauer pointed out that these extraneous costs had been caused by his own double-booking—perhaps he could ask Ghiringhelli for them! The tenor then signed his contract and went on to show Bauer the new costumes for *Gioconda* and *Tosca*, made by the famous Roman costume designer Petruzzi.

As a genuine best friend would do, Bauer then helped him pack his bags and escorted him to Malpensa on Tuesday, January 23. The fog on the way to the airport was so dense that Bauer feared their Alitalia flight would be canceled, but just as they arrived, the sun broke through.[2] Bauer couldn't help himself; he looked to the skies to see if God was there in a divine box, waiting for Corelli to arrive in New York in time for his first American *Tosca*, with Margaret Roberts. Though better known as Margherita Roberti, she had been born in Davenport, Iowa, and was making her Met debut that night by stepping in for

Leontyne Price, who had for some months been canceling a string of engagements on doctor's orders. (The reason for the cancellations is not definitely known, though the official version recorded in the Met's archives was that she had overworked herself to the point of total collapse.) At the second performance, even Birgit Nilsson came to Price's rescue, exchanging the mythical nebula of Wagner's *Walküre*, *Siegfried*, and *Götterdämmerung* Brünnhildes for Puccini's Tosca. When she entered her dressing room, she found a gift on the table: "Price had send me a bottle of Aquavit, with a note saying 'If I won't be there in person I will be there in 'spirit.'"[3]

February 1962: The World's Greatest Tenor and Enzo Ferrari

In February EMI released *Franco Corelli Sings Neapolitan Songs*, which had been recorded in July of the year before. The album cover showed Corelli posing in front of his brand-new 1961 Ferrari 250 GT Pinin Farina Cabrio, designed by Pininfarina himself. This shot probably sealed the deal between Franco and Enzo Ferrari, claims Marco Corelli: "Enzo was a fanatical fan of Franco and loved opera. When they met, they decided to mix business with pleasure.

Franco posing with one of his first Ferraris, a Pinin Farina. It was part of a promotional deal with Enzo Ferrari himself, who gave stars huge discounts on his cars in order to promote his brand. (Photo: Courtesy of Arrigo Michelini)

Corelli driving around Europe in a Ferrari was an excellent way of advertising among rich people. Franco would frequently trade in his car for a new model in order to continue being the fastest driver around."[4]

✦✦✦✦✦

With the Ferrari cover in hand and the influential critic Mario Morini putting in writing Del Monaco's opinion that "the youngsters [Corelli and Stella] weren't yet ready to be counted among the great singers,"[5] Franco decided it was time to claim his throne. He informed EMI that he would look for another record company unless they would subsequently promote him in their advertisements as "The World's Greatest Tenor." The alarmed assistant manager of the Met, John Gutman, intervened when Angel Records (EMI's classical outlet in America) begged him for help. Both EMI and the Met staff believed it would be not just counterproductive, but also a demonstration of extremely bad taste. Apart from that, Gutman immediately saw the disastrous effect this kind of advertising in their own programs would have on the Met's tenor roster: "Nothing but trouble."[6] With that, the matter was dropped. Corelli would have to content himself with the usual encouraging quotes from *The New York Times* or publications of lesser stature. As if to soothe the tenor's ego, *Opera News* then honored the reprise of the already legendary Cecil Beaton *Turandot* with the first full-color cover in fifteen years; the cover alone tripled the cost of the magazine.[7]

Louis Melançon's official role photo of Corelli as Radamès at the Met, February 1962. (Photo: Courtesy of the Metropolitan Opera Archives)

March 9–31, 1962: "Enzo Grimaldo, Principe di New York"

A lady asked me if I could tell her the story of the opera. That is a big order. It suffices to know that everyone is in love with the wrong person

and that infidelity, murder, arson, suicide, betrayal and adultery follow each other in breathless succession.
> Max de Schauensee, "Cast Headed by Franco Corelli Sparkles in *La Gioconda*," *Philadelphia Evening Bulletin*, February 19, 1964

Having presented a number of highly successful roles from his European repertoire to New York audiences, Corelli ventured on to more challenging projects. Instead of going on the Met's first desegregated spring tour, he presented himself to the nation on *The Ed Sullivan Show* with "Tu ca nun chiagne," after which he prepared himself for his first true American role debut as Enzo Grimaldo, Prince of Santafior, in Amilcare Ponchielli's *La Gioconda*. Though the production employed the old *Gioconda* sets, Corelli's three performances were highly successful. The part of Enzo seemed tailor-made for his voice, which had gained in warmth and melancholy while keeping its heroic ring undiminished, as can be heard in a thrilling fragment that survives of the finale from the March 9 debut with Zinka Milanov. (The complete *La Gioconda* CD issue [Grand Tier, ENGT-CD-2 #2/92] features the March 31 broadcast with Eileen Farrell.)

The three *Gioconda*s were followed by *The Bell Telephone Hour*, and on March 18 Corelli gave his first U.S. recital. The concert was a mix of arias and songs with piano accompaniment given before an enthusiastic audience in Dwight Morrow High School's Academic Hall in Englewood, New Jersey. The reaction of a young opera buff named Donald DiGrazia gives an interesting look at things from the American public's side. Says DiGrazia:

> We're Italians, my family, and we were all in love with opera. As for this Corelli guy, we knew him from the film all right! The *Tosca* movie with Caniglia and Guelfi! We couldn't believe our eyes when he suddenly appeared on the Met's

---

March 9, 24, and 31, 1962
Amilcare Ponchielli: *La Gioconda*
New York, Metropolitan Opera House
Zinka Milanov, Eileen Farrell [March 31] (*La Gioconda*), Franco Corelli (*Enzo Grimaldo*), Nell Rankin (*Laura Adorno*), Giorgio Tozzi (*Alvise Badoero*), Lili Chookasian, Mignon Dunn [March 31] (*the Blind Woman*), Robert Merrill (*Barnaba*), cond. Fausto Cleva

playbill, but for some reason we couldn't get to his debut and then, the first opportunity for me was this high school concert. My family couldn't go, because they were occupied, so I went alone: man, I couldn't believe it! There was the same great guy that we had seen in the movie! But that movie never prepared me for his true voice, I had no idea of the size of it until I heard him live! And once I heard it, I was hooked: this was everything I ever wanted from a tenor![8]

Licia Albanese chimed in a few days later when she became Franco's fourth *Tosca* of the season, after Roberti, Nilsson, and Zinka Milanov. She knew him personally from two earlier *Turandot* performances in which she had been his Liù and had become infatuated with him. Despite the fact that she sang but six opera performances with him during a brilliant career that brought her together with Gigli, Björling, Schipa, and Di Stefano, her most treasured memories were of the six nights and four recitals she sang with Franco: "He was my favorite on stage—his face and lips were so expressive. I once said to him: 'Franco, don't worry, when we have to kiss, I'll really kiss you because I love you.' 'Signora Licia,' he said, 'please don't dare to do that, because my wife is very jealous.'"[9]

Leaving his new fans either lovelorn or mesmerized, Corelli proceeded to conquer audiences in Philadelphia and Chicago. The Symphony Hall of Newark, New Jersey, accommodated his second U.S. recital, this time with a more challenging program of songs and arias from *Tosca, Fanciulla del West, Carmen, Rigoletto,* and *Fedora*. All that remained for him to perform before he could return to Europe was the April 7 broadcast of *Tosca*, for which Leontyne Price had suddenly regained her strength. Missing premieres and interim performances was not the same as giving up a national broadcast that carried one's voice and name to millions.

❖❖❖❖❖

With his American obligations behind him, Corelli arrived in Milan well rested. There he warmed up for his upcoming debut as Raul de Nangis with two *Turandot*s, in between which Loretta seems to have faced bigger problems:

> American women ask if a man is married before making a pass at him. In Italy the women do not ask. They do not care, married, not married. If they want a certain man, they ask for him. . . . In Italy I have to be present always, because

they invade the dressing room, these women. They see me there, but they pay no attention to me. Right in front of me they try to make assignations with Franco.[10]

Loretta recalled the story of a woman who came into Franco's dressing room three times in one night. The first time, the woman looked at him for three minutes, sighed, and left; the second time she took his hand before looking into his eyes, sighing, and departing once more. When she returned a third time and started crying while holding both Franco's hands, Loretta threw her out. She proceeded to read one of her husband's milder pieces of fan mail to the reporter: "You are my dream hero. When can I meet you? When can I spend time to tell you of my love for you?" Here the clever manager rises again, for few wives would have been able to produce as brilliant an answer as Loretta's, who replied to each: "You may not have my husband, but you may buy his records."[11]

Fortunately, the object of all that adulation was quite *tranquillo* about other women, interested only in studying. And besides, "She is always with me.... They would have to arrange it with her."[12]

May 12, 1962: *Denise*

While dealing with the obligations that came with his Milanese engagement, Corelli had the pleasure of seeing his second photo novel published. This time the subject was not an operatic one, but a genuine *fotoromanza* of the romantic

---

May 12–September 1, 1962

Denise

Photo novel for *Grand Hotel* (after Alexandre Dumas *fils*, adapted by F. Sergi)

Franco Corelli (*Andrea*), Leonora Ruffo (*Denise*), Mirella Uberti (*Adalgisa*), Carlo Cataneo (*Brissot*), Marcello Tiller (*Federico*), Sandro Pizzochero (*Alfredo*); director, Sirio Magni; producer, Arminda Tencalla; photography, A. Domingo; supervisor, Gino Fanano; scenographer, Tonj Camatta; costumes: Sartoria Werther; hairdresser: Silvano Rocchetti

"THE WORLD'S GREATEST TENOR" • 247

kind, titled *Denise*. Shortly before it started running in May, the Italian magazine *Grand Hotel* issued a complete version of the 1960 *Chénier*, which must have been the talk of the town in La Scala's dressing rooms. *Denise* hit the scene

An enchanting example of a page from *Denise*, with Andrea (Corelli) seducing Denise (Leonora Ruffo) into a kiss in the woods. (Photos: A. Domingo. Courtesy of *Grand Hotel*/Casa Editrice Universo)

in the middle of Corelli's *Ugonotti* rehearsals and was destined to stir the female hearts from where he had left them in *Chénier*, especially with regard to the kissing, which had been modest in comparison with the story line of *Denise*. The photo novel followed the Dumas *fils* novel of the same name, with a plot that runs along the average grotesque line of love, despair, and death. Adalgisa is pregnant with the child of Francesco, whom she leaves for a rich count when Francesco's father faces bankruptcy. When the child, Anna, is born, Adalgisa tells Francesco she had a miscarriage. Twenty-five years later Count Andrea (Corelli) finds the beautiful "orphan" Denise, who has been adopted by his administrator, Francesco, waiting in his bed upon his return from Africa. Andrea had planned to marry Anna, sister of his friend Fernando, but he succumbs instead to Denise's charms and decides to marry her instead. When Andrea learns that Fernando is Denise's secret lover, he demands a duel. Fernando is mortally wounded, and Adalgisa confesses to have blackmailed Denise into lying about being Fernando's lover so that Andrea would marry Anna, because Adalgisa's formerly rich husband is now facing huge debts. Fernando miraculously recovers, Anna runs off with a poor man, and Denise ends up in a loveless relationship far away. Andrea finally finds her pushing her invalid husband's wheelchair. Upon seeing Andrea, Denise is so shocked that she lets go of the wheelchair, which crashes into a tree. The impact miraculously cures her husband and he can walk again. He is so happy that he leaves the two former lovers to each other and goes off to travel the world.

Corelli and his Denise, Leonora Ruffo, were beautifully captured in the unabashedly romantic photography of A. Domingo, a true master of the genre. The castle and garden settings were splendid, Sartoria Werther made gorgeous realistic costumes, and Franco and Ruffo provided some hot-blooded kissing. One wonders not why he made this nonsense, but rather why he didn't make more of it.

May 28–June 12, 1962: Raul de Nangis

C2 is not a chemical formula indicating two different carbon molecules. No, it's just the nickname that the Americans gave to Franco Corelli. And while the singer humbly accepts this reference to Caruso, he would probably consider himself more the heir of Giacomo Lauri-Volpi, one of

the "Glories of Italy." And indeed it is to Lauri-Volpi that he always turns, when he performs in operas that were in the repertoire of the Maestro.
   Mila Contini, in "Timido ma bello il fusto della lirica," *Amica*, July 29, 1962

In their day Rossini, Donizetti, Bellini, and even Verdi saw their fame challenged by Meyerbeer, whose *Les Huguenots* was one of the most popular operas of the nineteenth century. But *Les Huguenots* vanished from the repertoire with the dawn of verismo, an operatic style that required a more realistic and down-to-earth subject matter. The famous grand operas were also becoming increasingly difficult to stage because of modern scenic requirements and the increasing rarity of tenors who could meet the vocal demands. The last great Raul de Nangis in the twentieth century had been Lauri-Volpi, who had caused a furor in the part in the Italian-language adaptation at the Arena di Verona in 1933. Once Corelli's *Gli Ugonotti* appeared on the La Scala playbill, expectations rose sky-high, as seen from the Caruso and Lauri-Volpi comparison in *Amica* quoted at the beginning of this section. The connection between Lauri-Volpi and Corelli is intriguing, because Corelli's lifelong friendship and work with Lauri-Volpi was supposed to have begun only in 1963. This article, however, is dated July 1962. Another from the same month by Mario Morini describes how Corelli, intrigued by Lauri-Volpi's earlier criticisms of his technique, wanted to study with the maestro.[13]

Lauri-Volpi himself denied that the two had studied together formally, but he mentioned that they had spoken frequently over the phone and that he had often heard Corelli sing in person. For someone who only knew his pupil from a vague number of telephone conversations, he was rather firm when asked his opinion of Corelli the man: "Here I have to say that I discovered a great artist

May 28 and 31; June 2, 7, and 12, 1962
Giacomo Meyerbeer: *Gli Ugonotti*
Milan, Teatro alla Scala
Franco Corelli (*Raul de Nangis*), Joan Sutherland (*Margherita di Valois*), Giulietta Simionato (*Valentina*), Giorgio Tozzi (*Count Saint-Bris*), Wladimiro Ganzarolli (*Count de Nevers*), Nicolai Ghiaurov (*Marcello*), Fiorenza Cossotto (*Urbano*), cond. Gianandrea Gavazzeni

and singer, but foremost also a man who has a quality that I have missed in others: modesty. A modesty that touches me and that makes him dear to me. I owe to him the fact that I partially started believing again in those currently active on the lyrical stage." Lauri-Volpi made no secret of the fact that their phone conversations had recently focused on Raul de Nangis: "That is very true and I am grateful for it. Here you have another example of his heart, his sensitivity, and the modesty he employs in serving art. I have wished him both the same success and the same intimate satisfaction that the part once brought to me."[14]

Corelli's reasons for consulting Lauri-Volpi are obvious. Lauri-Volpi had been the last great Raul and was the only tenor who could still draw upon an intact Meyerbeer tradition that went from Francesco Tamagno and Francesco Marconi to Mario and from there straight to Adolphe Nourrit and Gilbert-Louis Duprez.[15] An even more immediate line ran through Lauri-Volpi's teacher Antonio Cotogni (born in 1831),[16] the creator in Italy of Nelusco in the posthumous 1865 premiere of Meyerbeer's *L'Africana*. The question remains as to the precise extent of Lauri-Volpi's influence on Corelli's career. Certainly, as can be heard in the *Guglielmo Tell* rehearsals, Corelli experimented with Lauri-Volpi's technique, but he never effectively employed it onstage. Yet Morini paints an intriguing picture of Corelli consulting Lauri-Volpi in search of high notes.[17] Not only does this put their collaboration a full year earlier than previously believed, but it also suggests that Lauri-Volpi did more than mere psychological coaching. He instilled in Corelli an almost religious belief that he could deal with the remaining "limitations" of his voice: inflexibility and an insecure passage to the highest range. As long as he had the latter barrier in either his larynx or his mind, there could be no question of facing the demands of the

Most of the shots of Corelli as Raul de Nangis show him as a valiant knight, but the story actually concerns his humble family background, which leads the knights to humiliate him at the beginning of the opera in this rare photo from Act I. (Photo: Erio Piccagliani. Courtesy of the Teatro alla Scala)

"true" heroic repertoire, as defined by Rossini's *Guglielmo Tell* and the Parisian works of Meyerbeer, most notably *Les Huguenots*, which was revived for Corelli at La Scala on the evening of May 28, 1962.

✦✦✦✦✦

Rodolfo Celletti wrote a brief but accurate portrait of the *Ugonotti* performance in which he postulated that Corelli did not have the right sort of voice for that "impossible" role. Impossible, because Raul is conceived as an extremely young, dreamy, and pure character, which requires a brighter texture and a more flexible voice.[18] At the same time, the vocal demands (there is a thrilling D-flat in the Valentina-Raul duet) are such that few voices of the required clear and silvery timbre can successfully master them. In Celletti's opinion, the young Lauri-Volpi brilliantly qualified, whereas Corelli successfully tailored the part to his own vocal characteristics.[19] Instead of a young and dreamy Raul, he was an emotionally charged, heroic young nobleman with a voice forged on the anvils of Radamès, Enzo, Cavaradossi, Don José, and Calaf:

"Dillo ancor! . . . dì che m'ami. . . ." The ovation following the duet between Raul (Corelli) and Valentina (Giulietta Simionato) set a house record at La Scala. (Photo: Erio Piccagliani. Courtesy of the Teatro alla Scala)

> Corelli molds a Raul who moves from ardent and chivalrous to melancholy, and he is excellent in the love duet in the fourth act (despite the omission of a vocalise that rises to a D-flat). He gets over the difficulties of texture thanks to a potent voice which has an outstanding expansion, and is yet flexible and brimming with emotion. This is another achievement to be ranked next to the performances of Ernani and Poliuto, given by Corelli in that happy period at La Scala, but perhaps with one or two extra marks.[20]

The sheer emotional impact of Corelli's Raul is heard at the repeated "Dillo ancor" in the Act IV duet. There he captivated the audience with a voice that moved them so deeply that they hardly noticed the omitted high D-flat. Corelli and Simionato were rewarded with a full twenty-two minutes of applause, a mid-performance ovation unprecedented in the history of the theater. The astonishing Joan Sutherland, a young and sunny Fiorenza Cossotto, and the great Nicolai Ghiaurov shared in the glory of the night, one that stands as a landmark in the Meyerbeer revival that followed it. Celletti judged only Wladimiro Ganzarolli's Nevers and Giorgio Tozzi's Saint-Bris barely acceptable, but that didn't hamper the overall brilliance of the performance, masterfully conducted by Gianandrea Gavazzeni, who also made a number of much-discussed and often misunderstood cuts and restorations.[21] Joan Sutherland later rebuked Corelli for cutting his part at will. But in general Gavazzeni simply followed the score of the 1955 Lauri-Volpi revival. The recording of that performance was clearly Corelli's model, for he follows Lauri-Volpi's phrasing up to the very last *filature*, shading, and sob—playing the two recordings simultaneously sounds almost like stereo (until Act IV, which Lauri-Volpi did not sing).[22]

All in all, there are about twelve minutes missing from his part among the hour and a half Gavazzeni cut from the score. Sutherland's complaints should probably be attributed to the inexplicable cut of Corelli's part in his duet with the queen, from her "Ah! Si j'étais coquette" on. This robbed her of one of the crowning moments in her limited role. Still, Raul de Nangis stands as Corelli's greatest achievement up to this point in his career.

June 26, 1962: A Car Accident

Reluctant to fly and in love with automobiles, Corelli drove thousands of miles from theater to theater when he was singing in Europe. Apart from his recent taste for fancy sports cars, he had had a Mercury for years, and his stay in America had only made him more aware that big cars felt safer.[23] But one isn't always in control of what happens on the road. Fate caught up with the Corellis on June 26 as Franco drove the Mercury from Venice,[24] where he had performed in *Carmen*, to Enghien-les-Bains, near Paris, where he was to perform in *Andrea Chénier*. Near Sesto Calende, just after leaving the speedway for the Sempione highway, a truck showed up immediately in front of them, trying to pass a car. In a split-second reflex Corelli tried to find a passage in between,

PAUROSO INCIDENTE D'AUTO al tenore Corelli e alla moglie

Il cantante racconta come la sua vettura è stata investita da un autocarro presso Sesto Calende

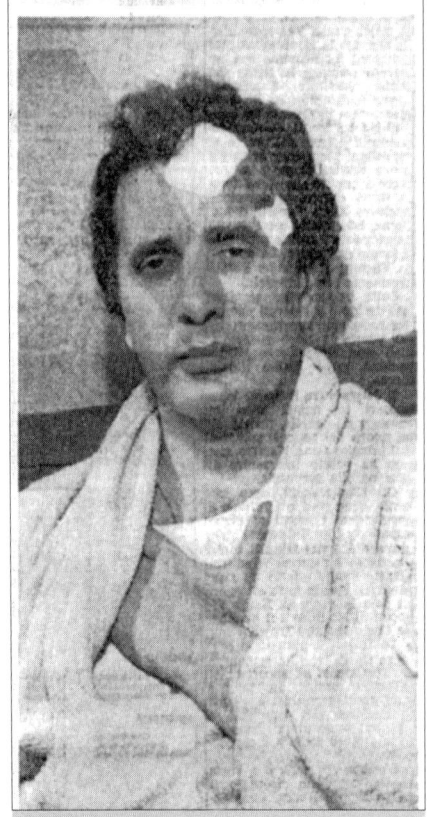

Corriere della Sera was there when Franco was confined to his bed after suffering injuries in a car wreck near Sesto Calende while on his way from Venice to Enghien-les-Bains. (Reproduced courtesy of *Corriere della Sera*/RCS Group)

but the two traffic lanes at kilometer marker 53 proved too narrow for three cars at once, and the truck hit the Mercury on the left side. The impact demolished the car from the left front to the back. The rear wheel on that side locked, and the car side slid into a ditch.

Both Corellis were briefly knocked out. When they regained consciousness, surprised to find themselves alive and with no more than minor injuries, Corelli managed to get the right-side door open, and, with the help of passersby, they were able to get out of the vehicle. They had only minor injuries. Looking at the wrecked car, Franco realized that if the truck had hit them just a few centimeters more to the middle, both he and Loretta would have been killed. Even more horrible to contemplate, if the impact had been less powerful, the car would have spun and slid sideways under the truck's trailer, which would have beheaded them. As it was, Corelli had bruises on his head and chest, which had taken the full impact of the steering wheel. Appearing at the famous casino of Enghien was now out of the question. The Corellis were taken to Milan, where Franco's favorite physician, a Dr. Dioguardi, prescribed him absolute rest for a full seven days. Corelli took a philosophical approach to the accident: "It's a blessing in disguise that it ended well after all."[25,]

July–September 1962: Back to Work

Enghien's *Chénier* was not the only casualty of the collision. It also interfered with part of the *Cavalleria Rusticana* recording for EMI, part of which Corelli dubbed in later over the orchestral tape. All in all it was an ill-fated recording from the start. The main problem was the casting. Initially, Lucine Amara had hoped to sing Santuzza, which would have complemented her earlier *Pagliacci* recording with Corelli.[26] That ambition was shattered when her career failed to bloom in the way EMI officials had hoped. Victor Olof ultimately engaged the established Victoria de los Angeles, who was more renowned for her *Faust* Marguerite than for her tame Santuzza, which put a damper on the overall effect of the recording: it has remained in the shadow of the more famous Callas–Di Stefano set.[27]

Despite his troubles, Corelli turned in a series of inspired *Trovatore* performances in Salzburg, with Leontyne Price and Herbert von Karajan at his side, between July and September of 1962. Working with Karajan provided Franco with a new experience and a new frontier. The essence of what generally stands as his quintessential Manrico was beautifully captured in the press: "His radiant voice, soft and focused at the same time, impresses as much in the lyrical *cantilene* as in heroic power. The *stretta* was all-surpass-

---

July 1962
Pietro Mascagni: *Cavalleria Rusticana*
Rome, Teatro dell'Opera (EMI recording)
Victoria de los Angeles (*Santuzza*), Franco Corelli (*Turiddu*), Adriana Lazzarini (*Lola*), Mario Sereni (*Alfio*), Corinna Vozza (*Lucia*), cond. Gabriele Santini

July 31; August 4, 11, 20, 25, and 30; September 14, 1962
Giuseppe Verdi: *Il Trovatore*
Salzburg, Neues Festspielhaus
Leontyne Price (*Leonora*), Franco Corelli (*Manrico*), Giulietta Simionato (*Azucena*), Ettore Bastianini (*Count di Luna*), Nicola Zaccaria (*Ferrando*), Laurence Dutoit (*Ines*), Siegfried Rudolf Frese (*Ruiz*), Vienna Philharmonic, cond. Herbert von Karajan

ing."[28] After that, German tour agencies flocked to offer him up to $10,000 per performance.[29]

August 8, 1962: A Home Run

Franco Corelli's inaugural performance at the 1962 Pesaro Summer Festival was a friendly gesture to some acquaintances who were involved with it. Surely, the fact that his uncles' Vincenzo Bellini Chorus was participating played a part in his accepting the invitation as well. Viero Corelli himself prepared the chorus for the performance. This was a highly charged performance for the tenor. Corelli was so nervous singing before his old friends that he actually sang the "Di quella pira" at pitch, instead of lowering it a half step, as was his custom. Furthermore, he was forced to cross swords with his very best friend, Carlo Scaravelli, who was entrusted with the part of Manrico's rival, Count di Luna.

Ever since Corelli's 1956 appearances in Pesaro he had kept in touch with Scaravelli, who was praised in the local papers for his pure voice, audible love for Verdi, and ability to deliver the required human and dramatic accents. Franco continued to discuss with Scaravelli the vocal challenges before him. Scaravelli's son Alessandro recalls how Franco would phone his father in the middle of the night from America, lamenting that he couldn't get his voice in the right place, that he didn't trust his breathing, and so on:

> They were on the phone for hours. My father was going to work at eight in the morning and it happened that he didn't get any sleep. He finished talking on the phone at seven, then he went to work, where Franco would call again: "Carlo, I improved, but I still believe that...." And my father would say: "Then

August 8, 1962
Pesaro, Palazzo dello Sport
Giuseppe Verdi: *Il Trovatore*
Giuseppina Tesi (*Leonora*), Franco Corelli (*Manrico*), Vittoria Calma (*Azucena*), Carlo Scaravelli (*Count di Luna*), Sergio Sisti (*Baspart*), cond. Nino Verchi

try this." Franco's reference point has always been my father, also because it was a way of being close to him, while being so far away. Those conversations were a telephone trip home, to Ancona, his friends and family.[30]

When asked why he had performed several times in Pesaro but never in Ancona, Corelli replied: "I would be very happy to perform in Ancona . . . [if] there [were] a theater, a stage to perform on. I will sing in Ancona as soon as the Teatro delle Muse reopens."[31]

Summer 1962: At Home with the Corellis

Because of his premature rise to fame he has always remained a little immature. . . . He was born before his time. He has been Corelli for years, but he never passed beyond his adolescence.
   Loretta Corelli, in Maurizio Chierici, "Il bel tenore sempre in burrasca,"
   Oggi Illustrato, January 23, 1964

Both Italian and American women's magazines continued to provide an interesting if somewhat fictional portrait of the Corellis in private. Yet their reporters posed questions that more serious journalists would hardly have dared to ask.[32] Loretta had by now emerged as Franco's most critical audience, his most trusted counselor, his most loyal supporter, and the most reliable brake on his temper. This "Adonis of opera," as *Amica*'s Mila Contini called him, would be lost without the woman who straightened his tie and who made sure he got enough sleep and attention. Ever since Franco was mocked by a passing bicyclist, she closed windows and curtains whenever he had to study.[33] Corelli commented intriguingly: "A true companion, for better or worse, as she knows me inside out."[34]

Wearing slippers, the top button of his shirt unbuttoned and his tie loosened, Franco tells Contini that when he is not singing he is the most normal man in town. He is superstitious, though; on performance days this Adonis will cross the street to avoid a black cat. And he always takes his good-luck charm to performances: Loris, his black poodle. Given to him by a female admirer when the dog was only a month old, Loris soon became the apple of Franco's eye: "He was all black and his little head popped up from a basket filled with roses. Loris is so used to the theater that he knows for certain that the show is over when

"THE WORLD'S GREATEST TENOR" • 257

the final applause has ended. Then all he wants is to leave."[35] (Sadly, according to Arrigo Michelini, Loris would later die after swallowing a ping-pong ball.)

An ordinary man, then? He has no doorknobs of gold, no trivial hobbies, and he has even forgotten the passions of his youth, when he used to make architectural drawings of boats. Watching television and reading detective novels and Dante's *Divina Commedia* (!) are his most frivolous activities. He devotes hours and hours each day to study, pacing through the house restlessly, singing a line here, a line there; walking to and from the piano, checking Loretta's opinion on his vocalizing, absentmindedly picking up objects at random and putting them back. Despite his success, he isn't at all sure he will go on singing for the rest of his life.[36]

Franco and Loretta enjoying a quiet moment together. (Photo: Walter Mori. Courtesy of the Mondadori Group)

✦✦✦✦✦

Corelli the man seems to have been trying to reconcile his career with his inner feelings, and these were surprisingly remote from the heroic characters he portrayed. His more sensitive side apparently yearned to express something more intimate, and so he told Bauer at last that he would do Des Grieux. The date of the meeting was August 16; the location, Munich; and the composer—Jules Massenet! Together with no fewer than six *Otello*s, *Manon* actually appeared on the Met's initial draft of his 1963–64 season, which documents his first recorded interest in both the lyric and the French repertoire (not counting his hints at a French *Carmen*). Present at the meeting was Corelli's brand-new "personal general manager," the Naples-born Aurelio Fabiani, also known as the founder and general manager of the Philadelphia Lyric Opera and a promoter of wrestling galas that Franco occasionally attended, especially when famous Italian boxers or wrestlers fought. The only fight in Munich was aimed at winning space for the eight television gigs that Fabiani had arranged for Franco, dates that interfered with his Met performance schedule. Bauer reported to Bing that the meeting had been conducted in the friendliest of tones. The Corellis hadn't even made demands with respect to the television dates; they simply "asked to see if it was possible."[37]

Summer 1962: Trouble in London

Throughout 1962 proposals went back and forth between EMI, their star tenor, and their diva, Maria Callas.[38] *Tosca* was one of the titles in his list of operas exclusively reserved to EMI, and he was expecting to record it with her in June 1962. Unfortunately, EMI had actually intended to use Alfredo Kraus for this recording, and they found themselves in an awkward position. Corelli subtly let EMI know that RCA was now also offering *Tosca* to him. If EMI had no need for his services in this opera, they surely wouldn't mind if he recorded it for RCA? English archive files aren't always accurate when it comes to emotions, but running through the cold description of the facts in EMI's records is a clear sense of panic. Their solution provides a revealing look at how some of the world's most prized or surprising record deals and recordings were born and how some would-be great ones were lost. In an attempt to appease Corelli, EMI offered their divo the opportunity to record *Il Trovatore* with Callas in the period offered by RCA for *Tosca*. Considering the way they made their offers, one wonders if the diva herself had even been asked. In the end, nothing came of these haphazard plans and counterplans, which included a Callas-Corelli-Giulini *Traviata*.[39]

Possibly Corelli let it all pass because he had his mind set on a greater challenge: *Otello*. Twice he actually asked EMI to set up a recording of *Otello* for him in London, with Carlo Maria Giulini and the Philharmonia Orchestra. He informed them that he would be free to record during September 1963, but EMI was very skeptical: he didn't yet know the part and did not intend to sing it in public until 1965 or 1966.[40] Corelli replied that EMI only needed to provide the main parts of the role as backing tracks, which he would overdub when he was ready. This was technically possible for EMI, although a headache for the engineers,[41] but it meant recording a complete *Otello* without a tenor on little more than the promise that he would fill in his part afterward. That proved too revolutionary for EMI's executives, and the project died.[42]

In turn EMI proposed a *Forza del Destino* recording to be released in 1963. Corelli took the bait, but in November EMI suddenly proposed *La Fanciulla del West* instead. Corelli countered with some ideas of his own: Puccini's *Manon Lescaut* and again *Otello*! (The exclamation point is from EMI's files.) Corelli's repeated insistence on *Otello* now convinced EMI he was ready, and they started to investigate the possibilities for the kind of setup Corelli had requested. But things were not going as either party desired. When Corelli subsequently asked to use one of his three contractual let-outs with a *Carmen* for RCA, EMI began to fear losing him completely and sent Victor Olof to talk things over with him. The surprising answer: "Corelli is happy with EMI and has no plans to defect to any other company."[43]

September 1962: Trouble in New York

After the satisfied Olof returned to London, trouble arose in New York, where Carlo Bergonzi was playing his part in the anti-Corelli campaign. Bergonzi felt mistreated by Bing, "who had always treated him as a second-rate tenor anyway, first as a filler for Del Monaco and now for Corelli." The proof: his wife had to beg for tickets that were almost standing room, whereas Mrs. Corelli was sitting in the orchestra section! Bing was at a loss; he had made Loretta swear that she would to keep her mouth shut about his generosity, but she instead used the ticket order to increase her prestige as the leading tenor's wife. Bing answered Bergonzi that if Loretta was sitting in the orchestra section, it was because her husband had the decency to buy his wife good seats. Meanwhile, he withdrew Loretta's ticket privileges. Bing's power play had no effect: when Loretta told Bauer that it would please Franco immensely if her seating arrangements were to be reinstated, they were. After all, a princess needed a decent seat![44]

With his wife newly restored to power, Franco suffered yet another attack from his archrival Del Monaco, who had given an interview to *Amica* that was filled with little poison arrows aimed straight at Corelli. Franco continued to tell Bauer he had also heard that Del Monaco planned to "accidentally" run into Bing in order to discuss a possible return to the Met. Next, Bing did indeed run into Del Monaco, who had "accidentally" booked a holiday on the same transatlantic cruise ship as he had, the *France*. Bing once more entered into serious negotiations with him,[45] with a by now predictable outcome: Loretta asked about the Met's plans for

Del Monaco. Bauer lied, claiming that he had heard nothing about any such plans. Loretta told him he'd better be right; naturally, they couldn't tell the Met whom to hire, but if Del Monaco ever returned to the Met, Bing would have to do without Franco.[46] Then, seemingly without stopping for breath, she demanded that all advertisements for Del Monaco's Decca recordings be removed from Corelli's Met programs and from the immediate vicinity of his Met performance posters. "Her husband" was irritated that Del Monaco's photo kept popping up in the context of Franco's own performances. When Del Monaco threatened to sue the Met on the grounds that the ban was an attack on his record sales, whereas they didn't harm Corelli's performances, Corelli observed that if he wanted his photo in the Met, all he had to do was to sing there himself.[47]

September 15–November 17, 1962: Great Singing, Lousy Opera

At intermission, his wife Loretta would barricade herself in his dressing room and scream at him, telling him everything he'd done wrong. She didn't shut up even when we were on-stage. I got so I would try to avoid going to extreme stage left or right, no matter what the blocking called for, because Signora Corelli was always in the wings, yelling at her husband in Italian and I'd have to concentrate like crazy to stay on track.

    Eileen Farrell on the 1962 *Chénier* run at the Met, in her autobiography
    Can't Help Singing, 1999

With only a single *Tosca* in Lugano left after the Pesaro performance, Corelli arrived well rested in New York for his imminent opening-night performance as Andrea Chénier. The "Improvviso" alone received a blasting twenty-minute ovation, according to the critic for the *New York Herald Tribune*, who hailed Corelli as "the new Caruso."[48] Harold C. Schonberg almost proved that claim when he wrote that neither Mrs. Farrell nor Mr. Corelli was daunted in the least by an eighty-plus-piece orchestra playing fortissimo: "They merely sing over them, and that is what they did in the Second Act duet. That B-flat was something to hear." Farrell was readily excused for having lost some of her former freshness, and Corelli's slight huskiness at the beginning (from a cold) soon disappeared. Merrill was instantly hailed as the likely successor to Leonard Warren's throne,

"THE WORLD'S GREATEST TENOR" • 261

vacant since the latter's tragic death onstage in March 1960. Even Cleva's conducting met with Schonberg's approval.

Since the performances left Schonberg without ammunition, he turned against the shabby, worn sets, which dated back to 1954. This was but the prelude to an attack on the opera itself: "Professionally pasted together without any real originality or much musical value." The half a dozen or so beautiful arias that he mentioned weren't enough to save Giordano from the *New York Times*'s axe. Not that the public cared; the performance and the opera were loudly cheered, confirms Donald DiGrazia, who went to applaud his new idol, this time bringing the whole family along:

A promotional shot of Corelli and Eileen Farrell in the Met's *Andrea Chénier*. Said Farrell: "During the reunion scene, Corelli grabbed me and kissed me right on the mouth." (Courtesy of the Metropolitan Opera Archives)

> My father, mother, Uncle Johnny, his wife, the whole bunch! Now Uncle Johnny, he had known Mario Del Monaco personally, but even he was impressed! At one point we all went backstage and for some reason it just clicked. Franco seemed to like the fact that we didn't come as individuals, but as a whole family. Our togetherness affected him and from then on we went to about each and every performance we could, continuing to see him backstage.[49]

October 15, 19, and 25; November 17, 1962
Umberto Giordano: *Andrea Chénier*
New York, Metropolitan Opera House (opening night)
Franco Corelli (*Andrea Chénier*), Eileen Farrell, Zinka Milanov [November 17] (*Maddalena di Coigny*), Robert Merrill, Anselmo Colzani [November 17] (*Carlo Gérard*), Rosalind Elias, Margaret Roggero [November 17] (*Bersi*), cond. Fausto Cleva

October 31, 1962: Meeting His Match

Corelli sang well, but not as well as I had.
   Louis Quilico, in Ruby Mercer, *The Quilicos*, 1991

Ruby Mercer's biography of the Quilicos is a detailed examination of the inner lives of opera singers, especially baritones. They are a proud race, but unfortunately the tenor and soprano usually take the solo bows when the curtain falls. Sometimes, though, the baritone, if he performed his evil part with grace, may be singled out as well.

But a baritone as great as Louis Quilico wouldn't mention those triumphs. His victories were defined by the times he outsang the tenor. Recalled Quilico:

> For his "Di quella pira," Corelli sang well, but not as well as I had. It was just one of those things that happen. Anyway, when we got to the end of the act, the stage director, Desiré Defrère, did a stupid thing. He decided that only Corelli would take a solo bow. So he went out and the public received him well. The second time too. But when he came out a third time the public screamed, "We want Quilico, we want Quilico!"[50]

The baritone gleefully recounts what (according to him) happened next. When they left the theater after the reception, those waiting there in line for the singers to come out cheered, "Oh, here comes Quilico, who stole the show from Corelli!" According to Quilico, this happened right in front of Franco and Loretta, who gave him a cold look. The very next day Quilico's contracts for recordings with Corelli and even for a non-Corelli project with Joan Sutherland were canceled. Because Sutherland recorded exclusively for Decca (apart from a single appearance with EMI in their 1959 *Don Giovanni*), Quilico can only be referring to the then upcoming RCA *Carmen* project, for that company was

---

October 31, 1962
Giuseppe Verdi: *Il Trovatore*
Philadelphia, Academy of Music
Lucille Udovick (*Leonora*), Franco Corelli (*Manrico*), Sandra Warfield (*Azucena*), Louis Quilico (*Count di Luna*), cond. Franco Patanè

still linked with Decca. According to Quilico, Corelli was the evil genius behind the cancellations: "Corelli had called the company and told them that 'If Quilico appears in any recording, I will not appear with you anymore.' So, because I had sung like an angel that night, it cost me two recordings!"[51]

November 9, 1962: The EMI Otello

The factors that lead a singer to perform well or to take on this or that role are very complex. Toward the end of 1962, Corelli was brooding over a number of things. Although his desire to persevere as Otello competed with such oddities as *Manon* and *Bohème*, there was one thing in favor of that Otello: it would mean bittersweet revenge on his now nearly mortal enemy. Just how adamant he was about settling the score is evident from a Philadelphia Lyric Opera program from November 9, 1962. Though the program was for a performance by another tenor, the opera's chairman, Aurelio Fabiani (also Franco's "general manager" at the Philadelphia Lyric and therefore effectively his employee's employee), made sure it included a full-page Angel advertisement for Franco's EMI recordings: "'Franco Corelli is the toast of the town. The tall and handsome tenor with the tall and handsome voice is regarded as the latter-day Caruso' (*New York Herald Tribune*). . . . 'One of the great living tenors' (*The New York Times*)." On page 22 another picture showed Corelli posing as Otello in an improvised costume. It was captioned: "CORELLI TO RECORD *OTELLO* ALBUM." Executives of Angel Records recently acknowledged plans to record the great tenor voice of Franco Corelli in Verdi's *Otello*, "one of Corelli's most famous

CORELLI TO RECORD "OTELLO" ALBUM
Executives of Angel Records recently acknowledged plans to record the great tenor voice of Franco Corelli in Verdi's "Otello", one of Corelli's most famous roles. Present plans of this world-wide recording firm call for a complete Angel album of Corelli's brilliant and exciting voice in the "Otello" role.

"Verdi's 'Otello,' one of Corelli's most famous roles." (Photo: Louis Melançon. Courtesy of the Metropolitan Opera Archives. Program reproduced by courtesy of the Philadelphia Lyric Opera)

roles. Present plans of this world-wide recording firm call for a complete Angel album of Corelli's brilliant and exciting voice in the *Otello* role."

The celebrated tenor in whose program that announcement was made was none other than Mario Del Monaco, and the opera advertised in the program was Mario's own Philadelphia *Otello*. One can imagine his reaction after Corelli's earlier veto of Del Monaco's advertisements in Corelli's Met programs. Giving Corelli more space in Mario's *Otello* program than Mario himself was already a daring act, but the deliberate insult of listing Otello as one of Corelli's most renowned roles was a deliberate attempt to drive him insane. Del Monaco surely would have gone mad, too—if he had ever seen the program. Those around him may have protected him from it, knowing his vulnerability on the C-word.

November 11, 1962: More Great Singing, Another Lousy Opera

The critic Raymond Ericson paraphrased Schonberg's notes on *Andrea Chénier* when he wrote a review of the celebrated Met premiere of *Ernani* with Corelli, Price, MacNeil, and Hines: "When an opera is not first-rate, there is one reason for its presentation—as a showcase for stellar singers." The audience disagreed, but his notion that the Met had nevertheless assembled just the right cast remains undisputed. On the vocal side, Ericson erupted in the sort of trumpeting about ringing and exciting voices that only American critics could write. He gladly forgave Corelli his exaggerated sobbing during the death scene, because his voice was irresistibly handsome and his singing in all that had come to pass before was extremely disciplined. Price sang superbly throughout, with agility and colorful *fioriture*: "Sometimes she

As Ernani at the Met, November 1962. (Photo: Louis Melançon. Courtesy of the Metropolitan Opera Archives)

> November 11, 14, and 22, 1962
> Giuseppe Verdi: *Ernani*
> New York, Metropolitan Opera House
> Franco Corelli (*Ernani*), Leontyne Price (*Elvira*), Cornell MacNeil (*Don Carlo*), Jerome Hines (*Don Ruy Gomez de Silva*), Margaret Roggero (*Giovanna*), Robert Nagy (*Don Riccardo*), Roald Reitan (*Jago*), cond. Thomas Schippers

lost her purity, but for the most part its beauty enriched the Verdian melodies and she provided some meltingly lovely moments in the final scene." Together with dramatic and thrilling singing from Hines and MacNeil, they largely compensated also for the production's odd and inconsistent sets.

November 13, 1962: Star Struck

Off-stage Corelli is like a schoolboy on holiday.
   Dick Owen, "He Started at the Top," *Coloroto Magazine*, October 14, 1962

With the added prestige of Franco's performances as Andrea Chénier and Ernani, the Corellis openly started to revel in their now-established fame and fortune. Franco (the man with no trivial hobbies) boasted to the press about his speedboat in star-studded Monte Carlo, which served to keep him in touch with the sea. Loretta chimed in, taking the female-fan legend one step further: "I 'find' fans for him. It is the womans who make a success, not the mans. Womans hold the world in her hands."[52] Franco matched that with *Coloroto*'s Dick Owen, adding that his favorite pastime after driving and singing was *amore*.[53] The *New York Post* balanced this human-interest factor with a few lines on his work in Milan with an eighty-one-year-old maestro, Arnaldo Schiavoni, with whom he searched the libraries for unjustly forgotten operas.[54] Said Corelli: "We search for the reasons. Is it because there was no tenor to sing them? If it is that, I look carefully through the score and try to conquer it. . . . In this way I brought back *The Huguenots* [and] *Poliuto*, and now I am to do *L'Africana* at La Scala."[55]

As Del Monaco's fans, during his Carnegie Hall recital of November 25, chanted "MDM back to the Met!," the Corellis left for Milan to claim their territory there as well, with Franco's unprecedented double opening of the Met and La Scala in the same season. In a photo in the December issue of *Look* magazine we see Corelli, in an impressive fur hat, waving goodbye to his American fans. The photo caption labeled him "a standout in a hair-seal topper (Cavanagh, $32)," with Franco striking a cloudy pose, his eyes fixed on imaginary troubles in a nonexistent studio sky. And yet, behind the questioning look, there is also the hint of a smile.[56]

December 7–30, 1962: A Memorable Double Date

Del Monaco was Del Monaco and he wanted to play the part of Del Monaco. Franco was a discreet man, while Del Monaco was a prima donna.
   Interview with Loretta Corelli, Milan, January 27, 2007

The Milanese theater had always been the foremost battlefield of rival prima donnas. The press had feasted for a decade on the Callas-Tebaldi feud, which culminated in Tebaldi's choosing to leave La Scala in 1954 and establish herself instead as the prima donna of the Metropolitan Opera, where she reigned unchallenged. However, after the Callas-Corelli *Poliuto* production in the 1960–61 season, little was heard of Callas professionally. With Callas on the wane and Tebaldi in America, the press turned to the *primi uomini*, the leading men: "Franco Corelli and Mario Del Monaco are the main rivals at the opening of the operatic season in Milan."[57]
   Del Monaco's situation was complex. Ten years earlier, when he was still in his prime, even a Corelli in top form would have had a tough nut to crack when faced with Del Monaco on his chosen ground. But since 1958–59 his voice had

---

December 7, 10, 13, 16, 20, 23, and 30, 1962
Giuseppe Verdi: *Il Trovatore*
Milan, Teatro alla Scala
Antonietta Stella (*Leonora*), Franco Corelli (*Manrico*), Fiorenza Cossotto (*Azucena*), Ettore Bastianini (*Count di Luna*), cond. Gianandrea Gavazzeni

lost flexibility and range owing to the unprecedented number of Otellos he had sung since 1950. With such former trump cards as Radamès, Calaf, and Andrea Chénier out of reach, his repertoire was mostly confined to Otello, Samson, Canio, and Don José. Normally there were escape routes for the losers in these battles, such as the one Tebaldi had taken to New York. But Corelli had not only defeated Del Monaco at La Scala, he had also shut him out of New York. The press thrived on the rivalry; *Sorrisi e Canzoni* went so far as to write that that they hoped both tenors would be "going at each other by all possible means!"[58]

That was precisely what happened. When the press questioned Corelli about the ongoing dispute, he insulted Del Monaco: "He has told the press that I ordered the Met not to spread his photograph, an accusation that is so ridiculous that it isn't worth discussing here. But I must admit that he is most sympathetic! Like all megalomaniacs."[59]

That was the atmosphere in which Corelli achieved his historic double opener.

Corriere della Sera focused on the audience, which discussed Franco's Manrico with as much gusto as the new sofas:

> "Is it true that these sofas were obtained on the black market? Does the blond hair look good on Corelli? Don't you think he looks as if he came straight out of an American college? Should Manrico be blond? Didn't Verdi create him as raven-haired?" Someone remembers an occasion where a standee shouted from the galleries: "You are the very soul of Verdi!" Elsewhere the "Pira" is discussed—will Corelli belt it out with gusto?[60]

When that last question was answered in the affirmative, Manrico, though a repeat performance from his 1959 run in the part at La Scala, confirmed Corelli's position as the dominant tenor in the coming decade. Ghiringhelli had spared no cost or effort to provide Corelli with optimal surroundings, as can be seen in the promotional photographs of the production. He also played the same fatherly role to his prized tenor as Bing did at the Met. For years now, it had been routine for Callas, Nilsson, Stella, Simionato, or Frazzoni to call for Ghiringhelli whenever the tenor wanted to run from the theater. Ghiringhelli would reassure the tormented Corelli, urging him on with the help of Loretta, the Corelli family (his father, brother, sister, and uncles often came to his aid at performances in Italy), and anyone else who might soothe Franco's nerves.[61] In this case it paid off very well, because the Milanese nobility, the ladies clad in jewel-spangled stoles, received Corelli's Manrico with the same unprecedented enthusiasm as Vienna had earlier. Full-page headlines that read "What a *Trovatore!*" or "Di quella pira, . . ." followed by such phrases as "inimitable," "passionate," and "to fall in love with," make further details superfluous. Milan kicked off the celebration of Verdi's 150th birthday in style.

CHAPTER 13 ❖ 1963

"Acclaimed the World's Greatest Tenor"

January 1963: *Otello* Defeated by the British Musicians' Union

Discussions of lost opportunities in the world of recordings often blame record companies for their stupidities. The singers themselves are just as often the cause of shattered projects. But sometimes neither of them is at fault. This was the case in the first and most promising chance to successfully record *Otello* with Corelli. After his repeated pleas to make arrangements that would give him relaxed recording conditions, EMI ultimately seized the opportunity, only to find themselves blocked by the British Musicians' Union in January 1963. The union argued that their rules would not allow them to record an opera by dubbing—that would violate the rights of the musicians.[1] With that, the *Otello* project was put on permanent hold, while *Andrea Chénier* and again *La Forza del Destino* came into view.[2] Still "perfectly happy," Corelli responded by informing EMI that he needed to be free to record with Joan Sutherland, Renata Tebaldi, Leontyne Price, and their very own house diva, Maria Callas.[3] At that moment, his list represented an interesting pick: Tebaldi was just about to cancel all her engagements, which led Bing to inquire whether Callas would be willing to take over her *Adriana Lecouvreur*s. Unfortunately for them, La Divina had just announced that she didn't want to sing opera any more for some time—if ever again.[4]

January 1963: Cheers for Cilea

I was as frightened as when I sang for President Kennedy.
Franco Corelli on the *Adriana Lecouvreur* premiere, in Christopher Howard, "Opera's Newest Tenor Is Sensational Success," *Diplomat*, January 1964

Cilea's opera had not been given at the Met since the days of Caruso. Bing's predecessor, Edward Johnson, loathed it so much that when he was forced to choose between his star soprano, Rosa Ponselle, and mounting *Adriana* for her, he preferred to let Ponselle walk out. That incident, which led Ponselle to give up her career at age forty-three,[5] had occurred exactly twenty-five years before Bing bowed for Tebaldi, giving her the much-desired premiere in this despised opera, which he judged a total failure. The gesture was doubtlessly Bing's greatest sacrifice to a singer ever, and when Tebaldi ultimately became indisposed because of overwork, there were no words sufficient to describe his despair. For any other opera they would simply have hired another soprano, but Bing was convinced that without Tebaldi he would be stuck with an unsellable stinker. Any other man would have turned to Magda Olivero at this point, but as has already been pointed out, Bauer considered her voice sour and utterly displeasing. They begged and pleaded with Tebaldi, who finally agreed to salvage the opening night and then see how far she could make it.

The January 1 premiere was a huge success with the public, though the critics once again judged the opera below Met standards. The agitated Tebaldi, Corelli, and Irene Dalis raised their voices in order to defend Cilea in a fifty-minute radio interview with Eric Salzman. Said Tebaldi: "*Adriana* may not be

---

January 1 and 28; February 1, 5, 9, and 13; April 14, 1963
Francesco Cilea: Adriana Lecouvreur
New York, Metropolitan Opera House
Renata Tebaldi, Mary Curtis-Verna [April 14] (*Adriana Lecouvreur*), Franco Corelli (*Maurizio*), Irene Dalis, Biserka Cvejic [February 1, 5, 9], Mignon Dunn [February 13] (*the Princess of Bouillon*), Anselmo Colzani (*Michonnet*), William Wildermann, Lorenzo Alvary [February 1] (*the Prince of Bouillon*), cond. Silvio Varviso

Franco Corelli at home studying in the early 1960s. (Courtesy of *Grand Hotel*/Casa Editrice Universo)

Right: Corelli as Pollione in Bellini's *Norma*, Verona, July 18, 1957. (Photo: Courtesy of the Arena di Verona)

Below: The brothers Franco and Ubaldo, as Cavaradossi and Sciarrone, bear a striking physical resemblance in the 1956 Gallone movie version of *Tosca*. (Still photo from film)

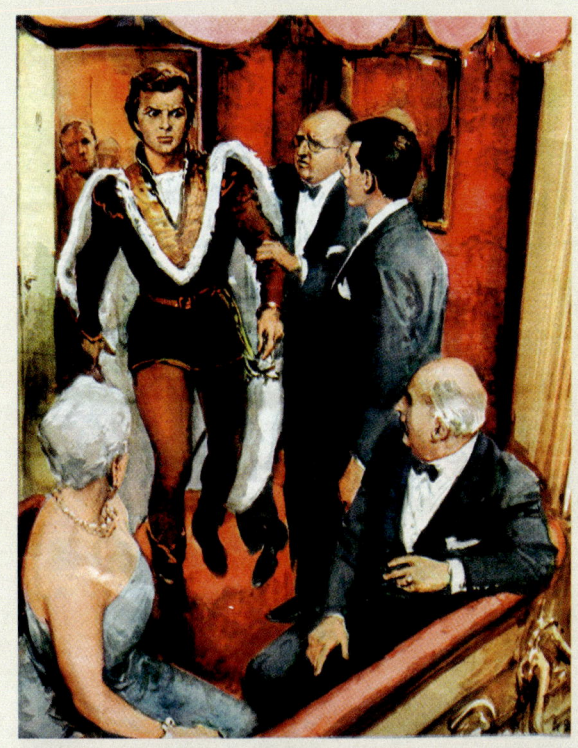

Left: *Grand Hotel*'s fanciful drawing of Corelli confronting Mario Improta after he booed Corelli during a Naples performance of *Il Trovatore*. Mario Falconi, *Tempo*, March 1, 1960. (Courtesy of *Grand Hotel*/Casa Editrice Universo)

Below: Corelli as Calaf in Verona, July 1958. (Courtesy of the Arena di Verona)

Top left: **Despite their heated arguments, Franco and Loretta were very much in love in 1964.** Says Arrigo Michelini: "There can be no doubt about that. Those who saw them only in their tempestuous moments did not have an accurate idea of their relationship." (Courtesy of Luigi Zoboli)

Top right: **Corelli in London, in May 1966, applying for a job at Her Majesty's court.** (Photo: Courtesy of Luigi Zoboli)

Middle: **Corelli visiting the DiGrazia apartment with John Ficarotta and his son, John Gary, April 1969.** (Photo: Courtesy of Donald DiGrazia)

Bottom: **Corelli and the DiGrazia family, in Miami, February 1966.** Said Donald DiGrazia: "By this time a genuine relationship had established, where I would bring my car around for every one of his performances." From left to right: Donald DiGrazia, Franco Corelli, and Donald's father, Dominique DiGrazia. (Courtesy of Donald DiGrazia)

OGGI ILLUSTRATO • 35

COLONNE ALTE 30 METRI New York. La facciata principale del nuovo Metropolitan. In primo piano, Corelli e la Tebaldi. L'inaugurazione del grandioso teatro d'opera è avvenuta con «Antonio e Cleopatra», su musica di Samuel Barber. Per dare un'idea dell'imponenza dello spettacolo e dell'ampiezza del palcoscenico (grande tre volte quello del vecchio «Met»), la trireme di Cleopatra, costruita con la consulenza di un archeologo, ha percorso sulla scena, azionata elettricamente, quasi quaranta metri. Le colonne di travertino che ornano la facciata principale del teatro sono alte una trentina di metri.

LA SALA PIÙ GRANDE DEL MONDO New York. Franco Corelli e Renata Tebaldi nella platea, che per ampiezza non è eguagliata da nessun altro teatro lirico; essa è capace di 3800 posti a sedere. La sera dell'inaugurazione una poltrona costava centocinquantamila lire. Sotto il palcoscenico è stato predisposto un montacarichi capace di sollevare al livello della scena pesi di ventitré quintali. Cinque ordini di palchi si affacciano sulla grande sala, che è stata costruita a forma di ferro di cavallo. Venti lampadari fanno corona a quello centrale, che è largo ben sei metri e che pesa undici quintali.

Corelli and Tebaldi showing off "their" new Met. (Photo: *Oggi Illustrato*, 1966. Reprinted by courtesy of RCS)

Enzo Grimaldo at the new Met, September 1966. (Photo: Louis Melançon. Courtesy of the Metropolitan Opera Archives)

Louis Melançon's official role photo of Corelli as Maurizio at the Met, September 1968.
(Courtesy of the Metropolitan Opera Archives)

Top left: Franco Corelli, Franco Enriquez, and Birgit Nilsson in *Turandot*, Macerata, July 4, 1970. (Photo: Courtesy of Birgit Nilsson)

Top right: Corelli practicing at his chalet in Cortina, August 1979. (Photo: Courtesy of Andrea Bucolier)

Bottom: Franco Corelli and Nicolai Gedda engaged in conversation; Viennese tenor gala, December 18, 1997. (Photo: Author)

the last word in opera, but I find it an interesting work also from a musical point of view, even though there are a few pages that leave something to be desired—but I find that even in Puccini. . . . What about the second act of *Bohème*?" Although he had resented singing Maurizio earlier in his career, Corelli jumped on Tebaldi's bandwagon. He couldn't understand why the opera had failed to please the Met in 1908—Caruso's only failure in his entire career there. With a wink to his illustrious predecessor, Corelli pointed to the work's triumphant current premiere: if it lacked something in the past, it apparently had that little something now![6]

When Salzman tried gently to poke a hole in their defense, the three artists pooh-poohed him. Corelli pointed out that all subsequent performances were sold out, which drew a haughty "See what I mean!" laugh from Tebaldi's lips. Changing the subject, Salzman asked whether there were other works of that epoch of interest. Tebaldi responded: "Giordano. And there is also Riccardo Zandonai with his *Giulietta e Romeo* and the famous *Francesca da Rimini*. One should know that opera because it's so beautiful!" "Which Tebaldi and I will do someday," said Corelli. Tebaldi was pleasantly surprised: "But Signor Corelli, why have you changed your mind? You always said no to that before!"[7]

❖❖❖❖❖

After her last *Adriana* on February 13, Tebaldi finally collapsed. She canceled her remaining *Adriana*s along with the entire remainder of her Met season. Mary Curtis-Verna stepped in for the final Met *Adriana*s on April 13 and found herself in one of the most memorable parts she had ever sung next to Franco: "Artistically it was probably the best thing I ever did at the Met. Varviso conducted so delicately and was so emotionally involved throughout that he gave you a magic carpet to sing on. And Corelli—there was an incredible electricity between us that evening."[8]

March 1963: "La Voce del Caprone"

In the spring of 1963 the EMI album *Franco Corelli in Opera and Song* (Italian title: *La Voce di Franco Corelli*) was released. It met with rave reviews. Concluded Bruno Slawitz: "In this album he gives a testimony of his enormous pro-gression and without a doubt it earns Corelli the right to take his place among the greatest tenors of all time."[9] However, one critical remark about his efforts simply has to be included here. The author, Del Monaco himself, was hardly a critic, but that couldn't lessen the fun when he started calling the Italian label that put out Corelli's recordings, La Voce del Padrone (His Master's Voice), "La Voce del Caprone" (the Voice of the Goat).[10]

This started the whole feud over again. An interview that Franco gave earlier about how happy he was in America and how well he got along with the most sympathetic Mr. Bing inspired Del Monaco to give a mirror interview to *Corriere Lombardo* titled "The Met? A Provincial Theater Compared to La Scala, Says Del Monaco." The interview appeared a few days before his imminent La Scala premiere as Don José, through which he hoped to regain his lost standing. Apparently he thought it wouldn't hurt to win the sympathy of the Milanese audiences. So he repeated that he left the Met because they couldn't afford him, adding that it was not a very satisfying theater to sing at, with respect to musical values: "Mostly they give routine performances. Totally incomparable to La Scala, which is the greatest theater in the world." So far his tirade was merely a barrage of defensive salvos, but his final words were curious in the light of his overall rant: "Nevertheless I will return to the Met next season."

Bing couldn't care less—he had never even heard of the *Corriere Lombardo* and already believed Del Monaco had lost his mind. Mario's frustration wouldn't have broken the fragile connection he still had to the Met's stage doors had he not chosen to introduce the passage quoted above by saying that these days "they" chose to let dogs sing in theaters (apparently even at La Scala). Whereas he, Del Monaco, sang the well-established repertoire, where the competition was fierce and the public critical, "they" now increasingly preferred to mount unknown operas that could easily be shortened and with key arias lowered. "Take for instance *Gli Ugonotti*. They shortened it by one and a half acts!"[11]

◆◆◆◆◆

While Bing was oblivious to something that was as obscure as the *Corriere Lombardo* was in New York, Corelli wasn't. The "Voce del Caprone" joke was already something he planned to avenge, but after the *Ugonotti* insult, he was not going to be satisfied until he had Del Monaco's balls. Aided by an election for Italy's most popular celebrities where he and Nicola Rossi-Lemeni came out on top of the opera scene,[12] he went to Bauer. Corelli spoke with him in the friendliest manner, agreed to any *Pagliacci* that Bing wanted for the 1963–64 season, and then reminded him of Bing's earlier promise that Del Monaco was not going to be in his plan for next season. Of course, Corelli wouldn't dream of dictating to Bing, but as it was, he was now only waiting for the first opportunity to knock Del Monaco down physically. That would obviously get him in trouble, and so he chose to protect himself from getting arrested by avoiding any theater where Del Monaco was also singing. Could Bauer please let him know the Met's plans for Mario as soon as possible? Then he, Corelli, could accept the lucrative offers that he had for the period he would otherwise have devoted to his good friend Mr. Bing.[13]

The Met pair tried to reassure Franco in general terms, hoping to get him to sign a fixed contract for a prolonged next season, but to no avail. In what was effectively the most brilliant soap opera of the 1960s, Bing ultimately lost his composure and brought his own vanity into the game, ranting that he was sick and tired of playing second fiddle to Ghiringhelli's lead. Why did Corelli always accept what La Scala wanted, even when Ghiringhelli happily engaged Del Monaco? Complained Bing to Bauer: "I find it difficult to understand, and, after the immense consideration and helpfulness that I have shown Franco in order to make it possible for him to oblige La Scala, both this season and next, I really feel it is not asking too much that he force La Scala to make their arrangements for once to help us."[14]

March 14–18, 1963: The Devil in Person

Poor Bing, playing second fiddle to Ghiringhelli and still having to see his prized trophy Corelli on the loose! Deeply insulted, Corelli organized yet another press conference, where he intended to speak about the situation up to and including the state of affairs at the Met. When a despairing Bauer tried to talk him out of it, Corelli made it clear that not only was he going on as planned, but he also expected Bauer to live up to his word. If he and Bing were telling him the truth about Del Monaco, they surely wouldn't mind confirming that at the press conference, where Franco expected his friend "Roberto" to stand beside him as the Met's official representative. The panicky Bauer remonstrated with him, but to no avail. Corelli, deeply insulted and mistrustful, demanded a vote of confidence: with me or against me? Ultimately, Bauer agreed on the promise that Franco would leave Bing out of the game, which he did. Bauer couldn't believe his luck. Even when he ran into journalists himself, who asked him about the reason for Del Monaco's prolonged absence from the Met, he got away with repeating Del Monaco's own statement that it was on "economic grounds." Some journalists doubted that this could be the case in a theater that could afford so many great singers at once, but they were left empty-handed with Bauer's simple reply: "No comment."[15]

The mysterious poster of the concert that was either given or planned with Mario Del Monaco and Carlo Scaravelli. It is not clear whether the concert ever materialized, but if it was at least intended, the link is clear: Scaravelli was a teacher whose singing career was restricted to local performances and the Bellini Chorus. Why would Mario Del Monaco appear in concert with him if not as a token of gratitude? (Courtesy of Alessandro Scaravelli)

Whether the vigor of Corelli's counterattack was inspired by an aching tooth that needed to be operated on or not,[16] it certainly was perfectly timed; the press conference occurred just a few hours before Del Monaco's crucial La Scala premiere as Don José in *Carmen*. Perhaps the whole situation that erupted from his initial attack on Corelli backfired when the moment of truth arrived, or perhaps he was simply indisposed (a claim made by Giulietta Simionato in Elisabetta Romagnolo's biography of Del Monaco), but either way, Del Monaco's Don José ended in disaster. The former King of Tenors received numerous catcalls, and riots erupted afterward when some angry *loggionisti* confronted him at the artists' exit because at the end of the opera he had shaken his fist at them. His wife, Rina, punched some women and trampled some hats, while her beleaguered husband threatened to use violence on whoever came near. Bauer told Bing: "I don't think we have to worry about Del Monaco anymore, as I can't see how he can ever return at La Scala after this." The reviews were predictably devastating.

Possibly the *loggionisti* were right—Mario should have controlled himself more onstage as well as off. But it was a sad and uncalled-for exit for one of the greatest dramatic tenors ever to grace the world's stages. To make clear to Ghiringhelli what his options were, Corelli refused to step in for Del Monaco, who had left all his remaining *Carmen* obligations behind. With that, Del Monaco's mockery of Corelli changed to unconcealed hatred. According to his son Giancarlo, Mario's endless outbursts actually led the boy to believe that Franco really was the devil in person. The Del Monacos lived very near the Corellis, so one day Giancarlo decided to knock on their door in order to see for himself what the devil looked like:

> I passed by their door, stopped, and rang the bell. A voice through the intercom asked: "Who is it?" I said: "Del Monaco." The door opened and I went up. When I entered Corelli said sternly: "Who are you? I expected someone else." I explained that I was Del Monaco junior, and they offered me a drink. They were most friendly to me, and Corelli didn't look a bit like the devil I had imagined. He was wearing slippers and was dressed in a dressing gown with a Japanese sort of print. After fifteen minutes or so I went back home. I was late, so they asked where I had been. My answer started the argument all over again.[17]

❖❖❖❖❖

In the past, when he had questions about vocal matters, Del Monaco would turn to his teacher, Arturo Melocchi, but Melocchi had died in 1960. And so, at his darkest hour, something incredible happened: supposedly Del Monaco asked Corelli for advice. According to Marco Corelli, Franco knew but one answer, and that was to recommend Mario to Carlo Scaravelli, who had once passed Melocchi's technique on to Franco himself. Said Alessandro Scaravelli: "Del Monaco then consulted my father. He was so grateful afterward that he invited my father to perform in a concert of arias and duets with him. I still have the poster."[18]

Giancarlo Del Monaco didn't recall his father asking Corelli for help and thought it very unlikely. On the other hand, he did not have an explanation for the poster for a German recital that billed Mario Del Monaco right next to Carlo Scaravelli in a joint aria and duet performance at the congress hall of the German Museum in Munich on May 11, 1963. According to Giancarlo, his father may well have consulted Scaravelli around that time, although he believed not much could be made of that: "My father consulted so many specialists in the field."[19]

March–April 1963: Spring Cleaning

Emerging victorious from all the ruptures in those first months of the winter, Franco decided it was time for general spring cleaning. He answered Bing's accusations of disloyalty by stating that he had refused some extra *Trovatore*s in Milan on the grounds that Del Monaco was singing there. La Scala had to get Umberto Borso to do them, which resulted in a number of empty seats. Bing's complaint about his tenor always doing what La Scala wanted was answered with a letter from the Italian Minister of Culture, who, at Ghiringhelli's instigation, scolded Corelli for spending too much time in America. With two months for La Scala and four at the Met, Bing surely had no reason to complain. Franco meanwhile had also informed Ghiringhelli that from now on he too had to choose between him and Del Monaco. There would be no Corelli in La Scala's planned 1964 tour to Moscow if Del Monaco were included.[20] Having settled his affairs in that arena, he settled a score with his record company as well. After all the failed plans, it was high time he and EMI landed some successful projects. When they discussed new possibilities in March, the usually fatal Shakespearean ides suddenly breathed life into their plans with *Tosca* and *Il Trovatore* (with Régine Crespin as the soprano lead). In addition, he was to record *Aida* (with Galina Vishnevskaya). Corelli welcomed the prospects but wanted some more important matters dealt with first. His primary grievances concerned the British tax authorities. He was so angry over their position that he demanded his U.K. contract be changed to an Italian one.[21]

The matter was settled when he signed up with Sandor Gorlinsky, who handled the royalties for him from then on.[22] A new exclusive agreement, this time a Swiss contract, was signed on April 10, 1963, guaranteeing four complete operas during the contract period of four years, as well as two solo LPs per annum. The reserved operas were now *Tosca, Il Trovatore, Aida, Otello, La Fanciulla del West, Manon Lescaut, Un Ballo in Maschera,* and *Turandot,* while his let-out clause was extended to five operas.[23]

April–June 1963: The Met Spring Tour

With Tebaldi indisposed, the planned Met Spring Tour performances of *Adriana Lecouvreur* were replaced by *Tosca,* after the usual discussions with Corelli.

Bing had wanted to replace the work with *Aida*, but Loretta maintained that Maurizio was sort of a "vacation role" for Franco, and she wouldn't have it exchanged with something as difficult as Radamès. The cities complained as well, with Boston asking whether it was given "a fair yodel in replacements" when comparing Tebaldi, a living legend, to Gabriella Tucci and Mary Curtis-Verna. The question was answered when the Met train finally left Boston and the papers looked back at "A Night of Full Glory by the Metropolitan." Thanks to the support of Bing and Bauer in his feud with Del Monaco, Boston's virile

April 16, Boston, John B. Hynes Civic Auditorium
April 23, Cleveland, Public Auditorium
May 23, Detroit, Masonic Temple Auditorium
Giacomo Puccini: *Tosca*
Gabriella Tucci, Mary Curtis-Verna [April 23, May 23] (*Tosca*), Franco Corelli (*Cavaradossi*), Anselmo Colzani (*Scarpia*), cond. Silvio Varviso

April 18, Boston, John B. Hynes Civic Auditorium
May 4, Atlanta, Civic Auditorium
May 11, Dallas, State Fair Music Hall
Ruggero Leoncavallo: *Pagliacci*
Eileen Farrell (*Santuzza*), Franco Corelli (*Turiddu*), cond. Fausto Cleva

May 17, Boston, John B. Hynes Civic Auditorium
May 25, Detroit, Masonic Temple Auditorium
Pietro Mascagni: *Cavalleria Rusticana*
Teresa Stratas (*Nedda*), Franco Corelli (*Canio*), Morley Meredith (*Alfio*), cond. Fausto Cleva

June 2, 1963
New York, Voice of Firestone (black-and-white telecast)
Mascagni: *Cavalleria Rusticana* "Intanto amici . . . Viva il vino spumeggiante," "Mamma, quel vino è generoso." Di Capua: "I' te vurria vasà." Puccini: *Turandot* "Non piangere, Liù." d'Annibale: "'O paese d' 'o sole." Firestone: "In My Garden"
Franco Corelli, cond. Wilfrid Pelletier

Cavaradossi subsequently became the "dashing Canio" of Atlanta and the savior of opera as, once more, Cavaradossi in Cleveland.[24]

These were the sort of headlines that made Bing so meek when it came to his champ's extravagant demands, although it should be noted that these reviews were balanced by an increasingly critical reaction to Corelli's acting. The *Cleveland Press*, for example, noted that he had but to open his mouth and the gorgeous sound came out, but added: "He doesn't bother to act very much—he doesn't need to."[25] To most, such details mattered but little. Local stories about the tour always emphasized extrinsic matters. Dallas marveled about "Big, Bad Tenor Corelli Picture of Calm, Charm,"[26] while Cleveland focused on its pre-Met party: "No matter what weather was outside Public Hall, in the pavilion it was spring."[27]

Springtime it was for the singers as well, who tried their best to turn the tour into a school class on holiday. Said Mary Curtis-Verna, Corelli's Tosca in Cleveland and Detroit: "We were like a family. The boys had a place where they would go in and play poker and there was always gossiping here and there. It was always a pleasure, a happy experience. And then when we'd go to Dallas in the South, we'd stay at a hotel that had a swimming pool. Of course, when you had a performance, you wouldn't show up at that pool but everybody else showed up. It was fun!"[28] With so many team-building activities going on in between performances, one wishes Franco could have relaxed a little more, especially because performance demands on tour were not the same as in New York. But he never showed up at any poker table or pool, even though he had once been a champion swimmer. As Curtis-Verna mentioned, his throat had become his bank, and he was all too aware of the risks of catching a cold. And so, while complaining about the primitive logistics, he either locked himself in his room with Loretta or, whenever there was enough time in between performances, headed straight back to New York. And he eventually contracted a cold anyway. It affected his performances during the last part of the tour, although it didn't prevent him from fulfilling his obligations. Neither did it affect his Voice of Firestone performance, broadcast nationwide on June 2.

June–July 1963: A Very Moribund *Chénier*

The June recordings in Milan of the album *Franco Corelli Sings Great Religious Songs & Arias* and in Rome of the complete *Andrea Chénier* were less easily

> June–September 1963
> Milan (EMI recording)
> *Franco Corelli Sings Great Religious Songs & Arias*
> Niedermeyer: "Pietà, signore." Schubert: "Ave Maria." Handel: *Serse* "Ombra mai fu." Tortorella: "Ave Maria." Wagner: *Wesendonck-Lieder* "L'ange." Verdi: *Messa da Requiem* "Ingemisco." Attributed to John Francis Wade: "Adeste fideles." Bach/Gounod: "Ave Maria." Mozart: "Ave verum corpus." Rossini: *Petite Messe solennelle* "Domine Deus." Bizet: "Agnus dei." César Franck: "Panis angelicus."
> Cond. Raffaele Mingardo
>
> June–July 1963
> Umberto Giordano: *Andrea Chénier*
> Rome, Teatro dell'Opera (EMI recording)
> Franco Corelli (*Andrea Chénier*), Antonietta Stella (*Maddalena di Coigny*), Mario Sereni (*Carlo Gérard*), Stefania Malagù (*Bersi*), Luciana Moneta (*Countess di Coigny*), Anna Di Stasio (*Old Madelon*), cond. Gabriele Santini
>
> 1963
> New York (Firestone recording)
> César Franck: "Panis Angelicus." Adolphe Adam: "O Holy Night."
> Cond. Joe Harnell

made than Corelli's impassioned singing suggests. He had not gotten over the cold he caught during the Spring Tour and managed to convince himself it was pneumonia. When his doctor told him it was just a neglected cold, he became convinced that it was cancer. With that perspective in mind, his emotional abandon in the religious arias is put in perspective, while his rendering of Chénier becomes an impassioned and utterly melancholic farewell to the world. Antonietta Stella was there to face the guillotine with him once again, though she suffered from some of his less romantic outbursts as well; there seems to have been no other recording during which Franco was this agitated.[29]

Upon his return to Milan, Franco spent two days with Bauer, with whom he balanced out his career: he hadn't had a holiday for five years and declared that he was suffering from a nervous breakdown. Intending to calm him down, Bauer and Loretta told him he was right—he deserved a break. The outcome was downright dramatic. Said Bauer: "He suddenly cancelled everything. (Busseto, Cannes, the recording of *I Puritani* in Florence and now also Salzburg.) As I said, there's absolutely nothing wrong with his voice, it's just his nerves."[30] Bauer had a point: the *Chénier* recording met with rave reviews, and even *Gramophone* judged Corelli to be "in sumptuous form."[31]

July–August 1963: The Mysterious Disappearance of *Guglielmo Tell*

If it is correct to place the following events around this time, it was a decisive month for Corelli's career. All evolves around the allegedly intended La Scala opening night with Corelli as Arnoldo in *Guglielmo Tell*. He continued his studies of the part over the summer while he was on his annual inhalation therapy in Salsamaggiore/Tabiani, just thirty-seven miles from Milan. There Corelli made a grave mistake:[32] instead of staying in Tabiani and letting the therapy do its healing work, he went back and forth to Milan, where he worked on *Tell* every night,[33] even though the intensive therapy required that he refrain from singing for a full twenty days to protect his throat.[34] The therapy softened the vocal cords; singing during this period would mean forcing them. According to Corelli, that was precisely what happened.[35] In the beginning he felt very good, because his throat was relaxed, but after some time his vocal cords began to swell, and he gave up on *Tell* altogether.[36] His friend Arrigo Michelini adds that Lauri-Volpi also played a part in Corelli's decision to bury Arnoldo and some other roles:

> Lauri-Volpi pointed out to him that for Arnoldo in *Tell* and Arturo in *I Puritani* you simply need a natural top, not a constructed one, as was Corelli's. Oh, he had the high notes, don't get me wrong, but they were not like Lauri-Volpi's, who hardly had to work for them! Franco's top was the result of meticulous study and hard work. But the main difference here was the style: Lauri-Volpi sang these parts with superb control of emission, in an old-fashioned style, balancing volume and dynamics, aiming for purity. Franco couldn't do that. He sang Arnoldo just as he had sung *Il Pirata*, *Poliuto*, *Ugonotti*, and all the other operas. Lauri-Volpi eventually pointed out to him that singing *Tell*,

Puritani, and also *Manon Lescaut* with Corelli's emotional involvement was bound to ruin his voice.[37]

Thus, Corelli's *Guglielmo Tell* piano rehearsals from 1961 now stand as both his last word on Arnoldo and a distant echo of what was lost in Tabiani.

◆◆◆◆◆

While on his cherished holiday in Cortina, Bauer managed to talk the Corellis out of visiting the Bings, who were staying in the same area—he even managed to escape from having to visit them himself. But he couldn't get out of Corelli's forty-five-minute tirade against the way the Met handled him these days. He smelled a plot against him by Sutherland, who was scheduled for a *Norma* run for which he wasn't considered, and complained about the way he was advertised. At the Met he suddenly felt like just a singer among singers, whereas Italian theaters were accustomed to asking him which soprano and conductor he desired for any given production. Corelli also complained about having to sing with small-voiced sopranos such as Stratas and Tucci; he had to hold back in volume opposite them, which made it look as if he were in decline. His preferred sopranos were Price, Nilsson, Farrell, Rysanek, Tebaldi, Milanov, and Sutherland. Under the circumstances, that last unsolicited recommendation surprised Bauer, who reported home that no one had to worry: "Obviously he has little at hand during his holiday and then he starts brooding over such trivia, to which the heat adds the rest. After three-quarters of an hour of this sort of talk, Loretta told me that it had been a delightful conversation and asked me to give you their best regards—she even wished me well with my leg."[38]

August–September 1963: The First Visit to Giacomo Lauri-Volpi

Besides being a singer, Giacomo Lauri-Volpi was also a renowned writer. Books, articles, and columns flowed from his pen in abundance. One column dealt with Corelli's first visit to Lauri-Volpi's home in Burjassot, near Valencia, Spain, in the late summer of 1963. According to Lauri-Volpi, Corelli was caught up in the middle of an artistic conflict regarding his vocal technique and his breathing. On top of that, he had developed a more general conflict of conscience about his merits that left him disappointed and pessimistic, despite all his achievements. Lauri-Volpi blamed the maddening world of modern opera for this, adding that it was almost inevitable that Corelli would eventually develop metaphysical doubts. At that point he quoted Dante's *Divina Commedia*, writing that Corelli threatened to stray from the narrow path before him: "He had no more control over certain quotes from famous books. And he arrived at a point where he could no longer count on himself and his future. That is when he decided to consult an old veteran, familiar with the golden age of bel canto. He arrived here in his Ferrari, symbol of existential hurry: hurry to learn, know, so he could decide if he would continue or stop."[39]

According to Marco Corelli, who remembers the story as Franco told it to him later in life, Franco greeted Lauri-Volpi, saying he had a problem with his voice. Lauri-Volpi shrugged his shoulders and asked him to sing, so he could hear what the problem was. When Franco finished, the older tenor shook his head: "And you are coming to me! I should be coming to you!"[40] These words are confirmed by the veteran, who, in his column, readily admits that his most important task was to exorcise his younger colleague's inferiority complex. To achieve this, he pretended to take Corelli at his word, bombarding him with morning sessions of tryouts, tryouts, and more tryouts, larded with imitations and discussions, and listening to examples. Said Lauri-Volpi:

> Fifteen days in a row, three hours a day, from eleven to two, he subjected me, with me accompanying on the piano, (the photo proves it) to the ungrateful task of singing the most renowned arias of my repertoire. From *Guglielmo Tell* to *Puritani*, from *Gioconda* to *Ugonotti*, from *Turandot* to the Puccinian *Manon*. Always with full voice, while being seated. And he repeated everything, perhaps a little shy at first, but with more suppleness and freedom thereafter. In the end he imitated me so perfectly, that anyone passing by wouldn't have been able to tell who of us was singing.[41]

✦✦✦✦✦

Corelli returned to the EMI studios to finish his religious arias album, which he had left unfinished in June. He actually had run through some of the arias (i.e., the Bach-Gounod "Ave Maria") with Lauri-Volpi, who himself had recorded a few of these titles in his younger years.[42]

November 18–27, 1963: *Carmen* and the Man Who Shot JFK

When Corelli approached EMI to let him record *Carmen* opposite Leontyne Price, with Herbert von Karajan conducting for RCA, Walter Legge had mixed feelings. He had hoped to record Corelli in *Carmen* for EMI opposite Maria Callas, but at the time there were no firm plans as far as Callas was concerned, and so Corelli, exercising the first of his three let-outs, accepted RCA's offer.[43] Legge was not the only one who felt ambivalent about this project, which somehow dragged half the recording industry into competition. A rupture over payments between Herbert von Karajan and Decca/RCA jeopardized their partnering, leaving a few orchestral pieces for Decca and the RCA *Carmen* to record. At the same time, Decca New York blew the whistle on the partnership with RCA and demanded that John Culshaw, producer of the RCA *Carmen*, get them a *Carmen* recording first. In a rush he assembled what his highly controversial and much-disputed autobiography *Putting the Record Straight* lists as an ill-fated recording. According to Culshaw, the right protagonists had already been hired by RCA, and with the leftovers the recording wouldn't even match the old one under Thomas Beecham. Culshaw even contemplated a stunt in getting Edith Piaf to record it, but finally settled for Regina Resnik as Carmen plus Joan Sutherland (minus her husband, Richard Bonynge, for once) as Micaëla. For the tenor part the Decca Classical boss, Maurice Rosengarten, wanted Giuseppe Di Stefano, whom he remembered as the greatest José he ever saw on stage. But before that could even be arranged, an unexpected volunteer appeared in Decca's Swiss office: "Del Monaco . . . was smarting because he had heard of the

> **November 18–27, 1963**
> **Georges Bizet: *Carmen***
> **Vienna, Sofiensaal (RCA recording)**
> Leontyne Price (*Carmen*), Franco Corelli (*Don José*), Robert Merrill (*Escamillo*), Mirella Freni (*Micaëla*), Monique Linval (*Frasquita*), Geneviève Macaux (*Mercédès*), Jean-Christophe Benoît (*Dancaïre*), Maurice Besançon (*Remendado*), Frank Schooten (*Zuniga*), Bernard Demigny (*Moralès*), Vienna Philharmonic, cond. Herbert von Karajan; producer, John Culshaw

RCA project with his much younger rival Corelli. . . . Del Monaco and his wife stormed into Zurich and created hell in Rosengarten's office. If only to get rid of them Rosengarten gave him the part."[44]

A risky detail was that Culshaw was the producer of both sets (the Decca set was completed first in a race to the market). The RCA effort started on November 18, with Corelli appearing in Vienna on time. Culshaw introduced him to a French language coach who was to follow him throughout in an effort to improve his pronunciation. Then he handed Corelli his recording schedule, whereupon the tenor wanted to know when the Flower Aria was due. Culshaw explained that he had put it in the middle to give him time to adapt to the Sofiensaal's acoustics. Then Loretta stepped in, much smaller than Rina Del Monaco but with the same kind of penetrating voice, and without even the most basic charm: "Ma Franco, e no singa da 'Flower Aria.'" Culshaw saw Franco's face begin to twitch in a way that became very familiar to the crew over the next few weeks whenever Loretta was around. When Culshaw asked where he wanted the Flower Aria to be scheduled, Loretta answered: "E maka da song when *I* say e maka da song. E no ready yet."[45]

The recording process went fairly smoothly with the team, minus Corelli, who mostly kept to himself. He simply did his job, belting out powerful notes in between rapid-fire conversations in Italian with Loretta, during which the French coach tried to listen in. But Franco refused to put his head in the French-language books, and the coach's efforts—she attempted to follow him into the control room while exaggeratedly mouthing the words and gesturing broadly—were wasted on him. Culshaw let it all pass. He allowed himself simply to be amused by the scene of the gesticulating voice coach running after Corelli with Loretta on her tail, waving her arms in the air and shrieking in Italian dialect at the top of her voice: "Anyone able to witness those exits would be forgiven for thinking he was in a madhouse."

Things proceeded in that fashion until the evening of Friday, November 22. Culshaw was celebrating Benjamin Britten's fiftieth birthday with colleagues in a restaurant. While discussing the performance of Britten's *Gloriana* (which was on in London at that moment in honor of the composer), a waitress came to their table and informed them that something had happened to President Kennedy. Reports were contradictory, so the group went back to the Sofiensaal, where they had a decent television set. On the way it became clear that there had been an assassination attempt, and by the time they arrived they knew that even if the president survived, he would be in a vegetative state. Culshaw's first thought was of Leontyne Price. Like other African Americans, she had had great hopes of the liberal president. Fearing she might be in shock and wanting to comfort her if necessary, he went looking for her. At the entrance of the State Opera he stumbled on an ashen-faced Corelli, who had interrupted his dinner, his mind set on exactly the same mission. Wrote Culshaw: "Whatever reservations I may have had about Corelli's behavior evaporated in that moment: he was a decent man trying to search out a colleague in trouble and offer what help he could."[46]

✦✦✦✦✦

Karajan was enraptured by Corelli for other reasons. Hearing the tenor's newfound vocal flexibility, he exclaimed: "What have you done? You are another Corelli. Magnificent." The answer may well be found in Lauri-Volpi's article "A lezione dal veterano," where he claims much of the credit.[47] With so much praise for Corelli as a singer and a human being, all seemed bound to culminate into a grand finale when the time finally came to record the Flower Aria. It was the very last piece left to record, at a moment where even the problem of the French was abandoned; any improvement would contradict with the parts already recorded. Then, like a jack-in-the-box, up popped Loretta, demanding an extra $1,000 because Franco had had to put so much extra effort into his French lessons! Culshaw burst out laughing, but at the head office all hell broke loose. Lawyers were put to work, and Culshaw feared getting caught in the middle. He had already had his fill of Rosengarten, who had wanted him to pay singers under the table, in cash. So when the head office wanted Culshaw to get Corelli to fulfill his contract as signed, he informed them that he was assigned to supervise only the recording, not the payments, and switched off his phone. The very next morning Corelli appeared in the best of moods, recorded a glorious Flower Aria, and proceeded to order champagne for the whole crew.[48]

✦✦✦✦✦

Vienna, and the $1,000 bonus wrung from RCA, inspired Corelli to settle any remaining scores with EMI as well. He informed EMI's Viennese representative, a Miss Meshkolitsch that:

1. He did not like the *Andrea Chénier* recording and would never record another opera; and
2. He had been offered *Il Trovatore* by Decca opposite Joan Sutherland. Why couldn't EMI make it with him using Gabriella Tucci, who had just sung it in Vienna with great success?

Apart from the fact that he had recently mentioned Tucci's voice as ill-matched to his own, the two statements in that order give a pretty clear picture of an overheated tenor's mind. Meshkolitsch seemingly had a ball with Corelli, simply following him wherever he wanted to go: *Tosca* with Crespin? *Aida* with Callas or Stella? *Il Trovatore* with Crespin or Stella? *I Puritani* with Mirella Freni? A popular recital album of Mario Lanza repertoire and a duet recording with Maria Callas? You name it!

A few days after the meeting with Meshkolitsch, Victor Olof dropped in. He reported from Vienna that the duet album with Maria Callas was still on, to be recorded in Paris by June 1964. *Il Trovatore* was on as well, to which now were added *Tosca* with Crespin, Gobbi, and Prêtre for July 1964 and *Aida* with Tucci (said Olof: "Much preferred to Crespin") and Schippers in September 1965. Olof saved the most interesting developments for the end: *Don Carlo* with Callas and Giulini some time in 1965, *Otello* with Tucci (according to Olof, "Again much preferred to Crespin") in 1966. At that stage Olof had already discussed the *Otello* plans with the conductor Sir John Barbirolli, but that name didn't stir much enthusiasm with Franco and Loretta:"Barbirolli's name is completely unknown to them, also, they say, he is unknown as an opera conductor in the USA."[49] Corelli's idea of "negotiations" is clear from his general ideas on the subject of conductors in what he clearly regarded as "his" recordings: he would accept Schippers, Giulini, Erede, or Santini and *basta*. Olof then pinned Giulini like a butterfly to *Otello*.[50]

November 26, 1963: Close Encounter with Giuseppe Di Stefano

Giuseppe Di Stefano, Callas's steady partner before Corelli gradually took over that role, was hired for a performance of Verdi's *Un Ballo in Maschera* by the Philadelphia Lyric Opera on the evening of November 26, 1963. Although well past his prime now, he garnered a mix of bad reviews with occasional performances that hinted at the great tenor he had been and still could be, in the proper repertoire. Despite his diminished powers, he managed to stay a public favorite, regardless of what the critics wrote. Like Del Monaco's, his name had acquired a legendary ring during the first postwar decade, when Italy was desperately looking for a new identity, for sons of whom it could still be proud. Di Stefano's Sicilian charm, his sunny appearance, and his loyalty to the Italian public continued to make him fierce competition there, even for a Corelli in top form. However, in Philadelphia, things were not what they had been in the Italian provinces, where Corelli had long since ceased to sing, and so it happened that Di Stefano's smiling eyes turned dark and angry when they saw page 4 of his very own *Ballo in Maschera* program. This page featured the usual full-page Franco Corelli ad, but with a slight deviation from the usual text, in which EMI presented him as *one* of the world's leading tenors. This time EMI had no say in the matter, because the page was Aurelio Fabiani's advertisement for Franco's upcoming performances in *Gioconda*, *Tosca* (which he ultimately canceled), and a very early *Roméo et Juliette*. The accompanying text contained precisely the lines Corelli had once demanded from EMI: "Franco Corelli, Acclaimed the World's Greatest Tenor."

The inferno that John Gutman had feared for the Met when Corelli had first demanded these lines now broke loose in Philadelphia, where Di Stefano erupted in an authentic Sicilian *tarantella tempestuoso*: "It's an insult! Who says Corelli is the greatest tenor in the world? A critic? That would be fine, but damned if it wasn't you, Aurelio Fabiani! You're his manager, aren't you. You really think Bing would ever print a program that claims Price or Nilsson [is] the greatest soprano in the world on a night that Tebaldi is singing?" According to a Flemish newspaper that printed an eyewitness account of the event, the crowd followed the fuming Di Stefano and his wife, Maria, all the way to the parking lot, begging him to reconsider. One moment he seemed to reconsider, the next he got into his car and threatened to drive off. Then a policeman intervened: "I beg you, Mr. Di Stefano: I was so happy to be assigned to work here tonight, which would give me the opportunity to hear you sing." Another voice promised him to pick up all the programs so that nobody would see the ad. Wrote the reporter: "The stage personnel then collected the programs, and Di Stefano appeared. But because of the bright stage lights, he couldn't see that afterward, the programs were redistributed."[51]

December 7–17, 1963: Another Car Crash

It is the first time I perform Cavalleria Rusticana *except for an experimental recital in Vienna. Strangely enough, whenever I inaugurate a season at La Scala I have to sing an opera that I've never sung before. This is my fifth inauguration, so this is my fifth first-time opera. Despite being a Sicilian bull, my Turiddu is sentimental. Together with the director we tried to polish Turiddu's character.*
   Franco Corelli at the *Cavalleria* rehearsals, on RAI Television, December 1963

On December 7 Corelli inaugurated a fifth La Scala season, this time as Turiddu in *Cavalleria Rusticana*. It was his fourth consecutive La Scala opening in a row and an unprecedented coup, but despite the jubilant reviews, Mascagni's one-act opera cannot be compared to the challenge of *Guglielmo Tell* or a dozen other operas that would have added more substantially to his laurels. Given the defensive way he minimized his Viennese *Cavalleria* debut in September in the RAI television interview quoted above (not even mentioning his Spring Tour performances in Minneapolis and Detroit earlier in the year), he must have sensed this himself. He treats the opera like Don José's contraband, smuggled into La Scala for three performances in preparation for the real fireworks of *Fanciulla del West* in January.

Although 1963 proved to be a turning point for Corelli in a number of ways, it turned out to be even more of one for another tenor. Like Franco, Mario Del Monaco was an enthusiastic driver, and six days after Franco's La Scala premiere Del Monaco suffered a nearly fatal car accident. He survived the impact but was severely injured, and it took him many months to recover. Bing suggests that Corelli might actually have sent his rival a letter of sympathy, stressing his personal grief over this tragic turn of events.[52] After all, this was not the way Corelli had dreamed of vanquishing his rival.

> **December 7, 10, and 17, 1963**
> **Pietro Mascagni:** *Cavalleria Rusticana*
> **Milan, Teatro alla Scala**
> Giulietta Simionato (*Santuzza*), Franco Corelli (*Turiddu*), Gian Giacomo Guelfi (*Alfio*), cond. Gianandrea Gavazzeni

CHAPTER 14 ❖ 1964

Toward a Lyric Repertoire

January 7–25, 1964: A Milanese Walkout

Every tenor thinks of himself as a prima donna.
   Antonietta Stella, telephone interview, May 25, 2006

In politics, scandals are seldom good, whereas in opera, anything that can stir things up seems to draw the crowds. Usually the scandals are clashes between singers and conductors, or between either one of them and the management. Not so at La Scala's *Fanciulla del West* premiere of January 7, 1963, where the soprano walked out on her tenor because she hadn't met him in rehearsal. The soprano was Antonietta Stella, and when La Scala's management issued a press release saying that she was suddenly indisposed, she duly informed the press of the disease that went by the name of Franco Corelli. Said Stella: "For me there exists a question of professional ethics and of artistic seriousness that prevents me from maintaining further relations with Signor Corelli." Beyond insisting that her personal prestige was at stake, she refused to comment further, which left the journalists with another hot-blooded case of "Corelli-itis." The *New York Post* ran the story under the resounding headline "Singer Exits, Can't Stand the Tenor."[1]

As it turned out, La Scala had little to complain about. Gigliola Frazzoni proved to be a more than able replacement who willingly followed Corelli's every move. By now Corelli had developed his own ideas about the parts in which he was considered the reigning divo, and after more than thirty performances in *Fanciulla del West*, Dick Johnson was clearly one of them—hence his skipping rehearsals. Last but not least, Loretta maintained that one could only sing so much, and the more demanding the repertoire, the shorter one's

> **January 7, 11, 19, 22, and 25, 1964**
> **Giacomo Puccini: *La Fanciulla del West***
> **Milan, Teatro alla Scala**
> Antonietta Stella [rehearsal only], Gigliola Frazzoni (*Minnie*), Franco Corelli (*Dick Johnson/Ramerrez*), Gian Giacomo Guelfi (*Jack Rance*), Piero De Palma (*Nick*), cond. Gianandrea Gavazzeni

career would last: "When you rehearse too much your best performance has already taken place in the rehearsal."[2]

In between performances, *Oggi*'s Maurizio Chierici confronted Corelli with his behavior, asking if there was a "pattern" in the string of incidents that had followed him around recently. First, there had been the fuss over his advertisement as "Greatest Tenor in the World" in Di Stefano's *Un Ballo in Maschera* program in Philadelphia; second, there was Del Monaco's suggestion in an interview that Corelli's high C was fake; third, Australian television had cut him from a special when Corelli wanted to use it to get back at a journalist who had offended him. Finally, there were two La Scala incidents: his clash with Gandolfi and now Stella's walkout. Chierici described the expressions on Corelli's face as he listened to the accusations: "At first he looks like he's been stung by a wasp, only to finish with a childlike expression of pure innocence on his face. . . . That is Corelli. Sweet, gentle, timid and emotional, but like a true Marchigiano he is also stubborn and easily provoked."[3]

In Corelli's defense, he had a brilliant excuse for missing the *Fanciulla* rehearsals: "Hey, I had a medical excuse. There can always be a day when I wake up without a voice. If I think about it, it drives me mad. . . . A little draft, a hint of dust can be enough. . . . My poor throat."[4]

As for the performance, Chierici noticed an improvement in Corelli's voice that pleased the tenor:

> Can you hear that my voice has changed? For months I have studied with Lauri-Volpi, and he has civilized my vocal production. I am a dramatic tenor with a loud but not very flexible voice. Now I have learned a way to capture certain notes of which I could previously only dream. Suddenly even *Bohème* is within my grasp. And it doesn't end there, because in two or three years from now I will risk *Otello*. How scared I will be that evening![5]

Before he could deal with *Otello*, there were first a few Dick Johnsons to deal with, which seem to have been settled by Loretta. As always, she'd lock herself in the dressing room with him, talking to him, preparing him, urging him on. Much that is unflattering about her can be, and has been, printed, but *Oggi* presents her as an angel who takes away all Corelli's fears and is very much in love with her beautiful husband, both as a man and as a singer. Said Loretta: "Please don't write about me. I speak only on behalf of my man. I don't want to step between him and his female admirers. I should never be in the picture. A picture? Please, no jokes!"[6]

February 29, 1964: Franco Corelli, tenore di grazie

Franco Corelli sang his first Rodolfo anywhere, and never at the Met has he seemed so at ease and so convincing. His was no wooden Indian portrait. He looked the part and moved with ardor and spirit. Then too it was wonderful to hear a lusty Radamès-Manrico voice in the part. Far from being overly heroic, Corelli's singing was wonderfully virile, and the emotions of the final act combined the exact amount of sobbing and singing. For my money there hasn't been such a Rodolfo since Björling.
John Ardoin, *Musical America*, April 1964

Just a few years earlier Corelli had described the role of Rodolfo as utterly unsuited to his huge voice. But when he was studying it in 1963, he told the *Newark Sunday News* that the part wasn't all that far from Maurizio in *Adriana Lecouvreur*, which he had sung numerous times to great acclaim.[7] Both

---

February 29, 1964
Giacomo Puccini: *La Bohème*
New York, Metropolitan Opera House
Franco Corelli (*Rodolfo*), Gabriella Tucci (*Mimì*), Elisabeth Söderström (*Musetta*), Frank Guarrera (*Marcello*), William Walker (*Schaunard*), Bonaldo Giaiotti (*Colline*), Fernando Corena (*Benoît*), cond. Fausto Cleva; stage director, Joseph L. Mankiewicz; sets and costumes, Rolf Gérard

arguments were true, but from 1964 on his work with Lauri-Volpi had indeed begun to bear fruit. And whereas Italy might not have embraced some of the more drastic changes this would ultimately bring about, Rudolf Bing wholeheartedly welcomed the idea of having Franco Corelli as Rodolfo in *La Bohème*. To Bing, having Corelli in *Bohème* simply meant that the Americans would get their all-time favorite opera with their current favorite tenor.

There the operatic world divided. American critics judged his Rodolfo a poetic, even great one. What he lacked in credibility—he certainly didn't sound like a poor starving *bohemièn*—he made up for with emotion and luscious voice, Rodolfo as a *grand signore* of noble allure. Corelli and those in his camp would point to Caruso and Jean de Reszke as well as to Lauri-Volpi himself, who had all given highly valued performances in *La Bohème*.

Corelli and Renata Tebaldi (as Rodolfo and Mimì) share a warm embrace, joined by Renata Scotto. (Photo: Courtesy of the Metropolitan Opera Archives)

Bing's American way of looking at opera also explains why he never pressed Corelli for anything out of the ordinary that would have brought his Met career up to par with his far more illustrious La Scala achievements. Bing merely suggested parts, but if Corelli refused them because he didn't feel ready for them, as with *Rigoletto, Otello, Manon Lescaut,* or a French-language *Carmen,* New York's audiences indulged themselves just as happily in his *Trovatore, Turandot, Don Carlo, Ernani, Aida,* or *Forza del Destino*. And if these operas weren't adding a jot to his repertoire, they were at one point all brand-new Corelli parts to New York. Not the opera, but the voice that brought it to life, was what mattered to Bing.

❖❖❖❖❖

Voice! One day it's there, the next it's gone. When the stage manager announced Corelli's cancellation of the March 3 *Tosca* in Philadelphia, a roar of boos erupted from the audience. But they stopped when Corelli himself was announced. He really couldn't sing, but he wanted to show his beloved Philadelphia audience, with which he had such a special bond, that he had prepared himself but had truly fallen ill. For his gesture of sincerity he received a veritable ovation and even ensured that his nervous understudy, Giovanni Consiglio, was cheered throughout the performance.[8]

◆◆◆◆◆

Philadelphia was not the only place where he felt very much at home at the time, for he had meanwhile acquired his own New York apartment at no. 16-A, 60 West Fifty-seventh Street. Another explanation for his suddenly relaxed attitude is found in an interview with the German opera magazine *Opernwelt*. There Corelli revealed that a recent visit to a yoga demonstration had awakened his interest in meditation as a possible solution for the continuing problems he had with his nerves. Wrote Giovanna Kessler: "Surely it is somewhat strange to enter the tenor's dressing room shortly before a performance and see him lying on the ground, eyes closed, legs up in the air."[9]

March 7, 1964: Where the Hell Is Franco Corelli?

The show was great, the audience went wild. Then came the moment where the "auto-da-fé" scene was due. Being a tenor, you cannot keep from participating even when you are a spectator. Awaiting the tenor's appearance, I nervously took hold of the armchairs. In vain, because the tenor did not appear in spite of the fact that this was a live broadcast!
    Jess Thomas, *Kein Schwert verhieß mir der Vater*, 1986

Like most other self-confident tenors at the Met, Jess Thomas seemed early on to develop an allergy to his rival and colleague Franco Corelli, to judge from Thomas's autobiography *My Father Never Promised Me a Sword*. Despite Thomas's endeavors in *Turandot, Aida, Don Carlo*, and *Tosca*, his fame rested largely on his German-language performances in Wagner and Strauss in theaters that were largely out of Franco's sights. However, Bing, his attempts to sign Thomas having been repeatedly rebuffed, happened to vent his anger to Thomas's friend and intermediary Irene Dalis: "Who the hell does Jess Thomas think he is, Franco Corelli?" Thomas relished Dalis's answer: "Well, no, he's

> **March 7, 1964**
> **Giuseppe Verdi: *Don Carlo***
> **New York, Metropolitan Opera House**
> Franco Corelli (*Don Carlo*), Leonie Rysanek (*Elisabetta di Valois*), Nicolae Herlea (*Rodrigo*), Irene Dalis (*Princess d'Eboli*), Giorgio Tozzi (*Philip II*), Hermann Uhde (*the Grand Inquisitor*), cond. Kurt Adler

better." Eventually Thomas joined the Met's roster and forgot all about Corelli until Bing blackmailed, forced, and cajoled him onstage to substitute for Corelli in the *Aida* of January 4, 1963. That Thomas was suffering from a serious inflammation of the throat (confirmed by the Met's doctor) didn't impress Bing, who simply promoted the occasion to "a matter of life and death!" When the shoes that fit Thomas went missing, a stagehand brought him Corelli's Calaf boots, which literally put the American tenor in Corelli's shoes. Of course, singing it in Italian was out of the question at this point in his career—apart from "Celeste Aida," he sang the Egyptian warrior in German!

Thomas's third encounter with the Bing-Corelli relationship came when he went out to see Irene Dalis in her signature part of Eboli, in the *Don Carlo* of March 7, 1964. Thomas was hardly prepared for what happened next: Franco didn't appear onstage at his cue in the auto-da-fé scene, where his presence was supposed to induce Elisabetta to erupt into the scene's opening line, "Qui Carlo! O ciel!" For those who knew the opera, it must have been odd enough to see her sing these words to no one in particular, but to leave King Philip's subsequent question about the identity of those kneeling before him unanswered, when Carlo should have said "They are deputies

Corelli as Don Carlo at the Met, March 1964. (Photo: Louis Melançon. Courtesy of the Metropolitan Opera Archives)

of Brabant and Flanders," had to have been shocking indeed. Thus it was that Thomas, even though he was in the house incognito, suddenly found a stagehand at his side begging him to run backstage, where Bing summoned him to take over, without even asking whether Thomas knew the part.

> He handed me a costume and pushed me toward the wardrobe. I firmly protested, refusing to cover. Then we reached the tenor's dressing room. Bing opened the door without knocking and left it open long enough for the tenor to see me with costume. Meanwhile he thanked me profusely, in a very loud voice. Then he closed the door and told me: "That should do the job." He had me wait there for a couple of minutes, until he returned with a broad smile on his face, shaking my hand and thanking me once again: "You can return to your seat now and enjoy the performance. The tenor has decided that he has miraculously recovered!"[10]

March 11–April 11, 1964: It Takes a Jew to Sing "O dolci mani"

When Corelli took on the role of Cavaradossi in 1964, he alternated it with Canio and Turiddu. The last two were never sung on the same night but were shared with the Turridus Arturo Sergi and Barry Morell and the Canios James McCracken and Richard Tucker.[11] Tucker was once very surprised to find his resented rival looking for him during Tucker's *Tosca* rehearsals. Corelli had a disarming request for his colleague: "Richard, would you do me a favor? Would you let me watch you sing 'O dolci mani'?"

Corelli was much in demand for *Pagliacci*, an opera where he was very much in his element, although he dreaded performing it. He feared the score and may also have disliked playing the heavy, and an older one to boot—until he discovered that U.S. audiences happily applauded a gorgeous Canio as well! (Photo: Louis Melançon. Courtesy Metropolitan Opera Archives)

> **March 11 and 20; April 11, 1964**
> **Ruggero Leoncavallo:** *Pagliacci*
> **New York, Metropolitan Opera House**
> Franco Corelli (*Canio*), Lucine Amara (*Nedda*), Nicolae Herlea (*Tonio*), Franco Ghitti (*Beppe*), Calvin Marsh (*Silvio*), cond. Fausto Cleva
>
> **March 22 and 30; April 8, 1964**
> **Giacomo Puccini:** *Tosca*
> **New York, Metropolitan Opera House**
> Renata Tebaldi, Mary Curtis-Verna [April 8] (*Tosca*), Franco Corelli (*Cavaradossi*), Tito Gobbi, Cornel MacNeil [April 8] (*Scarpia*), Fernando Corena (*the Sacristan*), cond. Fausto Cleva
>
> **March 25, 1964**
> **Verdi:** *Un Ballo in Maschera* "Teco io sto." **Puccini:** *Turandot* "Non piangere, Liù!"
> **New York, Bell Telephone Hour (color telecast)**
> Franco Corelli, Régine Crespin, Donald Voorhees
>
> **March 28 and April 2, 1964**
> **Pietro Mascagni:** *Cavalleria Rusticana*
> **New York, Metropolitan Opera House**
> Franco Corelli (*Turiddu*), Irene Dalis, Mary Curtis Verna [April 2] (*Santuzza*), Janis Martin (*Lola*), Lili Chookasian (*Lucia*), cond. Nello Santi

Tucker was so touched by this request that he hardly knew what to say. Then, out of the blue, he came up with the perfect answer: "To sing it right, Franco, you have to be Jewish." Corelli laughed, and Tucker, who had never seen the more humble side of the Anconetan tenor, started singing. From that point on they would be friends for life, although Tucker never really came to terms with his position as second best with Bing and the majority of the public.[12] Eventually he made peace with the idea that whereas you had to be Jewish to sing like Tucker, you had to be Italian to have the sort of good looks that Franco showcased in his *Bell Telephone Hour* appearance, where he looked like a god in the color telecast of the "Teco io sto" duet from Verdi's *Un Ballo in Maschera*.

April 14, 1964: Roméo in Philadelphia

Corelli, singing his first Roméo on any stage, was the essence of visual romance and brought vibrancy and ardor to this new part. Some of his work was naturally tentative, but repeated performances in a role for which he is obviously suited should bring assurance to his French diction and to his stage deportment.
   Max de Schauensee, "Philadelphia," *Opera*, August 1964

No correspondence on the matter has yet been found, but Rudolf Bing can't have welcomed the idea of his protégé's presenting a new role in the United States outside the Met, especially given Corelli's reluctance to add new roles to his repertoire. Bing's possessive and pragmatic attitude may partially account for the small number of roles Corelli would debut in the United States, where his earlier habit of testing new roles in a relaxed setting was virtually impossible to maintain. At the same time, European conditions were no longer optimally suited to his needs either, because Italian theaters were not likely to respond with much enthusiasm to the prospect of presenting Gounod's unpopular *Roméo* in French,[13] while the risk in France would have been too great because of the public's familiarity with the work and the language. Who other than his friend and manager Aurelio Fabiani could have provided Franco with carte blanche to test his French operatic studies in Philadelphia, at some distance from New York's more critical press and audience?

Those fortunate enough to obtain tickets for the *Roméo* tryout were lucky indeed, for there was only a single performance. Corelli arrived with his usual nerve troubles exacerbated by the fact that it was also his French-language debut onstage. He may not yet have been the poetic young hero one would imagine Roméo to be, but his fast, heated way of singing brought out the element of

April 14, 1964
Charles Gounod: *Roméo et Juliette*
Philadelphia, Academy of Music
Franco Corelli (*Roméo*), Gianna D'Angelo (*Juliette*), Agostino Ferrin (*Brother Laurent*), Peter Gottlieb (*Mercutio*), Nancy Williams (*Stéphano*), Mauro Lampi (*Tybalt*), cond. Anton Guadagno

grand opera in Gounod's distinctive score. Corelli may have forgotten a word or two, and his French may not have been nearly what it would become later on; nevertheless, the existing recording evidences an almost hypnotic performance. Fabiani arranged for Franco to be presented after the performance with a golden medal engraved with a portrait of Gounod. With this and another triumph in his pocket, he went home to prepare himself for his second Met Spring Tour.[14]

March 20–May 12, 1964: On the Road with Birgit and Renata

Franco Corelli was the iron man of the week. Monday night he sang the difficult role of Manrico in Il Trovatore. *Tuesday night his voice had the same ringing power and freshness when he sang the part of Radamès.*
    Oscar Smith, "Exciting Voices Enhance Met's *Aida*," Akron (Ohio) *Beacon Journal*, April 22, 1964

Singing Manrico on Monday evening and Radamès on Tuesday was not exactly Corelli's cup of tea. But he did it to save the day for Bing after both Carlo Bergonzi and Leontyne Price became indisposed just prior to their *Trovatore* performance, which was to open Cleveland's festive week with the Met. A panicked Bing went with his right-hand man in the United States, Robert Herman, up to Corelli's hotel room with a plan: they would knock on Corelli's door, fall to their

---

April 18, 1964
Giacomo Puccini: *Tosca*
Boston, John B. Hynes Civic Auditorium
Birgit Nilsson (*Tosca*), Franco Corelli (*Cavaradossi*), London (*Scarpia*), cond. Fausto Cleva

March 20, 1964
Giuseppe Verdi: *Il Trovatore*
Cleveland, Public Auditorium
Gabriella Tucci (*Leonora*), Franco Corelli (*Manrico*), Irene Dalis (*Azucena*), Mario Sereni (*Count di Luna*), cond. Thomas Schippers

March 21, 1964
Giuseppe Verdi: *Aida*
Cleveland, Public Auditorium
Birgit Nilsson (*Aida*), Franco Corelli (*Radamès*), Rita Gorr (*Amneris*), cond. Silvio Varviso

April 25, 1964
Giacomo Puccini: *La Bohème*
Cleveland, Public Auditorium
Franco Corelli (*Rodolfo*), Renata Tebaldi (*Mimi*), cond. George Schick

May 1, 1964
Giuseppe Verdi: *Aida*
New York, Metropolitan Opera House
Birgit Nilsson (*Aida*), Franco Corelli (*Radamès*), Irene Dalis (*Amneris*), cond. Silvio Varviso

May 5, 1964
Ruggero Leoncavallo: *Pagliacci*
New York, Metropolitan Opera House
Lucine Amara (*Nedda*), Franco Corelli (*Canio*), Anselmo Colzani (*Tonio*), cond. Fausto Cleva

May 8, 1964
Giuseppe Verdi: *Il Trovatore*
New York, Metropolitan Opera House
Gabriella Tucci (*Leonora*), Franco Corelli (*Manrico*), Regina Resnik (*Azucena*), Robert Merrill (*Count di Luna*), cond. Thomas Schippers

May 12, 1964
Giacomo Puccini: *La Bohème*
Atlanta, Civic Auditorium
Franco Corelli (*Rodolfo*), Renata Tebaldi (*Mimi*), cond. Schick

knees (as Birgit Nilsson had trained him to do to express his gratitude for her services), and beg. And so they did. However, they were on the wrong floor, and it was a bewildered elderly woman who opened her door to the two kneeling men.[15] Once they found the right room, their approach was more successful.

Together with Gabriella Tucci for Price, Corelli did what he always did when coming to the rescue—singing, conquering, and leaving the audience happier than they would have been with the original cast. (Sometimes, when Bing or the Met's stage manager, Ossie Hawkins, announced an indisposed tenor, one could hear the audience's disappointment turn into an ovation with the further announcement, "The replacement is . . . Franco . . . Corelli!")

The 1964 tour was a particularly successful one. The all-star cast included, besides Corelli, Rita Gorr, Anna Moffo, Birgit Nilsson, Leontyne Price, Regina Resnik, Joan Sutherland, Renata Tebaldi, Gabriella Tucci, Carlo Bergonzi, Richard Tucker, Fernando Corena, George London, Cornell McNeil, Cesare Siepi, and a number of others. For Corelli the tour started in Boston with a high-octane *Tosca* opposite Nilsson; Cleveland was treated to a dazzling *Aida* from the same two protagonists in a luscious production that had everything an opera could ask for, "including belly dancers."[16]

A relative novelty in the tour was the extension of the Metropolitan Opera season, which now overlapped with the tour because singers could simply travel back and forth by air. Even Corelli sang regular Met performances of *Aida*, *Pagliacci*, and *Il Trovatore* in between his tour engagements in Cleveland and Atlanta, where he finished the season with *La Bohème*.

June–July 1964: An Intriguing *Faust*

When Bing asked Corelli to take over some planned performances of *Faust*, Corelli refused on the grounds that the part was too light for his voice. Interestingly, he made that remark right in the middle of recording it complete, opposite Joan Sutherland.[17] The soprano seemed to have overcome her earlier negative feelings toward Corelli, although these quickly returned during the recording, which she remembered as a rather unhappy occasion. Like most of her other colleagues, she was annoyed with Corelli's attitude toward volume and high notes. In addition, Corelli had clearly reached a point where he believed that all those recordings and operas revolved around him. Her irritation peaked toward the end, when the recording threatened to collapse because Corelli had to leave before the final trio could be cut. Said Sutherland: "So he recorded it elsewhere later on and then had his lines glued over the master tape—that is why we sound so far apart instead of involved there."[18]

> June 1–18; July 9–10, 1964
> Charles Gounod: *Faust*
> London, Kingsway Hall (Decca recording)
> Franco Corelli (*Faust*), Nicolai Ghiaurov (*Méphistophélès*), Joan Sutherland (*Marguerite*), Robert Massard (*Valentin*), Margreta Elkins (*Siebel*), cond. Richard Bonynge

Nevertheless, Bonynge's concept brings out a whole new scope for the work. Despite the vagaries of all the principals' French diction, this *Faust* reveals an affinity with the world of grand opera. After all, libretto, music, and epoch situate the opera right between *Les Huguenots*, *L'Africaine*, and *Aida* and in the vicinity of the works of Daniel François Esprit Auber. The unstintingly heroic Marguerite and Faust are augmented by the equally overpowering Méphistophélès of Nicolai Ghiaurov, all captured so splendidly by Decca's engineers that EMI must have winced. Corelli's *Faust* recording for Decca may not be an historic recording, but it certainly defines the tenor for all he is worth as a thrilling and emotionally charged vocal phenomenon.

❖❖❖❖❖

Contract! It continued to be a game in which the players made up the rules as they went along. By now Bing simply wanted to keep Franco at the Met for the entire season and far away from La Scala and San Francisco, where Kurt Herbert Adler had offered Corelli a fine deal for the same season. Corelli was not going to open the Met, so he wanted to accept other offers. Bing hoped to foil Corelli's plan to go from San Francisco to La Scala by giving him his pick of almost anything in his repertoire, including the possibility of a debut in *Lucia di Lammermoor*. In addition, Bing played for months on Franco's pride and loyalty with respect to the plans for the festive closing season of the old Met and the even more festive opening season of the new Met at Lincoln Center, now scheduled for the fall of 1966. He pleaded with Franco not to commit himself to any theater for the entire duration of these two historical seasons: "It would be my hope that you would care to participate prominently in these two seasons."[19]

Bing threw Corelli another bone when he asked Bauer to tell Franco (with the highest degree of confidentiality!) that the *Turandot* film project they had recently discussed with him earlier was very likely to materialize. The plea for confidentiality was not directed at Franco. Said Bing to Bauer: "Loretta should keep her mouth shut."[20] Bauer replied promptly that he preferred to wait for Franco's return so that he could whisper it into his ear: "Should I write, then Loretta will definitely show the letter around, or accidentally forget to put it away, keeping it somewhere where it is likely to be found, in order to make some promotion with it."[21]

June 3–26, 1964: A Battle for Norma

A voice that resembles the sun.
  Le Figaro on Franco Corelli, quoted in Alexei Buljigin, *Prins v stranj Tjudes*, 2003

Few people are aware that 1964 brought Corelli's debut at the Paris Opéra in *Tosca* opposite Christiane Castelli and the great but very French baritone Gabriel Bacquier. Though the French press proclaimed it memorable, the impact of the debut was wiped out by the historic *Norma* that followed three days later, one of Maria Callas's few true opera performances in the 1960s. The fourth gala performance of *Norma* at the Opéra was the first of two featuring Franco Corelli substituting for Mario Del Monaco, who was still recovering from his injuries. The German *Opernwelt* subscriber and "critic without a cause" Martin-Wolfram Reinecke was in the audience and brought an intriguing German flavor to the usual Italian or Anglo-American reviews. Finally someone provided some balance to the otherwise universal acclaim of Franco Zeffirelli's utterly old-fashioned staging: Reinecke judged it horribly realistic and close to the way it must have been staged at the world premiere. Accustomed to more stylized performances (Germany was a front-runner in the modernization of operatic staging), it took him part of the overture to catch his breath again, only to receive the next shock when the Druids and Oroveso entered the stage in the tasteless costumes of the famous Marcel Escoffier: "Bearskin dresses and bearded masks that looked like leftovers from a Bayreuth performance in 1876."[22]

There was one single source of consolation for the shocked German spectator: Franco Corelli, who clearly had brought his own very fitted costume. Every possible prejudice one could have had against him was immediately overcome

> **June 3 and 22, 1964**
> **Giacomo Puccini: *Tosca***
> Paris, Théâtre National de l'Opéra
> Christiane Castelli, Régine Crespin [Jun 20] (*Tosca*), Franco Corelli (*Cavaradossi*), Gabriel Bacquier (*Scarpia*), cond. Georges Prêtre
>
> **June 6 and 10, 1964**
> **Vincenzo Bellini: *Norma***
> Paris, Théâtre National de l'Opéra
> Maria Callas (*Norma*), Franco Corelli (*Pollione*), Fiorenza Cossotto (*Adalgisa*), Ivo Vinco (*Oroveso*), Claude Calès (*Flavio*), cond. Georges Prêtre; stage designer and director, Franco Zeffirelli; costumes, Marcel Escoffier
>
> **June 15, 20, and 26, 1964**
> **Giuseppe Verdi: *Don Carlo***
> Paris, Théâtre National de l'Opéra
> Franco Corelli (*Don Carlo*), Nicolai Ghiaurov (*Filippo II*), Louis Quilico (*Rodrigo*), Suzanne Sarroca (*Elisabetta di Valois*), Rita Gorr (*Princess d'Eboli*), Huc Santana (*the Grand Inquisitor*), cond. Pierre Dervaux

by his entrance aria, which he sang so magnificently that Reinecke readily forgave him for passing over his high C (something no one else seemed to have noticed). After that, the stage was all Callas's, and she sang an introverted heroine with a new voice, bordering on the mezzo range and without her former agility in the high range. When a note in the first coloratura run didn't come out satisfactorily, the gallery immediately started to hiss, but she rushed through the cabaletta well enough, again with an unsung high C that went unnoticed. She left the stage to clamorous applause, repeated even more fervently after the Norma-Adalgisa duet and the trio with Pollione. When the fifth scene arrived, just when the audience was least prepared for it, Callas finally slipped. She lost her voice in one phrase, which brought ironic comments from the galleries. With a steely will she then repeated the phrase successfully, only to crack again a few bars later. The fans shouted "Brava Maria"; her enemies, "Callas au vestiaire" (Callas back to the closet). Shouts of "Viva Corelli!" followed, which was a euphemism for "Callas down!" The subject of all the commotion, accustomed to organized negative sentiments for over a decade, went on to give a shuddering account of her confession in "Son io," after which she sang the finale scene with her father (Ivo Vinco) and Pollione in a manner that made this night an historic one for its vocal and dramatic achievements.

Apparently, not all present were happy with the outcome, and to the astonishment of the European *beau monde* and the *fine fleur* of show business (including the Begum Aga Khan, Princess Grace from Monaco, Aristotle Onassis, Ingrid Bergman, Charlie and Oona Chaplin, Anthony Perkins, and Yves Saint-Laurent), the audience suddenly started to fight: "Educated gentlemen in tuxedoes turned into bitter enemies, fighting each other with raised fists; elegantly dressed ladies tore each other's hair from their heads and slapped each other's ears." The fighting ended only when the police interfered and separated the two camps as if they were soccer fans. Rudolf Bing was present in the audience and commented on the bedlam in the French press. He had never witnessed anything remotely like it at the Met or anywhere else: "That opera isn't possible without a woman like that. I have the feeling that tonight I witnessed a dream, in which the ancient tragedies were resurrected."[23]

The scandal merely confirmed Callas's continuing drawing power. He went to congratulate her—and it was then that the seed was planted for Callas's return to the Met.

Corelli with Maria Callas in *Norma*, Paris, June 6, 1964. (Photo: Courtesy of RCS)

June 25, 1964: The Shattered Callas-Corelli duets

Maria was an ideal partner. Never a note that was held too long, never a high note that was stolen. I never understood why they called her a tigress, because with me she was more like a lamb.

    Franco Corelli, in Marisa Rusconi, "La Callas e' un agnellino," *Tempo*, December 22, 1962

Just one day before the ill-fated Callas-Corelli duet recording session started, Loretta told Bauer the real reason Franco had refused to open the last season in the old Met with *Faust*. Bing had hired Georges Prêtre as conductor, and the Corellis, who had had tremendous difficulties with him over *Tosca* and *Norma* at the Opéra, felt they were sure to run into disputes with him. As far as the Corellis were concerned, Prêtre might be up to a French opera, but he didn't understand a jot of Italian opera. This was the attitude with which they entered EMI's studio in Paris on June 25 in order to make what was destined to be the record of the decade. Callas was the first to greet the Corellis (always together, even in the studio), followed by Prêtre himself.

This is as far as all the parties in the story can agree. To get to the bottom of events, one must recall Corelli's vengeful *Carmen* recording with Herbert von Karajan in November 1963, made on the let-out terms in his contract only because EMI couldn't promise him Maria Callas as his Carmen. After having lobbied Maria for years to do *Carmen* at the Met with him, the famous recording with Prêtre, Callas, and the miscast Nicolai Gedda as Don José suddenly materialized a good two weeks before the duet recordings started. (The duets were to be recorded in between.) The Corellis instantly suspected a plot against them, with Prêtre as the evil genius behind it.[24]

With that on their minds, the singers started warming up, which usually takes about an hour in all, during which the recording equipment isn't running.[25] In this case they had to make do with the space that was there, so all warmed up on their own, with the others present. Michel Glotz was the producer who supervised the recordings from the control room: "The orchestra was rehearsing with Mr. Prêtre and Mr. Corelli decided that he wanted to sing full voice. Plus Mrs. Corelli, who was in the control room with us, was all the time interfering with me, which I could not accept. I never accepted that the

> June 25, 1964
> Paris, Salle Wagram (EMI recording)
> Verdi: *Aida* "Pur ti riveggio"; *Un Ballo in Maschera* "Teco io sto"; *Don Carlo* "E dessa." Bellini: *I Puritani* "Fini . . . me lassa!"; *Il Pirata* "Vieni! Cerchiam pei mari." Donizetti: *Poliuto* "Donna! Malvagio! . . . Lasciando la terra."
> Maria Callas, Franco Corelli, cond. Georges Prêtre

wife of a singer would indicate to us what to do and what not to do, technically speaking. She was impossible, she was acting in an impossible way."[26]

The Corellis told a different story. There were problems between the tenor and the conductor. Prêtre had no clue as to what he was conducting: "When the recording started the tempi were wrong and Callas had first to tell him what the tempi are like!"[27] Glotz finally ordered the recording machines to be switched on for what was merely a test recording to adjust the balance and check the equipment and the positions of the singers. The duet tested was "Pur ti riveggio," from *Aida*. Recalled Glotz:

> Mr. Corelli sang full voice while the orchestra was rehearsing, even though I told him not to. Madame Callas was not singing full voice. When everything was ready to be recorded, Mr. Corelli said, "Well, I already sang, so I will not sing again, I will mark." At that point Madame Callas said, "Well, in that case, we shall not make this recording." That was the end of it. EMI knew perfectly well that it was against the will of Madame Callas to release this take, which she considered not to exist; the session was not even finished—everyone left before the end.[28]

That seems a sound explanation for the enormous difference between the tenor's output in this duet and Callas's thin voice, although Corelli maintained that Callas simply was not in good shape.[29] Still, the Corelli-Prêtre clash seems to have been the most immediate cause of the failed sessions: Victor Olof reported to EMI's headquarters that the recordings had "blown up after one session as Corelli had taken a violent dislike to Georges Prêtre—a dislike which is heartily reciprocated. Consequently we have canceled the remaining four sessions."[30]

❖❖❖❖❖

The relationship between Corelli and Prêtre never improved, and that cost the world some wonderful recordings as well as some spectacular performances, for Prêtre had become Callas's conductor of choice. Corelli's own view of the matter was typical. Whenever someone demanded that he diminish his volume, he felt as if they wanted to rob him of his glory, and so he reported "home" that Prêtre "tried his best to ruin his success." As for Prêtre, he started spreading the word that Corelli was unmusical, never came to rehearsals, and was altogether impossible. Poor Prêtre. He had just been hired by Bing for the Met's 1965–66 season, for which there was still one contract to be signed—Corelli's. Franco informed Bing that he was going to accept the offer from San Francisco for the 1965–66 season because he didn't want to run into Prêtre. Of course, Bing shouldn't read this as an attempt by his friend Franco to run the Met in his stead; it's merely a courtesy from a responsible artist. All poor Franco wanted to do was avoid a big fight, with all the unpleasant consequences. No, thinking about it, he actually preferred to divide his time between opening La Scala and singing in San Francisco and Chicago only, skipping New York altogether; a change of menu might be good for the Met's public.[31]

Corelli also said he had asked for rehearsals before the duet recordings, which Prêtre could not provide because he was running back and forth between his obligations in Paris and Vienna. Loretta then spelled it out: "It is Prêtre who doesn't come to rehearsals!" The matter meant so much to them (and would also influence the discussion over Prêtre at the Met) that Loretta summoned Bauer to their Milan apartment on June 29 so he could bear witness to a conversation with EMI's Peter Andry. They switched the phone to speaker mode so Bauer was able to listen in: "To make a long story short, after some embarrassment Mr. Andry confirmed that the recording could not go on because of Callas and that it was not possible to publish what had been recorded so far! So Loretta said to me, 'You heard it yourself.'"[32]

To top it off, the Corellis also claimed that Callas agreed with them, though she almost certainly did not, for she continued to record with Prêtre and without Corelli. Prêtre continued with her, but at the request of both Corelli and Crespin, he was immediately dropped as the conductor for their upcoming *Tosca* recording.[33]

June 1964: *Tosca* Lost, La Scala Lost

Once in the engineers' booth you can sit for a moment while you listen to the take you just did, but you're always tense, with a visceral fear that it wasn't good. . . . Everyone has this fear of failure, and superstitions that make you cross yourself, carry pastilles for a nervous cough, or furtively kiss a religious medallion; some travel with silent

> June 1964
> Giacomo Puccini: *Tosca*
> Paris, Salle Wagram (EMI recording)
> Régine Crespin (*Tosca*), Franco Corelli (*Cavaradossi*)

husbands who suffer by osmosis, or with annoying wives whom the engineers finally eject. Tebaldi knitted, Schwarzkopf isolated herself in a sort of telephone booth without a door, Horne did needlepoint, . . . Corelli stuffed himself with pills.
    Régine Crespin, On Stage, Off Stage: A Memoir, 1997

It is hard to imagine a more ill-fated project than EMI's plans for recording a Corelli *Tosca*. The choice of Régine Crespin was odd from the start. Her idiom was essentially French, and she could hardly be expected to match Callas in her signature role. Moreover, Crespin had been overworked and was not feeling well. After several days, she finally collapsed, which effectively ended the *Tosca* recordings. Sometimes it's really better to take pills.

Nearly an hour of music was captured at the recording sessions. They represent the last unpublished Corelli takes in EMI's archives.[34]

✦✦✦✦✦

During and after the *Tosca* recording session, negotiations continued with Bing, who was increasing the pressure on his unruly champ. Bing made it crystal clear that he would regard Corelli's singing in San Francisco and Chicago, combined with staying away from the old Met in the last season, as an insult. Bauer visited Franco in Rome and made it clear that his plans would jeopardize the *Turandot* film project. The film would be issued in precisely the season Franco was planning to stay away from the Met, in which case Bing might prefer to engage another tenor. Then Loretta spoke, saying that Franco now had signed contracts in San Francisco and Los Angeles; there could be no further discussion regarding those periods. Intriguingly, the only time he was still free was from the middle of November up to the end of December; apparently Ghiringhelli had just as hard a time as Bing in landing his favorite tenor for the fifth La Scala opening in a row. With the Met and La Scala in direct competition over Franco, there was no longer any question of sharing. Bing swiftly sent

Corelli a pre-contract for the *Turandot* film with a fee of $22,500, with shooting tentatively scheduled for June 1965 and a guaranteed fee of $5,000 should the final contract not materialize.

At this time Bauer was seriously ill. He required intensive treatment and major surgery, which left him confined to a hospital bed. The Corellis never left his side. Eventually the combination of pressure, pleading, money, the *Turandot* film, and their sympathy for their weakened friend bore fruit. Corelli ceded his fifth La Scala opening in a row in favor of six weeks at the Met with a revival of *La Fanciulla del West*, which Bing had tossed in as bait. *Fanciulla*, in which Franco was unrivaled, was a showpiece that Corelli very much wanted to bring to New York. Of course, Corelli still had no intention of running the Met in his friend Rudolfo's stead, but a letter from Robert Herman to Bauer makes it very clear who was effectively co-running the Met by July 1964: "We will somehow manage to switch *Fanciulla* into the period Mr. Bing requested. . . . The repertoire would be chosen from *Fanciulla*, *Chénier*, *Trovatore*, *Don Carlo*, *Lucia*, *Bohème*, and perhaps *Aida*. Naturally, we would not ask him to do all or nearly all these parts, but will select the ones which fit best into his schedule."[35]

Corelli's new "job" as co-director of the Met would normally have called for negotiations over a raise, but Bing was so desperate to keep him on board that he simply volunteered to increase Corelli's salary to an enormous sum, making his first-ever exception to the rule of all top fees being equal: "Let us show $3,250 per performance in the contract, and we will prepare a separate letter that he will receive $500 for each sung performance." Including 7 percent estimated tax, that totaled $45,000 net income for twelve performances,[36] which effectively sealed his status, long claimed though till now not substantiated, as the highest-paid tenor at the Met.

July–September 1964: Pilgrimage to Lourdes

The recording of *Il Trovatore* went ahead as planned in July and August 1964, with Gabriella Tucci replacing Crespin.[37] That left the Corellis free to visit their friend Lauri-Volpi in Burjassot, where Corelli continued to work on his vocal technique, with an emphasis on his breathing and attack.[38] Confident that he was back on track, Corelli and his wife undertook a most extraordinary journey to Lourdes in order to pray to the Madonna for Bauer's recovery. When they returned to Milan on the 25th of August and told Bauer of their pilgrimage, he was so touched he almost felt guilty over their feelings of genuine friendship and love for him.[39]

♦♦♦♦♦

Franco next went to Milan in preparation for his upcoming September performances in Moscow. He was to appear under the aegis of La Scala's adventurous tour to that (at the time) very mysterious and exotic Communist capital. Corelli's Russian biographer, Alexei Buljigin, recalled that posters bearing Franco's name were already on display in Moscow when Corelli arrived in Milan. He was to due to sing Calaf in the Soviet capital on August 8, but when the Milanese arrived on the square in front of the Bolshoi, their undisputed star tenor was absent.[40] Officially his cancellation was the result of a vexatious exhaustion; others suggested that the Met had paid him to stay home.[41] Both explanations are doubtful: he arrived rested in Milan and had no obligations at the Met or elsewhere that month. Reading between the lines of the Met's internal correspondence and taking into account Corelli's imminent future at La Scala, his cancellation seems to be the first sign of a breach in his alliance with Ghiringhelli, with whom he was having a disagreement about the choice of opera for La Scala's upcoming opening night.[42]

July–August 1964
Rome, Teatro dell'Opera (EMI recording)
Giuseppe Verdi: *Il Trovatore*
Gabriella Tucci *(Leonora)*, Franco Corelli *(Manrico)*, Giulietta Simionato *(Azucena)*, Robert Merrill *(Count di Luna)*, cond. Thomas Schippers

September–October 1958/Milan, September 1964
London (September 1964 dubbing of orchestral tracks used for another tenor's 1958 recording)
Verdi: *Un Ballo in Maschera* "Forse la soglia attinse . . . Ma se m'è forza"; *Il Trovatore* "Di quella pira"
Royal Philharmonic, cond. Eduardo Pedrazzoli

October 10, 1964: Billy Bigelow Bids Farewell to the Metropolitan

Del Monaco sent a special ambassador to see me to express his desire to return to the Metropolitan, if only for just one or two performances. He is singing Otello *and* Samson. *In view of the fact that Samson is now in our repertory for this and next season, and in view of the fact that Corelli does not do* Otello, *Del Monaco, if he has really recovered and is any good, is of increased interest to us. . . . If you do see Corelli, I think it might be useful if you just dropped a hint that I assume this silly feud is now over and that we would not expect any trouble from Corelli if Del Monaco should help out with one or the other* Samson *or possibly one or the other* Otello *neither of which Corelli does. If you do not see him, ask Roberto whether he could broach the subject.*
    Rudolf Bing to Robert Herman, October 2, 1964

While Herman contacted Franco, Bing lost no time in catching up with Del Monaco, who jumped at the chance to make peace by claiming that none of the allegations printed in the press had anything to do with him—they were all "manipulated."[43] Corelli's response was brilliant. He had the world at his feet. His voice was more flexible than ever, thanks to the inspiring new vocal insights Lauri-Volpi had given him in Burjassot. He was now able to truly negotiate Rodolfo, on the utterly lyric side of his repertoire, and still return to Manrico—which he proved in Chicago, where he debuted at the Lyric Opera in September. Moreover, his negotiations with the Met for the immediate future held the sort of challenges that any tenor would welcome at this point of his career, he proudly told a reporter from *Eva*. He spoke quite freely about himself and his immediate plans:

> I have the good fortune to—if you will allow me the indiscretion—hold one of the very first places in the operatic world. . . . The Metropolitan is an important theater to me, and . . . offers even greater challenges to me for next year, when I will perform in *Tosca* with Maria Callas and in *Rigoletto* with Joan Sutherland. . . . In between all these splendid novelties that America offers to me, there is also the exciting prospect of making color films for television. The first one will be *Turandot*, which will be filmed from June 8, 1965, onward. After that, *Il Trovatore* and *Andrea Chénier* will follow.

This little speech, though, ended with a bang:

> However, I will not return to the Metropolitan in 1966.

A bomb couldn't have been dropped less subtly: *Tosca* with Callas, the Duke of Mantua with Sutherland, a couple of films, and then—"*Addio*, Metropolitan!" At the apex of his career, he was ready for bigger challenges: "I am convinced that this is the perfect moment for me to make myself accessible to that immense public that could never be reached through lyric opera. It is my pleasure to confirm my debut on Broadway, where I will appear in *Carousel* early in 1966."

Corelli, Broadway, and *Carousel*—however it sounded, it was more than a whim. He was well aware of the pitfalls of the plan; but he was charmed by the idea and pointed to a number of great operatic artists that had appeared in musicals before him, such as Cesare Siepi and Ezio Pinza: "I don't feel like a traitor at all, although many people whisper that I'm lowering myself to the level of operetta." One can hear the pleasure he takes in revealing the novelty of the Broadway project; he even likes the music, having listened to the recording of the movie soundtrack: "It is melodic, a lovely work; you find yourself transported. And, as I am this incurably sentimental fool, my enthusiasm for the project got the better of me."

Rashly, he divulged the names of both ladies under consideration as his co-star—Barbara Cook or Caterina Valente—our carefree, insouciant hero had no preference. Perhaps that should be seen in the context of some motives not yet touched upon behind his sudden love for Rodgers and Hammerstein: "I won't deny that another reason for this decision is hidden in the fact that they offered me a rather enormous financial compensation. I have to confess something to you: if the lyric theater would ever pay me this much money, I would be inclined to leave everything behind after a mere three months, in order to live the rest of my days under the open, sunny Polynesian skies."[44]

❖❖❖❖❖

Corelli's voice would have added luster to the duet "If I Loved You"; to Billy Bigelow's solos, "Soliloquy" and "The Highest Judge of All"; and, to top it off, to the reprise of that evergreen "You'll Never Walk Alone." Of course, Rodgers and Hammerstein first had to rewrite the part: Billy Bigelow was and is a baritone, something Corelli curiously forgets to mention. What about the remaining *Carousel* contract matters? They were swept aside, trifling things he could easily fix upon his return to the United States. Studying the part almost seemed a joke; Billy Bigelow was like a summer holiday compared to the Chicago Manricos and the New York Dukes of Mantua that he had in mind as warm-up performances.[45]

No, there was only one tiny obstacle between Corelli and Broadway, and that was his virtually nonexistent comprehension of the English language. He even spoke of it as a point in his favor: "I am not the first operatic artist to appear in a musical, but I will be the first non-English-speaking tenor to appear in a leading role on Broadway." Over the summer he had had a record made of his speaking voice for *Carousel*'s producers, who assured him that his English could be tuned to perfection within the year that was left until the premiere. But in the end, Corelli was not completely optimistic: "If the perilous question of my English wasn't there, I would relax like a king."[46]

October 1964: *The King of Granada*

If the English lessons ever took place at all, they were not very successful. One problem was his lifestyle in New York, where the few friends with whom he kept in touch were all Italian-speaking. The Metropolitan Opera employed lots of Italian singers, and New York had had a large population of Italian Americans since the days of Caruso. Neither Corelli's private nor his professional life required him to speak English. It was Bing's good fortune that this limited Corelli's possibilities and prevented him from pursuing offers in the realm of other opera houses, musicals, and films, such as the one planned with Joan Fontaine and him as the successor of (again) Mario Lanza. This time there seemed to be no alternative: Lanza, for whom the script was written, had meanwhile died.[47] Said Corelli: "The provisional title is *The King of Granada*, a movie originally written for Mario Lanza. It is the first of all the scripts offered to me to be premiered."[48]

As with *Carousel*, he didn't see a cloud in the financial or contractual sky over the *King of Granada* project. There was really just one little detail to take care of: a screen test for Twentieth Century-Fox in London, due immediately upon his departure from Italy, where the audition was conveniently planned on his way to New York.[49]

Needless to say, the movie was never made, and when *Carousel* was revived in 1966, it was the role's creator, the baritone John Raitt, who triumphed as Billy Bigelow. The winner in all these lost opportunities was, as usual, Rudolf Bing. He wanted—and got—his box-office star on the top of the roster for the crucial reopening of the new Met at Lincoln Center, due in the very 1966 season that Corelli had publicly denounced in favor of his more trivial ambitions.

October 19, 1964: Plans, Plans, and More Plans

On October 19, 1964, EMI's Peter Andry suggested a *Turandot* recording to Corelli for July 1965 with Birgit Nilsson and Mirella Freni. He also mentioned *Otello* as a possibility, should Corelli be ready for it.[50] Meanwhile the Theater-

Corelli shops for Italian pastries on Manhattan's Bleecker Street. If Loretta's cooking had helped to soften his throat to the more elaborate realms of celestial phrasing, then her efforts were rewarded when Peter Gravina, Corelli's press agent, published his famous *Bel Canto Cookbook* in 1964, which featured Franco's favorite recipes. Said Loretta to Gravina about Franco: "Feeding him is like stoking a blast furnace." The *St. Louis Dispatch* followed up on the subject with a lovely illustrated article on the Corellis at home, in which two of Franco's three hobbies where thoroughly illustrated: eating and watching television (in spite of his limited understanding of the English language). (Photo: Louis Melançon. Courtesy of the Metropolitan Opera Archives)

Color Vision Corporation had reached an agreement with the Met over filming some operas with their stars, and Corelli accepted Bing's offer to film *La Bohème*. The option for the film was signed on November 6, and with a $25,000 fee (and a $5,000 guarantee in case the project did not materialize), things on the recording front seemed to be working out fine in regard to both financial matters and Franco's serious desire to leave something for posterity. In the meantime, a discussion of a planned *Forza del Destino* performance on April 17, 1965 (which was dropped in favor of another work), brought up interesting alternatives when Robert Herman suggested either *Lucia di Lammermoor* or *Simon Boccanegra* (Corelli had meanwhile backed out of *Rigoletto*, judging its tessitura too high).[51]

December 7–19, 1964: "Bark Better, Calaf!"

I truly hope that they will give me an illustrated card again, with the printed image of a beautiful dog and a good-luck wish on it, saying: "Try to bark better tonight!". . . . This is an established tradition at my Scala premieres, and these cards became my good-luck charm.

    Franco Corelli, as told to G. Fogliani, "Sto per conquistare Broadway,"
    Eva, October 15, 1964

More than once Corelli attested that stress helped him to peak. As unbelievable as it sounds, the one thing that got him in tune was once more his eternal rival, Del Monaco! The latter seemed to have copied Franco's tactics of the previous year by issuing press statements shortly before Corelli's opening night as

> December 7, 10, 12, 15, and 19, 1964
> Giacomo Puccini: *Turandot*
> Milan, Teatro alla Scala
> Birgit Nilsson, Amy Shuard [December 19] (*Turandot*), Franco Corelli (*Calaf*), Galina Vishnevskaya (*Liù*), Angelo Mercuriali (*Emperor Altoum*), Nicola Zaccaria (*Timur*), Renato Capecchi, Dino Mantovani [December 15, 19] (*Ping*), Franco Ricciardi (*Pang*), Piero De Palma (*Pong*), cond. Gianandrea Gavazzeni

Calaf in *Turandot*. Recovered from the accident and back in business, he suddenly spread word that Bing had engaged him as Samson for the 1965–66 season. Franco vented his anger to Bauer, now recovered from his illness, in a telephone tirade lasting about an hour, in which the tenor accused both Bauer and Bing of betrayal and foul play. With that he canceled his entire Met contract for the 1965–66 season. Bauer rushed over to his apartment and lied to him, saying that the whole story was an invention of Del Monaco's and contained not a grain of truth.[52]

Graziano Corelli with his cousin Franco in between acts at Franco's opening of La Scala, December 7, 1964. (Photo: Courtesy of Graziano Corelli)

Although Del Monaco was telling the truth about Bing's interest in him, the continuing premature announcements of his return to the Met started to work against him. With his prolonged absence, they started looking more and more like desperate cries. Corelli, on the other hand, was determined to prove his value, and when the thunderclouds gathered under Milan's December sun, he outdid himself in what Bauer judged his greatest Calaf of all.[53]

Perhaps his studies with Lauri-Volpi paid off here as well, although "just another Calaf" was not the opera he had had in mind with which to celebrate his fifth consecutive Scala opening. He blamed this on Ghiringhelli. With the Met solidly behind him, his position toward La Scala's intendant had changed fundamentally. In addition, the claques at La Scala and the Italian press who openly relished his quarrels with Del Monaco were bothering him more and more all the time.

❖❖❖❖❖

Caught in the middle of this quintessential moment in Corelli's career were the DiGrazias from New York. When Franco had learned that they were going to be in Europe around this time—Mrs. DiGrazia had been invited on a tour there with the International Ladies Garment Workers' Union—he said enthusiastically to Loretta: "Then let's invite the DiGrazias out for dinner in Milan!" Said Donald DiGrazia:

That was the first time from being backstage that he made the overture to us. We met him in front of the Duomo, which I have a beautiful picture of: me with my arm around him, my father, my mom; you know. From that time our relationship kind of changed. We became more close, although we weren't like real friends, unless you talked to my uncle Johnny, whom he called Giovanni! He was a jeweler and spoke Italian very well. We didn't; that would always be a barrier. But he liked us nevertheless. The fact that we operated as a family may have reminded him of the family he had at home, in Italy. He missed that; all he did in New York was singing, studying, or watching westerns on his television. In a sense, he was a lonely man.[54]

❖❖❖❖❖

Wearing the laurels from Milan, Corelli seized the opportunity to settle any remaining issues, such as how to avoid paying all those nasty American income taxes. Now that Gorlinsky had proved his usefulness with EMI, Corelli asked Bing to go through the agent as well. That, however, Bing vetoed: he refused to deal with Gorlinsky because of past experiences involving Callas and Tito Gobbi. To console Franco, Bing accompanied his letter with a $5,000 check as compensation for the collapse of the *Turandot* film project with the National General Corporation. Happy New Year![55]

CHAPTER 15 ❖ 1965

Mixed Emotions

January–March 1965: Money for Nothing

As I said, the shabbiness is unbelievable, but all is well and everybody seems happy.
  Rudolf Bing describing to Roberto Bauer his endless negotiations with the Corellis over a $50 raise, April 2, 1965

With a $5,000 "money for nothing" check, the New Year would indeed have started out well for anyone else, but not Franco. He had really hoped to do the film, for he had by now become aware of the importance of opera movies, both for one's imminent reputation and for posterity. The most inconvenient circumstance, though, was that he had accepted a single concert performance at Lewisohn Stadium for June 21, during the time scheduled for filming. He now faced a three-week period of doing nothing in New York while lucrative offers from Europe were beckoning.[1] Worse yet, word had reached him that Callas and Michel Glotz (whom he now counted among his mortal enemies) had obtained a large number of seats for Callas's claque at the scheduled Callas-Corelli *Tosca* at the Met, scheduled later in 1965. In response, Loretta demanded a minimum of twenty seats, so that "at least someone would applaud Franco as well."[2] The Corellis having got that off their chests, Franco went back to the United States, where he sang in a jubilee concert with Leontyne Price at the Academy of Music in Philadelphia. It was followed by his Met *Forza del Destino* obligations, which started on January 29. In the programs, EMI/Angel came up with a sweet compromise on his billing: "Conceivably the greatest tenor currently occupied in the business of Italian Opera." The *New York Post* reporter who was quoted here couldn't have come up with a

> January 23, 1965
> The Academy of Music 108th Anniversary Concert
> Philadelphia, Academy of Music
> Verdi: *Ernani* "Ernani, involami" (Price). Puccini: *La Bohème* "Che gelida manina"; *La Fanciulla del West* "Ch'ella mi creda" (Corelli). Verdi: *Aida* "O terra addio" (Corelli and Price)
> Franco Corelli, Leontyne Price, cond. William Steinberg; Van Cliburn (piano)

more flattering line if he'd been bribed.[3] Understandably, a tenor who was advertised like that had to be reckoned with. When Corelli's Met contract for the 1966–1967 season was signed on March 10, it was through Gorlinsky after all.[4] During the negotiations Corelli drove a very hard bargain. In the last round, they struggled over a raise of $50 per performance more for eleven tour performances. Bing, on the verge of collapse, caved: "As he will only be making approximately one hundred and seventy-five thousand dollars from the Metropolitan, he obviously feels very happy at these extra five hundred and fifty dollars! In return for this I made him give up one broadcast which was very important to us."[5]

Weary of eternally having to humiliate himself on behalf of guaranteed sold-out performances, Bing was overjoyed when the new tenor in town, Bruno Prevedi, debuted successfully on March 6 as Cavaradossi—a Corelli part! By March 25, after an equally successful Alvaro in *Forza del Destino*, he expressed the hope that Prevedi might be a successor to "the Corellis," who were getting more and more insufferable.[6] Then, just as Bing was about to sign the "divorce papers," the incredible happened: out of the blue, Corelli signed the contract, and a contract for the next season as well. He had run into trouble with Ghiringhelli, who wanted to let Bergonzi open the season. When Corelli raised the stakes, Ghiringhelli called his bluff, leaving the divo suddenly very eager to secure his income and reputation at the Met.[7] Bing jumped at the chance. Not only did he have Corelli locked in for two years to come, but finally he had emerged the winner in his battles with Ghiringhelli—battles he usually lost. His only concern was to hide his joy from Corelli. Bauer therefore was to write to the tenor that as usual, Franco had gotten everything he wanted: "It is important that you say that, because he told Robert Herman that 'as usual Mr.

Bing got everything he wanted,' and while this is more or less true, I don't want him in any way to feel that I am triumphant."[8]

March 19–25, 1965: Callas Returns!

Callas at the Met in Tosca: a triumph. The performance had already ended 25 minutes before and part of the audience was still applauding. The ushers had to intervene to show them out, they wouldn't leave and wanted to see her again.
  "Callas splendida spettatori in delirio," Il Giorno [Milan], March 21, 1965

Seven years of absence earned Callas a triumphant return to the Metropolitan Opera House. From the correspondence we know that Bing hadn't suddenly forgiven her for the breach of contract seven years earlier. They simply hadn't managed to realize any of their many plans since then until they finally got together on the terrace of a Parisian café after the Callas-Corelli *Norma* of 1964 to discuss the possibilities face to face. Naturally, both Callas and Bing designed her comeback with Corelli in mind, which almost started another tenor war when Richard Tucker demanded the first night. That fight was a lost cause; Bing called his bluff, and Tucker fell back into his role as second-best tenor.

The Met was sold out long in advance. Those who hadn't been able to obtain tickets ahead of time started lining up a whole week in advance, covering for each other when one needed a coffee break or some food. When black-market prices shot up to $800 on the day of the performance, Bing personally went down twice a day to hand the desperate Callas-Corelli-Gobbi fans coffee, as did

> **March 19 and 25, 1965**
> **Giacomo Puccini:** *Tosca*
> **New York, Metropolitan Opera House**
> Maria Callas (*Tosca*), Franco Corelli, Richard Tucker [Mar 25] (*Cavaradossi*), Tito Gobbi (*Scarpia*), Metropolitan Opera Chorus and Orchestra, cond. Fausto Cleva; stage director, Dino Yannopoulos; set and costume designer, Frederick Fox; Floria Tosca's costumes, Marcel Escoffier

his management.⁹ Old Met standees confessed that they hadn't seen a frenzy like this since the debut of Amelita Galli-Curci in 1918 or Geraldine Farrar's farewell in 1922.¹⁰ Of course, Donald DiGrazia's family was there as well, trying every trick in the true-fan book to get in:

> We couldn't get tickets, but we knew the ushers and tried to get in past the security, which was almost impossible because of the Callas factor. She had private security guys positioned all over the house, because she was afraid that Tebaldi fans would throw vegetables on her, which had happened in the past. Somehow we managed, though, with my mom actually occupying an empty orchestra seat, thanks to a befriended usher! She was so nervous and scared to be caught that she didn't remember a damned thing! But we were there! Of course we were there, are you kidding? How could we not be there? The return of Callas! My God!¹¹

⸫⸫⸫⸫⸫

Callas arrived three hours before the performance was to begin. Bing brought roses to her dressing room, where the famous reconciliation photos were taken of Callas and Bing in a warm embrace.¹² In the auditorium she was greeted by a long banner, unfolded by her fans, that read "Welcome home"—she had, after all, been born in New York. Whoever had jewelry to show off wore it to the occasion. The widowed Jacqueline Kennedy arrived in an aquamarine dress and white leather jacket, accompanied by her late husband's mother, Rose, and the rest of the Kennedy clan.¹³ Jackie looked absolutely gorgeous next to Bing, who proudly accompanied her to his box, where she was the guest of honor.¹⁴ When Fausto Cleva finally arrived in the

A beaming Corelli with Callas and Bing. Said Paul Jaretzki, Bing's associate artistic administrator: "Bing was crazy about Callas—in both meanings of the word." (Photo: Louis Melançon. Courtesy of the Metropolitan Opera Archives)

pit, the Met's general manager readily acknowledged who was in charge that night. Not he, Corelli, Gobbi, or even Callas—it was the fans. Franco started the show: his entrance aria, "Recondita armonia," was effectively the opera's opening number. He was audibly nervous, but his two-ticket claque (all the tickets Bing had granted Loretta, out of the twenty she had asked for) proved unnecessary: he was greeted with forty seconds of applause and bravos. From that moment on everybody held their breath in anticipation of the diva. When Franco opened the small door to the chapel through which Callas entered the scene, the house exploded. Cleva tried to continue but finally decided to lay down his baton until, a minute and twenty seconds later, the public was composed and ready for the rest.[15] Gobbi, already the quintessential Scarpia of the twentieth century, was likewise cheered when he first entered the stage. At the end of Act II the applause went on for over ten minutes; once it finished,

The torture scene in *Tosca*, with Callas acting the part in what stands as one of the legendary nights that defined opera in the twentieth century. (Photo: Courtesy of the Metropolitan Opera Archives)

so charged was the atmosphere that those in the audience would hardly leave their seats.

From that point on legend and reality diverge a little. According to *Corriere della Sera*, white, red, and green carnations were thrown onto the stage after Callas started blowing kisses at her fans. The roses are one thing, though they fell only during the one minute and forty seconds of applause after "Vissi d'arte."[16] However, for Callas, the most convincing actress in opera of the twentieth century, to step out of character in mid-performance is inconceivable. In fact, just as Callas had requested, the opera passed much as any other *Tosca* would, with loud applause for Corelli's "Vittoria!" and a three-minute ovation after "E lucevan le stelle."[17] Only at the opera's conclusion did the expected pandemonium come, with her fans roaring, "Brava Callas," "Callas more often at the Met!," and "Bravissima Callas!"[18] Before taking another six solo bows, she took six together with Corelli and Gobbi. Corelli was showered with roses from his numerous female admirers. Gallantly, under renewed applause, the erstwhile Cavaradossi picked up a rose and offered it to his beloved Tosca. Wrote Egon Stadelman: "He could afford it, as, from a musical point of view, the night had belonged to him."[19]

According to the reviews, the final ovation lasted about twenty-five minutes and stopped only when the ushers intervened to show the fans out—they wouldn't leave on their own.[20] The evening ended close to midnight, when fans knocked in approval on the windows of the limousine that took Callas to her hotel.[21] The critics' remarks were relatively mild regarding Callas's vocal condition, although Schonberg couldn't resist dissecting the *beaux restes* of the diva's voice. Still, even he acknowledged her triumphant return, and there could be no question as to whose night it had been as far as the audience was concerned.[22]

❖❖❖❖❖

One interesting point about the Corelli-Callas *Tosca* (available with fine sound on Ombra Records, OMB7008) is that it featured his most elaborate "E lucevan le stelle" *messa di voce* to date. His increasing indulgence in and security with this sort of playing to the gallery is confirmed in a report on his Public Hall Radamès with the Met in Cleveland. Not only did his last-minute appearance on the cast list help sell out the 8,402-seat auditorium, but it also constituted the first-ever reported example of his diminuendo on the B-flat of "Celeste Aida": "He took that climactic note somewhat softly, as it should be."[23]

June 1965: The Fifth Beatle

Franco's return to his native soil at the transition of May to June did not go unnoticed. He recalled his recent triumphs in *Musica e Dischi*, where he proudly mentioned that he was allowed to address Bing in a familiar and personal manner. Moreover, the American press had labeled him "the Fifth Beatle" because of his fans' hysteria, for which he would be eternally grateful: "The realization that many persons feel close to you, care for you, listen to your recordings, travel long distances just to hear you sing, stand up for you, is a very strange awareness for an artist. They force you to give the very best you possibly can and more. Only in that way you can reward them for all those testimonies of faith and love."[24]

It is quite clear that Corelli was both impressed with and genuinely fond of America. Interestingly, none of the three greatest things he recalled from his first three years there were of a musical nature. Instead, each and every one of them dealt with human signs of affection. The first was Bing's backstage embrace after his "Pira" in the *Trovatore* debut of 1961; the second was the meeting with the Kennedys after his Library of Congress concert in 1962; the third was the society hostess Elsa Maxwell rather surprisingly telling him that he was "her last true love" (she had written him a letter shortly before her death on November 1, 1963, and he kept it throughout his life).[25]

July–August 1965: Behind the EMI *Turandot*

Corelli's most successful song album was *Granada & Other Romantic Songs*, which he recorded in June 1965. Next to some melodious Italian-language evergreens, it contains very *joyeuse* interpretations of the Spanish title song and "Te quiero," a couple of French-language songs, including "Pourquoi fermer ton coeur?," and the English-language standards "I Love Thee," by Edvard Grieg, and "Because."

This summer was the time to hammer out at least one of his not-yet-completed EMI recording projects, and he settled on *Turandot*. This time, with Birgit Nilsson in the title role, the odds were particularly good that it would be a success; but in the end the project proved a difficult undertaking. The trouble started when the conductor, Sir John Barbirolli, refused to accept Corelli. That forced EMI to decide who was more important for the project. The answer was obvious, and so Francesco Molinari-Pradelli took over.[26] With that finally settled, Mirella Freni became indisposed. Fortunately, through Corelli's personal intervention Renata Scotto agreed to step in at the last minute.[27] In turn and each on his or her own grounds, Corelli, Nilsson, and Scotto found themselves in disagreement with the conductor.[28] Wrote Bauer: "Over the phone Loretta shouted to me that Molinari was a major jerk (which is correct) and that everyone ends up fighting with him (which unfortunately is also correct) and Franco would no longer sing with him."

Normally that wouldn't have mattered, but Molinari-Pradelli had also been engaged as the conductor for Corelli's upcoming opening night in San Francisco. While there was still plenty of time to mend fences for that, things were going from bad to worse at the summer recording sessions. There was not even any love lost between Franco and Nilsson, for Franco walked out long before they could even fall in love. Said Nilsson:

> I didn't sing with him. When I came from Bayreuth I didn't have more than two days, and he was sick and tired of it. "You can do your things and then I will do mine with earphones in London," he said. So it was a love at a distance, me at La Scala, he in London, where he mastered the dynamics the way he wanted. And that is why you can't hear my big notes there because his are way too overpowering."[29]

Regardless, Nilsson still offered to coach Corelli as Tristan, should he wish to sing it at her side.[30]

September 1, 1965: Cancellation of the San Francisco Opening

Corelli had had a hernia troubling him during performances for quite some time, and by September surgery could no longer be put off. The operation was scheduled to allow him to heal just in time to honor his September–October engagement at the San Francisco Opera, where he was due to open the season. Unfortunately, toward the end of September, while recuperating in Cortina, he slipped on a wet stone. He landed most awkwardly, injured his leg, and strained the barely healed surgical incision. A doctor confined him to two full weeks of immobility. That kept him away from San Francisco, where he was expected for rehearsals sometime between October 8 and 10. In view of Corelli's recent dispute with Molinari-Pradelli, Bauer went to great lengths to assure both Bing and Kurt Herbert Adler, San Francisco Opera's general director, that Franco was really confined to bed.[31]

Bing was in the loop mainly because he feared a breach-of-contract lawsuit from Adler, which might ban Corelli from appearing in the United States. His anxiousness to have Franco fulfill his obligations at the rival theater vanished, though, once he learned that the tenor was not only truly ill, but also following his doctor's orders so that he would be sure to arrive in shape at the Met.[32] Wrote Bauer to Bing: "We know that Franco is a hypochondriac. But why should we persuade him in this matter, when all we care for is that he arrives in shape to us in December."[33] Poor Adler, the next in line to put his fate in the hands of that friendly man, Roberto Bauer, who seems to have been either the only one with Franco's phone number or the only one who spoke Italian.

From both Bauer's statement and the time line, it is quite clear that Franco could have appeared at San Francisco's opening night (he was fit enough to travel from Cortina to Milan on October 6). The loss of San Francisco may not have seemed as important at the time as losing the Met or La Scala, but it is clear that opening the San Francisco season would have given his American career an enormous boost. As it was, he arrived just in time for a single, scarcely noted *Tosca* performance that proved to be Jess Thomas's finest hour, as Arthur Bloomfield wrote in *Fifty Years of the San Francisco Opera*: "Three different Cavaradossis appeared, [Sándor] Konya, Jess Thomas and Franco Corelli. The most intelligent and best presented one was the winning hero Jess Thomas."[34]

With San Francisco, Corelli chalked up another mark on his reputation for last-minute cancellations. On the whole this was undeserved: he rarely canceled and had more than once saved the day when colleagues fell ill. But as with Callas, audiences lined up days in advance for "Mr. Sold Out," paying whatever they had to. His cancellations were therefore the ones that were remembered. In the end, losing San Francisco proved disastrous for Franco personally as well; he was so depressed over the lost opportunity that his full recovery took many more weeks than the doctors had hoped.

October 1–12, 1965: On Low Cs and "Corelli-itis"

Why should we sing those high Cs while nobody was paying us for it? We were saving ourselves in rehearsal, naturally.
  Birgit Nilsson on Corelli's only recorded "Ti voglio tutto ardente," in which he takes Puccini's low option; interviews, April 10, 2005, and June 2005

One of the rare cases where a Corelli rehearsal was recorded by someone other than himself was an October 1965 *Turandot* rehearsal from Philadelphia. The portion recorded is from the Riddle Scene and provides a nice insight into his backstage routine. Whether because it was so soon after his operation, or because it was his usual practice at rehearsals, he sings the lower option on his stellar high-C phrase "Ardente" in "Ti voglio tutto ardente." Suddenly one can hear the difference between the singer with the C and the one without it. That sort of C made all the difference when Corelli negotiated with Bing over money, role, and opening nights, as Carlo Bergonzi was about to find out. Bergonzi had recently demanded to be included in next year's opening week of the new house. He also demanded that some of Corelli's festive *Gioconda*s be transferred to him, because Enzo Grimaldo was his best role. When Bergonzi didn't get what he wanted, he raised the financial stakes until Bing, fed up with this new case of "Corelli-itis," informed Bergonzi that he could take it or leave it.[35]

Just as Bergonzi accepted his new role as the Met's second fiddle, next to Tucker, Vickers, and company, Del Monaco once again knocked on the Met's doors. He practically begged Bing to let him have one or two performances at the Met in the context of an American tour he was going to undertake during the next year. He didn't even make financial

A regal Dick Johnson, aka Ramerrez, December 1965. (Photo: Louis Melançon. Courtesy of the Metropolitan Opera Archives)

> October 12, 1965
> Giacomo Puccini: *Turandot* (rehearsal)
> Philadelphia, Academy of Music
> Birgit Nilsson (*Turandot*), Franco Corelli (*Calaf*), Philadelphia Lyric Opera Chorus and Orchestra, cond. Anton Guadagno

or repertoire demands. Once Bauer and Bing discovered that Del Monaco's record company had demanded that he sustain ticket sales through a return to the Met, they finally had him where they wanted him.[36]

Alas, it was Corelli who ruled at the Met, and Montserrat Caballé saw the proof of it. While waiting her turn to be admitted into Bing's office the day after her Met debut on December 22, she heard a lot of high-pitched talking inside the general manager's office. Eventually the door opened, and a beaming Corelli emerged. When the Caballés entered, they found Bing playing nursemaid to Corelli's "exquisitely coiffured poodle."[37]

CHAPTER 16 ❖ 1966

The Best-Fed Tenor in the World!

January–April 1966: Magic

Until a few years ago, piano and legato were unheard in a Corelli performance; today, he can summon both when the mood and moment are upon him. True, he will on other occasions sob outrageously, but these outbursts are, after all, the birthright of the breed. You can take the tenor out of Italy, but never the Italian out of the tenor.
　　Emily Coleman, "Born to the Breed," *Opera News*, February 5, 1966

The dawn of 1966 shows the Corellis very much at home in New York. Bing's correspondence on Corelli diminishes by at least 90 percent. From Franco's side, 1966 held but a single request for a change of dates and one for his usual thirty-second cut in the first-act *Carmen* duet in a future performance. Even the former battles over the last dime were over, with the ritual question regarding tax deductions reduced to a single letter. Bing's legendary magic box may have helped out here after all: "If one pushed a little button, the box emitted loud human laughter. I used it with artists with whom I had friendly personal contact. So when Corelli came in to ask for a higher fee, unnoticeably to him I activated the little box. It broke the tension and things went more easily thereafter."[1]
　　With La Scala out, Franco devoted up to half a year to the Met instead of a few months. Freed from the need to study new parts and fully at ease with his routine, he even ceased his usual objections to switching operas from performance to performance. The year 1966 had him opening on January 3 with *Aida*, followed by *Fanciulla del West*, from which he went to *La Bohème* and then another *Aida* and *Fanciulla*. If that weren't enough, January also found him in *Tosca* and the Met's new production of *Andrea Chénier*. The *Aida* of January

22, with Martina Arroyo, Irene Dalis, John Macurdy, and Sherrill Milnes, was memorable for a very specific reason. Donald DiGrazia remembers receiving a phone call from Corelli one night at 1:30 A.M.: "Don, I started to figure out this pianissimo on the B-flat!" Recalled DiGrazia: "He was so excited! And then, of course, he did it!"[2]

That January 22 *Aida* was the first time his diminuendo on the B-flat in "Celeste Aida" was first captured. Taking down the B-flat from a full-voice attack to a pianissimo that ends with a *morendo* is a tricky thing to do with any voice, let alone one the size of Corelli's. Here he audibly struggles to bend his voice to his will, and though he ends a little flat, the diminuendo is there. Moreover, in the aria and the rest of the performance one can hear all that is hinted at in *Opera News* about his new vocal palette. He revels in dynamic changes, in taking back volume in passages to be sung *morbidezza* (with great delicacy). It is no longer the vocal attack in "Pur ti riveggo, mia dolce Aida" that we remember, but the heart-rending tomb scene, where his newfound lyrical qualities work magic. Whereas the B-flat in the *romanza* is the most generally renowned one, the delicate and ravishing B-flats in the tomb scene are the reference point for the connoisseur.

◆◆◆◆◆

Such versatile vocalizing despite a voice his size admittedly doesn't go well with the more mathematic principles of singing. Corelli's is the passionate, Italianate art of *smorzando*, the yearning intensity of certain phrases, which is more important to him than how he gets from A to B. He frequently indulges in excessive use of portamento and scoops to get back in line when he remembers that somewhere out there an orchestra is waiting for him. His intervals are often approximate, but that is to be expected from a voice that revs up like a B-52. Once it takes off, it answers to no law but the law of gravity. He lacks the vocal accuracy of Alfredo Kraus and Carlo Bergonzi, but they were not "born to the breed" in the same way as were Tamagno, Caruso, Zenatello, Pertile, Martinelli, Del Monaco, and Corelli—the last in the line.

March 1966: Unexpected Rivals and Fig-Stuffed Prosciutto

In the end, even a tenor born to the breed is but a human being. A persistent cold forced him to cancel his January 17 *Fanciulla del West* with Steber (herself replacing an indisposed Dorothy Kirsten) after Act I.[3] Defeat also struck in Miami, where the world's reigning Radamès had to bow before an unusual pair of *comprimari*: two trumpeting elephants that were the crowning glory in a triumph scene that also featured real camels and horses. Such splendors even surpassed Corelli's physique, although he was spared comparison with the heavyweight champion Cassius Clay, who passed on the offer to take a silent role as one of the soldiers in this sensational production. Not that Franco was easily defeated; he challenged the animals with another demonstration of his high B-flat pianissimo on the strength of Loretta's famous Fig-Stuffed Prosciutto and Fettucine, the recipe for which had been published recently in *Opera News*:[4]

Fig-Stuffed Prosciutto

¼ pound Italian prosciutto (about 8 thin slices)

8 small ripe figs

8 tablespoons gelatin, softened in lukewarm water

Peel and mash the figs. Place about a tablespoon of pulp (the size of a large walnut) in the center of each slice of prosciutto. Roll carefully into a cylinder. Arrange the rolls on a serving dish and sprinkle the gelatin over them. Chill thoroughly. Garnish with fig leaves or other greens, plus one or two whole figs if desired. Serves four.

Fettucine

1 pound fettucine noodles or other flat noodle about ½ inch wide

1 cup softened sweet butter (preferably whipped)

1 cup heavy cream

1 cup freshly grated Parmesan cheese, plus extra for garnish

⅓ cup freshly chopped parsley

Boil the noodles in six quarts of salted water till *al dente*. In a large porcelain or enamel skillet, melt the butter over low heat. Gradually add the cream, stirring constantly. Drain the cooked noodles, add them all at once to the butter-and-cream mixture, and toss gently for two to four minutes until the sauce is almost completely absorbed. Garnish with the extra cheese and parsley and serve immediately. Serves four.

March 1966: Well Compensated

Meanwhile, in London, EMI executives received a harsh reminder that they had double-crossed Corelli with their Callas-Bergonzi *Tosca* recording. The financial compensation they had offered didn't soothe Franco's hurt pride. Recording was as competitive a sport as was opening opera theaters, and Corelli didn't hesitate to sign up with Decca for the next two let-outs on his EMI contract. The *Faust* was perhaps not of much concern to EMI, but Decca's planned Corelli-Nilsson *Tosca* caused some panic. Their strategy was to offer Corelli a new three-year contract on the spot in order to keep him away from Decca and from RCA, who were both trying to sign him up for exclusive contracts of their own. EMI's offer consisted of *Aida* and a solo recording in 1967, and a very surprising doubling of his *Cavalleria Rusticana* and *Pagliacci* (this time with Callas) along with either a solo album or a duet recording with Nilsson in 1968. He was also free to choose one opera out of *Un Ballo in Maschera, La Fanciulla del West, Ernani,* or *Roméo et Juliette* and would be allowed another solo record for 1969. The list was impressive, but Corelli was not happy with the financial terms offered. EMI then exercised their option to extend the current contract by another year to 1968. That effectively prevented him from joining the competition, but it also left a big question mark for post-1968.[5]

March was not a very good month for contractual matters. Besides his failed negotiations with EMI, he was also found guilty of breach of contract in Milan with regard to two performances as Manrico in *Il Trovatore* that he was to have sung in Busseto. He had canceled this engagement immediately after the *Chénier* recording for EMI, when he became convinced that he was suffering from a nervous breakdown.[6] Corelli was sentenced to pay a 2 million lire ($2,300) fine and 324,305 lire ($520) in court costs.[7]

April 5, 1966
Umberto Giordano: *Andrea Chénier*
Philadelphia, Academy of Music
Franco Corelli (*Andrea Chénier*), Montserrat Caballé (*Maddalena di Coigny*), Dino Dondi (*Carlo Gérard*), Rita De Carlo (*Bersi*), cond. Anton Guadagno

April 5, 1966: Sabotage in Philly?

When I am angry I am not a person who loses my temper for everyone to see. Instead, I keep it bottled up inside me and somehow manage to channel it into my performance.

> Montserrat Caballé after the Corellis allegedly tried to sabotage her performance, in Robert Pullen and Stephen Taylor, *Montserrat Caballé: Casta Diva*, 1994

What did Franco do to Montserrat Caballé that made her announce she would never sing the part of Maddalena again?[8] Perhaps it wasn't even Franco, but Loretta. Incredibly, the diva entered her dressing room to prepare for Act I and discovered that all the elaborate lace trim had been ripped from her crinoline. In addition, the black velvet dress she had to wear for Acts II–IV had been hacked with scissors and her powdered white wig cut into pieces. When the general manager, Ray Fabiani, and Caballé's husband entered to see what was going on, they found her in a state of collapse, traumatized and in tears. Caballé initially refused to accept the idea that the couple from the dressing room next door was behind the attack (an idea apparently supported by or given in the presence of Fabiani, who was still Corelli's U.S. manager at the time). She changed her mind only when Franco and Loretta entered, apparently to see what all the commotion was about. According to Pullen and Taylor, "Signora Corelli advanced solicitously upon the vandalized wig, and to this day Montserrat bridles at the reminiscence of the strange tones with which the woman stroked the object, cooing 'povero perruchetto'—'poor little wiggy'—all the while."[9]

While the house waited, Caballé's husband rushed back to their hotel to get her *Traviata* wig. Meanwhile the wardrobe staff performed an *improviso* on the torn-up dresses and grabbed a stock replacement for the crinoline. That gave Loretta ample time to start Franco's pre-performance rituals, which had her "dancing attendance backstage on her increasingly hysterical husband, rubbing a crucifix up and down his throat to repeated cries of 'Madonna, Madonna.'" Caballé decided to settle the score onstage, but despite some ravishing high pianissimos the part was not very congenial to her talents.[10] Whether because of Andrea or Loretta, she parted from Philadelphia with the vow never to appear in the opera again—a promise she chose not to hold herself to.

April 16, 1966: Closing Time

The Met is dead! Long live the Met!
   Final words of Rudolf Bing's speech at the beginning of the Met's Farewell Gala

Whereas many American singers and members of the audience shed some tears, a good many European singers were looking forward to what lay ahead. Bing himself never understood the protests from some singers and conductors who wanted to preserve the old building. To him it was just a pile of bricks that stood between the Met and its entry into modern times. The backstage areas and indeed the stage itself were hopelessly inadequate to the more three-dimensional stage requirements of modern productions. Once more he played his trump cards, Corelli and Tebaldi—this time in a media campaign that had them modeling for magazines focusing on the splendors of the new house—and to lessen the pain he had scheduled an American opera, Samuel Barber's *Anthony and Cleopatra*, to open the new house. However, he also liked the idea of lowering the curtain on the old house with a big closing-night gala, both for the box-office appeal and to mark a historic moment. The roster of singers gave a fair overview of his sixteen-year tenure at the Met.

> April 16, 1966
> **Farewell Gala for the Old Met**
> **New York, Metropolitan Opera House at Broadway and Thirty-ninth Street**
> Featuring, in order of appearance, Anna Moffo, Charles Anthony, Robert Merrill, James McCracken, Anselmo Colzani, Cesare Siepi, Dorothy Kirsten, Regina Resnik, Thelma Votipka, Licia Albanese, Jon Vickers, Fernando Corena, Roberta Peters, Jan Peerce, Giorgio Tozzi, Régine Crespin, Leontyne Price, Renata Tebaldi and Franco Corelli, Sándor Kónya, Birgit Nilsson, Jean Madeira, Mary Curtis Verna, Kurt Baum, John Macurdy, Mario Sereni, Teresa Stratas, Eleanor Steber, Mignon Dunn, Blanche Thebom, John Alexander, Montserrat Caballé, Rosalind Elias, Zinka Milanov, Richard Tucker, Gabriella Tucci, Nicolai Gedda, Jerome Hines, and others

For the program, Franco granted Bing's request to sing the "Tu, tu amore? Tu?" duet from *Manon Lescaut* with Tebaldi, somewhere in the middle of the program. Bing might have hoped it would stir the tenor's enthusiasm for the opera as a whole, for he was convinced of Corelli's potential as Des Grieux. The evening turned out to be one of the theater's most memorable. Even those who were not present could get an almost firsthand experience through the LP release of the closing night, for each recording contained an authentic piece of the old Met: the original Met stage curtain, which was cut up in as many pieces as there were box sets issued. The VIPs feasted on more substantial memorabilia: one actually managed to get the toilet seat from the prima donnas' restroom![11]

❖❖❖❖❖

Having settled their business in America with a final Met Spring Tour appearance in Boston, the Corellis returned to Europe, where Franco began his summer obligations with a handful of ill-received *Turandot*s at Covent Garden. The critics judged the production underrehearsed and criticized the tenor's self-indulgent, static acting.[12] His mind at the premiere may have been less with Amy Shuard's praised Turandot than with Sir Laurence Olivier, whom he consulted with regard to next year's *Roméo et Juliette* at the Met. *Corriere della Sera* even reported that they might discuss an *Otello*, with Karajan conducting and Olivier directing.[13]

June–July 1966: Recording with Nilsson

Upon his arrival in Italy, Corelli appeared on television in an episode of Erberto Landi's *Continental Miniatures* that featured pop singers such as Milva and opera stars singing popular Italian songs.[14] Following his contribution on the show, the song "Munastero 'e Santa Chiara," he went on to Rome, where he started working on the EMI *Aida* recording with Nilsson and Zubin Mehta. The latter had been released by Decca to EMI specifically to replace Sir John Barbirolli.[15]

Despite the rave reviews that came in for the just-released Nilsson-Corelli *Turandot* recording, their *Aida* was not among EMI's most satisfying recording ventures. Nilsson was an impressive *Aida* on stage, but volume and dramatic impact matter less in recording; she lacked the required warmth and *Italianità*. The most discussed novelty in the set was Corelli's sustained diminuendo on

> **June 4, 1966**
> Galdieri: "Munastero 'e Santa Chiara"
> *Continental Miniatures* (telecast)
> Host: Erberto Landi
>
> **June, July, and August 1966**
> Giuseppe Verdi: *Aida*
> Rome, Teatro dell'Opera (EMI recording)
> Birgit Nilsson *(Aida)*, Franco Corelli *(Radamès)*, Grace Bumbry *(Amneris)*, Ferruccio Mazzoli *(the King of Egypt)*, Bonaldo Giaiotti *(Ramfis)*, Mario Sereni *(Amonasro)*, cond. Zubin Mehta
>
> **June 20–30, 1966**
> Giacomo Puccini: *Tosca*
> Rome, Accademia di Santa Cecilia (Decca recording)
> Birgit Nilsson *(Tosca)*, Franco Corelli *(Cavaradossi)*, Dietrich Fischer-Dieskau *(Scarpia)*, cond. Lorin Maazel

the "Celeste Aida" B-flat, which now reached hundreds of thousands instead of a few thousand in the theaters. Although it was not achieved artificially, as some critics suggested, the effect is indeed not very satisfying here because he clearly recorded it separately from the aria, with which it never really blended in the final edit.

Birgit Nilsson's experiences recording operas with Corelli continued to be among her least cherished memories of her "great friend," as is clear from the Decca recording of *Tosca* that followed EMI's *Aida*. This time his problems weren't just with Nilsson but also with Dietrich Fischer-Dieskau's odd Scarpia. Fischer-Dieskau's beautiful instrument lacked anything that remotely resembled the required "bite." Furthermore, his voice, never huge, simply couldn't be heard opposite Nilsson or Corelli and so had to be amplified. Nilsson understood this procedure, but Franco insisted that the difference in volume between him and Fischer-Dieskau remain audible in the recording. He started singing even closer to the microphone in order to make it impossible for the engineers to fix Fischer-Dieskau's volume. Fischer-Dieskau had to sing ever louder, to the point where he forced himself. Said Nilsson: "That *Tosca* is so loud I can't listen to it."[16]

September 22–November 29, 1966: New Met, New Cook...

Halfway through September the Corellis returned to the United States, where Franco was expected to sing the final duet of *Andrea Chénier* with Tebaldi in an episode of *The Ed Sullivan Show,* scheduled before his first performance, in *La Gioconda,* at the new Met. Long lines of people trying to get the few tickets that were to be sold on the day before the show were queued up in front of the Met's box office, and Franco was happy to step outside and hand out cups of hot coffee to those in line. (Thursday there were already 200 people waiting for the 175 tickets available, and the line grew even longer on Friday.)[17] Franco was in a very good mood, and even some of those inside benefited from his food and beverage services, to judge from the *Morning Star Tribune.* Corelli prepared himself for opening night with a cake-and-milk breakfast at 12:30 and "A Salad to Sing About." The main course was still made up of raw steak with lemon, but there were two surprising innovations in the menu. First, he was concerned with the calorie issue, and then, he claimed that he himself loved cooking. "I enjoy cooking. One of my favorites for days when I do not sing is my rice salad. I sometimes make it for Rudolf Bing. You would like to have my recipe? My pleasure. Here it is, I make it for six persons":

Franco's Rice Salad

4 cups cooked long-grain rice

2 large ripe tomatoes cut into bite-sized pieces

2 tablespoons capers

8 anchovies, diced

1 teaspoon fresh basil (or ½ tablespoon dried)

2 6-oz. cans tuna packed in oil

1 lemon, plus 3 or 4 thin slices

Salt and pepper to taste

6 pitted black olives

Toss all ingredients lightly until just combined. Garnish with olives and sprigs of fresh parsley.

Then, despite the fact that the childless Corellis don't have a large family to cook for, Franco gives Ida Bailey Allen his menu for

Monday Dinner for the Family
Franco's Rice Salad
Minute Steaks Pan-Grilled in Olive Oil
Zucchini Sauté Parmesan
Baby Carrots
Baked Potatoes (if desired)
Danish Apple Cake or Assorted Cheeses with a Basket of Fresh Fruit
Coffee, Tea, Milk

Franco gives Bailey one more recipe so that fans can re-create his menu:

Zucchini Sauté Parmesan
1½ pounds young zucchini (about 6)
¼ cup olive oil
1 clove garlic, peeled and minced
½ teaspoon salt and ⅛ teaspoon pepper
¼ teaspoon dried basil
¼ teaspoon oregano
⅓ cup grated Parmesan cheese

Cut the ends off the zucchini, then slice them crosswise into slices about ¼ inch thick. Fry them briefly with the garlic in hot oil. Sprinkle with salt, pepper, basil, and oregano. Fry about 10 more minutes, then sprinkle with grated Parmesan. Serves 6.[18]

❖❖❖❖❖

Owing both to the occasion and to his fine vocal projection, the *Gioconda* night proved to be one of the highlights in Corelli's career, and that called for a good meal afterward! In spite of the recent revelation of his newest passion in the press, his post-performance love affair with cooking was usually consummated in fancy restaurants, such as Quo Vadis, where the *maître* had created Chicken Crêpes Corelli—crêpes stuffed with mushrooms and poached breast of capon in a curry sauce, then glazed with béchamel sauce and served with more béchamel or curry sauce or a simple cream sauce—in honor of his distinguished guest.[19]

Chicken Crêpes Corelli

1 breast of capon

6 mushroom caps

½ pint curry sauce

8 crêpes

½ pint béchamel sauce [see recipe on p. 342]

3 egg yolks, beaten

1 cup heavy cream

Salt and pepper to taste

Poach the capon breast in rich chicken stock, remove from the poaching liquid, and dice after it is cool enough to handle. Simmer the mushroom caps in butter. Add the diced capon and the curry sauce and simmer 5 minutes. Remove from the heat.

Put 2 tablespoons of the capon mixture in each crêpe and roll it up. Into the hot béchamel sauce but off heat, add the egg yolks and a cup of heavy cream beaten to a stiff froth. Season to taste. Pour the sauce over the crêpes and serve.[20]

**September 22; October 10 and 18 (Philadelphia);
October 22 and 29; November 3, 10, 14, 23, and 29, 1966
Amilcare Ponchielli:** *La Gioconda*
New York, Metropolitan Opera House

Renata Tebaldi (*La Gioconda*), Franco Corelli (*Enzo Grimaldo*), Biserka Cvejic (*Laura Adorno*), Cesare Siepi (*Alvise Badoero*), Mignon Dunn (*the Blind Woman*), Cornell MacNeil (*Barnaba*), cond. Fausto Cleva; stage director, Margherita Wallmann; set and costume designer, Beni Montresor

During the first months of the season Corelli alternated Enzo with an equal number of Calafs with Nilsson as his Turandot, which presented a fine opportunity to test the acoustics of the new Met. The outcome was unexpected: the new acoustics proved so good that people wondered whether the stage was amplified (a discussion that had been going on since Lily Pons's appearances at the Met in the 1940s). Corelli denied it: "Acoustics today are different than a hundred years ago. The sound from a new building may not be better or worse—just different."[21]

September–December 1966: Välkki

Apart from an exciting single *Don Carlo* in Philadelphia, an *Ed Sullivan Show* appearance (in color) with three Italian songs, and a few more *Aida*s in December, the only novelty in the last three months of 1966 consisted of a change of partners in *Turandot*. Anita Välkki had sung Act III of *Turandot* with Corelli in a haphazard concert at the Met in March 1965, but her only complete stage performances with him were the ones of November 26 and December 20, 1966. Franco may or may not have remembered her from the earlier gala, but having had no rehearsals with her, he arrived at the stage rather skeptical. Nilsson was among the audience: "Välkki was a Norwegian soprano and an outstanding Turandot. But when she started to sing, he put up his hand behind his ear, pretending

A Philadelphia performance of *Don Carlo* on October 25, 1966, with Franco, in the title role, standing near Louis Quilico (Rodrigo). Opera's bitter rivalries usually petered out as fast as they had started, but this *Don Carlo* remains Franco and Quilico's only joint performance (apart from an earlier *Don Carlo* in Paris in 1964) since their *Trovatore* clash on October 31, 1962. Standing between them is Joseph Salvadori (the Sacristan). On the far right is the Philadelphia Lyric Opera's president, William B. Warden. (Courtesy of Franca Warden and the Philadelphia Lyric Opera)

> **November 26, December 20, 1966**
> **Giacomo Puccini: *Turandot***
> **New York, Metropolitan Opera House**
> Anita Välkki (*Turandot*), Franco Corelli (*Calaf*), Mirella Freni, Teresa Stratas [December 20] (*Liù*), cond. Zubin Mehta

he couldn't hear her. She saw that and gave him her 'Just you wait, mister' look. When she got to her high C, he suddenly had to set all sails up in order to keep up with her."[22]

Välkki was an exuberant Turandot. Her luscious voice, with its blazing edge, was far more beautiful than Nilsson's voice of cold steel, while the recording that the Corellis made of it from the backstage sound system suggests that she matched Nilsson's vocal power. Though only portions were recorded, they provide the best sound ever heard in any Corelli live recording. The beauty of both voices is fully conveyed, and despite its choppy character, this is the desert-island recording of Corelli in *Turandot*.

November 27, 1966: Corelli Sings Out . . . for Lasagna

Somewhere in Corelli's hectic performance schedule, his press manager found opportunities to further promote Loretta's cooking. On November 27 the *Newark Star Ledger* opened with a whole page titled "Corelli Sings Out . . . for Lasagna." When the appetizer (prosciutto with peeled lemon slices) has all been eaten it's party time with:

Lasagna Anconetana
1 pound lasagna noodles
½ pound each chicken livers, sweetbreads, and cooked chicken breast
8 tablespoons sweet butter
1 onion, finely minced
½ cup dried mushrooms
1½ cups chicken stock
1 heaping teaspoon tomato paste
cinnamon

*3 cups béchamel sauce [see recipe below]
prepared in two batches of 1½ cups each
2 tablespoons Madeira wine
Salt and pepper
1½ cups grated Parmesan cheese
1 truffle (preferably white, but black will do)*

Soak the dried mushrooms in water for about half an hour. Cut the chicken livers, sweetbreads and chicken breasts into tiny pieces. Sauté lightly in four tablespoons butter. Set aside. In the remaining butter cook the onion until transparent, then add the dried mushrooms. Add ½ cup of chicken stock and simmer for 15 minutes.

Add the tomato paste and a pinch of cinnamon. Add another ½ cup of broth and simmer for 10 minutes.

Add one cup of béchamel sauce, blend well, and add another ½ cup of broth that has been diluted with the Madeira. Add salt and pepper to taste. Simmer over low heat for 15 minutes. Stir in the cooked meats.

Meanwhile, cook the lasagna noodles in a large pot of salted water. The noodles should be *al dente*. Drain thoroughly.

In a large rectangular or square baking dish (preferably enamel) begin with a layer of lasagna noodles, then spoon several tablespoons of the sauce over them. Sprinkle with the Parmesan cheese and a few slices of truffle.

Repeat the process, alternating the lasagna with the sauce, cheese, and truffle. Sprinkle the top layer with cheese.

Allow the dish to stand in a cool place overnight, or at least six to eight hours, but do not refrigerate.

Add two tablespoons of grated Parmesan cheese to the second batch of béchamel sauce and pour this over the lasagna.

Place the dish in a hot oven (400°F) for about 15 to 20 minutes or until the top begins to form a golden-brown crust. Serves five.

Béchamel Sauce

*⅛ cup flour
⅛ cup butter
1¼ cups milk
Salt and pepper*

Melt butter over very low heat. Gradually stir in the flour and blend thoroughly. Add milk slowly and continue to stir until mixture is thick and smooth. Add seasonings.

The article continued with Loretta's recipes for Cheese Mushroom Salad and Granita di Caffe (coffee ice).[23]

December 24–31, 1966: Franco Corelli's Christmas

Christmas for me is always a simple festa. *We have the family together and we eat and drink and go to Midnight Mass together. I remember when I was just a boy waiting on Christmas for Baba Natale. We have also La Befana, who comes on January 6, the Feast of the Epiphany. La Befana is an old witch who comes in the night and fills all good children's stockings with toys and treats and all bad children's stockings with coal. I was very afraid many times that I'd wake up and find my stockings full of coal.*
    Franco Corelli, in Ann C. Eisner, "Franco Corelli's Christmas,"
    Tape Recording, 1966–67

We don't [often] have snow in Ancona. To my friends in New York I can only explain it as something that maybe resembles Christmas in Los Angeles.
    Franco Corelli, in Ann C. Eisner, "Franco Corelli's Christmas,"
    Tape Recording, 1966–67

Corelli earned his Christmas presents in Philadelphia, where he participated in a benefit concert for the victims of the flood that had ravaged Florence on

> December 15, 1966
> **Concert for the Flood Victims of Florence**
> **Philadelphia, Academy of Music**
> Cardillo: "Core 'ngrato." Di Capua: "O sole mio." Lara: "Granada."
> Franco Corelli, Renata Tebaldi, Licia Albanese, Flaviano Labò, and Bonaldo Giaiotti, cond. Anton Guadagno

November 4, when the Arno River rose above its banks. The water entered the city's historic center, destroying everything from private homes to historical sites and irreplaceable libraries. Many initiatives were launched among wealthy Italians to contribute to the reconstruction,[24] and Corelli was among them:

> I want to support my Florence. I say "mine," because Florence is the place where I began my career. I organized the charity concert together with Ray Fabiani. We found many people who wanted to help: the theater and the orchestra offered their support for free. Lots of singers joined the concert, first of all Tebaldi, but also Licia Albanese, Bonaldo Giaiotti, Flaviano Labò, and many other artists and musicians. The audience came in numbers. Everybody was happy about the evening, me included. Since Christmas approaches and I'll be flying to Florence for appearances there, I want to send a special greeting to the ones who mostly suffered from the flood.[25]

The benefit (during which Julie Andrews visited his dressing room)[26] left only a single Calaf and a final Radamès at the Met between the tenor and his native soil. It was there that he and Loretta celebrated Christmas with "Lasagna . . . Newyorkese!" This one was a lot easier to make than the Italian version, judging from the recipe provided by the Radiocorriere Torino.[27] With that recipe in hand, all seemed set to massage Franco into accepting *Luisa Miller* over pasta, as his Christmas dinner date, Roberto Bauer, was planning. Unfortunately, Loretta's delicious lasagna could not mask the bitter taste that the name of Thomas Schippers brought to Franco's palate, caused by a dispute over certain musical values in their recent Met *Aida*s. He would consider Verdi's Rodolfo only if the conductor agreed to make the customary Italian cuts. With that he unpacked his camera equipment in order to film the celebrations. Christmas gave him the opportunity to reflect on life in general: "I live in New York for about four months of the year. I like it very much. It is different from Italy. But not so different. Italy is changing. There are more cars. More people. Life moves faster. Perhaps it is a way of life that started in America, but it is now becoming the way of life all over the world."[28]

CHAPTER 17 ❖ 1967

Italy Greets the Prodigal Son

January 7–21, 1967: "Core 'ngrato"

At the second performance happened a thing I heard only once before in my life: the public simply did not leave the house, howled and screamed until the direction put a piano at the end of the opera on the stage and Franco had to sing "Core 'ngrato" as encore!! But the public invaded the stage and simply would not let him go off!
    Roberto Bauer, quoted by Paul Jaretzki to Geraldine Souvaine,
    January 27, 1967

After two years of absence, Corelli must have imagined his return to Italy would be somewhat different than it turned out. With respect to his *Forza del Destino* performances in Florence, the established critic Giorgio Gualerzi wrote that the tenor suffered from a slight indisposition that caused a sudden diminishing of his volume, affecting his performance (apart from the Act III aria "O tu che seno agli angeli" and the duet "Solenne in quest'ora").[1] If so, then the audience of the Teatro Communale proved most tolerant, clearly remembering his spontaneous and widely publicized fund-raiser held in Philadelphia the month before to benefit the restoration of the flood-ravaged city. But an earlier report in the *Corriere della Sera* declared the *Forza* premiere a true success, with Corelli the finest among his colleagues, which suggests that Gualerzi must have been writing about one of the three repeat performances.[2]

    That Corelli had arrived in Italy in stupendous shape, with his voice seemingly warmer and a deeper shade of bronze than ever before, is evident from the famous recording of the second Parma *Tosca* with the American-born and -bred Tosca of Virginia Copeland, better known as Virginia Gordoni, on January 21.

> January 7, 10, 12, and 15, 1967
> Giuseppe Verdi: *La Forza del Destino*
> Florence, Teatro Communale
> Franco Corelli (*Don Alvaro*), Ilva Ligabue (*Leonora di Vargas*), Giancarlo Luccardi (*the Marquis of Calatrava*), Piero Cappuccilli (*Don Carlo di Vargas*), Paolo Washington (*Priest Guardiano*), Biancamaria Casoni (*Preziosilla*), Giorgio Giorgetti (*Brother Melitone*), cond. Oliviero De Fabritiis
>
> January 19 and 21*, 1967
> Giacomo Puccini: *Tosca*
> Parma, Teatro Regio
> Virginia Gordoni (*Tosca*), Franco Corelli (*Cavaradossi*), Attilio d'Orazi (*Scarpia*), cond. Giuseppe Morelli
> (*Encore: Cardillo, "Core 'ngrato")

Here Corelli brings down the house as in the days of the great songbirds, who were carried from the theaters to their hotels on the shoulders of the audience. And yet, as far as one can tell from existing recordings, he never stepped so far out of line as he does in this fine example of sheer vocal exhibitionism and what some consider bad taste. He caresses every single note as if it were an entire aria and seems intent on surpassing Fernando De Lucia when it comes to rubato singing and embellishment. In addition, he presents his fans with a prolonged B-flat at the climax of "Recondita armonia," followed by a twelve-second A-sharp on "Vittoria!"

Finally, his "E lucevan le stelle" lasts almost twice as long as normal and presents the musical line broken in pieces (although some still speak of "hushed beauty" here). Admittedly, observations based on a recording are irrelevant to the actual warm-blooded live performance. The audience was spellbound by his unprecedented diminuendo on the high A in "Disciogliea dai veli," a ballet of notes in Cinemascope slow motion, with Cavaradossi conducting the conductor, Giuseppe Morelli. The latter takes his revenge when he either denies Corelli the rare encore he seems about to give after the unprecedented ovation following his "E lucevan le stelle" or cuts his applause short in an attempt to continue. At that point the public seems to silence the orchestra by outshouting it. Morelli is forced to stop until a high-spirited Corelli signals the public that their time will come. He finishes the opera and then, just as in the days of Nellie Melba, a piano is dragged onto the stage and Corelli sings "Core 'ngrato."

1967: Addio Ettore Bastianini

The Duke of Mantua had fascinated Corelli ever since his first attempt at the two cheerful arias in his Cetra days, no doubt inspired by Mario Del Monaco's 1954 recording. Corelli included the Duke's arias in a handful of concerts, most notably in 1966–67, in preparation for an assumption of the role at the Met. In the end he couldn't deal with his doubts regarding the Duke's tessitura and the stage requirements of the role; the careless, philandering Duke was at the opposite end of the spectrum from Corelli's usual romantic parts. The solution to this dilemma was presented at an impromptu press conference given in the euphoria following his triumphant return to Italy. He would sing the Duke . . . on the silver screen! An intriguing plan, but nothing ever came of it.

Corelli captured the Italian public's attention once more before he left for Portugal, when a special honor was awarded him by the mysterious Verdians of the Grotta Mafalda, an influential organization of notables who were famous for having intentionally limited their membership to twenty-seven, one for each of Verdi's operas. Corelli was given a gold medal for his efforts in the maestro's operas, and the title of "Honorary Member" was bestowed on him.[3]

Corelli took great pride in this most peculiar honor, but his mind was elsewhere. In the breaks between performances, he traveled up and down to visit his friend and colleague Ettore Bastianini, whose throat cancer had progressed to a critical stage. The disease had forced the baritone to end his career in the 1965–66 season, when he sang his last Marquis de Posa in Verdi's *Don Carlo*. He died on January 25, 1967, leaving the operatic world to mourn. Corelli remembered him in Marina Boagno's Bastianini biography as great company whenever he was on top of his emotions:

> I remember a Naples *Tosca* and a *Chénier* where he would tell joke upon joke over dinner. Others tried to retell these jokes later on, but lacking his particular style and coloring, they failed to have the same impact. And Bastianini was a great friend as well. I remember *Trovatore* in Berlin, where he had a bottle

of champagne brought to me in my dressing room, with an accompanying note: "You are a veritable cannon!" When I gave an improvised encore concert afterward, he acted as the impresario, refusing to sing himself.[4]

As it turned out, even Corelli was unaware of the true reasons behind Bastianini's vocal decline until the very end: "My colleagues and I, we thought of pharyngitis and believed it could be cured by the doctors that we recommended to him. At first he didn't answer, but later he called to thank me, while saying that there was no doctor who could cure him. Only after his death did Professor Perotta inform me of Bastianini's long fight against that terrible disease."[5]

February 15, 1967: The Final EMI Contract

On February 15, 1967, Corelli's EMI contract was finally renewed on an exclusive three-year basis, with a minimum of two operas and one solo LP. Curiously, the operas included the *Aida* already made, in addition to which he could choose from among *Un Ballo in Maschera*, *La Fanciulla del West*, *La Forza del Destino*, and *Roméo et Juliette*. From these negotiations he went straight to EMI's Kingsway Hall studios to begin recording the required solo recital album. From Corelli's enthusiasm and the vocal condition he demonstrated in the Parma *Tosca*s, one would expect swift and spectacular results, especially with a collection of arias truly worthy of his stature. Unfortunately, the recording sessions collapsed almost as swiftly as they had begun, and despite numerous attempts, they were never completed.[7]

The reasons for the collapse are rather clouded today, but from the results of his first attempts at the arias it appears that, despite his Parma triumph, he was not in the best of shape. The "Quando le sere al placido" from *Luisa Miller* (the only memento of his plan, which went unrealized, to sing in that opera at the Met around this time) does not do him justice, and the occasional lisp that can be heard in many of his other recordings is very pronounced here. Some uneasy moments elsewhere among these recordings may have had something to do with the uneven sound balance, whereas the *Rigoletto* aria demonstrates why he backed out of singing that opera onstage. The unfinished state of the album is further demonstrated by the "Che gelida manina," which is incomplete. Corelli fared better in the arias that were from his active repertoire, such as

> February 1967
> London, Kingsway Hall (EMI recording)
> Verdi: *Luisa Miller* "Oh! fede negar potessi . . . Quando le sere al placido"; *La Forza del Destino* "La vita è inferno . . . O tu che in seno agli"; *Macbeth* "O figli, o figli miei! . . . Ah, la paterna mano"; *Rigoletto* "La donna è mobile"; *Ernani* "Mercé, diletti amici . . . Come rugiada al cespite." Gounod: *Roméo et Juliette* "L'amour, l'amour . . . Ah! lève-toi, soleil." Massenet: *Le Cid* "Ah! tout est bien fini . . . Ô souverain." Puccini: *La Bohème* "Che gelida manina." Catalani: *Loreley* "Nel verde maggio."
> New Philharmonia Orchestra, cond. Franco Ferraris[6]

Verdi's *La Forza del Destino* and *Ernani* and Gounod's *Roméo*. The true gems, however, were two rarities among his repertoire, "Ah, la paterna mano" from Verdi's *Macbeth* and the unique "Nel verde maggio" from Catalani's *Loreley*. Macduff's aria has ring and authority, and the splendid Catalani sounds as if the massive Apennine Mountains are floating away on the Adriatic Sea.

✦✦✦✦✦

Despite the delay in the aria recordings, there was still plenty to enjoy when *Franco Corelli Sings "Granada" and Other Romantic Songs* received a well-promoted spring release "in response to overwhelming demand." It was accompanied by a nice quote from the *New York Herald Tribune*: "There is no tenor in modern times, Italian or otherwise, whose voice rings out with greater vibrancy, whose every tone carries with it emotion at white heat. The sounds he makes, seemingly without effort, are dazzlingly bright, urgent and communicative."[8]

February 1967: How Many Unpublished Chopin Études Do You Know?

Equally impressed with the "Prince of Tenors" was the *High Fidelity* reporter Conrad L. Osborne, who followed Corelli for a time "in and out of costume." Osborne is with him while he does his makeup and during his warm-ups before performances, humming with closed mouth or extending to E-flat above high

C. Intermittently Corelli clears his throat and bursts into a salvo of "bra-bri-bre-bro-bru"s on single tones before testing Calaf's opening lines: "Ah, padre mio, ti ritrovo!—trovo!—trovo!" When Mariano Caruso drops into the dressing room, the two tenors engage in a discussion of the positive effects of cortisone on the voice while comparing throats in the mirror. Osborne is charmed and puzzled by the colorful circus of friends and worshippers who somehow manage to get backstage at performances and readily succumbs to what he describes as the spontaneous nature of both Corellis. Aware of the ill-natured jokes at Loretta's expense, he gallantly comes to her aid: "I don't see anything odd or amusing in the joint front maintained by Corelli and his wife. Loretta is an attractive, extroverted person who seems more than happy with her lot. She is quite naturally devoted to the success and comfort of her husband, in an entirely un-selfconscious way, and does some of the talking for him, since she is bolder with her English."

Leaving the trivial spousal rituals for what they are, Osborne turns to Corelli's nature. He finds the tenor disarming, funny, and intriguing when he sits at the piano in his dressing room, whistling along with a tune. "E Chopin," explains Corelli. Says Osborne, doubtful: "Chopin? Really?" Replies Corelli: "Sure; it's an unpublished *étude*, completely unknown." While Corelli continues playing, the journalist's thoughts ponder the melody. Is it an Italian popular song? An unpublished Chopin *étude*? An "unpublished Chopin *étude*" by Franco Corelli, offered for the consideration of visiting music critics?

Corelli is in the best of spirits throughout, making fun of his press agent, Peter Gravina, who is from Naples and therefore is constantly referred to as a "gangster." Occasionally Corelli gulps down red wine poured into a tall glass of ice water, to Osborne's utter dismay. After they part, the reporter broods over his days with the uncomplicated-complicated "singer/musicologist," asking his readers: "How many unpublished Chopin études do *you* know?"[9]

April 27, 1967: Fighting over Giocondas

Corelli's performance techniques throughout 1967 reveal new shades to the heroic makeup of his voice. The texture begins to even out and becomes more suave, combining an even further diminished vibrato with increased use of vocal coloring, shading, and the spinning and swelling of single notes. In its most

> March 27, 1967
> Amilcare Ponchielli: *La Gioconda*
> New York, Metropolitan Opera House
> Renata Tebaldi (*La Gioconda*), Franco Corelli (*Enzo Grimaldo*), Rosalind Elias (*Laura Adorno*), Ruza Pospinov (*La Cieca*), Cornell MacNeil (*Barnaba*), cond. Fausto Cleva

pronounced form, this last aspect is displayed in the sublimation of the diminuendo to *morendo* on the B-flat of "Celeste Aida," an effect that will increasingly appear elsewhere in his repertoire. A fine example of this was presented at his final pre-tour performance of *La Gioconda* at the Met on March 27, in the *morendo* of the high B-flat that ends "Cielo e mar." The critic of the *Dallas Times Herald* was moved to write that Corelli impressed not so much through his loudness (duly noted) as through his vocal refinement.[10]

Paradoxically, that fine *Gioconda* also seems to have cost him the planned Decca recording of that opera (scheduled for July–August), according to Tebaldi's first biographer, Kenn Harris:

> Franco tried to outhold a high note with her at the finale of Act II, "Tu sei tradito." She looked at him and then blew him off the stage with that big voice of hers. During the curtain calls, he is supposed to have said to her: "Callas is a better Gioconda than you." She is supposed to have reciprocated with "Franco, Tucker is a better tenor than you." You couldn't prove it, but the first follow-up *Gioconda* should have had Corelli, but instead it had house tenor Barry Morell—for the broadcast! That summer she recorded the opera for Decca with Bergonzi, while it had been announced for Franco.[11]

April–June 1967: Thumbs Up and Spring Fever

It was 90 degrees outside in Atlanta when Franco knocked on my hotel door, asking for help. My Italian was limited then, but he had a dictionary and pointed to the words "sleeping suit." He had tried that trick in the shops before, but nobody understood him. So I went with him to Peachtree Street, to Davidson's department store, and they explained to me they wouldn't help him because they thought he was crazy. So I explained to them that he wanted these heavy pajamas, the flannel ones. He was afraid of the hotel's air conditioning and feared catching a cold. But all they had were silk and cotton, very light ones. So he ordered three sets of pajamas to wear on top of each other, and on the way out he bought about half a dozen silk ascots.

 Les Dryer (first violinist, Metropolitan Opera Orchestra), interview, New York, September 2, 2005

Corelli's problem with Atlanta's air conditioning was just one of the mishaps that befell the tenor at the beginning of the tour, when the Met troupe literally splashed into both a rainy *and* a snowy Boston. Corelli instantly caught a cold that forced him to give up his opening tour performance of April 18

April 21, Boston, War Memorial Auditorium
Aida with Leontyne Price (*Aida*), Franco Corelli, William Olvis (Acts II–IV) (*Radamès*), Nell Rankin (*Amneris*), cond. Thomas Schippers

April 24, Cleveland, Public Auditorium
La Gioconda with Tebaldi (*La Gioconda*), Franco Corelli (*Enzo Grimaldo*), Rosalind Elias (*Laura Adorno*), Belén Amparán (*La Cieca*), Cornell MacNeil (*Barnaba*), cond. Fausto Cleva

April 28, Cleveland, Public Auditorium
Aida with Leontyne Price (*Aida*), Franco Corelli (*Radamès*), Nell Rankin (*Amneris*), cond. Thomas Schippers

May 1, Atlanta, Fox Auditorium
La Gioconda with Renata Tebaldi (*La Gioconda*), Franco Corelli (*Enzo Grimaldo*), Rosalind Elias (*Laura Adorno*), Belén Amparán (*La Cieca*), Cornell MacNeil (*Barnaba*), cond. Fausto Cleva

May 8, Memphis, Ellis Auditorium
La Gioconda with Renata Tebaldi (*La Gioconda*), Franco Corelli (*Enzo Grimaldo*), Rosalind Elias (*Laura Adorno*), Belén Amparán (*La Cieca*), Cornell MacNeil (*Barnaba*), cond. Fausto Cleva

May 12, Dallas, Park Fair Auditorium
La Gioconda with Renata Tebaldi (*La Gioconda*), Franco Corelli (*Enzo Grimaldo*), Rosalind Elias (*Laura Adorno*), Belén Amparán (*La Cieca*), Cornell MacNeil (*Barnaba*), cond. Fausto Cleva

May 17, Minneapolis, Northrop Auditorium
La Gioconda with Renata Tebaldi (*La Gioconda*), Franco Corelli (*Enzo Grimaldo*), Nell Rankin (*Laura Adorno*), Belén Amparán (*La Cieca*), Cornell MacNeil (*Barnaba*), cond. Fausto Cleva

May 23, Detroit, Masonic Temple Auditorium
Turandot with Birgit Nilsson (*Turandot*), Franco Corelli (*Calaf*), Anna Moffo (*Liù*), cond. Zubin Mehta

May 26, Detroit, Masonic Temple Auditorium
La Gioconda with Renata Tebaldi (*La Gioconda*), Franco Corelli (*Enzo Grimaldo*), Rosalind Elias (*Laura Adorno*), Ruza Pospinov-Baldani (*La Cieca*), Cornell MacNeil (*Barnaba*), cond. Fausto Cleva

May 29, Philadelphia, Civic Center
Turandot with Birgit Nilsson (*Turandot*), Franco Corelli (*Calaf*), Gabriella Tucci (*Liù*), cond. Zubin Mehta

June 1, 1967
Concert
Providence, Rhode Island
Franco Corelli (singing Massenet: *Le Cid* "Ah ! tout est bien fini . . . Ô souverain." Verdi: *I Lombardi* "La mia letizia infondere." Puccini: *Tosca* "Recondita armonia." Cardillo: "Core 'ngrato." Di Capua: "I' te vurria vasà." Tosti: "L'ultima canzone," "A vucchella." Verdi: *Macbeth* "Ah, la paterna mano.") and Margherita Guglielmi, cond. Anton Guadagno

June 3, 1967
Amilcare Ponchielli: *La Gioconda*
Philadelphia, Civic Center
Renata Tebaldi (*La Gioconda*), Franco Corelli (*Enzo Grimaldo*), Rosalind Elias (*Laura Adorno*), Ruza Pospinov-Baldani (*La Cieca*), Cornell MacNeil (*Barnaba*), cond. Fausto Cleva

(coincidentally, a *Gioconda* with Tebaldi). On April 21, he sang Radamès to Leontyne Price's Aida, against his doctors' orders. They were vindicated when Franco had to relinquish the effort after Act I and let William Olvis finish the opera in his stead.[12]

Three days later Corelli proved fit enough for his next tour *Gioconda*, where he reconciled with Tebaldi. It was too late to salvage the Decca recording project, but not too late to save his throat, as Dryer's story attests. Corelli had a point there: numerous singers fell victim to the extreme climate changes on the Met Spring Tour. In the South, the combination of extreme heat and air conditioning set up a fry-and-freeze cycle that made singers very vulnerable.

What the press dubbed Corelli's "French poodle" Roméo was a novelty on tours.[13] (Photo: Courtesy of the Mississippi Valley Collection)

❖❖❖❖❖

Accompanying Corelli everywhere on the tour was a silver-grey miniature poodle called Roméo, who had succeeded Pippi after the latter died in Cortina, where he was buried.[14] Like his predecessor, the little dog (tethered by a red leash that matched his fancy silver-studded collar and called Roméo for the press but Pippi in private) was the cause of many travel inconveniences. Corelli's flight from Atlanta to Memphis was delayed because the pilot refused to take the dog until the airline administration allowed an exception to their rule. Corelli went to extravagant lengths to take care of his companion:

> In Detroit, Franco couldn't find the butcher shop to get the dog's favorite chopped meat. About an hour later, someone with a cart and a silver tray on it went to Corelli's room. On his way out I asked the servant what it was and he answered: "Would you believe it! This crazy guy had the chef grind up a filet mignon—for his dog!" After the performance, when I saw the empty tray with the little rose and the half-eaten filet mignon, I wanted to cry. Franco had had only a salad, whereas the dog's meal must have cost him twenty bucks! That was the most touching thing I ever saw. There was

a party that night, but he didn't attend; he seldom did. Instead, he went out walking the dog.[15]

Louise Ahrens, the reporter who broke the dog-on-a-plane story, also noticed a physical aspect of Corelli that had already struck Visconti during the *La Vestale* run at La Scala, one that had never before made it into the papers: his exceptionally long fingers.[16] The most striking feature of his hands, however, was his oddly long, curved thumbs, which Italians consider a sign of fortune in life—a sign that the person is destined to achieve something extraordinary.[17]

April 17, 1967: Benvenuti Versus Griffith

Throughout his career Corelli maintained an avid interest in sports. This was especially true when Italian athletes achieved notable success in the United States, now his second home since he settled into his West Fifty-sixth Street

On April 17, 1967, the Italian boxer Nino Benvenuti won the middleweight world championship in a legendary match against Emile A. Griffith. The fight between Benvenuti and Corelli over who was the greater fan of the other remained undecided. (Photo: Courtesy of Mondadori Group)

apartment. One of his favorite sports was boxing, and where America cherished the rise of the young Cassius Clay, Italian immigrants had two promising talents from their homeland on the rise in Sandro Mazzinghi and Nino Benvenuti.

Although his own boxing never went beyond a few visits to a gym in Ancona,[18] Franco enjoyed attending matches. And he was there on April 17, 1967, when Benvenuti, the Italian middleweight champion, came away from his first fight with the American champion Emile A. Griffith as the second Italian world champion.[19]

Franco loved sharing moments like this with his friends or fellow countrymen, such as the group of visiting Italian railway men he once picked up. Occasionally he took care of fellow Anconetans he didn't even know.[20] This was the Franco Corelli so dear to his intimate friends—friendly, quiet, polite, enthusiastic, and perhaps a little naive and easily manipulated.

◆◆◆◆◆

Franco's pride was legendary, and it is easy to see why he accepted an invitation to appear the following year at the Birmingham Festival: the program was built entirely around his appearance there, including a school program where his recordings would be used to teach the students. Never mind the money; the last aspect would probably have been inducement enough for him to sign the contract, which he did by the end of May.[21]

July–August 1967: Offers

Whereas some people use holidays to get away from business, Corelli usually wished to see Bauer or Bing over the summer. During previous vacations Bauer had always tried to keep Franco as far as possible from Bing, who was happy enough to have a few weeks without his singers, but by 1967 things had changed considerably. Bing and Franco's joint prosperous voyage was now in calmer seas, and Franco had a good reason for a visit. He wanted to discuss the possibility of another season opener with Bing and Ghiringhelli, who had offered him the La Scala opening of the 1967–68 season with *Ernani*.[22] The new relationship with the Met was exemplified by the fact that Franco actually consulted his benefactors first; and so Bauer joined the Corellis in Cortina on August 3. On Saturday, August 5, they arrived at the Bings' in the healthy Swiss mountain climate of Siusi. The outcome of their meeting was fairly positive, although Bing must have been a little miffed; after all, Corelli was already in his pocket for that period. However, the double date was a minor sacrifice to maintain friendly relationships. The main issue was how long Ghiringhelli would require Corelli's services. In the end, the three gentlemen and Loretta agreed to let Ghiringhelli have Franco for a maximum of forty-five days.[23]

August–September 1967: Appointment with Franco Corelli

Over the summer, Corelli took part in an utterly charming special shot on location for Italian television. First came Cortina, in the Dolomites, then Venice, and finally his Milanese home, where he alternated singing with a peek at his private photo albums. The show has been unavailable for so long that it was forgotten until it popped up recently at an exhibition.[24]

The climax of this lip-synched show appears when Corelli sits at a roulette table. The wheel gets a big spin, the ball rolls, and the tenor rises. Walking outside under neon lights, he suddenly starts contemplating *Otello*, an opera he

> August–September 1967
> Milan, Venice, Cortina
> "Appointment with Franco Corelli" (RAI television)
> Cairone: "Pourquoi fermer ton coeur"; Corelli welcomes the audience; Verdi: *Rigoletto* "La donna è mobile"; Corelli shows his private photo album; Bach/Gounod: "Ave Maria"; from his convertible Corelli watches old woman passing by in Italian landscape. Tortorella: "Mamma mia" (music runs under images of Corelli watching and driving away); Ponchielli: *La Gioconda* "Cielo e mar"; Corelli playing roulette, sings an a capella line of *Otello* ("E la gloria d'Otello..."); Verdi: *Otello* "Esultate"; Nightclub: Corelli dances to Sam the Sham & the Pharaohs' "Wooly Bully"; Grieg: "I Love Thee"; Corelli in front of La Scala; Verdi: *Il Trovatore* "Di quella pira." (All music dubbed from Cetra/EMI recordings)
> Host: Enrico Vaime

veramento never sang. He looks up and murmurs, "E la gloria d'Otello . . . e questo alfin, e questo alf—*Otello*! Why not?" The next shot presents him in Otello's full costume, watching his tuxedo-clad alter ego stepping onto the base of a column and singing "Esultate." Otello watches the concert performance from the side, alternately laughing and nodding his head in acknowledgment.[25]

Next Franco invites the television audience to a genuine and very smoky nightclub, where a herd of teenagers is dancing. While Sam the Sham and the Pharaohs sing "Harry told Matty / let's don't take no chance / let's not be L-seven / come and learn to dance / wooly bully, wooly bully . . . ," Corelli steps onto the dance floor and starts swinging with the teens . . . wooly bully! A pretty blonde bumps into him and asks him if he would sing for them. He succumbs to her charms, takes them to a more secluded room, and sings Grieg's "I Love Thee." Even before the show comes to its end with a staged "Di quella pira," the message is clear: "Mr. Esaurito" is back from his self-imposed exile and on his way to claim his rightful throne in Milan.

⟡⟡⟡⟡⟡

Having made a smashing impact on Italy's television audience, the path was clear for new adventures and greater things until his EMI *Aida* and Decca *Tosca* sets were released in the autumn of 1967. Despite earlier miscastings, his complete opera recordings had always brought him rave personal reviews and reached dazzling sales figures. Certainly there had been critics here and there who simply didn't like Corelli, but the *Gramophone* review of the recently released Corelli-Nilsson *Aida* echoed the criticisms published elsewhere: although Corelli was said to have been performing with the rest of the ensemble, he might as well have recorded his part later, for he hardly sounded involved. When a glitch in the recording process becomes that audible, there is clearly something wrong, which was confirmed when his Decca *Tosca* was judged "superfluous."[26]

At the same time, EMI London was suddenly confronted with disappointing record sales, and by November they concluded that Corelli had not fulfilled his potential for them. In the United States, Angel, EMI's principal opera market, agreed. For the first time one of Corelli's business partners doubted his value

Opposite page: To be or not to be; during the summer of 1967, Corelli was still tossing around the idea of *Otello*. (Author's photocollage taken from the television program "Appointment with Franco Corelli," RAI Milan, 1976)

ITALY GREETS THE PRODIGAL SON • 359

to them. With his last aria recital more or less abandoned, EMI/Angel found themselves married to a singer who, although still the leading tenor of his day, just wasn't delivering. They judged it high time to look for an alternative.[27]

Autumn 1967: A New Horizon

Few tenors stay at the top past 45. Some, through excessive high voltage use of their voices, don't last even that long. Abraded throat and vocal cords simply don't heal anymore, and the tenor finds he can hit high notes in the first act of an opera, but by the last act, though his stamina is as good as ever, he can barely sing at all.
  Robert Daley, "The Greatest Tenor," *Life,* **December 15, 1967**

EMI's quiet decision to look for another star tenor marks a turning point in Corelli's career. Claiming to be thirty-five clearly didn't cut it at forty-six, and although his performances were still very much in demand, he needed something more than a return to La Scala with a well-established part. Robert Daley's observation in *Life* that tenors are a special breed puts things in perspective: God didn't create male human beings to sing high Cs, and the advance of time makes it increasingly difficult to live up to recordings made years before. From that perspective alone, at a certain point new or little-known roles can be a wise addition to one's career. The Italian press sensed that things were about to change and announced Corelli in *Fedora* and *Francesca da Rimini* with Tebaldi, while *Werther* was scheduled for the Maggio Musicale Fiorentino of 1970.[28]

The busy forecast couldn't vanquish the need for an instant triumph, and his best chance for that was the upcoming Met premiere of Gounod's *Roméo et Juliette*. During his holidays Franco visited Verona, where he studied the historical sites where the original Romeo and Juliet supposedly lived and died: "The house is all covered with vines and there are an enormous amount of tourists. You have to stand in line to see Juliette's tomb and then the tomb is empty. But I am glad I went. Now I will play Roméo my way. . . . My Roméo will be hopelessly romantic because the music is sweet, like sugar, and also because I am hopelessly romantic." Loretta (smoking a pipe of Dutch tobacco) agreed: "Very romantic."[29]

September 1967: Roméo in New York

Roméo explodes one moment, cries the next, just like me.
  Franco Corelli, in Rex Reed, "Always Wondering: Can He Do It Again?,"
  The New York Times, September 17, 1967

Despite the fact that Roméo was not altogether new in Corelli's repertoire, it was treated as a role debut. Pages and pages in newspapers and magazines were devoted to this premiere, largely with Louis Melançon's imaginative shots of Freni swooning in Franco's embrace. The journalist Rex Reed decided to try the now-famous spaghetti that he saw simmering on the Corellis' stove while Franco explained to him why he refused the usual blond wig: "Where does it say Roméo must be blond?" Loretta, "the power behind the throne, the one that can handle him when no one else can," jumps in to challenge her husband: "Franco, I like you as a blond."[30]

Black, brown, or blond hair, *Roméo* being a French opera, one could be sure that Corelli would do it "his way." His Italianization of the score was as noticeable as his stunning looks next to the doe-eyed Freni, who brought an almost indecently fitting voice to her title role. Apart from his moments in the aria and the love duet, the duel scene proved an impressive highlight. It was set to great choreography, with Charles Anthony a priceless opponent. Harriet Johnson of the *New York Post* duly noted that Anthony lost only because he had to, for he was clearly the most skilled swordfighter onstage.[31]

Corelli couldn't complain; the morning after brought a review from Harold C. Schonberg that was all praise. The critic judged the performance a significant step in the tenor's career, precisely because he did not blast his way through the opera. His strengthened pianissimo

Corelli as Roméo. (Photo: Louis Melançon. Courtesy of the Metropolitan Opera Archives)

> September 19, 22, and 27; October 2, 7, 10, 16, and 26, 1967
> Charles Gounod: *Roméo et Juliette*
> New York, Metropolitan Opera House
> Franco Corelli (*Roméo*), Mirella Freni, Jeannette Pilou [October 7, 10, 16, 24] (*Juliette*), John Macurdy, Justino Díaz [October 10, 16, 26] (*Frère Laurent*), John Reardon (*Mercutio*), Marcia Baldwin (*Stéphano*), Charles Anthony (*Tybalt*), cond. Francesco Molinari-Pradelli; stage director, Paul-Emile Deiber

was duly noticed along the way: "In 'Ah, lève toi,' he took a stentorian B-flat and then tapered off to a diminuendo that was as pleasant as it was unexpected." Schonberg also noted the sob that constantly threatened to break through, but despite that, he believed Corelli's attempts to add a new dimension to his singing were paying off.[33]

⸙⸙⸙⸙⸙

The subsequent *Roméo* tour to Philadelphia, Seattle (where he had opened the season), and Hartford was nothing short of a triumph. The stunning B-flat diminuendo and his role portrait were never better, as the pirate recordings attest. For pure heroic ring and burnished tone quality, his greatest period was definitely from 1959 to 1963, but his greatest year for versatility was 1967.

The *Hartford Press* noted some remarkably complimentary features on the side, such as the fact that his latest reported scandal dated back nearly five years. Meanwhile, he was the disarming opposite of haughty while struggling to express himself in his newly acquired English.[34]

⸙⸙⸙⸙⸙

All this seemed to provide a perfect basis for a dream return to La Scala. The obstacles, however, proved insurmountable. According to both his friend Arrigo Michelini and Ghiringhelli's biographer Vieri Poggiali,[35] negotiations with La Scala went south when Corelli, inspired by his American *Roméo* triumphs, demanded that Gounod's second-best opera be mounted for him (previously they had discussed *Ernani*). Because it was not likely to be on La Scala's schedule for years to come, the white-haired intendant rejected Corelli's offer politely but unequivocally; he simply could not let a tenor dictate the house's repertoire and scheduling.[36] Additionally, Franco regularly insisted on having the Met house tenor Charles Anthony for the duel scene, after another Tybalt actually wounded him once.[37] And with Freni the apparently logical option for a La Scala Juliette, it would have looked as though the Met were taking over La Scala.

Pride played a major part on both sides of the Atlantic; Corelli's legendary La Scala debuts in major repertoire rarities would never be repeated at the Met and vice versa. Yet there was another side to the failing negotiations. Bing, Bauer, and the Corellis had agreed on a maximum absence from New York of forty-five days, while Ghiringhelli demanded that the prodigal son honor his native country by giving his countrymen the best of his craft. According to Earl Wilson's famous gossip column for the *New York Post*, La Scala wanted Corelli for seven performances at the fabulous sum of $7,000 each, but for that they required his services for a full sixty days. Corelli then demanded that Ghiringhelli make up the financial loss, for he was also to open the Met. Ghiringhelli said no, and Corelli walked out.[38] So far, so good for Bing and company, except for one little twist: Wilson mentioned that Corelli was making $5,000 a performance at the Met. If Bing hoped that the Met's other tenors would overlook that figure, Wilson

Mirella Freni and Corelli in the balcony scene of the Met's *Roméo et Juliette*, September 19, 1967. Unlike some other sopranos, Mirella Freni never found herself at odds with Corelli, whom she genuinely liked. According to Freni, they were occupied with the duets in much the same way ballet dancers are focused on their simultaneous entries and exits. Says Freni: "And when the balcony scene came, he would always end his aria 'Ah, lève-toi soleil!' with this big high C that he would take *sfumato* to *pianissimo*. And then, with his back to the audience, he would give me this tremendous smile, while looking up to me, above him, on the balcony with those beaming eyes, as if saying: 'Did you hear that!'"[32] (Photo: Louis Melançon. Courtesy of the Metropolitan Opera Archives)

made sure they would not: "The claims of friends that Corelli is highest paid will probably upset all the other male singers, each of whom has thought he was highest paid. Corelli let the cat out of the money bag." Labeling the tenor "the Caruso of today" added insult to injury, judging from the hand-drawn arrows pointing to the $5,000 and the claim to fame marked forcefully on the clipping in Bing's Met files.

But where would a gossip columnist such as Wilson get this news? And why not simply leave such gossip for what it was? Well, because Wilson apparently talked to Franco or to Jackie Kennedy after she bumped into Franco over mai tais and Bibb lettuce at Trader Vic's, where she was in the company of Cecil Beaton. The squealer, whoever it was, was well informed. Corelli's normal Met rate was now $4,000 plus $3,000 general travel expenses, but on tour and for the planned "*Carmen* in the Park" performances he had been granted $4,000 plus $550 expenses, plus $500 special expenses! That made his fee actually $50 higher than the $5,000 that Wilson reported. With such accuracy about a secret known to be safeguarded by the Met as if it were the U.S. Mint, one is inclined to believe the rest of the brief eighteen-line interlude as well.[39]

Now that the La Scala negotiations had been reduced to a matter of money and terms, the repertoire question regarding whether *Ernani* or *Roméo et Juliette* would be given was moot. Luckily, there was always EMI—the company immediately agreed to change course and insert an improvised *Roméo* recording with Franco and Freni. That effectively blocked Decca's planned *Roméo* recording and solved EMI's seemingly insurmountable casting problems with their own planned *Forza del Destino* recording.[40]

November 1967: Requiem

I will stop mourning the passing of my mother on the day that I sing a Requiem for her on the anniversary of her death.
   Franco Corelli, in "Sono il tenore più alto, ma voglio diventare il più grande," *Oggi*, March 12, 1959

The unique Requiem performance of November 14 did not count toward the promise Corelli had made upon his mother's death in 1950 because the Los Angeles performance did not occur on the anniversary of her death. Still, it was

> **November 14, 1967**
> **Giuseppe Verdi: *Messa da Requiem***
> **Los Angeles, Philharmonic Auditorium**
> Gwyneth Jones, Franco Corelli, Grace Bumbry, Ezio Flagello, Los Angeles Philharmonic, cond. Zubin Mehta

an interesting next-to-new addition to his repertoire; next-to, because he had already both recorded and starred in a filmed performance of the "Ingemisco," which leaves only the minor "Domine Jesu Christe" section as a true novelty.

Headlines in San Francisco and elsewhere took little notice of the Requiem performance until the pirates of Legendary Recordings issued it in a low-profile vinyl set in the 1970s. American fans who had access to such items went wild over it because the cast—Gwyneth Jones, Grace Bumbry, and Ezio Flagello under Zubin Mehta—made for a performance that is as wired as any Requiem will ever get.

◆◆◆◆◆

Meanwhile La Scala's loss was Parma's gain, since that city was happy with any single performance Corelli could spare. He celebrated his return to the Teatro Regio with a series of *Forza del Destino*s in the last weeks of December 1967. Regrettably, he arrived with a slight indisposition, which prevented him from delivering the sort of singing expected of him. However, much like the Florentine audience on his problematic *Forza* evening in January, the Parmesans accepted things they would not have tolerated from another tenor. Writing now for *La Stampa*, Giorgio Gualerzi could almost copy his earlier *Discoteca* review from January, because Corelli again regained his strength from the "La vita è inferno . . . O tu che seno agli angeli" onward, this time extending his resurrection well into the fourth act.[41]

CHAPTER 18 ❖ 1968–1969

The Years of Transition

January 11–23, 1968: Having a Ball with Verrett

The New Year opened with a few French-language *Carmen*s in Florence, which had the added attraction of Shirley Verrett in the title role. Verrett was left with a rather unflattering memory of the proceedings, in which Franco (still struggling with the aftereffects of the flu) showed up for rehearsals at will. Verrett suffered from the flu herself, yet Molinari-Pradelli demanded that she sing out during rehearsals. This resulted in a good old-fashioned clash when Verrett's husband asked the conductor if he hadn't heard her properly: "She said she is not singing." Recalled Verrett: "Silence followed. Someone in the chorus called out, 'Chi parla?' (Who speaks?) Another chorus member said, 'Il marito!' (The husband!)" Verrett couldn't believe her eyes when Molinari-Pradelli abruptly ended the rehearsal and she woke up the next morning to a raft of newspapers claiming the whole opera was being sung in French only because the mezzo had demanded it.[1]

> **January 11, 14, 18, 21, and 23*, 1968**
> **Georges Bizet:** *Carmen*
> **Florence, Teatro Communale**
> Shirley Verrett (*Carmen*), Franco Corelli (*Don José*), Antonietta Cannarile Berdini (*Micaëla*), Vladimiro Ganzarolli, Piero Cappuccilli [January 14, 18], Gian Giacomo Guelfi [January 21, 23] (*Escamillo*), Teatro Communale Chorus and Orchestra, cond. Francesco Molinari-Pradelli
> *Fund-raiser for the victims of the earthquake that struck Sicily on January 15

Corelli had a little more experience with the conductor he had so fervently reviled after the 1965 *Turandot* recording, although the very fact that he agreed to sing under his baton at all proves that all those emotions didn't necessarily last for life. Still, Molinari-Pradelli may have thought differently when (during the actual performance) at the Flower Aria Corelli suddenly switched to Italian. Verrett lost her concentration for a few moments, fearing that her colleague had forgotten the words. When it finally dawned on her that he was putting on a show, she realized that he had planned it: "I could see defiance in his eyes as he looked at me. But the joke was on him. The audience let him finish. Half of the people cheered, half jeered."[2]

There was clearly a story behind Verrett's story, for the jeerers had arrived "prepared" and unfolded a banner with the text "Vada a Berlitz" (Go to Berlitz). Some even threw vegetables on the stage, bringing the performance to a halt. Verrett seemed gleeful when she recalled the boos Corelli had received during his previous *Forza*s in Parma, even though she herself was merely trying to survive the *Carmen*s in spite of the flu. About Vladimiro Ganzarolli, who was mercilessly booed after he cracked at the end of his Toreador Song, Verrett added: "Some threw tomatoes and onions onstage at this poor man." That tribute was repeated after he cracked again during the reprise of the song in Act III, and the management replaced him with Piero Cappuccilli and Gian Giacomo Guelfi for the remainder of the performances. In the course of the *Carmen* run, Loretta accused Verrett's husband of having given her the middle finger. Regardless of the truth of the matter, the management strongly advised *il marito* to send Mrs. Corelli some flowers. Only when an earthquake killed hundreds of people in Sicily, on January 15, did the shocked cast unite for the final performance, the proceeds of which were donated to the victims. According to Verrett, all that was also very much what Italy and Italian opera were about in those days.[3]

January–March 1968: After the Muppets

After he recovered from the flu in Ancona, Corelli's February 1 arrival on New York's opera scene was accorded a six-page interview in *Music and Artists*.[4] Corelli criticized the absolute control granted to conductors, then presented his views on critics as a degeneration of the profession's seventeenth-century origins. Back then critics described what they witnessed, including a singer's success with the audience. Today, claimed Corelli, the critic presents only his own private opinion of a singer. If he had a fight with his wife, he may see the performance as all bad; if he feels very fine he may look at it differently.[5] With that off his chest, he was all set for a challenging Cavaradossi in a string of New York *Tosca*s. In the Philadelphia *Aida* he outdid himself in the B-flat diminuendo in order to convince the public that the ones in the recordings had been his own and not a sound engineer's, as had been suggested. Finally there was a March 3 performance on *The Ed Sullivan Show*. Corelli went on right after George Chakiris, Jane Powell, Paul Mauriat, and a group of hand puppets called the Muppets. Jim Henson's creations threw enormous quantities of fake $100 bills around the stage and toward the audience, which provided the perfect prelude to Corelli's performance of Torelli's "Tu lo sai." The piece was simply a short song, but it was broadcast in full color to millions of viewers (according to *Harper's*, an audience of 30 million),[6] and it made a bigger impact than a whole year of singing at the Met.

March 20, 1968: The Carnegie Hall Recital

Saturday night at the Metropolitan Gala, when others sang arias, you sang Neapolitan songs, and so the bravos and calls for encores went to Bergonzi and Tucker, not Corelli. Last night you got some of your "bravos," but not from the people who follow you from the Metropolitan. From them you got silence, laughter, anger, "boos," shouts of "basta" and "Sing opera" and cries of "Tucker."

> Letter from one Ronald Hollander, in the audience at Corelli's Carnegie Hall debut, to Franco Corelli, Erberto Landi, Rudolf Bing, the president of Angel Records, and *The New York Times*

It is not easy to please everyone. However, Ronald Hollander had a legitimate complaint about the level of the singing and the choice of songs presented to Corelli's loyal New York fans: "Are you an operatic tenor or a gondolier? . . . Did any [song] go above middle C? You should have served spaghetti and there should have been dancing. . . . And who needed Carnegie Hall? Your first New York concert should have been held in a pizza restaurant."

> March 20, 1968
> Franco Corelli in a Concert of Italian Songs dedicated to
> different Italian cities
> New York, Carnegie Hall
> Mayr: "La biondina in gondoleta" (Venice). Pigarelli: "La montanara" (Piedmont). Cesarini: "Firenze sogna" (Florence). D'Anzi: "Mattinata Fiorentina" (Florence). Traditional: "A la barcillunisa" (Sicily). Arona: "La campana di San Giusto" (Trieste). Tortorella: "Venezia no!" (Venice). Ranucci: "Arrivederci Roma" (Rome). Tagliaferri: "Piscatore 'e Pusilleco" (Naples). Cannio: "'O surdato 'nnammurato" (Naples). De Curtis: "Tu ca' nun chiagne" (Naples). Tosti: "A vucchella" (Naples). Silvestri: "Nanni (Na gita a li castelli)" (Rome).
> Cond. Anton Guadagno; presenter, Giovanni Martinelli

Corelli's choices, though, were less lightweight than they seem at first glance. While in Parma the year before, he had announced that he planned to turn the Carnegie Hall event into a musical tour through Italy: "I shall sing songs dedicated to Naples, Rome, Florence, Venice, Milan, Turin; and I shall see to it that Parma, the capital of melodrama, shall be included there as well." For this occasion, no less a composer than his early promoter Ildebrando Pizzetti was writing the one missing song about Parma,[7] which in the end was not sung. Judging from the *fiatis* in "A vucchella," the first of which threatens to slip away, Corelli was not in very good shape. In addition, the orchestra played as if they had just met. The press was favorable enough,[8] but inexplicably shortened songs as "Tu ca nun chiagne" hardly justified a full-price recital that cost $10 a ticket and lasted just thirty minutes. Still, it's a pity that EMI didn't grant Corelli's request to record the concert for release on LP, if only because of the unusual selection of songs that he only sang here, among which "La Montanara" truly stands out. EMI's reasons are as telling as (regrettably) understandable: apart from the costs, they doubted the extremely self-critical singer would approve the results for release.[9]

Tellingly, as Hollander predicted in his letter, Corelli's joint concert with Montserrat Caballé and Bonaldo Giaiotti on April 7 was not sold out. It was possible that a ticket price of $25 had something to do with this; however, the concert featured an array of interesting arias from all participants. Corelli sang arias from Verdi's *Macbeth*, Meyerbeer's *L'Africana*, and Massenet's *Le Cid*, and gave a fine rendering of "A vucchella" with a gorgeous filature in the middle, not to mention a thrilling "Vicino a te" from *Andrea Chénier* with Caballé.

Before any of Caballé's, Giaiotti's, or Corelli's arias could be appreciated, there was a full minute of silence in memory of Martin Luther King, Jr., who had been murdered on April 4, only three days before. Therefore this concert in effect represented the only political statement Corelli ever consciously made. The minute of silence may have inspired the trio onstage, because they surpassed themselves. Corelli, Caballé, and Giaiotti were wildly cheered and scored rave reviews.[10]

May 12, 1968: On Tour with Opera's Che Guevara

There is no clinical way of measuring Franco Corelli's temperament....
He has earned the reputation of a sort of operatic Che Guevara.
    William H. Honan, "A Champion Tenor Defends His Title,"
    The New York Times, February 8, 1970

There are reminiscences of Christoff and Corelli after their swordfight in the Teatro dell'Opera, there is the photo of Mario Improta with whom Corelli fought at the Naples *Trovatore*, but the photo by Flynn Ell for the *St. Paul Dispatch* surpasses them all. Here is Corelli engaged in full fisticuffs at Twin Cities Airport on Sunday, May 12. What happened? According to the Met makeup artist Victor Callegari, who witnessed the proceedings, a stagehand who owned a bag identical to Corelli's asked the tenor if he was carrying his own bag. Franco, not knowing that they had identical bags, assumed the stagehand was calling him a thief and exploded. After a high-pitched exchange in Italian at top volume, the two started throwing punches. But finally peace was established, and the public at Minneapolis's Northrop Auditorium prepared for a very passionate *Roméo*.[11]

❖❖❖❖❖

A handful of Met Tour performances in Detroit, Philadelphia, Memphis, and Dallas extended Franco's American season until June, when he concluded with his only two American *Carmen*s in Bing's "Met in the Park" project, offering

Corelli fighting a stagehand at Twin Cities Airport over a piece of misplaced luggage, May 12, 1968. (Photo: Flynn Ell for the *St. Paul Dispatch*. Courtesy of the St. Paul Pioneer Press)

free concert-format opera to the New York–area public. The first was given in Crocheron Park, Queens, the second in the Botanical Gardens in the Bronx. They may not count as historic *Carmen* performances, but they were certainly historic events. Corelli attracted more than 50,000 spectators, setting a Met record and breaking his own attendance record of 22,000 at Verona's Arena.[12]

June 1968: EMI's *Roméo et Juliette*

There is not any one French style. . . . I do not sing Roméo the way I sing Faust. Roméo is "piu amoroso"—sweeter. . . . You must leave out a portamento here and there, but each role is very personal.
    Franco Corelli on the myth of the "French style," in Jack Frymire,
      "Il piu semplice e il piu bello," *Music and Artists*, February–March 1968

With his "Met in the Park" concerts behind him, Corelli flew straight to Paris to record *Roméo et Juliette*.[13] He arrived in splendid voice. The pairing with Mirella Freni proved to be a very fortunate one, and the recording turned out to be one of his more successful studio ventures. He then took a holiday before visiting Lauri-Volpi in Burjassot in early August, where, as Bauer put it, he "had his voice checked." Around this time some papers quoted Mirella Freni's announcement that she would be singing Desdemona to Corelli's Otello, conducted by Herbert von Karajan. Corelli immediately denied it. He hadn't discussed it with Karajan and wouldn't consider the part at all in coming years.[14]

The payment arrangement between the Met, Corelli, and Gorlinsky was up for renewal in September, and once more Franco insisted that the Met pay Gorlinsky in full but without withholding any taxes. The idea was that the Met employed Gorlinsky, who then lent them the services of their "British" employee Franco Corelli. The arrangement was constructed in this way because British subjects were not subject to foreign tax withholdings. Bing had called the arrangement the "Swiss swindle," because the money would then be transferred to a Swiss bank account (so that taxes would not have to be paid in the United Kingdom). The Met refused to go along with it, saying that they could not violate U.S. law; if Gorlinsky was right, he and Corelli would be able to obtain a full refund of the withholdings through the Internal Revenue Service.[15]

September 18, 1968: On Rivals and Rivals

Human warmth between artists doesn't exist. Perhaps outside the performance, but on stage everybody is occupied with himself. All want to win and be the center of attention. I've seen first-class artists that completely freaked out over the modest success of a colleague, just because they wanted that last bit of applause for themselves. . . . There is no compassion between singers; they are competitors in a nerve-racking quest.
    Carlo Scaravelli on operatic rivalry, in "Private Recollections," mid-1960s

On the very day of Corelli's second opening of the Met season as Maurizio in *Adriana Lecouvreur*, some newspapers published photos of the young City Opera star Plácido Domingo, who was mistakenly identified in a caption as the Met's opening-night tenor. This blew Corelli's usual nerves sky-high. That morning he chewed the Met staff out over the phone, aided by Loretta, and in the evening, as the auditorium filled, he paced backstage as if "hexed."[16] The

> September 16 (season opener) and 21 ; October 29;
> November 4, 1968
> Francesco Cilea: *Adriana Lecouvreur* (season opener)
> New York, Metropolitan Opera House
> Renata Tebaldi (*Adriana Lecouvreur*), Franco Corelli (*Maurizio*),
> Irene Dalis (*the Princess of Bouillon*), Anselmo Colzani (*Michonnet*),
> Metropolitan Opera Chorus and Orchestra, cond. Fausto Cleva

event was intriguing for a number of reasons, foremost because of the chosen opera. Bing's contempt for the work was well documented. When asked about his sudden change of heart, he simply smiled and pointed to the box office; the public loved it! Suddenly it no longer mattered that *The New York Times* said it was like opening the Met with a real soap opera.

All such controversies were forgotten, however, when Tebaldi's longtime rival, Maria Callas, made an unexpected but very regal entry, to wild cheers from the audience, and took her seat in a center box. Then the stage manager, Ossie Hawkins, spotted her on the closed-circuit television backstage. Word spread from stage manager to singers, and the cast members all glanced at Tebaldi, who was rumored to fear Callas's "evil eye." When the curtain went up, Maria's fans once more started a salvo of bravos, now countered by the Tebaldi wing.[17]

The popular account of the birth of the Callas-Tebaldi feud is that a disagreement over encores during a joint 1951 concert in Rio de Janeiro escalated when Callas later reportedly stated that comparing her voice to Madame Tebaldi's was like comparing champagne to Coca-Cola.[18] If she ever really said that, then on this night the Coke certainly sparkled for critics from New York to Italy and Germany, who all judged Tebaldi to have surpassed herself, for she sang with a good deal of her former velvet. Corelli and Dalis were praised to the rafters as well, with Corelli looking extraordinarily handsome in a succession of dashing uniforms (on loan from the Rome Opera) while lavishing his beautiful tenor voice on Cilea's score. Unfortunately, Tebaldi's claque protested his post-performance solo curtain call, to which he replied by outlasting them in front of the curtain, after which he stomped off in fury to his dressing room.

Given that Bing was a cunning man with a good instinct for publicity, not to mention the fact that there were professional photographers present, it seems that he engineered an encounter between the sworn-enemy sopranos when he escorted Maria backstage to greet her friend Franco. On the way and according to plan, Callas ran into Tebaldi. All present froze and held their breath. To their amazement, they saw a weeping Callas embrace her smiling rival, then go on to smother Corelli's anger in her arms. Because all the attention was on the reconciliation photo, *Time* magazine teased the successful but unlucky tenor that it was sopranos' week at the Met: "Upstaged Again!"[19]

Tebaldi, Corelli, Bing, and Callas after the opening night of *Adriana Lecouvreur*, September 16, 1968. (Photo: Courtesy of the Metropolitan Opera Archives)

✦✦✦✦✦

Corelli's minor premiere misfortune turned into a major one when he became "indisposed" for his September 28 performance. On the afternoon of the performance, Domingo was rehearsing *Turandot* with Birgit Nilsson. While shaving at home in New Jersey afterward, he received a phone call from Bing, who asked how he felt. Domingo answered that he felt great. Wonderful, replied Bing, because Domingo was about to debut at the Met. Not in four days, as planned, but then and there: a few minutes earlier, at 7:20 P.M., Corelli had canceled. Domingo protested that he had sung three operas within the last seventy-two hours. Bing ignored his complaints and ordered the young tenor to come over immediately because the performance was about to begin. Domingo was convinced that Corelli had tried to pull a fast one by canceling so late, and he went to the Met with his mind set on revenge.

Despite his busy schedule in the preceding days, Domingo really did feel great. The added circumstantial adrenaline and unexpectedly warm welcome from the audience after Corelli's cancellation was announced provided the perfect fuel for a great performance.[20] Domingo's success, the audience's response to the substitution announcement, and the earlier photo mix-up awakened Corelli to Domingo's potential as a rival. Young singers were now popping up from everywhere, and they were trained in a modern vocal school where there was little room for tempo rubato or frivolous playing to the galleries. Domingo's entry into the ranks of the Met's tenor roster was followed by Luciano

Pavarotti's debut there (as Rodolfo in *La Bohème*) on November 11. Corelli had been accustomed to sitting on his throne and watching his rivals fall. The arrival of Domingo and Pavarotti on the scene changed all that. Even though his own Maurizio was judged to have been better than ever, Corelli had to start thinking about defending his throne.

❖❖❖❖❖

One has to suspect the hand of Peter Gravina in the stunning appearance of Franco and Loretta in the then-notorious magazine *After Dark*. The press manager made sure that there could be no misunderstandings with respect to his client's marital status, which meant that Loretta was to feature prominently in the pictures. In addition, the photography required something more outrageous than, say, a *Vogue* shoot. The interview brought the novelty that Corelli was now studying Massenet's *Werther*,[21] but the shock lay in Kenn Duncan's exquisite photographs of Franco and Loretta posing in an array of exotic furs, some from animals that were nearly extinct—Russian bear, seal, sea otter, mink, lamb, pahmi, even jaguar and ocelot—and most retailing for thousands of dollars.[22]

Left: Franco Corelli on the cover of *After Dark*, October 1968. *Right: Le pin-up boy* in a $5,000 jaguar coat. (Photos: Kenn Duncan. Courtesy of the New York Public Library)

October 23, 1968: Birgit *Tosca*

Was Franco difficult to sing with? Nilsson: "Not if you let him have everything his way."
   Birgit Nilsson to the author, interview, April 10, 2005

The *Tosca*s that Birgit Nilsson and Franco Corelli sang together are far less well-known than their *Turandot*s, but in 1968 the combination was considered powerful enough to merit a prestigious new production. Nilsson was well aware that she was not a warm, Italianate *Tosca*, but she loved to sing the part that she had once sung with Beniamino Gigli himself. Sadly, for those who thrive on vocal rivalry, there were few of *Turandot*'s vocal battles in the Nilsson-Corelli *Tosca*s, for as Nilsson observed, there was nothing to conquer: "In *Tosca*, we are in love from the start."

By this time their working relationship had developed into one of the legendary opera partnerships of all time. Nilsson had gotten to know Franco's habits, nerves, and stage rituals with Loretta, although they still puzzled her:

> There was always Loretta in the wings, sprinkling holy water on him. If he wanted it or if she wanted it, I don't know, but it really helped him. He was like a big child, and we were sort of afraid of each other. Before a performance he was running around like a lion in a cage and I tried to behave myself, so I was just sitting and reading *The New York Times*, but in reality I may have been even more nervous than he was—he once pointed out to me that I was reading that newspaper upside down.[23]

From there it went to Franco sending her flowers now and then, although his spontaneous nature guaranteed some backstage accidents and faux pas that are still cherished among those who witnessed and dined out on them. On one such occasion during the Met season, when all were gathered around the dining table after *Tosca*, Franco made an impromptu post-performance speech: "*Pubblico enthusiasta, applauso frenetico.* But it's unfair that the enthusiasm should be reserved to the singers, when the soul of this production has been the stage director. I bring a toast to him! *Come si chiama?* [What is your name?]" Well, "Come si chiama" was the renowned Otto Schenk. The opera authority

> October 4, 12, 15, 18, 21, and 24; November 27, 1968
> Giacomo Puccini: *Tosca*
> New York, Metropolitan Opera House
> Birgit Nilsson, Dorothy Kirsten [November 27] (*Tosca*), Franco Corelli (*Cavaradossi*), Gabriel Bacquier, William Dooley [November 27] (*Scarpia*), Metropolitan Opera Chorus and Orchestra, cond. Francesco Molinari-Pradelli; stage director, Otto Schenk

Marcel Prawy recalled the story in his own biography, continuing with Corelli's attempt to rescue the situation:

> "I have a big announcement to make. I am going to make movies. And they told me that I could pick the subject, the screenplay, the music and the director at will. I can choose the greatest director in the world. I can choose Zeffirelli, I can choose Strehler. I told them: Why do I need a great director? I can do with a little one like him there." With those words he pointed again toward "Come si chiama."[24]

◆◆◆◆◆

In between the Met *Tosca*s EMI made new plans for Corelli, settling again on *La Forza del Destino* and *Ernani* with Callas in Paris for July 1969. Their plans extended to 1970, when *Don Carlo* was to be recorded with Caballé, Milnes, and Verrett.[25] Well into December Franco sang one of his busiest seasons ever, ending with two concerts. One was a solo concert in New Orleans and the other a Christmas gala with Mirella Freni and Philip de la Torre celebrating the opening of the new Casa Italiana in Newark on December 18.[26]

Before leaving New York, Corelli took the opportunity to unveil a statue of Giacomo Lauri-Volpi at the Met. The bust, a creation of the Danish sculptor Johan Galster, was placed next to the one of Caruso and among other great artists. Karajan and Bernstein were present, along with dignitaries from the Danish community and New York society. Said Corelli: "Our own ambassador was there as well but it is quite telling that the bust was placed on the initiative of Danish opera fans, instead of fellow Italians. That confirms the saying 'Nemo propheta in patria' and this makes me a little bit sad."[27]

With his concerts and the Danish Lauri-Volpi fans behind him, he had ample time to celebrate Christmas *in patria*. From there he went to Nice for a final *Tosca*. He then planned to rest up before his return to the United States, where the prestigious revival of the Price-Corelli *Trovatore* was being prepared.

January–March 1969: Behind the Scenes of the Lost *Trovatore*

Corelli's plan had been to relax in Milan, celebrate the New Year with family and friends, and then fly on to Burjassot, where he wanted to restudy *Trovatore* with Lauri-Volpi.[28] But upon arriving in Ancona he found his father bedridden and, it seemed, terminally ill. Remo had had prostate surgery a year and a half earlier, but the operation had not been performed well, and now the problem had recurred and was more serious than ever. The specialists considered the old man too feeble to risk further surgery and were attempting a special recovery therapy. If the result was good, he would have another operation on February 1. In the meantime, Franco refused to move from his father's side, afraid of losing him without being able to say goodbye.[29] He had respected his father from childhood, but since the death of his mother in 1950, the emotional bond between Remo and his youngest son had deepened.[30]

Meanwhile, Bauer heard Franco practice Manrico and reported to Bing that he was in splendid vocal shape.[31] Unfortunately, Corelli ended up staying away until well into February, and that good condition was wasted on the Adriatic Sea: Bing was forced to replace him—with Domingo—for the *Tosca* broadcast of February 15. When Corelli delayed his return further, Domingo covered him in the *Trovatore* premiere of March 6.[32] To Corelli's dismay, some voices in the press suggested that he had withdrawn at the last minute so as to maximize Domingo's chances of failing. Domingo cordially rushed to his colleague's aid: "Corelli has constantly brought me good luck and if my father was ill I would stay with him, too. I think Corelli is probably doing the human thing."[33]

Bing took Corelli's absence surprisingly well, after Bauer had made it clear that the tenor's excuse was all sadly true. By now Bing could also afford to be reasonable, for the Met suddenly had a number of good alternates available,

Corelli visiting the DiGrazia apartment, April 1969, in a rare picture of his private life. Worries, lawsuits, reflections on his life as an opera singer—somehow all these facts take on somewhat more importance in a biography than they really were: in the end, his daily life went on as ever, as these rare pictures of his private life demonstrate. Back row: John and Helen Ficarotta and their son, John Gary. Seated, left to right: Loretta Corelli, Frances DiGrazia, Franco Corelli, Sandra DiGrazia, and Donald DiGrazia. (Photo: Courtesy of Donald DiGrazia.)

and he was able to use Corelli's indebtedness to get him to consent to the *Werther*s that Bing wanted for the 1970–71 season; but even so, his composure was remarkable. Unfortunately, the management of the Birmingham Festival, due to open on March 20, was less considerate. It had been built around Corelli, and the education program that they had set up for it had been running for months. Corelli postponed the decision about his appearance for as long as possible, but when Remo suffered an unexpected setback on March 11 and was transferred to a private clinic, Franco canceled his festival appearances as well. Bauer began to panic. He wrote Bing that the Corellis seemed serious and phoned him twice a day, but he couldn't exclude the possibility that Corelli's tax problems were behind his staying in Europe.[34]

Franco produced a medical affidavit from the Milanese doctor, Carlo Meano, on March 12, 1969, to counterattack the breach-of-contract suit with which the Birmingham Festival management was threatening him. The affidavit stated simply that his vocal cords were affected by an acute emotional crisis that had resulted in a grave depression, preventing him from singing for at least thirty days.[35] Shortly thereafter Remo, post-surgery, miraculously recovered enough for Franco to leave him in the hands of the family and return to the United States. Bing, desperate to get him before the public again, let him sing at the very first opportunity, which was the *Bohème* on April 4 with Radmilla Bakočević. It was a risky decision, prompted by both Corelli's and Bing's eagerness to pick up the pieces. Unfortunately, the medical document dictated thirty days, which brought Corelli in breach of contract with the Birmingham Festival.[36]

April 8, 1969: A Turbulent Tour

With rave reviews for the just-released EMI *Roméo* set pouring in, one might think that Corelli had reason to look forward to new recording projects. Instead, he picked his birthday as the moment to threaten EMI with nonrenewal of his contract. The reason was that they insisted on Lamberto Gardelli as conductor for the planned *Forza del Destino* recording. Though they kept it from him at the time, EMI then decided to end their relationship with Corelli, with the caveat that they be able to reengage him immediately should he ever be ready to record *Otello*. On June 17, just one week before the recording was due to begin,[37] Corelli walked out of the *Forza* production as expected when EMI insisted on Gardelli.[38] He claimed Loretta was ill and gave that as the reason for his indisposition, but EMI knew as well as anyone that medical affidavits were given out in Italy like aspirin. Rather than bothering with Corelli, they engaged the reliable Carlo Bergonzi.[39]

Corelli vented his anger to his spokesman, Gravina, who captured an echo of it in his article "Franco Corelli: A Voice Speaks." In it Corelli declares he is fed up with the operatic machinery of all sorts of other people deciding what roles should and should not be sung: "No matter which course the singer takes, it's a lost cause . . . as far as pleasing all is concerned." He didn't waste his time answering specific questions about repertoire—for example, Halévy's *La Juive* and Meyerbeer's *Le Prophète* and *L'Africana*. They were dismissed as mediocre works. *Tristan* was out as well; Corelli's interest in Wagner was restricted to *Lohengrin*. Corelli mentioned that *Lucia di Lammermoor* and *Werther* would reap him new laurels. Gravina readily jumped to his defense: "If he favors us with Edgardo in *Lucia* and Werther within the next seasons, we will have reason to be grateful and not carp about *Otello* or *William Tell*."[40]

With that, Franco left for the Met Spring Tour to Boston, Cleveland, Atlanta, Dallas, Minneapolis, and Detroit. With just *Bohème* and *Adriana Lecouvreur*, his program was not very challenging, but these performances brought in some of his best reviews ever. Under normal circumstances these would have helped him pick up his career again. But on May 8 a man emerged from among the line of fans waiting for autographs after *Adriana Lecouvreur* and handed Corelli a folded sheet of paper. "What is this?" Corelli demanded. "It's an order from the court," replied the man.

When she read the document Loretta began to spit fire, for it stated that Franco was being sued for $37,000 by the Birmingham Festival for breach of contract.[41]

THE YEARS OF TRANSITION • 381

July 16–20, 1969: Stargazer

You know what the two most important things are in the world today? You will say, "Love and Music." Yes, those too. But to me it is medicine and le stelle—space. I am so excited to look at the television set and to think that soon I shall see there the heavens as they look from the moon!
  Franco Corelli, in Jack Frymire, "Il piu semplice e il piu bello,"
  Music and Artists, February–March 1968

On July 20, 1969, the Apollo 11 spacecraft landed on the moon, and its door opened for Neil Armstrong to set foot on extraterrestrial soil. The very act surpassed anything human beings had ever achieved. Among other things, it was final proof that the world of literature and opera should never be taken lightly. Writers had envisioned traveling to the moon centuries earlier, and Haydn had composed a comic opera on the subject long before humans could fly. There can be little doubt that Corelli's mind, like that of everyone else on Earth, was in orbit in front of the television all through Apollo 11's four-day flight. Still, to put love and music after medical achievements and a man on the moon is quite something for a tenor to say, although the Apollo program clearly created an atmosphere of optimism. It confirmed Corelli's belief in the possibilities of science, just as Christiaan Barnard's first successful heart transplant a couple of years earlier had instilled in him even greater faith in medical research.

1969: Trouble in Paradise?

The stars, eternity, superhuman emotions—all those things were omnipresent in the heroes that featured in the librettos set to music by the likes of Verdi and Puccini, and they fascinated Corelli. His unexpected denial of love did not feature there, and this sideline may have had to do with a crisis in his marriage, which would lead to a temporary separation between Franco and Loretta. Franco is said to have had a mistress for some time,[42] and he may have also engaged in a brief affair with Renata Tebaldi.[43] One day in 1969, the doorman of Donald DiGrazia's parents' apartment informed him that there was a woman waiting in the lobby. Said DiGrazia:

Mom was still out, it was about midnight, we had been visiting family. And there in the lobby was Loretta, all wrapped up in a chair with her coat on, sleeping. When she woke up she started crying, saying that Franco had thrown her out. She had taken the little dog, and we hid her for the time being, afraid that Franco would knock our door down if he found out. I mean, we never saw any of it, but we had heard the stories of him chasing people along Broadway and all. We knew the stories about him and Loretta as well, but apart from this incident they always had seemed to be going along pretty well when we were around.[44]

Loretta stayed with the DiGrazias for about a month in all until she reconciled with Franco. Various sources confirm that when it came down to Franco's threats to leave her, she would know just what to say to dissuade him. And then there was the fact that ever since those first four *Carmen*s of his career, he was reluctant to step onto a stage without her standing behind him. This psychological factor should not be underestimated, to which the many examples elsewhere in this text may testify. Moreover, it would be unfair to deny the couple the obvious attachment they had to each other for a good eighteen years—and what marriage is ever without any troubles? Once they reconciled, though, one fundamental thing changed: after 1969, Loretta dropped very much out of the public eye. No longer did her recipes grace the papers, no more did she entertain journalists or feature in fashion-magazine shoots with her husband, and only on a limited number of occasions would she be audible in interviews.[45]

August 1969: EMI Says Goodbye

In August Corelli, in a last attempt to salvage his EMI career, suddenly suggested recording another album of popular songs. EMI quashed the idea. They had had their fill of his whims and considered his contractual obligations fulfilled. One outstanding recording (*Roméo*), two interesting ones (*Norma*, *Turandot*), three entertaining popular song albums, and one aria recital in nine years were not nearly enough. The rest fell short of expectations. The blame should be divided between the two parties. To begin with, the Corellis proved impossible to work with in terms of studio conditions and demands. And EMI had not only made some odd casting decisions, but also failed utterly to understand the man's psychology. Franco could be coached and coaxed—the Met team had proven that—but neither EMI nor Ghiringhelli at La Scala had a man with Roberto Bauer's unusual skills at hand.

✦✦✦✦✦

Franco dealt with this sudden change of plans in his own way. He went to Ancona to think things over. From his lodgings he would row out *a la barcilunisa* on the Adriatic Sea, singing "Because" with B-flats enthusiastic enough to be heard all the way to Yugoslavia.[46]

William H. Honan, who wrote these words in *The New York Times*, may have been exaggerating a little, but that Corelli was indeed in fine voice at the time is confirmed by his surprise appearance on the glittering Nana Mouskouri International Gala in the summer of 1969. Franco dashed into the Parisian television studio with a stentorian "O sole mio," after which he started "A vucchella." At the second verse, Mouskouri slightly opened her fragile lips, and a duet between the Queen of Candlelight with the black-rimmed glasses and the Prince of Tenors was born. This was a dream come true for the show's raven-haired star, who had once seen her hopes of becoming an opera singer dashed when she was kicked out of the conservatory, after a professor discovered that she was active in less-serious repertoire as well. Following the duet, the pair waltzed off through a hyper-romantic "'O marenariello," revealing that Franco was an excellent dancer. When I asked her about this in 2007, Mouskouri remembered the event in grand old Eurovision manner: "It was one of the greatest moments in my life. Harry Belafonte came over from the USA, and then also Franco Corelli. He was a great, magnificent singer and a wonderful personality." Thank you France; Italy, may we have your votes?

August–December 1969: Strike, Death, Salvation

Halfway through August, further adjustments to Franco's fall performance schedule were made. Bing was under great pressure from the unions, and strikes threatened by the Met's workers loomed ominously; Bing was forced to hustle with the program. Franco seized the opportunity to repay Bing for his understanding earlier that year and agreed to all and everything. No fewer than eight *Trovatore*s were suddenly inserted, as well as a number of *Aida*s. He was to sing in the premieres of *Andrea Chénier* on September 27 and *Il Trovatore* on October 3. Then came the Met general strike in September. It was unclear whether the Met would be able to open its doors at all for the 1969–70 season. Many singers were released from their contracts and found themselves forced to make other arrangements for the season. When the conflict was finally resolved and Tucker and Price opened with a haphazard *Aida* on December 29, the first half of the season was already lost, and some operas had to be dropped altogether. Here Franco proved himself a trouper, standing on the barricades right beside Bing, prepared to sing whatever was required.[47]

Bing made some friendly gestures of his own as well, finally allowing the dangerous Gorlinsky deal to pass. Instead of withholding taxes and having Gorlinsky ask for a refund, the Met now stopped making the 30 percent withholdings.[48]

◆◆◆◆◆

As if the illness of Franco's father, his legal problems, and the canceled September-to-December season hadn't been enough, the year had to end in the worst possible way for both Corelli and Bing when their friend Roberto Bauer died on December 21. Bing appointed Bauer's life partner, Otto Müller, as Bauer's successor, but despite his knowledge (he was a vocal coach) and the part he had played in Bauer's achievements, he couldn't possibly bring Bauer's fanatical enthusiasm and instinctive understanding of the singer's soul to the job.

CHAPTER 19 ❖ 1970–1975

Defending the Throne

January 8–February 2, 1970: A Champion Tenor Defends His Throne

Is this art? Well—yes. But not the sort that bears easy comparison to dancing with veils or playing the contrafagotto. The story of Franco Corelli singing Cav *at the Met has more in common with El Cordobés doing combat with a mean-spirited, 900-pound bull at the Plaza Monumental in Madrid.*
    William H. Honan, "A Champion Tenor Defends His Title,"
The New York Times, **February 8, 1970**

After canceling the first part of the season, the Met was sorely in need of an artistic triumph. Bing's hopes were set on the upcoming new *Cavalleria Rusticana* production with Franco Zeffirelli. Corelli agreed reluctantly, for he saw the part of Turiddu—and Mascagni's operas in general—as barriers upon which his voice would simply be battered: "As anyone knows *Cavalleria* starts with a veritable Chinese torture, the *romanza* that is generally known as the *Siciliana*: 'O Lola, ch'hai di latti la cammisa. . . .' It is short, lasting just a few minutes, but it forces the tenor to sing with full voice while standing behind the curtain. And worse, it is the first aria the public hears, without any possibility to warm up."[1]

    Arriving at the theater thirty minutes before he was due to hit the stage, Franco shot into Turiddu's costume and did his makeup. When the stage manager, Stanley Levine, called for his cue, Corelli started praying fervently to his deceased mother. He then patted his poodle Roméo, after which William H. Honan of *The New York Times* witnessed the tenor's pulse shoot from 58 to 130: "His teeth chattered, and his legs were quivering like mandolin strings."[2]

Left: Ready for the 1970s. (Photo: Epoca. Courtesy of the Mondadori Group) *Right*: Tenor pals Corelli and Tucker exchanging jokes about conductors shortly before their joint January 8, 1970, premieres of *Cavalleria Rusticana* and *Pagliacci*. (Photo: Louis Melançon. Courtesy of the Metropolitan Opera Archives)

Corelli was extremely worried because Bernstein had asked him to sing the Siciliana sostenuto—very slowly. Bernstein told him humorously: "You have the lungs of a camel, you'll be splendid."[3] When that also failed to help, Bernstein whispered into Corelli's ear that he had called for Domingo. A minute later Corelli marched to the stage. Said Bernstein: "The Metropolitan is the biggest psychiatric institution in New York."[4]

No one ever sees Turiddu's Siciliana performed. It is sung from backstage, on this night even from a little underneath. With Corelli were Honan; the floor manager, Stanley Levine; and the backstage conductor, Ignace Strasfogel. Claiming that he was indisposed, that he had no voice, and that he couldn't go

---

January 8, 12, 20, and 30; February 7; June 2 (Festival), 1970
Pietro Mascagni: *Cavalleria Rusticana*
New York, Metropolitan Opera House
Franco Corelli (*Turiddu*), Grace Bumbry (*Santuzza*), Nedda Casei, Judith Frost [January 20, 30; June 2] (*Lola*), Frank Guarrera, Walter Cassel [January 20, 30; February 7], Morley Meredith [June 2] (*Alfio*), Carlotta Ordassy, Jean Craft [June 2] (*Lucia*), cond. Leonard Bernstein; stage director and set and costume designer, Franco Zeffirelli

on, Corelli ripped his shirt open to show Levine a leather belt that he had girded around his waist; Levine had lent it to him once, and Franco feeling as though he could use some extra support under his chest, had worn it ever since. That is not surprising if one takes Honan's word for it that the tenor could inhale 300 cubic inches of air into his forty-seven-inch chest within two seconds, which brought his chest span to a good fifty inches. When Strasfogel signaled the harpist to start the Siciliana's dreamlike opening chords, Honan noticed that "Corelli, looking rather like the winged victory of Samothrace with one foot forward, chest thrown out and arms more or less dangling behind, opened his mouth wide, almost as if he were yawning, and out swam a gargantuan and voluptuous wail: 'O Lo-la, ch'ai di L-A-A-tti la cam-M-I-I-sa!'"[5]

All the way through Bernstein mouthed the words for him on the closed-circuit television monitor, indicating the pace and accents he wanted. Said Honan: "Almost as if to get even, the tenor's right arm began to beat time for the harpist."[6] Corelli's voice rose up to his first succession of A-flats with a silvery, bell-like tone. The second succession came out a little strident, and Honan saw that the tenor's head was beginning to spin. He clutched the harmonium for support, ending the aria with a difficult pianissimo on the last "Aha," after which he collapsed over the top of the instrument (a scene memorialized by a famous cartoon with the article): "There was an instant roar of applause from the house, yet the audience wasn't able to witness what was surely the most dramatic spectacle of the entire performance—Corelli sprawled across the harmonium rolling his head from side to side and gasping for breath like a fainting marathon runner." When Corelli rose, he left the room the way he had come, though Levine had warned him that he would be visible to some in the audience. Said Levine, schoolmarmishly: "That's my Franco." Honan caught up with his subject at the staircase ascending to his dressing room and heard Corelli grumble: "*Raaaaah! Eeeeeah!* Sostenuto! Sostenuto! Sosten-u-u-u-to!" The bravos from the backstage crowd in front of his dressing room, Bing's affectionate congratulations, uttered in a soft voice and accompanied by a loving pat on the tenor's sleeve, could not change his mood. He slammed his dressing-room door shut, feeling extremely miserable.[7]

What followed was one of the greatest triumphs in Corelli's entire career. Honan thought his first cry of "Mamma!" had the solidity of a church bell; his trick of changing tonal colors to suggest drunkenness was magnificent. Then he came to the section where he bade his mother farewell, not expecting to return from the fight: "[When he] implored mamma Lucia to be a mother to the girl he had made pregnant, Corelli's voice exploded in melodic sobs and gasps mingled with shimmering, golden A's, A-flats, and B-flats. They were the cries of a stricken animal, not in the least ethereal but virile and garlicky [sic]. The last of them—a ravishing A-flat—soared through the house like a great bird released from the stage."[8]

The next day there was much dispute over Bernstein's tempi and Grace Bumbry's Santuzza, but even Corelli's sworn enemy Alan Rich wrote that he "sang the hell out of it."[9] Bing readily admitted that his idol had saved the day and something of the season.[10] Corelli agreed: "I succeeded, but singing *Cavalleria* under Bernstein was a veritable heavyweight championship."[11]

February 1970: The Lost Requiem

When Bernstein and Schuyler Chapin, the vice president of Lincoln Center, set to work on two film projects, Chapin proved to be more effective than Bing, none of whose film projects ever materialized. Chapin set up a small company with Bernstein and took their plans for a film of the Verdi Requiem to the experienced producer Roger L. Stevens. He agreed to the cast—Franco Corelli, Josephine Veasey, Martina Arroyo, and Ruggero Raimondi—and a production budget of about $90,000. Now Chapin had just one worry left: Corelli. He feared the tenor would cancel the project at the last moment and was looking for a sound emergency understudy. Chapin explained his problem to Plácido Domingo and saw the young man's eyes sadden at the mention of Corelli's name. Domingo had been substituting for Corelli at the Met, Covent Garden, and La Scala since 1966. When Chapin approached him, Domingo felt that his days as a cover were behind him, although he agreed that working with Bernstein would be good for his career. Chapin decided to gamble: "Listen, Mr. Domingo, I think Corelli will back out of this and I think the film and the recording will be yours." He then offered Domingo Beethoven's Ninth Symphony on his own in a package deal, and the tenor accepted.

When Chapin arrived at St. Paul's Cathedral in London, where the Requiem was to be filmed, all seemed well, apart from some trouble with the unions over cassette rights for the recording. Even Corelli had arrived and was rehearsing, defying Chapin's misgivings. When the union problems were finally settled, Chapin retuned to the Savoy Hotel, where he heard "the most painful bleating" coming from Corelli's room. Said Bernstein's wife, Felicia: "It's been going on all afternoon. It's Corelli. He doesn't feel well." Bernstein entered: "Did you hear that?" Chapin nodded, and they agreed to have Domingo ready in the wings, in case the evening rehearsal was unsatisfactory. When Corelli showed up pale and perspiring, obviously not himself, Chapin secretly arranged for Domingo to fly in. He then faced the task of canceling Corelli. Fearing the tenor's reaction, Chapin went to bed, leaving the difficult phone call for the next morning. It was a lucky shot: Loretta woke him up the very next morning, hysterical and crying, to cancel the whole deal, film, recording, and performance: "We go back to Italy. Franco has such good memories of the Maestro he don't want anything to disturb this. Goodbye."[12]

Being forced by indisposition to give up Bernstein's recording of the Requiem must have been a major disappointment for Franco, who still linked that work with the promise made to his dead mother. Because the earlier Requiem in Los Angeles had been in a concert hall, the one at St. Paul's Cathedral would have brought his oath a step closer to fulfillment. Worse yet, both the Ninth Symphony recording and the Requiem film proved to be key to Domingo's early recording career. Whereas the *Cavalleria* coup had revitalized Corelli's career, the lost Requiem proved to be one missed recording opportunity too many.

March–April 1970: Corelli in Cape Town?

Apart from the mentioned victories and defeats in "combat," 1970 proved very much the aftermath of the mishaps that had plagued Corelli and Bing throughout 1969. Just how far Corelli went to help Bing, out of gratitude for his understanding when Franco's father was ill, is clear from the fact that Franco canceled his entire South African tour in order to sing in a number of *Roméo et Juliette* reprises during March and April. The Met readily made up for the breach-of-contract damage and had Gorlinsky transfer $22,000 in damages to the South Africans, who had booked Corelli for a number of concerts and theatrical performances. Once more Bing gained a few repeat *Roméo*s at the cost of Franco's international career.[13] The cancellation left only his hit-and-run raid on Paris, where he popped up for a single *Tosca* on March 4, as the most intriguing event in the months following his *Cavalleria* run. This performance is scarcely remembered today except for the reconciliation with Antonietta Stella, who was his Tosca. Stella maintains that the conflict over the 1963 *Fanciulla del West* premiere, where she had walked out on Corelli, had been exaggerated by the press: "Like every tenor he had a complicated character, which goes with the nature of having to sing such difficult roles. At times he could be irritable, but he was a good person at heart. After a while, we made up and our careers went on normally."[14]

✦✦✦✦✦

Back in New York, the Met's lawyers advised Bing to force Corelli into a settlement with the Birmingham Arts Festival. To begin with, they were pretty sure that it was a lost case and bad publicity, but they also worried over the upcoming Egenberg trial hearings, where a number of Met artists were summoned to testify in a case that concerned foreign income tax fraud. (Norman Egenberg, an accountant, had bribed a superior to falsify tax documents that netted huge tax refunds for some Met singers.) To have Corelli's questionable financial arrangements to avoid paying foreign income tax on display at a trial did not seem wise, so they settled the matter with the Birmingham Festival for $8,500, far less than the claim of $41,500. The check, of course, was the Met's, not Corelli's. Bing's champion tenor may well have pointed out that the only organization that benefited from his premature start was the Met itself.[15] So far, so good. But when the Egenberg trial started on June 2, it proved to be the beginning of a string of lawsuits with major consequences. The IRS finally ruled that all these alien Met singers had to pay income tax. Corelli, Nilsson, Tebaldi, and Konya, to name but a few, were all on the list of those whose cases were affected by the first ruling. The Met's lawyers handled it all pretty well from the viewpoint of damage control. They successfully downplayed the trials by minimizing exposure in the press, accomplished through a policy of trying to keep those on trial from personally attending the hearings.[16]

Difficult as the situation was, Bing also saw some opportunities in it and tried to capitalize on his now sincere personal friendship with Corelli. He planned to resign on April 22, 1972, and asked for a farewell present that no one would ever forget: Corelli's debut in *Otello* on April 3, 1972. *Faust* was scheduled as early as September 22, 1971, and *Rigoletto* was once more pending.[17] It was the chance of a lifetime.

July 4–11, 1970: Caught in His Own Web

There are no difficult phrases in Turandot. *It was the shortest role I ever sang. It has 300 bars while Isolde has 1,850 bars.*
   Birgit Nilsson, correspondence, April 4–6, 2005

Nilsson is really something, vocally speaking! She was an eagle, un apula, she was dominant, a voice that was so important, a voice that was really in the just point—very interesting. Also she is a beautiful colleague, with a fantastic sense of humor.
   Franco Corelli, "Opera Fanatic" broadcast, May 21, 1991

A fine taste of Nilsson's sense of humor is the story behind her surprise appearance for a series of *Turandot*s that the small but lovely mountain city of Macerata would never forget. The director of the theater, Carlo Perucci, had invited his childhood friend Franco Corelli to sing in this theater, located just twenty-five miles from Ancona, right next to Beniamino Gigli's birthplace, Recanati. Corelli didn't want to accept but couldn't bring himself to let a friend down. So he gave Perucci a riddle to solve, saying that he would gladly come provided that he arrange for an outstanding support cast—only Nilsson would do. Said Nilsson: "He knew that I would never accept to sing in a place called Macerata and considered the matter closed. But Perucci offered me so many 'good things,' including the fee, that I just had to accept!" Apart from the money, Perucci's promise that they would reside in her former partner Gigli's villa in Recanati proved irresistible for Nilsson and her husband. Of course, she had to go through some typical Italian fumbles before she could enjoy the whole thing:

> When the promised driver was not waiting for us at the airport I thought it was all a big mistake. I wanted to go back on the spot, but my husband said we might as well drive out there and find this Gigli villa ourselves, since we had already landed. It was a terrible trip; we couldn't find it and got lost. But . . . when we finally made it, it was fantastic! We were living in Gigli's bedroom and the villa: it was a castle![18]

"A castle" is also how Macerata's impressive Arena Sferisterio has been described. Originally it was erected as an outdoor sports arena for the odd ball-

> **July 4, 8, and 11, 1970**
> **Giacomo Puccini: *Turandot***
> **Macerata, Arena Sferisterio**
> Birgit Nilsson (*Turandot*), Franco Corelli (*Calaf*), Antonietta Cannarile Berdini (*Liù*), Antonio Zerbini (*Timur*), Carlo Scaravelli (*Ping*), cond. Franco Mannino; stage director, Franco Enriquez

game, until someone discovered that the acoustics were extraordinary. From then on incidental opera performances were organized. During the 1960s these performances started to become more frequent, and once the management began to engage first-rate singers, the festival rapidly rose in status. The Corelli-Nilsson *Turandot*s are among the most significant performances in Macerata's long operatic history. Judging from the photographs and surviving video fragments,[19] Corelli truly enjoyed himself here once he reconciled himself to the fact that he had been caught in his own web. After all, he was back in the arms of his family and friends in Macerata, where the Bellini Chorus participated and Carlo Scaravelli sang Pong. Due to both the acoustics of the Sferisterio and the way the valley descended from its auditorium, Corelli's voice was heard a mile down into the valley, an echo of which can be heard in the live recording and the filmed performance fragment of "In questa reggia."

Over the summer Franco began to rethink his new terms with the Met, which kept him stuck there for the greater part of the year. His doubts increased when he received a most peculiar invitation to Spain, where he was once more to be photographed with General Franco. That invitation effectively meant the end of the *Faust* project. Bing was furious and wrote that if being photographed with General Franco was that important,[20] he would gladly arrange for Corelli to be photographed with President Richard Nixon instead. Then again, wrote Bing: "Surely, a photographer doesn't take two weeks, so please reconsider that. It is of enormous importance to me personally, for my last season, to have you in the first week to do *Faust*. At least give us our first three *Faust*s; thereafter it will be difficult enough but we have a little more time and at least have the glamour of your presence in the opening weeks, which is vital for me."[21]

The combination of Franco and Franco won, and so the last Fascist dictator was partially responsible for, among everything else, the loss of Corelli's *Faust* and *Otello*. However, Corelli's schedule for January and February 1971 partially made up for this with *Lucia di Lammermoor* and the new production of *Werther*.[22]

August–December 1970: The Return to Verona and Vienna

Corelli did not return to New York until the end of December 1970. He was now starting to work seriously on reestablishing himself in Europe. Discussions with La Scala continued, but when they did not bear fruit he prepared his Arena di Verona comeback with a series of *Carmen*s. After a nine-year absence, his Don José received a warm welcome, although the performance as a whole was not on the highest level. Mignon Dunn readily discovered that singing Carmen in Italy was not the same as singing it to American audiences. She was crucified by a few very audible members of the audience shouting for "voice." These one or two persistent booers didn't show signs of stopping and may well have been hired to sabotage Dunn's appearance. Another part of the audience, annoyed by the disrupting catcalls, started shushing them. The fact that Italy's famous Carmen, Giulietta Simionato, was sitting on the front row, where Corelli presented his bouquet to her in homage, may not have helped Dunn either. Said Simionato: "He actually stepped down the stage and presented me his bouquet, saying, 'It's you, Signora, who deserves these flowers.'"[23]

Franco Corelli in his element at the Arena di Verona, August 1970. (Photo: Epoca. Courtesy of the Mondadori Group)

Dunn left the production after four performances to make way for Adriana Lazzarini. Her Carmen was, of course, well within the Italian tradition. The choice of Carmens was not the only error in judgment in this unfortunate run: during one of Dunn's performances a horse fell into the orchestra pit.

❖❖❖❖❖

Corelli's 1969 return to Vienna with a single *Tosca* was now being fortified by a string of highly acclaimed *Don Carlo* performances. The luxurious cast defined the generation that would dominate opera for years to come. Next to Nicolai Ghiaurov, Eberhard Wächter, Gundula Janowitz, Shirley Verrett (who came to value Corelli as a fine colleague during these performances),[24] and Martti Talvela in the principal roles, there were also Edita Gruberova as Tebaldo and Judith Blegen as the Heavenly Voice. The conductor, Horst Stein, a Karajan trainee, rolled out a magic orchestral carpet that purred like a Rolls-Royce engine. The roster of gilded, bronzed, and silvery voices performed to perfection. The critics considered it a quintessential *Don Carlo*, which meant something to Corelli, who had once feared the part in which he had involuntarily discovered the art of the diminuendo. However, in the sixteen years that had passed since, both his interpretation and his view of the part had changed considerably: "*Don Carlo* isn't all that difficult. It is an opera where the tenor may have to sing in all acts, but the arias are short. Really, the most important thing for Don Carlo is to look good."[25]

January 11–21, 1971: Edgardo di Ravenswood

In spite of all the beautiful music that Donizetti wrote for Edgardo di Ravenswood in *Lucia di Lammermoor*, it isn't the most logical choice for a tenor's tenth anniversary at an opera house. Neither Bing nor Corelli seems to have paid any attention to that in light of the upcoming *Werther* premiere. That debut received immense press attention, whereas the equally rare and unique Corelli *Lucia* debut went completely unpromoted. This was because Corelli merely stepped in for four performances in a running production that had employed a string of tenors from Sándor Kónya and Nicolai Gedda in early 1969 up to Plácido Domingo, Luciano Pavarotti, Giacomo Aragall, and even Richard Tucker in more recent months. The part of Lucia likewise was tossed

> **January 11 and 21, 1971**
> **Gaetano Donizetti: *Lucia di Lammermoor***
> **New York, Metropolitan Opera House**
> Roberta Peters, Gail Robinson [January 21] (*Lucia di Lammermoor*), Franco Corelli, John Alexander [January 21; Acts II & III] (*Sir Edgardo di Ravenswood*), Matteo Manuguerra (*Lord Enrico Ashton*), Leo Goeke (*Lord Arturo Buclaw*), Bonaldo Giaiotti (*Raimondo Bidebent*), Carlotta Ordassy (*Alisa*), Rod MacWherter (*Normanno*), cond. Carlo Franci

around among Roberta Peters, Anna Moffo, Joan Sutherland, and Gail Robinson. Peters was very attractive and one of the more frequently used Lucias in this production and therefore seemed to provide a sound context for Corelli's first operatic role debut since 1964. The tenor's premiere nerves should easily have been calmed by the conductor, Carlo Franci. He was not only the son of the famous baritone Benvenuto Franci, but also the very same conductor who had conducted Corelli's Edgardo "rehearsal" in the *Suprema Confessione* film from 1956!

Despite the low-profile debut, the press had shown up in droves—even the Italian press was there. Unfortunately, things did not go as planned. Surprisingly, Peters proved to be a very pale Lucia despite her experience, combining florid singing with a portrayal that was as imaginative as a potted plant. The press nearly annihilated her in the reviews,[26] and except for Bonaldo Giaiotti, the entire support cast failed, along with Franci, who gave one of the most uninspired readings of the score ever heard. Enter Corelli! His arrival on the stage as Edgardo was greeted by an unprecedented salvo of bravos. Opening-night nerves got the better of him, though, as was immediately apparent from his opening lines, where he assaulted his notes as if fighting for his life. Edgardo was supposed to secretly approach Lucia in the enemy castle's gardens; Corelli would have alarmed the whole castle and been arrested on the spot. The one thing that this particular performance proved is that he could still sing like a hurricane: he transformed the sextet "Che mi frena in tal momento" into a tenor solo with a chorus of five.

Judging from the outpouring of applause and bravos, which increased with each decibel Corelli added, his debut as Edgardo was an unprecedented triumph. But Franco knew better. How much he disliked his performance is clear from his second appearance, in which his interpretation turned around a full 180 degrees. With the superb Gail Robinson instead of Peters at his side,[27] Corelli suddenly proved inspired. "Aided" by a bad cold, he distributed his reserves more effectively, starting out in *mezza voce*, luxuriating in the words, softly spinning out notes, and bringing his beloved art of the diminuendo to the Act I duet. Here he proved those critics wrong who judged him too wooden a singer for the poetic role of Edgardo. Alas, this marvelous beauty couldn't last. Although Robinson didn't sing out, she nevertheless covered Corelli's voice in the unison sections, and after Act I Franco bowed out. John Alexander finished the performance, and when Franco gave up on the remaining two Edgardos in order to focus on the more important *Werther* premiere, Alexander took them over as well.

January 19–April 12, 1971: "Pourquoi me Réveiller"

It does not take great intelligence to learn a role. When the part is melodic it takes six days. Something like Stravinsky, well, it takes longer, maybe even twelve days.

> Franco Corelli, in "A Tenor in a Hurry 'Turns All the Knobs' and Finds a Teacher in Caruso," *High Fidelity*, **June 1962**

Werther! Corelli had contemplated the role ever since the late 1950s, when he recorded the two Cetra fragments from Massenet's second chef d'oeuvre. It turned out to be a lot more complicated than the average Stravinsky opera! Corelli's plans took shape in the second half of 1967; by 1968 he was actively studying the role. He then postponed his appearance until he felt obliged to soothe Bing. Bing considered the work too weak to give without his handsome star tenor; *Werther* was revived for Corelli alone. The idea was to bathe the opera in a romantic halo while still maintaining a realistic and credible human touch. Rudolf Heinrich provided an ideal visual setting for Corelli and Paul-Émile Deiber's stage direction.[28] Bing personally picked Christa Ludwig as Charlotte, and in January the team started working toward the prestigious premiere.

There are three stories to tell about the road toward the premiere. To begin with, Deiber soon drove Corelli crazy by demonstrating personally how Corelli should embrace and perform the stage kisses with Ludwig. Ludwig made no secret of it: "A ripe woman myself [she was forty-three], I nevertheless fell in love head over heels with a man who was a complete stranger to me; worse, he was my director."[29] Deiber's lighting concept turned out to involve reserving most of the spotlights for his *amourette*. This infuriated Corelli because the spotlights weren't immediately focused on him when he appeared on the stage, and at one rehearsal he simply walked offstage. Said Ludwig: "Paul-Émile's concept was to let him enter the light slowly, which would have been much more effective. But Corelli lost his temper, tore the wig off his head, cried out for Loretta, and started gathering his things and poodle in order to leave the theater. Only when Bing arrived and employed his famous diplomatic skills did the tenor calm down and return to the rehearsal."[30]

The second story about Corelli's *Werther* debut was of an altogether different nature: someone had called him up and written him anonymous letters threatening that something would happen to him if he sang the role. Apparently this person judged only Nicolai Gedda fit for it. Corelli took the threats very seriously, and to this day his opening-night cancellation remains clouded in mystery. Though he was not known to be indisposed, he canceled just minutes before the curtain rose, claiming that he suffered from a cold. Christa Ludwig had her doubts: "A mere fifteen minutes before the performance was due to begin, his fear for the role had overtaken him, and in spite of the fact that he

February 19 and 27; March 4, 9, 12, 18, 22, 27, and 31; April 7 and 12, 1968

Jules Massenet: *Werther*

New York, Metropolitan Opera House

Franco Corelli, Enrico Di Giuseppe [February 19; last-minute substitute] (*Werther*), Christa Ludwig, Rosalind Elias [March 18, 22, 27; April 7], Régine Crespin [March 31; April 7, 12] (*Charlotte*), Judith Blegen, Gail Robinson [March 22, 27, 31; April 12] (*Sophie*), John Reardon, Dominic Cossa [March 18, 22, 31; April 7, 12] (*Albert*), Fernando Corena, Donald Gramm [March 18, 22, 27] (*le Bailli*), cond. Alain Lombard, Martin Rich [March 4, 9, 12]; stage director, Paul-Emile Deiber; set and costume designer, Rudolf Heinrich

was already in full costume and with his stage make-up on, he exclaimed that he couldn't sing."[31]

Under great pressure and amid general panic, Corelli's cover, Enrico Di Giuseppe, was called upon to save the day. When Ossie Hawkins announced Corelli's sudden indisposition, some in the audience erupted in laughter, some applauded, and some booed, fed up with what they considered the divo's attitude. Ludwig adapted herself to the new situation by trading her high-heeled boots for ballet slippers and bending her knees as much as possible throughout in order to avoid looking ridiculous next to her very short new Werther. As it turned out, Di Giuseppe hardly needed the support; to his credit and quite unexpectedly, he found himself wildly applauded and scored a personal triumph, complete with fine press reports.

During the *Werther* rehearsals Corelli first learned what it was like to be "the fifth wheel," when Ludwig and stage director Paul-Emile Deiber fell madly in love. Perhaps Corelli's impassioned Werther was inspired by the director's ardent example in this photo, although Corelli seems to have his doubts here, not to mention the fact that the director's hand seems rather aimed at breaking the magic touch between Werther and Charlotte. (Photo: Courtesy of Christa Ludwig)

The third story behind the missed premiere is almost too bizarre to be true, but the eyewitness account of Bruno Sammartino, the Italian world wrestling champion, is supported by some stunning circumstantial evidence. It all began when Sammartino received a phone call from Loretta weeks before the premiere: "She told me about the threats and that they threatened to break his leg. At first I thought it was a joke, but she said it was very serious and asked if I could pick him up and stay with him throughout; then he would feel safe and would go on with it."[32] His own obligations prevented Sammartino from coming to all the performances, so he asked some wrestling friends if they could help Franco out. That puts into perspective an odd remark on the pirate recording from Corelli's Philadelphia *Carmen*, just three weeks before the *Werther* premiere. One can hear the astonished voice of the man operating the recorder noticing a very unexpected front-row visitor: Sammartino's good friend Robert Otto Marella, better known as Gorilla Monsoon. According to this version of events, Franco canceled the premiere because neither Sammartino nor Marella was able to attend.

Corelli's throat was instantly cured however, when Sammartino arrived at the theater for the second *Werther* in the company of two other enormous wrestlers. Sammartino positioned them strategically in the front row, within sight of Franco, and he personally kept an eye on the audience from the wings, which assured Franco a safe evening.[34] He arrived onstage with a voice pitched to kill. As was to be expected, some critics questioned his interpretation, and there was the obligatory mumble about his French pronunciation. The Swedish-born Nicolai Gedda certainly came a lot closer to the authentic French model, and Gedda's aggressive two-person claque protested loudly and clearly against what they considered the squandering of their idol's rightful part on Bing's favorite. (Even during the premiere with Di Giuseppe, the Gedda fan cried out for "Gedda!" after the Act II aria.)[35]

These cries for Gedda were repeated even more insistently at some of Corelli's subsequent performances, evoking memories of Del Monaco claque–ridden evenings in the San Carlo and La Scala,[36] but Bing couldn't care less: he knew that no more than a handful of those present were likely to have any knowledge of the French language at all, and with Ludwig as the Charlotte for the opening performances, authenticity was clearly not the aim of the production. Corelli and Ludwig were simply cast as two sumptuous voices that took over Massenet's score and turned it into a credible whirlpool of emotions. It was really a matter of style versus emotion, although Corelli's best evenings were those opposite the authentic and intimate Charlotte of Régine Crespin, when he had gained some onstage experience in the role. If the performances with Ludwig were thrilling for his stupendous vocal display, those with Crespin showed him at his artistic peak. His most disarming Werthers, however, were those he sang to Rosalind Elias's Charlotte. Her dark, grand voice blended well with his burnished timbre, and in

Corelli teaching Bruno Sammartino to sing a high C backstage in Philadelphia, prior to the *Werther* run. Said Sammartino: "I really liked Franco and am proud to have known him. He always let me visit him backstage and when he called upon me for help, when he received threatening letters prior to his Werther debut, I immediately offered my help."[33] (Photo: Courtesy of Bruno Sammartino)

spite of her heavy American accent, she brought a certain something to the role that inspired his more poetic side. What she lacked in style she made up for in beauty; she was by far the most attractive of his three Charlottes.

◆◆◆◆◆

If the *Werther* run served any purpose, it was to convince Goeran Gentele, Bing's appointed successor, that Corelli was indeed still "the Greatest Tenor in the World." When Gentele inquired about Corelli's demands, Robert Herman explained to him how they had been able to keep "Mr. Sold Out" glued to the house throughout the years:

> By making a higher guarantee than the number of scheduled performances. If he is going to sing thirty-two performances, we must guarantee forty-eight in order to have him agree to the $4,000 fee, which is far lower than he gets anywhere. If you wish to have us go ahead with the offer on that basis, please let me know and we will try to get a signed contract. Obviously, the above is very confidential. Only you, Mr. Bing and I will have this information.[37]

"We will try"—that about sums up Herman's views on ten years of marriage to Franco Corelli.[38] From Gentele's point of view, however, there was little to fear. He looked upon Corelli as one of the pillars for the coming years, and when the next film project was discussed—*Cavalleria Rusticana*, with Franco Zeffirelli directing—he readily granted Zeffirelli's request to do it with Corelli.[39] The most noticeable change produced by the shift in regime concerned the tour arrangements for the transportation of Roméo, the Corellis' poodle. Previously, with some makeshift arrangements and sweet talking of certain airplane captains, the dog had often been allowed on board. New regulations prevented this, and Bing went through some paperwork to explain to Loretta that she had to prepare to enjoy staying with the company, because she might have to travel with them on the charter plane in order to take the dog along.[40]

April–June 1971: Chiaroscuro

I have been trying for the last six years or so to color with my voice as a painter shades from red to—what is the English word for chiaroscura? Chiaroscuro. The B-flats in Aida—*I used to sing them forte. And a*

certain part of the audience prefers everything this way. But to shade is really more difficult. There is always the risk that the voice will break on a high diminuendo. Sometimes it does. If I can tell it will I do not attempt it. But if it breaks, this is not everything. There will be other notes.
    Franco Corelli, in Jack Frymire, "Il piu semplice e il piu bello,"
    Music and Artists, February–March 1968

When Corelli's voice gave out on his B-flat diminuendo in "Celeste Aida" during a Met spring tour performance in Detroit and at the opening of the Met's June festival,[41] some people thought they were hearing the first signs of decline. There is something to be said for this, but there are also good arguments against it. First of all, his now famous diminuendo was never one of his best weapons, and the risk involved in doing it was considerable. It was hard wrought and had eluded him occasionally before. As can be seen from Jack Frymire's quote at the top of this section, Corelli was aware of this from the start. The main problem with the diminuendo in Detroit is that it came at the wrong time and place, because On Stage! released this *Aida* early in the CD era, which made it a reference recording in the Corelli catalog (On Stage! 4708/2). Because the Met still actively fought copyright infringements then, On Stage! simply relabeled it with a more convenient 1968 date and pinned it down to a house less aggressive about defending its copyright (the Philadelphia Lyric). That made "the first signs of decline" seem to have come three years before they actually did.

But was Corelli in fact past his prime? That cannot be determined on the grounds of a single note that Theodore Stronging of *The New York Times* judged a mere miscalculation of breath, acknowledged by the tenor's gaze to the audience accompanied by a wry grimace. Stronging focused rather on "the other notes," belted out as usual.[42] Moreover, the road from the end of the Met season through the spring tour had garnered Corelli some valued laurels, beginning with a great Met *Bohème* premiere on April 4 (with Jeanette Pilou as Mimì) that had all the young love, dreaminess, and sentimental appeal the opera called for. *Il Progresso* recognized Corelli's Rodolfo for what it was, pointing to Puccini's own demands in defense of his interpretation:

> Rodolfo is close to Corelli's heart, close to his artistic temperament and close to the lyric-dramatic accents in his vocal makeup. It is precisely this intense and sorrowful focus, in combination with his vibrant voice, that lends the

scene where Mimì dies in his arms such an unbearable melancholy. There the gates toward the horizons of sentiment that Puccini asked for truly unfold in our hearts, giving his creatures an intense human appearance.[43]

Met Spring Tour 1971

April 23, Boston, John B. Hynes Civic Auditorium
Werther with Franco Corelli (*Werther*), Régine Crespin (*Charlotte*), Judith Blegen (*Sophie*), cond. Martin Rich

April 27, Cleveland, Public Auditorium
Werther with Franco Corelli (*Werther*), Régine Crespin (*Charlotte*), Judith Blegen (*Sophie*), cond. Martin Rich

April 30, Cleveland, Public Auditorium
Aida with Arroyo (*Aida*), Franco Corelli (*Radamès*), Dalis (*Amneris*), Sereni (*Amonasro*), cond. Fausto Cleva

May 6, Atlanta, Civic Center
Werther with Franco Corelli (*Werther*), Rosalind Elias (*Charlotte*), Joy Clements (*Sophie*), cond. Martin Rich

May 11, Dallas, State Fair Music Hall
Werther with Franco Corelli (*Werther*), Rosalind Elias (*Charlotte*), Joy Clements (*Sophie*), cond. Jan Behr

May 15, Dallas, State Fair Music Hall
Aida with Amara (*Aida*), Franco Corelli (*Radamès*), Irene Dalis (*Amneris*), Mario Sereni (*Amonasro*), cond. Fausto Cleva

May 21, Minneapolis, Northrop Auditorium
Werther with Franco Corelli (*W*), Rosalind Elias (*Charlotte*), Gail Robinson (*Sophie*), cond. Jan Behr

May 24, Detroit, Masonic Temple Auditorium
Werther with Franco Corelli (*Werther*), Rosalind Elias (*Charlotte*), Gail Robinson (*Sophie*), cond. Jan Behr

May 28, Detroit, Masonic Temple Auditorium
Aida with Arroyo (*Aida*), Franco Corelli (*Radamès*), Irene Dalis (*Amneris*), Mario Sereni (*Amonasro*), cond. Fausto Cleva

> **Met June Festival, 1971**
>
> May 31, 1971, *Aida* with Martina Arroyo (*Aida*), Franco Corelli (*Radamès*), Grace Bumbry (*Amneris*), cond. Fausto Cleva
>
> June 5, 1971, *Tosca* with Grace Bumbry (*Tosca*), Franco Corelli (*Cavaradossi*), Peter Glossop (*Scarpia*), cond. James Levine
>
> June 9, 1971, *La Bohème* with Raina Kabaivanska (*Mimì*), Franco Corelli (*Rodolfo*), Colette Boky (*Musetta*), cond. Fausto Cleva
>
> June 12, 1971, *Tosca* with Grace Bumbry (*Tosca*), Franco Corelli (*Cavaradossi*), Peter Glossop (*Scarpia*), cond. James Levine

After that, the wretched single note in *Aida* was drowned out by his most resplendent "Celeste Aida" diminuendo ever in Cleveland on April 30. And that was only Radamès, a part that went almost unnoticed in comparison to his revelatory Werthers on the tour, which proved to be the highlight of the season with critics and public alike. These performances were followed by his opening of the June Festival with *Aida*, after which a *Tosca* with Grace Bumbry became "historic" because of the Met debut of a twenty-eight-year-old conductor named James Levine. Levine was very well received, but Corelli's *sehnsucht* as the hapless Cavaradossi in the incandescent *Tosca* performance was probably due more to the effect his Tosca had on him than to the conductor.[43] He seldom commented on his private feelings, but a question about the most feminine singer onstage met with a decisive answer: "Grace Bumbry."[45]

The 1971 spring tour also was the source of a famous incident in which Loretta flew back to New York to get her forgotten bottle of holy water, which was crucial to any Franco performance. The Met deducted $341.99 from Franco's payment, which was billed as "transportation of Loretta."[46] In addition, they deducted loans made to Corelli on June 9, 1970 ($6,000); May 5, 1971 ($10,000); and June 21, 1971 ($20,000). Not that he had anything to complain about, with his earnings adding up to $168,975 over the 1970–71 season, but apparently his investments in stock and real estate were pretty much what they were when Ghiringhelli was helping him to bridge his temporary liquidity gaps.[47] With so much on his hands and with Goeran Gentele sharing Bing's view that he was still the greatest tenor in the world, Corelli's American future looked bright enough for a tenor who had just celebrated his fiftieth birthday.

October–November 1971: Franco in Tokyo

In the previous two years Corelli had sold 25,000 records in Japan alone, and when he landed at the Tokyo airport about 200 fans gave him a warm welcome and politely stood in line for autographs. His hotel rooms were filled with flowers, and in Osaka a policeman had to be stationed in front of his hotel room door to keep fans out. Corelli could do no wrong in Japan and even attached a good cause to his visit when he started a fund-raiser for the recovery of Venice. For this reason he added "Venezia, no!" to the program, a composition by his friend Luigi Tortorella, the porter-composer of the famous Hotel Bauer in that city. In the first two days the fund-raiser for the city known as La Serenissima brought in $3,000.[48]

The atmosphere of these concerts was captured in the NHK television broadcast of November 8, although Corelli was definitely not in the best of shape here. "Ô souverain, ô juge, ô père" was transposed down, and song codas were simplified. At other times he seemed fatigued, perhaps because of jet lag and a change of climate, although the public didn't seem to notice. Corelli was visibly touched by their tokens of appreciation, and the press followed the general enthusiasm, although they refused to grant Corelli the title "Prince of Tenors." As poetic and elegant as that sounded to Euro-American ears, in the Japanese Empire there could be no talk of a prince when there were higher

---

October 29, 1971, Tokyo, Koseinenkin Kaikan
November 1, 1971, Osaka, Festival Hall
November 5, 1971, Tokyo, Hibiya Kokaido
November 8, 1971, Tokyo, Koseinenkin Kaikan (NHK television broadcast)
November 12, 1971, Tokyo, Hibiya Kokaido
Conductor and pianist: Alberto Ventura

November 15, 1971, Seoul
Pianist: Alberto Ventura

November 17, 1971, Seoul (extra concert in open air)
Pianist: Alberto Ventura

titles vacant. Because Japan already had an emperor, Corelli was appointed "King."[49]

All this adulation and uninhibited praise may have contributed to some overenthusiasm on Corelli's part for the karate lessons he had been taking in between performances. After his last concert in the Hibiya Kokaido he felt confident enough to equal his black-belt instructor, who could break a wooden board with his bare hands. Corelli tried, but the board remained intact. His left pinky did not, however.[50] He arrived in Seoul with his hand bandaged and met with a welcome that was too hot to handle: fans who could not obtain tickets for his single concert there broke through the windows and stormed the theater. This spectacle ended in a concert that ended only after an hourlong final applause ovation, and then only after the star of the evening began to feel embarrassed by it and withdrew. To satisfy the disappointed fans who had not been able to attend and in gratitude for the ovation he received, Corelli agreed to give a second concert in the open air.[51]

December 29, 1971: A Santa Claus Belatedly Brings Parma a Tenor

And if you went to Parma! They were terrible, in Parma! "Loggionisti" came to hear the performance with the score! And they read it along with your singing! They understood all the notes, if they were placed correctly or not! To sing there was almost to die of fear.
    Magda Olivero, interview, Milan, January 12, 2005

The Parma audience was hard to please. They had not only a select group of favorite singers, but favorite composers as well. Their names were Verdi, Verdi, and Verdi. Starting with Bellini's *Norma* didn't guarantee a sold-out opening night. When you added the Dutch soprano Cristina Deutekom, who missed the dress rehearsal owing to illness, a replacement Adalgisa, and an established but indisposed tenor (Piermiranda Ferraro), things started looking pretty disastrous. The public showed no mercy to Ferraro, who gave up after Act II. He was replaced by the last student of Arturo Melocchi, Robleto Merolla, who arrived too late to save the performance. A miracle was needed to save the production run. Parma got one when Santa Claus dropped off at the Teatro Regio a belated Christmas present by the name of Franco Corelli. Suddenly there was tension in the air. The house was packed for the second performance.[52]

Corelli had not sung the part for a full seven and a half years, but he didn't want to turn down the desperate request for help from his friends in the Parma Theater management. The conductor, Antonino Votto, took a brief run through the score with his former protégé, who then began preparing himself psychologically.[53] Just before the curtain was to rise, Deutekom entered Corelli's dressing room and found him unable to communicate: "I wanted to wish him 'In bocca lupa,' but he was just sitting there, paralyzed, in his chair, with his wife, Loretta, beside him. She whispered something in his ear. Then she turned to me and said: 'Franco says hello too.'"[54] Deutekom feared the worst, but then:

> He entered the stage in his glittering Pollione tunic, made of copper. His sheer beauty already blinded me, but I completely lost myself when he started to sing! I could not believe that a human being was capable of producing such a sound. Really, I had to pull myself together, and I almost missed my cue staring at him like that. I sang with Pavarotti, Del Monaco, Aragall, but that night was on a different level. And all the while he was turning his back on the audience, asking for stage directions from us with his thumbs: "Left? Right? . . ."[55]

Deutekom's husband, Jaap, who was taping the performance, had his own Corelli moment in the auditorium: "When Corelli started to sing I had to adjust the recording levels, because the VU indicators shot into the red zone. That had never happened during a recording before."[56] The press was equally stunned. Apart from a few minor rhythmic slips, they couldn't find any fault with Franco's impromptu performance, which closed the circle that had started with his first Pollione there in 1954: "Humble study has made his voice and stage presence balanced, noble, flexible and powerful. . . . He sang with all the

---

December 29, 1971
Vincenzo Bellini: *Norma*
Parma, Teatro Regio
Cristina Deutekom (*Norma*), Franco Corelli (*Pollione*), Franca Mattiucci (*Adalgisa*), Maurizio Mazzieri (*Oroveso*), Mario Ferrara (*Flavio*), cond. Antonino Votto

perfection and intensity that has become his hallmark."[57] With that, the Teatro Regio finally had the tenor they had craved all along, for Corelli was the singer for whom the *Norma* revival had been planned in the first place.[58] Said Deutekom: "Corelli refused to take a solo bow, saying, 'This is *Norma*, and if I go out there, we will go together.' . . . So I took my curtain call together with him, but, naturally, I left him standing there to enjoy the applause on his own."[59]

January–April 1972: Springtime with Werther and Alvaro

Franco's Met season started with a mix of three not altogether satisfying *Forza* Alvaros[60] and seven great performances as Werther. The latter part was increasingly embellished with ethereal *mezza voce* singing and passages with exceptionally long spun *filature*. In certain passages, such as "Lorsque l'enfant" and the death scene, he reminds one of Giuseppe Di Stefano's communicative approach, which went straight to the heart. Corelli may still be loud enough elsewhere, but there is no denying that he wholly identified with the romantic, passionate, and lovelorn Werther to the point of indulgence. Together with his last three *Don Carlo* performances in April, these *Werther*s formed a touching farewell gift to his departing friend and champion, Rudolf Bing.

Bing's departure brought both risks and opportunities. When Paul Jaretzki went over his 1973 tour repertoire with Corelli, the tenor judged most parts unsuitable but offered to do Macduff in Verdi's *Macbeth*. Whereas Bing would likely have responded that he would love to have him in that small role for a quarter of his usual fee, Jaretzki recommended that Gentele accept the offer; Corelli's name might help sell this lesser-known opera to the tour audiences.[61]

With Leontyne Price in *La Forza del Destino*, January 21, 1972. (Photo: Louis Melançon. Courtesy of the Metropolitan Opera Archives)

1972: The Bing Farewell

The days of excitement are gone. And I miss them. But at least I am spared Franco Corelli's dog. He was so well trained that he would sit in his master's dressing room waiting for anyone who might reach for the paycheck. Then he would bite.

    Rudolf Bing on his tenure as general manager of the Met, in *A Knight at the Opera*, 1981

Bing's farewell gala was an event such as only the Met could provide. During his twenty-two-year tenure he had made as many enemies as friends. It was part of the job; not every singer has the courtesy to leave the stage with grace. Some artists, such as Mario Del Monaco, had their own reasons to be bitter and declined Bing's request to appear at the gala. Said Giancarlo Del Monaco: "I was there with my father when Bing called him, asking if he would conclude his farewell gala. But my father refused. By then, he hated Bing to the core, although that may well have been for the things that Roberto Bauer had hatched."[62] Another prominent absentee was Maria Callas.

Otherwise the assembly of artists read like a catalog of Bing's entire career: Teresa Stratas, Thomas Stewart, Paul Plishka, Ruggero Raimondi, Anna Moffo, Martina Arroyo, Joan Sutherland, Luciano Pavarotti, Cornell MacNeil, Dorothy Kirsten, Fernando Corena, Ezio Flagello, Montserrat Caballé, Plácido Domingo, Grace Bumbry, Régine Crespin, Mario Sereni, Lucine Amara, Cesare Siepi, Richard Tucker, Robert Merrill, Leontyne Price, Regina Resnik, Gabriella Tucci, Irene Dalis, James McCracken, Sándor Kónya, Rosalind Elias, Jerome Hines, Leonie Rysanek, and Jon Vickers. The best, however, was left for the end. Bing had increasingly built the house on the vocal pillars of Tebaldi, Corelli, and Nilsson, and they were to provide the climax. Franco wasn't able to give "Sir Rudolfo" the complete

Friends at last—Corelli and "Sir Rudolfo." (Courtesy of the Metropolitan Opera Archives)

farewell *Otello* that he had hoped for, but he promised at least a bite with "Già nella notte densa."

Before the gala came Bing's penultimate broadcast matinee—the third of Corelli's April *Don Carlo* performances. Sometimes it is hard to separate truth from legend, but according to Caballé, a hysterical Corelli bumped into her backstage right before "Tu, che la vanità." Blinded by stage fright, as he passed his elbow punched her in the stomach, leaving her dizzy. Her anger at Franco's outrageous and unapologetic behavior give fire to her aria and inspired her to hold her floating, conclusive note of the opera a little longer than normal, which drew out the audience's applause. Revenge![63]

With that behind him, Corelli walked toward his last obligation in the Bing era. Everybody had expected him to sing the *Otello* duet with Renata Tebaldi, but he appeared instead with Teresa Zylis-Gara. The audience was puzzled: where was Tebaldi? In fact, Tebaldi was in the middle of a vocal crisis that had forced her to stop singing from her last *Otello* in January 1971 until she accepted a few very lightweight Alice Fords in *Falstaff* in February 1972. After the last Alice on April 1, three weeks before the Bing farewell, she once more withdrew from the stage completely in order to rest and rework her voice. Zylis-Gara may not have brought the same air of nostalgia to the event, but she seduced both Franco and those present with the combined force of her physical presence and vocal beauty. In her arms, Corelli gave Bing a hint of what he had missed out on; the duet was arguably the highlight of the event. It was

April 22, 1972
Giuseppe Verdi: *Don Carlo*
New York, Metropolitan Opera House
Franco Corelli (*Don Carlo*), Montserrat Caballé (*Elisabetta di Valois*), Cesare Siepi (*Filippo II*), Sherrill Milnes (*Rodrigo*), Grace Bumbry (*Princess d'Eboli*), cond. Francesco Molinari-Pradelli

April 22, 1972
Rudolf Bing Farewell Gala
New York, Metropolitan Opera House (partial CBS telecast)
Verdi: *Otello* "Già nella notte densa"
Teresa Zylis-Gara (*Desdemona*), Franco Corelli (*Otello*), cond. Karl Böhm

scheduled just before the appearance of Birgit Nilsson, who was granted the honor of closing the Bing era with Salome's final scene, "Ah, du wolltest mich nicht deinen Mund küssen lassen, Jokanaan."

Bing's "female Corelli" proved inspired, presumably by the fulfillment of the general manager's promise: his head on a silver platter, which he had told her she could have if she sang Salome's finale at the gala. She found it on the piano in her dressing room, where Bing came to see her. Said Nilsson: "Farewell galas are farewell galas. Bing had been shedding some tears in my dressing room, as he didn't want to go. No, he didn't! He wanted to stay on!"[64]

✦✦✦✦✦

Bing was not the only general manager who resigned in 1972. La Scala faced even worse economic problems than the Met because of Italy's rampant inflation. The situation called for strong leadership. But that was something Antonio Ghiringhelli could no longer provide. He and his staff had been tried for embezzlement a couple of years earlier, and the trial turned him into a lame duck. In 1971 he was acquitted of all charges, but the proceedings had embittered him, and he was in poor health. This combination of factors urged him to announce his resignation, which made the 1972–73 season his final La Scala season.[65]

The odds for Corelli's return during the tenure of Ghiringhelli's successor, Paolo Grassi, weren't good. Not only had Grassi been Ghiringhelli's closest assistant for many years, but he was also focused on the modernization of repertoire and production values. Those were not processes in which Franco Corelli was likely to be very useful. Corelli's parts were also increasingly covered by the likes of Domingo and Pavarotti. Their eagerness, combined with the fact that they were a lot less difficult to handle, made things tougher for the aging Mr. Sold Out.

March–July 1972: The Highest-Paid Tenor in the World

The end of the Bing-Ghiringhelli era and the emergence of great new artists provides an opportunity to look into Corelli's status at that critical juncture. Such an investigation is best judged from the payroll. Officially, he was granted the top fee at the Met, which was $4,000 per performance for the 1971–72 season. This fee was also given to Caballé, Nilsson, Rysanek, Scotto, Sutherland,

Cossotto, Horne, Ludwig, Bergonzi, Gedda, McCracken, Thomas, Tucker, Vickers, Gobbi, Merrill, Ghiaurov, Siepi, and Karl Böhm, who was extremely popular in New York at the time. Only Nilsson was paid for anywhere close to the number of unsung performances Corelli was. Next came Sándor Kónya and James King, at $3,500 each, and Alfredo Kraus, who received $3,250. In fourth rank were Pavarotti and Domingo, with $3,000 each. Several ranks below them, the lowest-paid singers on the Met's roster were Rosalind Elias and Fedora Barbieri, who were paid $1,000 per performance.[66]

That made Corelli effectively "the highest-paid tenor in the world at the Met" with a gross total per season that was a very long way away from the 50,000 lire ($85) per month he had started out with at the Rome Opera.[67] Still, Corelli felt underrated, and, oddly, he asked Bing one last time for a raise. As always, Bing answered that he had done what he could and more, adding that Franco had to face the fact that neither Bing nor Robert Herman (who had resigned together with Bing) was any longer a member of the company. Bing was looking forward to meeting Franco and Loretta in Siusi, where he was spending his holidays once again. This time, genuine friendship was his only motive.[68]

July 18, 1972: A Tragic Accident

With money and other matters out of the way, the sincerity of Bing's friendship was finally beyond doubt, although the summer holidays would not bring all that Bing and Corelli had hoped for. Franco's Veronese appearance as Ernani on July 15 was glamorous enough,[69] but on July 18 his future changed unexpectedly. At approximately 3:00 P.M., 915 yards past the 217th kilometer marker off National Road SS. 125, in the immediate vicinity of the municipality of Arzachena near Cagliari, Goeran Gentele tried to pass the car in front of him. Just as he swung his car over, a vehicle appeared in the oncoming lane. Before Gentele had time to realize what was happening, his rented Fiat 125 crashed into the truck of Ottavio Mariotti. The Met's new general manager was dead on impact, as were his daughters Cecilia and Beatrice. His wife, Maritz, and daughter Janette were severely wounded but alive when Mariotti opened the doors of the Fiat with a crowbar. Francesco Azara, who was driving the car that Gentele had wanted to pass, returned to where the accident had happened and helped Mariotti get Maritz and Beatrice to the hospital.[70]

The news stunned the Met's board. They decided to let the assistant general manager, Schuyler Chapin, run the theater under their supervision. Chapin, unlike Gentele, was not a Corelli man, as can be deduced from the way he handled the affair of Bernstein's Verdi Requiem. Change was afoot. As if to demonstrate that fact, on the way back to Milan from Cortina Franco lost control of his Ferrari, spun toward the edge of a ravine, and stopped square on a milestone. Though unhurt, Franco vowed to limit himself to more sedate cars from then on. Some might argue about the speed possibilities of a BMW 735, but at least it seemed more secure and solid.[71]

August–September 1972: *Duetti d'amore*

The bomb has gone off: Franco Corelli is in love with La Tebaldi. There are an abundant number of photographs showing them together. Someone even confirmed that the two married in America a few months ago.
    Renzo Allegri, "Eco com'è nata la storia del mio flirt con la Tebaldi," *Gente*, August 1972

After a lifetime of keeping his private life very private indeed, Corelli's worst fear was realized when, during the course of 1972, an increasing number of publications began hinting at an affair. The woman was rumored to be Renata Tebaldi, who admittedly had plenty of opportunity, for she had spent quite a bit of time with her colleague, friend, and now assumed lover. At first the Corellis tried to ignore the story, but after a while some damage control was necessary. In between performances in Verona of *Aida* and *Ernani*, Renzo Allegri from *Gente* confronted the tenor in the presence of his wife: "Signor Corelli, is it true that you are secretly having a love affair with Renata Tebaldi?"

According to Allegri, Corelli almost cried, wringing his hands in despair for several minutes while gluing his eyes to the ceiling:

> In September 1970 I was in Ancona, where I attended a party near Sant' Arcangelo di Romagna. I was to receive an award there, and Tebaldi attended the ceremony. We had not seen each other for some time and it was a happy reunion. On that evening there were a number of pictures taken of us dancing together, as it was quite a sight to see two singers dancing at a village party.

A few weeks later we met again in Venice. Again there were pictures taken of us, now at the San Marco Square. Suddenly these pictures appeared in New York, with headlines that read that we were in love. Now you ask me if this is true or not. Well, look around you. I've been living in this hotel here for almost a month now together with my wife. We have a double bed, we dine together, and my wife answers all phone calls and opens my letters. If I had an affair, she'd be the first to know, and if I know her, she wouldn't exactly take it calmly.

Loretta, jumping at the chance to say something herself, emphasized that she was present at both photo occasions: "I even asked for some of them to be taken." Said Corelli: "I am deeply saddened by these rumors, also for Renata. I admire her, she is the greatest soprano in the world. We performed together in many operas and have always had mutual respect, and yes, we were attached to each other. And together we still have a number of plans for the future that will hopefully materialize sometime soon."[72]

In an attempt to change the subject, Allegri asked Corelli about his favorite pastime. The accused singer jumped at the chance: "I spend a lot of time with my wife." A very quiet life it must have been, with hardly more than four or five friends whom he trusted when it came to keeping confidences. His attempt was successful, though, and the story of his flirtation with Tebaldi officially ended (although some of Corelli's closest friends and family confirmed Kenn Harris's theory about a brief and uncomplicated affair around 1969, saying that the tenor had admitted

RENATA TEBALDI complimenta il tenore Franco Corelli dopo una recita della « Carmen » all'Arena di Verona: le rappresentazioni della « Carmen » hanno segnato il record d'incassi della stagione a Verona. Corelli ha colto grandi consensi impersonando Don José, una parte per la quale è considerato oggi forse il maggiore interprete.

One of the photos of Corelli and Renata Tebaldi that started the rumor of their alleged affair. This one was taken after a *Carmen* performance in the Arena di Verona and published in *L'Europeo* on August 20, 1970. Combined with a few other photos, it set the bomb off, although we found no other mention of this alleged affair than in *Oggi* (*L'Europeo* simply mentioned the facts). It's very possible that this was part of the pre-tour campaign—after all, Di Stefano and Callas had made their affair work to their advantage. (Reproduced courtesy of RCS)

> **August 24, 26–27, and 29–31; September 4, 1972**
> **Geneva, Victoria Hall (Decca recording)**
> **Great Opera Duets**
> Puccini: *Manon Lescaut* "Tu, tu amore ? Tu ?. . ." Cilea: *Adriana Lecouvreur* "Ma, dunque è vero?" Ponchielli: *La Gioconda* "Ma chi vien?. . . Oh ! la sinistra voce!" Verdi: *Aida* "L'aborrita rivale. . . Già i sacerdoti adunansi." Zandonai: *Francesca da Rimini* "No, Smaragdi, no!. . . Inghirlandata di violette"
> Renata Tebaldi, Franco Corelli, cond. Anton Guadagno

it to them). Yet the image he had so carefully nurtured of himself as a reclusive monk who lived on singing lessons was far from true. Loretta hardly ever gave him a chance to escape to the land of milk and honey, but after all, they had been separated for a number of months earlier in 1972. During this time he finally had had plenty of opportunity to do the thing most tenors do best, next to singing and eating their wives' spaghetti. The soprano he was seeing can be presented here only under a beguiling pseudonym; let's call her "Desdemona." Was it love? According to what Corelli told his friends in private, it seems to have been. Their stories about the way his eyes lit up when he told them about his daring acts in these days recalled the boyish candor of his reckless youth, when he roamed the streets of Ancona at night as the popular ringleader of the Archi district, running off with his Norma or Iride to wherever their parents couldn't find them.[73] The affair also lasted a relatively long time, with Loretta frequently returning to Europe.

That things had changed between Franco and Loretta was already clear from one of the little-known French radio interviews from the early 1970s. In it, the reporter recalls the story of how nice sweet Loretta is to her Franco and he to her, until she starts telling him how to answer. Suddenly he erupts, telling her to shut up—the question is for him, not her. There had been hints at their arguments in the press before, and their backstage feuds were legendary from New York to Milan, but that was all within the relative confinement of their private lives. In the French radio interview, all is made public. And yet, he wouldn't leave her, caught in the web of a love-hate relationship that was as destructive as it was fruitful. In the end, Franco always reconciled with Loretta, who wholly supported his ultimate attempt to recreate bygone vocal magic at the side of Renata Tebaldi. One of the two great operatic couples of the century (the other being Callas and Di Stefano) had big plans, starting with the recording of a planned album of, appropriately enough, love duets for Decca. With those recordings, Tebaldi finally put the horns—musically speaking—on her longtime partner Mario Del Monaco.[74]

The sessions were held in Geneva during the second part of August. Unfortunately neither Franco nor Renata was in particularly good voice. Tebaldi was audibly at the very end of her career and had been advised by Chapin and his staff to undertake mezzo parts,[75] as reflected in the "L'aborrita rivale" from *Aida* on this recording. Apart from that experimental recording and a few concert gimmicks, she just laughed at the very idea. Corelli, who had already noticed her decline in the early 1960s, proved uninspired by his partner's efforts in the Decca sessions. Despite the shortcomings of the "Inghirlandata di violette," it shows what could have been accomplished if they had executed their plan to sing it onstage earlier.

❖❖❖❖❖

Back in New York Corelli faced a wholly new sort of challenge, although he was totally oblivious to it. Rafael Kubelik, eager to confirm his new position as the Met's music director, was suggesting decisive changes to the artists' roster. Tucci and Moffo were under consideration for immediate replacement because they did not measure up to their prior fame.[76] Other singers whose contracts he would not like to renew included Robert Merrill, Lucine Amara, Jeanine Altmeyer, Lili Chookasian, Frank Guarrera, and, last but not least—Franco Corelli. The memorandum detailing all this was marked CONFIDENTIAL.[77]

Attempts to get a possible Corelli rival in the dramatic parts back to the Met seem to have begun shortly after Gentele's death. Because Domingo and Pavarotti were already on board and José Carreras was only just emerging in Europe, the only name fit for the task was . . . Mario Del Monaco! Chapin hoped to come to some agreement with the legendary singer, but his plan fell through when Albert B. Gins turned out to be a far less inventive assistant than Bauer had been to Bing; not one of the four invitations Gins cabled to Del Monaco and his son ever arrived. By November, when it was too late for the running season, Chapin and Kubelik had to deal with Corelli, who suddenly turned out to be an easy and agreeable partner in negotiations. No further problems on that front were ever reported. Regarding Del Monaco, Chapin and Kubelik had to content themselves with glittering newspaper reviews of sensational *Otello*s in, of all places, Brussels.[78]

Meanwhile Del Monaco saw Corelli in Verona in one of his August *Aida*s. Said Arrigo Michelini: "I was standing right behind him and watched him like a hawk, to see what he would do. But to my surprise he seemed genuinely impressed and applauded him enthusiastically."[79]

August–September 1972: *Duetti d'amore* Onstage

The Decca duet recordings were clearly made to promote the planned Tebaldi-Corelli tour, which was to take the two singers to three continents. Such adventurous plans, especially where Corelli was involved, generally called for low-profile tryouts. Therefore, from November to December the couple toured the United States from New Orleans to Memphis, San Antonio, and Columbus, and from Washington, D.C., to Philadelphia, long before the recording was even released. Out of the scope of the Met tour, Corelli and Tebaldi had to rely on local hosts and hostesses for logistics. An intriguing anecdote comes from San Antonio, where the diva and divo were greeted by two notable members of local society, an oil baron and his wife. They had agreed to host the stars and picked them up from their lodgings in the St. Anthony Hotel to take them to the concert hall. Corelli and Tebaldi, unaware of their hosts' status, took them for the organization's driver and his wife (brought along because of the extraordinary nature of his assignment) and hopped in the back of the car without even replying to the wife's words of welcome. As she got out of the Cadillac, Tebaldi leaned toward the driver's window and told him: "That is all, you may go."[80]

> November 27, 1972, Memphis, Music Hall Auditorium
> December 6, 1972, San Antonio, Theater for the Performing Arts
> December 10, 1972, Columbus
> December 15, 1972, Washington D.C., Performing Arts Society
> December 20, 1972, Philadelphia, Academy of Music
> Renata Tebaldi, Franco Corelli; pianists, Geoffrey Parson, Lawrence Smith [December 6]

The public and the press evidently recognized the singers' attitude for what it was: the concerts were obligations that inspired them even less than the recording sessions had done. The program had little to offer other than a selection of rather unchallenging songs and a bonus in the concluding *Tosca* duet. A trifling program like that may have served Tebaldi's vocal state at the time, but it was almost an insult to Corelli's vocal abilities, and the routine affair was no triumph. When the singers spotted the oil baron and his wife during a backstage line-up for autographs, Corelli suddenly turned to the man and said: "Get car now." The oil baron, appalled, walked out on the spot and drove off, leaving his wife stranded. She saved the situation by recruiting a driver with a drafty canvas-top Jeep. Corelli remained silent throughout the ride; Tebaldi acknowledged a compliment about the concert with a smile. Did they tip the driver?[81]

September–December 1972: A Belated *Roméo*

The Met had proposed a more challenging schedule (including *Lucia di Lammermoor* and *Il Trovatore*) for Corelli, but early on he had indicated that *Lucia* was not for him, and neither were the proposed two *Trovatores*.[82] *Norma* didn't materialize, and so the public was left once more with *Roméo et Juliette* and *Aida*. And even those were not easily won. Corelli was supposed to return to the Met for the premiere of *Roméo* on September 21, but when nothing was heard from him by the middle of the rehearsals, Chapin got George Shirley and William Lewis to cover. Corelli, who apparently didn't think too much of his obligations under the new management, arrived after the first *Roméo*, never having informed them that he would be absent.[83] He nervously entered Chapin's office and told him he had been ill and upset by Gentele's death. Chapin, not willing to make enemies at a first meeting, shook hands with him and expressed his sympathies. A few days later, Rudolf Bing, as Corelli's honorary ambassador on a mission, entered Chapin's office "just by chance, while passing by." His sole concern turned out to be Corelli's future: "You know, he is the *great* singer today and the only one I care about." Chapin assured him that he would do what he could to keep Corelli on board,[84] and when the tenor showed his good intentions by showing up for the *Aida* rehearsals while seriously preparing himself for the *Roméo* broadcast later on, things calmed down. Corelli's first Radamès on October 23 proved a huge success, confirmed by his first *Roméo*, on November 11.

Yet, despite Chapin's practical achievements at Lincoln Center and with the earlier Bernstein projects, his musical judgment seems to have been on an altogether different level than Bing's. Shortly after the *Aida* success, Corelli came into his office proposing to sing Macduff in *Macbeth*, a part consisting of one aria and a few moments in the ensemble. Chapin, apparently unaware of Corelli's previous discussion with Paul Jaretzki and not knowing that the Macduff aria "Ah! La paterna mano" had been on the tenor's concert repertoire for years, answered simply that he would love to have him and asked the tenor whether he would be able to learn it before the tour started. An eager Corelli answered: "Oh, yes, I would like to study now."[85]

January–March 1973: Ambassador Bing

In the middle of the dance around the chair of the vacant general manager's post, Rudolf Bing once more entered Chapin's office. He had but a single question: "Is Corelli returning next year?" Chapin was surprised; surely Bing knew of all the trouble they had had with Franco over the last season. Nevertheless, he was reengaged and given an impressive number of performances as well. "Ah, good," answered Bing, "I think he is one of our greatest artists."[86]

Corelli must have sensed that he had stretched the limit of his credit earlier, for he proved to be most gentle toward Chapin and his wife and was quick to save the day a couple of times with stand-in performances for indisposed tenors. Chapin, in turn, gradually started looking upon Corelli more positively. When he entered into negotiations with the comedian Danny Kaye over Gentele's original plans for a Mini Met and Kaye's fee was being discussed, he asked Chapin: "What do you pay Corelli?" A troubled but good-humored Chapin answered: "A lot, when I can find him."[87] Meanwhile, Corelli "prepared himself" for his Macduff debut in the upcoming spring tour.

Judging from his very limited performance schedule in the first three months of 1973 (two February *Carmen*s in Miami and Ft. Lauderdale, an *Aida* in New York, and three more *Carmen*s in Lisbon, where he also participated in a few *Tosca*s), Corelli was taking plenty of time to learn this "difficult" new part. Before the debut, however, there was still a *Roméo* at the Met, as well as a *Tosca* that was to be very meaningful for his career.

April 1973: "Vit-tooo-riiiiii-aaaaaaaaaa!"

At 6:00 P.M. I start vocalizing and singing parts of the role that is on. Often I record this in order to check and then I record it all again. Then I am off to the theater, nervous and agitated. ... If the opera of the evening belongs to the heavyweight category everyone stays as far away from Corelli as possible; the slightest disruption can irritate me then.

    Franco Corelli, in Giorgio Pillon, "Ho trovato in America la patria del bel canto," *Domenica del Corriere*, June 26, 1973

In *Sopranos, Mezzos, Tenors, Basses and Other Friends*, Chapin writes that he should have sensed an operatic disaster brewing after leaving the dressing room of his emergency Tosca, Dorothy Kirsten, who had stepped in at the last minute for an indisposed colleague. At the door of Corelli's dressing room, he found the tenor in a rage over some Italian political matter he had been arguing about with that evening's conductor, Carlo Felice Cillario. Said Corelli: "Maestro Cillario, he doesn't like me. We disagree about everything—tempi, politics, the world. I don't want to sing with him." Chapin comforted him: "Perhaps you won't have to. The Maestro will not be returning next year." Replied Corelli: "Ah, but we still have tonight."[88]

Chapin shrugged, thinking the heat might have exacerbated Corelli's usually fragile nerves. Soon, though, he found out otherwise; Cillario was covering Corelli's voice by having the orchestra play forte when the tenor sang. The first rupture occurred at the end of "Recondita armonia," where Cillario denied him his applause by forcing the orchestra to continue. An infuriated Corelli almost shouted his next line, "Fa il tuo piacere!"[89] The tenor tried to fight back when he arrived at his moment of glory in Act II at the end of "Vittoria!" Now he sang the note louder and held it longer than Chapin had ever heard before,

---

April 7, 14, 20, 24 (Boston); April 30 (Cleveland), 1973
Giacomo Puccini: *Tosca*
New York, Metropolitan Opera House
Dorothy Kirsten, Lucine Amara [April 14, 24] (*Tosca*), Franco Corelli (*Cavaradossi*), Tito Gobbi (*Scarpia*), Clifford Harvuot (*Angelotti*), Fernando Corena (*the Sacristan*), cond. Carlo Felice Cillario

preventing Cillario from continuing. In the ensuing passage Cillario increased the speed so as to force Corelli out of air by not giving him enough time to breathe properly, but the tenor kept up with him, and according to Chapin, the only reason further pandemonium was avoided was that Corelli had no part in the remainder of the act. The battle between tenor and conductor reached a climax when Cillario denied Franco his ovation at the end of "E lucevan le stelle." An infuriated Corelli flipped his overlong thumb to his teeth in disgust and ran offstage. The audience was left stunned, the orchestra still playing the ascending scale leading to Tosca's entrance, and Tosca herself bursting on stage to find it empty and the audience buzzing around in a mini uproar. Backstage, Chapin saw Corelli screaming at Charlie Riecker, teeth clenched, eyes bulging. There was no time for discussion. Chapin grabbed Corelli and pushed him back onto the stage, where he resumed his role.[90]

The real thriller happened only after the opera ended. Despite the clamorous applause, Corelli rushed toward the pit as Cillario was emerging from it and leaped at his throat. Chapin tried to get in between them but was no match for the two brawlers. All this happened against a background of frenetic bravos and booing from the audience, who had wanted to applaud Corelli earlier on. Not until Riecker and three strong stagehands arrived on the scene could they be separated. Just then Kirsten reappeared from her curtain call. Chapin then pointed Corelli toward his deserved triumph, and to his surprise the tenor walked out into the spotlight. Amidst the ovation that followed, complete with confetti made out of torn-up programs, Chapin suggested to Cillario that it was perhaps not a good night for a solo conductor bow.[91]

◆◆◆◆◆

Relations between Corelli and Cillario improved in the subsequent spring tour *Tosca*s, although the Cleveland performance of April 30 met with some unexpected but powerful offstage competition. No fewer than four television sets were set up in Cleveland's Pavilion so that the audience could listen to Richard Nixon's first Watergate speech. The Republican president claimed to be appalled by the actions of his own reelection committee with respect to the break-in at the Democratic Party headquarters in the Watergate Hotel. The speech came down to the fact that he, Nixon, had taken matters into his own hands, so now everybody could get back to work—the president would get to the heart of the matter. He finished by saying that he wanted his remaining (1,361) days in power to be the best in America's history, "because I love America."

The opera seems to have been arranged so that the speech would occur during the intermission, but when it extended beyond the duration of the break, a free double scotch was offered to those who preferred to watch the speech instead of Act II. That proved one temptation too many for some of the audience members, and onstage Tito Gobbi had to bow before a rival Scarpia for the first and only time in his career.[92]

May 15–21, 1973: Macduff

At the time he had a thing for Bumbry; that's why he agreed to sing those Macduffs.
    Marco Corelli, interviews, Ancona, January 28–30, 2007

Macduff! Schuyler Chapin had forgotten all about Corelli's desire to sing that role until Riecker informed him of the line-up for the touring *Macbeth*s. Suddenly Chapin, no longer interim but the new general manager of the Met, realized that this would be a very costly Macduff. Riecker quickly assured him that it wouldn't cost them a dime, because Corelli had to make up for the mess he had caused over the missed *Roméo* performances. Still, no one believed that Corelli was actually going to do it. When the Dallas Opera impresario Lawrence Kelly approached Chapin shortly before the first *Macbeth* there, it was to ask him where he planned to stand to make the announcement of Corelli's

> **Giuseppe Verdi:** *Macbeth*
> **May 15, 1973, Memphis, Municipal Auditorium**
> **May 18, 1973, Dallas, State Fair Music Hall**
> **May 21, 1973, Minneapolis, Northrop Auditorium**
> Sherrill Milnes (*Macbeth*), Grace Bumbry (*Lady Macbeth*), Ruggero Raimondi (*Banco*), Franco Corelli (*Macduff*), Rod MacWherter (*Malcolm*), cond. Francesco Molinari-Pradelli; stage director, Bodo Igesz; set and costume designers, Caspar Neher and Neil Peter Jampolis

cancellation. Chapin smiled mysteriously, in spite of the fact that deep down he suspected the same—until he spotted Corelli in wig and makeup. The tenor looked almost serene and asked his boss if he would be in the audience tonight. When Chapin said he would, Corelli replied: "Good! I sing well for you." Wrote Chapin:

> That night the opera lovers of Dallas had the surprise of their lives. There, onstage, were three major artists feeding on each other's excellence. Corelli was superb, both vocally and as an actor. When he appeared to announce Duncan's murder, his distress and horror were palpable; by the close of the first act, all that glorious music was being sung by three balanced, powerful voices. When the curtain came down, the theater erupted.[93]

Backstage Corelli actually grabbed one of Chapin's hands and held it in his own while the new man in charge told the tenor that he had liked the performance very much. But the true heart of the tenor's interest in Macduff was exposed when Chapin asked him to sing it at the Met too. That could only be done at a reduced fee, and Corelli immediately refused. Chapin contented himself with the fact that the trick of selling the opera through Corelli's presence had worked to perfection, although he regretted that the Met's home audience did not get to hear him in what Chapin considered to be one of his greatest artistic triumphs.[94]

One is inclined to accept Chapin's account here, but fear for a New York *Macbeth* without Corelli must have played a part in the request as well, for even with Corelli on the

Franco Corelli as Macduff, an odd role choice and an extremely rare photo in a role of which hitherto any visual testimony was believed to be nonexistent. Apparently it was taken during a full stage rehearsal (if not at the actual performance) in Memphis shortly before or on May 15, 1973. (Photo: Courtesy of the Mississippi Valley Collection)

roster the Memphis premiere attracted just enough public to fill about 60 percent of the house.[95] It was the public's loss, for the press judged *Macbeth* the highlight of the Memphis Opera Season.[96] In turn, the critic for the *Dallas Morning News* wrote of Corelli's Macduff: "The authority he brought to what is too often considered a secondary part, set many moments and scenes in a bright new perspective. And on his own terms, how he sang! It was like a brilliant youngster with the world ahead of him."[97] Minneapolis paid tribute to the tenor as well for proving himself a trouper in accepting such a minor part and enlivening it with his presence.[98]

May 1973: A Film at Last!

I believe that with the modern technical facilities, one can create a new operatic practice, not just in the theater, but also in the realm of television and film. These innovations are necessary if we want to interest the younger generations in opera.
    Franco Corelli, in Alfredo Mandelli, "Convince a metà la Carmen di vita,"
    Oggi, July 17, 1975

Filmed during 1972 and the beginning of 1973, the color telecast of *Andrea Chénier* rekindled the flame of Franco's career in Italy and beyond. At the time, filmed operas were still a rarity, and the impact was overwhelming. It fully achieved its goal, which was to create an interest in opera among the general public through the wider scope of film and television. The main question here is: Why did this one film materialize when all others since 1958 had fallen through?

For one thing, the producers of the *Andrea Chénier* film went to great efforts to convince their desired protagonist to cooperate. That was not too difficult; after all, Corelli had agreed to all proposed Metropolitan Opera film projects before, just as he had agreed to the Bernstein's Requiem project. All of them fell apart, but none through any fault of his own. The *Chénier* project materialized simply because the company behind it was solid (unlike with the Met projects) and because Corelli was available. He made few demands. They had to let him lose some weight, because he wanted to look the part to perfection. He also insisted that the costumes be tailored to his taste, which was influenced by Italian movies and books.[99]

> **May 25, 1973 (broadcast date)**
> **Umberto Giordano: *Andrea Chénier***
> **Milan, RAI (color telecast)**
> Franco Corelli (*Andrea Chénier*), Celestina Casapietra (*Maddalena di Coigny*), Piero Cappuccilli (*Carlo Gérard*), Giovanna Di Rocco (*Bersi*), cond. Bruno Bartoletti; director, Tito Capobianco

The film was well received, especially for the vocals, although in truth the singing doesn't approach the level of his previous EMI recording. Corelli's singing is still impressive nevertheless, which unfortunately can't be said of the production. The cardboard sets are rather shabby, and Corelli, despite his enthusiasm for the project, clearly fails to match his rival Del Monaco's earlier achievements. His acting is static and often limited to the notoriously commonplace tenor gesture of the raised right arm, fist clenched as if to squeeze the note out. According to Marco Corelli, that was not necessarily something born from within: "He could move himself well on the stage. But for the movie camera there are rules imposed by the direction, most of all for the movement."[100]

June 1973: America, the Homeland of Bel Canto

For ages the tenor has been living in America, where he is regarded as the true heir of Caruso. Thoughts about the Italian lyrical stage fill him with sadness: "Too many scandals before any given premiere. Here all is better."
   Giorgio Pillon, "Ho trovato in America la patria del bel canto," *Domenica del Corriere*, June 26, 1973

Corelli's status in Italy lessened with the dawn of the 1970s, in spite of a slight increase in the number of his performances there. His virtual absence from the Italian operatic scene after January 1965 had taken its toll, and his decision to distance himself from his native soil had remained a subject of much speculation. His increased Italian activities in the early 1970s may also be seen in the context of the approaching end of the Bing era, which clearly posed a threat that may have prompted him to spread his risk around. But once the new general manager's misgivings over the *Roméo* debacle were buried, the Chapin era turned into a most fortunate one for Corelli. Never before had he sung so many performances at the Met in one season, which quite unexpectedly made him the most reliable and constant artist on the foreign-singers roster.

Corelli's most remarkable comment about America is that it is not only his home, but also the home of bel canto: "Not only at that glorious, indestructible Metropolitan. There are hundreds of other theaters between Philadelphia, Baltimore, Memphis, Oklahoma City, Los Angeles, San Francisco . . . all with their own operatic seasons and concerts. . . . All is well handled, without irregularities; whereas, if I have to believe the Italian newspapers, there is never a premiere in Italy that doesn't start with a scandal." Corelli goes on to insinuate complaints about disloyal Italian audiences, organized claques, theater politics, young singers having to pay impossible sums for their own debuts, nepotism in the theater managements, critics publishing reviews of performances that didn't take place because the principal was changed at the last minute, the whole "second cast" business, and, finally, the rise of popular music, where eighteen-year-old girls earn millions of lire for singing vocally trifling music:

> I am glad for them, let there be no misunderstanding. But because these are public figures, one can only marvel over them. I believe I am a fairly successful singer myself. But how often can I perform? If I am lucky, about 50 times a year. And what do I receive for that in comparison with Mina, who can perform 365 times a year if she wants? And Mina, Milva, and Al Bano and company seem to own the entire press. Who writes about me [in Italy]? Only very rarely does the press of the Peninsula remember that there is still a Franco Corelli somewhere in the world.[101]

◆◆◆◆◆

Interesting as Corelli's opinions on the Italian theater may have been, the most striking aspect of Pillon's article was certainly the reflective spirit it exuded. Despite Corelli's busy performance schedule, there was not the slightest hint of future prospects that went beyond the usual Calaf, Rodolfo, Roméo, and the incidental Turiddu. They continued to sell out, just as they did when he first presented them to the American public, but this was clearly not the best way to ensure the sort of glorious end to a career that *La Juive*'s Eléazar had been for Caruso.

Gone with Corelli's dreams of completing the heroic repertoire were the days when he would invite journalists to his apartment in order to have his photograph taken—for instance, immediately after wrecking his car. He actually denied that certain notorious events in his career, to which he had attested many times before, had ever even happened. Glancing over all the scandals, infamous and less well known alike, on Corelli's path, Pillon wrote: "It is now impossible to check them with Corelli. From now on they simply belong to the trivial 'history' of our great tenor. Also because Corelli today is another artist than the man of ere. He has calmed down, his manners have improved; in short, he has matured."[102]

✦✦✦✦✦

As if he didn't want to be referred to in the past tense, Corelli immediately added another unbelievable affair to the ones that Pillon referred to, although this one never reached the press. Over the summer Corelli had entered into a dispute with his dentist, Nathaniel Wachtel, over an unpaid bill of $100. Wachtel had filed legal action against Corelli over this matter, and the tenor was ordered to pay. When August rolled around and he still hadn't paid up, Wachtel approached the Met. Chapin almost had to laugh. He wrote a letter to Franco and included copies of the legal documents the dentist had submitted, expressing his faith that this silly dispute would be resolved upon Corelli's return in October. To no avail; the matter was one of principle to Franco, and he simply refused to pay.[103]

✦✦✦✦✦

For better or worse, Loretta had been Franco's eyes and ears ever since that *Adriana Lecouvreur* back in 1952. Arrigo Michelini was present at the Met's June Festival, where Franco sang in two performances of *Tosca*: "His 'E lucevan le stelle,' normally the high point of his performance, did not come out so well. I was backstage with her and saw how her eyes filled with tears. I never discussed it with her, but I realized immediately that in that very moment she saw the end coming for him."[104]

July–August 1973: Escape from Manila

According to Kenn Harris, it was no coincidence that the haphazardly organized Callas–Di Stefano tour coincided with the long-planned Tebaldi-Corelli

> July 7, 1973, Cincinnati, Music Hall, cond. Anton Guadagno
> July 12, 1973, Ambler, Pennsylvania, cond. Ling Tung
> October 9, 1973, London, Royal Albert Hall; pianist, Gordon Jephtas
> October 14, 1973, Vienna, Großer Saal des Musikvereins; pianist, Gordon Jephtas
> October 23 and 27, 1973, Manila, New Music Center, cond. Tadashi Mori
> October 31, Manila, Araneta Coliseum, cond. Tadashi Mori
> November 7, 1973, Tokyo, Bunka Kaikan; cond. Tadashi Mori
> November 10, 1973, Osaka, Festival Hall
> November 14 and 17, 1973, Seoul, Sports Palace
> November 21, 1973, Tokyo, NHK Hall (television broadcast), cond. Tadashi Mori
> November 24, 1973, Mito, Ibaragi Kenritsu Bunka Center
> November 27, 1973, Hong Kong, Hong Kong Arts Center; pianist, So Hall Ieung

tour: "It was the last trick Callas would effectuate in order to pester Tebaldi." The clearly odd "coincidence" of the precisely matching dates after Callas had been retired for a full eight years suggests that Tebaldi's suspicions were not altogether unfounded, although the chronology leaves room for the opposite conclusion a well. To begin with, Callas and Di Stefano recorded duets for Philips five months before Corelli and Tebaldi recorded theirs for Decca. These Callas–Di Stefano recording sessions, however, coincided precisely with the beginning of the Tebaldi-Corelli tour in the United States (November 1972), which Callas must have noticed as she was concluding her master classes at the Juilliard School of Music in New York.

From then on that sort of coincidence occurred again and again. Both world tours were supposed to start in London's Royal Albert Hall, the Callas–Di Stefano one on September 22, 1973, and the Tebaldi-Corelli on October 9 (with two joint July concerts in Cincinnatti and Ambler as warm-ups).[105] When Callas became indisposed, that concert was postponed until after the beginning of the Tebaldi-Corelli concert, which then of course faced heavy competition from the rival concert still lingering in the air.

Another coincidence was the very design of the Callas–Di Stefano tour, which led them to the same places in Southeast Asia as Corelli and Tebaldi even though neither Callas nor her partner had ever been in most of them throughout either of their careers. That leaves a third possibility as well. Officially, the Corelli-Tebaldi undertaking was under the auspices of Columbia Artistic Management, but Corelli and Tebaldi's agent, Sandor Gorlinsky, had also arranged the Callas–Di Stefano tour. The whole rivalry may well have been a calculated promotional instrument.

If it bothered Tebaldi, who may have hoped to leave the stage gracefully as the reigning diva of the epoch, it didn't seem to faze Corelli. Whereas Tebaldi, Callas, and Di Stefano were singing only with the tarnished silver edges of their voices by now, Corelli was still the Met's undisputed champion. The *Chénier* film was perfectly timed to further promote his tour efforts, as was the release of his Decca duet album with Tebaldi.

Artistically the undertakings were both rather questionable, although that was not really the point. These were both farewell tours, even if Corelli might not have realized it at the time. Musically, Tebaldi came out ahead of Callas, mostly because she contented herself with an intelligent pick of easy songs and arias, whereas Callas tried to return as the diva of times past. As for the men, Di Stefano was at best a caricature opposite Corelli, even though the latter was hardly inspired throughout the tour, as can be seen from the Osaka Festival Hall broadcast of November 10. At times he seemed to be ashamed, as if performing an act of exhibitionism, clearing his throat between phrases while nervously fumbling with his hands.

Despite winning on the artistic aspects (the Callas–Di Stefano duet recordings weren't even released, owing to artistic flaws), the competition was a lost battle for the Tebaldi-Corelli coupling from the start. The Callas–Di Stefano venture stole most of the thunder in the international press thanks to the unrelenting focus on the return of Maria Callas, although the surviving videos show that audience response was divided equally between the competing couples. Wildly cheered and adorned with garlands of flowers, Corelli and Tebaldi went from London to Vienna and from there to the Philippines, Japan, Korea, and Hong Kong as if they were reigning sovereigns. It was a wild and exciting trip, with visits to the most exotic places. They had an adventurous stay in the Philippines, according to the account Corelli gave his family. In Manila they were received by the dictator Ferdinand Marcos and his wife, Imelda. Corelli recalled with glee how, during a private *soirée*, Imelda danced with him, then became so openly smitten that Loretta wanted to kill her. She and Franco excused themselves, escaped from the palace, and took the first plane out of Manila to Tokyo.[106]

January–March 1974: Settling Scores

The first months of 1974 were a turbulent time for the Metropolitan Opera. The uneasy truce between Chapin and Kubelik exploded in February, and Kubelik resigned. Meanwhile, economic crises were hitting the Met harder than ever before, and Chapin had to make ends meet despite falling attendance. While James Levine was chosen as Kubelik's successor and Pavarotti was being hailed as the new Caruso, the press started picking at the greed of the stars (although there weren't too many of them left at the Met). Peter Wynne from the *Sunday Record* put the Met's deficit at $5.9 million at the start of the season, a deficit created by the fact that two-thirds of the $75,000 cost of each Met performance went for singers and backstage personnel. With an average attendance rate of 91 percent, the Met could gross only about $50,000 per performance, and what was not made up for by gifts contributed to the deficit.

What we now know of the actual fees paid to the stars of that time shows that their salaries had only a slight effect on the Met's financial woes. If on an important night there were two singers being paid $4,000, with an added $1,000 to $3,000 for the other principals, that totaled just $12,000 at the most. Extras and expense money bumped it up to $15,000. For star-studded works such as *Gioconda*, *Don Carlo*, or *La Forza del Destino* an extra $5,000 may have been required. Some operas were more financially challenging, such as a *Robert le Diable*, *Les Huguenots*, or *Guillaume Tell*; still, these show that there still would have been a deficit even if no stars had been performing. Nevertheless, they may have inspired Chapin to deduct $136 from Corelli's paycheck in order to settle the score over his unpaid dentist bill, which now threatened to influence the whole operational activities of the company when the dentist threatened to sue the Met. He reasoned that the Met should pay in the tenor's stead because Corelli was effectively employed by the Met, in spite of the payment arrangement with Gorlinsky. Chapin and his legal advisors panicked. They thought it unwise for the Met's arrangement with Corelli to be looked into closely and paid Wachtel the sum due plus interest on the spot, which was then deducted from Corelli's very next fee. Like Bing before him, Chapin couldn't believe how a man as wealthy as Corelli could let things get so out of hand over $100.[107]

May–June 1974: A "Veiled" *Turandot*

The *Telegram* judged Corelli's spring tour performance as Calaf before an audience of 5,000 at John B. Hynes Civic Auditorium "Herculean,"[108] but according to the *Globe*'s correspondent, Richard Dyer, there were some bad vibes in Boston's air on the night of April 27. Where the *Telegram* critic may have been seduced by the audience's undiminished hysteria for Corelli, Dyer marveled over the tenor's preposterous behavior: "Sometimes, when the vowels and consonants were inconvenient, he dropped the impeding words of the text altogether; he even started to answer *Turandot*'s second riddle first." And that was not all, Dyer noticed: "During the third act for reasons of his own he simply wandered off the stage for a while; when he came back, ... at one point he seized Turandot's veil, as he's supposed to, and then used it to [wipe] his nose."[109] Others noticed the dropping of words and his leaving the stage at odd moments as well.[110] This habit of stranding his prima donnas during their solos was born of an increasing need to moisten his dry throat. Whenever he felt in need of water, he would leave the stage to get a drink or suck his sponges.[111]

April 27, 1974

Giacomo Puccini: *Turandot*

Boston, John B. Hynes Civic Auditorium (spring tour)

Elinor Ross (*Turandot*), Franco Corelli (*Calaf*), Edda Moser (*Liù*), cond. Gabor Ötvös

April 27, 1974

Giacomo Puccini: *Turandot*

New York, Metropolitan Opera House (June Festival)

Marion Lippert (*Turandot*), Franco Corelli (*Calaf*), Teresa Zylis-Gara (*Liù*), cond. Gabor Ötvös

May 17, 1974: Corelli in Mexico

Franco Corelli had been scheduled to debut in Mexico as Calaf on September 26 and October 12, 1963. He was also programmed in *Tosca, Carmen, La Gioconda,* and *Il Trovatore,* and the last-minute cancellation of his Mexican performances had greatly disappointed his fans there. Their second chance to see the tenor came in Mexico City on the evening of Friday, May 17, 1974. The concert was a substitute for Renata Tebaldi's, which had to be canceled due to a sudden indisposition. The agency of Carlo Morelli (a Chilean baritone and brother of the famous tenor Renato Zanelli) then hoped to obtain the services of Corelli, remembers Gilda Morelli. She was then president of the agency and the concert organizer. She and the agency's vice president, Rómulo Ramírez Esteva, went to New York, where the soprano Gilda Cruz-Romo (who had sung with Corelli in *Aida* and *La Forza del Destino*) introduced them to the tenor. Said Morelli:

> He accepted and was very friendly to us. I had asked the Instituto Nacional de Bellas Artes for some ornamental pillars so as not to have him on the stage

> May 17, 1974
> **Concert**
> **Mexico City, Cine Metropólitan**
> Andrea Falconieri: "Occhietti amati." Donizetti: "Me voglio fà na casa,"** "Lu tradimiento," "La conocchia." Bellini: "Malinconia, ninfa gentile."** Donizetti: "Amore e morto." Verdi: *Rigoletto* "La donna è mobile." Bellini: "Sogno d'infanzia," "Torna, vezzosa Fillide."* Massenet: *Le cid* "Ô souverain, ô juge, ô père." Di Capua: "I' te vurria vasà." Gaetano Lama: "Silenzio cantatore." Tosti: "L'ultima canzone," "'A vucchella." De Curtis: "Tu, ca' nun chiagne!" (Encores: Tortorella: "Addà turnà." Tosti: "L'ultima canzone." Cardillo: "Core 'ngrato." Denza: "Occhi di fata"); pianist, Miguel García Mora
>
> *The program mentions "Mille Cherubini in coro," but at the concert he sang Bellini's "Torna, vezzosa Fillide."
> **These two songs are otherwise unrecorded by Corelli, who sang them only on this occasion.

with just a piano. When he didn't like the way they were placed on the stage, he came to me and asked if it would be all right to arrange them differently. I wanted to call for someone to rearrange them, but before I could, Corelli was already moving these pillars all by himself. Then I discovered the human side of Franco.[112]

The tenor's surprise appearance created great excitement among opera fans in the Mexican capital, although some eyebrows were raised when the location proved to be the Cine Metropólitan instead of the famous Palacio de Bellas Artes. Enrique C. Lamadrid described the impact that the announcement had made on him in *La Mejor Revista de México*: "The educated part of the Mexican public faced a future event of deep significance and great transcendence in the musical world." In spite of the low-profile publicity for the spur-of-the-moment concert, all 3,000 seats in the auditorium were booked. Wrote Lamadrid: "It seemed as if the whole great musical elite of Mexico had made for itself an appointment to listen to one of the best tenors of the world: the great Corelli. And by our own testimony, it was. Corelli, exclusive star of the Metropolitan Opera House in New York, offered 18 magnificent interpretations."[113]

One might argue with Lamadrid over his description of Franco as "an orthodox singer who subjects himself to the demands of the composers whose scores he interprets," but otherwise his review is on target, to judge from the recording that remains of this concert:

> Franco Corelli possesses an easy, well-modulated voice of finished artistry. Besides, this superb artist knows to perfection how to use his middle voice and how to spin out a note. In short, Corelli is a textbook example of finished vocal artistry. . . . His incredible facility in all the registers, most notably the middle register, occasionally enables him to express a special sweetness, that marvelously accentuates his beautiful high notes, which are equally finished and impressive.[114]

Lamadrid regretted what was essentially a weak spot in both Corelli's solo concerts and the tour concerts with Tebaldi, namely, that he did not sing more arias from his celebrated stage repertoire. The Mexican public didn't hold it against him, though: "Drunk with his voice, the public requested him to give more and more, and he kindly agreed to sing three encores that made the audience rise from their seats. Overcome by emotion and enthusiasm, they gave him an ovation."[115]

✦✦✦✦✦

Corelli's surprise appearance in Mexico City was squeezed in between his final two Met Spring Tour appearances in *Turandot* (which makes it all the more puzzling why he didn't include, say, "Non piangere, Liù" or "Nessun dorma" in the Mexican concert, two arias the audience would surely have appreciated). Elinor Ross was his icy princess once more on May 25, after which Marion Lippert stepped in for the June Festival, which began on May 28. Lippert fared much less well there, and when Chapin came on stage before the third act, everyone assumed he would announce her indisposition. Instead, he asked consideration for Corelli, who had been his usual self throughout! That led the press to suspect that Corelli wanted to excuse himself from the general disaster around him. The bedeviled Chapin, who was held responsible for the Met's financial and artistic troubles, was practically hissed off the stage, and Lippert continued to be booed to the point where the public erupted in shouts to drown out the orchestra. Byron Belt of the *Jersey Journal* finished the job when he wrote that if this was her usual performance level, she deserved to be booed.[116]

The Summer of '74

Corelli and Tebaldi's first Viennese concert, on October 14, 1973, had been a tremendous success. When they approached the impresario Ilse Elisa Zellermayer to organize a second concert, she thought it too soon after the first but reluctantly agreed. The date was set for Friday evening, June 28, 1974, but when she discovered that Tebaldi planned on singing Amneris in the *Aida* duet, instead of the more popular "Pur ti riveggo" or "O terra addio," she started to have serious doubts. When only half the tickets had been sold by the evening before the performances, she lowered the prices, hoping to get at least some extra public to attend. On the day of the concert, she asked a taxi driver where Vienna's music-loving audience was. Replied the driver: "Friday is the beginning of the Sabbath, and the culture-minded Jewish public doesn't go out then."[118]

> **June 28, 1974**
> **Concert**
> Wien, Gesellschaft der Musikfreunde
> Scarlatti: "Toglietemi la vita ancor." Bellini: "Vaga luna che inargenti." Monteverdi: *Arianna* "Lasciatemi morire." Bellini: "Torna vezzosa Fillide," "Io chiedo al ciel." Alois Melichar: "Mille cherubini in coro." Verdi: *Rigoletto* "La donna è mobile;" *Macbeth* "Ah, la paterna mano;" *Aida* "Già i sacerdoti adunansi "(duet). Cardillo: "Core 'ngrato." Tosti: "L'ultima canzone." Puccini: *La Bohème* "O soave fanciulla" (duet).
> Renata Tebaldi, Franco Corelli; pianist, Eugene Kohn
>
> **July 13, 18, 21, and 27, 1974**
> **Georges Bizet: *Carmen* (Italian/French)**
> Macerata, Arena Sferisterio
> Grace Bumbry (*Carmen*), Franco Corelli (*Don José*), Franco Bordoni (*Escamillo*), Wilma Vernocchi (*Micaëla*), Carlo Scaravelli (*Moralès*), cond. Oliviero De Fabritiis

They fared better in Macerata, where Franco appeared for a few Italian-language Don Josés next to the sensational Carmen of Grace Bumbry, who managed to seduce her Italian partner in French. The added attraction for Franco here was of course being once again able to perform before and with his friends, for Carlo Scaravelli was scheduled to sing Moralès. Unfortunately, Scaravelli was no longer up to it, according to the management. So the general manager, Carlo Perucci, carefully approached Corelli and suggested that a replacement might be necessary. Corelli replied as was

Franco with his lifetime friend and teacher Carlo Scaravelli as Moralès, Macerata, July 1974. (Photo: Courtesy of Alessandro Scaravelli)

to be expected: without Scaravelli he did not feel up to Don José.[119] Scaravelli sang, and after that the Corellis had ample time to enjoy their freshly acquired Swiss *Fachholz* house in Cortina.

November 14–December 7, 1974: The Tide Turns

Guido Tartoni's description in *TV Radiocorriere* of Corelli as such a divo that "the sexually unchained subscribers of the Met lost their heads in the tight pants of his Roméo" sounds spectacular enough,[120] but when Joan Downs interviewed Corelli for her book *The Tenors*, she found quite the opposite. Corelli was seated on a green velvet sofa before a black marble table in his West Fifty-sixth Street apartment, and he spoke in a voice that scarcely betrayed his power as a singer. In the corner the television set, with the volume off, displayed the rapidly changing figures of the stock index. Downs described him as informally but expensively dressed in a white cashmere shirt, grey glen plaid slacks, and black shoes of thin glove leather while he told of his life, which was divided between singing and watching westerns on T.V.[121]

Press reviews continued to acclaim Corelli's singing, and in his 1974 Roméos he still negotiated three B-flats in "Ah! Lève-toi, soleil" alone, two B-naturals in the wedding scene, a B-natural and a high C in the duel scene, and another high C in the bedroom duet. However, as Franco himself attested, the high notes were now a little opaque and lacked their earlier brilliant focus.[122] They also tended to spread and were becoming shorter in duration. He had given up on the "Celeste Aida" diminuendo in October 1972, and with it went the B-flat diminuendo at the end of the *Roméo* aria. His tone in general lost some of its former bite, tending to dry up a little over the run of a performance. The press would increasingly notice sloppy phrasing and routine acting, such as during the experimental Metropolitan Opera fall tour

November 14, 23, 29; December 7, 1974

Charles Gounod: *Roméo et Juliette*

New York, Metropolitan Opera House

Franco Corelli (*Roméo*), Adriana Maliponte, Judith Blegen [December 7] (*Juliette*), cond. Henry Lewis in Cleveland. Wrote Farley Hutchins in the *Beacon Journal*: "He waits for his cues as he might a bus."[123]

Perhaps Corelli had sung in one *Turandot* too many; perhaps the whole operatic circus no longer provided a challenge for the man who had helped create the first part of the Met's fresh history at Lincoln Center. He now lamented *Lohengrin*, on his piano in Milan since 1968 but *verboten* to him because of the language barrier—he wasn't able to sing it in German. In addition, the Met could not grant him enough time to study *Manon Lescaut*, which left him once again with routine *Turandot*s and *Roméo*s. Downs asks him what he is still doing it for. Answered Corelli: "To refine the qualities I have in my voice—I don't know my voice, I have never heard it. For money? For glory? The glory doesn't exist. What is a moment of applause—a moment of happiness, maybe, because you can hold a note for ten seconds. If you can hold it for twenty seconds you can have as much applause as anybody can stand. . . . Why does the voice of Caruso exist on record today; *amor d'arte*? No. Because it is big money for RCA. There is no more *amor d'arte*."[124]

January 8–10, 1975: The Death of a Friend

On January 8, 1975, Robert Merrill and Richard Tucker woke up early in their hotel rooms in Kalamazoo, Michigan, where they were supposed to sing that night. That afternoon, at 4:35 P.M., Tucker's son received a phone call from a doctor telling him that his father had died of a massive coronary. Merrill was charged with putting the contents of Tucker's pockets into a plastic bag, which was still clutched in his fist when he arrived at New York's La Guardia Airport in a state of shock. New York's opera world mourned their local favorite, as did Franco Corelli. Ever since that *Tosca* rehearsal in 1964 he had maintained a close friendship with his esteemed colleague. On January 9, while saying goodbye to the body of his friend as he lay in state at the Riverside Chapel, he had been overcome with emotion: "When the moment came for him to view the body, Corelli looked at the lifeless form and sobbed loudly. When he approached Tucker's widow Sara to pay his respects, he said in a voice choked by tears, 'This is so cruel, so unfair! Richard loved life.'"[125]

The funeral was held on Friday morning, January 10, at the Metropolitan Opera. Franco and Loretta were sitting with Robert and Marion Merrill in the

Met's auditorium, where Tucker's catafalque and casket were waiting to be taken to the cemetery. The world had lost a great singer and Corelli, a great friend. They had shared many a moment of backstage gaiety, an echo of which was captured in their photographs together.[126]

✦✦✦✦✦

The months following Tucker's death proved to be historic ones for the Met, although Corelli played but a small part in them. With Bing gone, Magda Olivero was finally allowed to make her triumphant debut at the Met on April 3, when she sang *Tosca* to the Cavaradossi of James King. Four days later the City Opera star Beverly Sills was finally recognized at the Met in Rossini's *The Siege of Corinth*. Regrettably, the Olivero *Tosca* did not feature Corelli, and the Rossini opera was out of the scope of his repertoire. Franco therefore contented himself with alternating as Rodolfo and Roméo on the spring tour to Boston, Detroit, Atlanta, Memphis, Dallas, and Minneapolis. The Boston press welcomed him with the question as to "whether Franco Corelli, whose French pronunciation and cancellation record are equally notorious, will actually appear as Roméo."[127] He did and went on to fulfill his other tour obligations to largely winning reviews before embarking on the adventurous Met tour to Japan.

June 10–28, 1975: The Last *Bohèmes* with the Company

On May 25 the company left Minneapolis to go to Japan for a three-week tour with *La Traviata*, *La Bohème*, and *Carmen*. The Japanese paid for everything, including transportation of sets from the NHK Theater to the Bunka Kaikan, between which the performances were divided. The sets themselves were duplicates, made in Japan, of the original Met sets. The main draws of the tour were Joan Sutherland, Robert Merrill, Luciano Pavarotti, and Corelli. Still, the opening *Traviata* performance wasn't sold out, and Chapin resorted to asking his singers for help. He wanted and received their permission to have a performance taped and broadcast on Japanese television. It soon worked its magic. After the broadcast the public stormed the box office, and the tour turned into a triumphant procession of performances, with Corelli duly appearing for all his *Bohème*s. Said Chapin: "He was in good form, responding easily to the warmth of the Japanese audiences."[128]

> **June 10–13, 1975**
> **Giacomo Puccini:** *La Bohème*
> **June 10 1975, Tokyo, Festival Hall (Met Japan Tour)**
> **June 13, 1975, Osaka, Festival Hall (Met Japan Tour)**
> Franco Corelli (*Rodolfo*), Adriana Maliponte, Dorothy Kirsten [June 13] (*Mimì*), William Walker (*Marcello*), Gene Boucher, Russel Christopher [June 13] (*Schaunard*), Malcolm Smith (*Colline*), Mary Costa (*Musetta*), cond. Leif Segerstam
>
> **June 23 and 28, 1975**
> **Giacomo Puccini:** *La Bohème*
> **Vienna (Virginia), Wolf Trap Farm Park (Met spring tour)**
> Franco Corelli (*Rodolfo*), Renata Scotto (*Mimì*), John Reardon (*Marcello*), Russell Christopher (*Schaunard*), Justino Díaz, James Morris [June 28] (*Colline*), Mary Costa (*Musetta*), cond. Leif Segerstam

The most notable among Corelli's fans popped up rather unexpectedly—the Japanese Crown Prince (and acting emperor) Akihito. Chapin thanked him at length for the Japanese reception, telling him how wonderful everything was and how responsive the audiences had been. Finally, when he had to catch his breath, the Crown Prince took over and asked: "Is Franco Corelli going to sing?"[129] He was, and by the time the Met left the Bunka Kaikan it was Franco Corelli night: "Mr. Corelli, as Rodolfo, clearly delighted his Japanese audience with a powerful, emotional performance that brought him a prolonged ovation at the end."[130]

Outside the theater, though, Corelli was hardly recognized. Fortunately there was Loretta, who would introduce her husband to oblivious grocers in the area of narrow streets that James McCracken had dubbed "Smokey Alley": "You should know that my husband is the greatest tenor in the world."[131] On the flight back Chapin's wife celebrated her fiftieth birthday, and the soon-to-be-ex-general manager was truly touched when Corelli sought her out while boarding the plane, quietly presenting her with a lovely bouquet of white orchids: "I wish you all happiness, Signora Chapin." Said Chapin: "I thought to myself that I really wished him exactly the same."[132]

For Chapin, the flight back was marred only by his knowledge that his days as general manager were numbered.[133]

June 1975: Dear Colleagues

As you are no doubt aware, the Board of Directors of the Metropolitan Opera has decided on a major restructuring of this theater, including the elimination of the post of General Manager.
  Schuyler Chapin, June 26, 1975, in *Musical Chairs*, 1977

With those words Schuyler Chapin informed his former employees of the end of his short tenure at the Met. While he was in Japan, the Met's board had decided to let the theater be ruled by a consortium rather than by one man, dividing Chapin's responsibilities up among Anthony Bliss (general manager), James Levine (music director), and John Dexter (director of productions). Two days later Corelli sang his last Rodolfo with the Met at Wolf Trap Farm Park in Vienna, Virginia, before a noisy audience that featured President Gerald Ford; Vice President Nelson Rockefeller and his wife, Happy; and Senator Edward Kennedy.

The extent to which Chapin's departure troubled Corelli is unclear, but there were significant changes ahead that were bound to affect his future at the Met. To begin with, the theater was teetering on the brink of bankruptcy, and as early as February 1975 principal artists were asked to accept a pay cut or shorter contracts. With Bing gone, Gentele dead, Chapin fired, and Tebaldi out, Corelli's 1976 contract consisted of nothing but a single run of *Norma*s. It was to be a very prestigious new production, but Domingo and Pavarotti were now unmistakably on a par with Corelli, if not already taking over.

After a solo concert in Washington, D.C., Corelli performed his remaining European obligations at the Arena di Verona, where he featured in a series of *Carmen*s and two *Turandot*s.[134] The *Carmen*s met with a mixed reception, to which the two unfortunate *Turandot*s (with Lippert once more replaced, this time with both Hana Janku and Danica Mastilovic) added little to nothing. That left Corelli with something to brood over on his holidays.

Did the mountains of Cortina illuminate his soul? Did Lauri-Volpi tell him in Burjassot how to leave the stage with grace? Did Bing speak with him in Siusi about the future? Did he discuss this quintessential moment in his career with his unexpected new "friend" Mario Del Monaco, with whom he had sought to reconcile after his rival had so unexpectedly applauded him in Verona? They may all have played a part in Corelli's prolonged absence from the Met, which stretched well into *Norma* rehearsals in December.

December 1975: A *Norma* Dress Rehearsal

A fund-raising bazaar was organized for the Met at which everything from archival memorabilia to celebrities' costumes was on sale. Entrance was $2, but the catering was lavish; Lucine Amara was among the singers who served sandwiches.[135] Corelli did not attend. In fact, it had been impossible to locate him throughout, to the utter despair of the new management; the conductor, Gianfranco Masini; and the increasingly nervous Norma-to-be, Rita Hunter. She thought it high time to tune her voice with Franco's. That moment arrived when he showed up out of the blue at a late Act III orchestra rehearsal. According to Hunter, he sang his lines and then ran out with the words "Mamma mia, what a voice!"[136] He never returned to the Met stage, and John Alexander substituted for him at the premiere. There was some hope that he would appear at one of the subsequent performances with Sutherland, most notably the broadcast, but even that was not to be.

❖❖❖❖❖

There was no one single credible reason for Corelli's abrupt departure from the Met, unless we take his complaint of general fatigue at face value. Vocally, the recording of the rehearsal, made by Hunter's husband, shows him in fine, dark voice. It has been speculated that the tax problems he and other Met artists faced were behind his departure, although Loretta denied this.[137] Foreign singers were constantly looking for loopholes that would enable them to get back as much as possible of their deducted taxes. Some artists, including Corelli at one time, employed the services of Norman Egenberg.[138] The accountant's arrest on bribery charges eventually led to the imprisonment of some singers, while Birgit Nilsson escaped both arrest and paying by fleeing New York overnight, leaving behind all of her Met obligations (her last performance at the Met had been on April 2, 1975). Said Nilsson: "The arrest of Egenberg caused a

---

Beginning of December 1975
Vincenzo Bellini: *Norma* (Rehearsal)
New York, Metropolitan Opera House
Rita Hunter (*Norma*), Franco Corelli (*Pollione*), John Macurdy (*Oroveso*), cond. Gianfranco Masini

lot of problems for the Met's singers; for me myself, Freni, Tebaldi, Simionato, Corelli, and God knows who else. Of course Corelli had problems too, although I wonder how he came out of it. He was residing in America all the time, while I was hiding in Europe."[139] Corelli did remain in the United States, so it is unlikely that his tax problems were why he left the Met. On the other hand, Gabriella Tucci, who left in December 1972, pointed out another possibility, observing that a number of singers who had done well under Bing did not get along with James Levine: "He imposed other singers, preferring American artists."[140]

Marco Corelli reveals another reason for Franco's sudden departure from the stage: around this time the tenor developed prostate problems that eventually necessitated surgery. This had an enormous impact not only on Franco's private life, but also on his ability to sustain his voice with the necessary breath support.[141]

CHAPTER 20 ❖ 1976–1981

Dunque è proprio finita?

May–August 1976: The Final *Bohème*

Some day it will all be over. I will get up and know that the voice is no longer beautiful. I will stop. Never will I present an audience with a moment of pity.
   Franco Corelli, in Joan Downs, *The Tenors*, 1974

Corelli's American *Norma* walkout was followed by a rumored return to La Scala on May 13, 1976, when a new production of *Turandot* was to be premiered there. The occasion was prestigious: the jubilee commemoration of the world premiere fifty years earlier. Birgit Nilsson was foreseen as the protagonist, and a brave Montserrat Caballé, despite her bad memories of performing with Corelli, had accepted the role of Calaf's submissive slave girl, Liù. However, Corelli never showed up, and a doubtlessly relieved Caballé found Gianfranco Cecchele in his stead—for starters, because Nilsson canceled as well, which led to Caballé's assuming the title role and Elena Mauti Nunziata's stepping in as Liù. The event was then postponed from the 13th to the 16th when Caballé became indisposed. (Emma Renzi stepped in for Caballé in mid-performance but emerged triumphant.)[1]

Three months later, Corelli's return to the operatic stage during Torre del Lago's Puccini Festival in August 1976 came as something of a surprise. In the six months since his last performance, his name had suddenly entered the realm of living legends from the now mythical golden age of the '50s. Had these performances been a farewell, they would have been bathed in nostalgia, allowing audiences and critics alike to overlook any defects that time had cut

> **August 10 and 13, 1976**
> **Giacomo Puccini: *La Bohème***
> **Torre del Lago, Open Air Theater**
> Adriana Maliponte (*Mimì*), Franco Corelli (*Rodolfo*), Angelo Romero (*Marcello*), Giovanni de Angelis (*Schaunard*), Maurizio Mazzieri (*Colline*), Giovanna Santelli (*Musetta*), Torre del Lago Festival Chorus and Orchestra, cond. Nino Sanzogno

into those vocal cords that once seemed to have been made of molten bronze. Unfortunately, as a comeback appearance, the *Bohème*s proved disappointing. Corelli's timbre was a pale shadow of what the audience remembered, and a slow vibrato bordering on wobbling appeared in the large arcs of Puccini's most sculptured lines. As if that were not enough, in the first performance there was a distinct crack on his floating pianissimo on the A-flat at the end of "Della stagion del fior," near the very end of the third act. The audience whispered in shock and pity for the warrior who once had negotiated such notes as few had done before. He attempted the A-flat pianissimo on "Fior" again on the second night but quickly cut it short when it started to slip once again. The open-air festival did not have a curtain, but that night the curtain closed on Franco Corelli the tenor.

Even his cousin Marco agreed that he might have been better off had he left things as they were, although he saw some extenuating circumstances:

> Franco's nervous system was pushed beyond the limit, and in order to calm down he took too many tranquilizers in Torre del Lago. Apart from his physical condition, these tranquilizers and the potions he took to soften the muscles of his throat resulted in his having to push more than normal, and all that made his voice unsteady. You must realize that Franco burned himself up far more than others.... When he finished a performance, he was exhausted; he lost over a kilo in weight per performance. And it was never good enough for him; even if the public went into a frenzy, he still found defects! In the end he couldn't win that battle against his own standard. In the end pressure conquered him; when he came back to his dressing room after these *Bohème*s, he told me, "*Basta!* It's over. I'll never sing again."[2]

1977–1979: On Becoming a Living Legend

Little was heard of Corelli until March 1978, when word got out that he would make a surprise comeback as Maurizio in the upcoming Met run of *Adriana Lecouvreur*. This led to hundreds of phone calls and a run on the box office that brought back memories of days long past.[3] Unfortunately for the many fans who obtained tickets, either the rumor was just that or Corelli backed out at the last minute when he learned that people were waiting for him; heightened expectations weighed heavily on his tormented nerves. Still, the rumor brought him back into the limelight, and in the subsequent May 19 radio interview with George Jellinek he made it clear to the audience that he most certainly planned to return to the stage. His absence had been merely a much-deserved holiday, but now that all was well, the world could count on Franco Corelli once again. His plans involved roles in operas he had contemplated for decades without ever making his mind up about them, such as *Lohengrin*, *Un Ballo in Maschera*, and then *Otello*. *Ballo* was a sure thing, he said, citing offers from Rome, Naples, and Palermo. In this interview Corelli joked around in a way that was new for him, at least in public, such as when Jellinek complimented him on his looks in *Norma*. Said a laughing Corelli: "This is very important: the man that makes love to woman must be a nice man!" Jellinek was on his toes: "Especially the man that makes love to two women!" Corelli was so happy to be the center of attention again that he presented Jellinek and the radio audience with two previously unreleased recordings from the unfinished 1967 session: the incomplete "Che gelida manina" section from *La Bohème* and "Ah! La paterna mano" from *Macbeth*.

Following the Jellinek show, there were serious negotiations with La Scala, while there was word of October *Tosca*s in San Francisco and *Werther* and *Otello* at the Met, although neither project ever materialized. In 1978, over a cup of cappuccino (augmented by crème di cacao) with the journalist Lou Cevetillo in New York, he mentions two other reasons besides fatigue for his absence from the stage: "With my father being ill and my poodle Pipi [*sic*; Pippi] dying, I have not been in the best of spirits."[4]

Whereas Loris had been buried in the garden of a friend, the dentist Ernesto Stocchi in Parma, Pippi was buried in Cortina, where he had died the previous summer. However, the spring of 1978 brought new hope, said Corelli: "Now we have a new Pipi [*sic*; Pippi; this new Pippi was also called Schipi], and my father is better, and my outlook is better. Although I had not sung for seven months during my father's illness, I have begun again and I think that I will return soon."[5]

❖❖❖❖❖

In his dreams Corelli was still able to open La Scala, the Met, the Arena di Verona, the Teatro dell'Opera, and all the other theaters that were inseparably linked to his career. Sadly, the golden age of opera had vanished with his own last Rodolfo. Just a few months earlier, in May 1975, Mario Del Monaco bade farewell to the stage with a *Pagliacci* in Perugia. On September 16, 1977, Maria Callas died of heart failure in Paris. But the greatest blow for Franco was the death of his great friend and teacher Giacomo Lauri-Volpi on March 17, 1979. A few months later, on July 10, Antonio Ghiringhelli died, a man whose name seemed already to belong to some distant past.[6]

With their numbers diminished and bereft of the most illustrious names among them, the surviving stars of the epoch turned from mortals into living legends themselves, inevitably thrown back amongst each other. Di Stefano and Bergonzi came to cherish their former rivalry with Corelli as a sweet reminiscence of their glory days. Bergonzi continued singing, defying time, while Di Stefano lived out the fate he had predicted for himself of an aging singer forced to go on for the sake of money. Corelli continued to study and would occasionally discuss technique with Del Monaco on the phone. Did they ever meet in person after the 1950s? Del Monaco's son Giancarlo, then a celebrated stage director, maintains that the onetime sworn enemies established a sort of friendship in the end after Corelli called Del Monaco from Cortina (Alberto Del Monaco maintained that the first telephone calls dated back as far as 1970). There can be no doubt that Corelli had admired del Monaco from the start, and Giancarlo's claim that Franco, at the very outset of his career, had auditioned before the already famous Del Monaco may well be true.[7]

Once they were no longer competitors, their bond intensified, claims Giancarlo Del Monaco: "At times they cried on the phone, when talking about life, their careers, about the relativity of it all in the end. Those were not the usual sort of phone calls, but marathons that lasted for hours."[8]

> June 8, 1980
> Concert
> Madison, New Jersey, Fairleigh Dickinson University
> Tosti: "L'ultima canzone." Sicilian song: "A la barcillunisa."
> Franco Corelli

June 8, 1980: A Hit Record

All through these years of leisure, Corelli lived the life of a wealthy retiree. He would teach a bit, watch television, and go out for dinner with friends in New York, Milan, Monte Carlo, Rome, Cortina, Ancona, or Puerto Rico, where he owned homes. There was but one minor interruption when, in the middle of 1980, he suddenly appeared singing "L'ultima canzone" and "A la barcillunisa" in a surprise performance at Fairleigh Dickinson University in Madison, New Jersey. The occasion was an opera ball benefit organized by Mrs. Jerome Hines, also known as the soprano Lucia Evangelista. Even Luciano Pavarotti came to her aid in enlisting Franco to sing, calling him up and urging him on.[9] Those two songs hardly counted as a comeback, but the applause and the encouragement from friends and colleagues convinced him that he was still up to it, perhaps not in staged opera, but certainly on the concert platform.

This time he may actually have welcomed the pirates of Historical Recording Enterprises (HRE), who mysteriously obtained a copy of the two songs on tape. The live recording industry had meanwhile started to fill in a gap left by mainstream record companies, who for obvious reasons could not issue live recordings at will. HRE had already paid tribute to Corelli with an interesting three-LP tribute called *The Franco Corelli Collection, 1956–1973*. In addition, they welcomed the two new songs as the Holy Grail of opera, issuing them as a seven-inch single (HRE-SE-1) titled *The Return of Franco Corelli: First Public Appearance in Four Years*.

April 24, 1981: Triple Concerto

As was to be expected, Corelli went about his preparations for the concert with the utmost caution. He was well aware that the public expected "Nessun dorma," but right now he needed to regain some of his former confidence, and that required a

> April 24, 1981
> Concert*
> Newark, Symphony Hall (New Jersey State Opera)
> Massenet: *Le Cid* "Ô souverain, ô juge, ô père" (Tagliavini). Verdi: *Aida* "Ritorna vincitor!" (Zeani). Cilea: *L'arlesiana* "È la solita storia" (Tagliavini). Pennino: "Pecchè?" (Corelli). Tosti: "L'ultima canzone" (Corelli). Gambardella: "'O marenariello." (Corelli with piano). Billi: "E canta il grillo" (Corelli with piano). Di Capua: "I' te vurria vasà" (Corelli with piano). Lama: "Silenzio cantatore" (Corelli with piano). Sicilian song: "A la barcillunisa" (Corelli with piano). Tosti: "L'ultima canzone" (Corelli, encore)
>
> Virginia Zeani, Ferruccio Tagliavini, Franco Corelli, Klara Barlow, Nicola Rossi Lemeni, Jerome Hines; cond. Alfredo Silipigni; violinist, Erick Friedman; pianist, Alfredo Silipigni
>
> *The program given here is the section of the concert that is available on video/DVD; it is not known whether more songs and arias were performed.

repertoire that posed no real challenges. If only he could face an audience again, things might pick up from there. Because even a solo song concert might create too much pressure, the Hineses and the agent Tony Russo came up with the idea of inviting a few old friends to perform with him. The plan worked perfectly: none of them could possibly pose any threat to the star of the evening. The aged Ferruccio Tagliavini was in a deplorable vocal state, and Zeani sang with the *beaux restes* of her voice. That put a shy but surprisingly solid Corelli in the spotlight with a string of celebrated songs. The voice was still there; the timbre had regained depth, color, and security since the Torre del Lago *Bohème*s, and he could actually look forward to a successful comeback on the concert platform. The next question was: could he walk off with honors in his operatic repertoire as well?

May 9–June 9, 1981: The Return of "La Bella Voce"

There are rumblings of anticipation in the opera world these days, and they have nothing to do with the popular success, especially on television, of certain contemporary singers. The anticipation among true opera lovers is over the impending return of tenor Franco Corelli to the singing stage. The man once called "the greatest tenor currently occupied in the business of Italian opera" will be onstage at the Garden State Arts Center on Thursday, July ninth, and his return has roused interest in opera worldwide.

    Italian Tribune, June 26, 1981

After a three-song warm-up in a San Diego restaurant, no doubt in good company, Corelli finally appeared for his solo comeback concert, although the preparations were less thorough than one might have expected. Yet, even though there were only a few piano rehearsals, that didn't get in the way of the very favorable outcome. The concert was fascinating, with the tenor in a darker, fuller voice than he had exhibited during the last years of his active career. Sure, he transposed down in places, but the transposition in the *Cid* aria was habitual for him. The transposition of "Ch'ella mi creda" was more unusual, but he had lowered it before as early as March 18, 1962, when he made his American concert debut in Englewood, New Jersey. Certainly, his 1955 "Ch'ella mi creda" sounded fresher, but at sixty years of age he came off with more than average honors. Moreover, the clever insertion of "Niun mi tema" was enough to fuel discussions about a genuine Corelli *Otello* again, a discussion made all the

> May 9, 1981
> Concert
> San Diego, restaurant
> Three songs
>
> July 9, 1981
> Concert
> Holmdel, New Jersey, Garden State Arts Center
> Puccini: *La Fanciulla del West* "Ch'ella mi creda." Tosti: "La serenata." Massenet: *Le Cid* "Ô souverain, ô juge, ô père." Pennino: "Pecchè?" Verdi: *Otello* "Niun mi tema." Tosti "L'ultima canzone." Denza: "Occhi di fata." Tosti: "Sogno." Billi: "E canta il grillo." Sicilian song: "A la barcillunisa." Nutile: "Mamma mia, che vo' sapè?" Cardillo: "Core 'ngrato."
> Franco Corelli, cond. Alfredo Silipigni; pianist, Alfredo Silipigni

more understandable when listening to the recording. He gave Otello's death scene a very intense and imaginative sentimental edge that haunts the mind. Nonetheless, "Niun mi tema" is easily the least taxing part of that opera. It is very questionable whether he would have been able to sustain the same vocal splendor in full performance over heavy orchestral accompaniment, but this unexpected triumph left little doubt that Corelli had a few interesting years left in him on the concert platform.

November 1981: *L'ultima canzone*

Would you believe it? He came over!
Birgit Nilsson on Franco Corelli's surprise visit to the Swedish television gala in her honor, interviews, 2005–6

The Swedish Nilsson television tribute "This Is Your Life" was designed as a surprise show, the soprano kept unaware of the proceedings.[10] Said Nilsson: "I was sitting there recalling the past and came to Corelli. Just when I recalled how he always tried to hold the high notes, I heard his voice!" At first she thought it was a recording, but when it dawned on her that the pianist was playing live to a phrase from *Turandot*—"Il mio nome non sai . . . dimmi il mio nome . . . prima dell'alba, e all'alba morrio!" (Tell me my name before sunrise and I shall die)"—she realized that he was standing right behind her.

Corelli's mystery-guest appearance, complete with a live song performance, was the highlight of the evening. The selection of "L'ultima canzone" was perfect for the occasion, although Franco didn't

Corelli (right) with his Genoese friend Guido Ingaramo on the beach in Puerto Rico, where Franco had an apartment at the time. (Photo: Courtesy of Guido Ingaramo)

> **November 1981**
> **Birgit Nilsson TV Tribute**
> Stockholm (color telecast)
> Tosti: "L'ultima canzone" (Corelli). Sieczynski: "Wien, du Stadt meiner Träume" (Nilsson)
> Birgit Nilsson, Franco Corelli, with piano

realize that he was singing it for himself. There is little need to comment on this trifling, spontaneous song, sung after an exhausting trip through Copenhagen, Stockholm, and Malmö. The most striking element of his appearance is that he seems totally relaxed, suggesting a good sip of champagne with the crew backstage—or with Nilsson, if one doesn't buy the "surprise" part. According to the soprano, she knew about the plan to fly Corelli in but was told he had canceled at the last minute because he had been given the wrong kind of pills and felt ill. Said Nilsson: "So, if he looked a little tipsy, it may have been because of those pills! But whatever it was, he slept won-der-ful on that!"[11]

CHAPTER 21 ⟡ 1982–1989

Headed for the Future

1982–1983: A Last Salute to Mario Del Monaco

He was the best. The greatest. I envied his vocal emission, the type of voice. Often we had long telephone conversations about vocal technique. He could teach me a lot.... The truth is that we were both dramatic tenors, active in the same repertoire. Our rivalry was simply a professional confrontation.

    Franco Corelli on Mario Del Monaco at his funeral, in "L'ultima recita di Del Monaco," *Il Gazzettino*, October 20, 1982

Things change for people after a personal loss. Corelli had a tragic first encounter with that reality early in life when he lost his mother. It touched him again when he feared losing his father, first in 1968–69, then in 1977–78. When Del Monaco passed away in Mestre, Italy, on October 16, 1982, Corelli felt it deeply. He rushed to pay homage to his former rival in Lancenigo, near Treviso, where Del Monaco was lying in state. The priest memorialized the singer's career and personality. The silence afterward was broken by Del Monaco's voice singing Louis Niedermeyer's "Pietà signore" and César Franck's "Panis angelicus." It brought many to tears, as did the boy who followed with Orfeo's solo at the edge of the Elysian Fields. When the melody faded and the 3,000 mourners pres-

Corelli (far left) in Mario Del Monaco's funeral procession. (Photo: Author's collection)

ent regained their composure, Franco Corelli himself read the telegram sent by the president of the republic, Sandro Pertini. With his parting words vanishing in the air before family, friends, admirers, and colleagues such as Magda Olivero, Renata Tebaldi, and Fiorenza Cossotto, all paid tribute to Del Monaco's mortal remains for the last time.[1] Corelli wept bitter tears over the valiant warrior who was lying there motionless in the radiant costume of the character that had made him immortal—the Moor of Venice.

Afterward, when journalists asked him to comment on their rivalry, Corelli brooded over the past. Del Monaco had commented on the apparent reconciliation with Corelli in his very last television interview, in which he was already visibly weak and nostalgic to the point of tears. He singled out his friend Giuseppe Di Stefano, the greatest lyric tenor of his day. And then, for the first time ever, he mentioned his old enemy by name instead of a poisonous description: "I'd like to say that Corelli, who was also a great tenor, when he goes to Cortina d'Ampezzo, still telephones me now to ask how I'm feeling and to ask me advice on some vocal matters, because, like me, he's a fanatic about technique."[2] Corelli readily confessed that despite his improved relationship with his erstwhile rival, he had been awaiting the right time to resolve their remaining conflicts: "I had wanted to speak some more with him, to reconcile with him and tried to reach him a few days before he passed away; regrettably, I was too late."[3] The picture of Corelli weeping over Del Monaco's coffin is the only photo that has ever turned up of the two titans of postwar opera together.

1984: On Parting

Naturally singers with the status of Corelli and Del Monaco were sought after as teachers by other singers, both beginners and experienced performers. According to Del Monaco's pupil Nazzareno Antinori, in the end his illustrious maestro personally recommended him to the care of Franco Corelli: "According to del Monaco, Corelli was the only one capable of bringing me where I wanted to go."[4] Antinori took a number of lessons from Corelli, but although he spoke respectfully of them, they didn't quite match Del Monaco's. Corelli's work with him was more a matter of friendly advice—which is perhaps not surprising, for Antinori was already well on his way to the Arena di Verona when he went to Corelli.[5]

Others sought Corelli's help in order to solve particular problems, such as Neil Shicoff, who, according to Corelli, had problems with his *passaggio* in the early 1980s. There Corelli was on thin ice: the results of his work were likely to be tested immediately. Years later, a dispute arose over Shicoff's earlier vocal problems, which the emerging Met star supposedly blamed on Corelli rather than presenting him as the doctor who cured them. As it turned out, Shicoff never expressly said so, but the harm was done and the story followed Corelli for years to come.[6] In reflecting on his studies with Franco in *Gramophone*, Shicoff was rather vague regarding Corelli's merits as a teacher. Initially he had had high hopes: "Franco Corelli had the voice of the century, such an animalistic quality to the sound, such a connection between the voice and his heart and sexuality. So becoming his student, I was in total awe. To be near him in my late twenties was like a baseball player asking Babe Ruth how to swing a bat." Unfortunately, the teaching proved to be less impressive: "I learned mostly by osmosis, because he was often distracted. He would get up, sit down. Close the window, open it again—they were hardly perfect learning conditions. He used to speak of punching out a ball of sound, of air, from behind the teeth, and he'd demonstrate that." Shicoff considered the most important outcome of these studies to be that he came to emulate Corelli's obsessive pursuit of the quality of sound.[7]

Occasionally Corelli also revealed surprising insights, even to such well-established singers as José Carreras, who came to him in search of his proper *passaggio* after recovering from leukemia. Corelli investigated and came to a revealing insight: "You have no *passaggio*; yours is a natural voice, like Di Stefano's."[8]

Evaluations of Corelli's teaching, largely at the Jerome Hines Institute of Vocal Art in New Jersey, varied. There are as many enthusiastic reports of singers who maintained that he could forget about time when teaching as there are stories of students who left his classes disappointed. Corelli himself remained silent on the subject of his teaching in the 1980s, during which time the most important events of his life were the death of his father in 1983, followed by that of his best and lifelong friend Carlo Scaravelli, on February 2, 1984.[9]

✦✦✦✦✦

Whereas Franco taught mostly men, Loretta taught the women. As the wife of Franco Corelli and, reputedly, largely responsible for his career, she was quite a popular teacher herself. If one of her pupils arrived early, Franco would sometimes entertain her while Loretta was still teaching another elsewhere in the house. On two occasions this resulted in an affair, the first of which ended disastrously when Loretta investigated their unusually high telephone bills. An itemized bill revealed that a certain Swiss number appeared over and over; when she called it, her pupil Renée answered. Loretta confronted Franco with the bill and abruptly put an end to the relationship. When the girl died of leukemia a few years later, Franco was grief stricken. He was convinced that her illness was some kind of supernatural punishment; simple happiness apparently was not in the cards for him.[10]

CHAPTER 22 ❖ 1990–1994

"Opera Fanatic"

1990: Welcome to WKCR-FM Radio

Welcome, listeners from Easton and Langhorne, Pennsylvania, to western Massachusetts to "Opera Fanatic," WKCR-FM Radio 89.9 on the dial. I'm Stefan Zucker, listed in the Guinness Book of World Records *as the world's highest tenor. With us in the studio are Franco Corelli, Loretta Corelli, [and] Jerome Hines, as well as Bob Connolly and Leopoldo Mucci. Tonight is the result of five years of sacrifice to the devil on my part, and above all the perseverance of Jerry Hines, to whom I owe ten years of shoeshines.*
　　Stefan Zucker, opening lines of "Opera Fanatic" broadcast, February 3, 1990

With those opening lines, radio host and colorful opera buff Stefan Zucker set the tone for a four-year sequence of interviews with Franco Corelli. The context was an ongoing series of broadcasts that aimed to discuss the evolution of twentieth-century singing and tenor singing in particular, a subject with which Corelli was obsessed. His first appearance had been the immediate result of the indisposition of Alfredo Kraus for the broadcast of February 3, 1990. That provided the right low-profile circumstance: no advance promotion, no expectations, no audience apart from a small studio entourage of friends. Corelli proved high-spirited and, inspired by his friends in the studio and telephone calls from fans to the show, openly flirted with the idea of making a comeback.
　　The idea of a comeback was fueled by a comment from Michael Redmond, critic of the *Newark Star-Ledger*, who had recently heard the tenor vocalizing while visiting Jerome Hines's school for young singers, where Corelli

was teaching. Redmond had listened to him singing music from *Faust* and claimed that all the high notes were there in full splendor.[1] Corelli replied that having his voice at one moment no longer meant that he had it at his disposal at all times, but, from broadcast to broadcast, Zucker continued to try to get the tenor to perform again, or at least to record again. Corelli was vague, sometimes speaking from the heart, at others saying that he would need to have his voice of fifteen years earlier at his disposal.

At the time a surprise was in the air, but in the end the hoped-for miracle did not happen. Corelli's ambiguous remarks on a possible comeback stemmed largely from the regrets he had over his career. Looking back, he realized that he had lost the battle with Bing, that he had been before the same audience for too long in exchange for security and peace of mind. He had paid for these comforts with the loss of opportunities from Moscow to Buenos Aires, from Rio de Janeiro to South Africa, each and every one of which would have added a little to the importance of his career.[2] In retrospect, dominating the Met for fifteen years in a row seemed but slight compensation. His regrets extended to his poor choices of repertoire: "I should have liked to complete my art with some other operas that would have been interesting."[3]

As a small compensation, on December 8, 1990, Corelli was elected "Tenor of the Century" by the "Opera Fanatic" audience in a competition that had been going on for the greater part of the year. Although he smiles about the event and the outcome, Zucker makes a point when he elaborates on the reasons for Corelli's popularity: "Today, listeners long for Corelli's animal excitement and feel no one since measures up. Although most opera fans enjoy Pavarotti and Domingo, during the course of the voting and commenting here it's become plain they're not devoted to them. The support is broad but not deep."[4]

Corelli was noncommittal on the subjects of his successors and the Three Tenors. He claimed he had never really heard them, but he complimented Carreras on his beautiful tone color and Domingo on his fine legato. Corelli's vote, however, went to Luciano Pavarotti (despite the fact that he claimed to have never heard him in the theater either), for he had the best high notes.[5] While in Rotterdam for his farewell tour, "Big P." had some complimentary words for Corelli as well: "He was the greatest dramatic tenor who ever lived."[6]

1990–1994: Teacher

Throughout these years Corelli was actively teaching, and in the process of passing his knowledge on, he was making a genuine rediscovery of the music, which gave him immense satisfaction. At times it seemed that he enjoyed this aspect of teaching more than the teaching itself. With regard to his teachings, Corelli was very modest. He maintained that he took only advanced students and simply coached them in the art of phrasing, leaving their technique as it was.[7] That seems to have been a deliberate downplaying of his role, judging from the evaluation of his student Luigi Zoboli. Zoboli, a tenor, argued that his maestro definitely taught an actual method (one focused on the *passaggio*) and not just phrasing: "Franco taught to sing from the low note. He wanted you to sing with the larynx low. For six, seven months he made you study only to E or F. After that, he didn't want you to continue along the scale, but wanted you to go directly to D. From there, you had to go down. He had some phrases that helped here, like from *Tosca*, 'è brù-u-u' (from 'È bruna Floria'). He taught with the 'u,' as Melocchi had done."[8]

Zoboli's account also demonstrates that Corelli's life in the early 1990s did not revolve around those mere smatterings of "Opera Fanatic" broadcasts. He traveled, and his activities were not at all limited to the United States. Part of the year was still reserved for Italy, where he also taught a handful of pupils. According to Zoboli, there were four or five tenors, two baritones, and one bass, the Santo Domingo–born Mosé Franco.[9] Like Zoboli, Mosé Franco also developed a close friendship with Corelli during his seven years of study with the maestro: "He was a great Maestro, truly sympathetic and an extremely generous soul with whom I felt a deep bond. He guided me on my quest for technical perfection."[10]

The "Opera Fanatic" Extravaganzas

Running over four hours each, the "Opera Fanatic" broadcasts could be as much a long sit, as very revealing, or truly funny, such as when Corelli's banana diet became a topic. The health-obsessed Corelli was in high spirits and happy to talk about it: "I am dieting and this is a really good diet. It is composed in this way: two bananas and a yogurt in the morning, two bananas and a yogurt for lunch, two bananas and yogurt in the night, and plenty of water and coffee—absolutely without sugar. And I want to tell you that this diet really works."[11]

When the ensuing press coverage promoted the fad diet, Corelli was forced to refine the story on the next radio show: one should follow it for a few days only (otherwise it might be fatal!). In addition, Corelli warned of post-diet hunger, which could make one eat enough to gain back all the lost pounds overnight. Zucker, sounding more serious than ever, suddenly discovered a possible additional health risk: "Bananas, yogurt, and coffee—doesn't that give you diarrhea?"[12]

Another legendary aspect of the "Opera Fanatic" broadcasts was Zucker's occasional sex question, such as when Corelli asked (in Italian) if Zucker knew what the very handsome Miguel Fleta had done that made him lose his voice. Grinning, Corelli added that he himself had no clue. Zucker then explained it to the radio audience, saying that, as had been said of Giacomo Aragall, "He must have lost it in bed!" More seriously, Zucker proceeded to ask how having sex was incompatible with singing. Said Corelli: "Singing, as Gobbi said, is like sport. You must be strong to succeed. Francesco Merli once told me that if he would have been able to abstain from sex for one month in a row, he would have had a voice of steel."[13]

From that comment popped up another question: had Di Stefano lost his voice due to his frequenting women too much? Loretta immediately silenced Franco, who answered that he didn't know, because he was never "near" Di Stefano. Zucker replied: "Suppose it were true [that Di Stefano had many women], is that bad?" Responded Corelli: "Of course it is better than to go with the women than to go with the men! Ha, ha, ha!" Zucker: "Very well, but is sexual indulgence . . ." Corelli cut him short: "No, abuse is not good." High time for Zucker to draw his guest's attention to the fact that the larynx is only two and a half, three feet away from the nether regions: "What does one have to do with the other?" Said Corelli: "You need to be very strong in the theater, for dominate the nerves, for be sure of yourself."[14]

Loretta Corelli on "Opera Fanatic"

Loretta Corelli was present at most of the broadcasts and can frequently be heard making comments or suggesting answers to her husband. Besides having an urge to control the topics that Franco discussed, she had some taboos herself: when Zucker couldn't resist asking her about her father, she refused to come to the microphone and replied with "Basta!"[15] One time, on March 30, 1991, the Corellis walked away from the microphone in order to "discuss" something. Meanwhile, Zucker commented on what was going on between the couple: "There's a little rift between the two Corellis at the moment, none of us can quite figure out what's wrong, but they are having a little bickering. She said the wrong thing, irritating him. She's trying to calm him down and get him to stay, but he wanted her to leave, but instead he wants to leave. They're squabbling.... What are we supposed to play next?"[16]

Much has been said about the marriage of Franco and Loretta, but this picture, taken during a dinner with friends in 1988, clearly shows that despite their tempestuous characters, they were still very much a couple at the dawn of the 1990s. (Courtesy of Arrigo Michelini)

The rift was quickly mended, however—apparently she looked at him disapprovingly only because he was unable to find the right words in English. Time for some damage control from Zucker: "I've seen it before and ladies, most of you I think would cry in the face of it; on the other hand, most of you would be in ecstasy to be the recipient of what generally happens within moments afterwards. He can be very affectionate, holding her warmly, and it's lovely to behold."[17]

Of course, at times even Zucker decided to play it safe. When Loretta silenced her husband with an audible "Non parlare!" after a question about how the couple first got together, Zucker dropped the matter and announced "Nessun dorma," "Spirto gentil," "Come un bel dì di maggio," and "Bianca al par di neve alpin."[18]

1991: Meeting Gemma

The year 1991 started out badly. Corelli broke his wrist in two places and suffered from related complications for at least five months. Afterward he went to Europe for the summer, as usual, to manage his various possessions and affairs. With his semipermanent residence in New York, his Anconetan roots had faded into the distance, although he always kept his apartments in Milan and Ancona. Not that he ever used the latter, because whenever he returned he stayed in the comfortable Grand Hotel Palace in the heart of the city's center. In 1991, while visiting Ancona over the summer, he happened to meet Gemma Giacomini, the daughter of his adolescent love, Iride. He had asked after her before through acquaintances at the Bellini Choir, but Gemma couldn't bring herself to meet Corelli after her father died in 1990. His death brought back the jealousy she had harbored toward Franco when she was a child. Chance intervened in 1991. One day, while Gemma was working in a driver's license bureau, Franco suddenly showed up to renew his license. After some consideration, Gemma decided to tell him who she was: "He was so overwhelmed that he cried. He asked me about how my father had died and what my mother was doing. Later on he even talked on the phone with my mother. It meant so much to her to reconcile with him, because she was very ill herself."[19] Marcella Marchetti added: "In Iride's heart there has always been Franco, so much that, in her last years, she asked me to meet Franco, to put her mind at rest before dying."[20] Said Gemma: "Maybe we live in a different way today, or maybe it could happen to us as well, to find a love that you will never forget. It wasn't like nowadays, when you take a man, you leave him, you take one again."[21]

1993–1994: A New Pupil

After three years of taking Andrea Bocelli's phone calls, Marco Corelli couldn't possibly refuse to meet him when he phoned again to say he was in Ancona. When they met, Marco was surprised to hear the Bocelli voice: "It was not big, but there was something in it, and he had been phoning me so often that I couldn't refuse to put him in touch with Franco any longer. They met, and Franco became his teacher."[22] Bocelli recalled that he studied for about two hours a day with his new maestro, following him from Milan to Cortina. Initially he tried to imitate Corelli, but eventually he came to understand that he had to develop his own style. When Bocelli's calendar began to fill up, thanks to his status as a pop star, he developed a relationship with his teacher that recalls Corelli's friendship with Lauri-Volpi: "About twice a month I check up on my voice with him. That is very important because you can't hear your own voice when you sing. . . . I hear my faults and know my weaknesses and those I can discuss with Franco. As a colleague, he knows what bothers me. That gives me peace of mind and confidence."[23] Corelli's advice was not limited to technique and musical values but stretched well into Bocelli's developing career, giving his young protégé more than fatherly advice on how to deal with stardom.[24]

Summer 1994: Back Home

In 1994 Corelli gave some master classes with an audience (in cooperation with Stefan Zucker), but Franco's comments there were not great revelations, as was to be expected: the main interest of a public master class is usually to hear the star sing a few demonstrative phrases from unusual repertoire himself. The true buff cherishes hearing him murmur the opening line of the "Lamento di Federico" from Cilea's *L'Arlesiana* or some phrases of the *Pagliacci* prologue.[25]

The final master class, on June 17, ended Franco's collaboration with Zucker and marked the beginning of a new path. Following the death of a close American friend, a doctor, he decided to move back to Italy, where his Via Crivelli apartment once more became his main residence.[26]

CHAPTER 23 ⬥ 1995–2000

Silent Years

September 2, 1997: The Death of Rudolf Bing

For a few years little was heard of or from Corelli, but when Rudolf Bing died on September 2, 1997, mourners had expected Corelli to come to the funeral to pay his respects. Perhaps that was not entirely fair, for he no longer lived in New York, although he maintained an apartment there. Furthermore, there seems to have been little or no contact between the two men after Corelli was dropped from the Met roster. Yet Corelli, like a number of his former colleagues, did pay tribute to the man who once wrote that one of the duties for which he was grossly underpaid was keeping Corelli happy.[1] Corelli told *Opera News*: "Sir Rudolf and I felt both admiration and affection for each other, and we worked together in an atmosphere of trust, knowing that our word was our bond. When I was ill, he would come to my bedside as a father would, and when I went back onstage, he was there to encourage me. I treasure his memory and will miss him always."[2]

Bing's more recent history was an unhappy one. He had lost his wife, Nina (a former Russian ballerina), in 1981. After writing his second biography (*A Knight at the Opera*, 1983), he gradually fell victim to Alzheimer's disease. The tragic result was his marriage to a woman who seems to have been essentially a gold digger and who managed to ruin him before the marriage was annulled by an American court on the grounds of his mental incompetence at the time of the marriage. In 1989 Teresa Stratas and Roberta Peters arranged for him to be placed in the Hebrew Home for the Aged in Riverdale, New York. He died alone and in deplorable personal and financial circumstances—a sad ending for a man who once seemed invincible, remembers Bing's former assistant, Paul Jaretzki, one of the few people who occasionally visited his former boss throughout their post-Met years.[3]

> December 18, 1997
> Celebration of Tenors with Franco Corelli
> Vienna, Austria Center

1997: A Tenor Gala

At a time when no one even speculated about a comeback for the seventy-six-year-old tenor, the Viennese impresario Thomas R. Danieli announced a Viennese "Celebration of Tenors with Franco Corelli," which was sold to the world as Franco Corelli's return to the stage. Advertisements boasted that he would sing no fewer than four Italian songs. Danieli gathered a handsome supporting act consisting of a local favorite, Peter Dvorsky (replaced at the last minute by his brother Miroslav); the veteran Nicolai Gedda; the Wagner tenor Peter Seiffert; and two red-hot newcomers, Vladimir Galouzine and José Cura.

Fans flew in from as far away as the United States, Australia, and Japan in order to witness the miracle, but when they arrived at the theater the program had become a concert not "with," but "for" Franco Corelli. Corelli's brief speech and his decoration by the Austrian Minister of Culture were clamorously applauded, but all cheers for a song were silenced by a modest gesture. When Gedda and Cura invitingly held up the score of Sieczynski's "Wien, du Stadt meiner Träume" during the unison finale, the old panther extended his claw in defense, roaring mutely, pale as a ghost, and terrified of facing a concert hall filled with expectant fans. When I interviewed him the next day, he came up with a solid explanation for his sudden indisposition: "My dog was not allowed in the airplane from Milan to Vienna, and so I had to take the train over the Alps. I arrived in Vienna a broken man. How could I possibly have sung under such circumstances?"[4]

1998–2000: *Concorso* "Franco Corelli"

In Italy Franco found himself at ease with friends such as Andrea Bucolier, the dentist Stocchi, Guido Ingaramo, Luigi Zoboli, and Mosé Franco, to name but a few. Closer now to his family and his Ancona roots, he developed a plan to do something beyond merely passing time and teaching in private, much in

> **May 25–31, 1998 (1999, 2000)**
> *Concorso* "Franco Corelli"
> **Voice competition**
> **Ancona, Lazaretto**

line with the final outcome of his collaboration with Zucker. If master classes weren't a success, then maybe a voice contest would serve.

With that thought he finally arrived back home in the land of vocal plenty. Although he had drifted far from it, Franco still loved Ancona deeply. The beauty, the coast, the memories of nights filled with discussions of *canto* all made it the logical place to host the contest. The city welcomed the idea, seeing an opportunity to do something with Corelli's fame in tourism. That suited Franco—and why not, if it helped opera and the art of bel canto to survive? He also felt there was a need, for he was not impressed by the current level of singing and study. Young singers faced little competition at a time where a mere handful of high notes sufficed to create careers that they would never have approached in the 1950s. Nevertheless, he saw light on the horizon, although it didn't come from under blue Italian skies: "In Asia, in Korea, I found the preparedness to study as we did. There they have the discipline and though perhaps they are not yet at the top level, they are rapidly improving. The first Korean opera stars are emerging, and perhaps, why not, the next Otello will be born in Seoul."[5]

The first Corelli Vocal Competition was held in the courtyard of the Lazaretto, a mere hundred yards from where Franco was born. In the middle was a small chapel illuminated by blue beams of light. Stepping out unexpectedly from the dark into the well-lit arch of the chapel, surrounded by smoke, Franco appeared as a peaceful muse belonging to a world of myth.[6] Unfortunately, the city reduced its financial support for the competitions of 1999 and 2000, in addition to which there were some problems with sponsors. So Corelli, not used to budget cuts and improvising, closed the door on the vocal competition that had borne his name.[7]

In between, on August 20, 1999, his sister Liliana died. Corelli then came up with a number of different plans, such as giving a Requiem Mass in Ancona's Duomo in honor of his mother and father. Said Marco Corelli: "We spoke to all the authorities and they responded most enthusiastically. No, he wasn't going to sing there, he would have invited some famous colleagues who were still active and then lend his name to the evening. He would have liked that. But as soon as we left, they forgot all about it. After a while, Franco realized that there was no real interest in organizing such an event."[8]

CHAPTER 24 ❖ 2001–2002

New Life, New Muse

2001: Hypochondriac

Once I hugged him before he went to sleep, saying "Goodnight, Maestro, I'll see you tomorrow," to which he responded: "I hope!"
    Luigi Zoboli, interview, Genoa, November 16, 2006

How many people live happily into old age without worry or pain? Certainly not Corelli. For one thing, he was a born hypochondriac. His faith in the wonders of the medical world was such that when his mind was troubled in his last few years, he even consulted a psychiatrist. He was visiting Luigi Zoboli in Genoa and asked him to accompany him to the consultation. Once there, it was Loretta who answered the questions until the doctor demanded that the patient answer them himself. He arrived at the point where Franco had to recall his own life. Franco responded with a narrative that spanned 1952 to 1965. He then fell silent. When the doctor asked why he didn't speak of the thirty-seven years after that, Franco said there was nothing to tell. The psychiatrist then told him that there are two kinds of people: normal people and actors: "You were an actor once; now you are no longer an actor and must appreciate your life." Loretta scoffed; she was not looking for true paramedical answers but for words that would make things easier for Franco at that stage of his life. Said Zoboli: "That was her principal occupation when he grew old and frail."[1]

October 10, 2002: The Reopening of the Teatro delle Muse

When Anconetans long ago accused Corelli of having deserted them without even the honor of singing for them in their hometown (preferring the surrounding cities of Fermo, Pesaro, and Macerata), Franco had answered that in order to sing he needed a certain ambience. The only place in Ancona that suited his needs was the Teatro delle Muse, and it had been under reconstruction for the entire span of his career, plus close to twenty more years thereafter.

When it finally reopened on October 10, 2002, sixty years after Allied bombs had shattered its auditorium, Franco Corelli was the guest of honor, assisting Mayor Fabio Sturani with the ribbon-cutting ceremony.

✦✦✦✦✦

As great as his happiness may have been over that long-overdue union between himself and the theater of his first operatic dreams was the sorrow with which the year ended when, on November 22, his brother Bibi died.

CHAPTER 25 ◆ 2003

Tu che a Dio spiegasti l'ali

February–October 2003: "Le mort, le pauvre mort"

By the end of January 2003, Franco wanted to write his last will and testament, and Luigi Zoboli, who had substituted his tenor dreams for a more secure life as a magistrate, provided him with the necessary documents. On February 1 Franco called him from Milan, saying he had a terrible situation at hand with Loretta:

> He accused her of having hidden his last will, because he couldn't find it anywhere. After I arrived from Genoa, things calmed down a little, and I took Loretta back with me. Once in Genoa, she suddenly wanted to return to Milan, and I couldn't take her because it was three or four in the morning and I had to get to work the next day. She took a taxi back and then, at seven or eight in the morning, she called me to say that Franco was sick and in the hospital. When I arrived in Milan I found Franco in the psychiatric ward, acting very strangely. He wore a red jacket and spoke with me in English, telling me strange things about Russian people in the hospital who wanted to kill him.[1]

While Corelli stayed in Milan's Ospedale Policlinico, Zoboli puzzled over the question of how his friend could have lost his mind overnight: "I can only explain the sudden change by thinking that when he was brought to the hospital, they used too much force on him, which made him lose his senses. He broke a window in the hospital when he arrived; two policeman had to control him."[2]

His friends and family decided that the Ospedale Policlinico was not the best place for Franco, so Milan-based relative Graziano Corelli arranged for him to be transferred to the Casa di Cura, La Betulle, in Lomazzo. There he stayed in relative tranquility until spring. On March 27 Bucolier and Zoboli were visiting him with their wives and children when Franco suddenly collapsed and fell to the ground. His friends called for assistance, and an ambulance drove Corelli to the Ospedale Maggiore in Parma, where it became clear that he had suffered a heart attack. When he had recovered enough to leave intensive care, he was sent for observation to Parma's Ospedale Clinica. A week later he was transferred to a rehabilitation facility, the Casa di Cura Villa Maria Luigia, in Monticelli.

Franco's condition prevented him from attending the Met Guild Luncheon in his honor on April 25, but Loretta did the best she could to save the occasion by going to New York on her own, aided by a student because she wasn't able to walk without crutches. With Zucker and some other friends to lend a hand, she used the occasion to clean out the West Fifty-seventh Street apartment (the other apartment, the studio on the seventeenth floor, had been emptied in April 2002).[3]

In the agreeable spring weather Franco seemed to recover a bit, although he was still suffering from dementia. Both Luigi Zoboli and Guido Ingaramo recall that he appeared to believe that he was living in the 1960s, telling them, "If I cannot sing the *Trovatore* tonight, you must sing for me!" He stayed in Monticelli until Loretta took him to a Milanese home for the elderly, much to the dismay of his friends, who thought he would have been better off at home. Said Zoboli: "I think that the only thing that mattered to him was returning to his home. When a person has Alzheimer's, it is important to have the reference

February 2–12, Ospedale Policlinico, Milan
February 12–15, Casa di Cura, La Betulle, Lomazzo (Como)
February 15–19, Ospedale Sant'Anna, Como
February 19–March 7, Casa di Cura, La Betulle, Lomazzo (Como)
March 7–10, Ospedale Valduce, Como
March 10–27, Casa di Cura, La Betulle, Lomazzo (Como)
March 27–28, Ospedale Maggiore, Parma
March 28–April 3, Ospedale Clinica di Parma, Parma
April 3–June 17, Casa di Cura Villa Maria Luigia, Monticelli
April 25, Metropolitan Opera Guild's Sixty-Eighth Annual
Luncheon, given in Corelli's honor (attended by Loretta)

of home. Guido, Bucolier, and I told Loretta many times that Franco had to come home. But Loretta told us no, because she was afraid that he would hurt her." Her fears were not unfounded; the couple had had heated confrontations in the past, and now Loretta was confined to a wheelchair and Franco was no longer in full possession of his faculties. His friends and Marco remained in doubt, however, with respect to the choice of hospitals, which they considered inferior. What irritated them most was that Franco thought that it was all because they had no more money. Bucolier hinted at it, Ingaramo looked at the floor when asked, Marco Corelli fulminated against it, and Zoboli said some words that can't be put into print. He did say that they were certainly not poor. Said Zoboli and Marco Corelli: "They were rich!"[4]

❖❖❖❖❖

If Corelli really had to live out his worst fears, ending life as a poor man, that is indeed sad. But why should one blame Loretta to the extent that some have for many things in Franco's life, especially toward the end? About Loretta, so many contradictory statements can be found that it may be wise to return to the beginning of their relationship. What could she, a well-established *comprimaria* of film fame, expect from a handsome nobody on contract for $85 per month? A lad who was merely learning to sing without straining his throat to the point of collapse? They had fifty-three more years behind them when he refused to let her prepare his lunch in La Betulle.[5] But by then he was no longer himself. Besides, Franco's temper was as explosive as his voice had once been, and he yelled at her at least as often as she yelled at him. And then, how easy was it to be the wife of Franco Corelli?

Donald DiGrazia, whose family had lost contact with the Corellis after a *Bohème* in 1973, analyzed Loretta's relationship with Franco as one in which he was loved while she was tolerated. She knew that, and because she didn't want to lose her husband to the world, she may have resorted to ever more cunning ways to keep him. She is said to have once threatened to follow in the footsteps of Maria Di Stefano, who, after her husband dumped her for Callas

> June 17–August 14, Casa di Riposo Anni Azzurri, Milan
> August 14–?, Ospedale Policlinico, Milan
> ?–October 29, Casa di Riposo Anni Azzurri, Milan

Luigi Zoboli, Franco Corelli, and Andrea Bucolier at Monticelli, June 1, 2003. (Photo: Courtesy of Luigi Zoboli)

and divorced her, had settled the score by writing a vengeful book. Still, Guido Ingaramo maintains that the world wouldn't have had the divo Corelli without Loretta, at least not to the same extent or for so many years. Franco's colleague and friend Enzo Sordello agreed: "Since she pushed him all the time to do things, sometimes Corelli lost a little control and shouted at her. But she always encouraged his career and helped him survive."[6] Giorgio Gualerzi adds that for better or for worse, Franco's stage fright would have made him give up his career much sooner without Loretta.[7] Finally, they stayed together for nineteen years after Franco's career had ended. Clearly, their lives were inextricably linked.

❖❖❖❖❖

By the time Zoboli, Bucolier, and Ingaramo were able to help Franco draw up a new will to replace the one he thought he had lost, he was no longer able to write. A test showed that he could barely sign his name, so Zoboli wrote the text of the will, in which he left all his worldly goods to Loretta. Franco signed it with trembling hands, after which all present in the room witnessed it. Because Franco had not written the text himself and there was no notary present when it was signed, this last will proved invalid. That doesn't change the fact that in the very end he still chose to leave all to his wife, for better or for worse.

❖❖❖❖❖

Whereas Zoboli had found signs of recognition in the simple gestures Franco was able to make, Graziano managed to communicate with his nephew through music. Once, when he was just about to enter Franco's room, Graziano heard him improvising faintly on the vowel "A":

> I told him that that night's performance had been canceled and that he might take a break, but he continued his attempts; I told him to try his thrillers on the vowel "O" instead, but he somehow managed to let me know that he couldn't accomplish it on that vowel. The next day he asked to speak with me, but I couldn't make out what he wanted to tell me. In order to find a way to communicate with him, I reminded him that he had once promised to teach me the opening section of the *Otello* love duet. It was very late; the night was well under way, but he managed to produce the "Già nella notte densa, s'estingue ogni clamor" quite audibly.

After that he even remembered "Ah si, ben mio" from *Trovatore* and "Mia madre" from *Fedora*, but he refused to answer the three riddles while introducing Graziano to Turandot. Graziano was touched and surprised: "Of course, he didn't sing those arias, but aided by the melodies that he knew so well, he managed to pronounce the words quite clearly, whereas speaking was now almost impossible for him."[8]

On August 14 Corelli developed complications and had to be hospitalized. When he emerged partially paralyzed, life had played its last cruel trick. A few days later he was transported back to the Anni Azzurri nursing home, where he died on October 29 at 7:35 P.M.

When Corelli's friends arrived to give him *l'ultimo bacio*, they found the greatest Poliuto, Raul, Manrico, Calaf, and Radamès of the post–World War II era reduced to skin and bones, a spent candle with no wax to spare for the flame that once illuminated operatic stages from New York to Milan. On November 5 Corelli was cremated. On November 27, with the cold setting in, the urn containing his remains was placed in a small tile-sized crypt in the Galleria di Ponente Inferiore, pilaster 3.

CHAPTER 26 ◆ 2004–2007

In Memoriam

With Franco gone, the question arose as to what to do with his earthly remains. According to the Corellis, it had been his wish to be brought back to his native Anconetan soil (Marco Corelli even produced a document, dated July 16, 2001, in which he reserved a place at Ancona's main cemetery on behalf of his cousin). Such matters were not in the hands of the family, however, and Loretta decided that Franco's ashes should rest in Milan. There is something to be said for both places. Milan is of course where he lived and where he scored his greatest artistic triumphs. On the other hand, he is but a star among stars in the Cimitero Monumentale, whereas he would be the most prominent person in Ancona's central cemetery.

If he were to rest in Ancona, the city also might have a better chance of doing something with his memory, which might actually spur its musical culture and tourism. Although the city refused to rename the Piazza della Repubblica the "Piazza Franco Corelli," the Teatro delle Muse has definitely honored him. To begin with, they organized a concert honoring him in June 2004, with Juan Diego Flórez substituting for Andrea Bocelli. Giuseppe Taddei was there as well, recalling past times. He stressed the fact that he and Corelli were both devotees of expressing the precise meanings of words in singing. With that, he proceeded to demonstrate just how opera singers sounded way back when Franco started out:

Oh refrigerio! . . . la marina brezza! . . .	How refreshing! . . . The sea breeze!
Il mare! . . . Il mare! . . . quale in rimirarlo	The sea! . . . The sea! . . . to see it again
Di glorie e di sublime rapimenti	Brings back memories of triumphs

Mi si affaccian ricordi!—Il mare! . . . Il mare! . . .	And glory! The sea . . . the sea! . . .
Perché in suo grembo non trovai la tomba?	Why didn't I find a grave in its bosom?

Giuseppe Verdi, *Simon Boccanegra*

From January 2006 until well into May, the Teatro delle Muse also featured an intriguing audiovisual exhibition with a number of hitherto unknown Corelli documents from RAI television broadcasts of the late 1950s and 1960s. In May a bronze bust was placed halfway up the stairs leading to the auditorium, while a large painting of Franco as Andrea Chénier graces the conference hall of the theater. That painting captures to perfection what Renata Tebaldi once said of her celebrated stage partner: "It was worth the price of a ticket just to see him make his entrance."[1]

❖❖❖❖❖

Countless times Renata had sworn to either die for him or follow him on his path to the creator, be it as Tosca, Leonora di Vargas, Adriana Lecouvreur, Maddalena di Coigny, La Gioconda, or Mimì. She finally joined Franco, Mario, and Maria on her own journey into the unknown when she died on December 19, 2004. She was buried in the family chapel at the Mattaleto cemetery in Langhirano. Tragically, another colleague, Giuseppe Di Stefano, was mobbed by violent thieves at his home in Diani, Kenya, on November 30, 2004. Ever since Birgit Nilsson was reunited with Wotan on December 25, 2006, the operatic world has treasured the tidbits of information on Di Stefano's health and the occasional surprise appearances at celebrations of Giulietta Simionato and Magda Olivero. (When I met Olivero on January 12, 2005, age ninety-two, she asked me to arrive in the evening, because she liked to go shopping during the daytime!) And let's not forget Gabriella Tucci either—when she opened the door for me on January 18, 2005, I thought it was her daughter standing there. Then, when I asked her about her former career, she said I was lucky to catch her at home because she had just returned from a Japanese concert tour.

❖❖❖❖❖

On October 30, 2007, the Teatro delle Muse was renamed the Teatro delle Muse "Franco Corelli." Graziano Corelli has established a series of superb annual commemorations, including the two consecutive memorials in Milan (in 2004 and 2005), and one in Verona (on October 28, 2006). The most recent commemoration was held in Milan on October 28, 2007, in the Casa di Risposo per Musicisti "Giuseppe Verdi." There Magda Olivero recalled her visit to Franco during the last months of his life.

These events also brought Loretta back into the picture, for it was she who had inherited Corelli's fortune and, more important, his artistic legacy. Loretta is confined to her wheelchair and cared for by relatives and nurses around the clock. Consequently, she has been unable to take charge of the remaining collection of costumes, memorabilia, thousands of photos, and performance and practice tapes. But, contrary to rumors that have circulated on the Internet for years characterizing Loretta as a hawk who either guarded or burned his recordings, she has proven to be most generous toward Graziano Corelli, allowing photos and sound documents to be used in the events he has organized in honor of her husband. This was most notable in 2006 and 2007, when, during the commemorations and in her presence, a selection of his home rehearsals for *Poliuto* and *Trovatore* were played. On the first occasion, Graziano also answered the question that had puzzled the many fans who wondered why the great tenor's remains were being kept in such an unworthy resting place, a mere twenty-five-inch square of tile in the out-of-the-way left wing of the cemetery. It turns out that this was intended as a temporary interment site until a more

Franco's final resting place in a corner of the Galleria di Ponente Inferiore, pilastro 3. (Photo: Author)

appropriate place in Milan's famous Cimitero Monumentale could be found and a proper tomb erected. That moment arrived in mid-2007 when a bronze bust of the tenor was placed in a corner of the same Galleria di Ponente Inferiore, pilaster 3; until then the memorial tile had been on the opposite wall.

Finally he had a fitting monument, although the place still looked a bit unfinished, as can be seen in the photos. At the time of this writing it is also in need of some repairs, but the bust depicting him as Manrico (after the famous Fayer photo from Vienna) is a beautiful piece of art, both modest enough to reflect the humble, private Dario Corelli and yet also revealing a glimpse of the colorful, public Franco.

Colorful is the word here; he was colorful throughout, in his shyness, his anger, his despair, and often his behavior. He was also mysterious in his silences, in his retreating, and even in the years spent largely before his television set.

Epilogue

Standing before Corelli's memorial sculpture, we are transported back in time to the proud and stubborn child in the office of his father's lawyer; to the man who made a pilgrimage to Lourdes in order to pray for a friend; to the handsome, vain tenor who traded constantly on his looks; and finally, to the insecure artist who was his own harshest critic even at the height of his career, when he was freezing out his competition. Yet despite all the details—informative, trivial, colorful—revealed here of Dario "Franco" Corelli's life and career, Corelli remains as enigmatic to me as he was when I began my research. Learning how the pyramids were built doesn't take away the mysterious nebula surrounding them.

What makes a voice so unforgettable in the ears of millions? Not technique alone, certainly, or there would be many Carusos, Corellis, and Pavarottis on today's opera stages. No accumulation of facts will ever be able to explain the mystery that allows great voices to communicate from one heart to another. Perhaps the voice truly is an expression of the soul.

Night after night, Corelli brought one character after another to life onstage, clothing them in vivid, visceral flesh and blood, while leaving the real and private Franco behind in the dressing room. Standing before Corelli's bust in the twilight, we can imagine him as Manrico, fighting again before those famous, flaming pyres. How many battles did he endure as Calaf, Cavaradossi, Johnson, Radamès, Roméo, Turiddu, Werther? Werther! It is 1957 again, Franco and Loretta are in the Cetra studios, and on the recording he responds once more to her cruel parting lines, "Dividerci dobbiam" (We must part):

Ah! Perché m'han guardato	Ah! Why did thy eyes grace mine,
Gli occhi tuoi sì bei,	Those eyes so beautiful,
Gli occhi pieni d'amor,	Those eyes so full of love,
Gli occhi vostri, o gentil,	Those eyes of yours, so gentle,

E m'hanno innamorato?	That I lost my heart in them?
Come ormai posso dormir?	How could I ever sleep again?
Son riapparse le stele e il sol,	The stars and the sun may take their turns
Posson nel curvo ciel	In heaven
Refulgenti brillare,	Brilliantly radiating
Se è notte io più non so	so I don't know if it is night
Ver che fiammeggi il dì	And I don't care if it is day
Chè solo pensar	The only thought
Può questo cor,	Of this heart,
Bell'angelo, a te!	Is of you, O beautiful angel!

Jules Massenet, *Werther*

In Cetra's recording of that solo section we hear the pure heart and soul of Franco Corelli at his best. The voice rich in shades of copper with gilded highlights, brilliant on top, burnished and baritonal on the bottom, warm, luscious, and *squillante*; the expression desperate, impassioned, and deeply moving.

But finally, when night brings darkness to the Cimetero Monumentale, and we think back to the legendary tenor live onstage, the very last things that can be heard of him are Raul de Nangis's immortal, heart-rending plea, "Dillo ancor, si, tu m'ami" (Tell me again that you love me), and Poliuto's heavenly harps:

PAOLINA AND POLIUTO

Il suon dell'arpe angeliche	The sound of the heavenly harps
d'intorno a me già sento!	I can hear from within!
La luce io veggo splendere	I can see the light
di cento soli e cento!	of a hundred suns!
Di me, non ho che l'anima,	Of myself, nothing but my soul remains,
già son del nume al piè!	as I am prostrated at God's feet.
Eternamente vivere	Heaven has granted me
m'è dato in ciel con te.	eternal life with you.

Gaetano Donizetti, *Poliuto*

Appendix: Short Corelli Family Tree

Corelli family legend traces their line back to the famous composer Arcangelo Corelli (1653–1713). This being impossible because Arcangelo remained childless, the only possible line of descent would be through one of Arcangelo's brothers: Domenico Corelli (1647–1719), Don Ippolito Corelli (1643–1727), or Giacinto Corelli (1649–1719). Currently a gap of three generations remains to be bridged, in order to establish if there is indeed a direct line from one of these men to Carlo Corelli (b. ca. 1790/1800), the first established ancestor of the tenor Dario "Franco" Corelli.

Carlo Corelli (b. ca. 1790/1800), married Gertrude (dates unknown)
    Child: **Luigi Corelli (1821–?), married Antonia Puliti (1825–?)**
        Children (four known of eight):
            *** Augusto Corelli (1858–1923)**
            Francesco Corelli (adopted, dates unknown)
            Carlo Corelli (dates unknown)
            Ugo Corelli (1880–1960)

....

***Augusto Corelli (1858–1923), married Leonilde Sbarbati (1864–1946)**
    Children:
        Corrado (I) Corelli (1882–1882)
        Beatrice Virginia Corinna Corelli (1884–1887)
        Corrado (II) Attilio Fernando Corelli (1886–1966)
        ***Remo Pilade Adriano Corelli (1887–1983)**
        Corinna Elvira Adelia Corelli (1889–1968)
        Rossilla Quartilla "Bice" Corelli (1891–1975)
        Viero Dario Aldo Corelli (1894–1987)
            Child: Marco Corelli (b. 1946)
        Dora Alma Vanda Corelli (1896–1953)

....

***Remo Pilade Adriano Corelli (1887–1983), married Natalina "Adria" Marchetti (1889–1950)**
    Children:
        Ubaldo "Bibi" Corelli (1914–2002), married Elisa Rinaldi (1914–?), divorced 1972 (no children); remarried Alberta "Roberta" Baiocchi (b. 1934)
            Child: Francesca Corelli (b. 1968)
        Liliana Corelli (1916–1999), married Carlo Morichi (b. 1911)
            Child: Marco Morichi (b. 1939)
        Dario "Franco" Corelli (1921–2003), married Anna Laura "Loretta" Di Lelio (b. 1918) (no children)

Notes

CHAPTER 1: 1921–1925
1. Interviews and correspondence with Marco Corelli, Ancona, July 2004.
2. All opera titles are capitalized in accordance with the Metropolitan Opera practice. Hence, *La Bohème* rather than *La bohème*.
3. Interviews and correspondence with Marco Corelli, Ancona, July 2004.
4. Ibid.
5. Ibid.
6. There has been an ongoing dispute over Corelli's birthdate for several reasons. The Metropolitan Opera has more than once given the birthdate as August 4, which is explained by the mistake of reading the European "08-04-1921" (April 8, 1921) in the American way, as August 4, 1921. Further confusion was created by the tenor himself, who persistently tried to hide his true age, shaving off anywhere from two to ten years at every opportunity. The original birth certificate, as well as his military records and marriage certificate, reproduced in part here, ends this dispute. It is unlikely that *all* such documents could have been falsified.
7. The first handwritten proof that Franco referred to himself as such is found in his correspondence with the Maggio Musicale, beginning in 1949 (see chapter 6, n. 3). For this biography I have chosen to refer to him as "Dario Franco" until halfway through 1939, when he turned eighteen. After that he is referred to simply as Franco.
8. Interviews and correspondence with Marco Corelli, Ancona, July 2004.
9. Ibid.
10. Ibid.

CHAPTER 2: 1926–1939
1. Franco Corelli, in "Sulla scena sono un leone, ma prima . . . che paura!," *Arianna*, February 1961; interviews with Marco Corelli, Ancona, July 2006.
2. Interviews and correspondence with Marco Corelli, Ancona, July 2004.
3. Interview with Marcella Marchetti, Ancona, August 22, 2004.
4. Corelli, "Sulla scena sono un leone." In order to have been injured by both the shower of shot and the recoil, Franco would have had to have had the end of the barrel close to his face when the gun went off. This would explain the irregular scars that can be seen above his left eyebrow, while the scar from the recoil is very visible high on the right side of his forehead.
5. Interviews and correspondence with Marco Corelli, Ancona, July 2004.
6. Joan Downs, *The Tenors* (New York: Macmillan, 1974).
7. Interview with Marco Corelli, Ancona, August 16–17, 2004.
8. Interview with Marcella Marchetti, Ancona, August 22, 2004.
9. Interviews and correspondence with Marco Corelli, Ancona, July 2004.
10. Interviews and correspondence with Marco Corelli, Ancona, July 2004.
11. Interview with Giampieri Lamberto, Ancona, August 22, 2004.
12. Interview with Marcella Marchetti, Ancona, August 22, 2004.
13. Ibid.
14. Interviews and correspondence with Marco Corelli, Ancona, July 2004; radio broadcast of Franco Corelli singing "Or son sei mesi," 1955.
15. Interviews and correspondence with Marco Corelli, Ancona, July 2004.
16. Ibid.

17. Interview with Marco Corelli, Ancona, June 11, 2004.
18. Interview with Giuliani Solari, June 10, 2004.
19. Corelli, "Sulla scena sono un leone."
20. Franco Corelli, "Sono il tenore più alto ma voglio diventare il più grande," *Oggi*, March 12, 1959. In the booklet to *Corelli in Concert*, released by the Bel Canto Society (Bel Canto Society, D0091), Stefan Zucker writes that Corelli started to perform in the Fascist Youth Movement, Balilla, but this bare statement attributes far too much weight to his Balilla activities. In the March 12, 1959, interview in *Oggi*, Corelli himself says: "Until 1946, I had never sung seriously, unless you count my singing 'Fischia il sasso' in the Balilla." The Balilla was not an organization, but a name that applied to any youth organization at the time. It wouldn't have been possible for him to be active in sports without singing "Fischia il sasso." Or, for that matter, the "Giovinezza" and other obligatory Fascist songs of the time, such as the "Inno al Duce." The last was the "Inno di Roma," renamed. It therefore may well have been Corelli's "first Puccini" after his childhood episode at the lawyer Tambroni's office (see section titled "1932–1938").
21. Corelli, "Sulla scena sono un leone"; correspondence with Marco Corelli, Ancona, 2007.
22. Correspondence with Marco Corelli, Ancona, July 2004. In the early 1980s Marco spoke about Franco's childhood with Traù and Giordano Giaccaglia.
23. Interview with Gemma Giacomini (Iride's daughter), Ancona, January 18, 2005.
24. Interview with Giuliano Giaccaglia, Ancona, August 21, 2004. In the booklet to *Corelli in Concert* (Bel Canto Society, D0091), Stefan Zucker writes that Corelli told him he actually performed from 1938 onward. Zucker believes that he later denied the early performances in order to hide a history of thirteen years of unsuccessful attempts at singing. Not a single one of his friends, who have been very open with regard to his private life, has supported this view. If Franco said he gave "concerts" before the war at age sixteen, he had to have been referring to the fact that he occasionally performed for his friends, such as on the occasion that Giaccaglia mentions here.
25. Interview with Marcella Marchetti, Ancona, August 22, 2004.
26. This "lisp," a very slight swallowing of certain vowels, and also especially on certain sibilants, can easily be heard in any of the extensive "Opera Fanatic" radio broadcasts of the 1990s. Correspondence with Marco Corelli, Ancona, July 2004.

CHAPTER 3: 1940–1945

1. This date is deduced on the basis of Corelli's recollection, during a February 3, 1990 "Opera Fanatic" broadcast (Bel Canto Society, CZ1V), of attending a performance at the Teatro delle Muse with Gobbi in the days before Franco himself had begun singing. Gobbi's only Teatro delle Muse performance during this period is the one mentioned here; Marco Salvarani, *Le Muse: Storia del teatro di Ancona* (Ancona, 2002).
2. Interview with Gemma Giacomini, Ancona, January 18, 2005.
3. Interview with Alessandro Grati, Ancona, August 21, 2004.
4. Interview with Giuliano Giaccaglia, Ancona, August 21, 2004.
5. Ibid.
6. Interviews with Alessandro Grati, Ancona, August 21, 2004, and January 15, 2005.
7. French radio interviews, [ca. 1970–74]: "I never sang when I was a child. I only started singing when I had reached the age of twenty-one or twenty-two."
8. Interview with Alessandro Grati, Ancona, August 21, 2004.
9. Ibid.; military records of Dario Corelli, Mantua/Ancona, 1941.
10. I asked Alessandro Grati on two different occasions whether this story of a swimming champ's being exempted from military service on the basis of something that hardly seemed to fit his physical profile was really true or whether someone in the family had paid to get Franco discharged, but Grati kept to his story. Apparently, though an athlete, Franco was not cut out to endure the rigors of army life, including the Mantuan winter conditions. Interview with Marco Corelli, August 16–17, 2004.
11. Franco Corelli, in "Sulla scena sono un leone, ma prima ... che paura!," *Arianna*, February 1961; interviews with Marco Corelli, Ancona, July 2006.

12. Interviews and correspondence with Marco Corelli, Ancona, July 2004.
13. As told by Gemma Giacomini, Ancona, January 18, 2005.
14. E-mail correspondence with Jan Neckers, April 7, 2007.
15. Interview with Gemma Giacomini, Ancona, January 18, 2005.
16. Interview with Alessandro Grati, Ancona, August 21, 2004.
17. Interview with Giulani Solari, Ancona, June 10, 2004.
18. Interview with Alberto Podesti, Ancona, August 21, 2004.
19. Corelli, "Sulla scena sono un leone."
20. Ibid.
21. Interview with Gemma Giacomini, Ancona, January 18, 2005.
22. Interview with Alberto Podesti, Ancona, August 21, 2004.
23. Carlo Scaravelli, "Private Recollections," unpublished manuscript [ca. mid-1960s–79].
24. Ibid.
25. Interviews with Marco Corelli, Ancona, July 2004.

CHAPTER 4: 1946–1949

1. Interview with Gemma Giacomini, Ancona, January 18, 2005.
2. Interview with Gemma Giacomini, Ancona, January 18, 2005.
3. Interview with Marcella Marchetti, Ancona, August 22, 2004.
4. According to Gemma Giacomini, Iride never got over the separation: "Even though she married a few years later, she would think of Franco until the very end, perhaps also because his later fame meant she was often confronted with his image in newspapers and magazines. This bothered me for a long time, because I was very close to my father, and though my mother's affection for Franco didn't bother him, I could get enraged when I came across a picture of Franco in a magazine." Interview with Gemma Giacomini, Ancona, January 18, 2005.
5. Interview with Romolo Ricci, Ancona, August 21, 2004.
6. Interview with Marco Corelli, August 16–17, 2004.
7. Interview with Jan Neckers, Keerbergen, April 7, 2007.
8. Antonio Brancati, *I centodieci anni del Liceo Musicale Rossini (1882–1992), oggi Conservatorio in Pesaro* (Pesaro: Conservatorio di Musica "G. Rossini," 1992); letter, Marco Giannotti [director, Pesaro Conservatory], May 6, 2006.
9. Carlo Scaravelli, "Private Recollections"; letter, Marco Giannotti [director, Pesaro Conservatory], May 6, 2006.
10. Letter, Marco Giannotti, May 6, 2006.
11. French radio interviews, [ca. 1970–74].
12. "Opera Fanatic" broadcast, May 25, 1993 (Bel Canto Society, CZ10V).
13. Scaravelli, "Private Recollections."
14. French radio interviews, [ca. 1970–74]; "Opera Fanatic" broadcast, May 25, 1993 (Bel Canto Society, CZ10V). In the booklet to *Corelli in Concert* (Bel Canto Society, D0091), Stefan Zucker writes that Corelli told him on October 23, 2000, that he developed problems with his high notes due to an addiction to *pompino Bolognese*, which translates into oral sex Bolognese style. I feel that a discussion of sex and singing is legitimate. Moreover, with a man as popular with all the wrong girls as Franco was in the pre–birth control era, I am even inclined to believe the story about this alleged "addiction." However, to accept the suggestion that the loss of the tenor's top notes was due to this "overdose" rather than to singing with the wrong technique for his voice, I would have to hear it from Franco's own lips. Corelli liked a good joke, as can be heard in about any one of the eleven "Opera Fanatic" radio interviews that were broadcast between 1990 and 1994.
15. French radio interviews, [ca. 1970–74].
16. Interview with Alberto Podesti, Ancona, August 21, 2004; interview with Gemma Giacomini, Ancona, January 18, 2005.
17. Claudia Gentile, "Cantò da solo nelle Muse disastrate," *Il Messaggero*, November 5, 2003; interview with Marco Corelli, Ancona, June 11, 2004.

18. Interview with Marcella Marchetti, Ancona, August 22, 2004.
19. Interview with Giulani Solari, Ancona, June 10, 2004.
20. "He Spoke about Memories and Projects—Among the Ritual Stops, the Dom and Café Rico," unidentified newspaper [ca. 1988–90]. The family's reference to Bibi's early EIAR appearances may pertain to this period, where his name actually features in the EIAR chronology. His first appearance there was as a Maggiordomo in Pick Mangialli's *Notturno Romantico* (November 20, 1948), followed by Nicola in Umberto Giordano's *Fedora* (July 17, 1949); Gabriotto and the Maggiordomo in Vitorio Gui's *La Fata Malerba* (November 16, 1949); and finally, Uberto in Arrigo Pedrollo's *Primavera Fiorentina* (November 30, 1949). See Giorgio Gualerzi and Carlo Marinelli Roscioni, *50 anni di opera lirica alla RAI, 1931–1980* (Torino: ERI/Edizione RAI, 1981).
21. Interview with Alessandro Scaravelli, Ancona, June 11, 2004.
22. Interview with Marco Corelli, Ancona, August 16–17, 2004.
23. "He Spoke about Memories."
24. Interview with Alessandro Scaravelli, Ancona, June 11, 2004.
25. Franco regularly claimed that they went by train, but Davide Barbone, who told us this story himself, maintains that they went by car, as described here, perhaps because driving was cheaper than having to pay train and hotel fares for all. Telephone interview with Davide Barbone, January 30, 2007.
26. Franco Corelli, in "Sulla scena sono un leone, ma prima . . . che paura!," *Arianna*, February 1961.
27. Telephone interview with Davide Barbone, January 30, 2007.
28. French radio interviews, [ca. 1970–74]. With regard to identifying what Corelli actually sang, he recalls the arias and song differently on different occasions. The "Celeste Aida" is mentioned as early as 1961 in an interview with *Arianna*. In *Gente* Franco mentioned auditioning with "La strada del bosco" in Florence (see Renzo Allegri, "Ecco com'é nata la storia del mio flirt con Tebaldi," *Gente*, August 1972). He actually hummed the opening lines of "La strada del bosco" in an "Opera Fanatic" radio appearance of July 27, 1990, saying that it was the first song he had truly learned. "Giunto sul passo estremo" is mentioned in a French radio interview that dates back to the early 1970s, and he repeated his remark about choosing it for the low high notes in his interview sequence on the "Opera Fanatic" broadcast of May 25, 1991. My reconstruction follows these recollections, which were then combined with those of Davide Barbone, those of Franco as told to Marco Corelli, and those of Carlo Scaravelli as told to his son Alessandro. Finally, the insertion of the contest here, in February 1949, is based on the correspondence between Franco and Francesco Siciliani and Pariso Votto of the Maggio Musicale, made available to me in July and September 2007. In his first, undated letter of 1949, Corelli inquired after the beginning of the courses in 1949, which means that the events described in this chapter must have preceded it.
29. French radio interviews, [ca. 1970–74].
30. Scaravelli, "Private Recollections."
31. Interview with Robleto Merolla [Melocchi's last pupil], Pesaro, August 18–19, 2004.
32. Scaravelli, "Private Recollections"; Franco Corelli, "Opera Fanatic" broadcasts, February 3, 1990 (Bel Canto Society, CZ1V), and May 25, 1991; interview with Alessandro Scaravelli, Ancona, June 11, 2004; interviews with Marco Corelli, Ancona, July 2004.
33. Scaravelli, "Private Recollections."
34. Ibid.; interview with Alessandro Scaravelli, June 11, 2004; interviews with Marco Corelli, July 2004.
35. Correspondence with Moreno Bucci [archivist, Maggio Musicale], July 6, 2007.
36. Ibid.

CHAPTER 5: 1950

1. Correspondence with Moreno Bucci (archivist, Maggio Musicale), July 6, 2007.
2. Interview with Marco Corelli, Ancona, January 17, 2005.
3. Third French radio interview, [ca. 1970–74].

4. Franco Corelli, in "Sulla scena sono un leone, ma prima . . . che paura!," *Arianna*, February 1961.
5. Interview with Alberto Podesti, Ancona, August 21, 2004. From Gigli's (alleged) remark with respect to Franco's studies, we can assume that at this point he had not abandoned them altogether, although there is certainly room for speculation on this matter.
6. Letter, Corelli to Francesco Siciliani, January 28, 1950.
7. Interview with Marco Corelli, Ancona, January 17, 2005.
8. Interview with Mario Panzini, who acquired the recordings in the early 1970s, when Corelli discussed them with him. Corelli fumed, saying they weren't worth keeping, and even broke the disc of the "Recondita armonia" over his knees. When he began to do the same with the next disc, Panzini stepped in and snatched the recordings out of Corelli's hands. He told Corelli that if he didn't have any need for them, then he might as well give them to him, Panzini, for he valued them as the tenor's friend and admirer.
9. Letter, Corelli to Francesco Siciliani, November 27, 1950.
10. Correspondence with Moreno Bucci [archivist, Maggio Musicale], July 6, 2007.

CHAPTER 6: 1951

1. According to Marco Corelli, the fever caused by this exceptionally late case of the mumps was eventually judged to be the cause of his infertility. Franco loved children, and his childlessness caused him pain, but he was philosophical and very open about the subject among relatives, to whom he used to say, "When God gives you one thing, he takes away something as well, for balance."
2. Interview with Marco Corelli, Ancona, January 17, 2005.
3. That Dario/Franco was called "Franco" on a regular basis before he debuted is clear from his 1949–50 correspondence with Francesco Siciliani and Pariso Votto of the Maggio Musicale, letters that are always signed "Franco Corelli." The first known press mention of Corelli is in *Il Messaggero*, dated January 7, 1951, in an article listing "Franco Corelli" among the graduates of the Lirico Sperimentale.
4. Internal Spoleto interview with Franco Corelli, Spoleto, July 13, 1996.
5. Ibid.
6. Interview with Anita Cerquetti, Rome, January 14, 2005.
7. Internal Spoleto interview with Franco Corelli, Spoleto, July 13, 1996.
8. Interview with Anita Cerquetti, Rome, January 14, 2005.
9. Luigi Ricci was a vocal coach of the soprano Magda Olivero and had collaborated directly with Puccini.
10. Interview with Anita Cerquetti, Rome, January 25, 2005.
11. "Le 'promesse' prescelte," *La Nazione*, March 1951; French radio interviews, [ca. 1970–74].
12. Interview with Marco Corelli, Ancona, January 28–30, 2007.
13. French radio interviews, [ca. 1970–74].
14. Internal Spoleto interview with Franco Corelli, Spoleto, July 13, 1996.
15. Interview with Anita Cerquetti, Rome, January 25, 2005.
16. Lucia Danieli's voice has been preserved in the role of Suzuki in a studio recording of *Madama Butterfly* with Maria Callas as Butterfly, conducted by Herbert von Karajan (2-CD set, EMI 7479598,). In 2007 TIMAClub released a recital CD with a booklet that contains biographical info, a chronology, and a discography (Clama ML-52).
17. "Inviati speciali e critici d'arte," *Il Tempo*, August 28, 1951.
18. "Una Micaela che raramente ho incontrato nella mia carriera," *L'Unita*, August 29, 1951.
19. "Inviati speciali e critici d'arte," *Il Tempo*.
20. "Allo Sperimentale inaugurata la stagione," *Il Momento*, August 26, 1951.
21. "Inviati speciali e critici d'arte," *Il Tempo*.
22. In the booklet to the DVD *Corelli in Concert* (Bel Canto Society, D0091), Stefan Zucker writes: "Franco recalled on the radio program 'La barcaccia,' on RAI in Italy, how in 1951 he baby-sat me in Spoleto, where my mother was rehearsing, as was he. (In rehearsal she was Elvira, he a

substitute Ottavio.)." Corelli performed a number of operatic roles in the years following his debut, so he could have been a cover for just about anything at that time, but given the stress he felt over it, it is hardly likely that he would have been inclined to take on another role before his Spoleto or Rome debut. Furthermore, *Don Giovanni* was not performed at the Teatro Nuovo until the 1990s. In a telephone conversation with Zucker, he said that they rehearsed *Don Giovanni* in Spoleto, but the performance might have been in a small theater in Rome (and without Franco, who participated only as a cover).

23. "*Carmen* a Spoleto prima 'Sperimentale,'" *Il Messaggero*, August 27, 1951.
24. "*Carmen* trionfo al Nuovo," *L'Unita*, August 28, 1951. Andreotti served seven terms as prime minister before he was convicted by an Italian tribunal for his ties with the Mafia.
25. "Inviati speciali e critici d'arte," *Il Tempo*.
26. Ibid.
27. Ibid.
28. "Felice inaugurazione del Teatro Sperimentale," *Il Popolo*, August 1951.
29. "*Carmen* trionfo al Nuovo," *L'Unita*, August 28, 1951.
30. "Inviati speciali e critici d'arte," *Il Tempo*.
31. "Ieri a Spoleto successo della *Carmen*," *Il Momento*, August 28, 1951.
32. "Inviati speciali e critici d'arte," *Il Tempo*.
33. "Un nuovo grande successo per la seconda della *Carmen* di Bizet," *Il Messaggero*, August 31, 1951.
34. "Il compiacimento dell'On. Andreotti agli interpreti della terza della *Carmen*," *Il Messaggero*, September 9, 1951.
35. Interview with Marco Corelli, Ancona, June 11, 2004.

CHAPTER 7: 1952–1954

1. Enrico Fondi, "*Giulietta e Romeo* di Zandonai," *Il Paese*, February 1, 1952.
2. Alfredo Mandelli, "Convince a metà la Carmen di vita," *Oggi Illustrato*, July 12, 1975.
3. Ibid. The voice of Mercedes Fortunati was captured for posterity only in a live recording of Ildebrando Pizzetti's *Fedra*. The recording can be found on CD (2-CD set, Opera d'Oro, 1421).
4. Ennio Melchiorre, "*Giulietta e Romeo* all'Opera," *Avanti*, February 1952.
5. "*Giulietta e Romeo* di R. Zandonai al Teatro dell'Opera," *L'Osservatore Romano*, February 2, 1952.
6. Fondi, "*Giuliette e Romeo* di Zandonai."
7. Franco De Luca, "*Giulietta e Romeo*," *Giustizia*, February 1952.
8. V. S., "*Giulietta e Romeo* al Teatro dell'Opera," *Il Globo*, February 2, 1952.
9. G. Pan, "*Giulietta e Romeo* al Teatro dell'Opera," *Il Tempo*, February 1, 1952.
10. Fondi, "*Giulietta e Romeo* di Zandonai."
11. F. L. Lunghi, "*Giulietta e Romeo* all'Opera," *Il Giornale d'Italia*, February 2, 1952.
12. Melchiorre, "*Giulietta e Romeo* all'Opera."
13. "*Giulietta e Romeo* di R. Zandonai al Teatro dell'Opera," *L'Osservatore Romano*.
14. Interviews with Marco Corelli, Ancona, July 2004.
15. Interview with Loretta Corelli, January 26, 2007.
16. Interviews with Marco Corelli, Ancona, July 2004.
17. "Opera Fanatic" broadcast, February 3, 1990 (Bel Canto Society, CZ1V).
18. Ibid.
19. Franco Corelli, in "Sulla scena sono un leone, ma prima . . . che paura!," *Arianna*, February 1961.
20. Loretta's alleged problems with these facts are well documented and can readily be found online. The talk-show host Stefan Zucker wrote in the booklet for his DVD *Corelli in Concert* (Bel Canto Society, D0091) that she boasted about having obtained false birth documents.
21. Birth certificate, Loretta Di Lelio.
22. According to her birth certificate and her and Corelli's marriage certificate.
23. The films featuring Di Lelio in minor parts were released on the Bel Canto Society label. *L'Elisir d'amore* can be found on DVD (Bel Canto Society, 684) and *Lucia di Lammermoor* on VHS

(Bel Canto Society, 682S). In 1954 she sang Flora in a film version of *La Traviata*, which can be found on VHS (Bel Canto Society, 551).
24. Conversations with Luigi Zoboli, Graziano Corelli, and Marco Corelli, Genoa, Milan, and Ancona, July 2004, October 2006, and January 2007.
25. Interview with Loretta Corelli, January 26, 2007.
26. Marco Corelli maintains that they had never heard of Loretta until Franco introduced her to them during his performances in Pesaro in 1956.
27. Interview with Loretta Corelli, Milan, January 7, 2006. A biography is not the place to create saints or sinners. Much has been said in the press and on Internet forums about Loretta's character and her alleged obsession with keeping their personal relationship out from the public eye. Yet, when I interviewed her in 2004 and 2007, she spoke freely about their private life and acknowledged her role in his career right from the beginning.
28. Corelli, "Sulla scena sono un leone."
29. Based on the 1953 *Carmen* reviews from Rome.
30. "Opera Fanatic" broadcast, May 7, 1994.
31. *La voce republicana*, April 29, 1953.
32. V. T., "*Carmen* al Castello," unidentified newspaper, August 1, 1952.
33. Interview with Franco Corelli, Vienna, December 19, 1997.
34. Telephone interview with Giulietta Simionato, April 25, 2007.
35. "Opera Fanatic" broadcast, February 3, 1990 (Bel Canto Society, CZ1V).
36. Contracts between Franco Corelli and the Teatro dell'Opera, April 26, 1952, and July 24, 1952.
37. Letter, Roberto Bauer to Rudolf Bing, December 25, 1954.
38. Bing was indeed Austrian, but he was also Jewish, so at least he did not have to contend with accusations of Nazi collaboration, as some other conductors did when trying to break into the U.S. and British musical culture.
39. Rudolf Bing, *5000 Nights at the Opera* (New York: Doubleday, 1972).
40. Roberto Bauer, *Historical Records* (London: Sidgewick & Jackson, 1947).
41. Ilsa Elisa Zellermayer, *Drei Tenöre und ein Sopran* (Berlin: Henschel, 2000).
42. Bing, *5000 Nights*.
43. Corelli, "Sulla scena sono un leone." In the article the year mentioned is 1953, but Gabriella Tucci confirms and Metropolitan Opera records conclusively prove that it was 1952.
44. Interview with Gabriella Tucci, Rome, January 18, 2005.
45. Corelli, "Sulla scena sono un leone."
46. Carlo Scaravelli, "Private Recollections."
47. According to Alexei Buljigin, *Prins v stranj Tjudes* (Moscow: Agraf, 2003).
48. Corelli, "Sulla scena sono un leone."
49. S. C., "Cronache d'arte," *L'Osservatore Romano*, December 16, 1952.
50. G. Sciacca, "*Boris Godunov* all'Opera," *Il Quotidiano*, December 16, 1952.
51. Enrico Fondi, "*Boris Godunov*," *Il Paese*, December 15, 1952.
52. Ibid.
53. The GOP CD release gives February 23, 1952, as the recording date. Referring to the original LP release on HOPE 220, Alan Blyth mentions October 22, 1955, in the discography of the authorized biography by Atanas Bozhkoff, *Boris Christoff* (London: Robson Books, 1991). The earlier date is accepted here because it is confirmed in the memoirs of Rodzinski's wife, Halina (*Our Two Lives* [New York: Scribners, 1976]).
54. Gino Scaglia, "Roma, marzo . . .", *L'Ora del Popolo*, March 18, 1953; Ennio Melchiorre, "*Enea* di Guido Guerrini," *Avanti!*, March 12, 1953.
55. G. Pan, "*Enea* all'Opera," *Il Tempo*, March 12, 1953.
56. Melchiorre, "*Enea* di Guido Guerrini."
57. Scaglia, "Roma, marzo . . .", *L'Ora del Popolo*.
58. Ibid.; Melchiorre, "*Enea* di Guido Guerrini"; G. Pan, "*Enea* all'Opera"; and Giorgio Vigolo, "I gendarmi Virgiliani," *Il Mondo*, March 25, 1953.
59. Franco De Luca, "Successo all'opera dell'Enea di Guerrini," *Popolo di Roma*, March 12, 1953.

60. Telephone interviews with Antonietta Stella and Gian Giacomo Guelfi, both on May 25, 2006.
61. At the time of writing this recording was still unreleased. It features Mario Petri (*Enea*), Alfredo Mattioli (*Julo*), Floriana Cavalli (*Creusa, Didone, Lavinia*), Dora Minarchi (*the Sybil of Cuma*), and Renato Gavarini (*Turno*), cond. Arturo La Rosa Parodi.
62. Vigolo, "I gendarmi Virgiliani."
63. Giorgio Vigolo, "Passioni sfortunate," *Il Mondo*, April 22, 1953.
64. "*Norma* al Teatro dell'Opera," *Paese Sera*, April 10, 1953.
65. L. F. Lunghi, "*Norma* all'Opera," *Giornale d'Italia*, April 11, 1953.
66. Nino Piccinelli, "L'ultima sacerdotessa che infranse in voto travolta dall'amore," *Momento Sera*, April 10, 1953.
67. G. Pan, "*Norma* all'Opera," *Il Tempo*, April 10, 1953.
68. Vigolo, "Passioni sfortunate," *Il Mondo*, April 22, 1953.
69. A. P., "*Norma* all'Opera," *Il Globo*, April 10, 1953.
70. "*Norma* al Teatro dell'Opera," *Paese Sera*, April 10, 1953.
71. G. Pan, "*Norma* all'Opera."
72. Vigolo, "Passioni sfortunate."
73. "Opera Fanatic" broadcast, May 25, 1993 (Bel Canto Society, CZ10V); "Opera Fanatic" broadcast, May 7, 1994.
74. Vigolo, "Passioni sfortunate."
75. Sigrid Neef, *War and Peace at the Bolshoï Theatre*, booklet (3-CD set, Melodiya, 74321 29350 2, 1995); Sergio Sablich, "*Guerra e pace*," booklet (2-LP set, Fonit Cetra, DOC 77, 1986).
76. Rodzinski, *Our Two Lives*.
77. Ibid.
78. Ibid.
79. "Beniamino Gigli non canterà più a Spoleto," *Attualità*, September 1953.
80. M., "Il caso Gigli-Spoleto," *Corriere del Teatro*, September 8, 1953.
81. "Opera Fanatic" broadcast, February 3, 1990 (Bel Canto Society, CZ1V).
82. "Successo delle prime," *Giornale d'Italia*, September 8, 1953.
83. Buljigin, *Prins v stranj Tjudes*.
84. Mila Contini, in "Timido ma bello il fusto della lirica," *Amica*, July 29, 1962.
85. Elena Nicolai, *La mia vita fra i grandi del melodramma* (Parma: Editore Azzali, 1993).
86. Sol, "Festoso inaugurazione della stagione lirica," *Messaggero Veneto*, November 20, 1953.
87. Milan Petkov, "Maria Callas in Trieste," booklet, *Norma* (Divina Records, DV-3, 2000).
88. Lanfranco Rasponi, *The Last Prima Donnas* (New York: Limelight Editions, 1985).
89. Rodzinski, *Our Two Lives*.
90. Ibid.
91. Archipel Records released the same recording on CD (ARPCD 0130) with the missing portions inserted from different *Carmen* performances. It also contains two different cast lists and inaccurate location and date information on the insert.
92. "Gli spettacoli al 'S. Carlo,'" *A Napoli, Musica e Dischi*, date unknown.
93. Ibid.
94. G. Sciacca, "*Romulus* di S. Allegra," *Il Quotidiano*, January 29, 1954. Salvatore Allegra's *Romulus* received its world premiere in August 1952 at the Teatro Mediterraneo of Naples, followed by performances in Bari in January 1954.
95. G. Pan, "*Romulus* all'Opera," *Il Tempo*, January 19, 1954.
96. Sciacca, "*Romulus* di S. Allegra."
97. G. A. Canu, "*Romulus* di Salvatore Allegra," *Il Secolo*, January 29, 1954.
98. To date, the RAI *Romulus* recording of October 23, 1962, has never been released. It features Piero Cappuccilli (*Romolo*), Luigi Infantino (*Remo*), Anna Maria Frati (*Flora*), Paola Mantovani (*Tarpeja*), and Germana Paolieri (*Rea Silvia*), cond. Salvatore Allegra.
99. "*Romulus* di S. Allegra."
100. G. A. Canu, "Al Teatro dell'Opera *Don Carlo*," *Il Secolo*, March 6, 1954.

101. I. F. I., "Le prime all'opera *Don Carlo*," *D'Italia*, March 1954.
102. L. P., "*Don Carlo* all'Opera," *Il Paese*, March 5, 1954.
103. Vice, "*Don Carlo* all'Opera," *Paese Sera*, March 6, 1954. This can be observed in a few moments in the rendering of the Flower Aria from the 1953 live recording of *Carmen* (2-CD set, Archipel Records, ARPCD 0130; 2-LP set, Edizione Lirica, EL001-2), as well as in his earliest "Celeste Aida," from Naples, November 2, in 1955 (2-CD set, The Golden Age of Opera, GAO 116/17).
104. G. Sciacca, "All'Opera *Don Carlo*," *Il Quotidiano*, March 5, 1954.
105. "Opera Fanatic" broadcast, May 23, 1993 (Bel Canto Society, CZ10V).
106. Canu, "Al Teatro dell'Opera *Don Carlo*."
107. I. F. I., "La prime all'opera *Don Carlo*."
108. R. R., "*Don Carlo*," *Il Messaggero*, March 5, 1954.
109. Emme, "*Don Carlo* all'Opera," *Avanti!*, March 5, 1954
110. I. F. I., "La prime all'opera *Don Carlo*"; Canu, "Al Teatro dell'Opera *Don Carlo*"; Sciacca, "All'Opera *Don Carlo*."
111. S. C., "Cronache d'arte," *L'Osservatore Romano*, April 19, 1954.
112. P. Dl., "*Ifigenia in Aulide*," *Paese Sera*, April 20, 1954.
113. Nino Piccinelli, "Con il mito di *Ifigenia* Gluck volle rivelare la verità drammatica," *Momento Sera*, April 10, 1954.
114. F. L. Lunghi, "*Ifigenia* di Gluck all'Opera," *Giornale d'Italia*, April 18, 1954; Emme, "*Ifigenia in Aulide*," *Avanti!*, April 18, 1954; S. C., "Cronache d'arte."
115. "Opera Fanatic" broadcast, May 25, 1991.
116. Ibid.
117. Giorgio Vigolo, "Ifigenia in scatola," *Il Mondo*, April 27, 1959.
118. Giovanni Carli Ballola, "La grande révolution de La Vestale," in *"La Vestale" di Gaspare Spontini* (Milan: Teatro alla Scala, 1993).
119. Alfred Loewenberg, *Annals of Opera, 1597–1940* (London: John Calder, 1978).
120. Letter, Roberto Bauer to Rudolf Bing, May 24, 1954.
121. Ibid.
122. Ibid.
123. Letter, Roberto Bauer to Rudolf Bing, December 25, 1954.
124. A compilation of Fernando De Lucia's best recordings from 1902 to 1920, where the vibrato is apparent throughout, can be found on *Fernando De Lucia* (2-CD set, Bongiovanni, GB 1064/65-2).
125. Telephone interview with Giancarlo Del Monaco, August 24, 2005.
126. "Opera Fanatic" broadcast, February 3, 1990 (Bel Canto Society, CZ1V). The three earlier live recordings of *Guerra e pace*, *Carmen*, and *Agnese di Hohenstaufen* played no part in the matter at the time because they were not released until the 1970s, although *Guerra e pace* may have been a radio broadcast.
127. Corelli, in Jerome Hines, *Great Singers on Great Singing* (London: Victor Gollancz, 1983). The "physical force" mentioned by Corelli is put in perspective by his colleague Enzo Sordello, who performed with Corelli from December 1954 onward. Sordello recalled some experiments with Corelli himself: "Corelli's pronounced vibrato caused him stress on his diaphragm and he told me once that whenever he sang, the day after he couldn't walk even a hundred meters." Telephone interview with Enzo Sordello, October 14, 2006.
128. Interview with Arrigo Michelini, Modena, May 20, 2007.
129. Corelli, "Sulla scena sono un leone."
130. Ibid.
131. John Ardoin and Gerald Fitzgerald, *Callas* (London: Thames & Hudson, 1974).
132. Alberto Sinigaglia, "Intervista con Franco Corelli," in *Omaggio a Franco Corelli* (Milan: Teatro alla Scala, 2001); Franco Corelli, as told to G. Fogliani, "Sto per conquistare Broadway," *Eva*, October 15, 1964.
133. Sinigaglia, "Intervista con Franco Corelli."

134. Ibid.
135. Ardoin and Fitzgerald, *Callas.*
136. Ibid.
137. Ibid.
138. Arianna Stassinopoulos, *Maria Callas* (London: Weidenfeld & Nicolson, 1980.)
139. Freely drawing on Stassinopoulos, David Bret, in his more sensational *Maria Callas: The Tigress and the Lamb* (London: Robson Books, 1997), writes that after Visconti, Callas fell so in love with Bernstein that she became "putty in his hands. Her naivety for the time being would not allow her to recognize the fact that like Visconti, Bernstein too was homosexual, and that when he came to her apartment with friends such as the handsome tenor, Franco Corelli, there was much about life she had yet to learn." At a time where the only things known about Corelli were what was mentioned in his first biography (Marina Boagno and Gilberto Starone, *Un uomo, una voce* [Parma: Azzali Editore, 1990]; published in English as *Corelli: A Man, a Voice* [Dallas, Tex.: Baskerville, 1996]), in which Corelli is apparently born at thirty years of age, remains unmarried, and never meets any women; such imaginative statements, rife with innuendo, inevitably led to rumors among the emerging Internet community. Some members of the gay community eagerly claimed Corelli as one of their own; others may actually have confused him with the Colt label's early 1980s gay adult-film star of the same name (see http://www.francocorelli.com). Today, when so much of Corelli's childhood and his earlier and later relationships have been uncovered, discussion of this nonissue should end. Says Marco Corelli: "If he had been gay, I wouldn't have had a problem with it. But for forty years I talked with him, and only of women, never of men. Naturally, as women went crazy for him when he came on the stage, it also happened that men fell in love with him. Then, some of us have a psychology that wants the object of affection to become a member of the same group, in this case the homosexual camp. But Franco adored women; look at how he embraces them in his duets that have been preserved on film." Interview with Marco Corelli, Ancona, August 16, 2004.
140. Ardoin and Fitzgerald, *Callas.*
141. Contini, in "Timido ma bello"; Sinigaglia, "Intervista con Franco Corelli."
142. Bruno Slawitz, "L'inizio delle stagioni litiche in Italia, *Vestale, Elisir, David* e *Chénier* alla Scala," *Musica e Dischi*, date unknown; Franco Abbiati, "La *Vestale* di Spontini," *Corriere della Sera*, December 7, 1954; Mario Pasi, *Maria Callas: La donna, la voce, la diva* (Milan: I.M.I. Edizioni, 1981); Bardolfo [Eugenio Gara], "*La Vestale* nel fuoco e nell'arte," *Candido*, no. 51, 1954.
143. Letter, Roberto Bauer to Rudolf Bing, December 25, 1954.
144. Ibid.

CHAPTER 8: 1955–1957

1. V. T., "*La Fanciulla del West* accolta con grande successo," *Il Piccolo*, January 12, 1955.
2. Interviews with Marco Corelli, Ancona, July 2006.
3. Letter, Rudolf Bing to Roberto Bauer, March 4, 1955.
4. Letter, Roberto Bauer to Rudolf Bing, April 5, 1955.
5. *Diario de noticias*, April 30, 1955; *O Seculo*, April 30, 1955.
6. "Cronache Veronesi," *Il Gazzettino* (Venice), July 31, 1955, as quoted in Marina Boagno and Gilberto Starone, *Un uomo, una voce* (Parma: Azzali Editore, 1990); published in English as *Corelli: A Man, a Voice* (Dallas, Tex.: Baskerville, 1996).
7. Interview with Marco Corelli, August 16–17, 2004.
8. Interview with Arrigo Michelini, Modena, May 20, 2007.
9. "The San Carlo Opera Season," *Opera News*, December 26, 1955.
10. Giorgio Pillon, "Ho trovato in America la patria del bel canto," *Domenica del Corriere*, June 6, 1973.
11. Fernando L. Lunghi, "L'Opera ha aperto la stagione con il *Giulio Cesare* di G. F. Haendel," *Giornale degli spettacoli*, December 28, 1955.
12. Nino Piccinelli, "Alla presenza di Gronchi . . . ," *Momento Sera*, December 28, 1955.

13. U. D. F., "Giganti all'Opera di Roma per *Giulio Cesare*," *Tempo*, December 1955.
14. Lunghi, "L'Opera ha aperto la stagione."
15. Piccinelli, "Alla presenza di Grenchi. . . ."
16. Leo Riemens, "Sensazionele nieuwe tenor," *Luister*, [ca. 1956–57].
17. "Opera Fanatic" broadcast, May 7, 1994; unpublished broadcast.
18. Leo Riemens, "Zijn naam is Franco Corelli," *Luister*, [ca. 1956].
19. Interview (with assistance from Michael Delos) of Mary Curtis-Verna, Seattle, October 14, 2004.
20. John Ardoin and Gerald Fitzgerald, *Callas* (London: Thames & Hudson, 1974).
21. Ibid.
22. Ibid.
23. Ibid.
24. Rumors of an allegedly existing pirate recording of the Callas-Corelli *Fedora* started with the publication of John Ardoin's book *The Callas Legacy*, where he writes that "rumors of an existing transistor recording continue to exist, supposedly made by the wife of Franco Corelli." John Ardoin, *The Callas Legacy* (London: Gerald Duckworth, 1977). Ever since then the rumor has popped up again and again in slightly altered versions. Frank Hamilton, in his impressive online Corelli discography of 2002, lists it as "Private tape, now probably lost." Besides repeating Ardoin's line, with the addition of Corelli's denial of owning the tape, he explains his listing as follows: "For over sixteen years, none of Callas' *Fedora* was generally believed to be preserved in sound . . . but in the spring of 1973 an in-house tape, reported to be in very poor sound, was made available to a few tape collectors in Europe." Haunting indeed, but when asked by this author, Hamilton couldn't provide any firsthand witnesses who ever owned or personally heard this tape.

    In addition to Hamilton, the president of the Maria Callas International Club assured me once that Deutsche Grammophon was negotiating with La Scala over an in-house archival recording of *Fedora*. Then EMI was supposed to have negotiated buying the recording from the Corellis, but that turned out to be just another rumor when EMI asked this author if he had perhaps stumbled on this tape during his research in Italy. As a matter of fact, I almost did. Marco Corelli assured me that he knew a magistrate who had it. Unfortunately he had forgotten the magistrate's name, which might have served. He also assured me that the magistrate had made a copy for Franco. Even then, in the first half of the 1990s, Franco denied having a tape of *Fedora*: "I wish I had it, but there is no *Fedora*" ("Opera Fanatic" broadcast, June 9, 1990 [Bel Canto Society, CZ4V]). Loretta followed suit when I interviewed her in 2006: "I know people keep saying I have it, but it doesn't exist." Interview with Loretta Corelli, Ancona, January 27, 2006.

    That would have ended the matter had not Franco's close friend Luigi Zoboli personally assured me during one of my visits to him that he had actually heard the tape in Franco's house around 1997: "Loretta took it from the shelves with recordings. It was a small tape, very old, and there were only fragments on it, not the complete opera. She played the aria and part of the duet with Callas and it sounded very much as Franco sounded on his Cetra recordings of Loris's two arias"; interview with Luigi Zoboli, Genoa, November 16, 2006. Corelli's cousin Graziano, who has been responsible for the rediscovery of a number of Franco's private tapes, admitted that the tape may have existed once, but he had not come across it in the process of indexing the legacy; interview with Graziano Corelli, Milan, November 15, 2006. Finally, Loretta told me during my January 2007 interview with her: "Come back and we shall look for it together."
25. Ardoin and Fitzgerald, *Callas*.
26. "*Fedora* at the Milan Theater La Scala," *Corriere della Sera*, May 20, 1956.
27. Interview (with assistance from Michael Delos) of Mary Curtis-Verna, Seattle, October 14, 2004.
28. The dates given above for these recordings are those as stamped on the original Cetra vinyl pressings and not those of the official release entitled *Franco Corelli Arias, 1955–1958* (2-CD set, Warner Fonit, 5050466-3303-2-1). I have rejected the date provided in the Warner Fonit

booklet because I cannot see how a July 1, 1956, pressing could have been recorded in March–April 1957, as the CD booklet claims.
29. Bruno Slawitz, "Due secoli di stupenda musica," *Musica e Dischi*, June 1956.
30. Late in life he deeply regretted turning down the part of Percy in Donizetti's *Anna Bolena*, which suggests that he may have been the first choice for Callas's programmed La Scala premiere of May 14, 1957 ("Opera Fanatic" broadcast, May 25, 1991). Perhaps he feared another one-woman show, as with *La Vestale*. But he would have added glamour and presence to the role of Percy, who has some wonderful melodic moments, such as "Fin dall'età più tenera," and a number of splendid entries in the brilliant ensembles that dominate this exciting melodrama.
31. Interview with Marco Corelli, August 16–17, 2004.
32. In July 2006 I managed to obtain a worn 16mm copy of the film. It came in two large twenty-inch cans, with the Donizetti and Meyerbeer arias intact.
33. "Stasera sul palcoscenico dell'Arena," *Il Gazzettino*, August 9, 1956.
34. V. T., "*Aida* diretta dal m. o. Votto," *Il Piccolo*, November 15, 1956; G. C., "Unanimità di consensi per l'*Aida*," *Corriere di Trieste*, November 16, 1956.
35. Interview (with assistance from Michael Delos) of Mary Curtis-Verna, Seattle, October 14, 2004.
36. Bruno Slawitz, "Franco Corelli incide *Aida*, la sua prima opera completa," *Musica e Dischi*, June 1957.
37. Riemens, "Zijn naam is Franco Corelli."
38. Giancarlo Landini, "Verdi *Aida*," unidentified magazine, n.d.
39. Slawitz, "Franco Corelli incide *Aida*."
40. Interview with Marco Corelli, August 16–17, 2004.
41. Franco Corelli, "Sono il tenore più alto ma voglio diventare il più grande," *Oggi*, March 12, 1959.
42. Telephone conversation with Mrs. Marco Marchetti, April 10, 2005. Marchetti's refusal to discuss his childhood with Franco indicates that the rift was of some magnitude.
43. Interview with Alessandro Scaravelli, Ancona, June 11, 2004. If these duets were indeed made at the same time as Scaravelli's solo recordings, then it must have been long before 1956, perhaps even around the time of the recordings that Corelli made with his brother Ubaldo in 1950. It was unlikely that 78 rpm recordings would have been cut in 1956, given the easier alternative of recording on tape, which was the method Franco applied to record his own voice.
44. Robert Daley, "The Greatest Tenor," *Life*, December 15, 1967. With respect to this quote from *Life*, two things need to be mentioned. One, Corelli obviously points to a moment in one of his solo passages as the place where Nino Sanzogno actually may have stopped conducting, although it is more likely that he simply stopped giving cues. The second is that Corelli claimed he arrived at the dress rehearsal at the last minute, exhausted and completely unprepared, having come straight from Florence ("Opera Fanatic" broadcast, February 3, 1990 [Bel Canto Society, CZ1V]). This may be true, but before his *Pagliacci* obligations at La Scala, he was singing *Aida* at the same theater. If he came from Florence to do only the dress rehearsal, he definitely chose to skip the earlier rehearsals.
45. Daley, "The Greatest Tenor."
46. Ibid.
47. These dates are the ones stamped in the vinyl. The booklet of the CD release *Franco Corelli Arias, 1955–1958* (2-CD set, Warner Fonit, 5050466-3303-2-1) gives no date for this session, while other sources give later dates than those stamped on the disc itself. Note the absence of "Celeste Aida" in the February 6 session. The Cetra booklet attributes this recording to Arturo Basile, but the original LP, *Franco Corelli arie da opera di G. Verdi* (Cetra, LPC 55018) clearly indicates that this "Celeste Aida" was taken from the complete recording under Angelo Questa (3-LP set, Cetra, LPC 1262). All sources, including Cetra's CD release, give 1961 as the recording year for the highlights from *Carmen*, whereas the date stamped into the vinyl is April 18, 1957—the year in which it was also mentioned in Bruno Tosi, "Incontro con Franco Corelli," *Musica e Dischi*, August 9, 1957.
48. Tosi, "Incontro con Franco Corelli."
49. Ruy Coelho, "Últimas notícias espectaculos," *Diario de noticias*, April 26, 1957.

50. Tito Gobbi, *Tito Gobbi on His World of Italian Opera* (Long Acre: Hamish Hamilton, 1984).
51. Ibid.
52. "Vero," *The New Yorker*, February 4, 1961.
53. "Royal Opera House *Tosca*," Andrew Porter, *The Financial Times*, date unknown.
54. "After the Herculean Labors . . . ," *Time and Tide*, date unknown.
55. Porter, "Royal Opera House *Tosca*."
56. "Opera Fanatic" broadcast, March 3, 1990.
57. Philip Hope-Wallace, "Male Leads in *Tosca*," *The Guardian*, date unknown.
58. "Il tenore Franco Corelli fra i 'Papà del Gnocco,'" *Il Gazzettino*, July 18, 1957.
59. Interview with Marco Corelli, Ancona, June 11, 2004.
60. Luis Arrones Peón, *Historia de la ópera in Oviedo*, vol. 1 (Oviedo: Asociación Asturiana de Amigos de la Ópera, 1981).
61. Manuel Mairlot Salinas, *La voz de Asturias*, September 24, 1957; "Semitono," *Region*, September 24, 1957.
62. Mairlot Salinas, *La voz de Asturias*; "Mi-Sol-Do," *Region*, September 28, 1957; Florestan, *La Nueva España*, September 28, 1957.

CHAPTER 9: 1958–1959

1. The Flemish television producer Jan Neckers recalled that his colleagues told him stories of their celebration of that occasion in Flanders, to illustrate how extraordinary the broadcast was (e-mail correspondence with Jan Neckers, April 24, 2007).
2. Michael Scott, *Maria Meneghini Callas* (Great Britain: Simon & Schuster, 1991).
3. Ibid.
4. "Opera Fanatic" broadcast, March 3, 1990; "Opera Fanatic" broadcast, May 25, 1993 (Bel Canto Society, CZ10V).
5. There has been some misunderstanding about the moment she left the stage, which is sometimes given as after the end of Act I, whereas critics always point out that it was after Act I, Scene 1. However, it turns out that *Norma* was given that night in a version with four acts rather than the usual three. That night the opera ended after Act I.
6. Interview with Anita Cerquetti, Rome, January 14, 2005.
7. Franco Corelli, in "Sulla scena sono un leone, ma prima . . . che paura!," *Arianna*, February 1961. In the interview, Corelli actually mentions "Poliuto," but this is clearly an error because he wears no helmet there, whereas everybody readily recalls his prominent Pollione helmet.
8. "Il basso colpì il tenore con la spada di don Carlo," *Il Piccolo*, January 22, 1958.
9. Franco Corelli, "Sono il tenore più alto ma voglio diventare il più grande," *Oggi*, March 12, 1959; Aldo Falivena, "Corelli è un atleto in castigo," *Epoca*, August 27, 1961.
10. Corelli, "Sono il tenore più alto."
11. Tito Gobbi, *My Life* (New York: Doubleday, 1980).
12. Unidentified Italian newspaper, January 20, 1958; Corelli, "Sono il tenore più alto"; Falivena, "Corelli è un atleto"; "Opera Fanatic" broadcast, February 3, 1990 (Bel Canto Society, CZ1V).
13. Unidentified Italian newspaper, January 20, 1958; "Il basso colpì il tenore," *Il Piccolo*, January 22, 1958; Corelli, "Sono il tenore più alto."
14. Letter, Roberto Bauer to Rudolf Bing, January 21, 1958.
15. Letter, Roberto Bauer to Rudolf Bing, December 9, 1957.
16. "Opera Fanatic" broadcast, March 30, 1991 (Bel Canto Society, CZ7V).
17. Armando Cesari, *Mario Lanza: An American Tragedy* (Fort Worth, Tex.: Baskerville, 2004).
18. Conversation with Jan Neckers, Keerbergen, April 10, 2007.
19. To this day, the tapes remain without an index and unexamined in their entirety, but the Flemish critic Rudi van den Bulck, who discovered the "Granada" on Meesters's tapes, believes that the entire concert may well be on other tapes in the collection.
20. Bruno Slawitz, "*Il Pirata* di Vincenzo Bellini," *Musica e Dischi*, May–June 1958.
21. E. P., "*Il Pirata* di Bellini: La regia e le scene," *Corriere della Sera*, [May 1958]; John Ardoin and Gerald Fitzgerald, *Callas* (London: Thames & Hudson, 1974).

22. Franco Abbiati, "*Il Pirata* di Bellini," *Corriere della Sera*, [May 1958].
23. Rodolfo Celletti, "Un uomo chiamato tenore," *Discoteca*, June 1971.
24. Slawitz, "*Il Pirata* di Vincenzo Bellini."
25. Ibid.
26. Ardoin and Fitzgerald, *Callas*.
27. Corelli has said that he recorded numerous performances and rehearsals, although he never mentioned any specific performances before the December 1960 *Poliuto* rehearsals. For those who believe in the existence of the alleged *Fedora* recording, the thought of Corelli having recorded *Il Pirata* is a logical one, although, at the time of this writing, no such tape has surfaced. If at any given point he actually had a copy of *Il Pirata*, one can only speculate on his motives in keeping it for himself, although it is common knowledge that he was very much against the publication of pirated recordings in general. With respect to both the *Fedora* and the *Pirata* it has been said that the persistent interest in precisely these two titles bothered him, because he knew that if they were released they would probably be promoted as recordings of Callas rather than Corelli.
28. Letter, Franco Corelli and Loretta Di Lelio to "Enzo" [someone in management], ca. January 1958.
29. Lauri-Volpi had been very critical of his younger colleague, saying that if he continued to sing as he did, the world would soon have one fewer tenor and one more baritone. Mario Morini, "Raul De Lauri-Volpi a Corelli," *Corriere del Teatro*, May 1962.
30. Letters, Franco Corelli to Guido Sampaoli, [ca. August 1958]; Sampaoli to Corelli, August 9, 1958. Sampaoli's letter confirms Corelli's reluctance regarding the part of Loris. Because Sampaoli wanted to keep Franco for the season, he offered to give *Carmen* instead, while suggesting that Franco's *Trovatore* studies might result in a nice opening of the 1959 Caracalla season.

    In a telegram from March 1958, Corelli canceled his *Pagliacci*s, which suggests that the "flexibility" from Corelli's side had required some gentle pressure on Sampaoli's part.
31. Adone Zecchi, *La Scala*, December 1958.
32. Letter, Roberto Bauer to Rudolf Bing, October 26, 1958.
33. Letter, Rudolf Bing to Roberto Bauer, November 18, 1958.
34. Ibid.
35. Ibid.
36. Peter Dusek, interview with Franco Corelli (with interpreter Kristine Springer), "Opernwerkstatt," Austrian radio, October 8, 1989.
37. "Opera Fanatic" broadcast, presumably May 7, 1994.
38. Hines, *Great Singers on Great Singing*; "Opera Fanatic" broadcast, February 3, 1990 (Bel Canto Society, CZ1V). Those familiar with Hines's book will find here added details from Hines and Corelli as related in the "Opera Fanatic" broadcast.
39. C. Bianchi, "Non è più il 'terzo uomo della lirica Italiana,'" *Alba*, April 19, 1959.
40. Maurizio Chierici, "Il bel tenore sempere in burlasco," *Oggi*, January 23, 1964.
41. Interview with Magda Olivero, Milan, January 12, 2005.
42. Telephone conversation with Giancarlo Del Monaco, April 12, 2007; confirmed by various letters of Roberto Bauer.
43. Franco Corelli, "Sono il tenore più alto ma voglio diventare il più grande," *Oggi*, March 12, 1959.
44. Corelli, "Sono il tenore più alto."
45. Ibid.
46. Telephone interview with Giancarlo Del Monaco, August 24, 2005.
47. Franco Corelli, as told to G. Fogliani, "Sto per conquistare Broadway," *Eva*, October 15, 1964.
48. Interview, Marco Corelli, January 17, 2005.
49. Corelli, "Sulla scena sono un leone."
50. Letter, Roberto Bauer to Robert Herman, May 27, 1959.
51. Letter, Roberto Bauer to Robert Herman, May 12, 1959.
52. Letter, Roberto Bauer to Rudolf Bing, June 17, 1959.

53. Letter, Roberto Bauer to Rudolf Bing, June 23, 1959.
54. Ibid.
55. Interview with Gabriella Tucci, Rome, January 18, 2005.
56. Letter, Rudolf Bing to Roberto Bauer, July 3, 1959.
57. Letter, Roberto Bauer to Rudolf Bing, July 13, 1959.
58. EMI archives.
59. Letter, Roberto Bauer to Rudolf Bing, August 19, 1959.
60. Letter, Rudolf Bing to Roberto Bauer, October 6, 1959.
61. Letter, Rudolf Bing to Roberto Bauer, October 21, 1959.
62. Letter, Roberto Bauer to Rudolf Bing, October 27, 1959.
63. Florestan, *La Nueva España*, September 18, 1959; L. R., *El Comercio* [Gijon], September 18, 1959.
64. Letter, Roberto Bauer to Rudolf Bing, November 2, 1959.
65. Letter, Roberto Bauer to Rudolf Bing, November 17, 1959.
66. Letter, Rudolf Bing to Roberto Bauer, November 5, 1959.
67. Ibid.
68. Letter, Roberto Bauer to Rudolf Bing, November 17, 1959.
69. Letter, Roberto Bauer to Rudolf Bing, November 20, 1959.
70. Ibid.
71. Letter, Rudolf Bing to Roberto Bauer, November 26, 1959.
72. Letters, Roberto Bauer to Rudolf Bing, November 28, 1959; October 30, 1959; December 9, 1959.
73. Interview with Magda Olivero, Milan, January 12, 2005.
74. Unfortunately for Magda Olivero and her many American fans, Roberto Bauer was one of those who were allergic to her style. He judged her to be as unbearable as Adriana as she was in anything else he had heard her in before and singlehandedly kept her out of the Met while she was still in her prime. Letter, Roberto Bauer to Rudolf Bing, November 28, 1959.
75. Interview with Magda Olivero, Milan, January 12, 2005. Corelli himself repeatedly admitted to his use of sometimes rather experimental medications. Intriguingly, there is a discussion in an "Opera Fanatic" broadcast where he readily acknowledged his use of certain cocktails that were to be put directly on the vocal chords, just as he freely spoke about inhalation treatments. However, though it may not be common in singer's biographies, his fellow singer and radio guest Jerome Hines more or less suggested that this was common practice among singers. Apart from his own medicinal tricks for whenever he felt his vocal chords needed to be peppered, Hines mentioned the "Del Monaco cocktail," to which another guest added the "magic bag" of Enzo Sordello, filled with medicines. "Opera Fanatic" broadcast, March 3, 1990. Sordello recalled some experiments with Corelli himself: "I knew he went to a certain doctor often, but I think he went there mainly to get some psychological support. He also told me that he took quinine to feel better. I tried it too, but it wasn't my cup of tea. Quinine is for people with malaria!" Telephone interview with Enzo Sordello, October 14, 2006.
76. Letter, Roberto Bauer to Rudolf Bing, November 28, 1959.
77. Telegram, Roberto Bauer to Rudolf Bing, December 12, 1959.

CHAPTER 10: 1960

1. "Opera Fanatic" broadcast, May 25, 1991.
2. Letter, Roberto Bauer to Rudolf Bing, January 9, 1960.
3. Ibid.
4. Letter, Roberto Bauer to Rudolf Bing, January 13, 1960.
5. Letter, Roberto Bauer to Rudolf Bing, January 18, 1960.
6. Letter, Roberto Bauer to Rudolf Bing, March 22, 1960.
7. Mario Falconi, "Con spada e coruzza attacio' uno spettatore," *Il Tempo*, March 1, 1960.
8. Franco Corelli, in "Sulla scena sono un leone, ma prima . . . che paura!," *Arianna*, February 1961; interview with Bob Connolly, 2005.

9. Mila Contini, in "Timido ma bello il fusto della lirica," *Amica*, July 29, 1962.
10. "Opera Fanatic" broadcast, February 3, 1990 (Bel Canto Society, CZ1V).
11. Corelli, "Sulla scena sono un leone"; Falconi, "Con spada e coruzza."
12. Falconi, "Con spada e coruzza"; Contini, in "Timido ma bello."
13. Falconi, "Con spada e coruzza."
14. "Opera Fanatic" broadcast, February 3, 1990 (Bel Canto Society, CZ1V).
15. Falconi, "Con spada e coruzza."
16. Ibid.; "Opera Fanatic" broadcast, February 3, 1990 (Bel Canto Society, CZ1V).
17. Falconi, "Con spada e coruzza."
18. Ibid.
19. Quoted from Peter Dusek, interview with Franco Corelli (with interpreter Kristine Springer), "Opernwerkstatt," Austrian radio, October 8, 1989.
20. Roberto Bauer adds that one was sung fortissimo, the other piano—which is puzzling, because neither one of the high Cs in the second act can possibly be sung piano, not to mention that Corelli never took any high C piano. That was reserved for B-flats. Letter, Roberto Bauer to Rudolf Bing, March 22, 1960.
21. Letters, Roberto Bauer to Rudolf Bing, March 1960, and April 4, 1960. Bauer's remark is intriguing, because the alleged biting incident with Birgit Nilsson in Boston had not yet happened. Apparently Franco had a reputation, which may have inspired Bing later on—see the section on *Turandot*, Boston, April 19, 1961.
22. Martina Arroyo, speaker at the Metropolitan Opera Guild Annual Luncheon program, Waldorf-Astoria, New York, April 25, 2003.
23. Letter, Robert Herman to Franco Corelli, July 24, 1960.
24. By 1960, when Corelli began recording for EMI, the company was releasing almost all of its classical catalog in the United States on the Angel label, which by then was a division of Capitol, an American company EMI had acquired in 1953. But a few EMI classical recordings also appeared on the Capitol label in America, including Corelli's 1967 album *Granada*. Regardless of the labels on which they were eventually released, he recorded them for EMI, and therefore EMI is the reference used in this book.
25. Interview with Magda Olivero, Milan, January 12, 2005.
26. Interview with Marco Corelli, January 28–30, 2007.
27. Marisa Rusconi, "La Callas e'un agnellino," *Tempo*, December 22, 1962.
28. Letters between Roberto Bauer and Rudolf Bing, October–November 1960.
29. O. M., *Paris Match*, December 17, 1960.
30. Fedele D'Amico, "Martyrs in Milan," *Opera News*, March 4, 1961.
31. O. M., *Paris Match*.
32. Ibid.
33. Ibid.
34. Ibid.
35. Ibid.
36. Corelli, "Sulla scena sono un leone," *Arianna*, February 1961.

CHAPTER 11: 1961

1. Giuseppe Massera, "Una appasionata edizione del *Trovatore*," *Gazetta di Parma*, January 2, 1961; interview with Arrigo Michelini, Modena, May 20, 2007.
2. Alexei Buljigin, *Prins v stranj Tjudes* (Moscow: Agraf, 2003)..
3. Marco Corelli, Ancona, June 11, 2004; Luigi Zoboli, Genoa, January 27, 2007.
4. Interview with Loretta Corelli, Milan, January 27, 2007; interview with Marco Corelli, Ancona, June 11, 2004.
5. Marriage certificate, Dario Corelli and Loretta Di Lelio.
6. Ibid.
7. Form 4-15-54, for importing "a nonimmigrant alien of distinguished merit and ability," was signed on November 7, 1960, by Dario Corelli, who listed himself as having been born on April 8, 1923.

8. Interview with Loretta Corelli, Ancona, June 12, 2004.
9. Rudolf Bing, *5000 Nights at the Opera* (New York: Doubleday, 1972).
10. Dale Haven, "Met Star Has Manager Who Cooks," *New York Herald Tribune*, February 6, 1961.
11. Letters between Rudolf Bing and Roberto Bauer, October–December, 1960.
12. Interview with Marco Corelli, Ancona, June 11, 2004.
13. Trudy Viner, "Corelli Is Making Met Debut Tonight," *New York World Telegram and Sun*, January 27, 1961.
14. Though Price's debut was sensational, she was not the first African American artist to have graced the stage of the Met. That honor, as far as leading roles are concerned, belongs to Mattiwilda Dobbs, who debuted at the Met as Gilda in *Rigoletto* on November 9, 1956. In addition, she sang Lucia, Olympia, Oscar, and Zerlina at the Met before Price debuted there. Marian Anderson preceded Dobbs when she debuted as Ulrica on January 7, 1955, but that part was considered "fitting" in that it could be linked to the color of the singer's skin (the same goes for the baritone Robert McFerrin, who debuted as Amonasro on January 27, 1955). Some claims have been made that it was Price after all who graced the Met's stage as the first black artist ever: she sang "Summertime," from George Gershwin's *Porgy and Bess*, at a Metropolitan Opera Jamboree on April 6, 1953. However, that Jamboree telecast was not held at the Met, but at Manhattan's Ritz Theater.
15. "Skylark & Golden Calves," *Time*, February 3, 1961.
16. Ronald Eyer, "Il Trovatore," *Herald Tribune*, January 29, 1961.
17. "Skylark & Golden Calves."
18. Eyer, "Il Trovatore."
19. Bruno Tosi, "Franco Corelli è tornato in Italia: 'Mr. Esaurito' ci parla dell' America," *Musica e Dischi*, July 1965.
20. Harold C. Schonberg, "Opera: Two Debuts in *Il Trovatore*," *The New York Times*, January 28, 1961.
21. "Skylark & Golden Calves."
22. "Opera: Two Debuts in *Il Trovatore*."
23. Ibid.
24. Ibid.
25. Ibid.
26. Eyer, "Il Trovatore."
27. "Skylark & Golden Calves."
28. Bing, *5000 Nights*.
29. Interviews with Merle Hubbard and Herman Krawitz, New York, September 18 and 23, 2005.
30. Daley, "The World's Greatest Tenor."
31. "The Perilous Life of a Tenor," *New York Herald Tribune*, February 6, 1961.
32. Greg MacGregor, "Tenor Hurt at 'Met' but Sings Final Acts," *The New York Times*, February 5, 1961.
33. F. S., "Matinée Idol," *Opera News*, March 4, 1961.
34. Ibid.
35. Haven, "Met Star Has Manager Who Cooks."
36. F. S., "Matinée Idol."
37. "Vero," *The New Yorker*, February 4, 1961.
38. EMI archives, Tony Locantro, April 7, 2005.
39. Wriston Locklear, "Franco Corelli: His Road to the Metropolitan," *Musical America*, May 1961.
40. "Vero," *The New Yorker*.
41. Franca Cella, "Grandi voci," *Periodico di Cultura Musicale*, July 2002.
42. Comments by the author based on hearing the full tape of Franco Corelli's *Guglielmo Tell* studies, presumably dating back to the first half of 1961. Listening sessions: Milan, November 15, 2006, and January 27, 2007.
43. F. S., "Matinée Idol."

44. Franco Corelli, in "Sulla scena sono un leone, ma prima . . . che paura!," *Arianna*, February 1961.
45. Locklear, "Franco Corelli: His Road to the Metropolitan."
46. Haven, "Met Star Has Manager Who Cooks."
47. Chiara Milani, "Corelli, un ritorno tra gli applausi," *Il Piccolo*, October 25, 1999.
48. Telephone interview with Birgit Nilsson, April 10, 2005; correspondence with Nilsson, May–June 2005.
49. In the interview, Stokowski even stated he had written the Ricordi publishing house for a duplicate of the original autograph score, because he wanted to study the mistakes in it, beginning with the first act. Once he "fixed" those mistakes, he would continue to correct Acts II and III, even if it took hundreds of hours, because *Turandot* was potentially the master's greatest score. "What's Wrong with Opera," *Opera News*, February 24, 1962.
50. Franco Corelli, as told to G. Fogliani, "Sto per conquistare Broadway," *Eva*, October 15, 1964.
51. Ibid.
52. Telephone interview with Birgit Nilsson, April 10, 2005; correspondence with Nilsson, May–June 2005.
53. Interview with Merle Hubbard, September 23, 2005.
54. "Dates and Places," *Opera News*, February 25, 1961.
55. Interview (with assistance from Michael Delos) of Mary Curtis-Verna, Seattle, October 14, 2004.
56. "Il discorso di Kennedy," unidentified newspaper clipping.
57. Maurizio Chierici, "Il bel tenore sempre in burrasca," *Oggi Illustrato*, January 23, 1964.
58. Bruno Tosi, "Franco Corelli è tornato in Italia: 'Mr. Esaurito' ci parla dell' America," *Musica e Dischi*, July 1965.
59. Alvin H. Goldstein, "Big Man, Big Voice, Big Temper," *St. Louis Post-Dispatch*, April 19, 1961.
60. Letter, Rudolf Bing to Franco Corelli, March 30, 1961.
61. "Franco Corelli Sings First Don Carlo at 'Met,'" Eric Salzman, unidentified review, April 3, 1961.
62. Marjorie W. Sherman, "Party, Supper Dance Top Off Met Opera Opening," unidentified newspaper clipping, April 20, 1961.
63. John K. Sherman, "Met Audience Nearly Equals *Turandot*'s Glittering," *Minneapolis Star*, May 18, 1961.
64. Merle Hubbard, unpublished memoir; interview with Hubbard, New York, September 23, 2005.
65. Telephone interview with Birgit Nilsson, April 10, 2005.
66. Peter Dusek, interview with Franco Corelli (with interpreter Kristine Springer), "Opernwerkstatt," Austrian radio, October 8, 1989.
67. Birgit Nilsson, *La Nilsson: Mein Leben für die Oper* (Frankfurt am Main: Fischer Taschenbuch Verlag, 1999).
68. Dusek, interview with Franco Corelli.
69. Telephone interview with Birgit Nilsson, April 10, 2005.
70. Ibid.
71. Nilsson, *La Nilsson: Mein Leben für die Oper*; telephone interview with Birgit Nilsson, April 10, 2005; correspondence with Nilsson, May–June 2005.
72. Dusek, interview with Franco Corelli.
73. Telephone interview with Birgit Nilsson, April 10, 2005; correspondence with Nilsson, May–June 2005.
74. Nilsson, *La Nilsson: Mein Leben für die Oper*; correspondence with Birgit Nilsson, May–June 2005.
75. Dusek, interview with Franco Corelli.
76. Telephone interview with Birgit Nilsson, April 10, 2005.
77. "Corelli Gets Letters—But Prefers Wife, Music," *Cleveland Press News*, April 27, 1961.
78. Merle Hubbard, unpublished memoir; interview with Hubbard, New York, September 23, 2005.

79. Frank Daniel, "Met Idol Corelli Shivers Here," *Atlanta Journal*, April 28–29, 1961.
80. Patricia Deaton, "Opera Star's Diet," *Atlanta Constitution*, May 2, 1961.
81. Based on an interview with Merle Hubbard, New York, September 23, 2005.
82. Ibid.
83. Ibid.
84. Telephone interview with Birgit Nilsson, April 10, 2005.
85. Goldstein, "Big Man, Big Voice, Big Temper."
86. Based on an interview with Merle Hubbard, New York, September 23, 2005.
87. Ibid.
88. Telephone interviews with Birgit Nilsson, April 10, 2005 and June 2005. In her autobiography, written many years after the event took place, Nilsson separated the story of the piano from the story of the dog, believing the first one to have taken place in Philadelphia. Nilsson, *La Nilsson: Mein Leben für die Oper*.
89. Based on an interview with Merle Hubbard, New York, September 23, 2005.
90. Roger Dettmer, "Turandot Excellent," *Chicago American*, May 15, 1961.
91. Based on an interview with Merle Hubbard, New York, September 23, 2005.
92. Mark Beltaire, "Met Makes Big Impact," *Detroit Free Press*, May 22, 1961.
93. *Chicago Tribune*, May 24, 1961; *San Francisco Chronicle*; *Evening World Herald*; *Harrisburg Patriot*; *Baltimore Morning Sun*; *Toledo Times*; *Tulsa World*, May 24, 1961; "Bing and Grand Opera," *Alabama Star*, May 31, 1961.
94. Based on an interview with Merle Hubbard, New York, September 23, 2005.
95. Met internal correspondence, March–December 1961.
96. Letter, Robert Herman to Franco and Loretta Corelli, June 21, 1961.
97. Letter, Robert Herman to Roberto Bauer, May 24, 1961.
98. Letter, Robert Herman to Franco and Loretta Corelli, June 21, 1961.
99. Interview with Luigi Zoboli, Genoa, November 16, 2006.
100. Conversation with Andrea Bucolier, Como-Verona, October 28, 2006.
101. "Opera Tempo Was Slow, the Tenor's Temper Quick," *New York Post*, July 27, 1961.
102. Ibid.
103. Aldo Falivena, "Corelli è un atleto in castigo," *Epoca*, August 27, 1961.
104. Libera Danielis, *Opera*, November 1961; *Het Rijk Van de Vrouw*, undated magazine clipping.
105. Letter, Rudolf Bing to Franco Corelli, August 8, 1961.
106. Falivena, "Corelli è un atleto in castigo."
107. Ibid.
108. Ibid.
109. EMI archives, Tony Locantro, April 7, 2005.
110. Met office memorandum, July 24, 1961; letter, Roberto Bauer to Rudolf Bing, September 13, 1961. In 1964, when the *Cavalleria* tenor had to be replaced in Corelli's upcoming *Pagliacci* performances, it was a trembling Bauer who went to Corelli to ask if he would agree with Bing's suggestion to ask Bergonzi. Franco seemed surprised at the very question and said that it was up to the Met to schedule singers—he had nothing against Bergonzi. Bauer commented trenchantly, in a letter to Robert Herman dated January 7, 1964, "Not quite true!!" But the episode serves as circumstantial evidence that Corelli may have been serious when he suggested opening the Met along with Del Monaco. In the end, however, Bergonzi didn't sing; in performance Arturo Sergi and Barry Morell alternated in the part of Turiddu.
111. Letters, Roberto Bauer to Rudolf Bing, September 13, 1961; October 12, 1961.
112. Letter, Roberto Bauer to Rudolf Bing, October 12, 1961.
113. Ibid.
114. Alan Rich, "Mythless Corelli," *The Sunday Times*, February 11, 1962.
115. Ibid.
116. Letter, Roberto Bauer to Rudolf Bing, November 12, 1961.
117. Ibid.
118. James Drake, *Richard Tucker: A Biography* (New York: E. P. Dutton, 1984).

119. Daley, "The World's Greatest Tenor."
120. Drake, *Richard Tucker*.
121. Ibid.
122. Letter, Roberto Bauer to Rudolf Bing, October 12, 1961.
123. Letter, Roberto Bauer to Rudolf Bing, December 19, 1961; Metropolitan Office memorandum, December 19, 1961.
124. Metropolitan Opera memoranda, December 19, 1961, February 2, 1962.
125. EMI archives, Tony Locantro, April 7, 2005.
126. Josef Mossman, "Met Sends Its New Star to Shine on Opera Week," *Detroit News-Times*, May 20, 1961.
127. EMI archives, Tony Locantro, April 7, 2005. Locantro informed me that Corelli indeed recorded "two songs," but he couldn't confirm the release (mentioned in Marina Boagno and Gilberto Starone, *Un uomo, una voce* [Parma: Azzali Editore, 1990]; published in English as *Corelli: A Man, a Voice* [Dallas, Tex.: Baskerville, 1996]).
128. Bruno Slawitz, "Inaugurata la stagione lirica con la *Battaglia di Legnano*," *Musica e Dischi*, December 1961.
129. Ibid.
130. Letter, Roberto Bauer to Rudolf Bing, December 29, 1961.

CHAPTER 12: 1962

1. Letter, Roberto Bauer to Rudolf Bing, January 4, 1962.
2. Letter, Roberto Bauer to Rudolf Bing, January 23, 1962.
3. Telephone interview with Birgit Nilsson, April 10, 2005.
4. Interview with Marco Corelli, Ancona, August 16–17, 2004.
5. Mario Morini, unidentified magazine clipping [ca. January 21–27, 1962].
6. Letter, John Gutman to Rudolf Bing, Robert Herman and Mr. Robinson, February 23, 1962.
7. "This Week," *Opera News*, February 24, 1962; telephone interview with Birgit Nilsson, April 10, 2005.
8. Telephone interview with Donald DiGrazia, November 15, 2004; interview with Donald DiGrazia, New York, May 5, 2005.
9. *Classic Record Collector*, Winter 2006.
10. Hyman Goldberg, "Love That Man!," *New York Mirror Magazine*, May 13, 1962.
11. Ibid.
12. Fern Marja Eckman, "Closeup: Franco Corelli," *New York Post*, November 13, 1962.
13. Mario Morini, "Lauri-Volpi ha parlato: Corelli e' il mio Erede," *Settimana Radio TV*, June 3–9, 1962; "'Raoul' da Lauri-Volpi a Corelli," *Corriere del Teatro*, June 1962.
14. Ibid.
15. Francesco Tamagno's complete recordings can be found in superior sound on Truesound Transfers (TT-2425 and TT-2426); both feature fragments of Meyerbeer's *Le Prophète* and other grand operas by Rossini (*Guglielmo Tell*) and Massenet (*Hérodiade*). Marconi's complete recordings can be found on Symposium (CD 1069 and 1073); 1069 has two versions of Meyerbeer's "O paradiso" from *L'Africana*.
16. Antonio Cotogni's only verified recording is, incidentally, a duet with Francesco Marconi: Francesco Masini, "I mulattieri" (Symposium, CD 1069).
17. Morini, "Raul da Lauri-Volpi a Corelli"; Morini, "Lauri-Volpi ha parlato."
18. Rodolfo Celletti, "Un'eccezionale esecuzione alla Scala," booklet for Meyerbeer, *Gli Ugonotti* (3-LP set, Cetra Documents, DOC 34).
19. For the young Lauri-Volpi one has to turn to his 1929 recording of the aria "Bianca al par" and a good number of other recordings that are available on TIMAClub's complete Lauri-Volpi edition (5-CD set, Clama, CD 15).
20. Celletti, "Un'eccezionale esecuzione alla Scala."
21. Ibid.
22. Lauri-Volpi's Raul is available on CD (2-CD set, Living Stage, LS 4035132).

23. Franco Corelli, "Sono il tenore più alto ma voglio diventare il più grande," *Oggi*, March 12, 1959.
24. Interview with Marco Corelli, January 17, 2005.
25. "Pauroso incidente d'auto al tenore Corelli e all moglie," *Corriere della Sera*, June 27, 1962.
26. Interview with Lucine Amara, New York, May 16, 2005.
27. EMI's Corelli files.
28. Unidentified newspaper, "Ein idealer Troubadour," date unknown.
29. Letter, Roberto Bauer to Rudolf Bing, July 15, 1962.
30. Interview with Alessandro Scaravelli, Ancona, June 11, 2004.
31. "Corelli: 'Verrò ad Ancona quando riapriranno le Muse,'" unidentified newspaper clipping, August 1962.
32. Some authors have a priori called the writings of these women's magazines "romantic fantasies," linking these publications to the genre of gossip magazines as we know them today. This was certainly not the case with *Oggi*, *Amica*, *Eva*, *Grand Hotel*, and a string of others. The Corellis gave lengthy and substantive interviews to their reporters while posing extensively for their photographers in their private quarters, Franco's dressing room, and other places. In cases where their cooperation is obvious, I have been happy to quote from these magazines, if only because they sustain my argument that his life was by far not as secluded then as it seemed in recent years. Moreover, owing to the impact in Italy of, say, the very popular *Oggi* or *Amica*, he frequently used precisely these magazines when he felt he had something to say. For reasons of space alone, they provided a platform that allowed him to communicate with his fan base in a way that no serious newspaper could ever provide, which was another lesson learned from Maria Callas. In addition, these magazines were far ahead of their more serious rivals in the operatic field when it came to the most communicative element of the publishing industry, photography. Neither *The New York Times* nor the *Corriere della Sera* had room for full-page color photos then, which magazines and newspaper supplements provided lavishly.
33. Mila Contini, in "Timido ma bello il fusto della lirica," *Amica*, July 29, 1962; Giovanna Kessler, "Sterne am Opernhimmel," *Opernwelt*, February 1964.
34. Contini, in "Timido ma bello."
35. Ibid.
36. Ibid.
37. Letter, Roberto Bauer to Rudolf Bing, August 16, 1962.
38. Whereas the Metropolitan Opera kept meticulous notes of meetings, mostly due to the fact that Bing and Bauer corresponded daily on all matters regarding Italian singers, most EMI meetings were informal meetings with the producers or EMI representatives in the country concerned and were archived by means of summaries, which were eventually filed. They give a fascinating glimpse of what were often long and intense discussions. The same goes for internal EMI meetings concerning the company's strategy in negotiating with its artist, or the plans it had designed for him or her. EMI archives, Tony Locantro, April 7, 2005.
39. Ibid.
40. Ibid.
41. In a conversation between Tony Locantro and Peter Andry, who produced many EMI recordings at the time, Andry explained that although it was then technically possible to overdub a singer onto an existing orchestral track, it raised major problems for the engineers to get the sound levels right and achieve the right balance between voice and orchestra, especially when other singers were also involved. Overdubbing the whole of the role of Otello would have been quite a challenge.
42. EMI archives, Tony Locantro, April 7, 2005.
43. Ibid.
44. Letter, Roberto Bauer to Rudolf Bing, September 9, 1962.
45. Correspondence, Rudolf Bing with Roberto Bauer, September 14, 15, 17, 1962.
46. Letter, Rudolf Bing to Roberto Bauer, September 17, 1962.
47. Mario Morini, "Duello in si bemolle tra leone e coscia d'oro," Settimana Radio broadcast, September 30–October 6, 1962.

48. Harold C. Schonberg, "Opera: *Andrea Chénier* as an Opener," *The New York Times*, October 15, 1962.
49. Interview with Donald DiGrazia, New York, May 15, 2004.
50. Ruby Mercer, *The Quilicos* (Oakville, Ont., and New York: Mosaic Press, 1991).
51. Ibid. Two recordings seem a trifling matter, but Quilico's glorious voice didn't make it onto *any* recording until 1968, by which time RCA had apparently lost its fear of Franco's veto and hired him for their *Eracle* recording. In 1973 Ariola-Eurodisc required his services in *I Puritani*, after which Massenet's *Thérèse* for Decca completed his entire discography in opera. His Count di Luna remained unrecorded, although his rendering of "Il balen" can be heard on an interesting local Canadian CBC recital from 1985 (CBC, LP SM5043).
52. Here as elsewhere in both Loretta's and Franco's newspaper quotes one can observe grammatical mistakes. These were deliberately kept by the authors, presumably to add a little Italian-immigrant color. Fern Maria Eckman, "Closeup: Opera Star," *New York Post*, November 13, 1962.
53. Dick Owen, "He Started at the Top," *Coloroto Magazine*, October 14, 1962.
54. Ibid.; Contini, in "Timido ma bello."
55. Eckman, "Closeup: Opera Star."
56. "Toppers," *Look*, December 18, 1962.
57. Gioietta Ruffo, "Quest'anno a la Scala duello di 'primi uomini,'" *TV Sorrisi & Canzoni*, December 9, 1962.
58. Ibid.
59. Rusconi, "La Callas e'un agnellino."
60. "*Il Trovatore* inaugura la stagione della Scala in una fastosa cornice," *Corriere della Sera*, December 8, 1962.
61. Vieri Poggiali, *Antonio Ghiringhelli: Una vita per La Scala* (Urbino: QuattroVenti, 2004).

CHAPTER 13: 1963

1. According to Tony Locantro, in the period under discussion the power of the Musicians' Union was such that they could simply veto a project without giving any reason: "In this case they would probably have been suspicious that it was a means of recording an opera in a smaller number of sessions than normal, avoiding the usual retakes, and so they would have vetoed it on principle."
2. EMI archives, Tony Locantro, April 7, 2005.
3. Ibid.
4. Letter, Roberto Bauer to Robert Herman, February 27, 1963.
5. The story as told here is the popular one, but more critical observers have to admit that Ponselle was well past her prime when it came to high Bs and Cs. One of this book's readers, Jan Neckers, pointed out to me that her choice of the part of Adriana was made out of necessity rather than from an inborn affinity for the role, as Ponselle claimed afterward. When that option was withdrawn, she chose to resign gracefully rather than force herself into a repertoire in which she would no longer be able to excel.
6. Radio interview, Eric Salzman with Renata Tebaldi, Irene Dalis, and Franco Corelli, sometime after January 21, 1963.
7. Ibid.
8. Interview (with assistance from Michael Delos) of Mary Curtis-Verna, Seattle, October 14, 2004.
9. Bruno Slawitz, "La voce di Franco Corelli," *Musica e Dischi*, April 1963.
10. Letter, Roberto Bauer to Rudolf Bing, March 14, 1963.
11. Roberto Serafin, "Il 'Met'? Un teatrino in confronto alla Scala ha detto Del Monaco," *Corriere Lombardo*, March 10–13, 1963.
12. "Gala con premie ai dominatori," unidentified newspaper clipping, March 6, 1963.
13. Letter, Roberto Bauer to Rudolf Bing, March 14, 1963.
14. Letter, Rudolf Bing to Roberto Bauer, March 16, 1963.
15. Letter, Roberto Bauer to Rudolf Bing, March 14, 1963.
16. "Il dominatore della lirica messo k.o. da un dente," unidentified newspaper clipping, March 6, 1963.

17. Telephone interview with Giancarlo Del Monaco, August 24, 2005. The kimono mentioned appears in a photo published in *Grand Hotel*, January 9, 1965. Other photos in this publication go back to the end of 1960, when an insightful series of pictures was made in Corelli's Milan apartment for *Grand Hotel*. The kimono picture may have come from that photo shoot, or it may have been made sometime between 1960 and the end of 1964. Giancarlo was still in his teens, which places the event somewhere in the middle of the period of heightened antagonism between Del Monaco and Corelli (1961–63).
18. Interview with Alessandro Scaravelli, Ancona, June 11, 2004. Marco Corelli supports this account of events.
19. Telephone interview with Giancarlo Del Monaco, August 24, 2005.
20. Corelli got his way and canceled the Moscow tour at the last minute for other reasons (see chapter 14).
21. EMI archives, Tony Locantro, April 7, 2005.
22. Letter, Roberto Bauer to Rudolf Bing, January 5, 1966. Apparently Gorlinsky, an impresario who was also the agent of Callas, Del Monaco, and a string of other prominent opera stars, was brought in with an eye to taxes, rather than as a true agent. All future Met negotiations were always done directly with Corelli. The same goes for his negotiations with recording companies. The Philadelphia Lyric Opera's general manager, Ray Fabiani, seems to have handled his American television and local appearances.
23. EMI archives, Tony Locantro, April 7, 2005.
24. Oscar Smith, "Corelli Rescues Routine in *Tosca*," *Akron Beacon Journal*, April 21, 1963.
25. Frank Hruby, "Corelli Takes Top Honors in *Tosca*," *Cleveland Express*, April 23, 1963.
26. "Big, Bad Tenor Corelli Picture of Calm, Charm," *Dallas Times Herald*, May 8, 1963.
27. Marjorie Alge, "The Magic of the Met," *Cleveland Express*, April 23, 1963.
28. Interview (with assistance from Michael Delos) of Mary Curtis-Verna, Seattle, October 14, 2004.
29. Letter, Roberto Bauer to Rudolf Bing, July 31, 1963.
30. Ibid.
31. Philipe Hope Wallace, "Giordano: *Andrea Chénier*," *Gramophone*, date unknown.
32. Peter Dusek, interview with Franco Corelli (with interpreter Kristine Springer), "Opernwerkstatt," Austrian radio, October 8, 1989.
33. Franco Corelli, "Opera Fanatic" broadcast, February 3, 1990 (Bel Canto Society, CZ1V).
34. Letter, Roberto Bauer to Rudolf Bing, February 7, 1967.
35. Dusek, radio interview with Franco Corelli, October 8, 1989.
36. Franco Corelli, "Opera Fanatic" broadcast, March 3, 1990. Unfortunately, it was not possible to find conclusive proof regarding the exact moment when this inhalation course happened. Judging from Corelli's two radio interviews about the subject, it could have been anywhere between 1962 and 1975. The first interview was with Peter Dusek for Austrian radio on October 8, 1989, and there he links the episode to his ultimate farewell to the stage: "At the time I studied an opera that was extremely difficult but still rather congenial to my voice. However, I forced myself during an inhalation therapy in Tabiano, where I relaxed my vocal chords while studying this opera [*Tell*], which has many high Cs. My vocal condition afterward was no longer the same."

However, in an "Opera Fanatic" broadcast from February 3, 1990 (Bel Canto Society, CZ1V), Corelli mentions that it was "around" the time when he was singing *Poliuto* and *Gli Ugonotti*. He then remarks that he continued to sing for seven or eight more years, after which his voice was never the same. Further confusion was added early in 2006, when Zucker published a quote from Loretta on this subject in the accompanying booklet to the *Corelli in Concert* DVD (Bel Canto Society, D0091). The quote was made in the wake of the March 3, 1990, broadcast with Zucker and Franco, and in it Loretta dismisses the inhalation treatment damage as nonsense, claiming that the therapy had been in 1958. If this quote is not a misunderstanding—if Loretta means that Corelli started the Tabiano treatments in 1958—then it is clearly at odds with the facts, for there is conclusive proof in Corelli's correspondence with the Met that he went to Tabiano annually throughout the 1960s.

All in all, there are several reasons to place this episode around July–August 1963. For one, it is known from magazine interviews that he was studying *Tell* from early 1961 on. We also know from Bauer's letters to Bing that La Scala planned to mount it for Corelli sometime. In addition, Lauri-Volpi himself writes that Corelli came to visit him in his Spanish retreat for the first time in the autumn of 1963, in distress over an imminent vocal crisis. Giacomo Lauri-Volpi, "A lezione dal veterano," *Musica e Dischi*, 1969.

If Lauri-Volpi's account is accepted, the July–August 1963 date is the most likely. Firstly, it corresponds with the period during which he usually took his annual inhalation therapy (mentioned in a letter from Bauer dated February 7, 1967), following his June–July *Andrea Chénier* recording. He did not return to sing until September 26, 1963, skipping any summer festival appearances. Equally important is the fact that his announced plans for *Guglielmo Tell* and the heroic repertoire at La Scala never materialized. They ended with the May 1962 performances of *Gli Ugonotti*.

37. Interview with Arrigo Michelini, Modena, May 20, 2007.
38. Letter, Roberto Bauer to Rudolf Bing, July 31, 1963.
39. Lauri-Volpi, "A lezione dal veterano."
40. Interview with Marco Corelli, August 16–17, 2005.
41. Lauri-Volpi, "A lezione dal veterano." Lauri-Volpi's comment here is a bit self-serving. In his prime Corelli couldn't possibly have matched him in certain high-range roles, but by 1963 Lauri-Volpi was an old man with a toneless, hollow middle and forced, wobbling high notes. Apparently unaware of this, he relished in home sessions that demonstrated the singing of his day by merely belting out such things as a very shrieky high C in "Che gelida manina," but his self-indulgent comments in that particular video are best covered with the mantle of love: Corelli genuinely liked Lauri-Volpi, admired his career, and was clearly intrigued by his solid knowledge of vocal technique.
42. Ibid.
43. EMI archives, Tony Locantro, April 7, 2005.
44. John Culshaw, *Putting the Record Straight* (London: Secker & Warburg, 1981).
45. Ibid.
46. Culshaw adds that a couple of weeks later he met a woman who had been at the same civic dinner Corelli had attended. She commented on how gauche and typically Italian it was to leave a dinner like that; one simply can't always please everyone at the same time.
47. Lauri-Volpi, "A lezione dal veterano."
48. Culshaw, *Putting the Record Straight*.
49. EMI archives, Tony Locantro, April 7, 2005.
50. Ibid.
51. "Giuseppe Di Stefano was boos en wou niet zingen," *Gazet van Antwerpen*, November 29, 1963.
52. Letter, Rudolf Bing to Robert Herman, October 2, 1964.

CHAPTER 14: 1964

1. "Singer Exits, Can't Stand the Tenor," *New York Post*, January 7, 1964. Ever since, the dispute has remained over the question whether Corelli was the sole reason Stella walked out on La Scala or if there was something more personal. When she left the Met in 1960 on grounds of illness, she went on to perform at La Scala within a month. That brought on a breach-of-contract lawsuit, the result of which was that she was banned from American stages for a full two years (even though the Met was actually happy she had left, for she had received a number of bad reviews there). In addition to her having developed some sort of friction with Corelli over the *Fanciulla* rehearsals, the taxing part of Minnie may also have been ill suited to her vocal temperament. As it is, the walkout effectively ended her La Scala career.
2. Emily Coleman, "Born to the Breed," *Opera News*, February 5, 1966.
3. Maurizio Chierici, "Il bel tenore sempre in burrasca," *Oggi Illustrato*, January 23, 1964.
4. Ibid.
5. Ibid.

6. Ibid.
7. Alan Branigan, "Tenor on Way Up," *Newark Sunday News*, February 10, 1963.
8. Recording of the announcement, private print, Philadelphia, March 3, 1964.
9. Giovanna Kessler, "Sterne am Opernhimmel," *Opernwelt*, February 1964.
10. Jess Thomas, *Kein Schwert verhieß mir der Vater* (Vienna: Paul Neff Verlag, 1986).
11. See chapter 11, n. 116.
12. James Drake, *Richard Tucker: A Biography* (New York: E. P. Dutton, 1984).
13. When Gigli presented *Roméo* at La Scala in 1934, he did it in an Italian translation. The work was performed three times and was not revived there during Corelli's career.
14. Bruno Tosi, "Franco Corelli è tornato in Italia: 'Mr. Esaurito' ci parla dell' America," *Musica e Dischi*, July 1965.
15. Rudolf Bing, *5000 Nights at the Opera* (New York: Doubleday, 1972).
16. Fred Calland, "Corelli, Nilsson's *Aida* Dazzles," *Columbus Citizen Journal*, April 23, 1964.
17. Letter, Roberto Bauer to Robert Herman, June 18, 1964.
18. René Seghers, unpublished portion of an interview with Joan Sutherland published in *Luister*, June 2003.
19. Letter, Rudolf Bing to Franco Corelli, November 22, 1963.
20. Letter, Rudolf Bing to Roberto Bauer, June 21, 1964.
21. Letter, Roberto Bauer to Rudolf Bing, June 24, 1964.
22. Martin-Wolfram Reinecke, quoting Bing in the *Paris-Presse*, "Kampf um *Norma*," *Opernwelt*, June–July 1964.
23. Ibid.
24. There is no direct evidence to support this theory, but from the correspondence with EMI and Bauer concerning future recordings that didn't materialize, it is clear that the Corellis believed they were being plotted against. Corelli would usually act on his suspicions by counter-recording for other companies, producing direct rivals to those EMI sets that he regarded as his natural right in the first place.
25. E-mail correspondence with Tony Locantro, April 8, 2005.
26. Interview with Michel Glotz, April 12, 2005.
27. Letter, Roberto Bauer to Rudolf Bing, June 30, 1964.
28. Interview with Michel Glotz, April 12, 2005.
29. Letter, Roberto Bauer to Rudolf Bing, June 30, 1964.
30. EMI archives, Tony Locantro, April 7, 2005. In an "Opera Fanatic" broadcast (February 3, 1990; CZ1V) Corelli mentioned having also recorded part of the *Tosca* duet, which is a mistake. As can be seen on the program, *Tosca* was not due to be recorded, if only because it would interfere with EMI's imminent recording of the complete opera with Corelli and Crespin. Because there are indeed unpublished recordings from those sessions, which started immediately after the ruined Callas duets, Corelli mixed up the Crespin *Tosca* fragments with the Callas duet sessions (unless he warmed up with fragments from *Tosca*, but in that case the recorder would not yet have been running). E-mail correspondence with Tony Locantro, April 8, 2005.
31. Letters, Roberto Bauer to Rudolf Bing, June 30, 1964; July 18, 1964.
32. Ibid.
33. Letter, Roberto Bauer to Rudolf Bing, June 30, 1964; EMI archives, Tony Locantro, April 7, 2005; telephone interview with Michel Glotz, April 12, 2005.
34. EMI archives, Tony Locantro, April 7, 2005. Said Tony Locantro, a representative of EMI: "We know that about fifty minutes of music of the ill-fated *Tosca* with Crespin was recorded because there is a note in the file to that effect, but no trace could be found of those tapes. They may still turn up one day in the tape library in wrongly labeled tins, but that is a fairly slim chance now since all EMI's tapes were thoroughly checked about ten years ago when the company set up a massive computer database for all the master tapes it holds worldwide. Some lost treasures did turn up, but not the incomplete Corelli *Tosca*!"
35. Letter, Robert Herman to Roberto Bauer, July 24, 1964.
36. Ibid.

37. EMI archives, Tony Locantro, April 7, 2005.
38. Giacomo Lauri-Volpi, "A lezione dal veterano," *Musica e Dischi*, 1969.
39. Letter, Roberto Bauer to Paul Jaretzki, September 21, 1964.
40. Based on Alexei Buljigin, *Prins v stranj Tjudes* (Moscow: Agraf, 2003).
41. Marina Boagno and Gilberto Starone, *Un uomo, una voce* (Parma: Azzali Editore, 1990); published in English as *Corelli: A Man, a Voice* (Dallas, Tex.: Baskerville, 1996).
42. Internal Met correspondence, 1964–65.
43. Letter, Mario Del Monaco to Rudolf Bing, November 5, 1963.
44. Franco Corelli, as told to G. Fogliani, "Sto per conquistare Broadway," *Eva*, October 15, 1964.
45. Neither of these planned performances materialized.
46. Corelli, as told to Fogliani, "Sto per conquistare Broadway."
47. Piero Zanotto, "Corelli tenore bello sarà re di Granada," *Il Gazzettino*, November 2, 1964.
48. Corelli, as told to Fogliani, "Sto per conquistare Broadway."
49. Ibid.
50. EMI archives, Tony Locantro, April 7, 2005.
51. Contract between Franco Corelli and the Metropolitan Opera Association, November 6, 1964.
52. Letter, Roberto Bauer to Robert Herman, December 2, 1964.
53. Letters between Roberto Bauer and Rudolf Bing, January 5, 1965; January 7, 1965; January 9, 1965.
54. Interview with Donald DiGrazia, New York, November 15, 2004.
55. Letters, Rudolf Bing to Roberto Bauer and Franco Corelli, December 28, 1964.

CHAPTER 15: 1965

1. The letter from Bauer to Robert Herman of January 2, 1965, says "Lewisham" Stadium, an obvious error on the part of Bauer, who confused Lewisohn Stadium with a European venue. The concert never took place, presumably for the reason mentioned.
2. Letters between Roberto Bauer and Rudolf Bing, January 5, 1965, January 7, 1965, January 9, 1965.
3. Advertisement for Angel Records, *Opera News*, February 6, 1965.
4. Contract between the Metropolitan Opera Association and Franco Corelli, March 10, 1965.
5. Letter, Rudolf Bing to Roberto Bauer, April 2, 1965.
6. Letter, Rudolf Bing to Roberto Bauer, March 25, 1965.
7. Letter, Roberto Bauer to Rudolf Bing, July 9, 1965.
8. Letter, Rudolf Bing to Roberto Bauer, April 2, 1965.
9. Egon Stadelman,"Rückkehr der verlorenen Tochter," *Opernwelt*, April 1965.
10. Franco Occhiuzzi, "Ritorna trionfale della Callas," *Corriere della Sera*, March 21, 1965.
11. Interview with Donald DiGrazia, New York, November 15, 2004.
12. Stadelman,"Rückkehr der verlorenen Tochter."
13. "Callas splendida spettatori in delirio."
14. "Dopo 7 anni la Callas riconquista il Met," *L'Unita*, March 21, 1965.
15. Stadelman,"Rückkehr der verlorenen Tochter."
16. Occhiuzzi, "Ritorna trionfale della Callas."
17. Ibid.
18. Gene Gilette, "Trionfo della Callas al Met," unidentified Italian newspaper, March 21, 1965.
19. Stadelman,"Rückkehr der verlorenen Tochter."
20. "Callas splendida spettatori in delirio."
21. Gilette, "Trionfo della Callas al Met."
22. Harold C. Schonberg, "*Tosca*, Metropolitan Opera, New York," *The New York Times*, date unknown.
23. Ethel Boros, "Franco Corelli Packs Public Hall as Star of *Aida*," *The Cleveland Plain Dealer*, May 2, 1965. The things Boros writes about the performance are very specific. Unfortunately, they do not match the recording of the actual performance. Curtis-Verna is dead on pitch on

her B-flats in "O terra addio" and not flat, as suggested. In addition, Corelli does three excellent B-flat diminuendi there, which go unnoticed, even though they probably still talk about these diminuendi in Cleveland today. Also, the softening of the B-flat in "Celeste Aida" isn't really there. Therefore I assume Boros attended a rehearsal, which Corelli may have used to try out the B-flat diminuendo.

24. Bruno Tosi, "Franco Corelli è tornato in Italia: 'Mr. Esaurito' ci parla dell' America," *Musica e Dischi*, July 1965.
25. Ibid.
26. EMI archives, Tony Locantro, April 7, 2005.
27. Ibid.
28. Birgit Nilsson, despite writing in her autobiography that she never had an exclusive contract, had been under contract with EMI for several years starting from 1957, during which time she recorded several operatic recitals in London and a *Fanciulla del West* at La Scala. The contract was allowed to lapse and during the next few years she recorded extensively for other companies such as Decca/London and RCA. She returned to EMI for *Turandot* (1965), *Aida* (1966), and *Der Freischütz* (1969), all made under individual letter agreements. EMI archives, Tony Locantro, April 7, 2005.
29. Telephone interview with Birgit Nilsson, April 10, 2005.
30. EMI archives, Tony Locantro, April 7, 2005.
31. Letter, Roberto Bauer to Rudolf Bing, September 10, 1965.
32. Ibid.
33. Letter, Roberto Bauer to Rudolf Bing, September 13, 1965.
34. Jess Thomas, *Kein Schwert verhieß mir der Vater* (Vienna: Paul Neff Verlag, 1986).
35. Letter, Rudolf Bing to Roberto Bauer, October 6, 1965.
36. Letters between Roberto Bauer and Rudolf Bing, October 11, 1965, and November 14, 1965.
37. Robert Pullen and Stephen Taylor, *Montserrat Caballé: Casta Diva* (United Kingdom: Northeastern University Press, 1994).

CHAPTER 16: 1966

1. Rudolf Bing, *A Knight at the Opera* (New York: G. P. Putnam's Sons, 1981).
2. Interview with Donald DiGrazia, New York, November 15, 2006.
3. F. O., "Corelli trionfa al Met," *Corriere della Sera*, January 19, 1966.
4. Peter Gravina, "Artists in the Kitchen," *Opera News*, March 19, 1966. Corelli seems to have risen to the challenge.
5. EMI archives, Tony Locantro, April 7, 2005.
6. Letter, Roberto Bauer to Rudolf Bing, July 31, 1963.
7. "Franco Corelli condannato per inadempienza," *Il Piccolo*, March 27, 1966.
8. Max de Schauensee, "Philadelphia," *Opera News*, June 4, 1966.
9. Robert Pullen and Stephen Taylor, *Montserrat Caballé: Casta Diva* (United Kingdom: Northeastern University Press, 1994).
10. Schauensee, "Philadelphia."
11. Carlamaria Casanova, *Renata Tebaldi: La voce d'angelo* (Milan: Electa; 1981); published in English as *Renata Tebaldi: The Voice of an Angel*, trans. Connie Mandracchia DeCaro (Dallas, Tex: Baskerville, 1995).
12. Alan Blyth, "Slave-Girl Liù Steals the Show," *Gramophone*, July 1966; Stephen Walsh, "Covent Garden," *Music and Musicians*, July 1966; Colin Mason, P. H.-W., John Higgins, and D. F. B., unidentified newspaper clippings.
13. "Con *Turandot* di Puccini Corelli è tornato a Londra," *Corriere della Sera*, May 22, 1966.
14. "Franco Corelli questa sera in *Continental Miniatures*," *Il Progresso*, June 4, 1966.
15. EMI archives, Tony Locantro, April 7, 2005.
16. Telephone interview with Birgit Nilsson, April 10, 2005.
17. Review in unidentified newspaper with photo of Corelli handing around coffee, September 1966.

18. Ida Bailey Allen, "Let's Eat!," *Morning Star Tribune*, January 18, 1967.
19. Ibid.
20. Peter Gravina, *The Bel Canto Cookbook* (New York: Doubleday, 1964).
21. Ann C. Eisner, "Franco Corelli's Christmas," *Tape Recording*, 1966–67.
22. Telephone interview with Birgit Nilsson, April 10, 2005.
23. Caroline Cooke, "Corelli Sings Out . . . for Lasagna," *Newark Star Ledger*, November 27, 1966.
24. "Franco Corelli ha cantato a Firenze," *Corriere della Sera*, January 8, 1967.
25. Interview for American television, December 1966.
26. "Julie Andrews," *L'Europeo Milano*, January 12, 1967.
27. "Lasagne alla Newyorkese," *Radiocorriere Torino* [television viewing guide], October 22, 1966.
28. Eisner, "Franco Corelli's Christmas."

CHAPTER 17: 1967

1. Giorgio Gualerzi, *Discoteca*, February–March 1967.
2. "Franco Corelli ha cantato a Firenze," *Corriere della Sera*, January 8, 1967.
3. "Corelli sarà l'interprete di un nuovo film: *Rigoletto*," *Corriere della Sera*, January 24, 1967.
4. Marina Boagno and Gilberto Starone, *Ettore Bastianini: Una voce di bronza e velluto* (Parma: Azzali, 1991).
5. Ibid.
6. These recordings were not officially released until 2003, when they appeared under the title *Franco Corelli: The Unknown Recordings* (EMI 7243 5 62698 2 8). The CD featured added tracks from another unreleased session in which Corelli had dubbed "Di quella pira" and the *Ballo* aria onto orchestra tracks recorded as far back as 1958 (see the section on September 1964). The CD booklet has an asterisk indicating tracks 10 and 11 as the ones that were dubbed, but the notes suggest that tracks 9 ("Nel verde maggio") and 10 were the dubbed ones. I am grateful to Tony Locantro of EMI for providing the correct chronological information.
7. EMI archives, Tony Locantro, April 7, 2005.
8. Angel Records advertisement, 1967.
9. Conrad L. Osborne, "Franco Corelli In and Out of Costume," *High Fidelity*, February 1967.
10. Speight Jenkins Jr., "Corelli's Enzo Highlights *Gioconda*," *Dallas Times Herald*, March 31, 1967.
11. Interview with Kenn Harris, September 20, 2005.
12. Richard J. Cattani, "Spectacular *Aida*," *Christian Science Monitor*, April 22, 1967; Alta Maloney, "Leontyne Price Great in Met's *Aida*," *Boston Traveller*, April 22, 1967.
13. James Cortese, "Operatic Star Terms Success a 'Long Story,'" unidentified (Memphis, Tenn.) newspaper clipping, May 5, 1967.
14. Telephone interview with Arrigo Michelini, September 1, 2007.
15. Interview with Les Dryer, New York, September 2, 2005.
16. Louise Ahrens, "Molto Bello Memphis View Inspires Opera Star to Song," *Memphis Press-Scimitar*, May 8, 1967.
17. Interview with Marco Corelli, Ancona, March 21–23, 2006.
18. Interview with Marco Corelli, Ancona, January 17, 2005.
19. Antonangelo Pinna, "Benvenuti: Il match è mio," *Panorama*, September 28, 1967.
20. Interview with Marco Corelli, Ancona, January 17, 2005.
21. Letter, Mrs. Alan Drennen Jr. of the Birmingham Festival to S. A. Gorlinsky, May 31, 1968.
22. Jack Frymire, "Il piu semplice e il piu bello," *Music and Artists*, February–March 1968.
23. Letters between Roberto Bauer and Rudolf Bing, 1967.
24. The 1967 RAI special was presented at the audiovisual exhibition "Mostra per Franco Corelli," in Ancona's Teatro delle Muse, throughout the early part of 2006. The exhibition also featured a great deal of other forgotten footage from Corelli's Italian and American television appearances.
25. Enrico Vaime, "Appuntamento con Franco Corelli," *RAI Italy*, filmed August–September 1967.
26. A. P., "Verdi: *Aida*," *Gramophone*, November 1967.
27. EMI archives, Tony Locantro, April 7, 2005.
28. C. C., "Per Corelli una canzone di Pizetti," *Corriere della Sera*, December 30, 1967.

29. Rex Reed, "Always Wondering: Can He Do It Again?," *The New York Times*, September 17, 1967.
30. Ibid.
31. Harriet Johnson, "Words and Music," *New York Post*, September 20, 1967.
32. Telephone interview with Mirella Freni, May 22, 2007.
33. Harold C. Schonberg, "Opera *Roméo et Juliette* at the Met," *The New York Times*, 20 September, 1967.
34. Mary Campbell, "As Fame Increases, So Does Tenor's Tension," *Bristol Press*, November 8, 1967.
35. Interview with Arrigo Michelini, Modena, May 20, 2007.
36. Vieri Poggiali, *Antonio Ghiringhelli: Una vita per La Scala* (Urbino: QuattroVenti, 2004).
37. Interview with Charles Anthony, New York, September 2, 2005.
38. Earl Wilson, "It Happened Last Night," *New York Post*, February 19, 1968; Frymire, "Il piu semplice."
39. Wilson, "It Happened Last Night."
40. EMI archives, Tony Locantro, April 7, 2005.
41. Giorgio Gualerzi, *La Stampa*, December 27, 1967.

CHAPTER 18: 1968–1969

1. Shirley Verrett and Christopher Brooks, *I Never Walked Alone* (Hoboken, N.J.: Wiley and Sons, 2003).
2. Ibid.
3. Ibid.
4. Telegram, February 1, 1968.
5. Jack Frymire, "Il piu semplice e il piu bello," *Music and Artists*, February–March 1968.
6. Robert Kotlowitz, "The Fragile Ego," *Harper's*, June 1968.
7. C. C., "Per Corelli una canzone di Pizetti," *Corriere della Sera*, December 30, 1967.
8. Harriet Johnson, "Corelli Makes Carnegie Hall Debut," *New York Post*, March 12, 1968.
9. EMI archives, Tony Locantro, April 7, 2005.
10. Theodore Strongin, "Caballé, Corelli and Giaiotti Sing," *The New York Times*, April 1968; Douglas Watt, "Corelli & Co. a Winning Act," *New York News*, April 9, 1968.
11. Interview with Victor Callegari, New York, September 2, 2005.
12. Mary Campbell, "Corelli Will Sing in N.Y. Parks," AP Newsfeatures, June 1968.
13. EMI archives, Tony Locantro, April 7, 2005.
14. Letter, Roberto Bauer to Rudolf Bing, August 23, 1966. As late as June 10, 2006, Freni repeated that the offer was serious and that Karajan had wanted to do it with her and Franco, whom she called *stupido* for not doing it ("Mirella Freni alle Muse per Corelli," *Corriere Adriatico*, June 10, 2006).
15. Letter, Henry W. Lauterstein [one of the Met's lawyers] to Rudolf Bing, September 10, 1968; letter, Rudolf Bing to Sandor Gorlinsky, October 3, 1968.
16. "Sopranos' Week," *Time*, September 27, 1968; internal Met correspondence, September 1968.
17. Ibid.
18. Mark Campbell, "Bygone Days of Primadonna Rivalry Recalled at Met Opera," Associated Press, September 17, 1968.
19. "Sopranos' Week," *Time*; internal Met correspondence, September 1968.
20. Plácido Domingo, *My First Forty Years* (New York: Knopf, 1983).
21. William Como, "Mr. Opening Night," *After Dark*, October 1968.
22. Ibid., photos by Kenn Duncan. Fur was highly fashionable in the 1950s and the 1960s. The fact that some of these animals were exceedingly threatened by extinction merely added to a fur's price and prestige.
23. Telephone interview with Birgit Nilsson, April 10, 2005.
24. Marcel Prawy, *Erzählt aus seinem Leben* (Vienna: Kremayr & Scheriau, 2002).
25. EMI archives, Tony Locantro, April 7, 2005.

512 • NOTES

26. Unidentified newspaper clipping, January 9, 1969.
27. Franco Corelli, unidentified magazine interview, January 19, 1969.
28. Giuseppe Isozio, "Corelli a lezione (per *Il Trovatore*) da Lauri-Volpi," *Il Telegrafo* (Livorno), December 11, 1969.
29. Letter, Roberto Bauer to Rudolf Bing, January 29, 1969.
30. Interview with Marco Corelli, Ancona, January 17, 2005.
31. Letter, Roberto Bauer to Rudolf Bing, January 29, 1969.
32. Telegrams, Rudolf Bing to Franco Corelli, February 13–14, 1969; Rudolf Bing to Roberto Bauer, February 14, 1969.
33. Sally Hammond, "An Even Tenor and His Ways," *New York Post*, March 7, 1969; letter, Rudolf Bing to Franco Corelli, March 13, 1969.
34. Letter, Roberto Bauer to Rudolf Bing, March 11, 1969.
35. Carlo Meano, medical dispensation, March 12, 1969.
36. In the Superior Court of Fulton County, Georgia, Civil Action no. 65-45814, *Birmingham Festival of Arts Association Inc. vs. Franco Corelli*, added to a letter from April 14, 1970.
37. "Behind the Scenes," *High Fidelity*, October 1969.
38. EMI archives, Tony Locantro, April 7, 2005.
39. EMI archives, Tony Locantro, April 7, 2005; "Behind the Scenes," *High Fidelity*, October 1969.
40. Peter Gravina, "Franco Corelli: A Voice Speaks," unidentified magazine clipping, 1969.
41. Lane Carter, "Corelli Starred in Dramatic Scene in Atlanta Recently," *Birmingham News*, May 19, 1969.
42. The lady wished to remain anonymous, but she is known to me through the source, who asked me not to reveal his identity.
43. Interview with Kenn Harris, New York, September 2, 2005; interview with Luigi Zoboli, Genoa, November 16, 2006.
44. Telephone interview with Donald DiGrazia, New York, November 15, 2006.
45. It was tempting to quote Beverly Sills here, who in *Beverly: An Autobiography* (New York: Bantam, 1987) wrote that Loretta was rumored to have confronted Bing with the fact that her husband wouldn't have sex with her for three nights before he sang, and was too tired to have it for three nights afterward: "Since he's singing every fourth night, I want you to know that you have ruined our sex lives." However, Robert Merrill wrote almost exactly the same story eleven years earlier about Del Monaco's wife Rina and Bing. As Merrill was a lot closer to the fire, I am inclined to follow his version. (Robert Merrill with Robert Saffron, *Between Acts* [New York: McGraw-Hill, 1976].)
46. William H. Honan, "A Champion Tenor Defends His Title," *The New York Times*, February 8, 1972.
47. Rudolf Bing, *A Knight at the Opera* (New York: G. P. Putnam's Sons, 1981).
48. Letter, Lauterstein & Lauterstein to Robert Herman, October 20, 1969; memorandum, Lochlann B. Dey, October 28, 1969.

CHAPTER 19: 1970–1975

1. Giorgio Pillon, "Ho trovato in America la patria del bel canto," *Domenica del Corriere*, June 6, 1973.
2. William H. Honan, "A Champion Tenor Defends His Title," *The New York Times*, February 8, 1970.
3. Pillon, "Ho trovato in America."
4. Joan Peyser, *Bernstein: A Biography* (New York: Beech Tree Books, William Morrow, 1987).
5. Honan, "A Champion Tenor Defends His Title."
6. Ibid.
7. Ibid.
8. Ibid. There are no A's in that aria and only one B-flat.
9. Alan Rich, review, *New York Magazine*, January 9, 1970.
10. Rudolf Bing, *A Knight at the Opera* (New York: G. P. Putnam's Sons, 1981).
11. Pillon, "Ho trovato in America."

12. Telephone interview with Schuyler Chapin, March 16, 2005; quotes from Schuyler Chapin, *Musical Chairs* (New York: G. P. Putnam's Sons, 1977).
13. Letter, Lochlann B. Dey, Metropolitan Opera House, to Gorlinsky Promotions, March 23, 1970.
14. Telephone interview with Antonietta Stella, May 25, 2006.
15. Letter, Lauterstein & Lauterstein to Lipkowitz, Plaut, Salberg & Harris, June 10, 1970.
16. Letter, Lauterstein & Lauterstein, to S[andor] A. Gorlinsky, May 5, 1970.
17. Agenda for meeting with Corelli, June 19, 1970, Metropolitan office memo, June 24, 1970.
18. Telephone interview with Birgit Nilsson, April 10, 2005.
19. The film footage was shot by German television in the context of a Birgit Nilsson special. Because television required high standards in terms of sound and vision, studio shots of Nilsson were instituted, and the Macerata live soundtrack was substituted for the EMI studio production).
20. Interestingly, neither Corelli nor Bing seems to have had even the slightest awareness of the status of Francisco Franco, one of the last three noncommunist dictators in Europe, who was not accepted among democratic European politicians.
21. Letter, Rudolf Bing to Franco Corelli, October 13, 1970.
22. Corelli's schedule, January–April 1971, November 13, 1970.
23. Telephone interview with Giulietta Simionato, April 25, 2007.
24. Shirley Verrett and Christopher Brooks, *I Never Walked Alone* (Hoboken, N.J.: Wiley and Sons, 2003).
25. French radio interviews, ca. 1970–74.
26. Donal Henahan, "Soprano Miscast as Met's Present Lucia," *The New York Times*, January 13, 1971; Speight Jenkins, "Unhappy Day for Lucy at the Met," *Dallas Times Herald*, January 17, 1971; A. Fedele, "Prestigiosa *Lucia* al Met," *Il Progresso Italo-Americano*, January 13, 1971.
27. Manuela Hoelterhoff, "*Lucia* Enhanced by Top Soprano," *Hofstra Chronicle*, February 18, 1971; Mary Campbell, "*Lucia* Singer Triumphs," *Baltimore Morning Sun*, January 25, 1971; Allen Hughes, "Lucia Sung Here by Gail Robinson," *The New York Times*, January 20, 1971.
28. Letter, Rudolf Bing to Emily Deiber, April 30, 1969.
29. Christa Ludwig and Peter Csobádi, . . . *Und ich wäre so gern Primadonna gewesen: Erinnerungen* (Berlin: Henschel, 1994).
30. Ibid.
31. Ibid.
32. Telephone interview with Bruno Sammartino, January 31, 2006.
33. Ibid.
34. Ibid.
35. Richard Covello, "Out of Chaos," *The New York Times*, March 3, 1971.
36. The shouts of "*Bravo*, Gedda!" are very audible on the Melodram recording of March 27 (Melodram CM 27088) and the unreleased pirate recording of March 31. Some caution is needed here, however, because most other recordings don't give the applause after "Pourquoi me réveiller" uncut. At this point one is reminded of Corelli's remarks regarding organized anti-Corelli claques in Naples and Milan, whose heckling is not audible, either because the applause was cut off before they could be heard, or because these particular performances went unrecorded. But from Corelli's comments throughout it is clear that this practice was part of the reason he stayed away from Italy in the second half of the 1960s.
37. Letter, Robert Herman to Goeran Gentele, March 17, 1971.
38. Ibid.
39. Letter, Herman Krawitz to Goeran Gentele, March 31, 1971.
40. Letter, Rudolf Bing to Loretta Corelli, April 14, 1971.
41. Theodore Stronging, "Sparkling *Aida* Opens June Festival at the Met," *The New York Times*, June 1, 1971.
42. Ibid.
43. A. Fedele, "Fascino del *La Bohème*," *Il Progresso Italo-Americano*, April 7, 1971.
44. A. Fedele, "Met: Incandescente '*Tosca*' con la Bumbry e Corelli," *Il Progresso Italo-Americano*, June 9, 1971.

45. Stefan Zucker, "Opera Fanatic" broadcast, May 7, 1994.
46. Letter, L. B. Dey to Robert Herman, June 9, 1971.
47. Statement of final accounting, 1970–71 season, June 21, 1971.
48. P. S., "Corelli dal Giapone aiuta la Serenissima," *Corriere della Sera*, November 23, 1971.
49. Ibid.
50. "Per Franco Corelli karate' sfortunato," *Corriere della Sera*, November 17, 1971.
51. P. S., "Corelli dal Giapone aiuta la Serenissima."
52. Alfredo Mandelli, "Gesù bambino ha portato un tenore," *Oggi Illustrato*, January 15, 1972.
53. Ibid.
54. Joost de Man, unpublished interview with Cristina Deutekom, Amsterdam, January 2000; conversation with Jaap Deutekom, Amsterdam, November 14, 2007
55. Ibid.
56. Ibid.
57. Mandelli, "Gesù bambino ha portato un tenore."
58. Mario Posi, "L'opera a Macerata," *Corriere della Sera*, July 5, 1971.
59. Cristina Deutekom with Paul Korenhof, *Een leven met muziek* (Baarn: Bosch & Keuning, 1988).
60. Peter G. Davis, "Price and Corelli in *Forza* at Met," *The New York Times*, January 23, 1972.
61. Letter, Paul Jaretzki to Ross D. Smith and Richard Cisek, April 28, 1972; letter, Hugo Dixon to Jaretzki, April 28, 1972.
62. Telephone interview with Giancarlo Del Monaco, August 24, 2005.
63. Robert Pullen and Stephen Taylor, *Montserrat Caballé: Casta Diva* (United Kingdom: Northeastern University Press, 1994).
64. Telephone interview with Birgit Nilsson, April 10, 2005.
65. Jay Shir, *A Tale of Four Houses* (London: Harper Collins, 2003); Vieri Poggiali, *Antonio Ghiringhelli: Una vita per La Scala* (Urbino: QuattroVenti, 2004).
66. Confidential handwritten memo, no date attached, indicating payments agreed upon with all singers in the 1971–72 season.
67. Radio interview with George Jellinek, May 19, 1977.
68. Letter, Rudolf Bing to Franco Corelli, June 17, 1972.
69. "Lirica a Verona," *Il Gazzettino*, July 12, 1972.
70. Maritz Gentele later denied that Goeran had been trying to pass, but Mariotti, Azara, and the driver of a passing mail truck who witnessed the accident testified otherwise. No one could explain how Gentele could have failed to see the truck at that hour, in bright sunlight with an unrestricted view. Mariotti testified that the glaze of the sun shining on the asphalt must have blinded him. (Regiment of the Carabinieri of Cagliari, N. 307/1 of the Judicial Report, Arzachena, July 31, 1972.)
71. Interview with Marco Corelli, Ancona, January 17, 2005.
72. Renzo Allegri, "Eco com'è nata la storia del mio flirt con la Tebaldi," *Gente*, August 1972.
73. Interview with Luigi Zoboli, Genoa, November 16, 2006.
74. Allegri, "Ecco com'é nata la storia."
75. Schuyler Chapin, *Sopranos, Mezzos, Tenors, Bassos, and Other Friends* (United States: Random House, 1995).
76. Cable to Rafael Kubelik and Henry Lewis, October 18, 1972.
77. Met office memorandum, September 25, 1972.
78. Letter, Albert B. Gins to Chapin, November 24, 1972.
79. Interview with Arrigo Michelini, Modena, May 20, 2007.
80. "Enzo Adorato" (screen name of Charles Handelman), "My Only Encounter with Tebaldi," e-mail to Opera-L mailing list, December 23, 2004, http://www/opera-l.org.
81. Ibid.
82. Metropolitan office memorandum, March 17, 1971.
83. Interview, Schuyler Chapin, March 16, 2005; Chapin, *Musical Chairs*.
84. Chapin, *Sopranos, Mezzos, Tenors, Bassos*. In his earlier book, *Musical Chairs*, Chapin describes another meeting with Bing that has some similarities to the one mentioned here but takes place at a different time.

85. Ibid.
86. Chapin, *Musical Chairs*.
87. Ibid.
88. Chapin, *Sopranos, Mezzos, Tenors, Bassos, and Other Friends*.
89. The private recording of the performance largely supports Chapin's reading, although the "Fa il tuo piacere" is not shouted at the top of Corelli's lungs.
90. In *Sopranos, Mezzos, Tenors, Basses, and Other Friends*, Chapin made the end of the story a little more colorful than it really was. There Chapin rushes backstage to find Corelli and Riecker, while Tosca was already singing the duet lines all by herself. That left him no time for discussion, so he pushed Corelli onstage. Chapin may well have pushed Corelli back onto the stage, but that would not have been possible if he were not already backstage, because it is very unlikely that he could ever have made it from the auditorium to the Met's backstage area in just thirty seconds. The pirate recording leaves no room for mistakes at this point: Corelli doesn't miss a beat, and the duet starts as it should, with Cavaradossi's "Franchigia a Floria Tosca." Chapin, *Sopranos, Mezzos, Tenors, Bassos, and Other Friends*.
91. Ibid.
92. Mary Strassmeyer, "First Night Drama: *Tosca* Nixon," *The Cleveland Plain Dealer*, May 1, 1973.
93. Chapin, *Sopranos, Mezzos, Tenors, Bassos, and Other Friends*.
94. Ibid.
95. Robert Jennings, "Material of *Macbeth* Transcended by Talent," *Tennessee Commercial Appeal*, May 16, 1971.
96. Louis Nicholas, "*Macbeth* Proved to Be Highlight of Memphis Opera," *The Tennessean*, May 20, 1971.
97. John Ardoin, "Met Sparkles in Staging of Both *Macbeth, Tosca*," *Dallas Morning News*, May 20, 1973.
98. John H. Harvey, "Metropolitan Opera's *Macbeth*, Though Flawed, Shows Genius," *St. Paul Dispatch*, May 22, 1973.
99. Interview with Marco Corelli, Ancona, August 16–17, 2004.
100. Ibid.
101. Pillon, "Ho trovato in America." The singers he mentions were the current hot Italian pop singers.
102. Ibid.
103. Correspondence, August 7, 1973–March 21, 1974.
104. Interview with Arrigo Michelini, Modena, May 20, 2007.
105. Interview with Kenn Harris, September 20, 2005.
106. Interview with Marco Corelli, January 17, 2005.
107. Correspondence, August 7, 1973–March 21, 1974.
108. Raymond Morin, "5,000 Hear Met Perform Puccini's Elaborate *Turandot*," *Worcester Telegram*, May 3, 1974.
109. Richard Dyer, "Metropolitan Closes Season with *Turandot, Rigoletto*," *Boston Evening Globe*, May 1, 1974.
110. Ellen Pfeifer, "Opera Review," *Boston Advertiser*, May 1, 1974; Louis Snyder, "Met Opera's Varied Tour Fare," *The Christian Science Monitor*, May 1, 1974.
111. Joan Downs, *The Tenors* (New York: Macmillan, 1974).
112. Telephone interview with Gilda Morelli and Juan José Arias Dávalos, April 14, 2007.
113. Enrique C. Lamadrid, "Extraordinaria fue la presentación del eminente tenor Franco Corelli, en un cine de esta Capital," *La mejor revista de México*, May 1974.
114. Ibid.
115. Ibid. Corelli's Mexico City recital was forgotten until this publication. Juan José Arias Dávalos provided the program, the review, and the recording (made by his father). Arias Dávalos still remembers his father's enthusiasm: "It caused a sensation in our musical world and constituted one of the most important artistic events of the year. I am very happy that these facts are now finally where they belong, back into the chronology and the story of both Corelli's life and the history of opera in Mexico."

116. Byron Belt, "*Turandot* Booed at Met," *Jersey Journal*, May 29, 1974.
117. Interviews with Marco Corelli, Ancona, January 28–30, 2007.
118. Ilsa Elisa Zellermayer, *Drei Tenöre und ein Sopran* (Berlin: Henschel, 2000).
119. Interview with Alessandro Scaravelli and Marco Corelli, Ancona, June 11, 2004.
120. Guido Tartoni, "Il Divo," *TV Radiocorriere*, May 19–25, 1974.
121. Joan Downs, *The Tenors* (New York: Macmillan, 1974).
122. Bruce Badger, e-mail correspondence, June 4, 2006.
123. Farley Hutchins, "Met's Lesser Lights Fare Well in Turandot," *Akron Beacon Journal*, September 21, 1974.
124. Downs, *The Tenors*.
125. James Drake, *Richard Tucker: A Biography* (New York: E. P. Dutton, 1984).
126. Ibid.
127. Ellen Pfeifer, "It's Metropolitan Opera Week," *Boston Herald Advertiser*, April 20, 1975.
128. Chapin, *Sopranos, Mezzos, Tenors, Bassos, and Other Friends*.
129. Harriet Johnson, "A Prince in Tokyo Asks, 'Is Corelli Going To Sing?,'" *New York Post*, June 11, 1975.
130. Richard Halloran, "Ovation for Corelli Marks Successful Tokyo Stand," *The New York Times*, June 11, 1975.
131. Ibid.
132. Chapin, *Sopranos, Mezzos, Tenors, Bassos, and Other Friends*.
133. Chapin, *Musical Chairs*.
134. It has been said that he only accepted the Calafs at the last minute in order to save the day for the Arena, when a colleague became ill, but Jan Neckers, who attended the performances, pointed out to me that the programs with Corelli's name were available starting in early July.
135. Johanna Fiedler, *Molto Agitato* (New York: Nan A. Talese/Doubleday, 2001).
136. Rita Hunter, *Wait 'til the Sun Shines, Nellie* (London: Hamish Hamilton, 1989); telephone conversation with Mairwyn Thomas (Hunter's daughter), January 10, 2003.
137. Interview with Loretta Corelli, January 27, 2007.
138. Norman Egenberg, "Tax Schedule for Franco Corelli," 1962.
139. Telephone interview with Birgit Nilsson, April 10, 2005; correspondence with Nilsson, May–June 2005.
140. Interview with Gabriella Tucci, Rome, January 18, 2005.
141. Interviews with Marco Corelli, Ancona, January 28–30, 2007. The exact date of the surgery was not known to Marco and may have been as late as 1977, in which case the problem would have occurred around the time he left the Met.

CHAPTER 20: 1976–1981

1. Liner notes to *Emma Renzi: A Tribute* (Claremont, G SE 785075); Robert Pullen and Stephen Taylor, *Montserrat Caballé: Casta Diva* (United Kingdom: Northeastern University Press, 1994).
2. Interviews with Marco Corelli, August 16–17, 2004, and January 28–30, 2007.
3. Lou Cevetillo, "Vocal Scoops," *Yonkers Herald Statesman Sunday Magazine*, March 26, 1978.
4. Lou Cevetillo, "Will Corelli Come In from the Cold?," *Yonkers Herald Statesman Sunday Magazine*, February 26, 1978.
5. Ibid.
6. Vieri Poggiali, *Antonio Ghiringhelli: Una vita per La Scala* (Urbino: QuattroVenti, 2004).
7. Telephone interview with Giancarlo Del Monaco, in the presence of his uncle Alberto, August 24, 2005; Alberto was sitting next to Giancarlo and can be heard in the background giving the answers to some of the questions.
8. Telephone interview with Giancarlo Del Monaco, August 24, 2005.
9. "Opera Fanatic" broadcast, February 3, 1990 (Bel Canto Society, CZ1V).
10. Mark Schiavone, Gilberto Starone, and Stephen R. Leopold, who together compiled the first Corelli videography, mention that this television show was a celebration of Nilsson's birthday. Hamilton used the November date as well but omitted the reference to her birthday, which is

understandable: she was born on May 17, 1918. The show is clearly designed in the format of the television series *This Is Your Life*.
11. Telephone interviews with Birgit Nilsson, April 10, 2005, and June 2005.

CHAPTER 21: 1982–1989

1. Giuliano Marchegini, "L'ultima saluto a Del Monaco ascoltando ancora la sua voce," *La Stampa*, October 20, 1982.
2. Mario Del Monaco, in his last interview (1978), on "Del Monaco, the Singing Volcano," DVD (Bel Canto Society, 0123).
3. Rainer Stiller, "Der letzte könig der Tenöre," *Bunte*, October 1982.
4. Interview with Nazzareno Antinori (with assistance from Chiara Liuti), December 2005.
5. Antinori's voice can be heard in a *Tosca* CD (Arts, 447158-2) and a *Madama Butterfly* DVD (Arena di Verona, 4509-00220-2).
6. "Opera Fanatic" broadcast, May 12, 1990 (Bel Canto Society, CZ3V); "Opera Fanatic" broadcast, July 21, 1990 (Bel Canto Society, CZ5V).
7. Neil Shicoff, "Tenor Neil Shicoff on His Teacher, Franco Corelli," *Gramophone*, September 2007.
8. Interview with Luigi Zoboli and Guido Ingaramo, Genoa, November 16, 2006.
9. Interviews with Marco Corelli, Ancona, March 21–23, 2006.
10. The affair with Renée was confirmed by no fewer than three different sources, all within Corelli's immediate circle, but we respect their wish to remain anonymous. Their identity, however, is known to the publisher.

CHAPTER 22: 1990–1994

1. "Opera Fanatic" broadcast, February 3, 1990 (Bel Canto Society, CZ1V).
2. Corelli mentions Buenos Aires and Rio de Janeiro in the "Opera Fanatic" broadcast of March 3, 1990. Moscow and South Africa follow from the text elsewhere in this book.
3. "Opera Fanatic" broadcast, May 25, 1991.
4. "Opera Fanatic" broadcast, December 8, 1990, (Bel Canto Society, CZ6V).
5. "Opera Fanatic" broadcast, February 3, 1990 (Bel Canto Society, CZ1V).
6. Interview with Luciano Pavarotti, Rotterdam, April 15, 2005.
7. "Opera Fanatic" broadcast, May 12, 1990 (Bel Canto Society, CZ3V); "Opera Fanatic" broadcast, May 25, 1991.
8. Interview with Luigi Zoboli, Genoa, November 16, 2006.
9. Ibid.
10. Mosé Franco, http://www.mosefranco.com, accessed October 15, 2007.
11. "Opera Fanatic" broadcast, June 9, 1990, (Bel Canto Society, CZ4V).
12. "Opera Fanatic" broadcast, July 21, 1990 (Bel Canto Society, CZ5V).
13. "Opera Fanatic" broadcast, May 12, 1990 (Bel Canto Society, CZ3V).
14. "Opera Fanatic" broadcast, May 25, 1991.
15. "Opera Fanatic" broadcast, February 3, 1990 (Bel Canto Society, CZ1V). Curiously, when I visited Loretta in Milan on January 7, 2006, she spontaneously pointed out to me the painting of her father, which was placed in front of Franco's famous portrait as Don José. She mentioned her beloved father's name with great pride and deep respect. No doubt she had a complex personality, but there is much more to the story of Franco and Loretta than the simplistically negative image she acquired in part because of a few uncontrolled outbursts in a few ill-conceived radio interviews. Her "Basta!" here may have been modesty, or an echo of her previous obsession with hiding her true age, which follows from Harold Rosenthal's account in his book *My Mad World of Opera* (London: Weidenfeld & Nicolson, 1982).
16. "Opera Fanatic" broadcast, March 30, 1991 (Bel Canto Society, CZ7V).
17. Ibid.
18. "Opera Fanatic" broadcast, February 3, 1990 (Bel Canto Society, CZ1V).
19. Interview with Gemma Giacomini, Ancona, January 18, 2005.
20. Interview with Marcella Marchetti, Ancona, August 22, 2004.

21. Interview with Gemma Giacomini, Ancona, January 18, 2005.
22. Interview with Marco Corelli, Ancona, June 11, 2004.
23. Christian Peters, *Andrea Bocelli* (Naarden, The Netherlands: Strengholt, 1999).
24. Ibid.
25. Franco Corelli, master class, Florence Gould Hall, Alliance Française, New York, hosted by Stefan Zucker, May 2, 1994.
26. Interview with Marco Corelli, Ancona, January 17, 2005.

CHAPTER 23: 1995–2000

1. Rudolf Bing, *5000 Nights at the Opera* (New York: Doubleday, 1972).
2. "The Last Great Impresario," *Opera News*, November 1997.
3. Interviews with Paul Jaretzki, New York, September 18 and 29, 2005; conversations with John Pennino, New York, September 18 and 29, 2005.
4. Interview with Franco Corelli, Vienna, December 19, 1997.
5. Ibid.
6. Interview with Marco Corelli, Ancona, June 11, 2004.
7. Ibid.
8. Ibid.

CHAPTER 24: 2001–2002

1. Interview with Luigi Zoboli, Genoa, November 16, 2006.

CHAPTER 25: 2003

1. Corelli was increasingly forgetful from the early 1990s on. Giulietta Simionato told me that when she went to the presentation of his Scala book, *Omaggio a Franco Corelli*, in 2001, she had the feeling that he didn't recognize her. Telephone interview with Giulietta Simionato, April 25, 2007.
2. Interview with Luigi Zoboli, Genoa, November 16, 2006.
3. E-mail correspondence with Stefan Zucker, September 4, 2007.
4. Graziano Corelli, who saw Franco through his various moves in the last months of 2003, maintained in a personal communication (May 17, 2007) that most of the choices were made on the basis of availability and proximity to where Loretta was living.
5. According to Marco Corelli, Luigi Zoboli, and Guido Ingaramo.
6. Interview with Enzo Sordello, October 14, 2006.
7. Telephone interview with Giorgio Gualerzi, May 20, 2006.
8. Interview with Graziano Corelli, Milan, November 15, 2006.

CHAPTER 26: 2004–2007

1. Carlamaria Casanova, *Renata Tebaldi: La voce d'angelo* (Milan: Electa; 1981); published in English as *Renata Tebaldi: The Voice of an Angel*, trans. Connie Mandracchia DeCaro (Dallas, Tex: Baskerville, 1995).

Index

Dario "Franco" Corelli does not have an entry in this index; his name is abbreviated as "FC" in the entries of people related or connected to him. In some cases, only one name of a person was known; in such cases, an identifier is given, as in "Norma (FC's first girlfriend)." Names of operas are given as they appear in the book, meaning that *Gli Ugonotti* is given along with the original French title *Les Huguenots*, whereas *L'Africana* appears only as such.

Abbiati, Franco, 151
Adami, Giuseppe, 216
Adler, Kurt Herbert, 208, 221, 224, 294, 301, 326
Aeneas, 1
Ahrens, Louise, 355
Akihito (crown prince and emperor of Japan), 483
"A la barcillunisa" (Sicilian song), 369, 446–448
Albanese, Francesco, 91, 92
Albanese, Licia, 208, 245, 334, 343, 344
Al Bano (Albano Carrisi), 425
Alexander, John, 334, 395, 396, 440
Allegra, Salvatore, 81–82
  Romulus, 81–83
Allegri, Renzo, 412–413
Altmeyer, Jeannine, 415
Alva, Luigi, 124
Amara, Lucine, 183–184, 199, 208, 215, 217–218, 221, 224, 254, 296, 299, 402, 408, 415, 419, 440
Amparán, Belén, 118–119, 137–139, 352–353
Anderson, Marian, 499n14
Andrea Chénier (photonovel), 187–188, 248
Andreotti, Giulio, 49, 488n24
Andrews, Julie, 344
Andry, Peter, 307, 314
Angeli, Adolfo, 67–68
Anthony, Charles, 208, 215, 217–218, 221, 224, 334, 361–363
Antinori, Nazzareno, 452
Aoyama, Yoshio, 208, 210
Appiani the Elder, Andrea, 98
Aragall, Giacomo, 394, 406, 458
Ardoin, John, 99, 115, 151, 291
Armstrong, Neil, 381
Arroyo, Martina, 183–184, 330, 388, 402–403, 408
Azara, Francesco, 411

Bacquier, Gabriel, 302–303, 377
Bakočević, Radmila, 379

"Munastero 'e Santa Chiara," 335–336
Balilla (Fascist youth movement), 15, 484n20
Barbarossa. *See* Frederick I
Barbato, Elisabetta, 82, 85, 93, 102
Barber, Samuel
  Antony and Cleopatra, 334
Barbieri, Fedora, 70–72, 74–75, 79, 107–108, 142, 154, 158, 166, 171, 180–181, 234, 411
Barbirolli, John, 286, 324, 335
Barbone, Davide, 36–38, 486n25, 486n28
Barnard, Christiaan, 381
Barrymore, John, 200
Bastianini, Ettore, 74–75, 137, 148–151, 158, 162, 165, 167, 171, 174–175, 178, 183–184, 192–193, 226–227, 234, 237, 254, 266, 347–348
Bauer, Roberto, 63, 90, 92, 100–101, 103, 145, 155–156, 166–173, 175–179, 182, 197, 231–233, 235–236, 239–241, 257–260, 270, 272–274, 277, 279–281, 301–302, 305, 307–310, 316, 318–319, 325–326, 328, 344–345, 356, 363, 372, 378–379, 383–384, 404, 408, 415, 497n74, 498n20, 501n110, 503n38, 506n36, 507n24
Beaton, Cecil, 207–210, 243, 364
Bechi, Gino, 37
Beecham, Sir Thomas, 283
Beethoven, Ludwig van, 388
  Ninth Symphony, 388
Behr, Jan, 402
Belli, Adriano, 48
Belli, Gioacchino, 76
Bellini, Vincenzo, 70–71, 150–152, 249
  "Malinconia, ninfa gentile," 431
  Norma, 62, 70–72, 78–79, 95–97, 104, 126, 136, 141–143, 168, 188–189, 192, 281, 302–305, 320,

405–407, 414, 417, 439–440, 442, 444
  I Puritani, 55, 151, 225–226, 280–282, 286, 305
  "Torna, vezzosa Fillide," 431, 434
Belt, Byron, 433
Benedetti, Maria, 56, 82, 85
Benois, Nicola, 97, 114, 150–151, 192
Benvenuti, Nino, 355–356
Bergman, Ingrid, 80, 304
Bergonzi, Carlo, 26, 126, 138, 155, 166, 177, 195–196, 259, 300, 319, 327, 330, 332, 351, 368, 380, 411, 445, 501n110
Berlioz, Hector, 90
Bernstein, Felicia, 389
Bernstein, Leonard, 377, 386–389, 412, 418, 423
Bertelli (Maestro), 47–48
Berti, Guido, 22–24
Biagi (bass player), 29
Bing, Nina, 462
Bing, Rudolf, 62–63, 90, 92, 100–101, 103, 145, 155–156, 166, 168, 169–173, 175–176, 178–179, 198–199, 201–202, 208–209, 211–216, 221–226, 228, 231–237, 239, 241, 258–260, 267, 269–270, 272–274, 276–278, 281, 287–288, 292–298, 300–302, 304–305, 307–309, 311, 313, 314–322, 324, 326–329, 334–335, 356–357, 363–364, 368, 370, 372–374, 378–379, 383–385, 387–390, 392, 394, 369–397, 399–400, 403, 407–411, 415, 417–418, 424, 430, 437, 439, 441, 456, 462, 489n38, 498n21, 503n38, 512n45, 513n20, 514n84
Bixio, Cesare Andrea, 37
  "La strada nel bosco," 37, 486n28
Bizet, Georges
  Carmen, 12, 36, 41, 47, 48–51, 60–61, 76–81, 93, 104, 113,

118–119, 127, 131, 135–139, 179, 183–184, 195, 226–228, 231, 236, 239, 252, 257, 259, 262, 274, 275, 283, 292, 305, 329, 364, 366, 367, 370–371, 382, 393–394, 398, 413, 418, 423, 431, 434, 437, 439, 491n103
Björling, Jussi, 111, 126, 234, 245, 291
Blanc, Giuseppe, 15–16
  "Inno del balilla" ("Fischia il sasso"), 15, 484n20
Blegen, Judith, 394, 397, 402, 435
Bliss, Anthony, 439
Bloomfield, Arthur, 326
Boagno, Marina, 106, 177, 347
Bocelli, Andrea, 460–461, 474
Böhm, Karl, 409–411
Boito, Arrigo, 65
  Mefistofele, 38, 126–127
Bonardi, Liduino, 62–63, 101, 156, 166–168, 175
Bonocore, Alberto, 111–112
Borgnognoni, Lucio, 36
Borkh, Inge, 80, 165
Boros, Ethel, 508n23
Brancati, Antonio, 33
Brando, Marlon, 96, 100
Bret, David, 492n139
Britten, Benjamin, 81
  Gloriana, 284
Brosio, Manlio, 211
Bucchi sisters, 5
Bucolier, Andrea, 204, 463, 469–471
Buljigin, Alexei, 132, 302, 310
Bumbry, Grace, 336, 365, 386, 388, 403, 408–409, 421, 434
Buzzi-Peccia, Arturo, 111
  "Lolita," 111–112

Caballé, Montserrat, 328, 332–334, 369–370, 377, 408–410, 442
Caesar, Gaius Julius, 1
Cairone, Renato
  "Pourquoi fermer ton coeur?," 236–237, 324, 357
Callas, Maria, 55–56, 61, 64, 70–72, 74, 78–79, 90–91, 95–100, 114–117, 126, 141–143, 145, 150, 152, 172, 174, 179, 188–194, 197, 226, 229, 231, 232, 239, 254, 258, 266–267, 269, 283, 286, 302–308, 311–312, 317–318, 320–323, 326, 332, 351, 373–374, 377, 408, 413, 415, 426–428, 445, 470, 492n139, 493n24, 496n27
Callegari, Victor, 370
Campanini, Carlo, 25
Caniglia, Maria, 56, 118–120, 126, 244

Canova, Antonio, 98
Capecchi, Renato, 74, 148, 157, 315
Cappuccilli, Piero, 346, 366–367, 424
Capuana, Franco, 56, 155
Cardillo, Salvatore
  "Core 'ngrato" ("Catari"), 225, 343, 345–347, 353, 431, 434, 448
Carreras, José, 415, 453, 456
Carteri, Rosanna, 73, 74–75, 112–113, 153, 157
Caruso, Enrico, 4, 42–43, 111, 206, 248–249, 260, 270, 271, 292, 313, 330, 364, 377, 396, 424–425, 429, 436, 478
Cassidy, Claudia, 222
Castelli, Christiane, 302, 303
Catalani, Alfredo, 65, 349
  Loreley, 349
  La Wally, 154
Cecchele, Gianfranco, 442
Celletti, Rodolfo, 151, 162, 251–252
Cerquetti, Anita, 46–48, 55, 78, 142–143, 163
Cevetillo, Lou, 444
Chakiris, George, 386
Chaliapin, Feodor, 65
Chapin, Schuyler, 388–389, 412, 415, 417–422, 424, 426, 429–430, 433, 437–439
Chaplin, Charlie, 304
Chaplin, Oona, 304
Cherubini, Luigi, 90
  Medea, 96
Chiari, Walter, 25
Chierici, Mario, 49
Chierici, Maurizio, 160, 256, 290
Chookasian, Lili, 244, 296, 415
Christoff, Boris, xv, 65, 68, 79, 86, 89–90, 108, 110, 130–132, 143–146, 148–149, 186, 370
Cialdini, Enrico, 2, 3
Cilea, Francesco, 91, 173–174
  Adriana Lecouvreur, 56–57, 111–112, 173–176, 186, 225–226, 269–271, 372–375, 380, 426, 444, 475
  L'Arlesiana, 447, 461
Cillario, Carlo Felice, 419–420
Cionci sisters, 30
Clay, Cassius (Muhammad Ali), 331, 356
Cleva, Fausto, 199, 244, 261, 277, 291, 296, 298–299, 320–322, 339, 351–353, 373, 402–403
Coleman, Emily, 329
Colzani, Anselmo, 74, 91, 104, 107, 115, 119, 136, 138, 166, 261, 270, 277, 299, 334, 373
Connolly, Bob, 455
Consiglio, Giovanni, 293

Contini, Mila, 249, 256
Cook, Barbara, 312
Corale "Croma," 5, 14, 36
Corale "Giuseppe Verdi," 2
Corale "Vincenzo Bellini," xvi, 14
Corbucci, Sergio
  Suprema Confessione (film), 120–121, 395
Corelli, Antonia Puliti (great-grandmother of FC), 2, 481
Corelli, Arcangelo, 2, 481
Corelli, Augusto (grandfather of FC), 2–6, 14, 481
Corelli, Beatrice Virginia Corinna (daughter of Augusto and Leonilde, died in infancy), 3, 481
Corelli, Carlo (great-great grandfather of FC), 2, 481
Corelli, Carlo (great-uncle of FC), 481
Corelli, Corrado (I) (son of Augusto and Leonilde, died in infancy), 3, 481
Corelli, Corrado (II) Attilio Fernando (uncle of FC), 3–5, 11, 14, 47, 51, 481
Corelli, Corinna Elvira Adelia (aunt of FC), 3, 5, 34, 481
Corelli, Domenico (brother of Arcangelo), 2, 481
Corelli, Dora Alma Vanda (aunt of FC), 3, 4, 46, 481
Corelli, Francesco (adopted great-uncle of FC), 2, 481
Corelli, Franco (stage name of erotic performer unrelated to FC), 492n139
Corelli, Gertrude (great-great grandmother of FC), 2, 481
Corelli, Giacinto (brother of Arcangelo), 2, 481
Corelli, Graziano (grandson of Ugo Corelli, cousin of FC), 316, 468, 472, 475–476
Corelli, Ippolito (brother of Arcangelo), 2, 481
Corelli, Leonilde Sbarbati (grandmother of FC), 2, 24, 28, 481
Corelli, Liliana (sister of FC), 4, 8, 11–12, 16, 34, 41, 44–45, 47, 51, 464, 481
Corelli, Loretta Di Lelio (wife of FC), xvi, 52, 54–59, 61, 63, 65, 66, 68, 77–78, 86–87, 102–104, 113, 116, 122–123, 125–127, 131–133, 136–138, 140, 145, 153, 155, 163–166, 172, 174, 188, 195–197, 202–205, 207, 213–215, 217–219, 222, 224, 230, 233, 245–246, 253, 256–257, 259–260, 265–267, 277–278,

280–281, 284–286, 289, 291,
302, 305, 307–308, 314, 316, 318,
322, 325, 331, 333, 341, 343–344,
350, 357, 360–361, 367, 372,
375–376, 379, 380–382, 389,
397, 398, 400, 403, 406, 411,
413–414, 426, 429, 436, 438,
440, 453–455, 458–459, 466,
468–472, 474, 476, 481, 488n20,
493n24, 505n36, 512n45, 517n15
Corelli, Luigi (great-grandfather of
FC), 2, 481
Corelli, Marco (cousin of FC),
xiii–xv, 5–6, 8, 32, 36, 43–44,
105, 120, 136, 195, 226, 242,
275, 282, 421, 441, 460, 464,
470, 474, 487n1, 489n26,
492n139, 493n24
Corelli, Natalina "Adria" Marchetti
(mother of FC), 4–7, 9–12,
16–17, 31, 34, 41, 43–44, 59,
159, 364, 378, 385, 389, 451,
464, 481
Corelli, Remo Pilade Adriano
(father of FC), 3, 4–6, 8–9,
11–14, 26–29, 32, 41, 43, 47, 51,
378–379, 384, 389, 444–445,
451, 453, 464, 478, 481
Corelli, Rossilla Quartilla "Bice"
(aunt of FC), 3–5, 481
Corelli, Ubaldo (brother of FC; aka
Aldo Corelli, Bibi, Aldo Relli),
4, 6, 8, 11, 16–17, 25, 29–30, 36,
41–43, 51, 120, 467, 481, 486n20
Corelli, Viero Dario Aldo (uncle of
FC), 3–6, 11, 14, 24, 28, 32, 47,
51, 255, 481
Corena, Fernando, 74, 291, 296,
300, 334, 397, 408, 419
Corradi, Nelly, 58
"Coscia d'Oro" ("Golden Thighs";
nickname for FC), 72, 230
Cossotto, Fiorenza, 178, 249, 252,
266, 303, 411, 452
Cotogni, Antonio, 250
Crespin, Régine, 165, 276, 286,
296, 303, 307–309, 334, 397,
399, 402
Crociani, Giovanni, 108
Cruz-Romo, Gilda, 431
Culshaw, John, 283–285
Cura, José, xv, 463
Curtis-Verna, Mary, 113–114,
116, 122, 210, 211, 270–271,
277–278, 296

Daley, Robert, 125, 360
Dalis, Irene, 199, 219, 270,
293–294, 296, 298–299, 330,
373, 402, 408
Danieli, Lucia, 48–51, 165, 487n16
Danieli, Thomas R., 463

David, Jacques-Louis, 98
Deaton, Patricia, 218
De Curtis, Ernesto, 236
"Tu ca' nun chiagne!," 225, 244,
369, 431
De Fabritiis, Oliviero, 82, 93, 102,
113, 119, 166, 185, 231, 234,
246, 434
Defrère, Desiré, 262
de Gaulle, Charles, 167
Deiber, Paul-Émile, 362, 396–398
de la Torre, Philip, 377
Del Monaco, Alberto, 445
Del Monaco, Giancarlo, 94, 164,
275, 408, 445
Del Monaco, Mario, 26, 39, 79,
81, 94–95, 103–104, 106–107,
111–112, 120, 122, 145, 149,
154–156, 162–164, 169,
172–173, 178–179, 190, 193,
205, 232–235, 243, 259–261,
264–267, 272–277, 283–284,
288, 290, 302, 311, 315–316,
327–328, 330, 347, 399, 406,
408, 415–416, 424, 439, 445,
451–452, 497n75
Del Monaco, Rina Filipini, 274,
284, 512n45
de los Angeles, Victoria, 222, 231,
254, 308, 343, 364–365, 389,
425
De Luca, Franco, 54, 68
De Lucia, Fernando, 94, 346,
491n124
DeMille, Cecil B., 15
Denise (photonovel), 246–248
Denza, Luigi, 431, 448
"Si tu m'aimais," 236–237,
502n127
De Palma, Piero, 74, 113, 131, 142,
157, 162, 185, 189, 192, 227,
290, 315
de Reszke, Jean, 292
De Rosa, Nora, 138–140
de Schauensee, Max, 244, 297
Deutekom, Cristina, 405–406
Dexter, John, 439
Di Capua, Eduardo
"O sole mio," 236, 343, 383
Di Costanzo, Pasquale, 180–181
Di Giuseppe, Enrico, 397–399
DiGrazia, Dominick,
DiGrazia, Donald, 244, 261, 316,
321, 330, 379, 381–382, 470
DiGrazia, Frances, 316, 379, 382
DiGrazia, Sandra, 379
Di Lelio, Loretta. See Corelli,
Loretta Di Lelio
Di Lelio, Umberto, 57–59, 517n15
Di Marco, Ofelia, 49–50, 68
Di Stefano, Giuseppe, 26, 112,
117, 122, 126, 136–138, 145,

154–157, 163–164, 168, 181,
193, 213, 229, 245, 254, 283,
286–287, 290, 407, 413, 415,
426–428, 445, 452–453, 458,
470, 475
Di Stefano, Maria, 470
Dobbs, Mattiwilda, 499n14
dogs of Franco Corelli. See Loris,
Roméo, Pippi I, Pippi II
Domingo, Plácido, 372, 374–375,
378, 386, 388–389, 394,
410–411, 415, 439, 456
Donizetti, Gaetano
Anna Bolena, 494n30
L'Elisir d'Amore, 58, 136–137,
173
La Favorita, 111, 148, 225–226
Lucia di Lammermoor, 58, 117,
121, 126, 315, 380, 393–396
Poliuto, 184, 190–195, 204–206,
224, 251, 265–266, 280, 305,
472, 476, 479
Dow, Dorothy, 92
Downs, Joan, 435–436, 442
Dryer, Les, 352, 354
Dumas, Alexandre, Jr., 246, 248
Duncan, Kenn, 375
Dunn, Mignon, 224, 244, 270, 334,
339, 393–394
Duprez, Gilbert Louis, 193, 207,
250
Duval, Franca, 118–120
Dvorsky, Miroslav, 463
Dvorsky, Peter, 463
Dyer, Richard, 430

Egenberg, Norman, 390, 444
Eisenhower, Dwight D., 26
Elias, Rosalind, 261, 334, 351–353,
397, 399, 402, 408, 411
El Cordobés (Manuel Benítez
Pérez), 385
Ell, Flynn, 370–371
Enriquez, Franco, 118–119, 150, 392
Ercolani, Renato, 76, 157, 161,
175, 183
Erede, Alberto, 19, 286
Ericson, Raymond, 264
Escoffier, Marcel, 302–303, 320
Esteva, Rómulo Ramírez, 431

Fabiani, Aurelio "Ray," 257–258,
263, 287, 297–298, 333, 344
Falconi, Mario, 180
Falivena, Aldo, 228–230
Farrar, Geraldine, 321
Farrell, Eileen, 244, 260–261,
277, 281
Fernandi, Eugenio, 221
Ferrari, Enzo, 242
Ferraro, Piermiranda, 405
Ferrauto, Augusto, 20

Ficarotta, John, 379
Ficarotta, Mrs. John, 379
Ficarotta, John Gary, 379
Filippeschi, Mario, 58, 188
Fischer-Dieskau, Dietrich, 336
Fitzgerald, Gerald, 99, 115
Flagello, Ezio, 219, 224, 265, 408
Fleta, Miguel, 9, 53, 458
Florez (doctor), 139
Flórez, Juan Diego, 474
Flynn, Errol, 200
Fogliani, G., 315
Fondi, Enrico, 54
Fontaine, Joan, 313
Ford, Gerald R., 439
Fortunati, Mercedes, 52–54, 488n3
Fox-Kelly Impresarios (Carol Fox & Lawrence Kelly), 103
Franci, Benvenuto, 395
Franci, Carlo, 121, 395
Franco, Francisco (general of Spain; "El Caudillo"), 14, 139, 392
Franco, Mosé, 457, 463
Franck, César
 "Panis Angelicus," 279, 451
Frazzoni, Gigliola, 112–113, 124, 138, 175, 177–178, 267, 289–290
Frederick I (Holy Roman Emperor; "Barbarossa"), 238
Friedrich Wilhelm III (king of Prussia), 90
Freni, Mirella, 283, 286, 314, 325, 341, 361–364, 371–372, 377, 441, 511n14
Frymire, Jack, 371, 381, 401

Galli-Curci, Amelita, 321
Gallina, Giacinto, 76
Galouzine, Vladimir, xv, 463
Galster, Johan, 377
Gambardella, Rachele (aunt of FC), 28
Gandolfi, Romano, 195–196, 290
Ganzarolli, Wladimiro, 249, 252, 366, 367
Gara, Eugenio, 100
Gardelli, Lamberto, 380
Gari, Giulio, 208, 211, 223
Gavazzeni, Gianandrea, 108, 115, 162, 167, 178, 231, 237–238, 249, 252, 266, 288, 290, 315
Gedda, Nicolai, xv, 305, 334, 394, 397, 399, 411, 463
Gencer, Leyla, 165–166, 192, 194–195
Gentele, Beatrice, 411
Gentele, Cecilia, 411
Gentele, Goeran, 400, 403, 407, 411–412, 415, 417–418, 439, 514n70
Gentele, Janette, 411
Gentele, Maritz, 411, 514n70

Gentile, Claudia, 35
Gentile (Maestro), 38
Ghiaurov, Nicolai, 249, 252, 301, 303, 394, 411
Ghiringhelli, Antonio, 63–64, 95, 97, 125, 152, 156, 171, 175, 177, 191, 195, 231–234, 236–238, 241, 267, 273–274, 276, 308, 310, 316, 319, 356–357, 362–363, 383, 403, 410, 445
Giaccaglia, Giordano, 17, 22
Giaccaglia, Giuliano, 17, 21
Giacchetti, Rolando, 36–37
Giacomini, Gemma, 18, 31, 459–460, 485n4
Gibson, Alexander, 133–134
Gigli, Beniamino, 5, 25, 36, 42–43, 49, 56, 75–77, 146, 150–151, 174, 179, 191, 245, 376, 391
Gigli, Rina, 76
Gin, Albert B., 415
Giordano (Ancona pastry shop), 36
Giordano, Umberto
 Andrea Chénier, 3, 39, 42, 64, 113, 121, 126–127, 129, 177–178, 183, 186, 225, 252, 260–261, 264–265, 267, 269, 278, 279, 286, 311, 329, 332, 337, 370, 384, 423–424, 475
 Fedora, 42, 62, 114–117, 126–127, 138, 140, 245, 360, 472, 493n24, 496n27
Gioventù Italiana Littorio, 16
Giulini, Carlo Maria, 258, 286
Glotz, Michel, 305–306, 318
Gluck, Christoph Willibald von, 70, 87–88, 90
 Alceste, 90
 Ifigenia in Aulide, 87–89
 Ifigenia in Tauride, 90
 Orfeo ed Euridice, 451
Gobbi, Tito, 20, 56, 58–59, 86, 93–94, 113, 130–131, 144, 147–149, 183, 286, 296, 317, 320, 322, 323, 411, 419, 421, 458, 484n1
Goldstein, Alvin H., 220–221
Gordoni, Virginia, 345–346
Gorilla Monsoon (Robert Otto Marella), 398
Gorlinsky, Sandor, 276, 317, 319, 372, 384, 389, 428–429
Gorr, Rita, 204, 299, 300, 303
Gounod, Charles
 "Ave Maria," 279, 282, 357
 Faust, 300–301, 305, 371, 390, 392, 456
 Roméo et Juliette, 287, 297–298, 332, 335, 348–349, 360–364, 369–371, 380, 382, 389, 417–418, 421, 424–425, 435–437, 478

Grace, Princess of Monaco (Grace Kelly), 190, 304
Graf, Herbert, 90, 192
Grassi, Paolo, 410
Grati, Alessandro, 22–24, 26, 31, 484n10
Gravina, Peter, 314, 350, 375, 380
Grieg, Edvard
 "I love thee," 324, 357, 358
Griffith, Emile, 355–356
Gronchi, Carla, 108, 167
Gronchi, Giovanni, 108, 142, 167, 192
Grotta Mafalda, the, 347
Gruberova, Edita, 394
Guadagno, Anton, 297, 328, 332, 343, 353, 369, 414, 427
Guagni, Angelo, 52, 54
Gualerzi, Giorgio, 345, 365, 471
Guarrera, Frank, 208, 215, 217–218, 221, 224, 291, 386, 415
Guelfi, Gian Giacomo, 68, 82, 84–85, 91–92, 102, 119, 122, 127, 129, 134, 148, 154, 180, 185, 244, 288, 290, 366–367
Guerrini, Guido
 Enea, 62, 66–70
Gui, Vittorio, 65–66, 91, 107, 130–131
 La Fata Malerba, 486n20
Gutman, John, 243, 287

Halévy, Jacques Fromental
 La Juive, 380, 425
Hamilton, Frank, 493n24
Hammerstein, Oscar. See Rodgers & Hammerstein
Händel, Georg Friedrich, 108, 123, 279
 Eracle, 157–159
 Giulio Cesare, 108–110, 123, 158
Harris, Kenn, 351, 413, 426
Haven, Dale, 202, 207
Hawkins, Ossie, 300, 373, 398
Heinrich, Rudolf, 396, 397
Henson, Jim, 386
Henze, Hans Werner
 Boulevard Solitude, 88
Hepburn, Audrey, 100
Herman, Robert (Bob), 156, 173, 298, 309, 311, 315, 319, 400, 411
Hines, Jerome, xv, 157–159, 264–265, 34, 408, 447, 453, 455
Hines, Lucia Evangelista, 157, 159, 446–447
Hitler, Adolf, 14, 19, 28
Hollander, Ronald, 368, 369
Homer, 1
Honan, William H., 370, 383, 385–387
Honegger, Arthur
 Jeanne d'Arc au Bûcher, 80

INDEX • 523

Horne, Marilyn, 308, 411
Hubbard, Merle, 210, 214, 217, 219–224
Hudson, Rock, 60
Hunter, Rita, 440
Hurley, Laurel, 222
Hutchins, Farley, 436

Improta, Mario, xv, 180–181, 370
Ingaramo, Guido, 449, 463, 469–471
Ingres, Jean Auguste Dominique, 98
"Inno al Duce," 484n20
"Inno di Roma," 484n20

Janku, Hana, 439
Janowitz, Gundula, 394
Jaretzki, Paul, 321, 345, 407, 418, 462
Jellinek, George, 444
Johnson, Edward, 270
Johnson, Harriet, 361
Jones, Gwyneth, 365

Karajan, Herbert von, 183–184, 208, 254, 283, 285, 305, 335, 372, 377, 394
Kaye, Danny, 418
Kelly, Lawrence, 421
Kennedy, Edward, 439
Kennedy, Jacqueline Bouvier, 211–212, 321, 324, 364,
Kennedy, John Fitzgerald, 211, 212, 270, 284, 324
Kennedy, Rose, 321
Kessler, Giovanna, 203, 293
King, Martin Luther, Jr., 224, 370
King of Granada (film script), 313
Kirsten, Dorothy, 331, 334, 377, 408, 419–420, 438
Kónya, Sándor, 334, 394, 408, 411
Kraus, Alfredo, 136, 258, 330, 411, 455
Kubelik, Rafael, 415, 429

Lama, Gaetano
 "Silenzio cantatore," 128, 236, 431, 447
Lamadrid, Enrique C., 432
Lamberto, Giampieri, 12
Landi, Erberto, 335–336, 368
Lanternari, Fausto, 27, 29
Lanza, Mario, 147, 286, 313
Lara, Agustín
 "Granada," 111, 148, 150, 324, 343, 349
Lauri-Volpi, Giacomo, 25, 36, 55–56, 94, 153–154, 179, 248–252, 280–282, 285, 290, 292, 309, 316, 372, 377–378, 439, 445, 460, 496n29, 506n37, 506n41

Lazzarini, Adriana, 104, 153, 155, 254, 394
Leoncavallo, Ruggero, 65
 La Bohème, 164
 Pagliacci, 76–77, 93–95, 104, 118, 120, 124–127, 136–137, 153–154, 168, 179, 183–184, 223, 235, 239, 241, 254, 267, 273, 277–278, 295–296, 299, 300, 386, 445, 461
Levine, James, 403, 429, 439, 441
Levine, Stanley, 385, 387
Ligabue, Ilva, 160–161, 346
Limarilli, Gastone, 39, 238
Lippert, Marion, 430, 433, 439
Liszt, Franz, 90
Locantro, Tony, 504n1, 507n34
Lollobrigida, Gina, 58, 142
London, George, 300
Loris (dog), 214–215, 222–223, 256–257, 444
Lualdi, Adriano, 66
Ludwig, Christa, 188, 396–399, 411

MacNeil, Cornell, 162, 265, 296, 339, 351–353, 408
Macnez, Umberto, 33
Macurdy, John, 330, 334, 362, 440
Magni, Giovanni (uncle of FC), 46
Malipiero, Giovanni, 81, 126
Mancini, Caterina, 77, 86, 95, 144
Mangialli, Pick, 486n20
Marchetti, Caterina (aunt of FC), 10, 16
Marchetti, Giuseppa "Nonna Peppa" (grandmother of FC), 6
Marchetti, Marcella (cousin of FC), 9, 11–13, 34, 460
Marchetti, Marco (cousin of FC), 9, 12, 17, 123
Marchetti, Natalina "Adria." *See* Corelli, Natalina "Adria"
Marchetti, Vera (aunt of FC), 9
Marchetti, Vitaliano "Taglià" (uncle of FC), 6, 8–9, 13
Marconi, Francesco, 250
Marcos, Ferdinand, 428
Marcos, Imelda, 428–429
Marie Antoinette (queen of France), 88
Mario (tenor), 250
Mariotti, Ottavio, 411
Marschner, Heinrich
 Der Vampyr, 90
Martí, Bernabé (husband of Monserrat Caballé), 333
Martinelli, Giovanni, 111, 330, 369
Martini (violinist), 29
Mascagni, Pietro, 3, 56, 91
 L'Amico Fritz, 20
 Cavalleria Rusticana, 22, 126–127, 168, 232, 254, 277,
 288, 296, 332, 385–390, 400, 501n110
 Guglielmo Ratcliff, 117
 Iris, 122
 Isabeau, 52, 82
 Lodoletta, 126–127
 Parisina, 82
Masini, Gianfranco, 440
Massenet, Jules
 Le Cid, 394, 353, 370, 431, 447–448
 Manon, 257
 Werther, 102, 126–127, 360, 375, 379–380, 393–394, 396–400, 402–403, 407, 44, 478, 479
Mastilovic, Danica, 439
Matačić, Lovro von, 158, 183
Mauriac, Paul, 368
Maxwell, Elsa, 190, 209, 324
Mazzinghi, Sandro, 356
McCracken, James, 235, 334, 408, 411, 438
McFerrin, Robert, 499n14
Meesters, Frans, 150, 495n19
Mehta, Zubin, 335–336, 341, 353, 365
Melachrino, George, 148
Melançon, Louis, 198
Melba, Nellie, 347
Melchiorre, Ennio, 66–67
Melocchi, Arturo, 39, 275, 405, 457
Menotti, Giancarlo, 81
Mercer, Ruby, 262
Merli, Francesco, 458
Merolla, Robleto, 405
Merrill, Marion Machno, 436
Merrill, Nathaniel, 208–209, 210, 216
Merrill, Robert, 199, 219, 244, 260–261, 283, 299, 310, 334, 408, 411, 415, 436–437, 512n45
Merzi, Camilla, 105, 195
Meshkolitsch, Mrs., 285–286
Meyerbeer, Giacomo, 90, 162, 249, 251–252
 L'Africana, 121, 123, 250, 265, 370, 380
 Le Prophète, 226, 380
 Robert le Diable, 429
 Gli Ugonotti / Les Huguenots, 123, 172, 184, 204–205, 225–226, 231, 245, 248–252, 272, 280, 282, 301, 429, 472, 479
Michelini, Arrigo, 105, 257, 280, 362, 416, 426
Micheluzzi, Mafalda, 52, 54, 93
Milanov, Zinka, 133–134, 244–245, 261, 281, 334
Milva (Maria Ilva Biolcati), 335, 425

Mina (Mina Mazzini), 425
Moffo, Anna, 208, 300, 334, 353, 395, 408, 415
Molinari-Pradelli, Francesco, 104, 148, 227, 325–326, 362, 366–367, 377, 409, 421
Monina, Gino, 27
Monina, Iride, 17–20, 23–27, 29, 31–32, 35, 414, 460
Monina, Maria, 31–32
Montresor, Beni, 339
Morell, Barry, 295, 351
Morelli, Carlo (Carlo Zanelli), 431
Morelli, Gilda, 431
Morelli, Giuseppe, 76, 346
Morichi, Attilio (uncle of FC), 10, 16
Morini, Mario, 243, 249–250
Moroni, Tullio, 19
Mouskouri, Nana, 383
Mozart, Wolfgang Amadeus
  Don Giovanni, 262, 487–488n22
  Idomeneo, 119
Mucci, Emidio, 82, 85
Mucci, Leopoldo, 455
Müller, Otto, 384
Munteanu, Petre, 65–66
Muppets, the, 367–368
Mussolini, Benito, 5, 14–15, 19–21, 26, 28, 53, 66
Mussorgsky, Modest
  Boris Godunov, 64–66
  Kovantchina, 131–133

Nache, Maria Luisa, 155, 171
Navarrini, Nuto, 25
Neri, Giulio, 71, 104, 107, 122, 142, 144
Nicolai, Elena, 77–79, 86–87, 89–90
Niedermeyer, Louis
  "Pietà, Signore," 279, 451
Nilsson, Birgit, xv, 61, 156–157, 181–182, 197, 208, 210–211, 213–221, 223–224, 242, 245, 267, 281, 287, 298–300, 314–315, 324–325, 327–328, 332, 334–336, 340–341, 353, 358, 374, 376–377, 390–392, 408, 410–411, 440, 442, 449–450, 475
Nixon, Richard M., 392, 420
Norma (FC's first girlfriend), 16, 59
Nourrit, Adolphe, 193, 250
Novelli, Ugo, 140
Nunziata, Elena Mauti, 442

Olivier, Sir Laurence, 335
Olof, Victor, 254, 259, 286, 306
Olvis, William, 352, 354

Onassis, Aristotle, 141, 190, 304
Oncina, Juan, 137
Osborne, Conrad L., 349–350
Owen, Dick, 265
Oxilia, Nino
  "Giovinezza," 15

Pampanini, Silvana, 142
Pan, G., 54, 66, 70, 72
Panone, Alfredo, 147
Panzini, Mario, 36, 43
Pasero, Tancredi, 65
Pavarotti, Luciano, 357, 394, 406, 408, 410–411, 429, 437, 439, 446, 456, 478
Pavlova, Tatiana, 114–115
Pavoni, Rinalda, 33–34
"PeCorelli" (insulting nickname for FC), 94, 104, 163–164, 173
Peña, Fernandez, 138
Penno, Gino, 162, 179
Pergolesi, Giovanni Battista, 2
Pertile, Aureliano, 11, 36, 43, 94, 111, 191, 330
Pertini, Sandro, 452
Perucci, Carlo, 391, 434
Peters, Roberta, 395–396, 462
Petri, Mario, 107–108, 110, 123, 144–145
Petruzzi (costume designer), 241
Piaf, Édith, 283
Picchi, Mirto, 74–75
Piccinelli, Nino, 110–111
  "Canción moresca," 111–112
  "La montanara," 369
Pillon, Giorgio, 49, 424–426
Pinza, Ezio, 201, 312
Pippi I (dog), 354
Pippi II (dog), 444–445
Pirazzini, Miriam, 65–66, 68, 79, 122, 136, 142, 153
Pizzetti, Ildebrando, 38, 42, 70, 369
Pizzi, Massimo, 14
Plishka, Paul, 408
Pobbe, Marcella, 89–90, 104, 130–131, 186, 188
Podesti, Alberto, 27, 29, 35
Podesti, Francesco, 14, 27, 29
Poggi, Gianni, 138, 362
Poggiali, Vieri, 362
Poli, Afro, 52, 54, 119
Polignac, Pierre de (prince of Monaco), 190
Ponchielli, Amilcare
  La Gioconda, 42–43, 57, 225–226, 241, 244, 282, 287, 327, 337–340, 350–354, 357, 414, 429, 431, 475
Pons, Lily, 340
Ponselle, Rosa, 96, 270, 504n5
Porto, Luigi Da, 52
Poussin, Nicolas, 71

Powell, Jane, 368
Prandelli, Giacinto, 126
Prawy, Marcel, 377
Prêtre, Georges, 286, 303, 305–307
Price, Leontyne, 154, 198–201, 208, 242, 254, 264–265, 269, 285, 287, 298, 300, 319, 334, 352, 354, 378, 384, 407–408
Prokofiev, Sergei, 81
  Guerra e Pace / War and Peace, 72–74, 93
Protti, Aldo, 76–77, 104, 124, 153, 171
Puccini, Giacomo, 5, 86
  La Bohème, 3, 164, 230–231, 263, 271, 290–292, 299–300, 309, 311, 315, 319, 329, 349, 375, 379–380, 401, 403, 425, 434, 437–438, 442–445, 447, 470
  Edgar, 117
  La Fanciulla del West, 28, 102–103, 109, 111–113, 184–186, 245, 259, 288–291, 309, 319, 327, 329–330, 332, 348, 390, 434, 438–439, 448, 478
  Madama Butterfly, 42, 58, 189, 286
  Manon Lescaut, 62, 169, 173, 184, 189, 205, 225–226, 259, 276, 281, 292, 335, 414, 436
  Suor Angelica, 119
  Tosca, 42, 93, 106–107, 111, 118–120, 131–132, 134, 137, 147–149, 154, 168, 171, 185–186, 225, 234, 241–242, 244–245, 258, 260, 276–278, 286–287, 292–293, 295–296, 298, 300, 303, 305, 307–308, 311–312, 318–320, 322–323, 326, 332, 336, 345–348, 353, 358, 368, 376–378, 390, 394, 403, 417–420, 426, 431, 436–437, 444, 457, 475, 478
  Turandot, 5, 9, 81, 111, 131, 134, 146, 148–149, 153–154, 156–157, 160–161, 164–165, 171, 173–174, 181–184, 189, 205, 207–211, 214–218, 221–222, 224–226, 243, 245, 251, 267, 276–277, 282, 293–294, 296, 301, 308, 310–311, 314–317, 324, 327–328, 335, 340–341, 344, 350, 353, 367, 374, 376, 382, 391–392, 425, 430–431, 433, 436, 439, 442, 449, 472, 478
Pullen, Robert, 333

INDEX • 525

Quilico, Louis, 262–263, 303, 340

Radice, Attilia, 49, 119
Raimondi, Gianni, 118
Raimondi, Ruggero, 388, 408, 421
Rainier III (prince of Monaco), 190
Raisa, Rosa, 9
Rameau, Jean-Philippe, 88
Rasponi, Lanfranco, Count,
    220–221
Ravel, Maurice, 52
Redmond, Michael, 455–456
Reed, Rex, 361
Reinecke, Martin-Wolfram,
    302–303
Renée (pupil of Loretta Corelli),
    454
Renzi, Emma, 442
Resnik, Regina, 283, 299–300,
    334, 408
Ricci, Luigi, 47
Ricci, Romolo, 32
Rich, Alan, 230, 241, 388
Riecker, Charles, 221, 420–421
Riemens, Leo, 110, 112, 123, 131
Rinaldi, Elisa, 16
Rizza, Gilda Dalla, 53
Roberti, Margherita (Margaret
    Roberts), 137, 162, 171, 241, 245
Robinson, Gail, 395–397, 402
Roch, Manuel, 49
Rockefeller, Margaretta Murphy,
Rockefeller, Nelson, 439
Rodgers, Richard, *See* Rodgers &
    Hammerstein
Rodgers & Hammerstein
    Carousel, 312
Rodzinski, Artur, 66, 73–75, 80–81
Rodzinski, Halina, 72–75, 80
Roméo (dog), 354, 385
Romney, George, 224
Romney, Lenore, 224
Ronchi, Fabio, 138–139
Rosengarten, Maurice, 283–285
Rosenthal, Harold, 192
Ross, Elinor, 430, 433
Rosselini, Ida (Mrs. Umberto Di
    Lelio), 57
Rossi-Lemeni, Nicola, 97, 123, 162,
    167, 272, 447
Rossini, Gioacchino, 2, 90, 190, 249
    Aureliano in Palmira, 2
    *Guglielmo Tell / Guillaume
    Tell / William Tell*, 172,
    184, 204–207, 250–251,
    280–281, 288, 380, 429
    Riccardo e Zoraide, 2
    Semiramide, 135
    The Siege of Corinth, 437
Rotelli, Ivo, 27, 29
Rousseau, Jean-Jacques, 88
Ruffo, Leonora, 246–248

Russo, Tony, 447
Rysanek, Leonie, 221, 281, 294,
    408, 410

Sammartino, Bruno, 398–399
Sampaoli, Guido, 45, 53–55, 101,
    143–144, 153–154, 496n30
Saint-Laurent, Yves, 304
Saint-Saëns, Camille
    Samson et Dalila, 100, 204, 267,
    311, 316
Salzman, Eric, 212, 270, 271
Sam the Sham & The Pharaohs
    "Wooly-Bully," 357–358
Santì Reginelli, 10
Santini, Gabriele, 56, 71, 86–87, 89,
    142, 144, 180, 254, 279, 286
Savarese, Ugo, 80–81, 178
Scaglia, Gino, 67
Scaravelli, Alessandro, 36, 38, 124,
    255, 275, 372, 392, 434–435,
    453
Scaravelli, Carlo Federico, 29–20,
    33–34, 36–40, 47, 64, 123–124,
    255–256, 274–275, 372, 392,
    434–435, 453
Schenk, Otto, 376–377
Schipa, Tito, 226, 245
Schippers, Thomas, 265, 286,
    298–299, 310, 344, 352
Schonberg, Harold C., 198–200,
    210, 260–261, 264, 323,
    361–362
Schumann, Robert, 90
Schwarzkopf, Elisabeth, 158, 308
Scoponi, Mario, 47
Scott, Hazel, 148, 150
Scotto, Renata, 227, 292, 325,
    410, 438
Seiffert, Peter, xv
Serafin, Tulio, 154, 188–189
Sereni, Mario, 199, 254, 279, 298,
    334, 336, 402, 408
Sergi, Arturo, 295
Sevitzky, Fabien, 226–228
Shicoff, Neil, 453
Shirley, George, 417
Shuard, Amy, 315, 335
Sieczynski, Rudolf
    "Wien, du Stadt meiner
    Träume," 450, 463
Siepi, Cesare, 300, 312, 334, 339,
    408–409, 411
Sills, Beverly, 437, 512n45
Simionato, Giulietta, 60–61, 79–81,
    104, 123, 174–175, 227–228,
    249, 251–252, 254, 267, 274,
    288, 310, 393, 441, 475
Simioni, Renato, 216
Slawitz, Bruno, 117–118, 122–123,
    152, 238, 271
Smith, Oscar, 298

Sordello, Enzo, 97, 124, 138, 471,
    491n127, 497n75
Spatafora, Emanuele, 49, 51
Spontini, Gaspare, 2, 90, 159
    Agnese di Hohenstaufen, 90–92,
    96, 100
    La Vestale, 91, 95–100, 114,
    120, 355
Starone, Gilberto, 177, 237
Steber, Eleanor, 330, 334
Stein, Horst, 394
Stella, Antonietta, 68, 104, 107, 117,
    144, 153–154, 183, 237–238,
    243, 266–267, 279, 286,
    289–290, 390
Stellari, Gian, 111
Stevens, Roger L., 388
Stewart, Thomas, 408
Stocchi, Ernesto, 444, 463
Stokowski, Leopold, 73, 208–210,
    215, 217–218, 226, 500n49
Strasfogel, Ignace, 386–387
Stratas, Teresa, 208, 277, 281, 334,
    341, 408, 462
Strauss, Richard, 81, 293
Stravinsky, Igor, 52, 396
Strehler, Giorgio, 377
Stronging, Theodore, 401
Sturani, Fabio, 467
Sullivan, Ed, 244, 337, 340, 368
Sutermeister, Heinrich
    Raskolnikov, 118
Sutherland, Joan, xiv, 182, 249,
    252, 262, 269, 281, 283, 286,
    300–301, 311–312, 395, 408,
    410, 437, 440

Taddei, Giuseppe, 26, 80, 237, 474
Tagliavini, Ferruccio, 126, 447
Tajo, Italo, 58, 74
Talvela, Martti, 394
Tamagno, Francesco, 191, 207, 250,
    330, 502n15
Tamberlick, Enrico, 191
Tambroni, Fernando, 13, 103
Taranto, Vito De, 65–66, 119, 185
Tartoni, Guido, 435
Tassinari, Pia (Mrs. Ferruccio
    Tagliavini), 60, 80, 126–127
Taylor, Stephen, 333
Tebaldi, Renata, 61, 74, 147–149,
    174–175, 178, 183–184, 211, 226,
    231, 239, 240, 266–267, 269,
    270–271, 276–277, 281, 287,
    292, 296, 299–300, 308, 321,
    334–335, 337, 339, 343–344,
    351–354, 360, 373–374, 381, 390,
    408–409, 412–417, 426–428,
    431–434, 439, 441, 452, 475
Thomas, Jess, 293–295, 326, 441
Torelli, Giuseppe
    "Tu lo sai," 368

Tortorella, Luigi, 225, 279, 357, 431
"Venezia, no!," 369, 404
Toscanini, Arturo, 4, 9, 99–100
Tosti, Francesco Paolo
    "A vucchella," 236, 353, 369, 370, 383, 431
    "L'ultima canzone," 353, 431, 434, 446–449, 450
Tozzi, Giorgio, 244, 249, 252, 294, 334
Trajan (emperor of Rome), 1
Traù, Gastone, 12, 17
Trinelli, Edgardo, 126
Tucci, Gabriella, 63, 167, 171, 277, 281, 286, 291, 298–299, 310, 334, 353, 408, 415, 441, 475
Tucker, Richard, 234–235, 295–296, 300, 320, 327, 334, 351, 368, 384, 386, 408, 411, 436–437

Udovick, Lucille, 91–92, 154, 157, 160, 262
Umberto II (crown prince and king of Italy), 33, 53, 164–165

Valente, Caterina, 312
Välkki, Anita, 340–341
Vallaure, Don Julio, 138–139
Vanvitelli, Luigi, 12
Varviso, Silvio, 270–271, 277, 299
Veasey, Josephine, 388
Verdi, Giuseppe
    Aida, 30, 37, 45–48, 77–78, 85, 104–107, 112, 126, 132, 153–154, 168, 171, 173–174, 184, 189, 197–198, 219–221, 224, 226, 234, 243, 251, 267, 276–277, 286, 292–294, 298–301, 305–306, 309, 319, 323, 329–332, 335–336, 344, 348, 351–352, 354, 358, 368, 383–384, 400–403, 412, 414–418, 431, 433, 435, 447, 472, 478, 486n28, 491n103, 494n44, 494n47, 508–509n23
    Un Ballo in Maschera, 11, 117, 169, 276, 286–287, 290, 296, 305, 310, 332, 348, 444
    La Battaglia di Legnano, 237–239
    Don Carlo, xv, 62, 85–87, 100, 122, 129, 143–145, 149,
        189–190, 212, 139, 265, 286, 292–294, 303, 305, 340, 347, 377, 394, 407, 409, 429
    Ernani, 126–127, 161–163, 167, 251, 264–265, 292, 319, 332, 349, 356, 362, 364, 377, 411–412
    Falstaff, 173, 409
    La Forza del Destino, 122, 127, 148–149, 168, 183, 211, 259, 269, 292, 310, 315, 318–319, 345–346, 348, 349, 364–365, 367, 377, 380, 407, 429, 431
    I Lombardi, 117, 126, 211, 353
    Luisa Miller, 344, 348–349
    Macbeth, 349, 353, 370, 407, 418, 421–423, 434, 444
    Messa da Requiem, 44, 279, 364–365, 388, 389, 412, 423, 464
    Nabucco, 173
    Otello, 52, 99, 104, 126–127, 203–205, 207, 232–233, 235, 257–259, 263–264, 267, 269, 276, 286, 290–292, 311, 314, 357, 358, 372, 380, 392, 409, 416, 444, 448–449, 464, 472, 503n41
    Rigoletto, 117, 126, 204, 245, 292, 311–313, 315, 347–349, 357, 390, 431, 434
    Simon Boccanegra, 52, 130–133, 189, 315, 475
    La Traviata, 58, 117, 119, 258, 333, 437
    Il Trovatore, xv, 41, 58, 92, 123, 126–127, 129, 146, 154–155, 164–166, 168, 170–171, 173–174, 179–181, 184, 189, 195–196, 198–201, 206, 210, 233–234, 254–255, 258, 262, 266–268, 276, 286, 291–292, 298–300, 309–311, 313, 324, 332, 340, 347, 357, 370, 378, 383–384, 417, 431, 469, 472, 476–478, 499n14
    I Vespri Siciliani, 119
Verrett, Shirley, 366–367, 394
Vickers, Jon, 204, 235, 327, 334, 408, 411
Vigolo, Giorgio, 70–72
Vinco, Ivo, 102, 160, 303–304
Visconti, Guido, Duke, 98
    Visconti, Luchino, 97–100, 191, 355, 492n139
        Ossessione (film), 25
Vishnevskaya, Galina, 276, 315
Vittorio Emanuele III (king of Italy), 32–33
Vogelsang, Alfred, 49
Votto, Antonino, 56, 79, 95, 97, 104, 107, 113, 122, 150, 153, 157, 165, 182, 192, 208, 406

Wachtel, Dr. Nathaniel, 426, 430
Wächter, Eberhard, 394
Wagner, Richard, 65, 70, 81, 90, 230, 242, 279, 463
    Lohengrin, 380, 436, 444
    Tristan und Isolde, 80, 123, 325, 380
Wallmann, Margherita, 108, 110, 339
Warden, Franca, 340
Warden, William B., 340
Weber, Carl Maria von
    Der Freischütz, 90
Weissmuller, Johnny, 15, 19
Welitsch, Alexander, 80
Werther, Sartoria, 186, 246, 248
Wilson, Earl, 363–364
Wynne, Peter, 429

Zaccaria, Nicola, 162, 189, 192, 254, 315
Zandonai, Riccardo, 52
    Francesca da Rimini, 52, 54, 271, 360, 414–415
    Giulietta e Romeo, 52–56, 59, 112–114, 128, 271
Zanelli, Renato, 431
Zeani, Virginia, 123, 447
Zeffirelli, Franco, 302–303, 385–386, 400
Zenatello, Giovanni, 330
Zerbini, Antonio, 65–66, 68, 122, 175, 237, 392
Ziino, Ottavio, 47, 49, 51–52, 54, 76, 153, 160
Zoboli, Luigi, 457, 463, 466, 468–472
Zucker, Stefan, 455, 465, 458, 459, 461, 464, 469, 484n20, 484n24, 485n14, 487n22, 505n36
Zuffi, Piero, 98, 108, 110, 150–151
Zylis-Gara, Teresa, 409, 430